FUNCTIONAL ANATOMY
of Speech, Language, and Hearing

FUNCTIONAL ANATOMY
Of Speech, Language, And Hearing
A PRIMER

William H. Perkins, Ph.D., & Raymond D. Kent, Ph.D.

A COLLEGE-HILL PUBLICATION
Little, Brown and Company
Boston/Toronto/San Diego

Artwork by Kyle Perkins; design by Christopher Perkins

College-Hill Press, Inc.
A Division of Little, Brown and Company (Inc.)
34 Beacon Street
Boston, Massachusetts 02108

First printing, November 1985
Second printing, August 1986
Third printing (revised), June 1987

Library of Congress Cataloging in Publication Data

Main entry under title:

Perkins, William H. (William Hughes), 1923-
   Functional anatomy of speech, language & hearing.

1. Speech — Physiological aspects.
2. Voice — Physiological aspects.
3. Hearing — Physiological aspects.
4. Anatomy, Human.   I. Kent, Raymond D.   II. Title
QM251.P47   1986   612'.78   85-17081

ISBN 0-316-69940-3
Printed in the United States of America

Contents

Preface

This textbook is dedicated to the prevention of drowning. It emphasizes how the speech mechanism works rather than the anatomical detail of how it is constructed. What students with little background in anatomy and physiology must struggle to swim through first is a new lingo, the foreign language of muscles and nerves. Descriptions of how the speech and hearing mechanisms operate, which are inherently easy to comprehend, can seem frighteningly formidable until the language in which they are presented has been mastered. Shifting metaphors, then, this book is mainly concerned with the forests of anatomical functions of speech. These forests can be virtually impenetrable for the neophyte if terminological foliage on anatomically detailed trees is too abundant.

We have attempted to reduce this problem in several ways. Recognizing that mastery of new terms is, in itself, a formidable task (and one that is not likely to be the main basis of your interest in the anatomy of speech), we will couch as much of this text in plain English as is possible. Where "in front," for example, will suffice for "anterior," or "below" for "inferior," the more familiar term will be used. The objective is to communicate the idea to the beginning student (who may have little background in anatomy, physiology, acoustics, or phonetics) with as much facility as can be mustered.

For those, however, who want to know anatomical terms, selected lists of relevant ones are provided in Appendix B. Many of these terms are readily deciphered if their roots, prefixes, and suffixes are understood. Also, many general terms occur frequently enough to warrant special listing; they also are in Appendix B.

That a picture is worth a thousand words is nowhere truer than in learning anatomy. If a speech structure can be visualized, it will be much easier to remember and to understand its function. Because we will need to visualize many structures

in the head and chest as if we could open the body and look inside, Figure P–1 gives the three planes, and related spatial terms, by which a structure can be visualized and described.

Another strategy that can reduce your memory load is to bear in mind a few simple principles when studying muscles. By knowing these principles, you can *figure out* what muscles do rather than *memorizing* what they do:

1. Muscles only pull, they never push.
2. Muscles can pull on one structure which pushes on another.
3. Unless diverted, muscles always pull in a straight line between their two attachments, that is, between their points of origin and insertion.
4. Direction of muscle pull can be diverted by any structure that acts as a pulley.
5. For every muscle force pulling in one direction, there are opposing muscular forces pulling in the opposite direction.
6. To determine the muscle or muscles that produce a particular movement, look first for muscles that pull in the direction of the movement, or that have their direction of pull changed by a pulley.

This textbook is not a definitive analysis of our subject. It is an interdisciplinary up-to-date tale of how the anatomical structures function physiologically to produce the acoustic signals of speech. We present only as much anatomy, physiology, and acoustics as is necessary to understand how the equipment functions to produce and understand speech.

Traditions of scholarship mandate referencing sources of all of our information. Tempted as we were to honor this mandate, we decided against it. Our primary objective is to present as sophisticated an account as we can and still make it readable. We feel that citations of sources would intrude on this objective. As an alternative, we have provided selected readings in Appendix A.

FIGURE P-1
ANATOMICAL PLANES

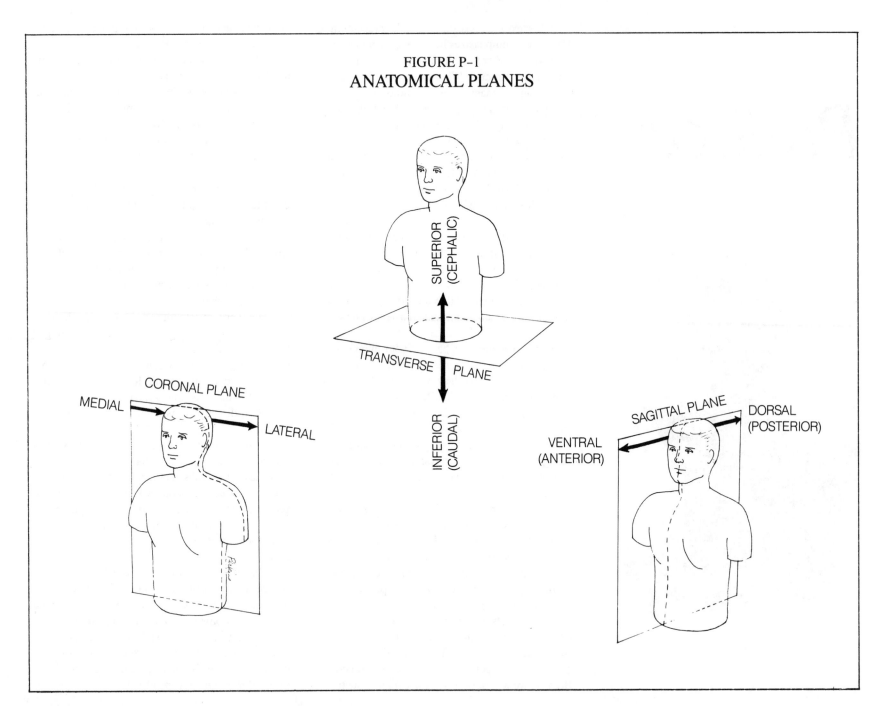

The reader will observe that some pages have more than the usual amount of white space. These spaces resulted from our attempts to keep the texts and illustrations as closely matched as possible. It can be frustrating to flip pages when the illustration and relevant text are on different pages of a book. We decided that more white space was better than flipping pages.

ILLUSTRATION ACKNOWLEDGMENTS

A purpose of this text is to present anatomy of the head, neck, and chest wall in a manner that will clarify speech, language, and hearing functions of these structures. For this, we chose line drawings to highlight the essential anatomical features discussed in the text.

For the artist to illustrate each feature required selecting a point of view, such as from above, or behind, or from one side. To do this we gathered all of the models, photographs, and drawings of a feature we could find. Because there can be considerable variation in how a structure is displayed in these sources, we required that at least two be in agreement. Accordingly, the artist worked from a minimum of two, and usually many more, sources in preparing each figure in his own style, to the extent that style can be revealed in a line drawing.

In one sense, then, these are original drawings; in another sense they are derivative. Because each figure would have to carry multiple credits, sometimes more than half a dozen, we have chosen to acknowledge our sources collectively, as follows:

Borden, G., and Harris, K.: *Speech Science Primer.* Baltimore, Williams & Wilkins, 1980.

Brash, J., and Jamieson, E.: *Cunningham's Textbook of Anatomy* (8th Ed.). New York, Oxford University Press.

Daniloff, R., Schuckers, G., and Feth, L.: *The Physiology of Speech and Hearing.* Englewood Cliffs, N.J., Prentice-Hall, 1980.

Denes, P., and Pinson, E: *The Speech Chain.* New York, Doubleday, 1973.

Dickson, D., and Maue-Dickson, W.: *Anatomical and Physiological Bases of Speech.* Boston, Little, Brown and Company, 1982.

Hirano, M., Kurita, S., and Nakashima, T.: The structure of the vocal folds. *In* K. Stevens and M. Hirano (Eds.), *Vocal Fold Physiology.* Tokyo, University of Tokyo Press, 1981.

Hudspeth, A.: The hair cells of the inner ear. *Scientific American, 248:* 54–64, 1983.

Kahane, J., and Folkins, J.: *Atlas of Speech and Hearing Anatomy.* Columbus, Ohio, Charles E. Merrill, 1984.

Kapit, W., and Elson, L.: *The Anatomy Coloring Book.* New York, Harper & Row, 1977.

Ladefoged, P.: *Elements of Acoustic Phonetics.* Chicago, University of Chicago Press, 1962.

Lieberman, P.: *Speech Physiology and Acoustic Phonetics.* New York, Macmillan, 1977.

Minifie, R., Hixon, T., and Williams, F.: *Normal Aspects of Speech, Language and Hearing.* Englewood Cliffs, N.J., Prentice-Hall, 1973.

Moore, P.: Otolaryngology and speech pathology. *Laryngoscope, 18:*7, 1968.

Netter, F.: *The Ciba Collection of Medical Illustrations. Volume I, Nervous System; Part I, Anatomy and Physiology.* West Caldwell, N.J., Ciba, 1983.

Palmer, J.: *Anatomy for Speech and Hearing.* New York, Harper & Row, 1984.

Schneiderman, C.: *Basic Anatomy and Physiology in Speech and Hearing.* San Diego, College-Hill Press, 1984.

Scientific American, Volume 241, September 1979.

Stevens, S., Warshofsky, F., et al.: *Sound and Hearing.* New York, Time, 1965.

Strong, O., and Elwyn, A.: *Human Neuroanatomy.* Baltimore, Williams & Wilkins, 1948.

Zemlin, W.: *Speech and Hearing Science: Anatomy and Physiology.* Englewood Cliffs, N.J., Prentice-Hall, 1981.

Self-Study

The spirit of Trudeau's *Doonesbury* cartoon was a major incentive for writing this text. Having taught this material for years, we were peevishly aware that scribbling pencils during lectures short-circuit the brain. What we sought, and have attempted to provide, is a text that "teaches itself." Thus, the *review glossary* at the end of each chapter is intended to provide you with an "ideal" set of notes. These are the notes you would have taken if the instructor highlighted the content on which you would most likely be examined for that chapter. Ergo, if your examinations are based on this textbook, you would be better advised to keep your pencils quiet and your minds in gear during lectures. The notes have already been taken for you.

The self-study materials are organized to help you move successfully from one level of mastery to another. Working backwards, we prepared a brief account of how each speech system works for the *self-study tests of understanding*. We removed key terms which you should be able to figure out if you have a reasonable grasp of how the system functions. More than rote memory will be required for this test — some thinking will be needed. The key words are from the review glossary for that chapter. To carry understanding further, a clinical exercise is also included. These tests are also at the end of each physiology chapter.

Similarly, at the end of each anatomy chapter is a *Self-Study Test of Speech Function*. To master it requires knowledge of the functions served by the various anatomical structures described in the chapter.

Obviously, you will need to know what the terms in the glossary mean before being tested for function or understanding. To help you determine how well you have mastered these terms, a *Self-Study Test of Terminology* is also provided for each chapter.

Finally, for the anatomy chapters, *Self-Study Drawings* are provided. These are materials with which to improve your visualization of the structures. It is much easier to remember anatomical terms if they are related to structures you can visualize than if you have only written descriptions of them. To aid in this visualization an easy and effective technique for facilitating learning is coloring. (Two dozen or so different-colored transparent felt-tip pens and pencils will be needed.) The purpose of coloring is to provide you with a visual connection between the name of a structure or concept and what that name refers to. By this color coding, you can tell at a glance what is related to what. To aid in this color-linkage of terms to their anatomical or physiological connections, all of the names used in the chapter are listed in a review glossary, with brief descriptions, at the beginning of each study section. All terms to be color coded are on these lists.

These study materials at the end of each chapter are intended to help you sort out and organize the main information in the chapter. They are not intended to provide a comprehensive review of all the details that may appropriately be included on an examination. They are to help you identify the forests, so to speak, so that you will have a better grasp of where the trees of each chapter belong. Instructions for use of the study materials are provided with each of them. Answers are given in Appendix E.

May we offer, now, some important advice. Use this functional-anatomy subject matter as only an example of the much bigger life-long problem you will face: mastery of new facts in an age of information explosion. You will constantly face the necessity of remembering essential details with which to understand and think about modern life. The skills you use to understand the information in this textbook will be skills of value in coping with countless demands on your memory for the rest of your life. Functional anatomy of speech lends itself ideally to honing of information-mastery skills. Even though we have pared as much detail away as we justifiably could, we realize that students encountering anatomy for the first time may still feel overwhelmed.

In truth, if you attempt to memorize all of the terms as your chief learning strategy, then in all likelihood you *will* be overwhelmed. Worse yet, you will have a head full of isolated, and hence useless, information. Fortunately, your memory bank can accommodate just as many chunks of large-denomination ideas as it can small-coin pieces of information. If you stuff it with pennies and nickels, you will soon run out of storage for any more. But if you organize and store information in large denominations, then one big-bill idea can give you ready access to a multitude of small-coin details.

Our advice, therefore, is to skim each chapter in search of a few big organizing ideas on which to hang a multitude of details. Avoid the desperation tactic of trying to read with an attempt to remember each isolated topic by itself. Keep skimming until you have a sense of what the chapter is about.

An economical way of doing this is to use topic headings as a guide. Start with a chapter title. Skim the topics and illustrations in that chapter until you have a clear understanding of what it is about. Then go to the first major heading. Skim the section it applies to until you understand clearly what that heading means. Proceed in the same manner with each subheading. Then move to the next major heading and skim your way through it and all of its subheadings. By the time you finish the chapter by following this procedure, you will be thinking about the information instead of trying to memorize it. You will find that the facts are linked together in an associational network. Save your use of memorization for what you can't reach by association, and when you do use it, try to link

whatever you're memorizing to as much other information as possible.

To find out if you do have a sense of the main issues in the anatomy chapters, turn to the self-study speech-function test for each chapter. There are only relatively few functions to remember (and our purpose in knowing anatomy is to understand how these functions are accomplished), so learn anatomical details in terms of the speech functions they perform. Once you've mastered the speech-function test, then turn to the self-study test of understanding at the end of the associated physiology chapter. Only after you grasp the sense of what these two tests are about should you concentrate on details in the terminology tests. Otherwise, you will have to store all those details separately instead of gaining access to them through a few big functional ideas.

With your "notes" already taken (in the review glossaries), and with self-instructional materials available to guide your preparation for examinations, you are free to listen to lectures for their interest and enjoyment. You are also free to read this textbook for what we hope will be interest and enjoyment. It is in that spirit that we wrote it. Read each chapter the first time in this spirit and you are likely to discover that with little effort, you will find a framework on which to hang details. Who knows, you may even discover that all of this can be fun.

William H. Perkins
Raymond D. Kent

SECTION ONE

Speech Muscle Systems and Acoustics

CHAPTER ONE
Preview

The marvel of speech is that it seems so simple. No reasonably normal infant will fail to learn a natural language. This despite having parents who, even if they tried to teach the rules of language, probably do not know them. Unless an infant is virtually deaf, severely retarded, or locked away in isolation from human sound and affection during the growing years (appallingly, this does occur occasionally), speech will be acquired, at least to some extent.

Why is this commonplace feat remarkable? Because its simplicity belies depths of complexities. What is it that is so special about humans? Until recently, it was taken for granted that they alone were equipped to speak. But our nearest neighbors in the animal kingdom are proving to be not so different from humans. Apes can think, and they can be taught rudimentary forms of human language. A number of animals, notably mynah birds, can produce human-sounding speech. A recording one of the authors made of a "talking" dog has been mistaken regularly for the speech of a handicapped child.

If other animals are equipped to make the sounds of speech, or to think thoughts that they can "map" in language, then why are humans alone in the ability to acquire speech naturally? Is it be-

cause they have bigger brains? If so, then chimpanzees, with 1,500 gram brains, should be more verbal than Walt Whitman, whose brain weighed only 1,300 grams, but less talented than Lord Byron with his 2,300 gram brain. Were brain size sufficient, 50 ton sperm whales would be linguistic giants to match their bulk; their brains weigh 4,000 grams. Honey bees, on the other hand, should have not an iota of abstract communicative ability. Yet, bees have a dance language with which they can communicate 40,000,000 abstract distinctions about the distance, direction, type, quality, and odor of pollen.

Considering how ill-suited much of the human speech equipment is for its task, the fact that we speak at all is all the more remarkable. For one thing, we produce high-speed speech with low-speed equipment. When speaking at normal rates, the different sounds flow from our mouths at about 14 per second. Yet, few of us can make our lips, tongue, or jaw move faster than seven times per second. For another thing, attempts to build equipment that will automatically recognize speech have been undertaken for almost half a century. Despite great progress, even the largest computer cannot match a human's performance. In fact, back in the days of vacuum tubes, it was estimated that a computer that could simulate a person's ability to recognize speech would occupy the entire Empire State Building. Yet, we accomplish this task routinely with only a portion of a neural mechanism consisting of about 100 billion parts with multiple interconnections packaged in a container about the size of a large grapefruit.

Investigation of this unique ability is in its infancy or, at best, early childhood. That we are far from having complete knowledge of how our speech equipment functions should not be surprising. Why should not man's most complex achievement, speech, offer an even greater challenge than deciphering our simplest instant of existence as a fertilized egg? Only in recent decades have we learned that, in this simplest state, the past experiences of our species are transmitted by molecular DNA codes that are estimated to contain as much information as a thousand printed volumes, each the size of a volume of the Encyclopaedia Britannica; and all packed into an egg one millionth the size of a pinhead. If this is the problem basic to understanding the simplest beginnings of life, may not speech be even more complex if we are to unravel it completely?

What we have now, and will be discussing in this primer, are current impressions of what the final answers are likely to be. On casual observation, speech seems to involve little more than moving lips and tongue. This notion was so prevalent, historically, that impaired speech was assumed to be caused by "tongue-tie," at least until a few decades ago. Not only has that explanation gone the way of phlogiston and other antiquated concepts, but in addition the more discoveries that are made, the more speech appears to be a "mystery wrapped in an enigma." There is nothing about it, presumably, that cannot be unwrapped, but many layers remain.

A few general remarks about language are in order. In its barest sense human language is a set of rules and a vocabulary of lexical items (words).

The number of languages in the world is estimated to be between four and five thousand. The minority of these are written as well as spoken, and of those that are written a fraction are standardized, that is, have a variety or form that is commonly accepted for formal writing and speech. The language in which this book is written is in the minority of human languages if only because it *can* be used to write a book. In human history, spoken language emerged before written language, and so it does in the child as well. Aside from a few limited gestures, our first use of language is through the modality of speech, which remains the most flexible, most readily available, and most exercised form of language expression. Mastery of a language involves acquisition of a large amount of information, but because this process begins early in childhood, it is easy to underestimate the knowledge acquired and very difficult to make this knowledge explicit (that is, to explain how we actually talk). Fortunately, explicit or formal instruction is rarely needed, as children simply learn the language spoken around them. It has been calculated that children between 4 and 6 years may be learning five to seven words per day, yet they cannot be said to be engaged in arduous linguistic scholarship. Happily, language acquisition usually comes about easily and relatively rapidly.

How does speech develop in the child? Most writers on the subject describe the process in terms of stages. Vocalization itself begins very early, typically with the birth cry. The sounds produced in the first month are usually described as vegetative (grunts, gurgles, hums, breathy noise) but, as any parent can testify, the infant cries and produces vowel-like sounds. This earliest stage is called the *phonation stage*. Between 2 and 3 months the infant's sounds change to include a large number of cooing or gooing vocalizations. These are formed of a nasalized vowel preceded by a *k*- or *g*-like consonant. This stage may be called the *gooing stage*. At 4 to 6 months the infant's sound repertoire increases markedly to include normal nonnasal vowels, trills (such as the raspberry or Bronx cheer), squeals, growls, yells, and babbles composed of alternating consonants and vowels. As will be discussed later, this stage of development, called the *expansion stage*, corresponds to a time of significant alteration in oral anatomy, in which the infant's oral structures change from a chimpanzee-like form to a distinctively human form. Shortly after the expansion stage comes the *stage of reduplicated babble*, characterized by strings of repeated sounds, such as ba ba ba, dee dee dee, dah dah dah. These repeated strings are conspicuous in the development period of 7 to 11 months. Initially, these babbling sequences are basically the repetition of a given syllable, such as da da da. Eventually, this simple repetition is followed by more contrastive babbles, such as ba ba bee bee doo. This contrastive babble is thought by some to be a springboard to first words.

The child's first word typically appears toward the end of the first year (between 10 and 13 months) and two-word combinations are noted between 15 and 21 months. By the time children reach the second birthday, they are likely to have a vocabulary of at least 50 words. For most people, vocabulary continues to increase throughout life, although the peak growth is in early childhood. The child's mastery of speech sounds continues until 6 to 8 years, during which time the difficult sounds *r*, *l*, *s*, *sh*, and *th* are mastered by most children.

Vocalization is one of the first voluntary behaviors in development. Some scientists regard vocalization as the earliest and most effective means of discovery of self. Before infants can roll over, sit up, or crawl, they can utter sounds at will and, through cry and other sounds, solicit parental attention. A scientist who has investigated the relations between development of the brain and behavior commented that mammals differ behav-iorally from reptiles in three major ways: (1) mammals nurse their young; (2) mammals play; and (3) infant mammals produce an isolation call. The third point gives an animal kingdom perspective on the species-unique behavior of speech. Throughout our lives, our voices are a distinctive attribute, part of our personal identity. With speech we interact socially, confess our emotions and attitudes, and make known most of our needs and desires. Our reliance on this remarkable faculty of speech is best appreciated when we are forced to do without it. Some persons never develop the power of speech, others lose it through disease or accident. Although this book is not directed immediately to meet these clinical needs, it is written in part to provide a background of understanding from which such applications can take form. As part of that background, tables of fetal development are given in Appendix C.

SPEECH: AN OVERLAID CIRCLE

Consider what happens when you speak. What you say always begins with a thought. A thought can be expressed in various ways, one of which is with speech. Sometimes a gesture will suffice, sometimes a drawing, sometimes writing. When a language is used, it "maps" the idea, so the idea exists independently of the form in which it is expressed. If it is to be spoken, it must first be organized by the speech networks of the brain according to linguistic rules. Not until the words in the intended sentence are arranged in a sequence that will say what you intend to say will your brain be ready to select the sequence of sounds to be spoken. After all, you have to know the word you are trying to say before you know the movements to make to say it.

Talking begins when the brain sends about 140,000 signals per second to the hundred or so speech muscles in the head, neck, and chest wall.

These muscles will produce sound waves that will meet about a dozen requirements. It is probably not by accident that we learn speech naturally by ear. True, sign language can be learned, writing can be learned, reading can be learned, but they are not acquired naturally. They are learned by eye, for which we have no natural capacity for acquisition.

Design Features of Speech

Because language is learned naturally by ear, not by eye, the following dozen requirements apply exclusively to communication by ear:

1. Speech must be loud enough to be heard and be broadcast omnidirectionally, but it must be received directionally so that the speaker can be located. In effect, speech is for all to hear, but is to be understood only by tuning into the message of a single speaker at a time.
2. Speech sounds must fade rapidly. Otherwise, they would blur into each other and impair intelligibility.
3. The system for generating speech must be capable of reproducing speech that is heard. Without this requirement we could not learn the language of our culture.
4. Feedback of the sound spoken must be available to provide a check on the accuracy of what was said and how it was said.
5. The sounds of speech must not be reflexive. If belches, sneezes, and coughs were used, we could never be certain that what we heard was a "map" of an idea rather than a manifestation of biological upset or bad manners.
6. Differences among the sounds of speech must be distinct enough that a change from one sound to another in a word is sufficient to change meaning. The difference between "p" and "b," for instance, is enough for "*p*it" and "*b*it" to have different meanings.
7. All of the words of a language must be capable of being spoken with a limited number of speech sounds arranged in different combinations. About 40 are used in American English to produce its entire vocabulary.
8. The words of a language must have meaning. When the sounds used to make words do not obey the linguistic rules by which ideas are converted into speech, the result is meaningless babble. "Rose," when spoken "orse," is nothing and certainly does not mean "rose."
9. The meaning of words must be arbitrary. Meaning is not embedded in any inherent quality of a word; little things do not require little words, for example, nor does the sound of a bell require that "ding dong" be the name of the object.
10. A spoken language must have rules capable of being transmitted from one generation to the next. This means that language maps meaning with grammatical rules by which words are arranged to produce sentences and phonological rules by which sounds are arranged to produce words.
11. A language must make it possible to talk about things that need not be present in space or time. This requires the ability to hold several thoughts in mind simultaneously while their relationship is being worked out.
12. A language must provide the capacity to generate novel statements. This is the capacity to speak and understand statements that have never been made before.

The Circle

To meet these design requirements for speech requires, first of all, a *nervous system* that can encode ideas in linguistic forms which culminate in the control of speech muscles. The *respiratory* muscles of the chest wall must be able to generate

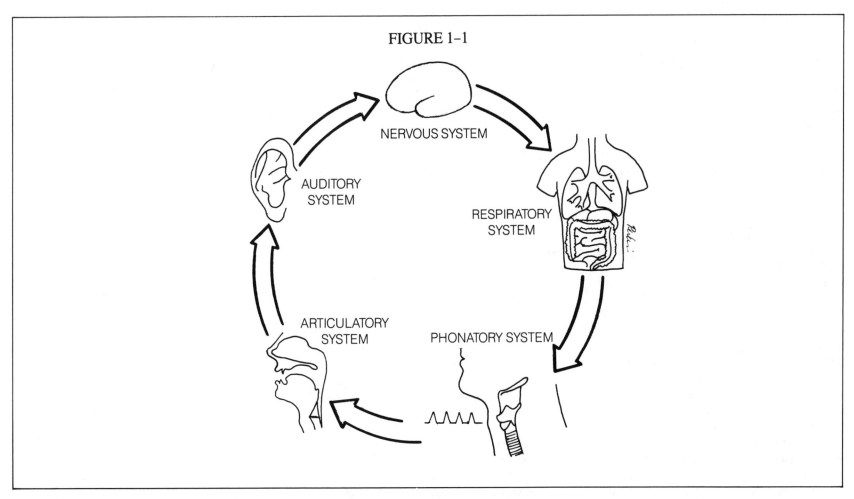

FIGURE 1–1

sufficient air pressure to drive the sound generator. The *phonatory* muscles of the *larynx* (the voice box) must generate enough vibratory energy for speech to be easily heard at a distance. The *articulatory* muscles of the vocal tract (the throat, mouth, and nose) must expend this vibratory energy rapidly so that the various sounds of speech that are shaped will fade quickly and not blur into each other. The *auditory system* of the ear must transform the acoustic waves of speech sounds into neural signals so that speakers can monitor their own performance and listeners can focus on the speaker of interest. Finally, coming a full circle, the auditory system, as it extends from the ear into the brain, must respond selectively to the special features of speech by which it is decoded so that the meaning of the message can be understood (Fig. 1–1).

Thus, as you can see, speech is a circular process, whether listening to oneself or to someone else. Either way the message that is generated reaches the ear, whether as feedback to provide guidance to the speaker or as information in a circular exchange with another speaker. The complexity of this communicative circle is suggested by a glimpse of the many disciplines whose members have produced the body of knowledge we have drawn on for this primer: neuroanatomists, neurophysiologists, neurolinguists, neuropsychologists, speech physiologists, respiratory physiologists, laryngeal physiologists, auditory physiologists, phoneticians, acousticians, and speech-language pathologists.

Overlaid Functions

Not long ago, speech was thought to be an "overlaid function." It has been self-evident that, to speak, we use equipment that was "designed" for basic biological survival — breathing, swallowing, chewing, and the like. Even though it is true that we "borrow" the lungs, larynx, throat, mouth, ears, and parts of the brain when we speak, it is also true that this equipment has been specially adapted to serve speech functions in humans. The more this equipment has been studied, the more special it appears to be.

When breathing quietly — or even heavily, after exertion, for example — exhalation takes about as long as inhalation. This breathing pattern requires no thought. It is a reflexive response to the respiratory needs of the moment. But when speaking, the pattern shifts automatically. We inhale quickly in preparation for speech, and then slowly expend the air while speaking on exhalation. As long as an individual is talking, this respiratory pattern is effortless and efficient. Try using it when not speaking, though, and it is neither automatic nor efficient. It requires voluntary effort to maintain, and we typically become light-headed from hyperventilation or run out of breath from hypoventilation. Speech obviously borrows the breathing mechanism, but it uses it in its own special way.

The same is true of using the larynx. Biologically, the vocal folds form a valve that closes tightly to build pressure for coughing or sneezing and to protect the lungs from food and liquid when swallowing. For speech, however, the folds open and close more than a dozen times per second in a phrase such as "put it off." For "p," they open to let air through without vibration, for "u" they close and vibrate, and so on. It is not just the speed with which they open and close that is remarkable; even more, it is the delicate precision with which they close. They do not jam shut tightly as for coughing or swallowing. They come just close enough together to vibrate, not just at any speed, but at exactly the speed and stiffness required to produce the pitch and loudness needed for each syllable. So, the larynx, also borrowed for use in talking, operates in a very special way for speech.

Moving up the vocal tract to the throat and mouth, the pattern of specialization for speech continues. The equipment with which we chew and swallow, when used for talking can be shaped to form so many resonating cavities, air-channel constrictions, and air-channel stoppages that over 160 speech sound positions are available for vowels and consonants. No language uses all of these positions; English uses fewer than one fifth of them, some languages use more, and some use less. Still, the range available accounts for the diversity of sounds heard in the various languages of the world.

We continue on to the ear, which evolved from adaptation of the organ of balance to include the function of hearing. (Strange as it may seem, we detect changes of our position in space with the same type of equipment with which we detect sound. This accounts for why the ear and the balance mechanism are joined together, are filled with the same fluids, have the same type of sensory detectors, and share the same nerve into the brain.) We need look no farther than the ear canal to find one reason why our ears are specially tuned to detect speech. This canal resonates best at speech frequencies. Beyond this, there are probably other reasons that have not yet been discovered.

Finally, we reach the brain, which has specialized networks not only for understanding speech, but also for producing it. Interestingly, one of the leading theories of speech perception points up the circularity of the speech-communication process. Called the *motor theory of speech perception*, it says, in effect, that we

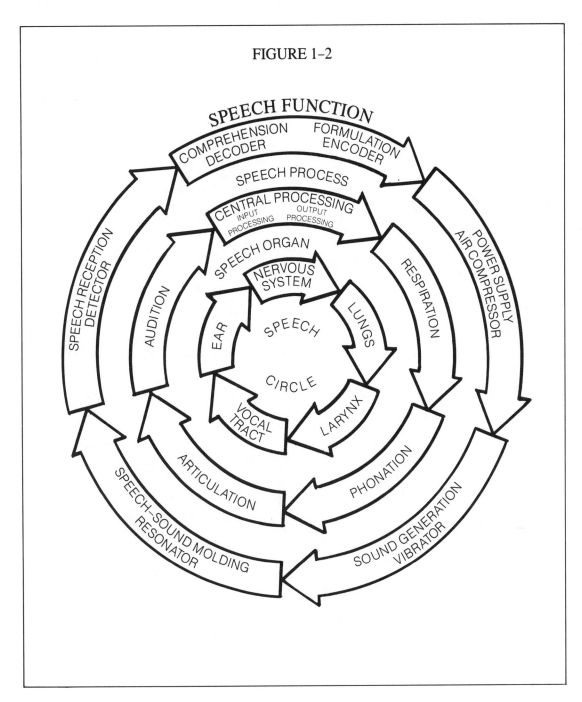

FIGURE 1-2

decipher the speech we hear by referring back to the speech movements that would be necessary to produce what we heard.

Speech, being a circular process, begins and ends with the brain. Therefore, unless we are to explore it twice, which would be inefficient to say the least, we should either begin our exploration with the brain, or end with it. We have chosen to end with it. We will begin, then, with respiration (Fig. 1-2). It is the power supply for phonation, the generator that feeds "raw" sound into the vocal tract for molding into the sounds of speech. From the mouth, the sound waves are received in the ears where they are converted to neural signals for processing by the brain. It is in this order that this primer is organized.

CHAPTER ONE

Self-Study

Preview

Review Glossary: Preface

Planes
  Coronal: The plane dividing the body into front and back parts
  Sagittal: The plane dividing the body into right and left parts
  Transverse: The plane dividing the body into upper and lower parts
Positions
  Anterior (ventral): Closer to the front of the body
  Posterior (dorsal): Closer to the back of the body
  Superior (cephalic): Closer to the head
  Inferior (caudal): Closer to the feet
  Medial: Closer to the midline of the body
  Lateral: Closer to the side of the body

Review Glossary: Chapter 1

Nervous system for speaking: The system that controls speech formulation and production
  Central processing: The neural operations by which ideas are formulated and mapped in linguistic form
  Output processing: The neural operations by which linguistic rules are converted into speech movements
Respiratory system for speaking: The system that generates air pressure for speech
  Respiration: The process by which air is compressed in the lungs to provide power for speech
Phonatory system: The sound generation system
  Phonation: The laryngeal process by which vocal fold vibration generates sound
Articulatory system: The system by which speech sounds are molded
  Articulation: The vocal tract and laryngeal processes by which vowels and consonants are produced
Auditory system for reception of speech: The system by which speech vibrations are detected
  Audition: The processes in the ear by which sound waves are converted into neural signals
Nervous system for speech comprehension: The system for decoding and comprehending speech
  Input processing: The neural operations by which auditory signals are recognized as speech
  Central processing: The neural operations by which the meaning of speech is comprehended
Pre-speech stages of vocal development: The stages of vocalization that emerge prior to development of speech
  Phonation stage: Vegetative grunts and noises, cries, and vowel-like sounds
  Gooing stage: Cooing or gooing vocalization
  Expansion stage: Vowels, trills, squeals, growls, yells, and babbles associated with a change from chimpanzee-like vocal tract to a human form
  Reduplicated babble stage: Strings of repeated syllables

Self-Study Drawings

Coloring Instructions

1. Using terms from the Glossary, write the names of the planes in *A* through *C* and the names of positions in *D* through *I* on Drawing P–I.
2. Write the names of the speech systems in *J* through *N* on Drawing 1-I.
3. Write the appropriate terms for speech organs, processes, and functions in *a* (Nervous System) through *q* on Drawing 1–II.
4. Color each plane (*A–C*) and the matching term in the Glossary with a different light-colored felt-tip pen.
5. Color each arrow (*D–I*), (*J–N*), (*a–q*) and the matching term in the Glossary with a different dark-colored felt-tip pen.
6. Check your answers in Appendix E.

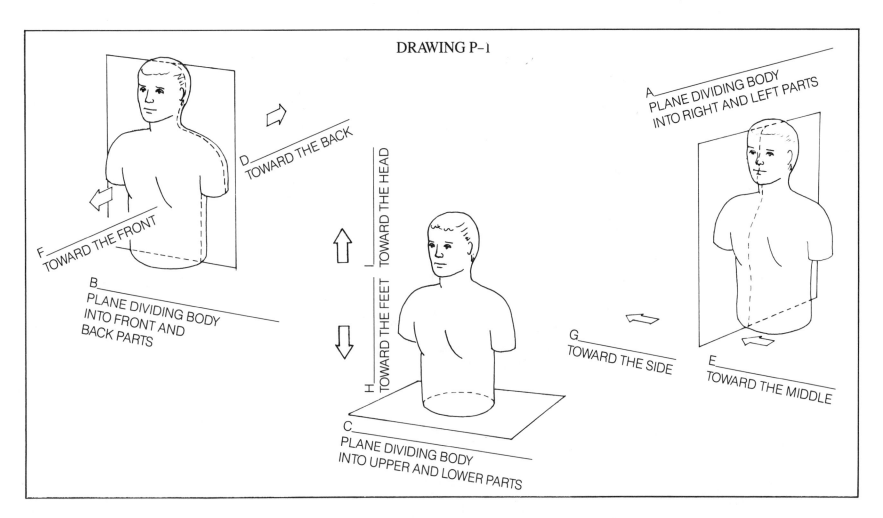

DRAWING P–1

D. TOWARD THE BACK

F. TOWARD THE FRONT

B. PLANE DIVIDING BODY INTO FRONT AND BACK PARTS

A. PLANE DIVIDING BODY INTO RIGHT AND LEFT PARTS

I. TOWARD THE HEAD

H. TOWARD THE FEET

C. PLANE DIVIDING BODY INTO UPPER AND LOWER PARTS

G. TOWARD THE SIDE

E. TOWARD THE MIDDLE

DRAWING 1–I
PROCESSES OF SPEECH

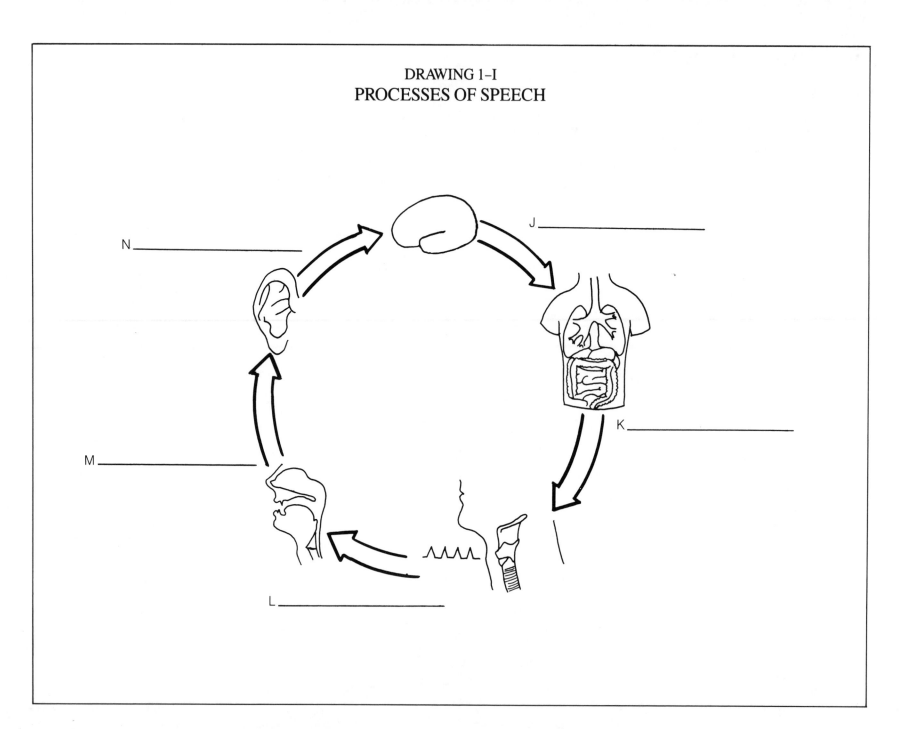

N _____

J _____

K _____

M _____

L _____

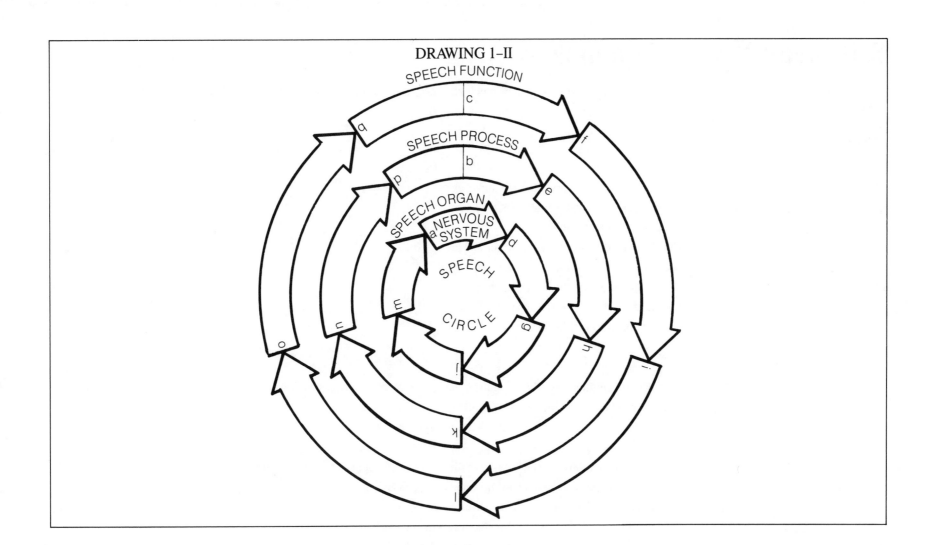

DRAWING 1–II

Self-Study Test of Terminology

Self-Study Instructions: These questions can be used to help you assess how much you have retained from studying the Review Glossary. Answers are given in Appendix E.

Preface

(1) _____ The position closer to the front of the body

(2) _____ The plane dividing a body into front and back parts

(3) _____ The position closer to the midline of the body

(4) _____ The position closer to the head

(5) _____ The plane dividing the body into upper and lower parts

(6) _____ The position closer to the side of the body

(7) _____ The position closer to the back of the body

(8) _____ The plane dividing the body into right and left parts

(9) _____ The position closer to the feet

Chapter 1

(1) _____ The neural operations by which linguistic rules are converted into speech movements

(2) _____ The sound generation system

(3) _____ The system by which speech vibrations are detected

(4) _____ The neural operations by which auditory signals are recognized as speech

(5) _____ The neural operations by which ideas are formulated and mapped in linguistic form

(6) _____ The neural operations by which the meaning of speech is comprehended

(7) _____ The system by which speech sounds are molded

(8) _____ The processes in the ear by which sound waves are converted into neural signals

(9) _____ The system that controls speech formulation and production

(10) _____ The system for decoding and comprehending speech

(11) _____ The system that generates air pressure for speech

(12) _____ The vocal tract and laryngeal processes by which vowels and consonants are produced

(13) _____ The processes by which air is compressed in the lungs to provide power for speech

(14) _____ The laryngeal processes by which vocal fold vibration generates sound

CHAPTER TWO
Respiratory Anatomy

Imagine an organ of the human body that could almost stretch over a tennis court. Waves of air blow across this surface 15 to 20 times every minute of every day. A thin layer of blood circulates through this organ to exchange oxygen and carbon dioxide with the air. Each wave of oxygen-rich air is closely followed by a wave of oxygen-depleted air that carries off carbon dioxide picked up from the film of blood. The rate of ventilation changes with exercise and is occasionally interrupted, but not for long.

The expansive surface in this imaginary scene is not the respiratory organ of a bizarre giant but rather an ordinary human lung. If the lung tissue with all of its myriad tiny air sacs could be stretched out, it would virtually cover a tennis court. This huge surface contained within the thorax is the interface between blood and air, the means by which oxygen and carbon dioxide are exchanged to maintain life.

But, in addition to this vital function, the respiratory system has come to perform another important role. It is the source of the air pressure and flows that are the power of speech. Humans have exploited this air-pumping system for a secondary purpose, using the moving air to generate sounds in the air passages that lie between the lungs and the air outside the body. Sound can be produced either on incoming air *(ingressive sounds)* or on outgoing air *(egressive sounds)*. The sounds of English are normally egressive, which means that our task in understanding what the respiratory system does in speech is essentially (1) to explain how air is drawn into the lungs to become a potential source of energy for sound production, and (2) to discuss how the egressive flow of air is valved to generate sounds.

Speech sounds are vibrations. To generate the energy in the form of air pressure needed to produce the vibrations of speech is the task of respiration. For this, we use respiratory equipment "borrowed" from the equipment we breathe with to stay alive. It includes the rib cage, diaphragm, abdomen, and the contents of the abdomen and rib cage, particularly the lungs.

OUTLINE

CHEST WALL
Inspiration
 Rib Cage
Expiration
 Rib Cage Muscles
 Abdominal Muscles
 Passive Forces

SELF-STUDY
Review Glossary
Self-Study Drawings
Self-Study Test of Terminology
Speech Functions of Respiratory Muscles

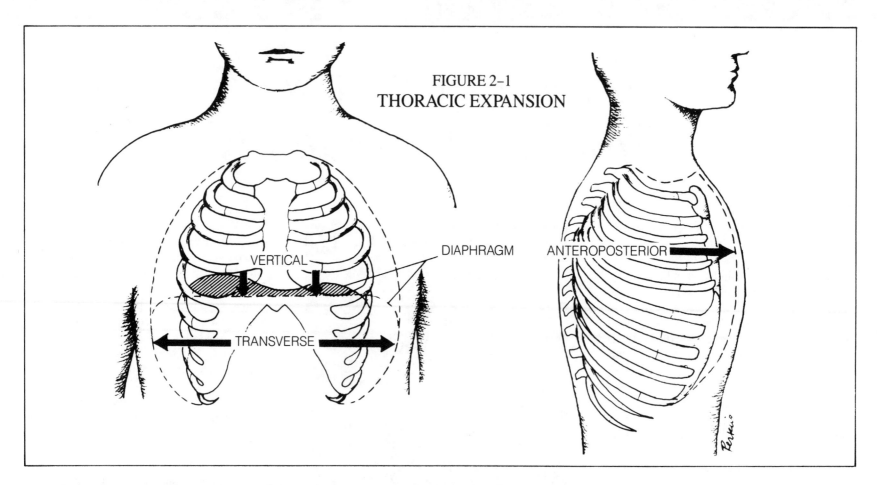

FIGURE 2–1
THORACIC EXPANSION

When breathing for life, we inhale and exhale in order to move oxygen into the lungs and carbon dioxide from them. For speech, we capitalize on this inhalatory-exhalatory (inspiratory-expiratory) ability by making the chest function as a pressure pump. Before pressure can be increased, the lungs must be inflated. This is accomplished by creating a partial vacuum which requires expansion of the volume of the chest. The chest can be expanded in three dimensions: vertically, transversely (sideways), and anteroposteriorly (front to back) (Fig. 2–1). Vertical expansion is achieved by lowering the diaphragm, which is the floor of the chest cavity. Lateral and anteroposterior expansion result from raising the rib cage.

FIGURE 2–2
DIAPHRAGM
ABDOMINAL MOVEMENT

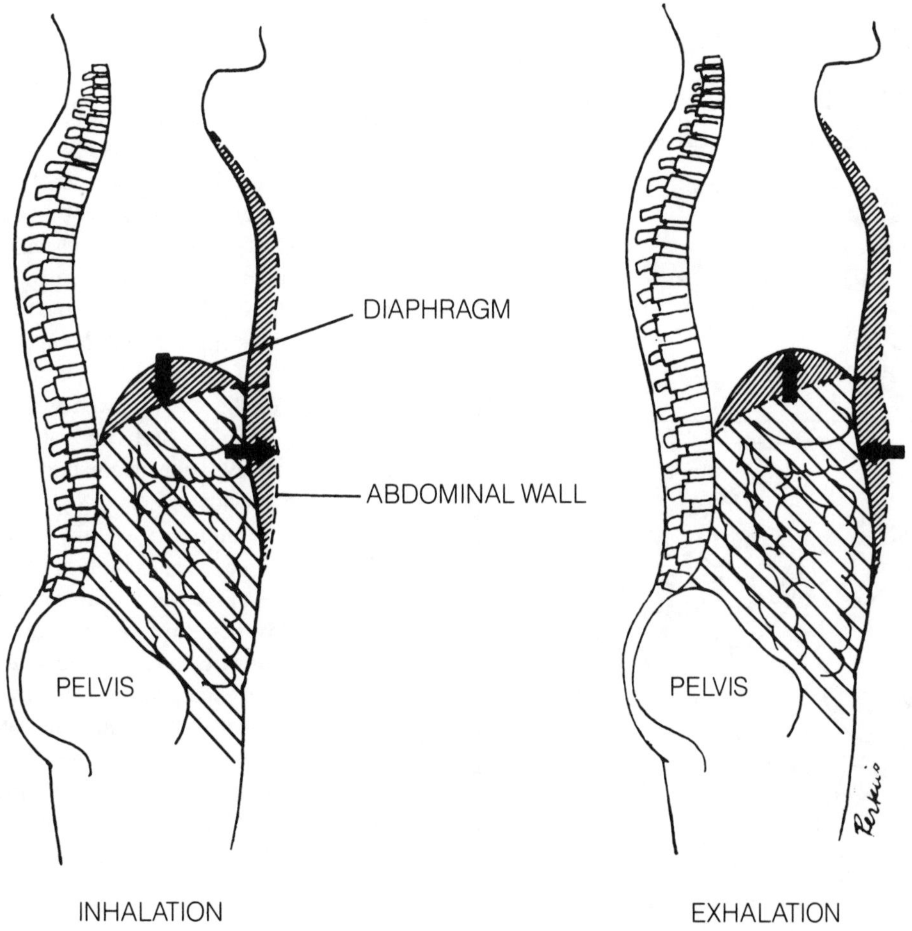

DIAPHRAGM

ABDOMINAL WALL

PELVIS

PELVIS

INHALATION

EXHALATION

To build exhalatory pressure, the lungs are squeezed by lowering the rib cage and pushing the diaphragm upward with abdominal force. Herein we encounter one of our simplifying principles. If muscles can only pull when contracted, how is it possible to *push* the diaphragm upward? The answer is not an exception to the principle; the upward push is accomplished by muscular contraction not of diaphragmatic muscles but of abdominal muscles. The reason this arrangement works is because the abdomen contains so much fluid it is virtually incompressible. Thus, when it is squeezed by abdominal wall muscles, the resultant visceral pressure pushes upward against the undersurface of the diaphragm, which is the roof of the belly (Fig. 2–2).

With this overview, you can see that to understand how respiratory pressure for speech is controlled, we must understand how the rib cage is raised and lowered, how the diaphragm is pulled down and pushed up, and how the lungs inflate and deflate.

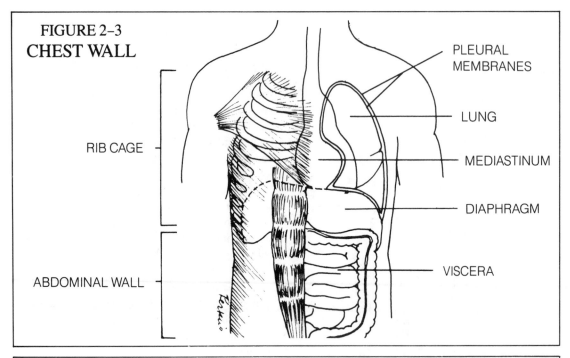

FIGURE 2–3
CHEST WALL

RIB CAGE

ABDOMINAL WALL

PLEURAL MEMBRANES

LUNG

MEDIASTINUM

DIAPHRAGM

VISCERA

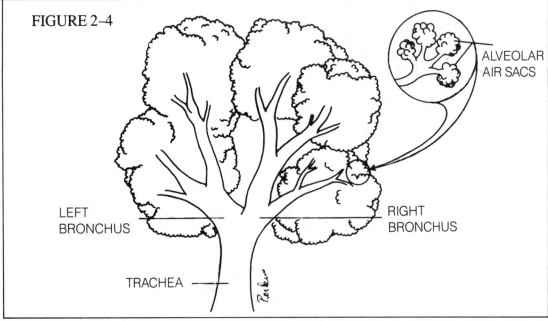

FIGURE 2–4

ALVEOLAR AIR SACS

LEFT BRONCHUS

RIGHT BRONCHUS

TRACHEA

The respiratory pump consists of two major units, the chest wall and, within it, the pulmonary system. The *chest wall* is composed of the rib cage, the diaphragm, the abdominal wall, the abdominal viscera, and the muscles of the chest and abdomen. Within the rib cage is the *thoracic cavity,* which contains, in addition to the pulmonary system, the *mediastinum* (it includes mainly the heart, blood vessels, and the esophagus) and the two thin, air-tight *pleural membranes* in which the lungs are encased (Fig. 2–3).

The *pulmonary system* consists of the network of tubes leading from the *trachea* (windpipe) to the *alveolar air sacs* at the outermost reaches of the lungs. The lungs are arranged in lobes, three on the right, two on the left. You can visualize this arrangement by imagining a tree turned upside down, the trunk being the trachea, the major branches being the right and left *bronchi,* which continue to branch into three main limbs on the right, and two on the left, followed by branching into smaller and smaller limbs until at the ends of twigs are the leaves, the alveolar air sacs. Figure 2–4 shows the tree analogy.

Just as the pulmonary system is arranged like an upside down tree, so is its biological function reversed. Leaves of the tree absorb carbon dioxide and give back oxygen; alveolar air sacs pass oxygen into the blood stream on inhalation and release carbon dioxide on exhalation. Each of these air sacs is like a tiny balloon. Because they are lubricated, the surface tension makes the air sac resist inflation, as does a balloon. This is an important dynamic force to which we will return in our discussion of how air pressure is generated for speech.

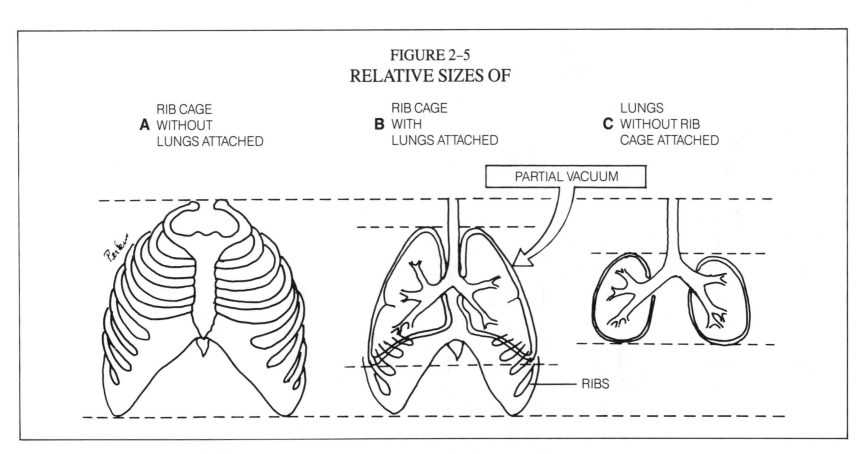

FIGURE 2-5
RELATIVE SIZES OF

A RIB CAGE WITHOUT LUNGS ATTACHED

B RIB CAGE WITH LUNGS ATTACHED

C LUNGS WITHOUT RIB CAGE ATTACHED

PARTIAL VACUUM

RIBS

Before concluding this discussion of the structure of the pulmonary system, we should note that if the lungs were removed from the thorax they would collapse until almost completely deflated. Conversely, thoracic volume would increase. Because lungs and thorax are attached by pleural linkage, they resist these opposing tendencies, so the lungs do not collapse completely, nor does the thorax expand excessively. The force that makes the lungs stick to the chest wall was once thought to be surface adhesion of the lubricant between the inner pleural membrane, in which the lungs are wrapped, and the outer membrane, which adheres to the rib cage. (With this arrangement, the lungs do not rub directly against the ribs; instead, the lubricated pleural membranes rub against each other, which is why infected pleural membranes rubbing together make breathing painful). Instead of the pleural membranes sticking like two wet glass surfaces, it is now known that they are held together by suction. A negative pressure (similar to a partial vacuum) within the two pleural cavities sucks the lungs against the ribs on both sides of the chest (Fig. 2-5). As can be seen in Figure 2–6, this negative intrapleural pressure varies with lung volume.

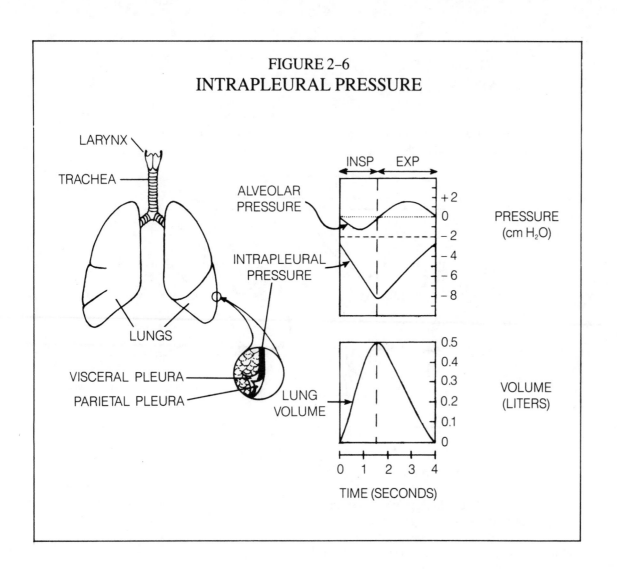

FIGURE 2–6
INTRAPLEURAL PRESSURE

We will now consider the muscular arrangements of the chest wall that are used for inspiration and expiration. For inspiration this involves raising the rib cage and lowering the diaphragm. Unless one stands on one's head—in which case gravity helps—inhalation is accomplished entirely by muscular contraction. Expiration, on the other hand, involves both passive forces, such as gravity, and contraction of abdominal as well as rib cage muscles.

Inspiration

Rib Cage. The thorax is formed by 12 pairs of *ribs* attached by cartilage to the 12 thoracic *vertebrae* of the backbone. In front, the upper 10 ribs attach by cartilage to the *sternum* (breastbone), whereas the lowest two are unattached or "floating ribs." Notice in Figure 2–7 how the lower ribs slope downward from their connection to the sternum, much in the fashion of a bucket handle. It is by virtue of this bucket-handle effect that the ribs move outward laterally when they are raised.

The upper ribs, by contrast, are hinged in such a way that they do move forward a bit when raised, much like a pump handle, but they do not provide nearly as much expansion as is achieved with elevation of the lower ribs (Fig. 2–8). It is for this reason that so-called "clavicular breathing," which emphasizes upper chest elevation, is considered inefficient. This type of breathing gets its name from the *clavicle* (collar bone), which runs from the sternum to the *scapula* (shoulder blade) to complete the thoracic skeleton (Fig. 2–9).

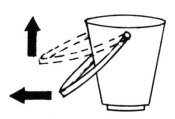
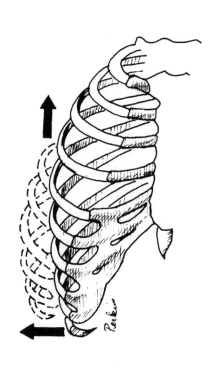

FIGURE 2–7
LATERAL THORACIC EXPANSION

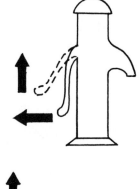
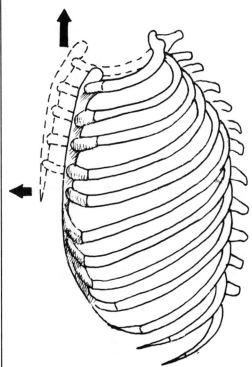

FIGURE 2–8
ANTEROPOSTERIOR THORACIC EXPANSION

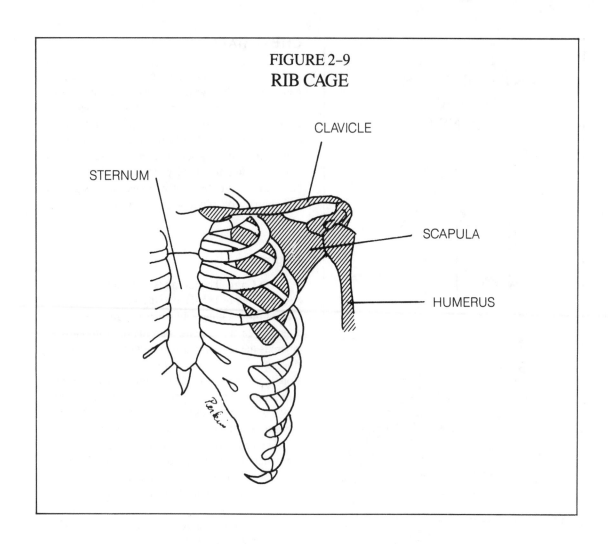

**FIGURE 2–9
RIB CAGE**

CLAVICLE

STERNUM

SCAPULA

HUMERUS

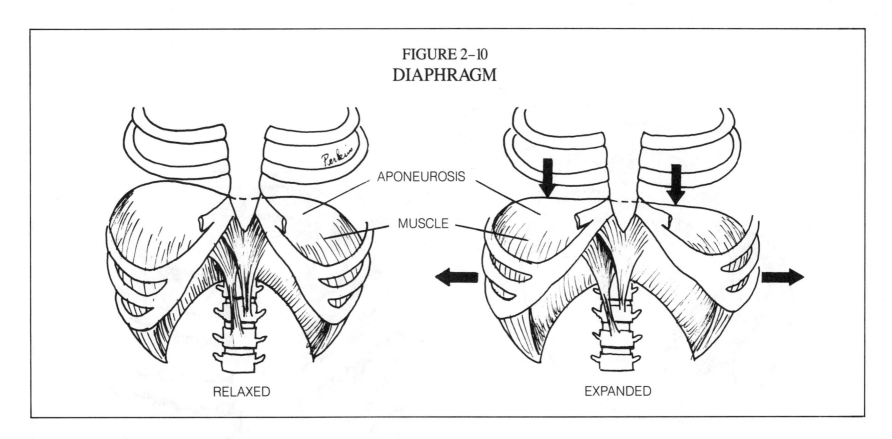

FIGURE 2–10
DIAPHRAGM

APONEUROSIS

MUSCLE

RELAXED

EXPANDED

The *diaphragm* is a flat sheet of muscle and tendon (sometimes called the *diaphragmatic aponeurosis* or *central tendon)* connected to the lower border of the rib cage (Fig. 2–10). The arrangement resembles the attachment of a trampoline bed (central tendon) by springs (rim of muscles) to a frame (lower border of the thorax). The diaphragm is shaped like an inverted bowl. When the rim muscles contract, they flatten the domes on each side, thereby achieving vertical expansion, and pull up on the lower ribs, moving them outward. This combined action accounts for most of the increased thoracic volume that occurs on inspiration.

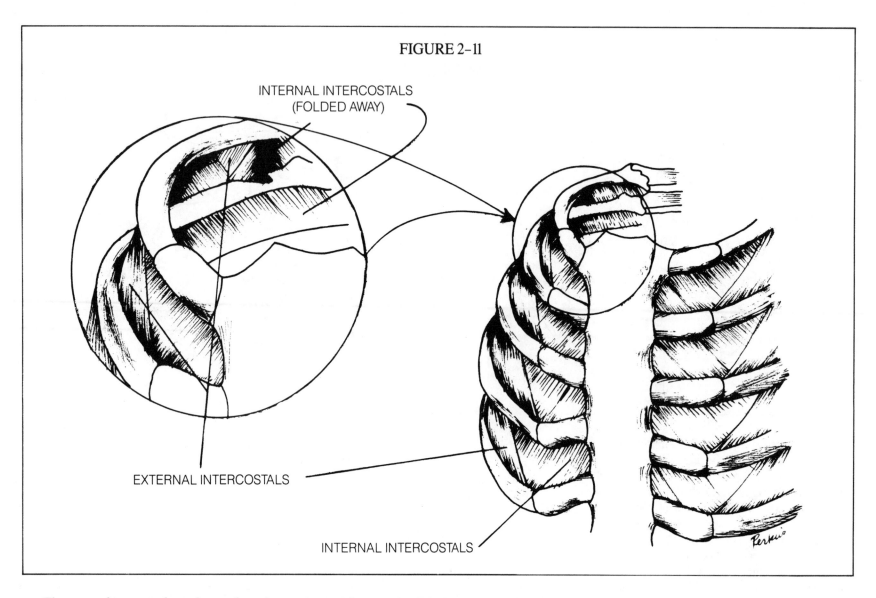

FIGURE 2-11

INTERNAL INTERCOSTALS
(FOLDED AWAY)

EXTERNAL INTERCOSTALS

INTERNAL INTERCOSTALS

The *external intercostal* muscles run from the lower border of one rib to the upper border of the rib below, filling the outside of the 11 spaces between the ribs (Fig. 2-11). Those who are sparerib lovers have had a culinary encounter with this delicious muscle, along with its counterpart, the internal intercostals. (Whether or not the internals participate in inhalation, or exhalation, or both, is a matter of conflicting evidence.) Without doubt, however, the external intercostal muscles function as if they were in a single sheet of muscle pulling all of the lower ribs toward the first rib, which, in turn, is attached to the first thoracic vertebra and to the base of the skull. After the diaphragm, the external intercostals are the next most important muscles of inhalation.

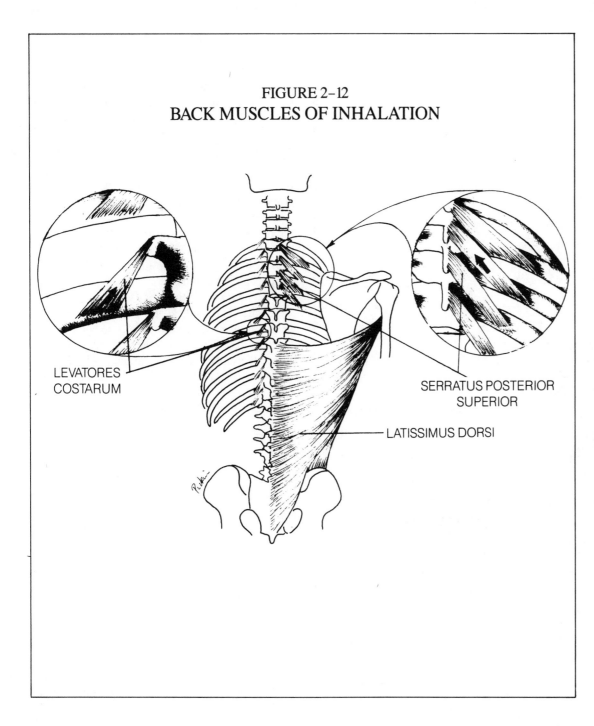

FIGURE 2-12
BACK MUSCLES OF INHALATION

LEVATORES
COSTARUM

SERRATUS POSTERIOR
SUPERIOR

LATISSIMUS DORSI

Depending on how vigorous the breath, other accessory muscles often assist in raising the rib cage. Because they differ in size, angle, and place of attachment, the amount of upward pull they exert on the ribs and how much expansion results from that pull also differ. We will consider them not in order of importance, but from back to front of the rib cage.

The *levatores costarum* (rib elevators) are a series of 12 small muscles, each of which inserts into the rib just below the vertebra from which it originates. As you can see from Figure 2-12, when contracted they pull up on the ribs, but the power of this pull is weakened by their small size and by their points of insertion, which provide poor leverage for lifting the ribs.

The *serratus posterior superior* muscles are flat muscles slanting down from the neck (lower cervical and upper thoracic vertebrae) to insert into the second through fifth ribs. These muscles are somewhat larger than the levatores costarum and have a little better angle of insertion to lift the ribs for inhalation. The name of this muscle reveals several things: "serratus" describes the serrated appearance of the edge of the muscle; "posterior" implies that an *anterior* serrated muscle will also be found; and "superior" tells you that an *inferior* serrated muscle exists. Although lifting the upper ribs does not result in much thoracic expansion, it does stabilize the upper ribs for the pull of the external intercostals which, as we just discussed, provide the major force for raising all of the ribs.

Although it is now doubted that the *latissimus dorsi* is involved in respiration, it has traditionally been considered a muscle of inhalation. It is a large, flat muscle originating from the upper arm just below the armpit. It fans downward to insert into lower back vertebrae, with some fibers inserting into the lower ribs. When the humerus (upper arm bone) is braced, contracting of these rib fibers could conceivably assist in expanding the lower thorax.

Respiratory Anatomy

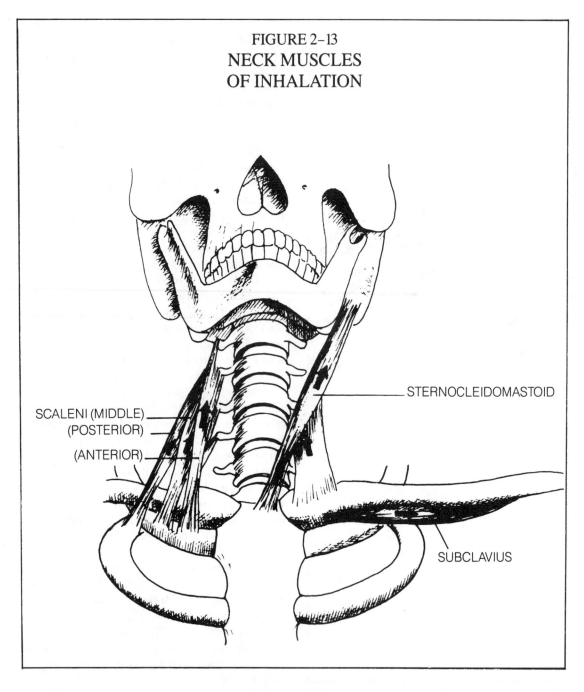

FIGURE 2–13
NECK MUSCLES
OF INHALATION

SCALENI (MIDDLE)
(POSTERIOR)
(ANTERIOR)

STERNOCLEIDOMASTOID

SUBCLAVIUS

Having explored the back muscles of inhalation, we will now continue on the front side from the neck down. Two relatively large muscles originating from the skull and neck join with the serratus posterior superior to help provide a stable point of origin from which the external intercostals can pull (Fig. 2–13). One is the *sternocleidomastoid*, which descends from behind the ear and subdivides to insert into the clavicle and sternum. The other is the scalenus group of three muscles: the *scalenus anterior, medius,* and *posterior.* They originate from the cervical vertebrae to insert into the first and second ribs. Although these are muscles of head balance, when the head is fixated they provide the major force for raising and stabilizing the upper chest of inhalation.

Another muscle that assists in raising the upper chest is the *subclavius.* It runs slightly downward from the collarbone (the clavicle) to insert into the first rib near the sternum. Contribution of the subclavius to inhalation is not great, thanks to its relatively small size, poor angle of pull, and the fact that the clavicle must be anchored for it to pull upward at all.

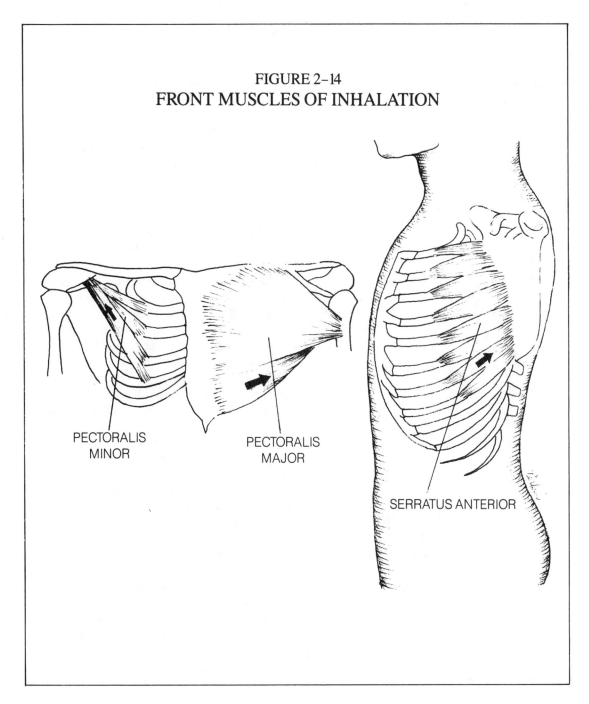

FIGURE 2-14
FRONT MUSCLES OF INHALATION

PECTORALIS
MINOR

PECTORALIS
MAJOR

SERRATUS ANTERIOR

The *pectoralis major* is the large upper chest muscle originating from the humerus that fans out to insert into the sternum and clavicle. With the upper arm in a fixed position, the pectoralis major assists in drawing the sternum and its ribs upward (Fig. 2-14).

Deep to the pectoralis major (beneath it) is the *pectoralis minor.* Also fan-shaped, it originates from the scapula and inserts into the second through fifth ribs. For it to raise these ribs, the scapula must be stabilized.

Finally, the *serratus anterior* is a large muscle originating from the scapula that fans down and around the chest to insert into the upper nine ribs. With the scapula anchored, this muscle is a relatively powerful rib raiser.

FIGURE 2–15
INTERNAL RIB CAGE
MUSCLES OF EXHALATION

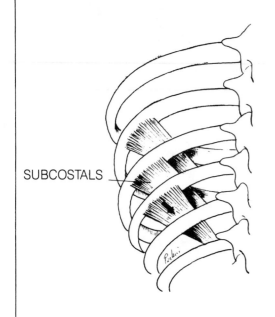

OUTSIDE VIEW
OF BACK WALL
OF LOWER
SIX RIBS

SUBCOSTALS

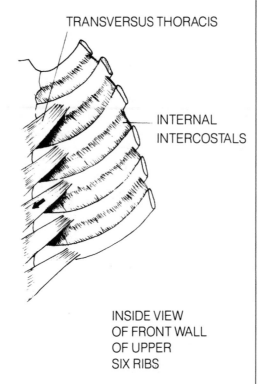

TRANSVERSUS THORACIS

INTERNAL
INTERCOSTALS

INSIDE VIEW
OF FRONT WALL
OF UPPER
SIX RIBS

Expiration

Unlike inspiration, which is accomplished entirely with active muscular contraction, expiration involves interaction of passive forces with muscular activity. These active forces are from rib cage muscles and abdominal muscles as they work in opposition to the diaphragm. Thus, three relatively independent forces interact for exhalation: passive forces, active diaphragm-abdomen forces, and active rib cage forces. Let us continue where we left our discussion of inhalation—with rib cage muscles of exhalation.

Rib Cage Muscles. The internal intercostals, like the external intercostals, fill the spaces between the ribs (except in back) on the inside of the chest (Fig. 2–15). Although similar, the internal intercostals connect the ribs at opposite angles to the external intercostals. These two sets of muscles have been thought by some to work in opposition to each other, as apparently they can. Whereas the external intercostals pull upward from the spine, skull, neck, and fixated upper ribs, the internal intercostals are thought to pull down from the pelvis through their connection with abdominal muscles. Evidence also suggests that the intercostals brace the lower ribs to prevent their collapse.

The *transversus thoracis* sweeps upward and outward from the lower part of the sternum to insert into the second through sixth ribs. It is a flat muscle lying along the inside front wall of the chest. Its upper fibers, which run vertically and obliquely, assist in pulling the chest downward.

Along the lower inside back wall of the thorax are the *subcostal muscles*. They originate from the lower ribs near the vertebral attachment and run outward and up to insert into ribs one or more higher. The net effect of their action is to pull the lower ribs, which move like bucket handles, inward and downward.

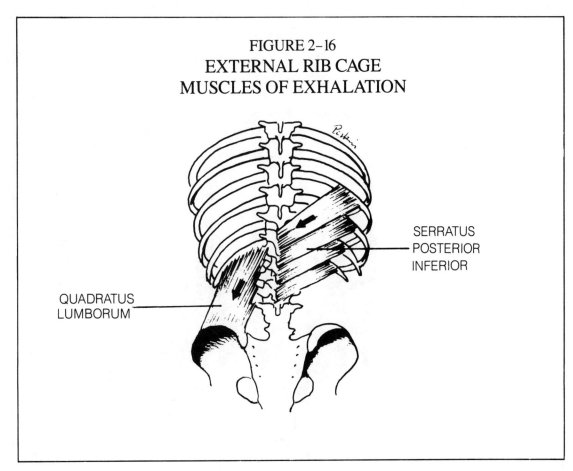

FIGURE 2–16
EXTERNAL RIB CAGE
MUSCLES OF EXHALATION

SERRATUS
POSTERIOR
INFERIOR

QUADRATUS
LUMBORUM

Next, we come to another serrated back muscle, the *serratus posterior inferior* (Fig. 2–16). It slants upward and outward from lower thoracic and upper lumbar vertebrae to insert into the lowest four ribs. It has the size, angle of pull, and leverage to depress the lower ribs with strong force.

Similarly, the *quadratus lumborum* pulls downward strongly on the lowest floating rib from its attachment along the upper border of the hip (coxal bone). It is a flat, vertical muscle in the posterior abdominal wall.

Abdominal Muscles

The muscles of the abdominal wall are generally considered to provide the major active force in exhalation. Because they must be strong enough to move the torso into its various positions, such as rising from lying on your back to a sitting position, they are large, powerful muscles. Their major contribution in breathing is to compress the viscera that push up on the diaphragm to displace 60 to 80 percent of the volume of air exhaled. They have a major role, however, in pulling down on the thorax, so they also function as rib cage depressors as well as abdominal compressors.

The *rectus abdominis* is a large, vertical ribbon of muscle that runs from the front of the pelvis (coxal bone) along the midline of the belly to the sternum and lower ribs (Fig. 2–17). It is limited in how much compression it can apply to the viscera because it can only pull in a straight line between its attachments. Nonetheless, its downward pull on the sternum provides a powerful exhalatory force.

The *external oblique* is a large, flat muscle that arises from the lower eight ribs and sweeps downward and forward. The posterior fibers descend vertically to the crest of the coxal bone, whereas the other fibers slant obliquely forward toward the midline. There they insert into the tendinous sheath, called the *abdominal aponeurosis,* that covers the rectus abdominus. Because the oblique fibers slant from the ribs across the belly, they contribute to exhalation by pulling down on the thorax, while simultaneously compressing the viscera.

Beneath the external obliques are the *internal obliques.* This thinner muscle is the middle layer of abdominal muscles. The course of its fibers is the opposite of external fibers. The internal obliques originate along the upper border of the coxal bone and fan outward and upward, more or less at right angles to the external obliques, to insert at the midline into the abdominal aponeuro-

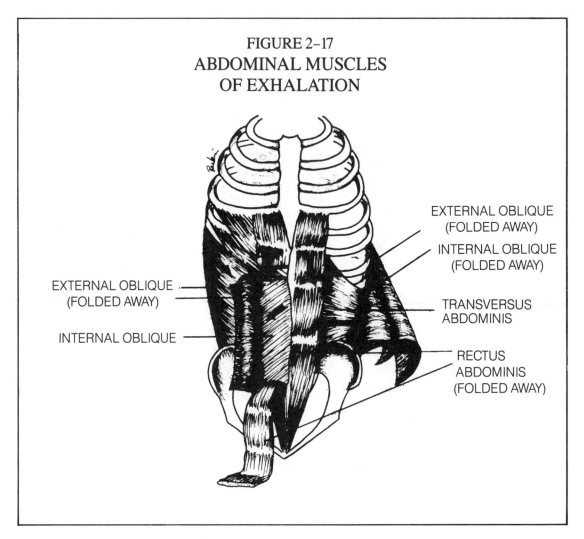

FIGURE 2–17
ABDOMINAL MUSCLES
OF EXHALATION

EXTERNAL OBLIQUE
(FOLDED AWAY)

INTERNAL OBLIQUE
(FOLDED AWAY)

TRANSVERSUS
ABDOMINIS

RECTUS
ABDOMINIS
(FOLDED AWAY)

EXTERNAL OBLIQUE
(FOLDED AWAY)

INTERNAL OBLIQUE

sis and the cartilages of the lower ribs. Just as the external obliques pull down on the thorax and squeeze the viscera, so do the internal obliques.

The deepest layer of abdominal muscles is the *transversus abdominis.* Its horizontal fibers sweep from the vertebrae in the back of the abdomen around to its insertion into the abdominal aponeurosis. It attaches above to the lower border of the ribs (the cartilages of the lower six ribs) and below

to the upper border of the pelvis (coxal bone). Like a corset, it can compress the viscera with more power than any other muscle. This corset action, to which the fibers of the internal and external oblique muscles contribute, is made possible by their attachment to the abdominal aponeurosis. Because all of these abdominal muscles are paired, when contracted they pull in a tug-of-war fashion on opposite sides of the abdominal aponeurosis.

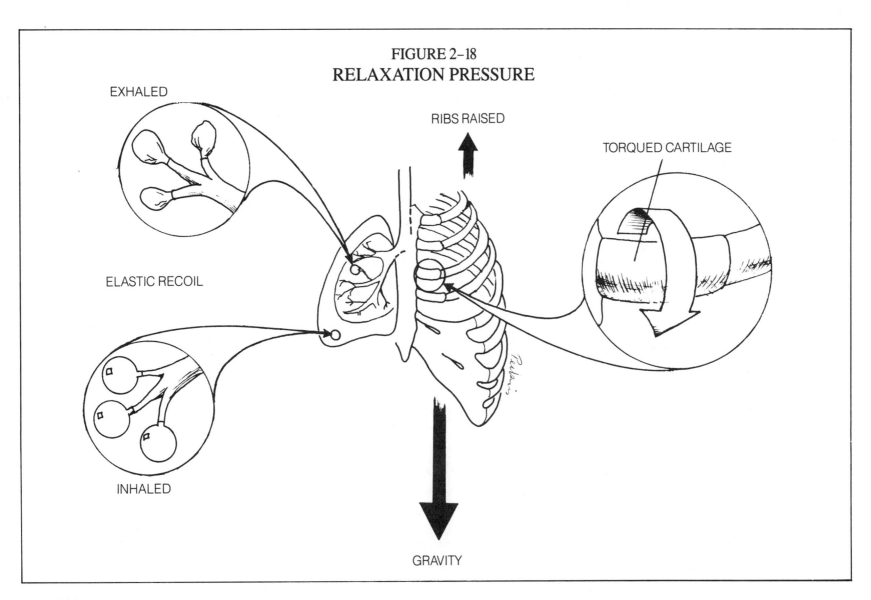

FIGURE 2–18
RELAXATION PRESSURE

EXHALED

RIBS RAISED

TORQUED CARTILAGE

ELASTIC RECOIL

INHALED

GRAVITY

Passive Forces. With inspiration, the rib cage is raised against the force of gravity, the cartilages attaching the ribs to the vertebrae and sternum are twisted, the viscera are compressed, and mainly, the alveolar air sacs in the lungs are inflated against the resistance of surface tension of the fluid covering these alveoli. The greater the inhalation, the greater the resistance to be overcome by contraction of inspiratory muscles. When these muscles relax, the passive forces of *gravity, untorquing* of rib cartilages, and, above all, *elastic recoil* of the lungs and abdomen work to deflate the lungs, pull the rib cage downward, and push the diaphragm upward. During speech, the effect of these forces is to build pressure in the lungs, called *alveolar pressure.* The portion of alveolar pressure that results from passive forces is called *relaxation pressure* (Fig. 2–18).

Respiratory Anatomy

CHAPTER TWO
Self-Study
Respiratory Anatomy

Review Glossary

Chest wall: The rib cage and muscles, diaphragm, abdominal wall, and abdominal viscera

    Rib cage: The 12 ribs and their attachments to the sternum and thoracic vertebrae

    Sternum: Breast bone

    Diaphragm: the partition of muscle and aponeurosis that separates the thoracic and abdominal cavities

Diaphragmatic aponeurosis: The fibrous connective tissue forming the domes of the diaphragm, to which the circle of muscles arching upward from the lower ribs attach

Abdominal wall: The abdominal muscles and ligaments that form the abdominal cavity

Abdominal viscera: The organs of the abdomen

Abdominal muscles (presented from superficial to deep):

    Rectus abdominis muscle: Extending from pubis to sternum and lower ribs, and contained in the fibrous connective tissue of the abdominal aponeurosis, it pulls the rib cage down

    External oblique muscle: Extending upward and outward from pelvis to lower eight ribs, it pulls the rib cage down

    Internal oblique muscle: Extending upward and inward from hip bone to lowest three ribs and abdominal aponeurosis, it pulls lower ribs down and compresses viscera

    Transversus abdominis muscle: Extending horizontally from lower ribs, lumbar vertebrae, and hip bone to abdominal aponeurosis, it compresses viscera

Chest muscles of inhalation (presented from lowest to highest):

    Latissimus dorsi muscle: Large back muscle extending from hip bone, lower vertebrae, and ribs to upper arm; it is of dubious importance to speech

    External intercostal muscles: Extending from the rib above to the rib below, they function as a single sheet of muscle to pull lower ribs upward toward the first rib

    Levatores costarum muscles: A series of small muscles extending from vertebrae to the ribs just below, they pull upward with little leverage or strength

    Serratus anterior muscle: Fanning down and around the chest from the scapula, this large muscle pulls the chest upward

    Pectoralis major muscle: Large upper chest muscle that pulls against humerus to draw sternum and its ribs upward

    Pectoralis minor muscle: Extending from shoulder to upper ribs, it raises the ribs

    Serratus posterior superior muscle: Extending downward and outward from vertebrae to upper ribs in back, it pulls the chest upward

    Subclavius muscle: Extending from clavicle to first rib, this short muscle pulls upward slightly

    Sternocleidomastoid muscle: Extending from skull to sternum and clavicle, it pulls chest upward

    Scalenus (anterior, medial, posterior) muscles: Extending from neck vertebrae to first and second ribs, they pull chest upward

Chest muscles of exhalation (presented from lowest to highest):

    Quadratus lumborum muscle: Extending from hip bone to lowest rib, it anchors this floating rib against pull of diaphragmatic muscles

    Serratus posterior inferior muscle: Extending upward and outward from vertebrae to lowest four ribs, it pulls these ribs downward

    Internal intercostal muscles: Extending from bottom of one rib to top of rib below, they are thought to pull rib cage down and stiffen lowest ribs

    Subcostal muscle: On the inside of the rib cage, they extend upward and outward from lowest to higher ribs to pull them downward and inward

Clavicle: Collar bone

Scapula: Shoulder blade

Thorax: Chest cavity

    Mediastinum: Space containing heart, blood vessels, and esophagus

    Pleural membranes: The air-tight membranes within which the lungs are sealed

    Pulmonary system: The network of tubes from the windpipe to farthest reaches of lungs

        Trachea: Windpipe

        Bronchi: Subdivisions of the trachea to right and left lungs

Lung: The organ, containing three lobes on the right and two on the left, that inflates with inhalation (inspiration) and deflates with exhalation (expiration)

    Alveolar air sacs: Terminal sacs in lungs where inflation and deflation occur

    Alveolar pressure: Pressure in the lungs

Relaxation pressure: The passive exhalation force that increases with extent of inhalation

    Elastic Recoil: Deflation force from inflating air sacs

    Untorquing of ribs: Resistance of rib cartilage to twisting as ribs are raised

    Gravity: Downward pull as ribs are raised

Ingressive sound: Sound produced on inhalation

Egressive sound: Sound produced (normally) on exhalation

Self-Study Drawings

Coloring Instructions: For all further exercises, you may need to supplement definitions in the Glossary by reviewing the more elaborate discussions in the text.

1. Put the appropriate term in all lettered blanks. *A* through *H* in Drawing 2–I.
2. Using a light-colored felt-tip pen, color in the right half of the drawing to which the term for *A* refers in Drawing 2–I.
3. Using different colored pens, color in the left half to which terms for *B* and *C* refer in Drawing 2–I.
4. Using different colored pencils, color in the right half to which terms for *D* through *H* refer in Drawing 2–I.
5. Fill in the terms for *I* through *Z* and *a* through *d* in Drawings 2–II and 2–III.
6. Color the arrow for *I* with a new color, and the three chest arrows with the same color used for *L* through *R* arrow in Drawing 2–II.
7. Color the *a* through *d* arrow with a new color, and the two chest arrows with the same color used for the *S* through *Z* arrow in Drawing 2–III.
8. Fill in the terms for *e* through *g* in Drawing 2–IV.
9. Using different pencils, color the drawing and the terms for *e* through *g* in Drawing 2–IV.
10. Color terms in the Glossary with the same colors used for those terms on the drawings. For terms, such as *A,* color that term and draw a vertical line in the margin as far as the subheadings for the terms extend. This color-coding technique is to help you visualize what terms mean and how they are related.
11. Check your answers in Appendix E.

DRAWING 2–I

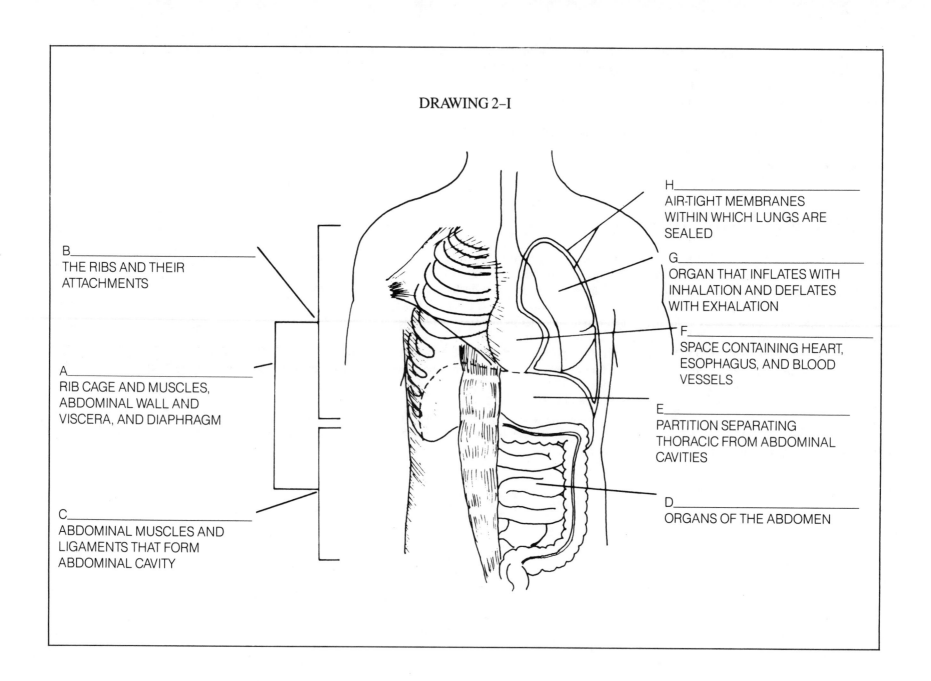

H_____
AIR-TIGHT MEMBRANES
WITHIN WHICH LUNGS ARE
SEALED

G_____
ORGAN THAT INFLATES WITH
INHALATION AND DEFLATES
WITH EXHALATION

F_____
SPACE CONTAINING HEART,
ESOPHAGUS, AND BLOOD
VESSELS

E_____
PARTITION SEPARATING
THORACIC FROM ABDOMINAL
CAVITIES

D_____
ORGANS OF THE ABDOMEN

B_____
THE RIBS AND THEIR
ATTACHMENTS

A_____
RIB CAGE AND MUSCLES,
ABDOMINAL WALL AND
VISCERA, AND DIAPHRAGM

C_____
ABDOMINAL MUSCLES AND
LIGAMENTS THAT FORM
ABDOMINAL CAVITY

Functional Anatomy of Speech, Language, and Hearing

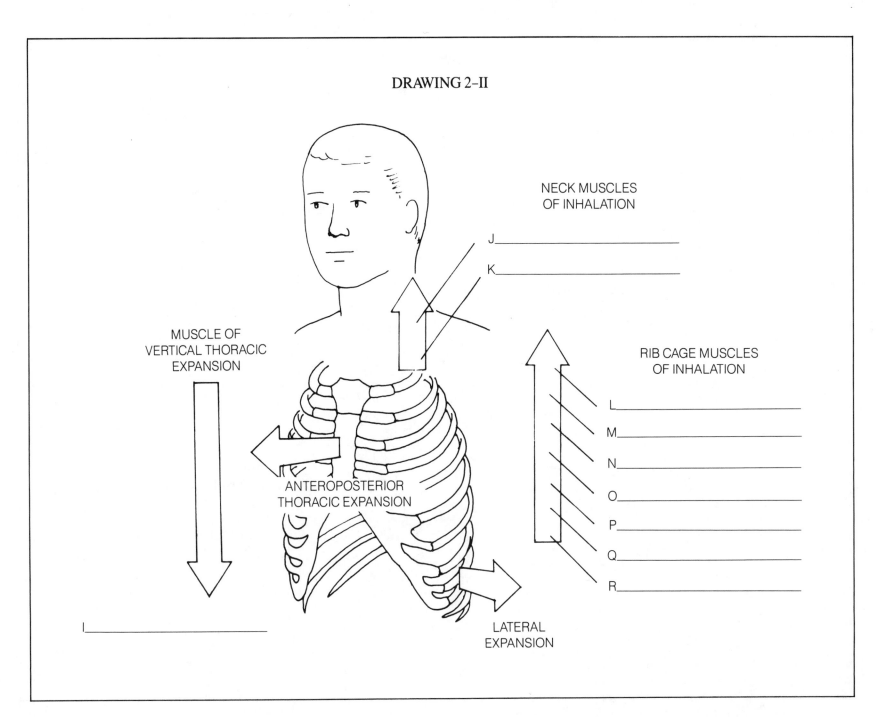

DRAWING 2–II

NECK MUSCLES
OF INHALATION

J_____

K_____

MUSCLE OF
VERTICAL THORACIC
EXPANSION

RIB CAGE MUSCLES
OF INHALATION

L_____

M_____

N_____

O_____

P_____

Q_____

R_____

ANTEROPOSTERIOR
THORACIC EXPANSION

LATERAL
EXPANSION

I_____

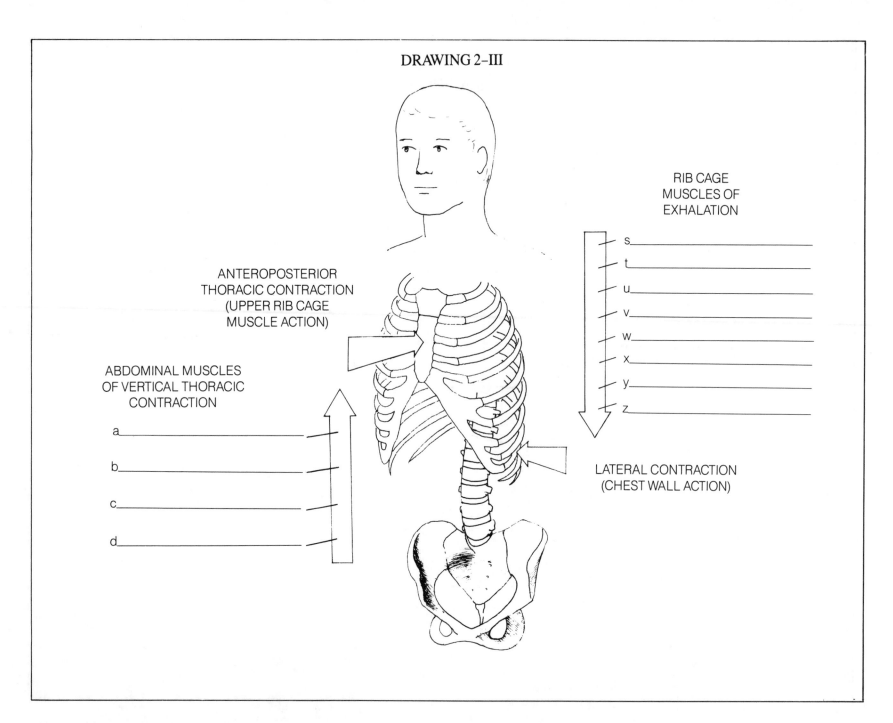

DRAWING 2–III

RIB CAGE
MUSCLES OF
EXHALATION

s_____
t_____
u_____
v_____
w_____
x_____
y_____
z_____

ANTEROPOSTERIOR
THORACIC CONTRACTION
(UPPER RIB CAGE
MUSCLE ACTION)

ABDOMINAL MUSCLES
OF VERTICAL THORACIC
CONTRACTION

a_____
b_____
c_____
d_____

LATERAL CONTRACTION
(CHEST WALL ACTION)

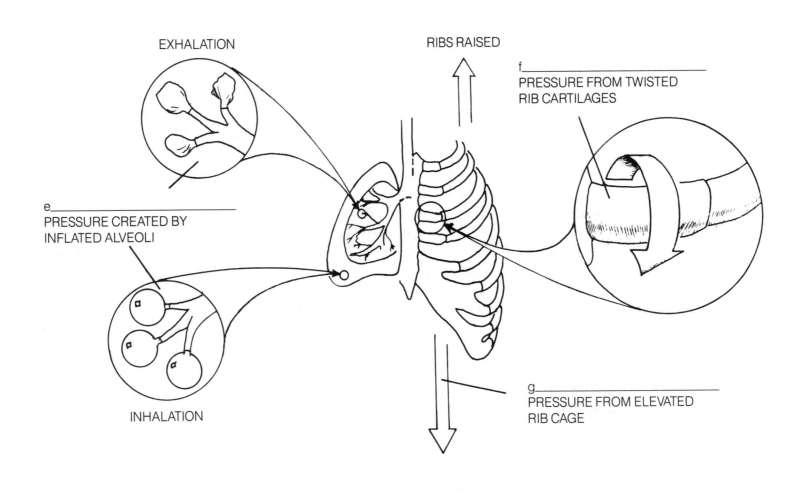

DRAWING 2–IV

ELEMENTS OF RELAXATION PRESSURE

EXHALATION

RIBS RAISED

f_____
PRESSURE FROM TWISTED
RIB CARTILAGES

e_____
PRESSURE CREATED BY
INFLATED ALVEOLI

INHALATION

g_____
PRESSURE FROM ELEVATED
RIB CAGE

Self-Study Test of Terminology

Self-Study Instructions: These questions can be used to help you assess how much you have retained from studying the Review Glossary. Answers are given in Appendix E.

(1) _____ The 12 ribs and their attachments to the sternum and thoracic vertebrae

(2) _____ The abdominal muscles and ligaments that form the abdominal cavity

(3) _____ Extending from pubis to sternum, and contained in the fibrous connective tissue of the abdominal aponeurosis, it pulls the rib cage down

(4) _____ Extending upward and inward from hip bone to lowest three ribs and abdominal aponeurosis, it pulls lower ribs down and compresses viscera

(5) _____ Extending from hip bone to lowest rib, it anchors this floating rib against pull of diaphragmatic muscles

(6) _____ Large back muscle extending from hip bone, lower vertebrae, and ribs to upper arm, it is of dubious importance to speech

(7) _____ Extending from rib below to rib above, they are thought to pull rib cage down and stiffen lowest rib

(8) _____ The rib cage and muscles, diaphragm, abdominal wall, the abdominal viscera

(9) _____ The partition of muscle and aponeurosis that separates the thoracic and abdominal cavities

(10) _____ The organs of the abdomen

(11) _____ Extending upward and outward from pelvis to lower eight ribs, it pulls the rib cage down

(12) _____ Resistance of rib cartilage to twisting as ribs are raised

(13) _____ Extending horizontally from lower ribs, lumbar vertebrae, and hip bone to abdominal aponeurosis, it compresses viscera

(14) _____ Extending from the rib above to the rib below, they function as a single sheet of muscle to pull lower ribs upward toward the first rib

(15) _____ Extending upward and outward from vertebrae to lowest four ribs, it pulls those ribs downward

(16) _____ On the inside of the rib cage, they extend upward and outward from lowest to higher ribs to pull them downward and inward

(17) _____ Fanning down and around the chest from the sternum, this large muscle pulls the chest upward

(18) _____ Extending from shoulder to upper ribs, it raises the ribs

(19) _____ Extending from skull to sternum and clavicle, it pulls chest upward

(20) _____ Collar bone

(21) _____ Chest cavity

(22) _____ Subdivisions of the trachea to right and left lungs

(23) _____ Outermost tips of lungs where inflation and deflation occur

(24) _____ The passive exhalation force that increases with extent of inhalation

(25) _____ The network of tubes from the windpipe to farthest reaches of lungs

(26) _____ Downward pull as ribs are raised

(27) _____ Fanning out from upper arms to sternum, it draws sternum upward

(28) _____ Sweeping upward and outward inside the chest from sternum to upper ribs, it pulls chest downward

(29) _____ Extending from clavicle to first rib, this short muscle pulls upward slightly

(30) _____ Extending from first thoracic vertebra to first rib, they pull chest upward

(31) _____ Breast bone

(32) _____ The organ, containing three lobes on the right and two on the left, that inflates with inhalation and deflates with exhalation

(33) _____ Space containing heart, blood vessels, and esophagus

(34) _____ Shoulder blade

(35) _____ Windpipe

(36) _____ Pressure in the lungs

(37) _____ The air-tight membranes within which the lungs are sealed

(38) _____ Deflation force from inflating air sacs

(39) _____ A series of small muscles extending from vertebrae to ribs just below, they pull upward with little leverage or strength

(40) _____ Extending downward and outward from vertebrae to upper ribs in back, it pulls the chest upward

(41) _____ The fibrous connective tissue, forming the domes of the diaphragm, to which the circle of muscles arching upward from the lower ribs attach

Speech Functions of Respiratory Muscles

Self-Study Instructions: This test can be used to help you assess how well you understand the speech functions of respiratory muscles. Terms to be filled in are from the Review Glossary. Answers are given in Appendix E.

Speech Functions	*Muscles*
Inhalation (thoracic expansion)	Neck
Pulls sternum upward and outward	(1) _____
Pulls first ribs upward and outward	(2) _____
	Chest (front)
Pulls laterally to assist in drawing sternum and its ribs upward	(3) _____
Pulls upward and laterally to raise second and fifth ribs	(4) _____
Raises upper eight ribs	(5) _____
	Chest (back)
Pulls all 12 ribs upward	(6) _____
Pulls second through fifth ribs upward	(7) _____

Pulls all lower ribs toward first rib

Pulls downward to expand thorax vertically

Exhalation (generates pressure)

Pulls downward on lower four ribs

Pulls downward on lowest floating rib

Pulls downward and inward on lower ribs

Pulls downward on upper ribs

Pulls ribs down and stiffens lowest ribs

Pulls sternum downward

Pulls lower eight ribs downward

Pulls lowest three ribs downward and compresses
viscera

Compresses viscera

Chest (front and back)

(8) _____

(9) _____

Chest (back)

(10) _____

(11) _____

Chest (inside back)

(12) _____

Chest (inside front)

(13) _____

Chest (inside front and back)

(14) _____

Abdominal

(15) _____

(16) _____

(17) _____

(18) _____

CHAPTER THREE
Respiratory Physiology

Breathing to stay alive is, of course, the fundamental purpose of respiration. The fact that in our evolution we have commandeered this equipment for speech purposes (hence the idea that speech is an *overlaid function*) does not mean that the original biological purpose has been abandoned. If you doubt this, try talking after running up several flights of stairs. Although using the same mechanism, the respiratory patterns are very different when breathing for life and breathing for speech — so much so, in fact, that no one uses the pattern for speech except when speaking. Understanding respiration for speech is easier if you understand how we breathe for life, so that is where we will begin.

BREATHING DURING THE LIFE SPAN

For most of us, the first breath occurred as our heads were born. The initial expiration came about as pressure from the birth canal squeezed the thorax. This compression accomplished two important goals. First, it expelled amniotic fluid from the lungs. Second, it set the stage for the first inspiration, which resulted largely from the elastic recoil of the compressed thorax. During the next few minutes, chemical changes in the blood influenced the respiratory center in the brain, which brought

about a regular respiratory pattern. Actually, full efficiency of respiration is not achieved for several days or weeks because it takes this long for all of the alveoli to be expanded.

A number of changes occur in respiratory anatomy and physiology from infancy to adulthood (fetal airway development is summarized in Appendix C), but it is sufficient for our purposes to point out only three of these for now. The first is an increase in the capacity of the lungs, which can be measured as *vital capacity* (the volume of air inspired after a maximal expiration). As Figure 3–1 shows, vital capacity increases fairly regularly with age so that a young adult has 3.5 to 5 times the lung volume of a 5 year old child. Vital capac-

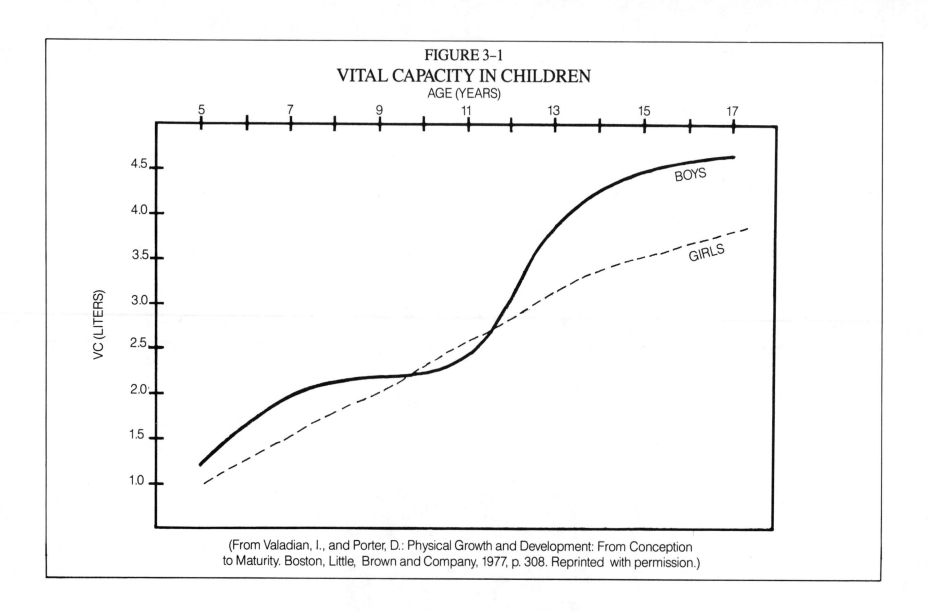

FIGURE 3-1
VITAL CAPACITY IN CHILDREN
AGE (YEARS)

(From Valadian, I., and Porter, D.: Physical Growth and Development: From Conception to Maturity. Boston, Little, Brown and Company, 1977, p. 308. Reprinted with permission.)

ity depends largely on the volume of lung tissue, which can be estimated from the circumference of the chest. An individual's peak vital capacity usually is reached in the late teens or early twenties. Thereafter, it decreases, along with a reduction of diaphragmatic action. With advanced age, the lungs and bronchi sink to a lower position in the thoracic cavity. *Residual volume* (the volume of air that remains after a maximal expiration) increases with age, which means that a smaller volume of total air is available for the exchange of oxygen and carbon dioxide. However, these changes, unpleasant as they may sound, usually do not impair the respiratory function of older persons for most activities.

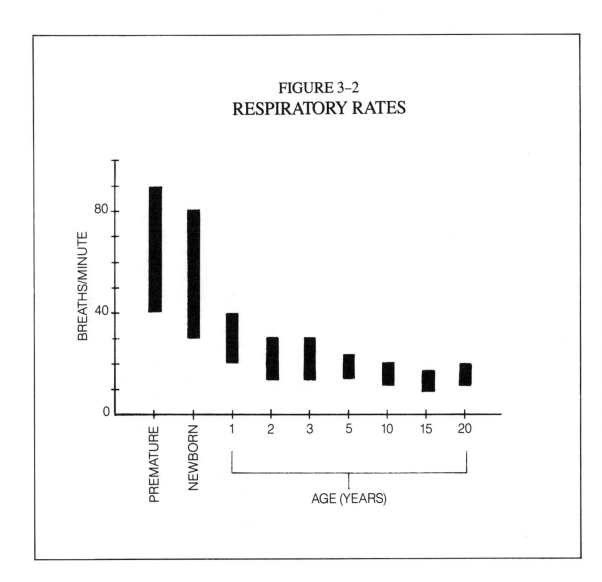

FIGURE 3–2
RESPIRATORY RATES

Changes also occur in breathing rates as a function of age. Figure 3–2 illustrates that premature and newborn infants have high rates, between 30 to 90 breaths/minute, whereas a lower and fairly stable rate of about 10 to 22 breaths/minute is established during late childhood and early adulthood. The rate of respiration is determined by lung capacity and the efficiency of respiratory exchange, both of which are greater in the older child or adult than in the infant. Irregularity in breathing rate is not uncommon in the infant.

A final developmental change is one of increased size of the respiratory structures, including the larynx and trachea, as well as the lungs themselves. A newborn has a trachea that is one third as long as the adult's and one fourth the diameter. Also, the cartilaginous rings of the trachea are soft in the infant, and the airway is overlaid by less tissue than in the adult. The consequences of these differences should be noted. First, tracheal and bronchial sounds are louder in children than in adults. Second, children are bothered more than adults by tracheal inflammation, which constricts further an already narrow passage. Infants and adults breathe differently in other ways as well, and we will return to this topic in a later chapter.

You probably have heard of babies who "turned blue" because of strenuous crying, breathing difficulties, or just holding their breaths. Technically, this condition is known as *cyanosis*. The blue (or gray) color of the skin occurs when the oxygen level in the arteries falls below a certain level.

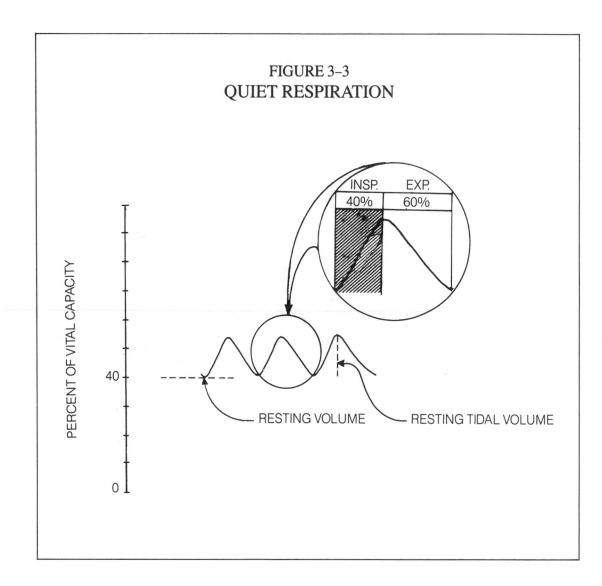

FIGURE 3–3
QUIET RESPIRATION

INSP. 40% EXP. 60%

PERCENT OF VITAL CAPACITY

40

0

RESTING VOLUME   RESTING TIDAL VOLUME

BREATHING FOR LIFE

You have doubtless observed that you breathe differently when sitting quietly reading than after playing several sets of tennis. The former is *quiet respiration*; the latter, *forced respiration*.

Quiet Respiration

Breathing while resting is an exercise in economy of effort. It reflects minimum departure from the resting volume a person reaches after a quiet breath. At this volume, a relaxed balance exists between the tendency of the thorax to expand and of the lungs to collapse. To observe where this balance occurs, take a deep breath, then relax and note how far the chest contracts. Next, exhale maximally, then relax and note how far the chest expands. This balance point will be at about 35 to 40 percent of your vital capacity (the total amount of air available for use). By and large, *quiet inspiration* reflects the volume of air that can be inhaled from a resting level with contraction of the diaphragm and external intercostal muscles. *Quiet expiration*, on the other hand, is a passive process resulting from elastic recoil of lungs and abdomen. When passive expiratory forces reach the resting level, the respiratory cycle is ready to be repeated. The durations of quiet inspiration and expiration are not very different, inspiration taking 40 percent of the cycle and expiration 60 percent. The volume of air moved is called *resting tidal volume* (Fig. 3–3).

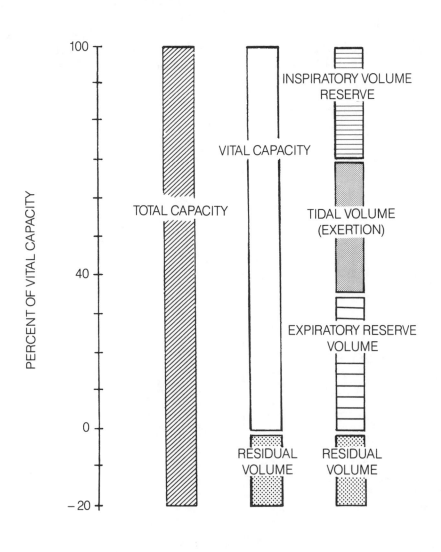

FIGURE 3–4
RESPIRATORY VOLUMES

PERCENT OF VITAL CAPACITY

100

40

0

−20

TOTAL CAPACITY

VITAL CAPACITY

INSPIRATORY VOLUME RESERVE

TIDAL VOLUME (EXERTION)

EXPIRATORY RESERVE VOLUME

RESIDUAL VOLUME

RESIDUAL VOLUME

Forced Respiration

When energy requirements demand more air exchange in the lungs than can be managed by quiet respiration, muscular support is recruited for both inspiration and expiration. Forced inspiration is accomplished with accessory muscles of inhalation assisting the diaphragm and external intercostals. Forced expiration is accomplished with active forces of abdominal and thoracic exhalatory muscles that supplement the passive forces of expiration. Any expiration that goes beyond the resting level (the level at which passive forces are depleted) will involve forced expiration. Of course, the deeper a person breathes, the more muscles will be recruited for forced inspiration and expiration. The time spent inhaling and exhaling is about the same as it is in quiet breathing.

Before we turn to speech respiration, we need to clarify the terms used to describe lung capacities and lung volumes. The most useful measure of overall functional lung capacity is *vital capacity* (Fig. 3–4). This is the maximum usable volume of air that can be inhaled and exhaled. Rarely does a person breathe so deeply as to reach the limits of

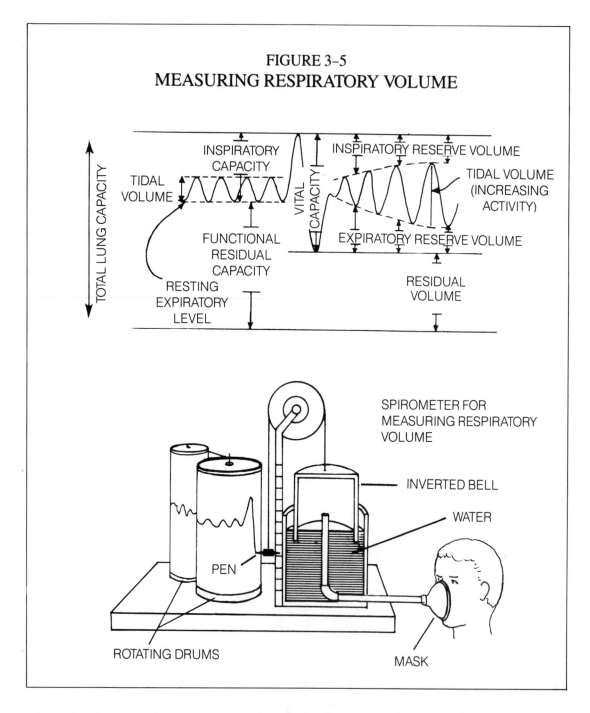

FIGURE 3–5
MEASURING RESPIRATORY VOLUME

vital capacity. To the extent that this limit is not reached when inhaling, there is *inspiratory reserve*. If the limit of vital capacity is not reached when exhaling, the volume remaining is *expiratory reserve*. The volume of air actually used, regardless of how deep the breath, is *tidal volume*. After maximum expiration, however, almost one fourth of total lung capacity will remain as *residual volume* (Fig. 3–5). This is the air in the pulmonary tubing that cannot be forced out without opening the chest and deflating the lungs completely.

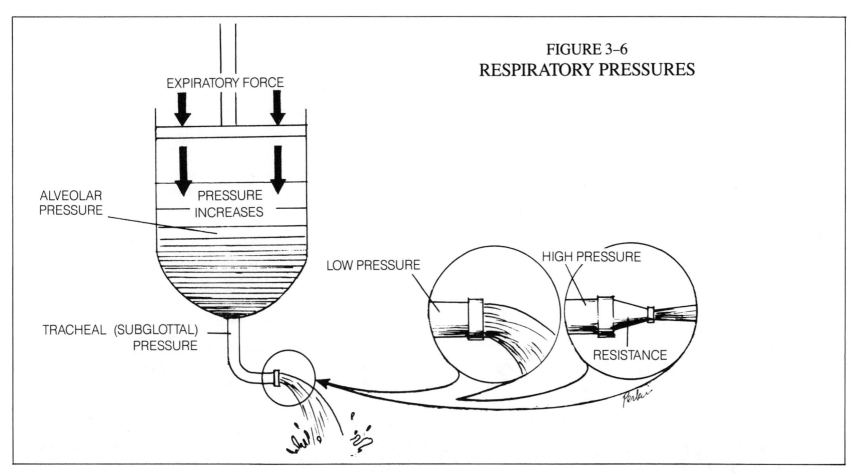

FIGURE 3–6
RESPIRATORY PRESSURES

EXPIRATORY FORCE

PRESSURE INCREASES

ALVEOLAR PRESSURE

TRACHEAL (SUBGLOTTAL) PRESSURE

LOW PRESSURE

HIGH PRESSURE

RESISTANCE

BREATHING FOR SPEECH

The same respiratory equipment and measures of air volume and lung capacity apply when breathing for speech as when breathing for life. The difference is in how and why they are used. For life, the objective is to move oxygen-laden air into and carbon dioxide out of the lungs. Any resistance to the air stream interferes with this purpose, so free air flow is to be facilitated when breathing to live.

For speech, the purpose of respiration is quite different. What is needed is air under pressure, which can force the vocal folds to vibrate or can expel a burst of air in a sound like "p." To achieve pressure requires that air flow be resisted.

Pressure Requirements

Loudness

If you produce a soft tone followed by a loud one, you can observe the increased pressure needed to increase loudness. For speech, then, we need to resist the flow of air just enough to produce the desired sounds at the desired loudness.

You can achieve the necessary pressure for speech two ways. One is by adjusting the expiratory force of the respiratory pump. The other way is by adjusting airway resistance (this will be the subject of the next chapter). Both are essential if pressure is to be generated. What they affect is the pressure in the air reservoir, the lungs. This is *alveolar pressure*. The resulting pressure that builds up in the trachea below the vocal folds is usually called *subglottal pressure*. It is variations in airway resistance to expiratory forces that determine pressure (Fig. 3–6).

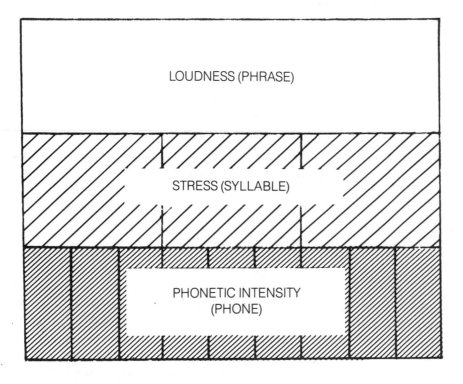

FIGURE 3–7
PRESSURE REQUIREMENTS AND DURATIONS

LOUDNESS (PHRASE)

STRESS (SYLLABLE)

PHONETIC INTENSITY
(PHONE)

Stress and Articulation

If speech consisted of a sustained monotone, all that the respiratory pump would need to generate would be a steady alveolar pressure sufficient to maintain the loudness of the phrases. But monotony, which tends toward constant loudness and equal stress on all syllables, is the hobgoblin of expressiveness. For speech to sound interesting, stress must vary from syllable to syllable. Variations in *stress* are made with adjustments in pitch, loudness, and duration of the syllable. Loudness of the syllable, particularly, varies with changes in alveolar pressure, probably produced by small contractions of the respiratory muscles.

In addition to variation in stress, continuous speech also varies in intensity from sound to sound. Vowels are generally more intense than consonants, and some consonants, such as "s," are more intense than others, such as "f." These variations in intensity from sound to sound are controlled, to some degree, by changes in airway resistance that alter *intraoral pressure*, but probably not alveolar pressure. If you say "too," for instance, pressure rises when you block the air stream for "t" and it falls when the tongue is released from the roof of the mouth.

Thus, three aspects of speech require control of pressure (Fig. 3–7). First, the loudness level of the phrase is controlled by the interaction of all passive and active expiratory forces. Second, more or less superimposed on this overall level are variations in stress from syllable to syllable. These result from small expiratory contractions or relaxations of expiratory muscles which produce momentary changes in alveolar and subglottal pressures. Third, variations in intensity from sound to sound occur within the syllable. These result mainly from instant-to-instant changes in airway resistance that cause momentary fluctuations in intraoral pressure.

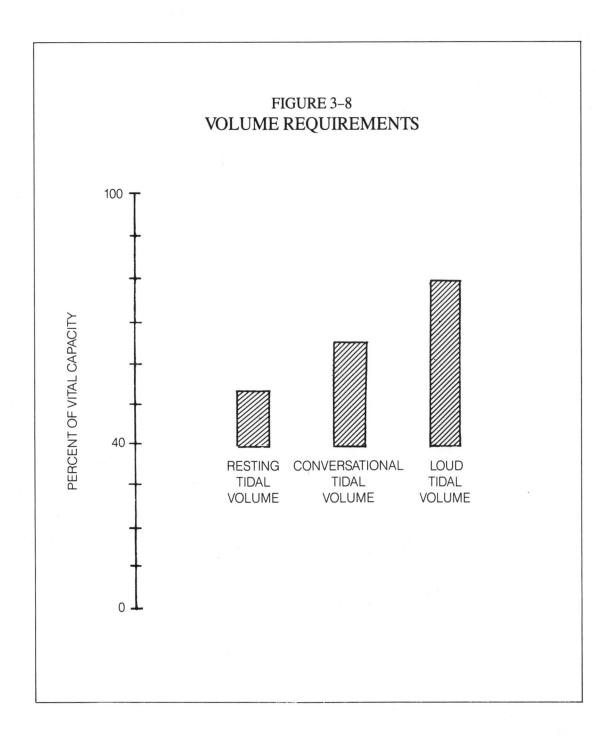

FIGURE 3–8
VOLUME REQUIREMENTS

PERCENT OF VITAL CAPACITY

100

40

0

RESTING
TIDAL
VOLUME

CONVERSATIONAL
TIDAL
VOLUME

LOUD
TIDAL
VOLUME

Volume Requirements

Beyond requiring reasonably steady alveolar pressure, speech breathing differs from quiet breathing in several other ways. For one thing, it requires greater volumes of air. Quiet breathing uses 10 to 15 percent of vital capacity, whereas conversational speech uses around 25 percent and loud speech around 40 percent. These differences in volume are achieved mainly by the amount of air inhaled above resting volume (recall that resting volume is at about the 40 percent level of vital capacity) (Fig. 3–8). Thus, for quiet breathing people inhale up to 55 percent of vital capacity and exhale until relaxed at the 40 percent level. For conversation, deeper inhalation, in the vicinity of 60 to 65 percent of vital capacity, is used. For loud speech, inhalation rises to about the 80 percent level.

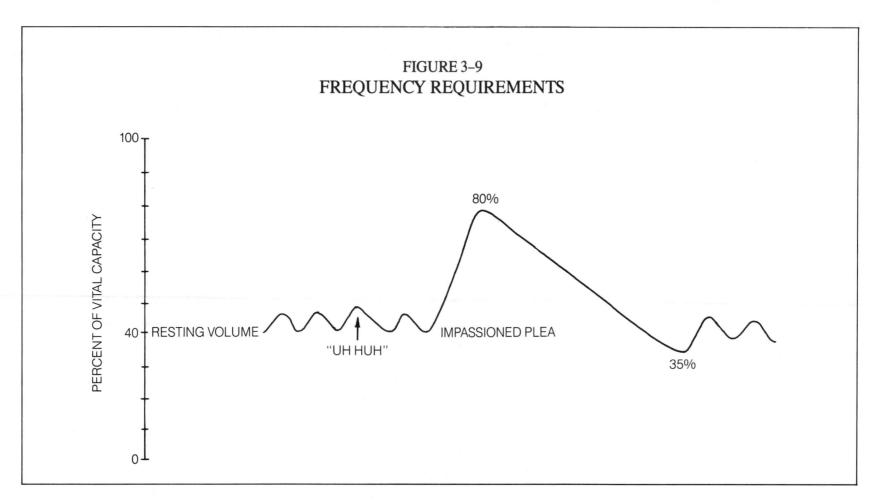

FIGURE 3-9
FREQUENCY REQUIREMENTS

Frequency Requirements

Another difference is in the frequency with which we breathe. Most people inhale and exhale 10 to 20 times per minute when breathing quietly. This rate is determined by our need for oxygen. For speech, the length of a breath depends on how much we choose to say in a phrase. To grunt approval, "uh-huh," will not take much longer than quiet breathing, but give any of us a chance to make a crushing statement in a loud argument and we will likely run out of air before we let go of our point. To sustain such a long, loud phrase will require a deep inspiration of air, which we will continue to use past the resting volume level down to forced expiratory levels, usually not lower than 35 percent of vital capacity (Fig. 3-9). The duration of most of what we have to say falls between these extremes.

Functional Anatomy of Speech, Language, and Hearing

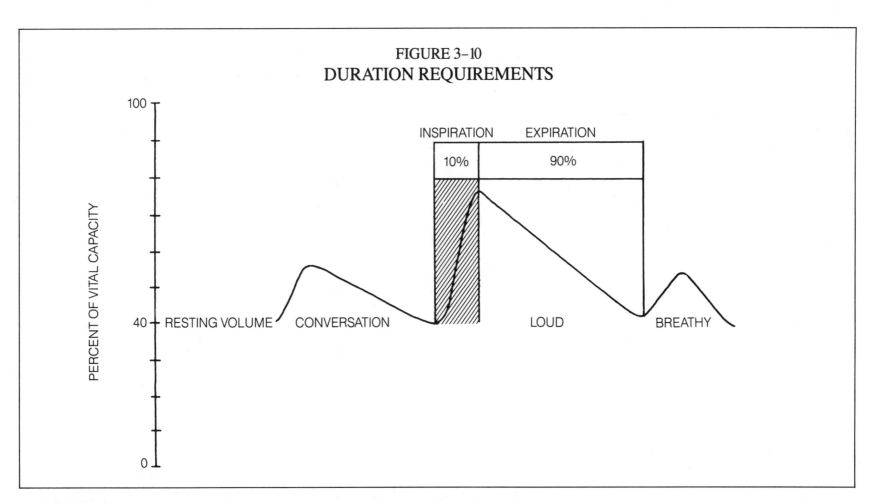

FIGURE 3–10
DURATION REQUIREMENTS

Duration Requirements

Still another difference between breathing for life and breathing for speech is in how quickly we inhale. Whether resting or after heavy exercise, we spend almost as much time inhaling as exhaling. You can observe how this reflexive pattern changes sharply, though, if you prepare to produce sound, whether to whisper, argue, sing, or converse. Without thinking, you will take a quick breath and spend a longer time producing sound on exhalation. About 10 percent of the respiratory cycle will be spent inhaling and 90 percent exhaling (Fig. 3–10). Duration of expiration will depend on how breathy the tone is, and to some extent on how loud it is. For example, you will have to use shorter phrases if you whisper (which offers relatively low resistance to airflow) than if you use full voice. The fact that quick inspiration and long expiration is a very unnatural way to breathe to stay alive points to the evolutionary adaptation of respiration that has been made in humans to accommodate speech.

RESPIRATORY MECHANICS OF SPEECH

We have studied how the respiratory pump functions for life. What remains is to understand how these functions are adapted to meet the special requirements of speech. The answer, basically, lies in understanding how the pressure requirements of speech are met without compromising fundamental life-sustaining requirements. This answer involves control of two components of speech expiration: (1) effects of changes in lung volume during the phrase and (2) active expiratory forces needed to maintain required alveolar pressure for the phrase.

Relaxation Pressure and Lung Volume

Recall that the deeper the inspiration, the greater the resistance of elastic lung tissue and air sacs against greater stretching and inflation. Their elastic recoil from inspiration, supplemented by gravity and untorquing of rib cartilages when the chest is raised, results in relaxation pressure, the passive expiratory force.

Remember, too, that the louder and longer the phrase to be spoken, the greater the volume of air that will be required. As volume increases, so does depth of inspiration. And, as inspiration increases, passive resistance of elastic recoil force mounts, which results in greater relaxation pressure. In fact, elastic recoil forces are so strong (above 60 percent vital capacity) that they exceed the alveolar pressure needed for speech (Fig. 3–11).

You can see for yourself what happens when relaxation pressure exceeds the necessary alveolar pressure by performing a simple experiment. Imagine that you are sitting next to your special friend. Now inhale deeply and prepare to say softly, "You excite me." As soon as you have said it as you normally would (whether or not you would

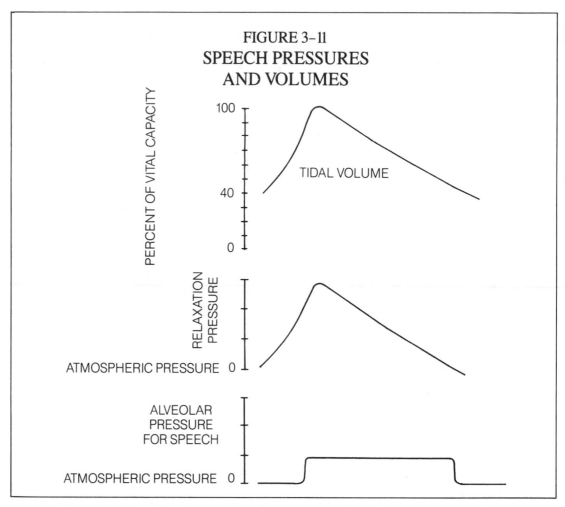

FIGURE 3–11
SPEECH PRESSURES
AND VOLUMES

normally make such a statement is another matter), immediately hold your breath. Then relax. You will note that when you relaxed, a quick expiration occurred until your resting volume level was reached (this is the 35 to 40 percent of vital capacity level). Thus, even after speaking, some relaxation pressure remained. Now repeat the experiment, taking another deep breath, but this time hold your breath before you start to speak instead of afterward. Relax and use no muscular effort to control expiration while speaking what presumably would be a soft seductive message. Relaxation pressure will do all of the expiratory work for you, so much of it in fact that you will probably blow your friend's ear off until about half way through "excite" and the rest will hardly be heard. If you rely only on relaxation pressure for loudness, you will often start with too much and end with too little.

Maintaining Alveolar Pressure for Speech

We are now ready to confront one of the many paradoxes about speech. Obviously, we inhale with inspiratory and exhale with expiratory muscles. Speech, of course, occurs on exhalation, so common sense tells us that we will use exhalatory muscles to speak. The paradox is that at the beginning of speech both inspiratory and expiratory muscles are often used. Conversely, expiratory muscles are also used to some extent during inhalation.

If you have not already detected the answer to this puzzlement, it is not far to find. Your experiment demonstrated part of it. When you began to speak, relaxation pressure was too high for the alveolar pressure needed for the loudness of your phrase. To offset excessive relaxation pressure, active inhalatory muscular contraction continued to lift the rib cage until relaxation pressure was reduced to about the necessary alveolar pressure level (Fig. 3–12). This reduction in relaxation pressure occurred as air was expended during speech. As air flow continued, lung volume and elastic recoil decreased, as did the need to counteract relaxation pressure with inspiratory muscles. Thus, the muscular force needed to check relaxation pressure varied from instant to instant during speech. If you had inhaled less than 60 percent of vital capacity, relaxation pressure would not have exceeded the required alveolar pressure for speech, so active checking of passive exhalatory force would not have been required. This points up the general principle of speech breathing: For any given alveolar pressure needed for speech, a different balance of active and passive muscular forces will be required to maintain that pressure at each lung-volume level.

This explains why active force is required to offset passive relaxation pressure at the beginning of an utterance. But why should inhalatory and exhalatory muscles be used simultaneously during

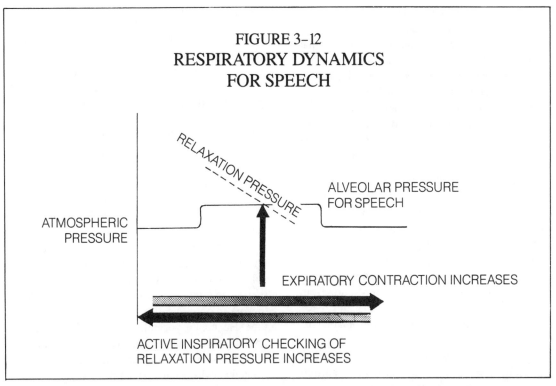

FIGURE 3–12
RESPIRATORY DYNAMICS
FOR SPEECH

RELAXATION PRESSURE

ATMOSPHERIC PRESSURE

ALVEOLAR PRESSURE FOR SPEECH

EXPIRATORY CONTRACTION INCREASES

ACTIVE INSPIRATORY CHECKING OF RELAXATION PRESSURE INCREASES

speech inhalation as well as exhalation? You can see for yourself how this arrangement works by stiffening your abdominal muscles as if you were going to shout, but, instead, keep them tense and speak softly. What you will have done is to escalate the size of the inspiratory force required to offset relaxation pressure by opposing it with active exhalatory muscular force. The effect is to give you more precise control over the alveolar pressure you need for speech. Professional speakers and singers, who pay considerable attention to breathing, are especially likely to use a respiratory pattern such as this.

Another variation which most of us use in a long, loud statement, is to continue speaking after relaxation pressure falls below the desired alveolar pressure level. To do this requires progressive recruitment of more and more expiratory muscles

until your air supply is exhausted as you squeeze out the last gasp. At this point, when you relax your active exhalation, the chest wall and lungs will rebound to the relaxed position of about 35 to 40 percent of vital capacity (VC), thereby demonstrating that negative relaxation pressure builds rapidly as exhalation drops below 35 percent VC just as positive passive force builds rapidly as inhalation exceeds 60 percent VC.

The special requirement of speech that we have considered so far is how to maintain loudness. The manner in which the respiratory machinery meets this requirement, while meeting the oxygen needs of life, determines how most of the other speech requirements are met:

- The volume of air inhaled will be affected by length of the phrase, loudness and breathiness of the tone, and the need for oxygen.

- The frequency of inspiration, a flexible requirement, is a determinant of the volume that must be inhaled. The more frequent the breaths, the smaller the volume needed per breath, but the shorter the phrases will be.
- The other flexible requirement is duration of the phrase. It is the other side of the coin from frequency of inhalation. The longer the phrase must be, the farther apart the breaths must be.

The remaining requirements of stress and articulation involve what can be thought of as refined adjustments superimposed on the respiratory mechanics of loudness control. As discussed earlier, stress of a syllable appears to be accomplished with a little pulse of alveolar pressure applied by a brief contraction of expiratory muscles and shut off, presumably, by opposition from the inspiratory muscles. These changes in stress tend to occur from syllable to syllable at a rate of about six per second.

Articulation requirements, on the other hand, are met by how much intraoral pressure is permitted to squirt air from the reservoir (the lungs), where it is held under alveolar pressure. You can visualize this process with a garden hose. Turn the water on to slightly more than a trickle, plug the end of the hose with your thumb until you can feel pressure, then release it. Water will squirt out and quickly return to a trickle as the pressure at the end of the hose falls. This pressure change, corresponding to intraoral pressure fluctuations in the mouth, would have virtually no effect on pressure in the city reservoir (alveolar pressure in the lungs). Articulatory changes occur at a rate in the vicinity of 14 per second. Thus, the driving power for speech from moment to moment is coordinated to meet the slow-changing pressure requirements for loudness, the moderately fast pressure changes for stress, and the high-speed changes for articulation.

Summary and Discussion

We can summarize the current understanding of speech breathing as follows. An utterance is initiated at about 60 percent vital capacity (VC). The speaker talks on the exhaled air until a level of about 35 to 40 percent VC is reached. A speaker may exhale more air for an utterance — that is, to a volume less than 35 to 40 percent VC — but this does not seem to be a very efficient way of breathing for speech. One reason for the efficiency of the 60 percent to 35 percent range for speech breathing is that within this range the *active forces* provided by the contraction of the respiratory muscles and the *passive forces* provided by elastic recoil of the respiratory structures work together in the same direction. In contrast, if an utterance uses lung volumes greater than 60 percent VC or less than 30 percent VC, the active and passive forces will have to work in opposing directions at least some of the time. Hence, the normal range of volumes used to produce speech satisfies the requirements of biological efficiency, or the least muscular force needed to exhale a given volume of air.

During the exhalation phase on which speech is produced, expiratory muscle activity occurs in both the thorax and abdomen. For the inspiratory refilling between utterances, a degree of expiratory muscular activity persists in both thorax and abdomen, but a rapid and forceful contraction of the diaphragm makes for a net inspiratory effect. This pattern of events was described only recently and is at odds with the earlier understanding that the abdominal muscles rarely participate in breathing for conversational speech.

There is another advantage to simultaneous activity in the inspiratory and expiratory muscles. The advantage comes when a speaker needs to stress a syllable in an utterance. For example, imagine that a speaker wants to say the sentence, "The blue whale is not only a large mammal, it is *the* largest." When the speaker comes to the word *the*, he or she needs to say this word with special emphasis or stress. Usually, a stressed syllable is produced with an increase in subglottal pressure, which is the pressure developed at the highest point in the respiratory system — the trachea just below the larynx. This increase in pressure is generated by a pulsatile increase in the activity of the respiratory muscles. Such a pulsatile increase is more easily produced when required if both the inspiratory and expiratory muscles are active, for the brief increase in activity is then just a matter of adjusting the relative amounts of inspiratory and expiratory activity, at any level of lung volume.

We can think of the respiratory "problem" of speech as having two "solutions." The first, a *volume solution*, uses a continuous change in muscular effort to maintain a constant pressure even as the passive forces change in magnitude as lung volume changes. That is, the active forces are adjusted to compensate for changing passive forces, and thus provide for a constant air pressure throughout the utterance. The second solution is the *pulsatile solution*, in which pulse-like increases in respiratory muscle activity meet the need for brief pressure increases, such as those that occur for stressed syllables. The volume solution and pulsatile solution give us the flexibility and efficiency of our breathing apparatus.

As an additional step in understanding the mechanics of the respiratory system, consider the case of a person who has a completely paralyzed respiratory system as the result of a spinal cord injury. Some persons with such a paralysis live on a rotating bed which moves in the fashion of a teeter-totter. When the foot of the bed is low, the head is high, and vice versa. The rotating bed makes respiration possible for the paralyzed person in the following way. When the person's head is higher than the feet, gravity pulls downward on the abdominal contents and on the diaphragm, which separates the thoracic and abdominal cavities. The downward pull on the diaphragm draws air into the lungs as the alveolar pressure is reduced relative to the atmospheric pressure. Then the foot of the bed elevates relative to the head, forcing the abdominal contents and diaphragm in the opposite direction to push air out of the lungs. The occupant of the bed can speak on the expired air only during this phase, when the feet are higher than the head.

Ventilatory capacity is a function of age, sex, and body size, but it also is determined by such factors as exercise and voice training. Research has shown that physical exercise can substantially moderate the reduction of vital capacity that accompanies the aging process in most individuals. Strenuous exercise helps to develop and maintain ventilatory capacity. Studies of trained singers have shown that even when their total lung capacity is equal to that of nonsingers, there are differences in the subdivisions of this capacity. The trained singers had larger values for vital capacity and lower values for residual capacity. These differences work hand in hand. If the trained singer can reduce the residual volume (the amount of air that remains in the lungs following a maximal exhalation) this will naturally lead to increased values of vital capacity — even though the total lung capacity is unchanged.

CLINICAL POSTSCRIPT

The science of speech, like any other science, is incomplete. Although some is known, much more remains to be known. The path to discovery often is indirect and may seem to take some unlikely detours. Occasionally, a fundamental question may be answered not from study of the normal person but from study of the person with a certain kind of impairment. In this postscript, we will consider an example of this path of discovery as it relates to the study of speech breathing.

At one time there were two views about the role of the respiratory system in speech. One hypothesis was that the respiratory system produced discrete pulses of air for each syllable in speech. The other hypothesis was that the respiratory system functioned more like a bellows, delivering a fairly constant flow of air into the upper airway of the speech system. As one approach to deciding between these hypotheses, scientists examined the speech of a person in an iron lung, which was used to ventilate patients with poliomyelitis affecting the respiratory muscles. It was discovered that the person in an iron lung could produce apparently normal speech, even though the iron lung did not produce pulses of air but rather acted more like a bellows to generate a steady flow of air. Moreover, the speaker in the iron lung was able to stress words or syllables on request.

Although this simple experiment did not reveal how the respiratory system functions in a normal speaker, it did provide some arresting information to those who argued that discrete respiratory pulses were necessary for the production of speech. As discussed in this chapter, the actual role of the respiratory system in normal speech is more complicated than either of these two hypotheses and is, in fact, rather like their combination. The volume solution provides a continuous change in muscular effort through an utterance, in a manner similar to the way in which a bellows provides a relatively constant flow of air. The pulsatile solution, which is superimposed on the volume solution for any task of speech production, provides for brief efforts of the expiratory muscles. The pulsatile solution is adapted to the requirements to produce stress on syllables. The speaker in the iron lung was part of the history of research on speech breathing. The success of this speaker in producing satisfactory speech despite a paralyzed respiratory musculature is testimony to the adaptability of speech production. The iron-lung patient, like the patient on the rotating bed, is capable of generating speech on the force of air provided by an external mechanical device.

CHAPTER THREE
Self-Study
Respiratory Physiology

Review Glossary

Overlaid function: Superimposing of functions (such as speech and language) on mechanisms that evolved for breathing, feeding, hearing, and thinking

Respiration: Movement of air into and out of the lungs

  Quiet respiration: Breathing when at rest

  Forced respiration: Breathing with exertion, requiring muscular effort on exhalation as well as on inhalation

  Inhalation (inspiration): The portion of the respiratory cycle in which air is sucked into the lungs

  Exhalation (expiration): The portion of the respiratory cycle in which air is forced out of the lungs

  Active force: Contraction of respiratory muscles

  Passive force: Elastic recoil of respiratory structures

Pressure: The result of compression of air in the lungs, which provides the source of power for speech

  Relaxation pressure: Compression resulting from gravity, untorquing of ribs, and elastic recoil of alveoli

  Alveolar pressure: Pressure measured within the lungs

  Subglottal (tracheal) pressure: pressure measured within the trachea below the vocal folds

  Intraoral pressure: Pressure measured within the mouth

  Pressure requirements: Pressures needed to meet loudness requirements for phrases, stress requirements for syllables, and phonetic intensity requirements for speech sounds

Volume: Amount of air in the lungs

  Vital capacity: Maximum volume of air that can be exhaled following maximum inhalation

  Inspiratory reserve: The difference between the volume of air inhaled and the maximum volume that could be inhaled

  Expiratory reserve: The difference between the volume of air exhaled and the maximum volume that could be exhaled

  Tidal volume: The volume of air actually exhaled

  Resting tidal volume: The volume of air exhaled in quiet respiration

  Residual volume: Air remaining in the lungs after a maximum exhalation

  Volume requirements: Amounts of air required for breathing and for various levels of loudness

  Frequency requirements: The rate at which inhalation and exhalation are required for breathing and for loudness and phrasing

  Duration requirements: The length of time of the inhalatory phase and of the exhalatory phase of the respiratory cycle for breathing and speech

Speech breathing problem

  Volume solution: Active forces are adjusted to compensate for changes in passive forces as lung volume changes

  Pulsatile solution: Brief pressure increases are generated for syllable stress by changing the relative levels of inspiratory and expiratory activity

Self-Study Test of Terminology

Self-Study Instructions: These questions can be used to help you assess how much you have retained from studying the Review Glossary. Answers are given in Appendix E.

(1) _____ Superimposing of speech and language functions on mechanisms that evolved for breathing, feeding, hearing, and thinking

(2) _____ Compression of air in the lungs which provides the source of power for speech

(3) _____ Pressure measured within the lungs

(4) _____ Amounts of air required for breathing and for various levels of loudness

(5) _____ The length of time of the inhalatory phase and of the exhalatory phase of the respiratory cycle for breathing and speech

(6) _____ Amount of air inhaled, exhaled, or in the lungs

(7) _____ The difference between the volume of air exhaled and the maximum volume that could be exhaled

(8) _____ Breathing with exertion, requiring muscular effort on exhalation as well as on inhalation

(9) _____ Compression resulting from gravity, untorquing of ribs, and elastic recoil of alveoli

(10) _____ The portion of the respiratory cycle in which air is forced out of the lungs

(11) _____ Movement of air into and out of the lungs

(12) _____ Pressure measured within the trachea below the vocal folds

(13) _____ Pressure needed to meet loudness requirements for phrases, stress requirements for syllables, and phonetic intensity requirements for speech sounds

(14) _____ Maximum volume of air that can be exhaled following maximum inhalation

(15) _____ The rate at which inhalation and exhalation are required for breathing and for loudness and phrasing

(16) _____ The volume of air actually exhaled

(17) _____ Air remaining in the lungs after a maximum exhalation

(18) _____ The difference between the volume of air inhaled and the maximum volume that could be inhaled

(19) _____ The portion of the respiratory cycle in which air is sucked into the lungs

(20) _____ Breathing when at rest

(21) _____ The volume of air exhaled in quiet respiration

(22) _____ Contraction of respiratory muscles

(23) _____ Adjustment of active forces for changes in passive forces as lung volumes change

(24) _____ Changes in inspiratory and expiratory activity to generate brief pressure increases for stressed syllables

Self-Study Test of Understanding

Self-Study Instructions: This test can be used to help you assess how well you understand the content of this chapter. Terms to be filled in are from the Review Glossary. Answers are given in Appendix E.

You are to give a speech before your class at a university in Southern California where sunshine is the norm and a slight sprinkle jams freeway traffic for miles. An unexpected rain has produced predictable results, you have an audience of only two — a brave student in the front row and your professor in the back.

To calm yourself while waiting to begin, you concentrate on breathing easily. This means using (A) _____, in which about 40 percent of the (B) _____ cycle is devoted to (C) _____ and 60 percent to (D) _____. The amount of air used in this type of breathing is (E) _____. The (F) _____ of air remaining after each breath is about 40 percent of (G) _____, which is the maximum amount of air that can be exhaled following maximum inhalation. This 40 percent level is the rest position at which the expansion force of the rib cage and contraction force of the lungs are in balance.

Standing now behind the lectern, still breathing as a biological function, you inhale to begin speaking, which shifts control of respiration to the (H) _____ of speech. As a result, differences in breathing occur in (I) _____ (in that you inhale quickly and exhale slowly), (J) _____ (in that you take longer breaths less often) and (K) _____ (in that you take deeper breaths than when breathing quietly). The deep breathing requires (L) _____, which raises the (M) _____ of air available and makes long phrases possible. It also reduces (N) _____, the volume of vital capacity still available following inhalation.

As you inhale for your speech, the student just in front of you catches your eye, so you address the opening statement to her. Being close by, you automatically use a reduced loudness level which requires that (O) _____ in the trachea must be lower than it would be to speak to your professor in the back of the room. To adjust (P) _____ (the extent to which air molecules are compressed) requires adjusting (Q) _____ pressure in the lungs with chest wall adjustments.

Having inhaled deeply for speech, you have raised the rib cage, which gravity pulls down on, torqued the cartilages that attach the ribs to the sternum and vertebrae, and inflated the alveolar air sacs, which, being elastic, recoil against inflation. The result of these passive exhalatory forces is (R) _____, which contributes to the (S) _____ for loudness, syllable stress, and phonetic intensity. As a result, the balance of active respiratory forces favors inhalatory muscular contraction during the beginning of speech, when passive exhalatory forces are greatest. As these forces decline, the balance shifts progressively from inhalatory to exhalatory muscular contraction to maintain the necessary pressure for speech.

Unaccustomed as you are to public speaking, you conclude the talk, return to your seat, and heave a great sigh of relief that expends your entire (T) _____, leaving only (U) _____, which is the air that remains after this maximum exhalation.

Clinical Exercises

These exercises allow you to test your knowledge of respiratory physiology as it relates to clinical application. Fill in the blanks with the word or words that best complete the statements.

Tommy is a 13 year old boy with cerebral palsy. Cerebral palsy is a neurological condition resulting from brain damage that occurs before, during, or shortly after birth. Because of this condition, Tommy's respiratory function is impaired relative to that of normally developing children. If we wanted to determine Tommy's maximum usable volume of air, we would measure the (a) _____, which would be obtained by asking him to exhale all the air he can and then take in the largest breath he can. Typically, this task is repeated three to five times, and the largest value is taken as the measurement to be reported. We know that this respiratory volume varies with age, so we would compare the values recorded for Tommy with those shown in Figure (b) _____ (find the appropriate figure in this chapter). This figure tells us that a normally developing boy should have a value of about (c) _____. If the value we measured for Tommy is 2.0 liters, Tommy's value is (d) _____ (greater than, equal to, or less than) the normally expected value for a boy his age.

From this one measure, we have some idea of the amount of air that Tommy is able to control for speech and other tasks. One speech task often used in clinical testing is vowel prolongation. This task simply requires that the subject being examined produce as long as possible a vowel such as "ah." We might expect from the measure we just made that Tommy would have a maximum vowel phonation time that is (e) _____ (longer than, equal to, or shorter than) the value obtained for neurologically normal boys his age.

Additional information on Tommy's respiratory function can be obtained from other measures. For example, if we suspected that his inspiratory musculature was impaired more than his expiratory musculature, we would expect to see a reduced value for (f) _____. Or, if we wanted to test whether Tommy could adjust the amount of air he breathes for increases in physical effort, we would measure changes in (g) _____. Another measure of possible interest is breathing rate. The appropriate comparison data for normal values are contained in Figure (h) _____. We would expect from this figure that Tommy's rest breathing rate would be about (i) _____ breaths per minute.

If you study Figure 3–5, it is apparent that each of the capacity measures is made up of two or more (j) _____ measures. For example, total lung capacity consists of (k) _____, (l) _____, (m) _____, and (n) _____. Inspiratory capacity consists of (o) _____ and (p) _____.

CHAPTER FOUR
Phonatory Anatomy

The larynx, or voice box, might be likened to a valve that connects the respiratory system to the airway passages of the throat, mouth, and nose. Its valving capabilities are many. On the one hand, it can close tightly, as when we lift a heavy object, to make the thorax rigid with compressed air. Or it can accomplish the explosive movements of a cough, expelling mucus and irritants at great velocity into the airway that lies above. On the other hand, the larynx can valve the air stream so as to produce finely controlled vibrations of two fleshy cushions called the vocal folds. The control of this system is sufficiently fine that trained singers can sing an intended pitch accurately even on the first few cycles of vibration, before they have had an opportunity to hear the result. For people like vocalists, radio announcers, and teachers, the larynx is pressed into long and demanding use. The vocal folds vibrate thousands of times each day, beginning with the birth cry and continuing through a lifetime of speech.

Phonation is the generation of voiced sound. It is accomplished with the *larynx* (voice box), which is attached to the top of the trachea, and is the outlet of the respiratory pump into the upper airway. The larynx is a valve that has evolved to prevent anything but gas, preferably air, from

entering the lungs. It also serves as a pressure device for such biological activities as coughing, sneezing, elimination, and the like.

Two functions of the larynx have been borrowed for speech. One is the ability to open in order to produce about half of the consonants, the half that are *voiceless sounds*. These sounds are made with bursts and hisses of noise. The other function is the ability of the lowest level of the valve (the true vocal folds) to close just enough to vibrate when air pressure pushes against it. These vibrations produce *voiced sounds*, the tones that characterize vowels and semivowels particularly. It is the ability to control the rate and manner of vibration of this valve that accounts for our ability to control pitch, loudness, and, to some extent, quality.

LARYNGEAL ANATOMY

Superficially, the larynx is relatively simple in its construction. Its framework consists of five relatively large cartilages and about half a dozen pairs of muscles that move these cartilages into different positions. The entire larynx, which is attached to the top of the trachea, is suspended by

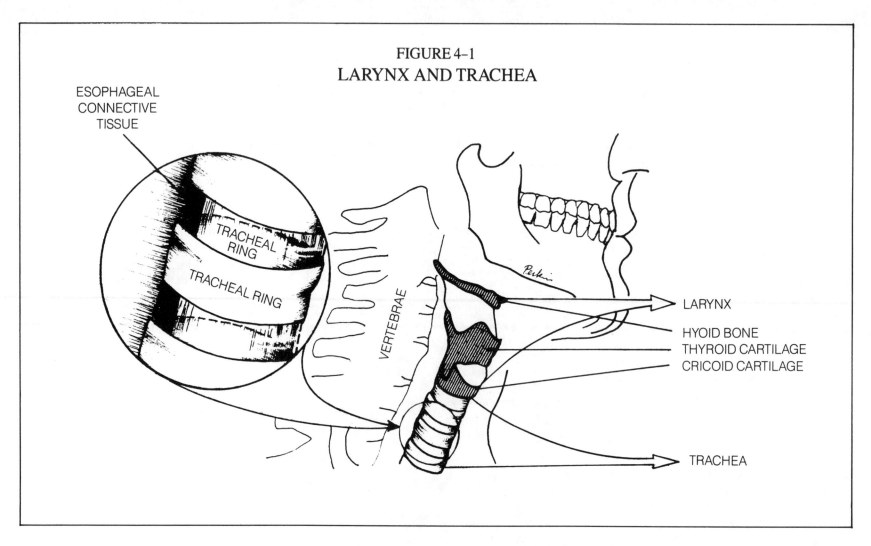

FIGURE 4–1
LARYNX AND TRACHEA

ESOPHAGEAL CONNECTIVE TISSUE

TRACHEAL RING

TRACHEAL RING

VERTEBRAE

LARYNX

HYOID BONE
THYROID CARTILAGE
CRICOID CARTILAGE

TRACHEA

ligaments and a few muscles that connect it to the base of the tongue above and the sternum below.

It is the intricacy of its microstructure and its vast potential for patterns of adjustment and vibration that make it so pivotal for speech. We will approach the edge of these complexities closely enough that interested students can peer over for a glimpse, and delve into them if they wish, but we will attempt not to fall over this precipice.

Laryngeal Cartilages

The *cricoid cartilage* is the foundation of the larynx, to which the other cartilages attach (Fig. 4–1). The cricoid, a Greek name meaning "ring-like" (this cartilage resembles a signet ring), is in actuality the uppermost tracheal cartilage. Because it forms a complete circle, with the signet portion

located in back, it differs from the other tracheal rings, which are all incomplete circles; their posterior openings are filled with flexible connective tissue because the esophagus is squeezed between the trachea and the spine, as you can see in Figure 4–1. Were it not for the flexible back wall of the trachea, which permits a bolus of food to push into the tracheal space during swallowing, you would not be able to swallow anything past your throat.

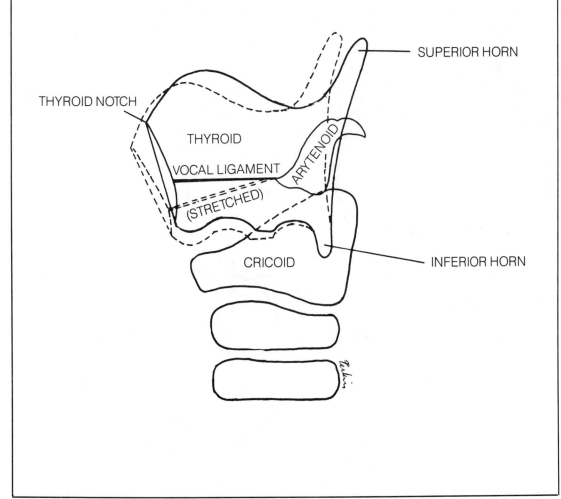

FIGURE 4–2
LARYNGEAL CARTILAGES

SUPERIOR HORN

THYROID NOTCH

THYROID

VOCAL LIGAMENT

ARYTENOID

(STRETCHED)

CRICOID

INFERIOR HORN

The largest and most prominent of the laryngeal cartilages is the *thyroid cartilage*. It is like a wing-shaped shield (its name derives from the Greek word for shield), and is best known for its anterior prominence, the "Adam's apple" (*thyroid notch*). In back, it sweeps both up in a *superior horn* and down in an *inferior horn*. It is this lower horn that provides a pivotal attachment to the cricoid which permits these two cartilages to rock back and forth in relationship to each other. This ability to tilt the thyroid forward and the cricoid backward is the basis for changing the length of the vocal cords in pitch adjustments. As you can see in Figure 4–2, when these two cartilages are pulled toward each other, the vocal folds are lengthened; when tilted apart, the folds are shortened.

The *arytenoids*, a pair of small cartilages shaped roughly in the form of a pyramid, are mounted opposite each other on the rim of the signet portion of the cricoid cartilage. Traditionally, the arytenoids appeared to have three motions when viewed two-dimensionally in a laryngeal mirror: rotating, rocking, and sliding. Careful investigation has revealed that these apparent motions are, in reality, the result of only two movements, *rotation* and *gliding* (Fig. 4–3), which occur together.

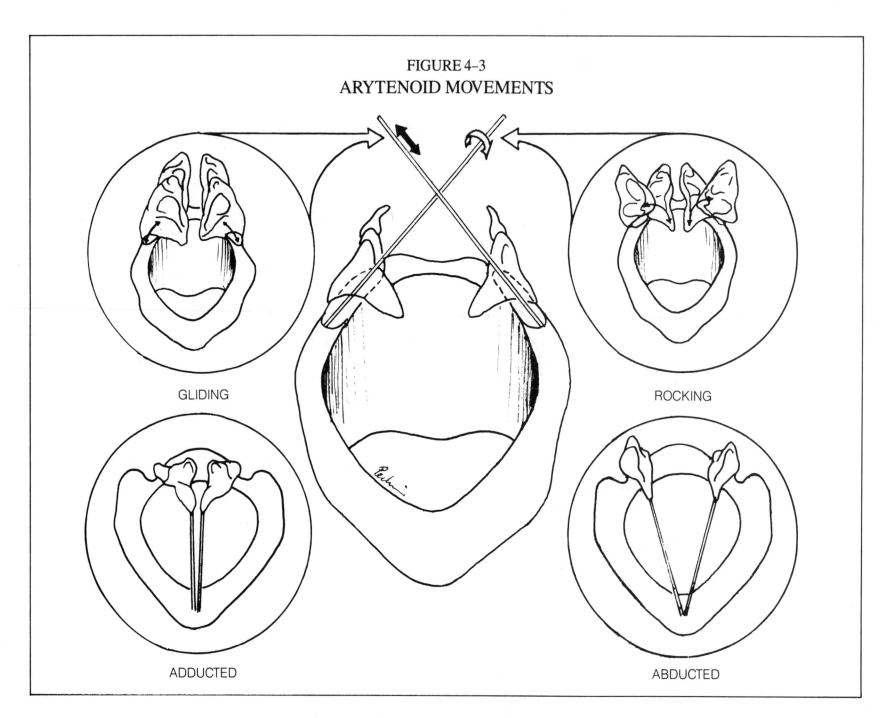

FIGURE 4–3
ARYTENOID MOVEMENTS

GLIDING

ROCKING

ADDUCTED

ABDUCTED

FIGURE 4-4

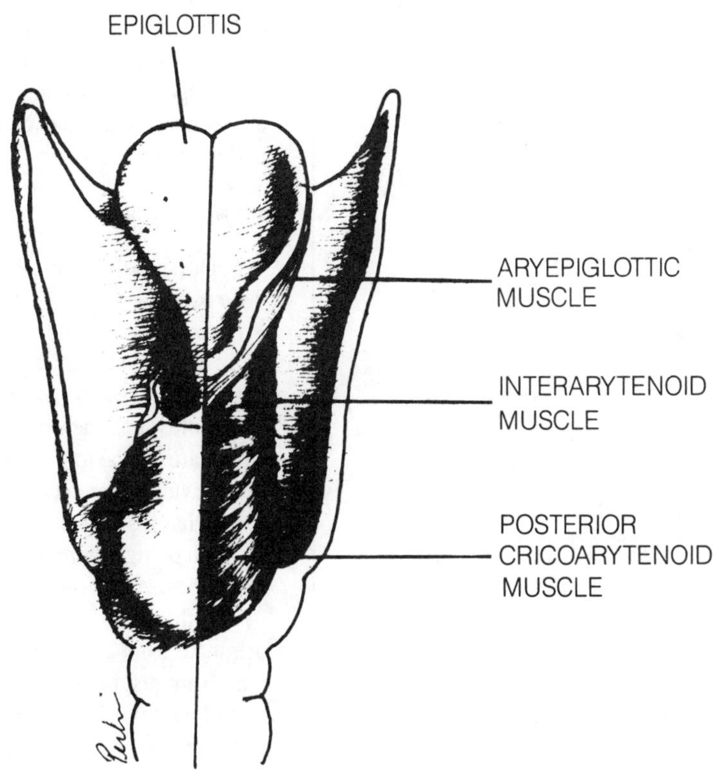

EPIGLOTTIS

ARYEPIGLOTTIC
MUSCLE

INTERARYTENOID
MUSCLE

POSTERIOR
CRICOARYTENOID
MUSCLE

When the arytenoids *rock*, their front sides tilt toward or away from each other. When they *glide*, their back sides slide toward or away from each other. With these two movements, the vocal folds can be *abducted* (opened) for voiceless sounds (or breathing) or *adducted* (closed) to a variety of phonatory positions.*

Each arytenoid has two *processes* (prongs), one projecting forward, the other laterally. The anterior one is the *vocal process*, to which the vocal folds attach. The lateral projection is the *muscular process*, to which several of the muscles responsible for rotation and gliding attach. The upward projection is the *apex*.

The *epiglottis* is the least important of the main cartilages of the larynx. It seems crucial in animals that rely heavily on the sense of smell, but some maintain it is all but useless in humans. Be that as it may, it is a leaf-shaped flap that fans out above its stalk-like attachment to the thyroid cartilage, just below the thyroid notch (Fig. 4-4). One thing it does provide is the anterior wall of the tube leading from the vocal folds to the throat.

*Strictly speaking, *abduct* means to draw away from the median plane or line, and *adduct* means to draw toward the median plane or line. For the vocal folds, however, the terms "open" and "closed" allow students to visualize the action more clearly.

Phonatory Anatomy

FIGURE 4–5
TRUE VOCAL FOLDS

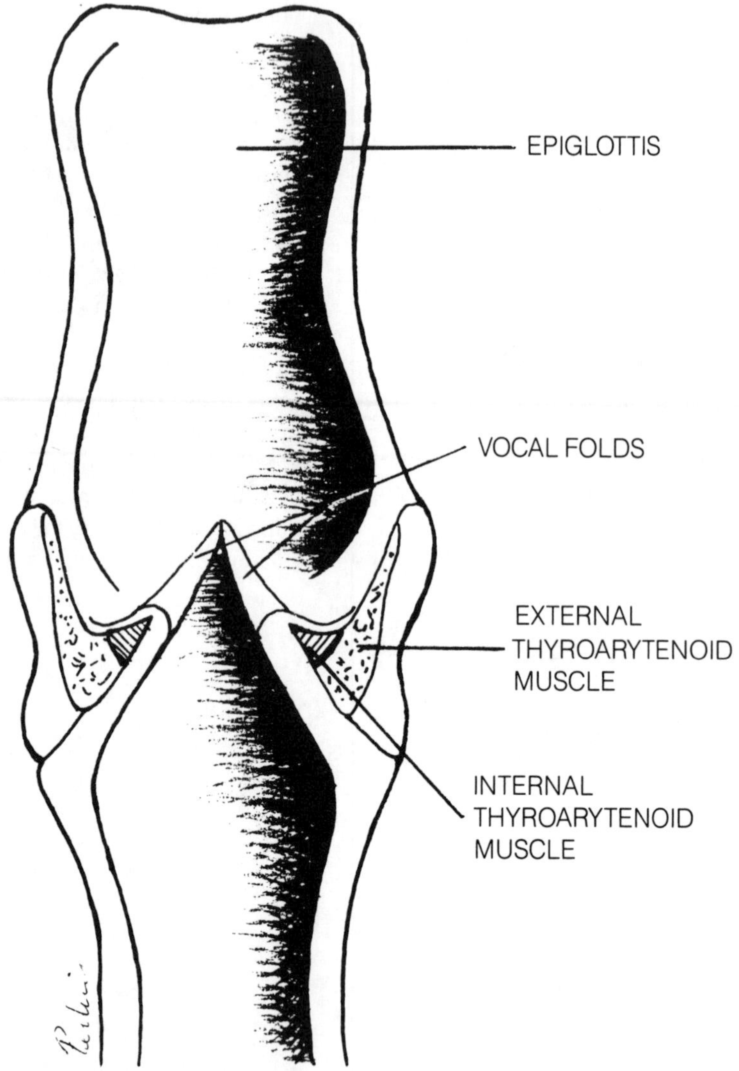

EPIGLOTTIS

VOCAL FOLDS

EXTERNAL
THYROARYTENOID
MUSCLE

INTERNAL
THYROARYTENOID
MUSCLE

Intrinsic Laryngeal Muscles

In the interest of simplicity, we will limit this discussion to *intrinsic laryngeal muscles*, those pairs of internal muscles of the larynx that abduct and adduct the vocal folds and are directly involved in phonatory adjustment. (All come in pairs, with one exception, the transverse arytenoid, which will be noted later.) Admittedly, the *extrinsic laryngeal muscles*, the outside muscles by which the larynx can be raised or lowered, are also of importance to laryngeal performance. Still, they will be discussed later when they can be more easily understood.

Vibrator Muscles

The muscles that are set into vibration to produce sound are part of a larger pair of muscles, the *thyroarytenoids*. This large, complexly twisted muscle is usually described as consisting of two parts: the *internal thyroarytenoids*, which are the vocal folds, and the *external thyroarytenoids*, which are lateral to the vocal folds. Altogether, the thyroarytenoid protrudes into the upper airway to form what resembles a cathedral arch, the tip of the arch being where the vocal folds meet when they vibrate, as shown in Figure 4–5.

Both parts of each thyroarytenoid muscle originate from a narrow vertical attachment running from just below the thyroid notch to the bottom of the thyroid cartilage. The difference in the two parts of the thyroarytenoid depends on where they insert into the arytenoid cartilage. The internal thyroarytenoid inserts into the vocal process, the external part into the muscular process. These external fibers do not participate directly in vocal fold vibration. The effect of their contraction apparently is to shorten and adduct the vocal folds, thereby closing the muscular glottis.

Functional Anatomy of Speech, Language, and Hearing

FIGURE 4–6
VOCAL FOLD ACTION

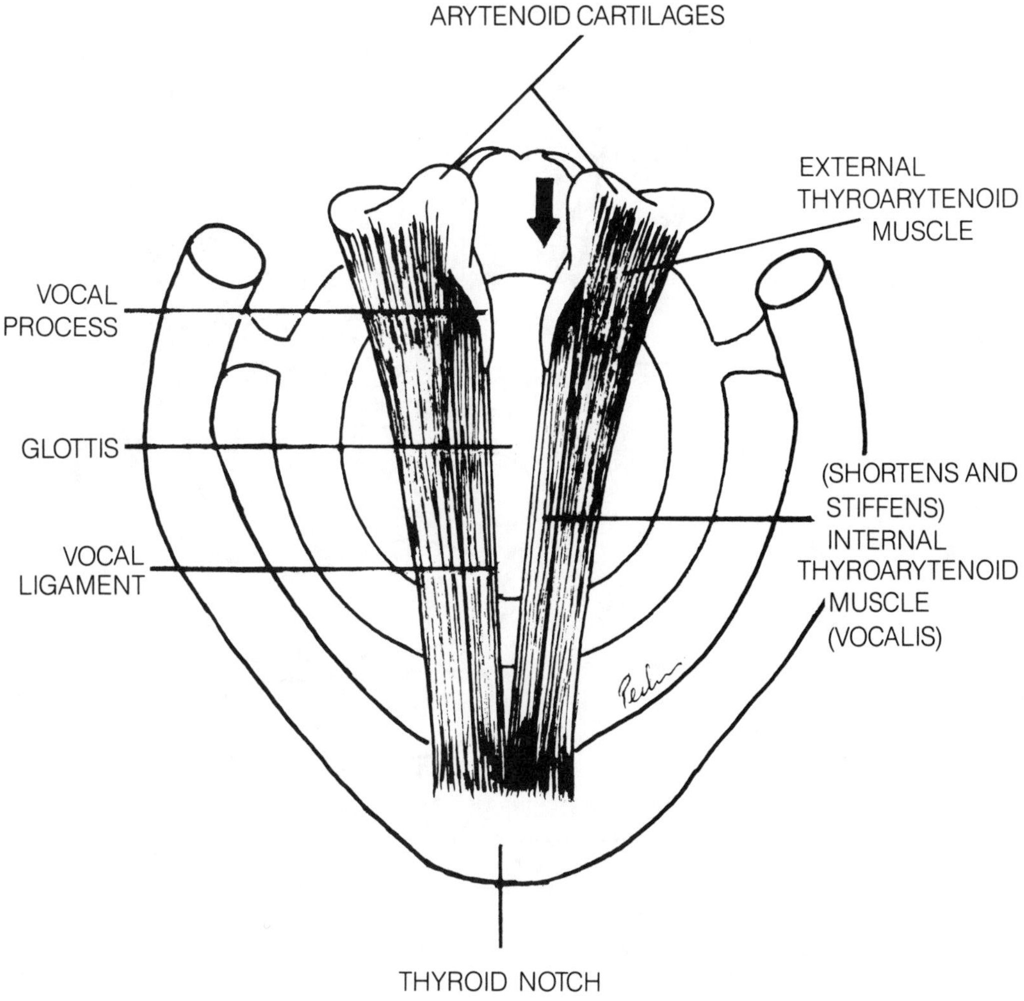

ARYTENOID CARTILAGES

EXTERNAL
THYROARYTENOID
MUSCLE

VOCAL
PROCESS

GLOTTIS

(SHORTENS AND
STIFFENS)
INTERNAL
THYROARYTENOID
MUSCLE
(VOCALIS)

VOCAL
LIGAMENT

THYROID NOTCH

Vocal Folds. The internal thyroarytenoids are the vibratory positions of the vocal folds, also called *vocal cords*. This paired muscle, which is directly involved in phonatory vibration, is usually referred to as the *vocalis*. The action of this muscle when it contracts is to pull the vocal process, to which it attaches, into a straight line toward the thyroid notch, the point of origin (Fig. 4–6). This action shortens the vocal folds and adducts them, provided they were abducted. Probably, though, it is antagonistic to medial compression, the reason being that by pulling the vocal processes straight forward, they are prevented from being squeezed together.

Another important effect of vocalis contraction is that it *stiffens* the vocal folds. This stiffening action is independent of vocal fold length. Paradoxically, common sense says that the more the folds are lengthened, the more they will be stretched, and the more they are stretched the more tense they will become. In point of fact, the effect of lengthening a muscle is to thin it and stiffen it, but not tense it like a violin string. Muscles are tense only when contracted, and when they contract, they shorten. As you will soon discover, another muscle lengthens the vocal folds and thereby thins them.

Glottis. The glottis is a space, not a structure. It is the space between the vocal folds. Accordingly, the *glottal edges* are the edges of the vocal folds that make contact when adducted. Under this condition, the glottis is said to be closed. When abducted, the glottis is open. Similarly, vocal fold vibration is often referred to as *glottal vibration*.

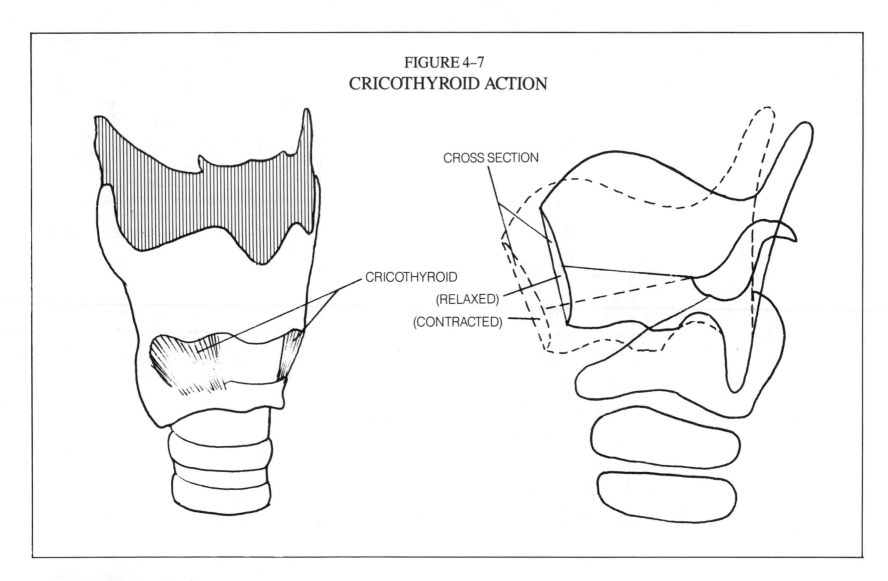

FIGURE 4–7
CRICOTHYROID ACTION

CROSS SECTION

CRICOTHYROID

(RELAXED)

(CONTRACTED)

Vocal Fold Lengthening Muscles

The *cricothyroid muscles*, as the name implies, originate from the front of the cricoid cartilage and insert into the lower border of the thyroid cartilage. Their contraction is responsible for pulling the two cartilages together, thereby lengthening and stiffening the vocal folds (Fig. 4–7).

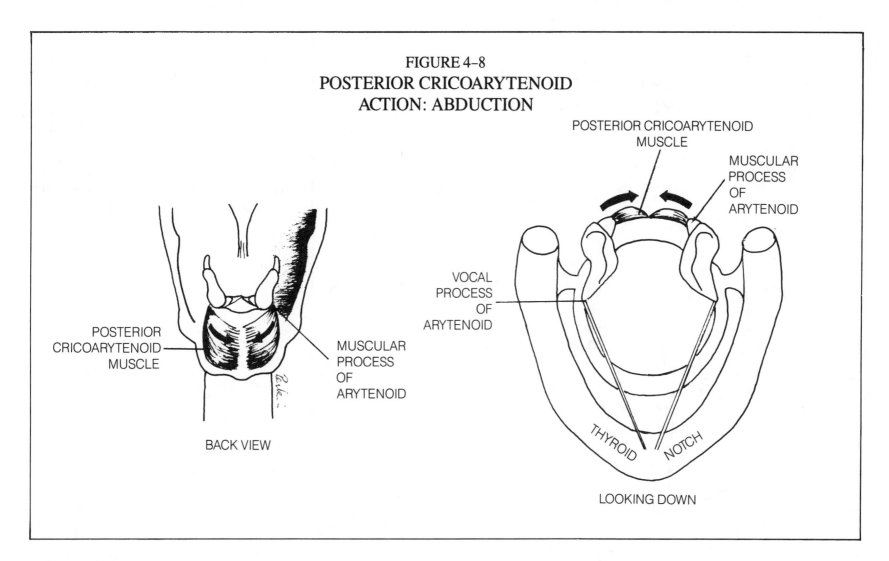

FIGURE 4–8
POSTERIOR CRICOARYTENOID
ACTION: ABDUCTION

POSTERIOR CRICOARYTENOID
MUSCLE

MUSCULAR
PROCESS
OF
ARYTENOID

VOCAL
PROCESS
OF
ARYTENOID

POSTERIOR
CRICOARYTENOID
MUSCLE

MUSCULAR
PROCESS
OF
ARYTENOID

THYROID NOTCH

BACK VIEW

LOOKING DOWN

Abductor Muscles

The *posterior cricoarytenoids* are flat muscles
arising from the back wall of the cricoid cartilage.
They insert into the muscular processes of the
arytenoid cartilages. They are the major muscles
responsible for rocking and gliding the arytenoids
apart. Hence, they are the major muscles that
abduct the vocal folds (Fig. 4–8).

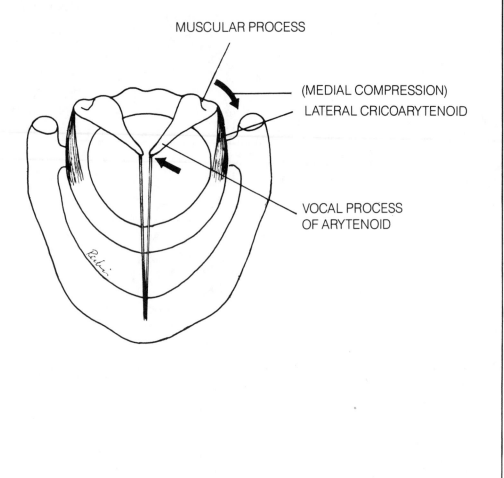

FIGURE 4–9
LATERAL CRICOARYTENOID
ACTION: ADDUCTION

MUSCULAR PROCESS

(MEDIAL COMPRESSION)
LATERAL CRICOARYTENOID

VOCAL PROCESS
OF ARYTENOID

Adductor Muscles

The *lateral cricoarytenoid* muscles arise from the lateral borders of the cricoid cartilage and they, too, insert into the muscular processes at the outside corners of each arytenoid cartilage (Fig. 4–9). They pull in essentially the opposite direction from the posterior cricoarytenoids and so, predictably, their effect is also opposite. They adduct the arytenoids, and can also squeeze the anterior tips of the vocal processes tightly together in a condition of medial compression.

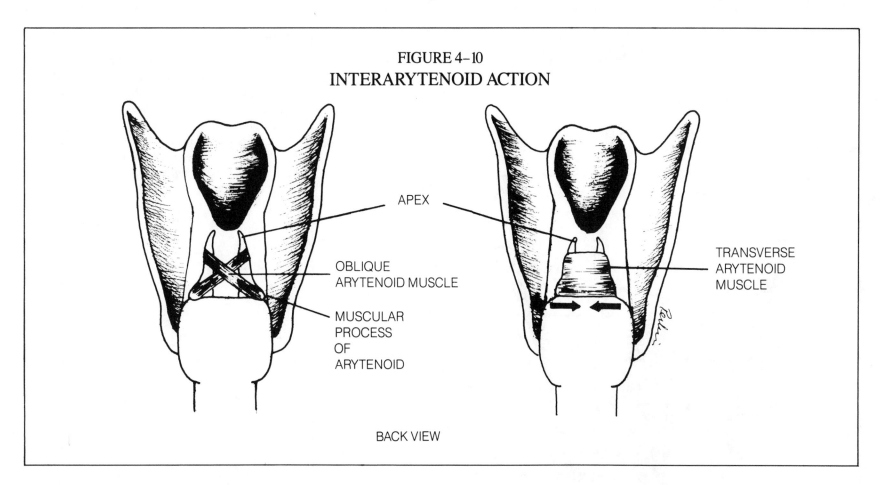

FIGURE 4–10
INTERARYTENOID ACTION

APEX

OBLIQUE
ARYTENOID MUSCLE

MUSCULAR
PROCESS
OF
ARYTENOID

TRANSVERSE
ARYTENOID
MUSCLE

BACK VIEW

The *interarytenoids*, the name generally given to the muscles that pull the posterior medial borders of the arytenoids together, are formed by two muscles, the *transverse arytenoid* (the only intrinsic laryngeal muscle that is not paired), and the *oblique arytenoids*, a crisscrossed pair of muscles (Fig. 4–10). The transverse arytenoid extends horizontally across the backs of the pair of cartilages. It pulls their middle edges together from bottom to top. The oblique arytenoids, on the other hand, extend from the muscular process of one arytenoid to the apex of the other. Their action is to pull the upper tips of the arytenoids together.

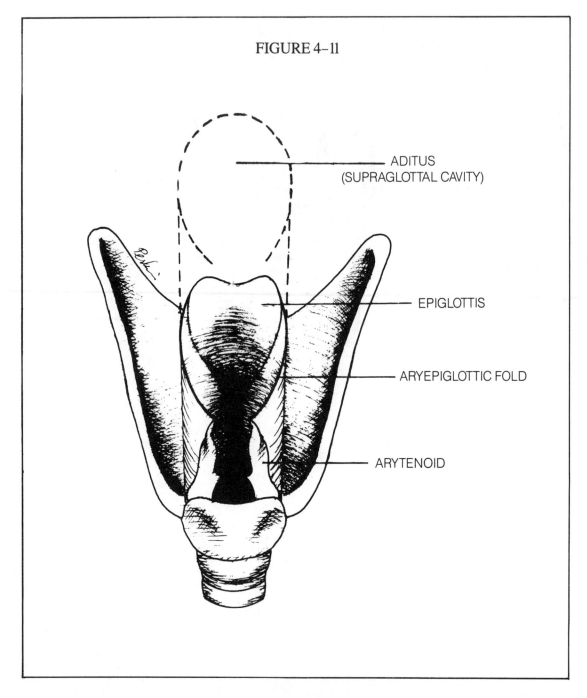

FIGURE 4-11

ADITUS
(SUPRAGLOTTAL CAVITY)

EPIGLOTTIS

ARYEPIGLOTTIC FOLD

ARYTENOID

Supraglottal Cavity

The tube extending upward from the level of the glottis through which the air stream from the larynx enters the throat is referred to by several names: *aditus*, *laryngeal collar*, *laryngeal cavity*, and *supraglottal cavity*. Of these, the latter is the most descriptive. This cavity is formed anteriorly by the epiglottis, posteriorly by the arytenoids, and laterally by the *aryepiglottic folds* (Fig. 4-11).

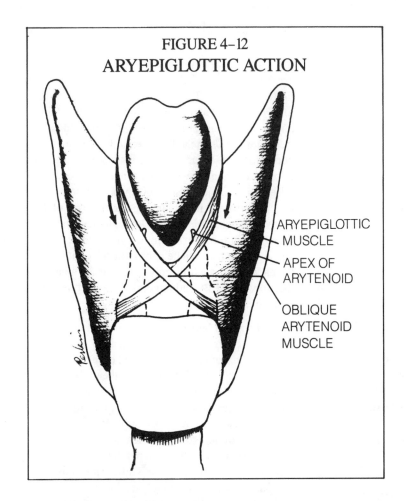

FIGURE 4–12
ARYEPIGLOTTIC ACTION

ARYEPIGLOTTIC MUSCLE

APEX OF ARYTENOID

OBLIQUE ARYTENOID MUSCLE

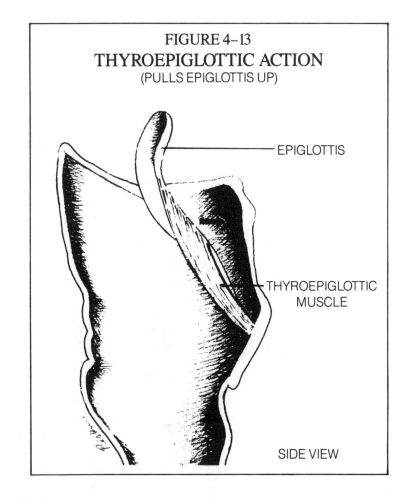

FIGURE 4–13
THYROEPIGLOTTIC ACTION
(PULLS EPIGLOTTIS UP)

EPIGLOTTIS

THYROEPIGLOTTIC MUSCLE

SIDE VIEW

Embedded within these membranous folds are the *aryepiglottic* muscles. They appear to be a continuation of the oblique arytenoid muscles which, after inserting into the arytenoid cartilages, extend upward and forward to insert into the epiglottis (Fig. 4–12). Contraction of the aryepiglottic muscle, probably coupled with the oblique arytenoids, tends to tilt the arytenoids against the epiglottis and to pull the epiglottis down, possibly assisted by a push from the base of the tongue. To pull the epiglottis back up, the *thyroepiglottis* must contract (Fig. 4–13).

Laryngeal Membranes and Ligaments

Although the muscles just discussed move the laryngeal cartilages in relation to each other, it probably goes without saying that these cartilages are attached to joints, are held together by ligaments, and are covered with membranes. In the interest of maintaining our focus on vocal function, we will consider only those ligaments and membranes that you are most likely to encounter in understanding phonation.

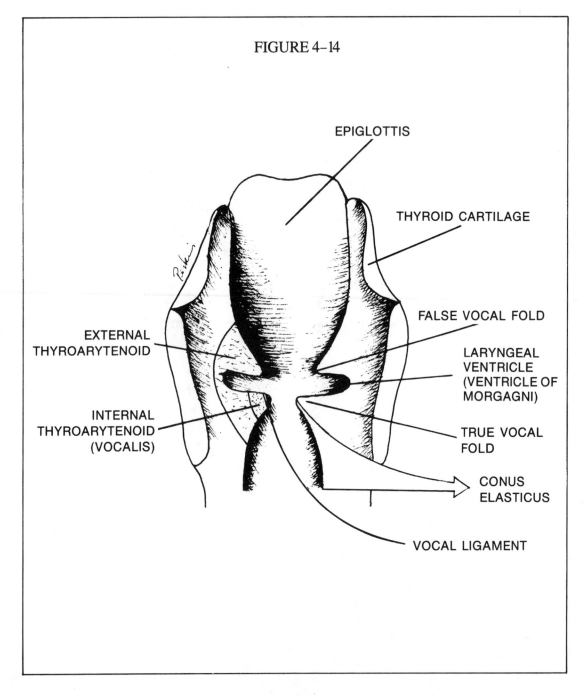

FIGURE 4–14

EPIGLOTTIS

THYROID CARTILAGE

FALSE VOCAL FOLD

EXTERNAL THYROARYTENOID

LARYNGEAL VENTRICLE (VENTRICLE OF MORGAGNI)

INTERNAL THYROARYTENOID (VOCALIS)

TRUE VOCAL FOLD

CONUS ELASTICUS

VOCAL LIGAMENT

Membranes

False Vocal Folds. Above the true vocal folds are the *false vocal folds*, also called *ventricular folds* (Fig. 4–14). They consist mainly of thick folds of mucous membrane that protrude into the airway, but not as far as do the true vocal folds. Accordingly, when the folds are adducted for phonation, these true folds are visible below the false folds when viewed in a laryngeal mirror. The false folds originate just below the attachment of the epiglottis and insert into the lateral edges of the arytenoids below the apex. Although they contain a few fibers of the external thyroarytenoid muscle, and although they can be approximated enough to be made to vibrate, this only occurs under abnormal conditions. By and large, they are soft, passive structures.

Laryngeal Ventricle. Between the false folds above and the true folds below is a deep indentation in the mucous membrane wall of the larynx, a ventricle (it is from this name that the term "ventricular folds" comes). This is the *laryngeal ventricle*, sometimes called the *ventricle of Morgagni* for the anatomist who gave it his name. It extends almost the full length of the vocal folds, and is bounded laterally by the external thyroarytenoid muscle. Within the ventricle is a liberal supply of mucous glands to provide lubrication of the true folds. The ventricles also serve as spaces into which the folds can move when vibrating.

Conus Elasticus. A broad elastic membrane covers the entire inner wall of the larynx. The lower portion of this membrane, the conus elasticus (named for the cone-shaped arch formed below the true folds), extends from the glottal edges to the cricoid cartilage. It is covered with mucosa, which can move somewhat independently from the glottal edge in ways essential to vibration.

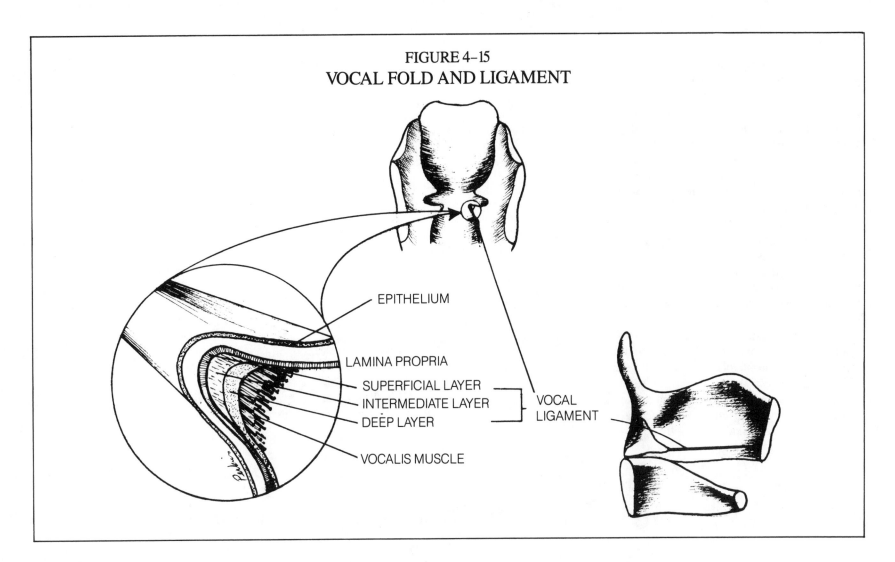

FIGURE 4–15
VOCAL FOLD AND LIGAMENT

EPITHELIUM

LAMINA PROPRIA

SUPERFICIAL LAYER

INTERMEDIATE LAYER

DEEP LAYER

VOCAL LIGAMENT

VOCALIS MUSCLE

Vocal Ligament

What is known as the *vocal ligament* is actually an integral part of the mucosal cover of the vocalis muscle called the *lamina propria*. As can be seen in Figure 4–15, the lamina propria consists of a superficial layer, almost gelatinous, that provides a loose connection between the outer epithelial covering of the glottal edge and the *intermediate* and *deep layers* of the lamina propria that attach to the vocalis muscle. The intermediate layer, containing elastic fibers (like rubber bands), blends into the deep layer containing collagenous fibers (like threads). Together these two layers form the vocal ligament, which is shown by itself at the lower right in Figure 4–15. The effect of this arrangement permits the mucosal membrane to vibrate more or less independently of the vocalis muscle, which vibrates synchronously, but not as vigorously. This explains the impression under some conditions that the vocal folds, when seen vibrating in ultra-slow motion, appear to be like flags flapping in the breeze.

Summary

This chapter provides a picture of the framework of the larynx and its internal parts that are most essential to generate voice. Its structure is deceptively simple. The cricoid cartilage is the foundation. Pivoting on it is the thyroid cartilage in front, and gliding and rotating on the upper back edge are the two arytenoid cartilages. (The fifth large cartilage, the epiglottis, attaches to the thyroid cartilage, but it is of little direct importance to vocal fold vibration.) The muscles that move these four main cartilages, and the dynamic interplays of forces among them that produce laryngeal movements, are what make phonation so difficult to comprehend. The cricothyroid muscles tip the thyroid cartilage forward, thereby stretching the thyroarytenoid (the vocal folds), which pull against the arytenoids (held in position by several cricoarytenoid muscles). It is the balance of forces among the posterior and lateral cricoarytenoids as they pull against the internal and external thyroarytenoids that is particularly complex. Still, each of the relatively few laryngeal muscles and cartilages is reasonably easy to understand as a structural element when it is considered by itself.

CHAPTER FOUR
Self-Study
Phonatory Anatomy

Review Glossary

Larynx: The structure at the entrance to the trachea that functions as a valve biologically and as the source of voice for speech

  Laryngeal cartilages: The cartilages forming the framework of the larynx

    Cricoid: The signet ring–shaped cartilage at the top of the trachea that is the foundation of the larynx

    Thyroid: The wing-shaped cartilage that is hinged to the cricoid by its inferior horns on which it pivots; the thyroid notch (Adam's apple) is in the midline of the top edge of this cartilage

    Arytenoid: A pair of pyramidally shaped movable cartilages that glide and rock on the top back edge of the cricoid

      Vocal process: An anterior projection of the arytenoid to which a vocal fold attaches

      Muscular process: A lateral projection of the arytenoid to which abductor and adductor muscles attach

      Apex: The upper tip of the arytenoid

    Epiglottis: A leaf-shaped cartilage, attached to the thyroid cartilage below the thyroid notch, that can be pulled up or down to help close the laryngeal airway

Abduction: Movement of the arytenoids that opens the vocal folds

Adduction: Movement of the arytenoids that closes the vocal folds

Medial compression: The adductory contraction that squeezes the vocal processes of the arytenoids together

Extrinsic laryngeal muscles: The sternothyroid muscle and the thyrohyoid muscle that originate outside the larynx but insert into it (See *Infrahyoid muscles*, Chapter 6 Review Glossary)

Intrinsic laryngeal muscles: Muscles that originate and insert within the larynx

  Posterior cricoarytenoid muscle: The pair of muscles on the back of the cricoid that attach to the muscular processes of the arytenoids to abduct the vocal folds

  Interarytenoid muscle: The transverse and oblique arytenoid muscles that attach to the backs of the arytenoids to pull them together

  Aryepiglottis muscle: The pair of muscles each of which extends from the apex of an arytenoid to the epiglottis to pull it down (aryepiglottics are upward continuations of oblique arytenoid muscles.)

  Thyroepiglottis muscle: The pair of muscles extending from thyroid cartilage to epiglottis that pull the epiglottis up

  Lateral cricoarytenoid muscle: The pair of muscles extending from the lateral upper edges of the cricoid to the muscular processes of the arytenoids that medially compress the vocal processes

  Cricothyroid muscle: The pair of muscles extending upward and backward from the upper border of the cricoid to the lower border of the thyroid that tilt the cricoid up toward the thyroid cartilage, thereby lengthening the vocal folds

  Thyroarytenoid muscle: The pair of muscles extending from thyroid cartilage to arytenoid cartilage that adduct and shorten the vocal folds

    External thyroarytenoid muscle: The segment of thyroarytenoid muscle that inserts into the lateral front portion of each arytenoid to close the muscular glottis

    Internal thyroarytenoid (vocalis) muscle: The vibrating segment of thyroarytenoid muscle that inserts into each vocal process; vibratory rate (pitch) can be controlled by length, thickness, and stiffness of the vocalis (the true vocal fold)

    Conus elasticus: The elastic membrane covered with mucosa that can move separately from the vocal cord during vibration and that covers the inner wall of the larynx from edge of the vocalis to the cricoid cartilage

    Lamina propria: The mucosal-ligamentous cover of the vocalis muscle

      Vocal ligament: The thread-like collagenous fibers of the deep layer of the lamina propria

False vocal folds (ventricular folds): The thick folds of mucous membrane protruding into the airway above the true folds

Laryngeal ventricle (ventricle of Morgagni): The lubricating indentation between true and false folds

  Aditus (laryngeal collar, laryngeal cavity, supraglottal cavity): The airway above the true vocal folds, formed by the aryepiglottic folds (suspended from the aryepiglottic muscle) and the epiglottis to which they attach; this cavity is the uppermost laryngeal valve (the false and true folds are the middle and lower valves) that can be closed for such activities as swallowing and opened for breathing and phonation

Phonation: Laryngeal generation of voice

    Voiced sounds: Speech sounds produced when the vocal folds vibrate

    Voiceless sounds: Speech sounds produced when air flows through (nonvibrating) vocal folds

    Glottis: The space between the vocal folds

    Glottal vibration: Opening and closing of the glottis when the vocal folds are adducted for phonation (voice)

Self-Study Drawings

Coloring Instructions

1. Identify cartilages and processes *A* through *E* on Drawing 4–I and *S*, *T*, *V*, and *Y* on Drawing 4–IV. Using pencils, color processes *D* and *E* differently on Drawing 4–I.
2. Identify *H* in Drawing 4–I, *I* in 4–II, and *R* in 4–III by whether each represents abduction, adduction for phonation, or adduction with medial compression.
3. Identify muscles *F* and *G* that produce action *H* in Drawing 4–I, muscle *K* that produces action *I = 1 in Drawing 4–II, and muscles N* through *Q* that produce action *R* (*O* and *P* together are called *N*) in Drawing 4–III.
4. Using different pens, color answers *F*, *G*, and *H* in Drawing 4–I the same, answers *I* through *M* on Drawing 4–II the same, and answers *N* through *R* on Drawing 4–III the same.
5. Identify the muscle *J* that lengthens the vocal folds in Drawing 4–II, *U* that opens the aditus, and *X* that closes the aditus, and color each with a different pen in Drawing 4–IV.
6. Identify *M* and color it with a pencil in Drawing 4–II.
7. Identify spaces *L* in Drawing 4–II and *W* in Drawing 4–IV and color with different pens.
8. Color terms in the glossary with the same colors used for those terms on the drawings.
9. Check your answers in Appendix E.

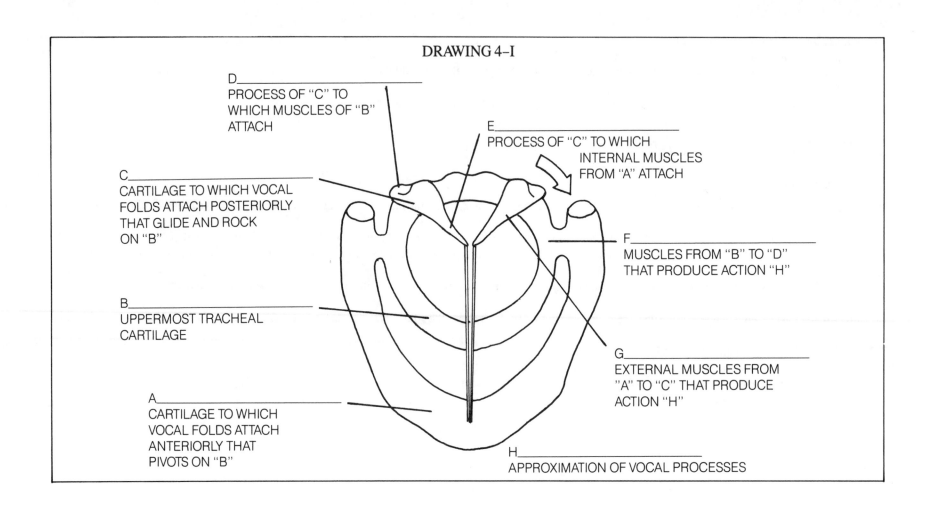

DRAWING 4–I

D_____
PROCESS OF "C" TO
WHICH MUSCLES OF "B"
ATTACH

E_____
PROCESS OF "C" TO WHICH
INTERNAL MUSCLES
FROM "A" ATTACH

C_____
CARTILAGE TO WHICH VOCAL
FOLDS ATTACH POSTERIORLY
THAT GLIDE AND ROCK
ON "B"

F_____
MUSCLES FROM "B" TO "D"
THAT PRODUCE ACTION "H"

B_____
UPPERMOST TRACHEAL
CARTILAGE

G_____
EXTERNAL MUSCLES FROM
"A" TO "C" THAT PRODUCE
ACTION "H"

A_____
CARTILAGE TO WHICH
VOCAL FOLDS ATTACH
ANTERIORLY THAT
PIVOTS ON "B"

H_____
APPROXIMATION OF VOCAL PROCESSES

DRAWING 4–II

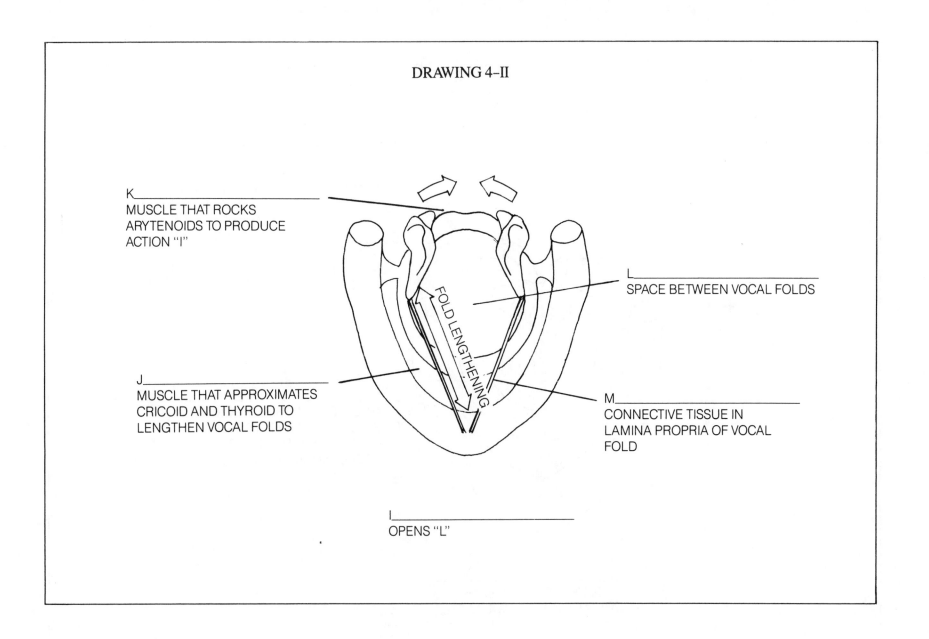

K_____
MUSCLE THAT ROCKS
ARYTENOIDS TO PRODUCE
ACTION "I"

FOLD LENGTHENING

L_____
SPACE BETWEEN VOCAL FOLDS

J_____
MUSCLE THAT APPROXIMATES
CRICOID AND THYROID TO
LENGTHEN VOCAL FOLDS

M_____
CONNECTIVE TISSUE IN
LAMINA PROPRIA OF VOCAL
FOLD

I_____
OPENS "L"

DRAWING 4–III

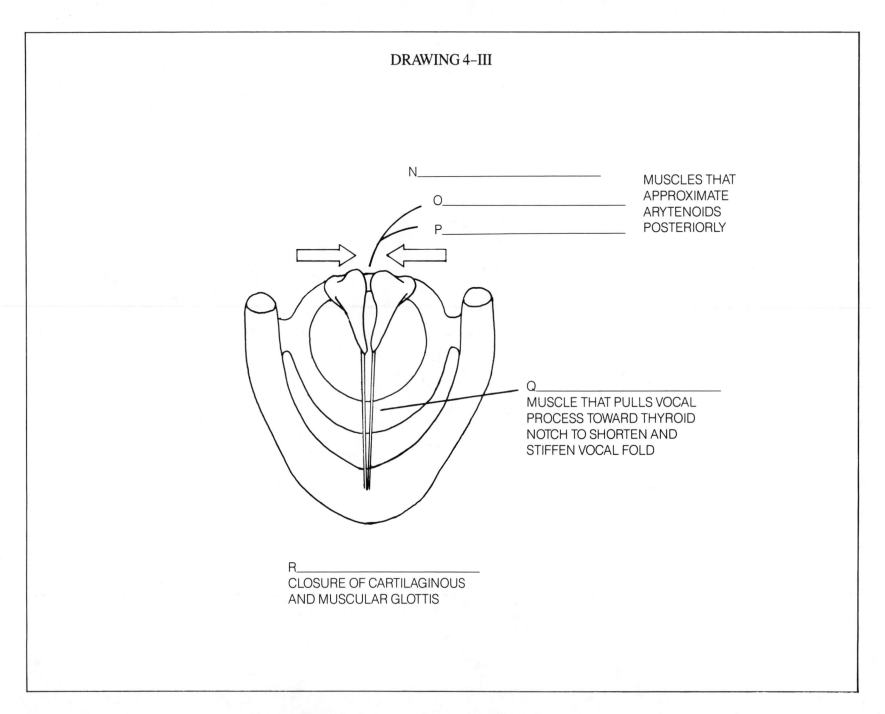

N_____ MUSCLES THAT
                          APPROXIMATE
O_____ ARYTENOIDS
                          POSTERIORLY
P_____

Q_____
MUSCLE THAT PULLS VOCAL
PROCESS TOWARD THYROID
NOTCH TO SHORTEN AND
STIFFEN VOCAL FOLD

R_____
CLOSURE OF CARTILAGINOUS
AND MUSCULAR GLOTTIS

DRAWING 4–IV

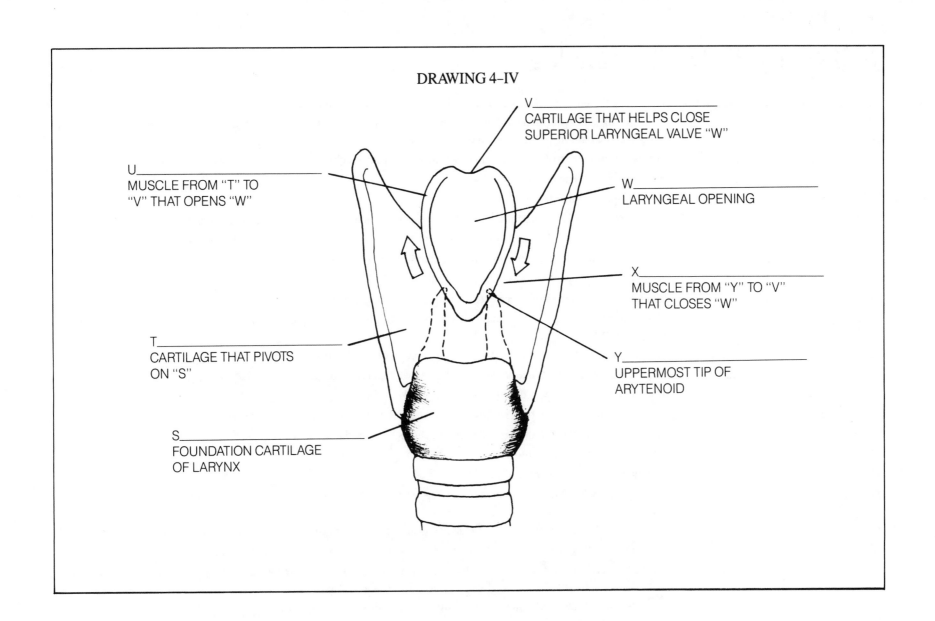

V_____
CARTILAGE THAT HELPS CLOSE
SUPERIOR LARYNGEAL VALVE "W"

U_____
MUSCLE FROM "T" TO
"V" THAT OPENS "W"

W_____
LARYNGEAL OPENING

X_____
MUSCLE FROM "Y" TO "V"
THAT CLOSES "W"

T_____
CARTILAGE THAT PIVOTS
ON "S"

Y_____
UPPERMOST TIP OF
ARYTENOID

S_____
FOUNDATION CARTILAGE
OF LARYNX

Self-Study Test of Terminology

Self-Study Instructions: These questions can be used to help you assess how much you have retained from studying the Review Glossary. Answers are in Appendix E.

(1) _____ The wing-shaped cartilage that is hinged to the cricoid by its inferior horns on which it pivots; the thyroid notch (Adam's apple) is in the midline of the top edge of this cartilage

(2) _____ An anterior projection of the arytenoid to which a vocal fold attaches

(3) _____ The upper tip of the arytenoid

(4) _____ The cartilages forming the framework of the larynx

(5) _____ A pair of pyramidally shaped movable cartilages that glide and rock on the top back edge of the cricoid

(6) _____ The sternothyroid muscle and the thyrohyoid muscle that originate outside the larynx but insert into it

(7) _____ The transverse and oblique arytenoid muscles that stretch to the backs of the arytenoids to pull them together

(8) _____ Movement of the arytenoids that opens the vocal folds

(9) _____ The pair of muscles each of which extends from the apex of an arytenoid to the epiglottis to pull it down

(10) _____ A leaf-shaped cartilage, attached to the thyroid below the thyroid notch, that can be pulled up or down to help close the laryngeal airway

(11) _____ A lateral projection of the arytenoid to which abductory and adductory muscles attach

(12) _____ A signet ring–shaped cartilage at the top of the trachea that is the foundation of the larynx

(13) _____ Movement of the arytenoids that closes the vocal folds

(14) _____ The pair of muscles on the back of the cricoid that attach to the backs of the arytenoids to abduct them

(15) _____ The adductory contraction that squeezes the vocal processes of the arytenoids together

(16) _____ Muscles that originate and insert within the larynx

(17) _____ The mucosal cover of the vocalis muscle

(18) _____ The pair of muscles extending from the lateral upper edges of the cricoid to the lower border of the thyroid cartilage that lengthens the vocal folds

(19) _____ The segment of thyroarytenoid muscle that inserts into the lateral front portion of each arytenoid to close the muscular glottis

(20) _____ The pair of muscles extending from thyroid cartilage to epiglottis that pull the epiglottis up

(21) _____ The elastic membrane covered with mucosa that can move separately from the vocal cord during vibration and that covers the inner wall of the larynx from edge of the vocalis to the cricoid cartilage

(22) _____ The thick folds of mucous membrane protruding into the airway above the true folds

(23) _____ The vibrating segment of thyroarytenoid muscle that inserts into each vocal process

(24) _____ The pair of muscles extending from the lateral upper edges of the cricoid to the muscular processes of the arytenoids that medially compress the vocal processes

(25) _____ The thread-like collagenous fibers of the deep layer of the lamina propria

(26) _____ The pair of muscles extending from thyroid to arytenoid cartilages that adduct and shorten the vocal folds

(27) _____,_____ Opening and closing of the glottis when the vocal folds are adducted for phonation (voice)

(28) _____ The airway above the true vocal fold formed by the aryepiglottic folds and the epiglottis to which they attach

(29) _____ The space between the vocal folds

(30) _____ The lubricating indentation between true and false folds

Vocal Functions of Phonatory Muscles

Self-Study Instructions: This test can be used to help you assess how well you understand the speech functions of the phonatory muscles. Terms to be filled in are from the Review Glossary. Answers are given in Appendix E.

Vocal Function	*Muscles*
Abduction for voiceless sounds	(1) _____
Adduction for phonation	
Pulls arytenoids together to close cartilaginous glottis	(2) _____
	(3) _____
	(4) _____
Pulls vocal cords together to close muscular glottis	(5) _____
	(6) _____
	(7) _____
Medial compression of vocal folds	(8) _____
Adjustments for pitch, loudness, and quality	
Stiffness	(9) _____
Length	(10) _____
Mass	(11) _____
Opens aditus	(12) _____
Closes aditus	(13) _____

CHAPTER FIVE
Laryngeal Physiology

LARYNGEAL PHYSIOLOGY

Valving for Life

Like breathing for speech, use of the laryngeal valve for speech is, in many ways, another overlaid function. To see evidence of the priority which biological needs still hold over speech, try sneezing and talking at the same time, or try to speak after you are half way through swallowing. Because we can "borrow" the larynx for phonation only to the extent that it is not being commandeered for biological functions, we had best have a brief glimpse of the mechanics of these functions.

Breathing

When breathing for life, the airway must be open. For this purpose, the three valves of the larynx must all be open: the supraglottal cavity, the false vocal folds, and the true vocal folds. The true vocal folds, however, can be opened to either of two positions, depending on how heavily a person needs to breathe. For quiet respiration, the cords abduct to the *intermediate position*; for forced respiration, they abduct to the *lateral position* (Fig. 5–1).

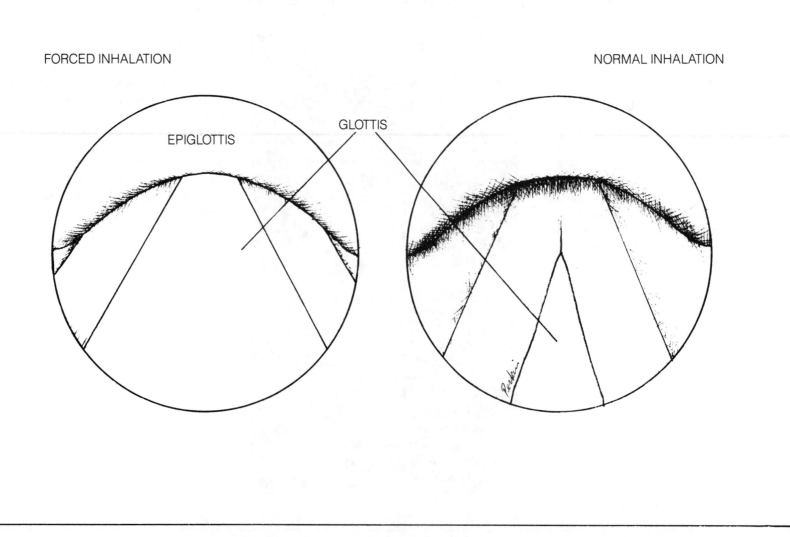

FIGURE 5–1
GLOTTAL OPENINGS FOR
BREATHING

FORCED INHALATION

NORMAL INHALATION

GLOTTIS

EPIGLOTTIS

Swallowing

The major task of the larynx in swallowing is to guard against entrance of any substance into the airway that would be harmful to the lungs. This includes fluids as well as solids. After all, the lungs are not equipped to digest food, and if the alveolar air sacs fill with fluid, as they do in pneumonia, you literally drown in your own juice. To keep from inhaling what belongs in the stomach, we have evolved a reflexive mechanism for swallowing that pulls the larynx up against the base of the tongue and squeezes the arytenoid cartilages against the epiglottis (Fig. 5–2). This action effectively closes the laryngeal inlet to the supraglottal cavity and pulls the top of the esophagus open to receive the bolus as it is swallowed.

Pressure Activities

Sneezing, coughing, defecating, childbirth, lifting — all require alveolar pressure. Generating such pressure not only requires compression of air by the respiratory pump, it is equally dependent on how tightly the laryngeal valve can be closed to resist the escape of air. Without airway resistance, thoracic compression produces only expulsion of air. The fact that you can build such high pressure that blood vessels throb while you turn red with exertion is evidence of how much the three laryngeal valves, especially the true vocal cords, can resist escape of air under high alveolar pressure.

Valving for Speech

Speech requires modified use of the laryngeal valve for its biological activities. Breathing adjustments of the larynx are modified least, but the swallowing reflex prevents speech altogether, so this reflex must be suppressed in order to speak; we cannot swallow and talk at the same time. It is modification in pressure functions of the larynx that most clearly reveals evolution at work. These functions have been changed significantly for speech, so much so that were we to use the laryngeal valve as it is used for biological reflexes, as in lifting a piano, say, speech would be all but impossible.

Clearly, we have inherited a pressure reflex that has evolved solely for the unique requirements of speech. Instead of being jammed so tightly together that air flow is shut off, the vocal cords adduct just enough to be set into vibration. The amount of resistance they offer permits a little air flow with voice, considerably more with a breathy tone, and nothing but air flow with a whisper. In fact, laryngeal resistance for voice is so refined that it can be controlled to produce changes in pitch and loudness from syllable to syllable many times per second to serve our expression of ideas and emotions.

Mechanics of Voiceless Sounds

For voiceless consonants (such as the first sounds of words like *pad, tad, cad, fad, sad*), the laryngeal valve is opened so that air can flow unobstructed into the throat and mouth. There it can be resisted partially or completely with the tongue or lips. The particular voiceless sound produced will depend on how completely the air channel is constricted or blocked and where in the channel the obstruction occurs.

Whispering. Although whispering involves air flow through the larynx in which voice is not produced, the vocal folds nevertheless offer considerable resistance to the air stream. Were it not for the friction noise set up by this resistance, the air would flow noiselessly through the glottis and a whisper would be inaudible.

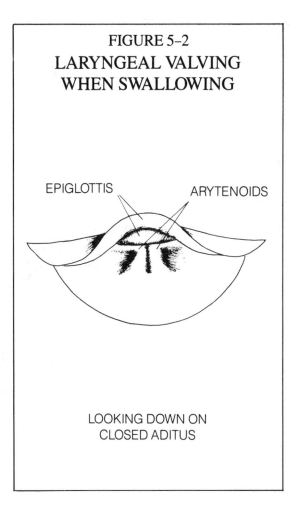

FIGURE 5–2
LARYNGEAL VALVING
WHEN SWALLOWING

EPIGLOTTIS   ARYTENOIDS

LOOKING DOWN ON
CLOSED ADITUS

FIGURE 5–3
THE GLOTTIS

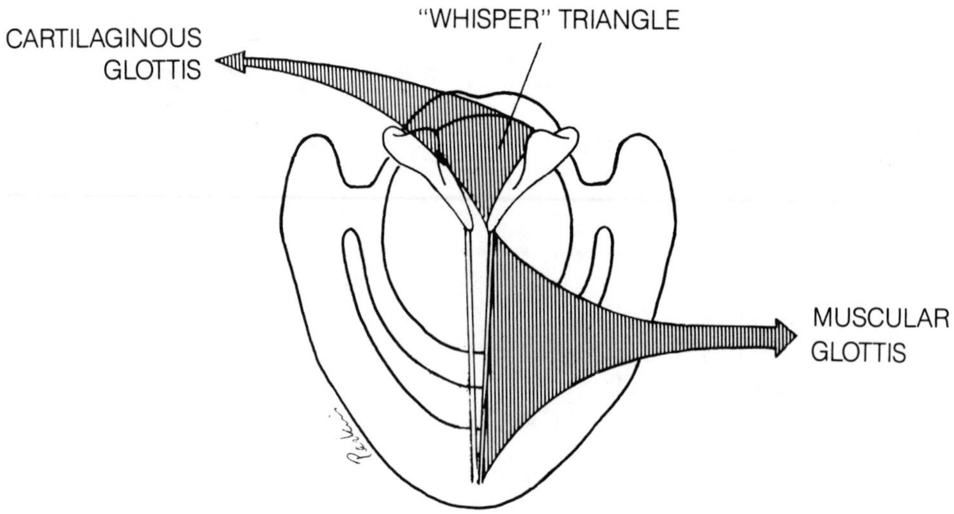

For the vocal folds to resist the air stream without vibrating and still permit air flow requires a special whisper adjustment. The vibrating glottal edges that border the vocalis muscle (the *muscular glottis*) are stiffened and positioned far enough apart to prevent vibration, but the vocal processes are toed in (by contraction of the lateral cricoarytenoids). At the same time, the *cartilaginous glottis* (the portion of the glottis bordered by the arytenoid cartilages) is separated posteriorly to form a glottal chink, sometimes dubbed the "whisper triangle." This adjustment permits air to flow through the glottis without setting the vocal folds into vibration (Fig. 5–3).

Mechanics of Glottal Vibration

To investigate how the vocal folds function for speech has required some remarkable technology. Because the folds frequently vibrate several hundred times per second, they appear only as a blur in x-rays or if their image in a laryngeal mirror is photographed. One of the earliest solutions to this problem was to use *high speed cinematography*, in which a 100 foot reel of film can be run through a special camera in less than a second. At speeds which can be upwards of 4,000 frames per second (compared with 24 frames per second in a conventional camera), the rapid movements of the vocal folds can be studied in ultra-slow motion.

Other approaches have been used to obtain information about laryngeal functions. Air flow has been measured with a *pneumotachograph*, which only requires wearing a specially designed face mask. Other procedures have involved punctures and probes. Electrodes have been inserted into laryngeal muscles, even into the vocalis during vibration, to determine patterns of muscle contraction with the technique of *electromyography*. Subglottal pressure has been measured by puncturing the trachea with a large, hollow needle, and by slipping a miniature microphone the size of the tip

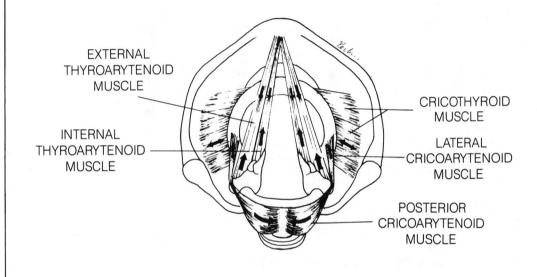

FIGURE 5–4
INTRINSIC LARYNGEAL MUSCLES

EXTERNAL THYROARYTENOID MUSCLE

INTERNAL THYROARYTENOID MUSCLE

CRICOTHYROID MUSCLE

LATERAL CRICOARYTENOID MUSCLE

POSTERIOR CRICOARYTENOID MUSCLE

of a pencil through the nose and down into the larynx. The folds have been photographed with flexible fiberoptics cables, also fed into position through the nose.

To avoid such invasions, with their distortions of the speech being studied (to say nothing of their effects on the subject), alternative techniques have been developed. They range from the relatively straightforward *laryngograph*, which measures changes in current through the larynx when the glottis opens and closes, to *stroboscopic laminography*. The latter is a complex form of radiography in which bursts of x-rays are timed to the vibratory rate in order to produce slow motion x-ray pictures of the vocal folds in action.

It is from measures such as these, and from more recently developed sophisticated acoustic analyses (which are as noninvasive as is possible), that the following synopsis has been derived. This research has revealed only some of the laryngeal adjustments of speech. Much remains to be discovered, particularly about which muscles produce which adjustment.

One of the main reasons that voice physiology is so difficult to understand is that the vocal folds are held in dynamic balance by so many different combinations of muscles pulling in so many different combinations of directions. An increase in vocalis tension, for example, if it is not to shorten the folds, must be opposed by increased cricothyroid contraction, along with a readjustment of the balance of forces on the muscular processes by the posterior and lateral cricoarytenoids and the external thyroarytenoids (Fig. 5–4). Rarely, if ever, can laryngeal movement be appropriately explained by the action of individual muscles. At the very least, they act in pairs, and usually in complex groups.

Vibratory Cycle. To understand how voice is produced requires that you understand a single vibration of the vocal folds, the *glottal cycle*. It is the basic building block of voice. Generally, it is described as beginning when subglottal pressure overpowers fold resistance just enough for the

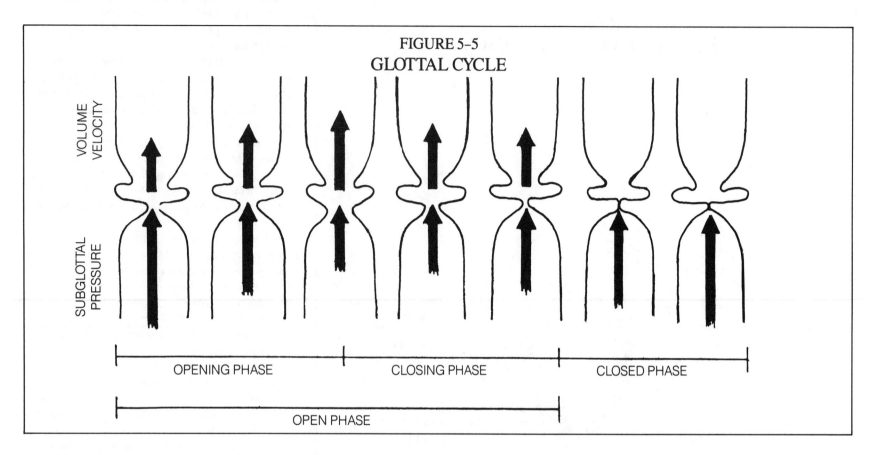

FIGURE 5-5
GLOTTAL CYCLE

VOLUME VELOCITY

SUBGLOTTAL PRESSURE

OPENING PHASE   CLOSING PHASE   CLOSED PHASE

OPEN PHASE

vocal folds to first start to blow open. They continue to blow apart during the *opening phase* until the escape of air reduces subglottal pressure enough for fold resistance to overpower air flow. At that point, the *closing phase* begins as the folds move toward each other. It ends as soon as the glottis is closed (or as nearly closed as it will get during the cycle). During the remainder of the cycle, the glottis is closed while subglottal pressure builds up to start the entire cycle over again (Fig. 5-5).

Two ratios have been devised to describe features of this cycle. The *speed quotient* (SQ) is the ratio of the durations of the opening phase to the closing phase. Note that during both of these phases, the glottis is open. The ratio of the duration of this period of openness to the duration of the entire cycle is the *open quotient* (OQ). In normal voice, the period of openness is followed by a closed phase in which the folds are together. During this closed phase, subglottal pressure rises. In some types of voice, however, as in production of a breathy tone, the glottis never closes completely. When this happens, there is one long *closing* phase, but the *closed* phase never occurs. In these instances, SQ reveals more about the glottal cycle than OQ.*

The closed phase is a period during which the vocal folds absorb the impact of their collision when they slam together. Presumably, the duration of this period of closure depends on how forcefully the folds collide, and how absorptive the folds are of this force. Were the vocal folds like two steel balls, they would hit and immediately bounce apart. There would be no closed phase when they were together for any period. Instead, they are *compliant*, more like rubber balls. The more compliant they are, the more they absorb the impact, and the longer they remain closed (Fig. 5-6).

*You may have discovered that there are two conditions under which the glottis is opened. One is when the arytenoids are abducted for breathing and voiceless sounds, the other is when the arytenoids are adducted for phonation and the cords are blown open by subglottal pressure. During a glottal cycle the arytenoids remain adducted in a phonatory position.

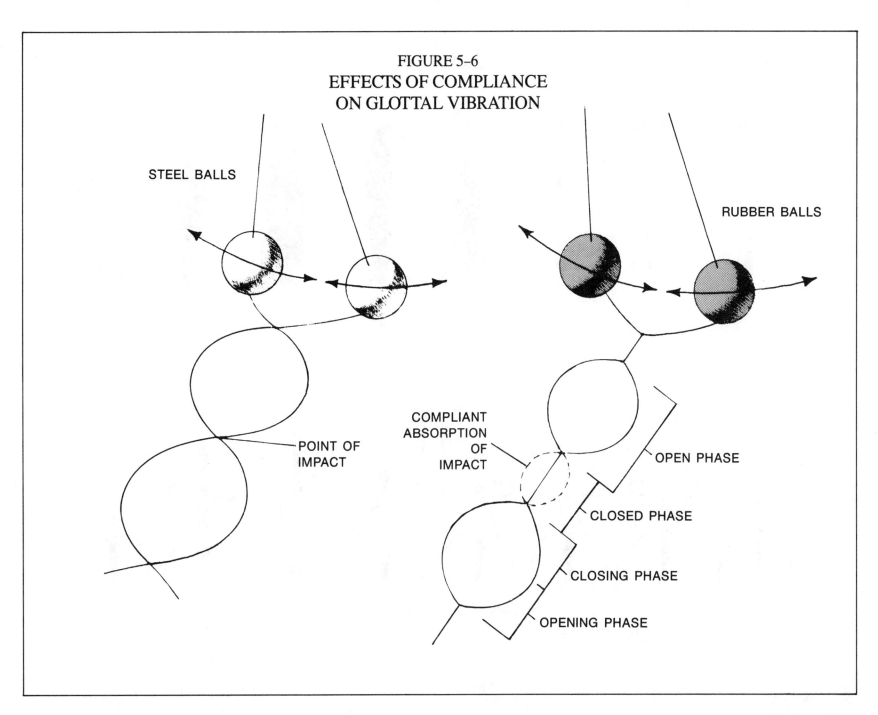

FIGURE 5–6
EFFECTS OF COMPLIANCE
ON GLOTTAL VIBRATION

STEEL BALLS

RUBBER BALLS

POINT OF
IMPACT

COMPLIANT
ABSORPTION
OF
IMPACT

OPEN PHASE

CLOSED PHASE

CLOSING PHASE

OPENING PHASE

FIGURE 5–7

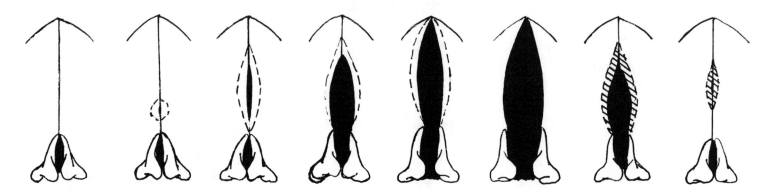

SPREAD OF GLOTTAL OPENING

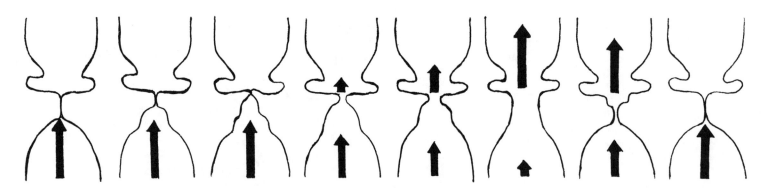

VERTICAL PHASE DIFFERENCE

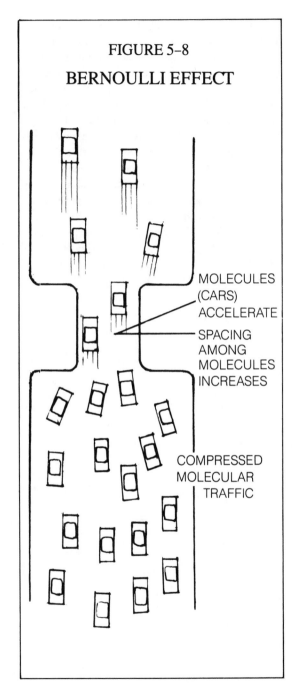

FIGURE 5–8

BERNOULLI EFFECT

MOLECULES (CARS) ACCELERATE

SPACING AMONG MOLECULES INCREASES

COMPRESSED MOLECULAR TRAFFIC

Not only can the vocal folds vary in compliance (and hence in how absorptive they are of impact force), they also vary in complexity of vibratory motion. They begin the opening phase by blowing upward and outward. They open from bottom to top and close from bottom to top. This creates what is called a *vertical phase difference*, as is shown in Figure 5–7. They also typically open from back to front and close from front to back, as in Figure 5–7. But in some people the motion is reversed; the opening spreads from front to back, and closes from back to front. Still another vibratory complexity is the motion of the mucous membrane covering the true folds. This loosely attached membrane tends to undulate in waves during phonation like jelly being shaken. In fact, the mucosa apparently vibrates more than the vocalis muscle, and the mucosa may be more essential to phonation than the muscle, which seems to function mainly to control shape of the vocal fold. All of these motions are difficult to study, so their effects on voice are not well understood. Yet, enough is known from computer simulation of phonatory motions to know that vibration would not occur at all were it not for vertical phase differences in the vocal folds, particularly in the mucosa, during the glottal cycle.

Vibratory Forces. What are the forces that operate in a glottal cycle that determine when and where the vocal folds will separate, how quickly they will open, how quickly they will close, and how long they will remain closed? The best unified answer to this question is the *aerodynamic-myoelastic theory* of phonation. The essence of this theory is that glottal vibration is a result of the interaction between aerodynamic forces and vocal fold muscular forces.

The aerodynamic forces at work in phonation make sense only if you understand the so-called *Bernoulli effect* (the effect of the Bernoulli principle bearing the Swiss scientist's name). Your life is full of encounters with this effect which, if you have thought about them, may seem puzzling. It is the effect that gives "lift" to an airplane wing, and that pulls air out of a car window when a wind-wing is open.

Stated briefly, the Bernoulli principle (which physicists call the venturi effect) is that, as velocity of a gas or liquid increases, pressure decreases. This principle is not difficult to grasp if you think of the trachea and laryngeal airway as being analogous to a freeway, and of the molecules of air as analogous to cars on the freeway. Add to this analogy the knowledge that the closer together molecules are compressed, the higher the pressure. Now all you need do is to recall that the closer together the cars are, the slower they move (Fig. 5–8). Conversely, the faster they move (the faster the air velocity) the farther apart they will be spaced (the lower the pressure). Thus, the faster the air flows through the glottis, the farther apart the molecules, so the less force they will exert against the vocal folds to push them open.

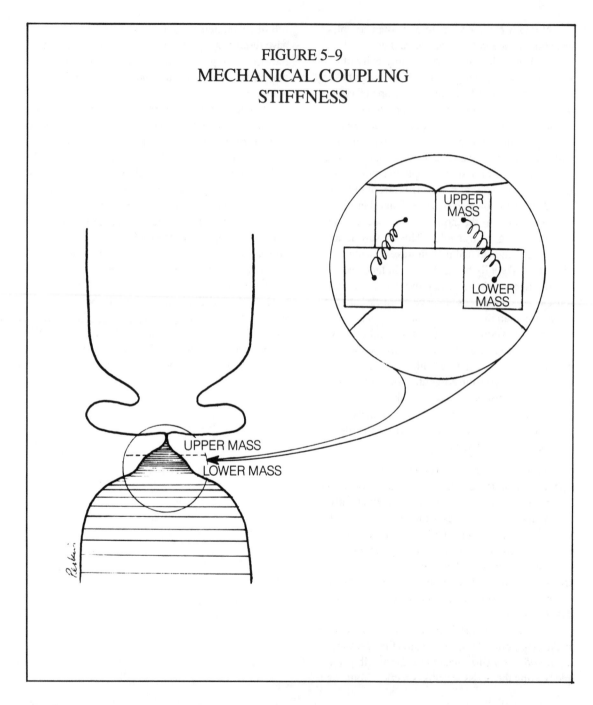

FIGURE 5-9
MECHANICAL COUPLING
STIFFNESS

UPPER MASS

LOWER MASS

UPPER MASS

LOWER MASS

The opposing myoelastic (muscular and elastic tissue) forces also need some explanation. We commented earlier that phonation would not be possible were it not for the vertical phase difference between the upper and lower portions of the vocal folds. The reason this is so has to do with the fact that the glottal edge, particularly the loose mucosal covering, functions as if it were two separate but interconnected masses, one below the other. (In reality these two masses are the upper and lower portions of the mucous membrane and the underlying vocalis muscle, and because these portions are attached, when the lower portion is pushed aside by air pressure, the upper portion is necessarily dragged along with it.) The strength of the connection between these two masses is the *mechanical coupling stiffness* (Fig. 5-9).

Another muscular force needing explanation is often called longitudinal tension, but more recently has been termed *stiffness*. Some maintain it results from stretching the vocal folds. Others point out that except for the vocal ligament, which some think becomes tense when stretched, elongation of the vocalis muscle merely thins it. In this view, the tension of the vocalis is a matter of how much it contracts. Whatever the case, the effect of "longitudinal tension" is to stiffen the folds and increase their resistance to being pushed outward and upward by air pressure. In addition to the resistance resulting from stiffness is the resistance resulting from *mass* (thickness of the vocalis muscle). The more mass in the cords, the more force required to move them apart.

Finally, the *viscous forces* of vocal fold tissues determine how well they dissipate force applied to them. If you filled a plastic bag with molasses and drove your fist into it, it would offer more resistance than if it were filled with water. The reason, of course, is that molasses is more viscous than water. Similarly, the more viscous the vocal folds, the more they decrease the velocity of any movement they are forced to make, and hence the more resistance they offer to aerodynamic forces.

Putting these aerodynamic and myoelastic forces together, vocal fold vibration can be understood as the result of dynamic interchanges of *intraglottal pressure* between the folds that forces them apart and their mechanical resistance to this pressure. At the beginning of the glottal cycle, intraglottal pressure (which is approximately the same as subglottal pressure) exceeds atmospheric pressure above the folds, so it forces open a small glottal chink, usually posteriorly, as it escapes. Air flows through this chink as the molecules move upward from a standstill in the trachea to high velocity through the glottis. (Returning to our freeway analogy in Figure 5–8, it is like breaking out of a traffic jam and accelerating quickly as the space between cars increases.) As air molecules accelerate and move farther apart, pressure against the upper portion of the folds decreases, but remains high against the lower portion, where the molecules are still compressed in a "traffic jam." Thus, the upper glottis is not blown open by pressure so much as it is dragged open by the stiffness of the mechanical coupling of the upper to the lower portion of the folds. It is against the lower portion that intraglottal pressure forces the folds apart.

The aerodynamic force continues to open the glottis, thereby increasing volume velocity and mechanical resistance of vocal fold tissues to wider displacement. When this resistance exceeds intraglottal pressure, the glottis begins to close. Because the lower portion of the fold drags the upper portion open, the lower also leads the upper in closing. As the folds close, air flow velocity through the glottis increases, thereby reducing intraglottal pressure (the Bernoulli effect); thus, the folds gather momentum as they move toward closure. When they collide, the duration of closure, before the cycle will be ready to repeat itself, will depend on how rapidly the force of the impact is dissipated by viscous forces and how rapidly intraglottal pressure builds up to overcome glottal resistance.

Mechanics of Voice Control

Voice can be controlled for pitch, loudness, and quality. In addition, the register in which it is produced can also be controlled. Our task now is to examine how the aerodynamic and myoelastic forces are regulated for these different vocal characteristics.

Register. The mode of adjustment of the larynx by which voice is produced is traditionally called the *register*. It is a controversial term, especially among singers who are inclined to claim that there are numerous registers, and then argue at length about how to differentiate one from the other. An indisputable fact about registers, though, is that they make a profound difference in quality, pitch range, and loudness.

The two registers for which there is clearest physiological distinction are usually identified by singers as *chest* and *falsetto* (Fig. 5–10). You have encountered the transition from chest to falsetto if your voice has "broken" when you have tried to sing a high pitch, or have yodelled. For those who have experience with chest and falsetto adjustments, the difference in quality is unmistakable, and the range of pitches possible in the two barely overlap.

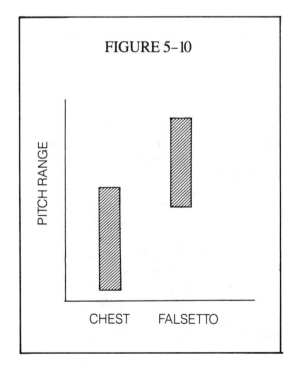

FIGURE 5–10

PITCH RANGE

CHEST   FALSETTO

Compared to singing, speech uses a relatively restricted range of fundamental frequencies and a restricted mode of laryngeal vibration. Ranges of fundamental frequencies for singing are about 80 to 700 Hz for men and 140 to 1,100 Hz for women. Almost all speech is produced with one *register*, which is defined as a mode or combination of modes of laryngeal vibration. The *modal register*, which is the register used for speech, is distinguished from *falsetto register* and *pulse register*, among others.

The modal register produces relatively low fundamental frequencies. (It is also called *chest* or *heavy* register.) Physiologically, this register is associated with vocalis muscle activity, which keeps the vocal folds short in length, and cricothyroid muscle activity, which increases to produce higher fundamental frequencies. Generally, for modal register, the vocal folds are short and thick, stiffness of the vocal folds is relatively low, amplitude of vibration is large, the folds tend to come together completely during the closing phase, the signal generated is rich in harmonics, and the conversion of muscular-aerodynamic energy to sound energy is efficient.

The falsetto register (also called *light* register) produces a higher range of fundamental frequencies. In this register, the vocalis is lax and the cricothyroid activity adjusts the length of the vocal folds, with longer, hence thinner, folds producing higher frequencies. Compared to modal register, falsetto register has not only longer and thinner vocal folds but also stiffer folds, a small amplitude of vibration, incomplete closure of the folds, fewer higher harmonics, and a lesser efficiency in converting the energy from the lungs into sound energy. Vocal fold vibration in the falsetto register has a shutter-like appearance in which the tense folds move rapidly and with a small excursion.

The pulse register is also called *vocal fry*, *glottal fry*, or *glottal roll*. This is a very low-frequency register and often sounds rough or deep. It is used infrequently for either speech or singing. It is characterized by short, thick, and lax vocal folds and sometimes by a complex vibratory pattern in which the folds come together twice in each closing phase.

Physiologically, a popular explanation of the difference between chest and falsetto adjustments hinges on whether elongation of the vocal folds is opposed by the vocalis muscle or the vocal ligament. Presumably, contraction of the vocalis would provide a relatively thick glottal edge. With such thickness, the two layered vibratory dynamics discussed earlier would operate. If elongation is opposed by the stretched vocal ligament, then the vocal folds would come close to functioning as a taut vibrating fold. The glottal edge would be thin (which it seems to be in falsetto), and the resistance to air pressure would be reduced, so the folds would barely close before they blew open again (which also seems to be the case). Pitch would be raised by stretching the ligament to increase longitudinal tension, and by medially compressing the folds, thereby shortening their vibratory length (a strategy used with string instruments for raising pitch).

This is an attractive account, but it is probably wrong. The dubious part of this popular explanation is that the ligament can be stretched taut enough to perform as a vibrating cord. To be taut would require that it be lengthened to its limit. Research has shown, though, that the folds never come close to reaching their maximum potential length during phonation, even in falsetto register (Fig. 5–11). What does appear to happen is that only the mucosal edge vibrates. Although ligament tension does not seem to be the answer, whatever it turns out to be will have to explain why the folds perform as if the ligament were being stretched.

FIGURE 5-11
VOCAL LIGAMENT LENGTH

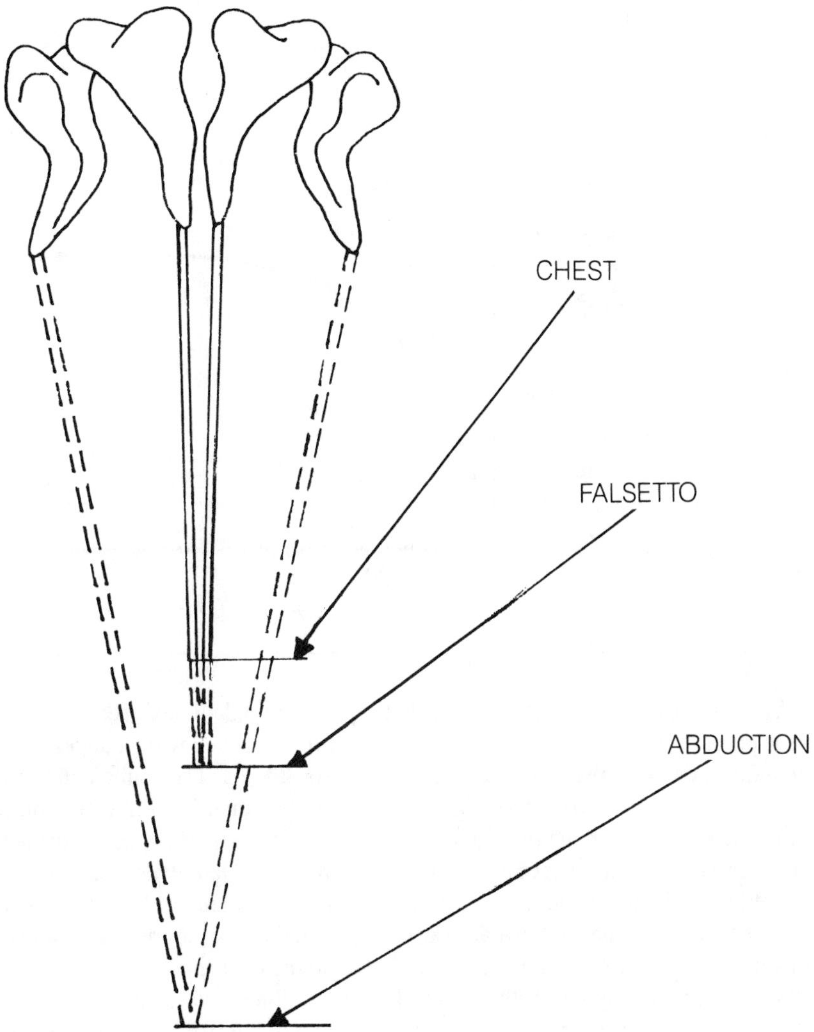

CHEST

FALSETTO

ABDUCTION

Pitch. Obviously, what we hear as the "pitch" of the voice differs among speakers. Within a family, the father has the lowest pitched voice, the mother has a higher pitch, and a very young child has an even higher pitch. Older children have intermediate pitches. Especially after about the age of 11 or 12, males have a lower vocal pitch than females. In men, the range of *fundamental frequencies* in speech (fundamental frequency is the physical correlate of perceived pitch) is about 80 to 240 Hz, with a mean value of about 125 Hz. A baby in the first two or three months of life has a mean fundamental frequency of about 400 Hz, but the range is as great as 100 to 1,200 Hz. Because of these differences in fundamental frequency, speakers are perceived to have different pitches. These differences are related primarily to the size of the larynx and especially to the size of the vocal folds. As the larynx grows, the fundamental frequency tends to decrease. The most rapid changes in the size of the larynx occur during adolescence — especially in males. As the larynx grows relatively rapidly in size, the voice breaks, skips, and seems generally unsteady. The adolescent whose voice is changing is testimony to the relationship between fundamental frequency and the size of the larynx.

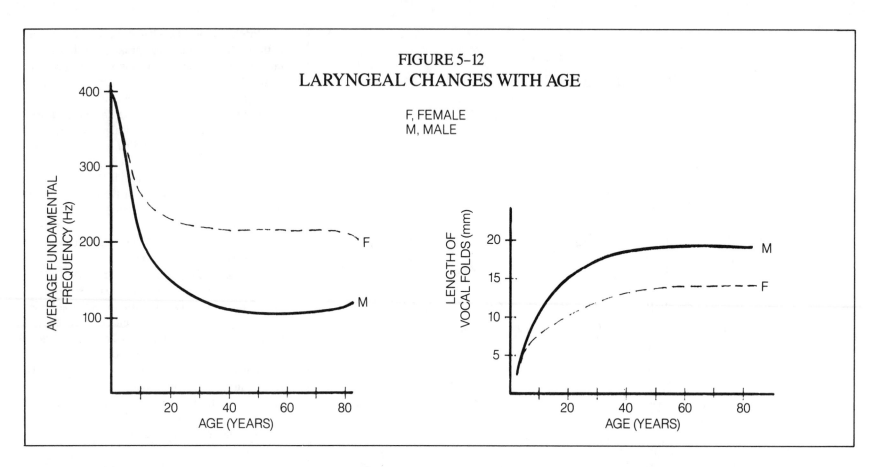

FIGURE 5–12
LARYNGEAL CHANGES WITH AGE

F, FEMALE
M, MALE

A speaker's average fundamental frequency is strongly affected by age and gender. As shown in Figure 5–12, the average fundamental frequency changes markedly during the first 20 years of life and then assumes relatively stable values throughout adulthood. Infants vary greatly in their mean fundamental frequencies, but the figure of approximately 400 Hz may be taken as representative for about the first year of life. Thereafter, the fundamental frequency falls steadily until the adult value is achieved. For males, a particularly large change occurs during adolescence, at which time the laryngeal structures increase markedly in size. A male-female difference in fundamental frequency is apparent by the age of 12 years, but it is after that age that the average curves depart from one another. Eventually, the female reaches an average value of 225 to 250 Hz, about one octave higher than that of the male, for whom the average is about 125 Hz. Limited data also suggest that there are gender differences in the geriatric years. The fundamental frequency declines somewhat in aging women but tends to increase in aging men. The quality of the voice changes as well with advanced age, such that the age of a speaker can be judged with some accuracy even from tape recordings of prolonged vowels.

You can see in Figure 5–12 that the changes in mean fundamental frequency during the life span are correlated with changes in the length of the vocal folds. The young child has vocal folds that are less than 5 millimeters (mm) long (about one fifth of an inch), whereas the adult male has a vocal fold length approaching 20 mm (about four fifths of an inch). It is also apparent that most females have shorter vocal folds in adulthood than do most males.

Singers frequently use *vibrato*, or a modulation of the fundamental frequency. Vibrato is a kind of physiologic tremor that causes the fundamental frequency to vary up and down over a small range a few times per second. Vibrato is an aes-

FIGURE 5-13
VOCAL FOLD THICKNESS

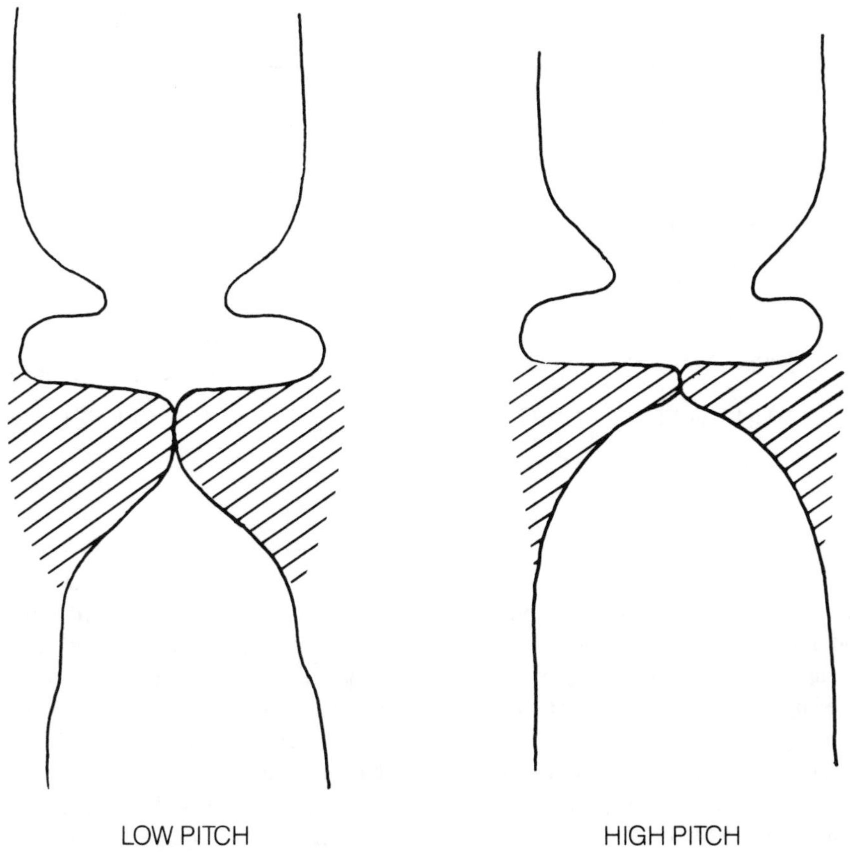

LOW PITCH   HIGH PITCH

thetic use of fundamental frequency modulation. An undesirable modulation, pathological vocal tremor, occurs in some speakers with various voice disorders. Their speaking voices sound wavering or quavering.

Fundamental frequency of the voice is determined physiologically by the rate at which the vocal folds vibrate. More technically, this is the number of times per second the glottal cycle is repeated. What we will consider now are the muscular force adjustments that can be made to oppose aerodynamic forces and thereby control vibratory rate.

Bear in mind that the shorter the glottal cycle, the greater the number of cycles that can occur per second. Thus, any adjustment that shortens the glottal cycle will raise the fundamental frequency. Let us start with myoelastic adjustments.

An obvious place to begin would appear to be with vocal fold length. As has been noted, the pitch of the voice is generally higher in women than men, although there is some overlap. The reason almost certainly is that the folds are longer in men than women. That length alone is not the explanation becomes apparent when we recall that to increase pitch, the folds are lengthened, not shortened. Whatever role vocal fold elongation plays in pitch control, it must be through its effect on some factor other than length. One possibility is that longitudinal tension is increased as the folds are elongated, but we have seen that the analogy to a vibrating string is probably not even true of the vocal ligament, let alone the vocalis muscle. That leaves thickness of the vocal folds — that is, their mass. Here we find a genuine possibility. Not only are the folds longer in men than women, they are also thicker. Moreover, the effect of lengthening them to raise pitch thins their mass (Fig. 5-13). In fact, vocal fold thickness correlates better with fundamental frequency than does length. So far, so good. The problem with mass as the major explanation is that it does not vary enough to account for the range of pitches we can produce.

What is the major explanation, if not length, longitudinal tension, or mass? It would appear to lie in the stiffness of the folds resulting from lengthening and contraction of the thyroarytenoids, especially the vocalis portion. You can see for yourself how these factors operate. Flex your arm and notice how contracting and relaxing the biceps does not change its thickness particularly, but the muscle does stiffen more and more as it is contracted. Now extend your arm and observe how thickness of the biceps diminishes. When the biceps is fully elongated, contracting it alters only its stiffness, not its thickness. For the finale of this demonstration, push against the biceps when it is contracted and when it is relaxed. With contraction, you cannot push the muscle to the side (its stiffness resists displacement). You can also observe in passing that the arm can rest comfortably in any position, whether extended or flexed, in which the muscles are relaxed. Still, an elongated muscle when relaxed is somewhat stiffer than when shortened, so stiffness is in part a result of vocal fold lengthening.

We have laid the foundation for what probably happens when fundamental frequency is increased. We start with the folds in vibration at any given rate. This means that subglottal pressure exceeds supraglottal pressure (the atmospheric pressure above the glottis); otherwise, no aerodynamic force would be overpowering mechanical resistive forces enough to cause the folds to vibrate. If vocalis contraction is increased, the folds will stiffen and be more resistant to being pushed as far apart, thereby shortening the opening phase. Then, when they collide at closure, they will be more resistive to impact, so the period of closure will be shortened. The net effect will be to shorten the glottal cycle, thus increasing fundamental frequency, but within limits probably imposed by the mass of the folds. To thin this mass will require lengthening

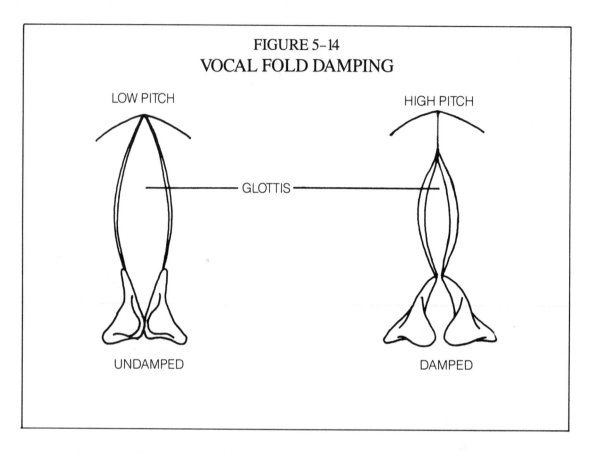

FIGURE 5-14
VOCAL FOLD DAMPING

LOW PITCH

HIGH PITCH

GLOTTIS

UNDAMPED

DAMPED

them, which is accomplished by contraction of the cricothyroid muscles. Within the fundamental frequency limits of any given mass, pitch is probably fine-tuned by vocalis contraction. At the highest frequencies, glottal length is probably shortened by medial compression of the vocal folds, thereby damping vibrations of the posterior portion of the folds as shown in Figure 5-14. With a shorter glottis to open and close from back to front or from front to back, glottal cycles will also be shortened; hence, pitch will be raised.

To reduce fundamental frequency from high pitches, the folds must be shortened, thickened, and relaxed. By necessity, shortening requires contraction of some portion of the thyroarytenoids.

If this portion is the vocalis, then stiffness will be traded off against thickness, which it probably is for some pitch adjustments. For lowest pitches, the external thyroarytenoids must provide the contraction so that the vocalis can be relaxed as well as thickened and shortened.

Definitive research on pitch control is still to be done. The foregoing description is as probable as any. At least it matches the observable changes in the vocal folds as pitch is changed. When fundamental frequency is in the lower mid-pitch range, the folds appear thick and relaxed. Vertical phase differences between upper and lower portions of the glottal edge are prominent. As pitch is raised, the rounded, thick glottal lips become stiffer and thinner, until at high pitches, the glottis is little more than a slit, only the edges of the folds vibrate, and complete closure does not occur. Although subglottal pressure increases with pitch for many, this is not a necessity; it need not vary with pitch. The only aerodynamic requirement is that it provide sufficient force to oppose mechanical forces in a vibratory interchange.

Loudness. If Bishop Berkeley's proverbial tree fell in the forest and no one heard it, would it create a sound? The answer, of course, is "yes." The crash would generate acoustic waves which would radiate in all directions, whether or not anyone were around to respond to the vibrations. The force of the crash would be reflected in the *intensity* of the sound, that is, in the amount of energy of the vibrations. If anyone had been around to hear the tree fall, what they would have perceived in response to that intensity would have been the *loudness* of the sound. In brief, loudness is the listener's response to the amount of energy in a sound.

Three methods of generating energy for speech are used. Two take the form of noise. One involves friction for sounds like *s* and *f*. The noises for sounds like *p* and *t*, however, are made with explosive bursts of air released by the tongue or lips. The third method of generating energy produces tone. Because tones have more intensity than the noises we use for speech, they give syllables carrying power. Syllables do not have to contain noise consonants, but they do have to contain a tone. The particular tone typically takes the form of a vowel — which means "voice," and which is what humans produce when they generate tone. Thus, the remainder of this discussion of loudness will deal with how we control vocal intensity.

The reason voice has so much more energy than noise is because it is produced by a repetitive series of glottal pulses. Each of these pulses is similar to the one you produce for the sound *p*. If you put your hand in front of your mouth, you can feel the force of the puff of air, as well as hear it. Produce *p* softly and loudly. Observe how loudness varies with the volume and velocity of air you can feel against your hand with each puff. You can see that *volume velocity* of the air stream determines intensity of the acoustic vibration. For voice, about 50 to 1,000 of these puffs are generated each second — the rate is the fundamental frequency which, you will recall, is heard as the pitch. Because there are so many more pulses per second than in a consonant like *p*, there is much greater intensity. Although the amount of energy increases with fundamental frequency, it is the amount of energy in the glottal pulses that is the major determinant of loudness; so the more frequently pulses occur (the higher the fundamental frequency), the greater the energy.

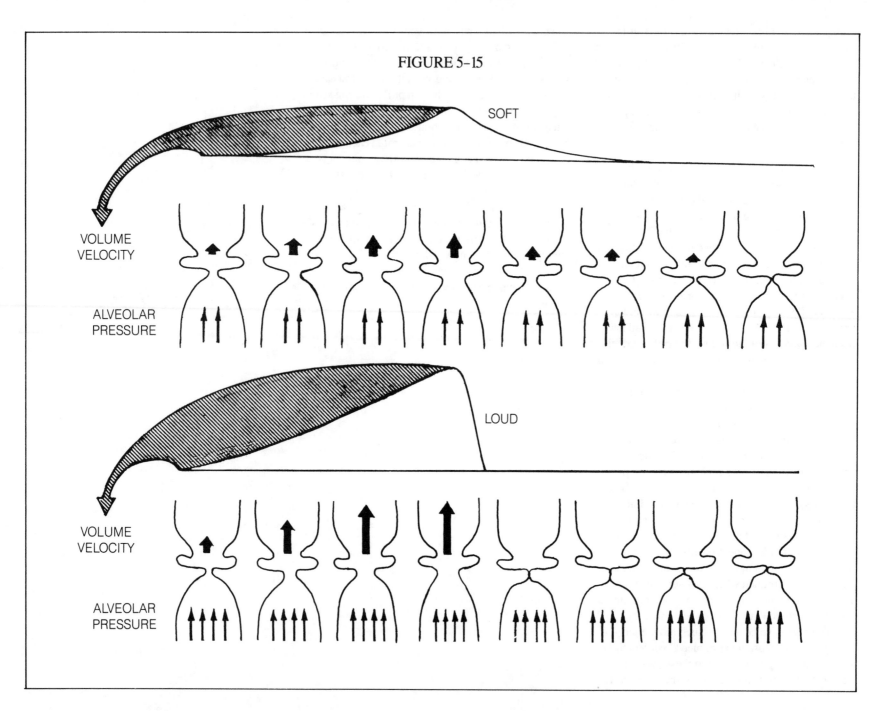

FIGURE 5-15

SOFT

VOLUME
VELOCITY

ALVEOLAR
PRESSURE

LOUD

VOLUME
VELOCITY

ALVEOLAR
PRESSURE

Functional Anatomy of Speech, Language, and Hearing

Thus, we are back again to the glottal cycle, this time with a view to how it controls loudness. It should be evident that the greater the volume velocity of each glottal pulse, the greater the loudness. Not surprisingly, volume velocity is directly related to alveolar and subglottal pressures. The higher the pressure, the greater the volume of air that will escape, and the greater the velocity with which it will escape. We would think that loudness would also vary with *glottal area* (how far apart the folds are blown), but this is not necessarily the case. Loudness is the result of the amount of acoustic energy generated by the glottal pulse, which is not necessarily a function of how much air escapes through the glottis (Fig. 5–15). Actually, a major factor responsible for loudness is the abruptness with which volume velocity of air flow in the glottis is shut off by fold closure at the end of each glottal cycle. Abrupt termination creates a partial vacuum above the folds after they close, which sets up a relatively powerful acoustic disturbance somewhat like a mini-thunderclap. Control of volume velocity of air molecules for a soft tone is not unlike a fire drill; for a loud tone, like escape from a conflagration. Air molecules are likened to people, and pressure is the difference between a drill and an emergency demanding a hasty exit. In a drill, people may stroll out leisurely (low pressure and low volume velocity). In a conflagration, the pressure to escape will be great (high alveolar and subglottal pressures), and the people will be shoving to escape (high-volume velocity). This much about loudness is reasonably certain.

What we do not know with much certainty are the laryngeal mechanics that control volume velocity. What is known is that intensity increases as alveolar and subglottal pressures increase. Predictably, glottal resistance also increases with intensity. After all, pressure cannot rise any higher than there is resistance to oppose air flow. The other factor known with reasonable certainty is that the louder the tone, the longer the vocal folds will remain closed during a cycle. This factor seems sensible; the longer the folds are closed, the more resistance they offer, hence the greater the pressure before they are blown open in the next cycle.

What seems to vary is air flow and glottal area. With some people, perhaps most, air flow and glottal area increase with loudness. But neither of these conditions is *necessary* for increased loudness. Some persons show no increase in air flow, and some may actually decrease glottal resistance and the duration of glottal closure.

What is not known well enough to warrant conclusions is what the laryngeal adjustments are that increase glottal resistance and the duration of glottal closure. Even more puzzling is how loudness can be controlled separately from pitch. Admittedly, pitch and loudness typically rise and fall together. But they need not, and many times do not. The puzzle arises from the fact that the interaction of glottal resistance and air pressure seems to be the key to the control of pitch as well as loudness. But how they are controlled to change one without the other gives us a glimpse of the complexity beyond the edge of our knowledge.

Quality. The aspect of voice about which least is known is the one that is most difficult to describe: *quality*. For lack of a better definition, it can be thought of as the distinctive characteristic of a tone, exclusive of its pitch and loudness. Acoustically, it can be defined, but trying to describe voice quality as we hear it has been an exercise in futility — with one exception. Speech sounds of a language differ by virtue of quality, and that difference is stable enough that different sounds in different words signify different meanings. Those differences in quality, however, are primarily due to resonator adjustments in the throat and mouth.

For that matter, resonance plays an important part in any voice quality, for reasons we will examine in Chapter 8. Aside from breathiness, harsh-

FIGURE 5–16
BREATHY VOICE

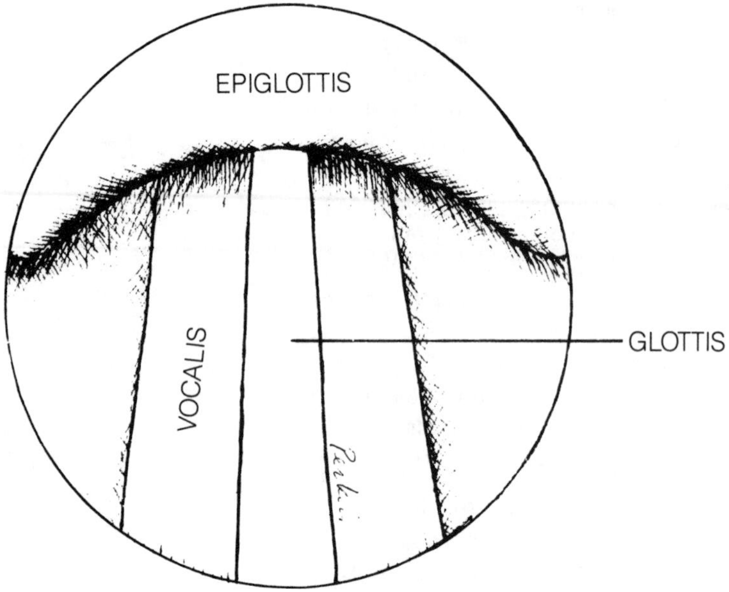

EPIGLOTTIS

VOCALIS

GLOTTIS

ness, and hoarseness, attempts to describe good or bad voice quality have met with remarkably little agreement. In view of the fact that these three qualities, for which there is some agreement, are mainly dependent on differences in laryngeal function, we will limit this discussion to them.

Breathiness is a quality that results from a glottal adjustment in which the folds offer enough resistance to be set into vibration by the air stream, but not enough to prevent a high volume of air from escaping with low velocity (Fig. 5–16). At least two laryngeal adjustments can result in breathiness. In one, the front of the folds are approximated closely enough to vibrate and thereby generate tone, whereas in back, a glottal chink is left open through which air escapes to an excessive extent. The size of the chink determines the extent of breathiness.

In the other adjustment, fold resistance is apparently so low that the folds are blown widely apart by relatively low pressure. The result is an excessively large glottal area in each cycle through which large volumes of air flow at low velocities. With either adjustment, the folds will barely close to build up pressure, so the voice will be breathy, will be soft or weak, and will consume excessive volumes of air for the intensity of sound produced.

Harshness, sometimes called *roughness*, is the quality often associated with a "gravelly" voice. It is a quality that can be heard in weak or loud voices. The cause is irregularity in vocal fold vibration. This results from glottal cycles that vary irregularly from one cycle to the next in duration, intensity, or both. The greater the irregularity, the rougher the voice. When duration is irregular, it has been called *pitch perturbation*, or, more sportively, *jitter*. When intensity varies irregularly, it is called *shimmer*. By contrast, a clear tone is one in which the duration and intensity of one glottal cycle are about the same as of the one before it and the one that follows.

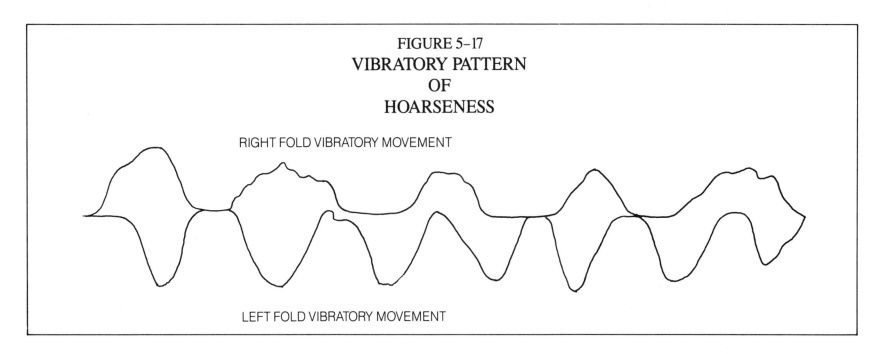

FIGURE 5–17
VIBRATORY PATTERN
OF
HOARSENESS

RIGHT FOLD VIBRATORY MOVEMENT

LEFT FOLD VIBRATORY MOVEMENT

Hoarseness is the quality that combines both breathiness and harshness. It results from irregular vibratory patterns in which air leakage is excessive (Fig. 5–17). Although hoarseness can be produced with a normal larynx, it is usually considered to be the early warning sign of laryngeal pathology. Any abnormal condition of the vocal folds, such as a tumor or paralysis, will tend to cause aperiodic vibration. The reason is that if one fold has more mass (the tumor adds mass) or is stiffer than the other (the paralyzed fold cannot contract and become stiff), the two folds will not vibrate at the same rate. Therefore, they will not always collide with each other when they close, the result being breathiness as well as roughness, which together are heard as hoarseness.

CLINICAL POSTSCRIPT

Because of various medical conditions, but especially cancer of the larynx, some individuals lose their vocal folds and their voices. However, they are not doomed to a life of mutism, for substitute voices are possible. One type of pseudo-voice is esophageal speech, in which the speaker swallows air that is trapped in the esophagus. When the individual desires to speak, he or she releases the esophageal air in a kind of belching action and forms speech sounds from this outflowing air. This manner of speaking may sound laborious, but an accomplished esophageal speaker can produce several syllables on one air release. An alternative to this natural type of voice generation is the artificial larynx, a mechanical vibrator that produces a tone that approximates the human voice. The alaryngeal speaker (speaker without a larynx) typically holds the vibrator close to the neck and then produces speech powered by the energy that is

transmitted through the neck wall and into the vocal tract. A third type of pseudo-voice is a prosthetic device in the form of a tube that is inserted into a surgically created opening between the trachea and the esophagus. For speaking, air is routed from the lungs through the prosthesis, which produces sound by means of a razor-thin slit in the end that extends into the esophagus. The other end of the tube is at the trachea. During breathing, a valve prevents air from entering the prosthesis to produce sound.

With these three types of pseudo-voice, together with experimental surgical procedures of laryngeal reconstruction, it is possible for most alaryngeal individuals to produce speech for general purposes. Continued improvements in these techniques are likely to yield better voice with less inconvenience to the individual. Losing one's vocal folds is still a serious matter, but voice rehabilitation permits the alaryngeal person to reenter the world of speech communication.

CHAPTER FIVE
Self-Study
Laryngeal Physiology

Review Glossary

Laryngeal adjustments: Adjustment of the larynx for biologic and phonatory functions

   Biological adjustments: **Abduction** of vocal folds in the lateral position for forced respiration and in the intermediate position for quiet respiration; **adduction** with all three valves (true folds, false folds, and aditus) close the larynx for swallowing and high pressure requirements

  Voice adjustments: Adduction of vocal folds for tone production and whispering

   Whisper adjustment: An adjustment in which the *muscular glottis* (formed by the vocalis muscle) is stiffly resistant to vibration and the *cartilaginous glottis* (formed by the vocal processes) is open to permit turbulent air flow

   Phonatory adjustment: An adjustment in which glottal vibrations can be controlled for tone production

    Aerodynamic-myoelastic theory: The theory that explains phonation as the interaction of air flow with muscular resistance

    Aerodynamic factors: Factors of laryngeal air flow and pressure

     Volume velocity: The volume and velocity of air through the glottis

     Bernoulli (venturi) effect: Reduction of pressure as velocity of air flow increases

     Glottal pulse: The jet of air released through the glottis with each vibratory cycle

     Subglottal (tracheal) pressure: Pressure below the vocal folds

     Intraglottal pressure: Pressure between the vocal folds

     Supraglottal pressure: Pressure above the vocal folds

    Myoelastic factors (glottal resistance): Factors of laryngeal muscular resistance to air flow

     Compliance: The extent to which the vocal folds absorb impact

     Damped vibration: Stiffening of the vocalis muscle that reduces the functional length of the vibrating glottis

     Length: Length of the vocal folds

     Mass: Thickness of the vocal folds, which decreases as length increases

     Stiffness (longitudinal tension): Resistance of the vocal folds to deformation that results from vocalis muscle contraction and lengthening, which is a determinant of compliance

     Mechanical coupling stiffness: Resistance of the upper and lower masses of the vocal folds to independent movement

     Vertical phase difference: Extent to which upper and lower masses of the vocal folds vibrate separately

     Viscosity: Resistance of the vocal folds to deformation resulting from fluids in the vocalis muscle; a determinant of compliance

  Vibratory (glottal) cycle: A cycle of vocal fold vibration from the time the glottis begins to open to the next time the glottis begins to open

   Open phase: The duration of the glottal cycle during which the vocal folds are open

    Opening phase: The phase during which the glottis opens

     Glottal area: The area of glottal opening

    Closing phase: The phase during which the glottis closes

   Closed phase: The phase during which the glottis is closed

   Open quotient (OQ): The ratio of the duration of the open phase to the duration of the glottal cycle

   Speed quotient (SQ): The ratio of the durations of the opening phase to the closing phase

Loudness: Perception of the intensity of voice determined mainly by volume velocity of glottal pulses

Pitch: Perception of fundamental frequency of voice determined by glottal vibration rate

Quality: Perception of the distinctive characteristics of a sound, exclusive of pitch and loudness; phonatory determinants are not well understood

Jitter: Irregular changes in duration of glottal cycles from one cycle to the next

Shimmer: Irregular changes in intensity of glottal pulses from one cycle to the next

Self-Study Test of Terminology

Self-Study Instructions: These questions can be used to help you assess how much you have retained from studying the Review Glossary. Answers are given in Appendix E.

(1) _____ The theory that explains phonation as the interaction of air flow with muscular resistance

(2) _____ Adduction of vocal folds for tone production and whispering

(3) _____ Adjustments of the larynx for biological and phonatory functions

(4) _____ Reduction of pressure as velocity of air flow increases

(5) _____ Resistance of the upper and lower masses of the vocal fold to independent movement

(6) _____ Stiffening of the vocalis muscle that reduces the functional length of the vibrating glottis

(7) _____ Pressure below the vocal folds

(8) _____ Abduction of vocal folds in the lateral position for forced respiration and in the intermediate position for quiet respiration; adduction with all three valves (true folds, false folds, and aditus) closes the larynx for swallowing and high pressure requirements

(9) _____ An adjustment in which the muscular glottis (formed by the vocalis muscle) is stiffly resistant to vibration and the cartilaginous glottis (formed by the vocal processes) is open to permit turbulent air flow

(10) _____ Factors of laryngeal air flow and pressure

(11) _____ Extent to which upper and lower masses of the vocal fold vibrate separately

(12) _____ Thickness of the vocal folds, which decreases as length increases

(13) _____ Pressure above the vocal folds

(14) _____ The duration of the glottal cycle during which the vocal folds are open

(15) _____ An adjustment in which glottal vibrations can be controlled for tone production

(16) _____ The extent to which the vocal folds absorb impact

(17) _____ A cycle of vocal fold vibration from the time the glottis begins to open to the next time the glottis begins to open

(18) _____ The phase during which the glottis is closed

(19) _____ The ratio of the duration of the open phase to the duration of the closed phase

(20) _____ Resistance of the vocal folds to deformation that results from vocalis muscle contraction and lengthening, which is a determinant of compliance

(21) _____ The ratio of the durations of the opening phase to the closing phase

(22) _____ Length of the vocal folds

(23) _____ The phase during which the glottis opens

(24) _____ Factors of laryngeal muscular resistance to air flow

(25) _____ Resistance of the vocal folds to deformation resulting from fluids in the vocalis muscle; a determinant of compliance

(26) _____ Perception of the distinctive characteristics of a sound, exclusive of pitch and loudness; phonatory determinants are not well understood

(27) _____ Pressure between the vocal folds

(28) _____ Perception of fundamental frequency of voice determined by glottal vibration rate

(29) _____ The volume and velocity of air through the glottis

(30) _____ The phase during which the glottis closes

(31) _____ Perception of the intensity of voice determined mainly by volume velocity of the glottal pulse

(32) _____ The area of glottal opening

(33) _____ The jet of air released through the glottis with each vibratory cycle

(34) _____ Irregular changes in intensity of glottal pulses from one cycle to the next

(35) _____ Irregular changes in duration of glottal cycles from one to the next

Self-Study Test of Understanding

Self-Study Instructions: This test can be used to help you assess how well you understand the content of this chapter. Terms to be filled in are from the Review Glossary. Answers are given in Appendix E.

The phone rings. After acknowledging that you are the person sought, the anonymous voice says, "You've just won the state lottery." Stunned, you whisper, "Me?" Then you shriek, "Me?!"

To produce the whispered "Me," the muscular glottis is adducted and stiffened to prevent the vocal folds from vibrating while the air stream is set into turbulent flow through the open (A) _____ glottis. Elated, but disbelieving, you activate the biological respiratory reflex, which abducts the folds, you inhale deeply, and then activate the (B) _____ adjustment by closing the glottis in preparation for hoarsely shrieking the question, "Me?!"

It is spoken with an upward inflection, which means that (C) _____ rises as the glottal vibration rate increases the fundamental frequency of the voice. It is spoken loudly, which means considerable (D) _____ of air through the glottis. And it is spoken hoarsely, which means that the duration and intensity of the (E) _____ vary irregularly from one (F) _____ to the next. These aperiodic variations are called (G) _____ and shimmer.

Each glottal cycle can be divided into two phases, the (H) _____ phase and the (I) _____ phase, during which (J) _____ pressure in the trachea increases to activate the next glottal cycle. The ratio of duration of open phase to duration of glottal cycle is the (K) _____. The open phase, in turn, can be subdivided into (L) _____ phase and closing phase, which describe the glottal aperture from initial opening to maximum (M) _____ to closure of the aperture. The ratio of these two phases is called the (N) _____.

The forces operating to produce glottal vibration are described by the (O) _____ theory of phonation. The energy that forces the vocal folds to vibrate involves (P) _____ factors. This source of energy derives from respiratory pressure, which when measured in the lungs is alveolar pressure. It is (Q) _____ resistance to airflow that provides a basis for pressure. Without resistance, air would flow unimpeded so there would be no pressure. Only when (R) _____ pressure is less than subglottal pressure will the vocal folds be set into vibration.

At the beginning of a glottal cycle, (S) _____ pushes the lower masses of the opposing vocal folds away from each other. As the upper folds are also finally dragged apart enough to create a small aperture, a jet of air begins to escape. The velocity of this air flow causes the pressure pushing on the upper folds to decrease. This happens because of the (T) _____. As a consequence of these interactions, there is a (U) _____ between the upper and lower vocal fold masses. Because these masses all belong mainly to the vocalis muscle, they exhibit (V) _____ by resisting separate movements. Thus, the upper masses are dragged along through their vibratory cycles largely by movements of the lower masses.

A characteristic of the vocalis muscle that cannot be adjusted by the speaker but that contributes to its resistance to air flow and to the (W) _____ with which it absorbs impact (thereby determining duration of the closed phase in a glottal cycle) is the viscosity of this muscle. Vocalis muscle characteristics that can be adjusted for regulation of pitch, loudness, and quality include (X) _____ (adjusted by contraction of the cricothyroid muscle), (Y) _____ (adjusted by lengthening or shortening the vocal folds), and (Z) _____ (adjusted by contraction of the vocalis muscle).

Clinical Exercises

These exercises allow you to test your knowledge of laryngeal function as it relates to clinical application. Fill in the blanks with the word or words that best complete the statements.

Mrs. L., a 48 year old woman, complains of a voice disorder. She describes a history of vocal fatigue and hoarseness. She also believes that her vocal pitch is too low. Measurements of her speaking fundamental frequency indicate a mean value of 150 Hz. From comparisons with normative data in this chapter, your conclusion would be that her fundamental frequency is (a) _____ (lower than normal, about normal, higher than normal). She is capable of a range of fundamental frequencies in a singing task of about 120 to 360 Hz. This range is (b) _____ (smaller than normal, about normal, larger than normal). From listening to her voice, it is apparent that her complaint of hoarseness is justified. Hoarseness is a combination of two voice qualities. One of these, (c) _____, is also called roughness. The other, associated with excessive air flow through the vocal folds, is called (d) _____. The first of these can be related to irregularities in either the durations or (e) _____ of the glottal pulses in each cycle. If the duration of successive glottal cycles changes in an irregular fashion, then we might expect variations in the fundamental frequency of the voice as well, because the fundamental frequency in hertz is determined by the number of (f) _____ occurring in a unit of time.

Examination of Mrs. L's vocal folds by a laryngologist (a physician specializing in diseases of the larynx) revealed a growth on her left vocal fold. This growth prevented the folds from making complete closure along their length.

Mr. J., a 56 year old man, also complained of a voice disorder. One of the characteristics of his vocal disorder was that he often produced phonating sounds upon inhalation. For these sounds to occur, the vocal folds must be in an (g) _____ (adducted, abducted) state during inhalation. Laryngeal examination revealed that this man had vocal folds that were paralyzed in a midline position. (h) Draw a sketch of the vocal folds to show what this position would look like.

CHAPTER SIX
Articulatory Anatomy

VOCAL TRACT

Physiologically, *articulation* means a joining of structures loosely to allow movement. In speech analysis it has come to mean the modification of the air stream into the various sounds of speech. This air stream will either have been set into vibration to generate voice when it passed through the larynx, or it will have flowed through the open glottis unimpeded for a voiceless sound. The tube in which this modification will occur, the *vocal tract*, consists of the throat, mouth, and nose (Fig. 6–1). The sounds formed in this tube will be made in any of the three ways discussed briefly in the last chapter: by exploding the air stream with bursts of pressure, by constricting it to generate turbulence, or by resonating it to shape different qualities of tone. Our task now is to determine how the vocal tract is designed to accomplish these three types of articulation.

We turn now to a complete set of organs that we can collectively term the articulators, or vocal tract. When we think about the act of speaking, these are the organs that usually come to mind: the tongue, the lips, the jaw, and — less likely to be known to the layman — the velopharynx and the pharyngeal cavities (the throat). The fastest of

these organs, the tongue, can perform simple repetitive movements at rates up to about 10 per second. Thus, if you try to say the syllable "tuh" repetitively as fast as you can, you should be able to produce a sequence of 7 to 10 in 1 second. We might take this rate of simple repetition for our fastest articulator to be the maximum for sound production. However, if we determine the rate at which speech sound segments are uttered during many ordinary conversations, we discover the surprising result that the rates are in the range of 10 to 14 per second. How is it that a system which can manage 10 simple repetitions in its fastest component can produce complexly changing sequences of sounds even faster than this same, apparently maximal, rate? This is one of the puzzles we must solve in our attempt to understand speech.

Development of the Vocal Tract

A major feature of the human vocal tract is the right angle formed by the craniovertebral junction (the angle of the upper throat where the spine joins the skull). The general orientation of the head and neck is vertical (that is, aligned with the long axis of the body), but the base of the cranium and the vocal tract are bent sharply relative to this axis.

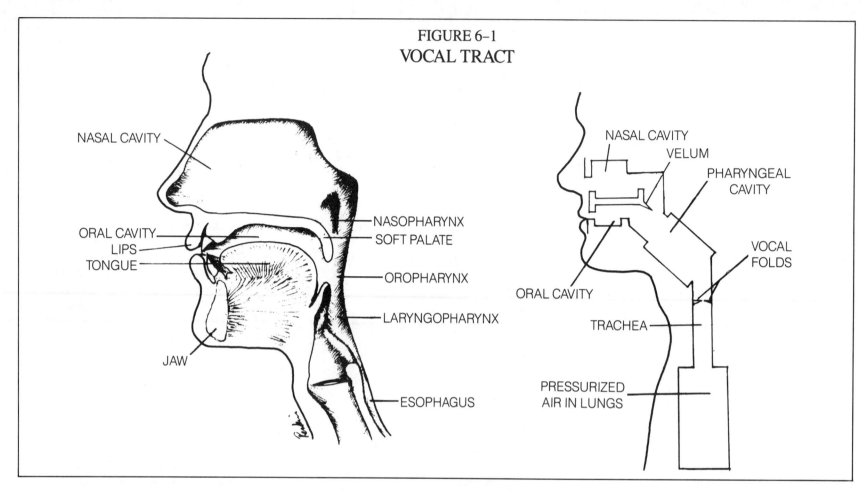

FIGURE 6–1
VOCAL TRACT

NASAL CAVITY

ORAL CAVITY

LIPS

TONGUE

JAW

NASOPHARYNX

SOFT PALATE

OROPHARYNX

LARYNGOPHARYNX

ESOPHAGUS

NASAL CAVITY

VELUM

PHARYNGEAL CAVITY

ORAL CAVITY

VOCAL FOLDS

TRACHEA

PRESSURIZED AIR IN LUNGS

This sharp bending is distinctive of the human species and it is an important characteristic of the sound production apparatus of humans. The right-angle orientation contrasts with the typically elongated skull of other species, in which the oropharyngeal tract is only slightly bent. The shape of the human head preserves two highly desirable properties: (1) an essentially horizontal orientation of the special sense organs (sight, smell, and hearing) and the feeding apparatus, and (2) a straight continuity between the brain stem and the spinal cord. It is generally considered that the evolution of the

human head derives from three major influences: The first is erect bipedalism, or walking on two legs. The second is a large brain, which requires a large cranium, or bony case, for the brain. The third is a modified oral apparatus, as already described.

It is easy to overlook some of the advantages of this geometric arrangement. A particularly important one is that humans, alone among the animal species, can readily and completely close the nasal cavity while maintaining an open oropharyngeal tract. In other species (and in very young

human infants) the ability to close off the nasal tract is nonexistent or only partly effective. The capacity to separate the nasal and oropharyngeal tracts makes possible a major phonetic distinction — nasal sounds such as the consonants in the word *meaning*, and the oral, non-nasal sounds that make up the balance of the English sound system — and an essential phonetic skill, the ability to impound enough pressure to produce speech sounds.

But how and why should the right-angle craniovertebral relationship develop in the human infant? First, the how. Basically, the neonate is

Functional Anatomy of Speech, Language, and Hearing

born with a nonhuman oropharyngeal anatomy, similar to that of a monkey or chimpanzee. (Fetal vocal tract development is summarized in Appendix C.) The epiglottis is relatively high in the pharynx, high enough to touch the soft palate. The larynx also is positioned quite high, which gives the oropharyngeal channel a gradual bend. Sometime before the sixth month of life, the infant's larynx moves inferiorly, away from the tongue and soft palate. The epiglottis moves inferiorly with it, so that both epiglottis and larynx eventually are positioned deep within the laryngopharynx. With these changes, the infant's vocal tract assumes the right-angle configuration described earlier. Clearly, then, the infant's oral and pharyngeal anatomy is drastically remodeled during the first half year of life.

But what is the functional significance of the early anatomy, before about 6 months of life? Apparently, this infantile anatomy allows respiration and feeding to occur simultaneously. If you've ever watched an infant nursing or taking milk from a bottle, you might have noticed that the infant rarely stopped to breathe. The reason is that the infant's head anatomy permits feeding to continue even while respiration proceeds. Thus, the infantile anatomy protects the infant against choking. Things change with the adult, who must interrupt respiration for a half-second to 4 seconds during every swallow. But the adult also gains the ability to close off the nasal tract at will. The importance of this ability to speech is indicated by a coincidence of two phenomena: the infant's ability to close off the nasal tract and the appearance of a period of babbling called the expansion phase, during which sound production increases markedly. Humans have lost the capacity to eat and breathe simultaneously, but they have gained an important valving function for speech.

The most difficult part of describing the vocal tract is in deciding where to begin. We could, and will, start with vocal tract cavities. These cavities run from the glottis in the larynx to the lips or the nose. It is in the cavities formed within this pharyngeal-oral-nasal tube (throat, mouth, nose) that determine the qualities of tone that are resonated. These cavities are shaped mainly by the tongue, lips, jaw, and soft palate. But these are the same structures that are used in the same places in the same tube for constrictions and stoppages of the air stream. Thus, one group of structures is not used exclusively for one articulatory process, like resonance, and another group for constrictions or stoppages. All aspects of articulation use the same structures, but they are used in different ways.

Cavities

The major subdivisions of the vocal tract that participate in articulation are the *pharyngeal cavity* (throat), *nasal cavity* (nose), and *oral cavity* (mouth). Because the nasal cavity can be shut off from the remainder of the vocal tract by the soft palate, it is separate and functions in speech only as a resonator. The boundary between the oral and pharyngeal cavities, however, is purely arbitrary, at least so far as articulatory function is concerned. Some singers are persuaded that sinus cavities also resonate the voice, and perhaps these bony spaces are set into vibration by sound energy passing through the bones of the skull. We will give them only a brief peek, and will mention in passing that they lighten the skull (hollow bone is lighter than solid bone) and are the site of certain disease conditions, such as sinusitis.

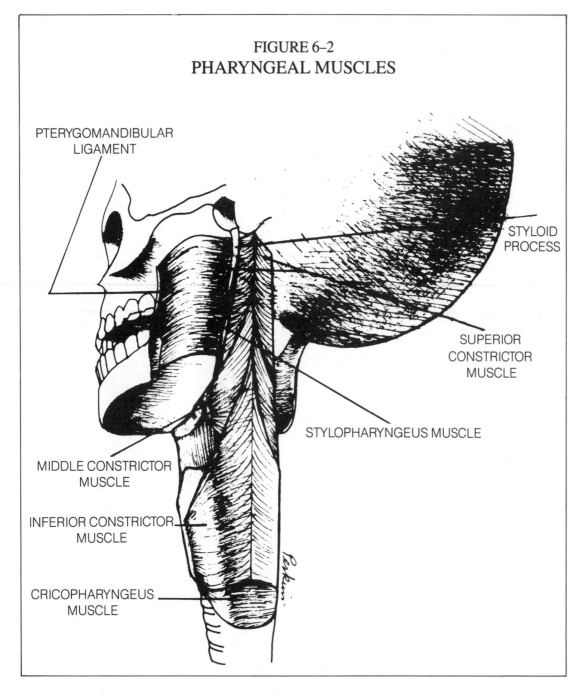

FIGURE 6–2
PHARYNGEAL MUSCLES

PTERYGOMANDIBULAR
LIGAMENT

STYLOID
PROCESS

SUPERIOR
CONSTRICTOR
MUSCLE

STYLOPHARYNGEUS MUSCLE

MIDDLE CONSTRICTOR
MUSCLE

INFERIOR CONSTRICTOR
MUSCLE

CRICOPHARYNGEUS
MUSCLE

Pharyngeal Cavity

Continuing upward from where the air stream leaves the laryngeal inlet (the supraglottal cavity), the air emerges into the *pharynx*. This vertical tube opens into the mouth in front and into the nose at the top. It is described anatomically in three sections.

The *laryngopharynx* extends from the laryngeal and esophageal openings upward to the level of the hyoid bone at the base of the tongue. This level is just out of sight below the back of the tongue.

The next level is the oropharynx, which extends upward from the laryngopharynx to the soft palate. This is the portion of the pharynx you can see when you look in the mouth behind the posterior faucial pillars that arch upward from the back of the tongue to the soft palate. This faucial arch marks the anterior border between the oropharynx and the mouth.

The highest level, the *nasopharynx*, continues upward from the soft palate to the base of the skull and provides the entrance to the nasal cavity, terminating where the median septum, separating the two chambers of the nose, ends in the back of the nose.

Pharyngeal Muscles. Three large, thin muscles wrap around the sides and back wall of the pharynx. They are fan-shaped and overlap from bottom to top, much like shingles (Fig. 6–2).

The lowest and strongest is the *inferior constrictor*. It arises mainly from both sides of the thyroid cartilage to wrap around the lower to mid sections of the pharynx. Although not part of the inferior constrictor, but just below it, the *cricopharyneus muscle* originates largely from the cricoid cartilage and encircles the neck of the esophagus to squeeze it closed.

Overlapped by the inferior constrictor and above it is the *middle constrictor*. From its narrow

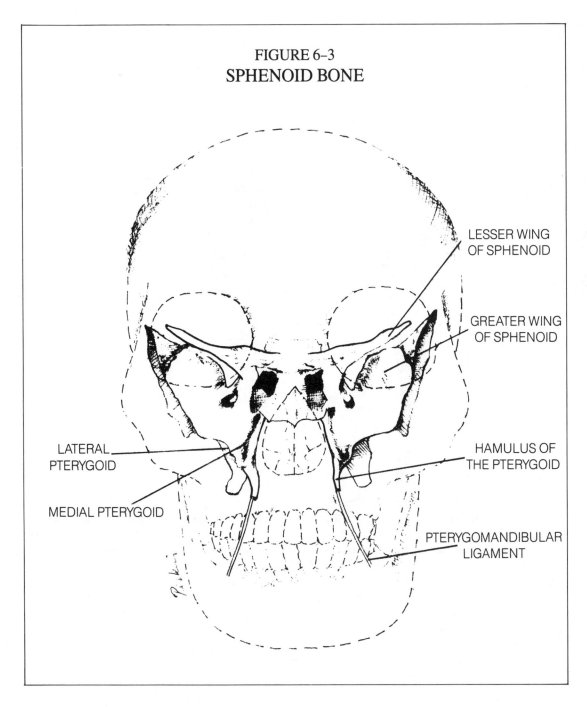

FIGURE 6–3
SPHENOID BONE

LESSER WING
OF SPHENOID

GREATER WING
OF SPHENOID

HAMULUS OF
THE PTERYGOID

PTERYGOMANDIBULAR
LIGAMENT

MEDIAL PTERYGOID

LATERAL
PTERYGOID

attachment to the horns of the hyoid bone, it sweeps upward and downward to encircle the pharynx. Also inserting into the pharyngeal wall is the *stylopharyngeus* arising from the *styloid process*, a bony prong below the ear, and the *salpingopharyngeus*, which attaches to the opening of the eustachian tube. Neither has much importance to speech.

The most complex and weakest of the pharyngeal constrictor muscles is the *superior constrictor*. It arises largely from the bony framework for the soft palate that forms the side walls at the back of the nasal cavity (the medial pterygoid plate, the hamulus of the pterygoid that projects downwards from it, and the pterygomandibular ligament that extends downward to the jaw). The superior constrictor wraps around the upper pharynx, almost reaching the base of the skull, but not quite.

Sphenoid Bone. The bone in the base of the skull forming the roof of the pharyngeal and nasal cavities is the *sphenoid*. Viewed head on, it resembles a bat in flight with its legs extended (Fig. 6–3). The wings are, indeed, called the *greater wings of the sphenoid*, and what appear to be large bat ears are the *lesser wings*. Within the body of the sphenoid are two cavities, the *sphenoid sinuses*. It is the "legs," however, that are of functional significance for speech. These are the *medial* and *lateral pterygoid plates* at the back of the nasal cavity.

Jutting down from each medial pterygoid plate is a small hook-like projection, the *hamulus of the pterygoid*. The significance of this pair of hooks is twofold. First, it is the upper attachment of the *pterygomandibular raphe* (ligament) which attaches to the jaw below. The importance of this ligament is that it connects the lower front border of the superior constrictor to the cheek muscle, the *buccinator*. The other point of significance of the hamulus is that it serves as a pulley for the tendon that stretches the soft palate taut.

Articulatory Anatomy

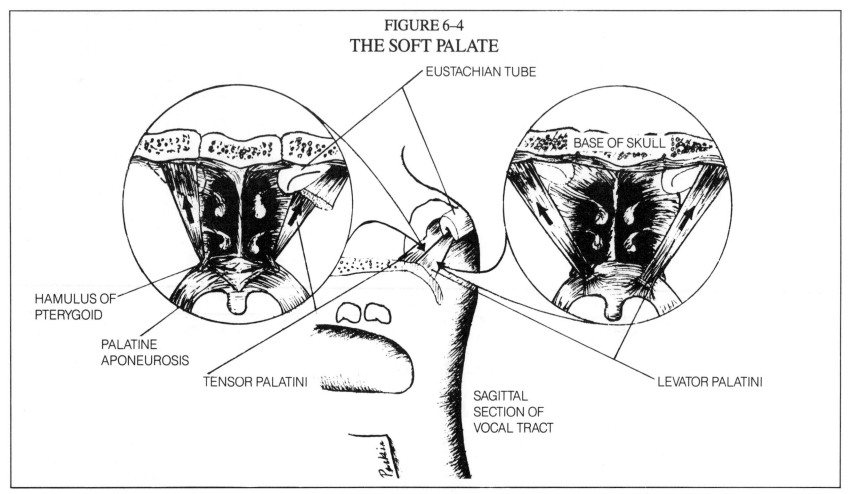

FIGURE 6–4
THE SOFT PALATE

EUSTACHIAN TUBE

BASE OF SKULL

HAMULUS OF PTERYGOID

PALATINE APONEUROSIS

TENSOR PALATINI

SAGITTAL SECTION OF VOCAL TRACT

LEVATOR PALATINI

Soft Palate. The *velum*, better known as the soft palate, hangs as a flexible muscular flap from the hard palate (Fig. 6–4). It is attached by the *palatine aponeurosis*, a sheet of flattened tendon that serves as the fibrous framework of the soft palate to which the velar muscles attach. They can pull it up, pull it down, or stretch it taut.

The velum is stretched by the pair of *tensor palatini* muscles. Each originates above the palate, at the opening of the *eustachian tube*, from the medial pterygoid plate. The tendon of the tensor

palatini muscles descends and hooks around the hamulus of the pterygoid. From there, it flattens out to form the palatine aponeurosis. Thus, contraction of this pair of vertical muscles is converted into a horizontal tug-of-war on the palatine aponeurosis by the pulley effect of the tendon hooked around the hamulus. It also permits the ears to "pop" when it pulls open the auditory tube.

Elevating the velum is the pair of *levator palatini* muscles. Originating above and behind the soft palate, near the origin of the tensor palatini

and extending downward roughly parallel to the tensor, the levator inserts directly into the aponeurotic "skeleton" of the velum. Thus, it is the pair of muscles that pulls the palate up and back against the pharyngeal wall with an assist from the tensor. The point of closure is against the *adenoids* (more technically, the *pharyngeal tonsil*). It is this *velopharyngeal* action that closes the nasal cavity from the pharyngeal cavity.

FIGURE 6–5
VELAR DEPRESSORS

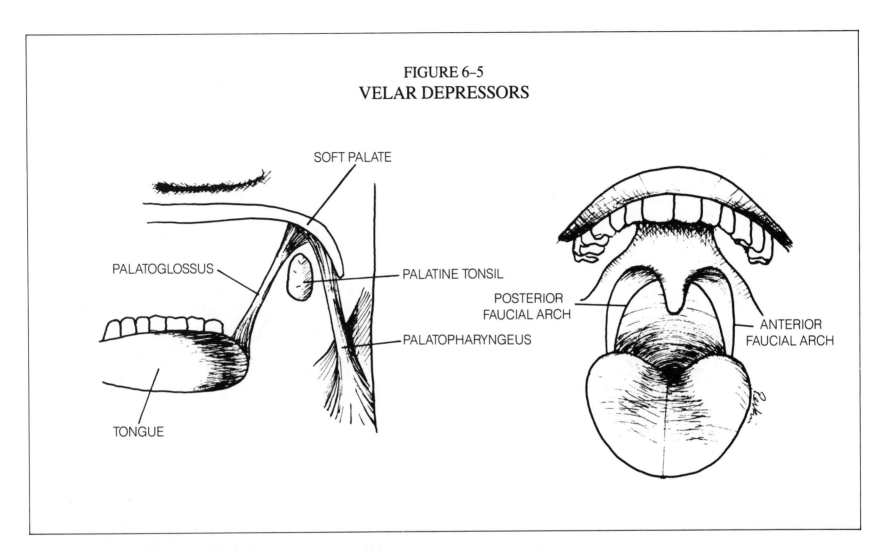

SOFT PALATE

PALATOGLOSSUS

PALATINE TONSIL

POSTERIOR FAUCIAL ARCH

PALATOPHARYNGEUS

ANTERIOR FAUCIAL ARCH

TONGUE

Two muscles pull the velum down, thereby opening the airway from pharynx to nose (Fig. 6–5). The *palatopharyngeus* arises from the palatine aponeurosis and inserts into the pharyngeal wall, forming the posterior *faucial arch*. The *palatoglossus* also arises from the aponeurosis, but it inserts into the tongue, forming the anterior faucial arch. Between these faucial pillars are the *palatine tonsils*, more popularly known merely as "tonsils."

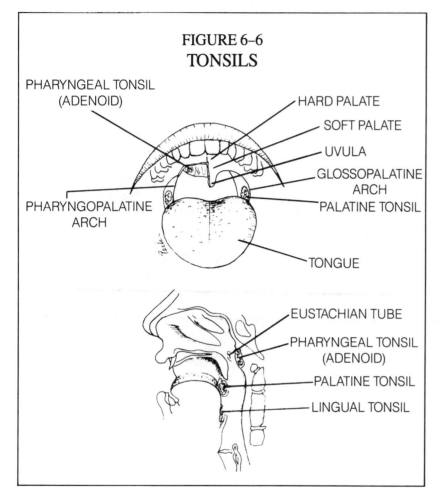

FIGURE 6–6
TONSILS

PHARYNGEAL TONSIL (ADENOID)

HARD PALATE

SOFT PALATE

UVULA

GLOSSOPALATINE ARCH

PALATINE TONSIL

PHARYNGOPALATINE ARCH

TONGUE

EUSTACHIAN TUBE

PHARYNGEAL TONSIL (ADENOID)

PALATINE TONSIL

LINGUAL TONSIL

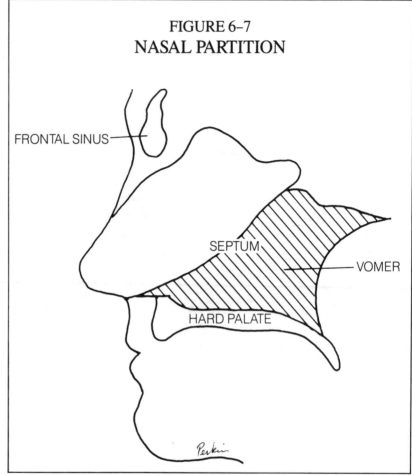

FIGURE 6–7
NASAL PARTITION

FRONTAL SINUS

SEPTUM

VOMER

HARD PALATE

The *pharyngeal*, *palatine*, and *lingual tonsils* form a *tonsillar ring* (also called Waldeyer's ring), a band of lymphoid tissue that encircles the opening of the digestive and respiratory tracts (Fig. 6–6). This ring is formed in its upper and back portion by the pharyngeal (adenoid) and tubal tonsils of the nasopharynx (lymphoid nodules located at the lip of the eustachian tube). The lateral portions of the ring are composed of the palatine tonsils situated at the entrance into the oropharynx. The ring is completed below by the lingual tonsils located at the base of the tongue. The lymphoid tissue reaches its maximum growth at about 10 years of age and typically begins to atrophy (become smaller) at puberty.

Nasal Cavity

The nasal cavity is actually two cavities separated in the middle of the nose by the *septum*, which is cartilage in front and bone (mainly the *vomer*) in back (Fig. 6–7). The roof of these two tubes is the base of the skull, and the floor is the hard palate. The *frontal sinuses* are above this roof. These nasal tubes are elaborated along the side walls with channels so as to resemble a labyrinth. Three scroll-like turbinates, the *superior*, *medial*, and *inferior concha*, project out from the nasal walls. They have far more biological function for warming and humidifying air than they have for speech.

Respiratory Epithelium. The respiratory tract is lined extensively with mucous membrane. In fact, this membrane reaches from the lungs to the nasal vestibules; only the pharynx is without this lining. The thickness of the mucosa varies roughly in proportion to the force of air flow; the membrane is relatively thick on the turbinates and septum, where the force of flow is great.

The function of the respiratory mucous membrane is to condition the inspired air. As the air moves from the nares to the conchae (turbinates) a distance of about 10 cm or 4 inches, the air is cleaned, moistened, and warmed. Cleaning is accomplished primarily as particulate matter sticks to the mucus and becomes embedded in it. This process is capable of removing nearly all dust and bacteria. Material not removed in this way can be expelled by sneezing (a reflexive series of muscular actions triggered by irritation of the respiratory mucous membrane). Airborne bacteria are killed by an enzyme (lysozyme) that is powerful enough to keep the posterior half of the nose nearly sterile.

The relative humidity of the inspired air is 75 percent or more by the time it flows into the pharynx. To support this humidification, evaporation within the nasal tract occurs at the rate of approximately 1,000 ml of water in 24 hours. The secretory control normally is precise enough so that ample water is available to humidify the air without causing nasal drip. However, when air is moved quickly at low temperatures, excessive amounts of water may be supplied. It is for this reason that you may experience nasal drip when you exercise vigorously in cold air, as when jogging in the winter.

Temperature regulation is achieved by rapid submucosal blood flow within the turbinates and septum. The heavily vascularized nasal tract is capable of warming the air to about 36° C (96.8° F). Warming the 500 cu ft of air we breathe each day can require 70 calories when the outside air temperature is 20° C (68° F).

Ciliary action keeps the mucous blanket in continuous motion, thereby restoring the nasal tract's ability to clean the inspired air. The mucous blanket is transported to the pharynx, where it is swallowed. Gland secretion renews the mucous blanket at least two to three times per hour. The tiny cilia are 5 to 7 micrometers in length and stroke at a rate of about 700 to 1,000 per minute. A remarkable feature of the cilia is that they will continue to contract even when the cells to which they are attached are torn apart. The millions of cilia that line the nasal passages cooperate to produce a highly coordinated movement pattern in which the ranks stroke in unison and the files in sequence. This pattern causes a smooth, continuous transportation of the mucous blanket and prevents the cilia from interfering with one another. Ciliary movement in the direction of mucous flow is rapid and powerful (the power stroke). During the slower recovery motion the cilium bends. The duration of the power stroke to the recovery motion is 1:3, the same ratio as that of a swimmer's arm stroke. The mucous load carried by the cilia is several hundred times thicker than the cilia are long, which indicates the power of ciliary movement.

The motion of the cilia is slowed or stopped by a variety of factors, including chilling, drying, or exposure to cocaine, cigarette smoke, ammonia, and formaldehyde. The ciliated cells also fall victim to viruses causing colds and influenza. As the cells are damaged they float freely in the copious, thin secretion characteristic of colds.

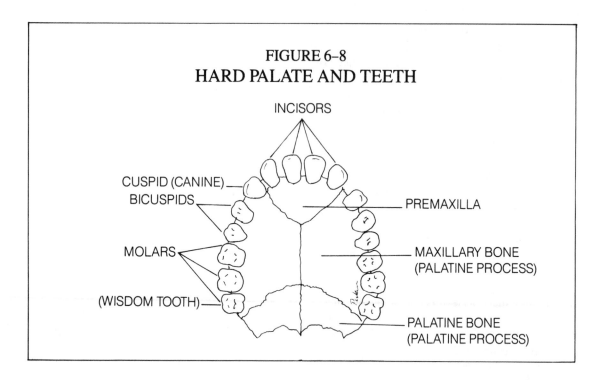

FIGURE 6–8
HARD PALATE AND TEETH

INCISORS

CUSPID (CANINE)

BICUSPIDS

MOLARS

(WISDOM TOOTH)

PREMAXILLA

MAXILLARY BONE
(PALATINE PROCESS)

PALATINE BONE
(PALATINE PROCESS)

either side, a cleft lip will result. It is because the premaxilla joins the alveolar ridge under one side of the nose or the other that a cleft never occurs in the middle of the lip, but always off to one side.

Posterior to the maxillary bone is the *palatine bone*, the horizontal portion forming the back of the hard palate. Lest you become confused by similar terms, the *palatine process* is the name of the horizontal portion of both the maxillary bone and the palatine bone which forms the hard palate. The palatine bone attaches to the back edge of the maxillary bone. In turn, the soft palate attaches to the back edge of the palatine bone.

Hard Palate. So far as speech is concerned, the hard palate is related more to the mouth than to the nose. Anatomically, however, the hard palate belongs as much to the nose, being its floor, as it does to the mouth for which it is the roof. Therefore, we will cover this topic in our transition from nasal to oral cavity.

The hard palate is formed by portions of two faucial bones, the *maxilla* and the *palatine bone* (Fig. 6–8). The segment of the maxilla that forms the palate can be subdivided into the *alveolar process*, the *palatine process*, and the *premaxilla* (containing the upper *incisors*). The alveolar process is also called the *alveolar ridge* and the *gum ridge*. It contains the sockets from which the upper *molar*, *bicuspid*, and *cuspid* teeth grow. In fetal development it is the bony portion of the *primary palate*. Above it in the front of the cheek bones are the *maxillary sinuses*.

The palatine process of the maxillary bone, the *secondary palate*, is the shelf that grows from the alveolar process in the early weeks of fetal development. It begins its growth vertically, straight downward. Probably pressure of the developing tongue molds the palatine process into its horizontal position. By the eighth week after conception, if all goes well, this thin shelf of bone will fuse at the midline of the palate with the shelf from the other side. Actually, it is a three-way fusion because the nasal septum must arrive at the place of fusion at the same time that the palatine processes arrive. If any of these three structures fail to fuse, a cleft palate will result.

The *premaxilla*, a small wedge of bone containing the four upper front incisor teeth, becomes an integral part of the hard palate at the time the palatine processes are fusing in the midline. If the premaxilla fails to fuse with the maxillary arch on

Functional Anatomy of Speech, Language, and Hearing

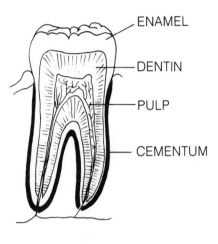

FIGURE 6-9
CROSS SECTION OF A TOOTH

ENAMEL

DENTIN

PULP

CEMENTUM

Dentition

A tooth is a living structure composed of layers of hard and soft tissues. The outermost layer is the enamel, which by virtue of a high concentration of crystalline mineral salts is the hardest substance in the body. Underlying the enamel is the dentin, a bone-like substance that forms the bulk of the tooth. The high elasticity of dentin makes it an excellent supporting structure for the hard but brittle enamel, much as a golf ball has a pliable core surrounded by a hard and resistant surface. Dentin has nerve endings sensitive to thermal and mechanical stimulation, especially at the boundary between the dentin and the enamel. Dentin is produced by the dental pulp located in a central chamber and associated canals. The pulp is soft tissue and contains nerve fibers that transmit signals for pain and vascular tone. The pulp chamber is lined with odontoblasts, the formative cells of dentin. The part of the tooth not exposed in the oral cavity is covered by cementum, which extends from the enamel boundary to the root apices (Fig. 6–9).

Each tooth inserts into a socket in the alveolar process of the mandible or maxilla. The tooth is anchored by the periodontal ligament, a complex organ of connective fibers, blood vessels, nerves, and formative elements for cementum and alveolar cortical bone. Groups of collagenous fibers distribute the forces of tooth contact or chewing to the cementum and alveolar bone. The transmitted forces cause resorption or deposition of cementum and alveolar bone, which is the basis for the clinical practice of orthodontia. The alignment and position of the teeth can be adjusted by appropriate application of forces.

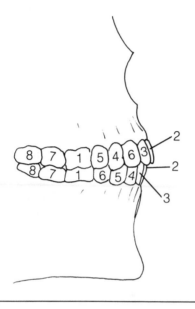

FIGURE 6–10
SEQUENCE OF ERUPTION
OF ADULT DENTITION

As is readily apparent from the smiles of many first-graders, the child's first dentition is not permanent. The first set of teeth, called the *deciduous*, temporary, primary, or milk teeth, normally erupt (appear in the mouth) between 6 months and 24 months and are shed between 6 years and 12 years. The normal timetable is shown in Table 6–1, and the sequence of eruption is shown in Figure 6–10. The child's first set of teeth totals 20, in contrast to the complete adult set of 32. Each quadrant, or half of a dental arch, in the deciduous dentition includes a central incisor, a lateral incisor, one cuspid (canine), and two molars.

The *permanent teeth* erupt over the considerable developmental span of 6 years (central incisors) to 17 or more years (third molars, or "wisdom teeth"). The approximate ages of eruption are shown in Table 6–1.

It might be asked why humans, unlike animals such as cats, dogs, and horses, should have two sets of teeth. One likely reason is that teeth that would fit in a child's mouth would not be large enough, or have sufficient capacity to grow, to serve the needs of an adult. Evolution has given to the human a relatively short oral cavity, quite different from the oral cavity that fits within the elongated skull of most animals. Space is at a premium in the human oral cavity. The deciduous teeth serve the eating purposes of the young child but then, as facial growth proceeds, they are shed to make way for the larger and more numerous adult teeth.

Table 6–1. Approximate Ages of Eruption of the Teeth

Deciduous Teeth		*Permanent Teeth*	
Lower central incisors	6–9 months	First molars	6 yr
Upper central incisors	8–10 months	Central incisors	7 yr
Upper lateral incisors	8–10 months	Lateral incisors	8 yr
Lower lateral incisors	15–20 months	First premolars	9 yr
First molars	15–21 months	Second premolars	10 yr
Canines	15–20 months	Canines	11–12 yr
Second molars	20–24 months	Second molars	12–13 yr
		Third molars	17–25 yr

UPPER	2	—	1	—	2	—	3
LOWER	2	—	1	—	2	—	3

Incisors _____ Canines _____ Premolars _____ Molars _____

DENTAL FORMULA FOR ADULT OR PERMANENT DENTITION ON ONE SIDE

UPPER	2	—	1	—	2
LOWER	2	—	1	—	2

Incisors _____ Canines _____ Molars _____

DENTAL FORMULA FOR DECIDUOUS (TEMPORARY OR PRIMARY) DENTITION ON ONE SIDE

Occlusion can be defined as the contact between the upper and lower teeth. *Malocclusion* refers to an abnormality of occlusion. Three major classes of malocclusion are recognized. A *Class I malocclusion* is characterized by a proper alignment of the dental arches but misalignment of one or more individual teeth. In a *Class II malocclusion* the upper (maxillary) dental arch protrudes over the lower (mandibular) dental arch. A *Class III malocclusion* is the opposite of Class II: The lower dental arch protrudes past the upper dental arch. It has been estimated that in over 90 percent of the population occlusion deviates from the ideal, but clinical treatment is unnecessary for many of these people because the deviations do not interfere significantly with appearance or function. It seems useful to think of occlusion in a dynamic sense, as striking a balance between injury (such as wearing of the teeth) and repair.

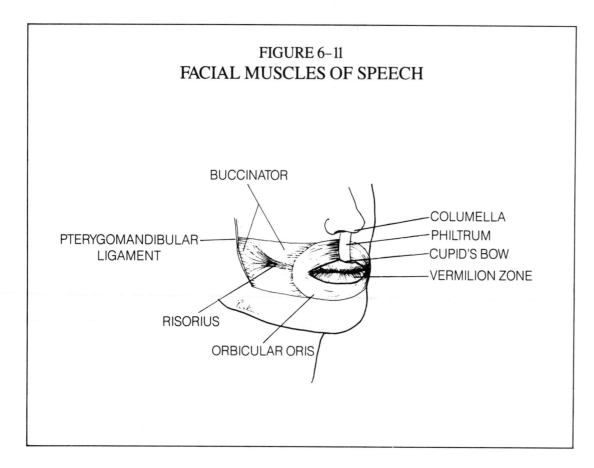

FIGURE 6-11
FACIAL MUSCLES OF SPEECH

BUCCINATOR

PTERYGOMANDIBULAR
LIGAMENT

COLUMELLA
PHILTRUM
CUPID'S BOW
VERMILION ZONE

RISORIUS

ORBICULAR ORIS

face is the *vermilion border*, also called the *prolabium*, with the *cupid's bow* in the middle of the upper lip. The indentation above the cupid's bow is the *philtrum*. Above it is the *columella*, the fleshy partition between the nostrils. In cleft lip, the philtrum is disconnected from the rest of the lip.

A number of facial muscles insert into the lips to pull them at angles and vertically for various facial expressions. The extrinsic lip muscles of importance to speech, however, are those that spread the lips, as in smiling. There are two of these. The *risorius* is superficial both anatomically and functionally. Anatomically, it is just below the surface of the skin. Functionally, it is relatively weak and can only assist in spreading the lips. The major transverse muscle of importance is the *buccinator*. Its fibers insert into the corners of the mouth to pull and stretch the lips. Thus, with the connection of the orbicular oris to the pair of buccinator muscles in front, and the connection of the superior constrictor to the buccinators in back, a continuous ring of muscle encircles the throat and mouth.

Oral Cavity

The boundary of the *oral cavity* in back (where it is continuous with the pharyngeal cavity) is the posterior faucial arch. The boundary in front is the incisor teeth and lips. Laterally, teeth and cheeks form the side walls. The tongue serves as the floor, but it is so flexible that this floor can be elevated firmly against the palatal roof. It is the capacity of the tongue to change the size and shape of the air channel in the mouth, and of the lips to change the exit from the mouth, that gives the oral cavity such importance in the molding of speech sounds.

Lips and Cheeks. The principal muscle of the cheeks is the *buccinator* (Fig. 6-11). It originates from the pterygomandibular raphe, the same ligament to which the superior constrictor muscle attaches. The space between the teeth and cheeks is the *buccal cavity*. Normally, this cavity has no significance for speech, although it is by squeezing air through this cavity that "Donald Duck" sounds are produced.

The muscle of the lips is the *orbicularis oris*. It is an oval ring encircling the mouth that functions as a sphincter to purse the lips. The lips have identifying landmarks. The reddish mucosal sur-

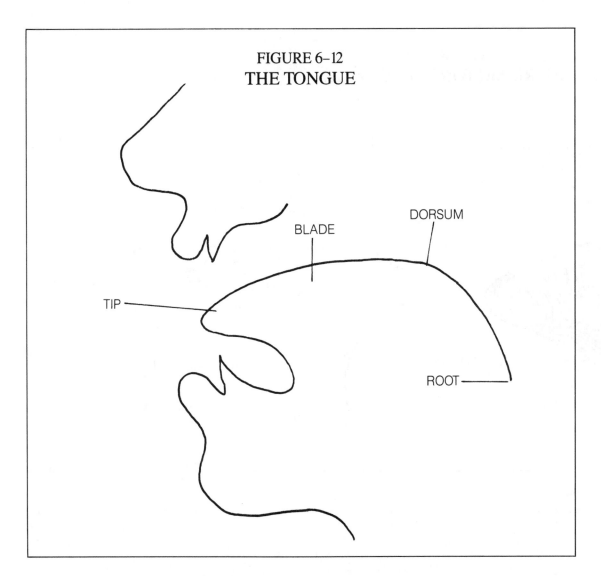

FIGURE 6–12
THE TONGUE

DORSUM

BLADE

TIP

ROOT

Tongue. The tongue is pulled into its various positions in the oral cavity by four *extrinsic lingual muscles* and is shaped into various contours by four *intrinsic lingual muscles*. The extrinsic *glossal* (another name for tongue) muscles originate outside of it and insert into it. The intrinsic muscles have both origin and insertion within it. The tongue is described from front to back as *tip*, *blade*, *dorsum*, and *root* (Fig. 6–12). The tip can protrude between the teeth. The blade can be arched against the alveolar ridge, the front of the dorsum against the hard palate, and the back of the dorsum against the soft palate. The root is the base of the tongue.

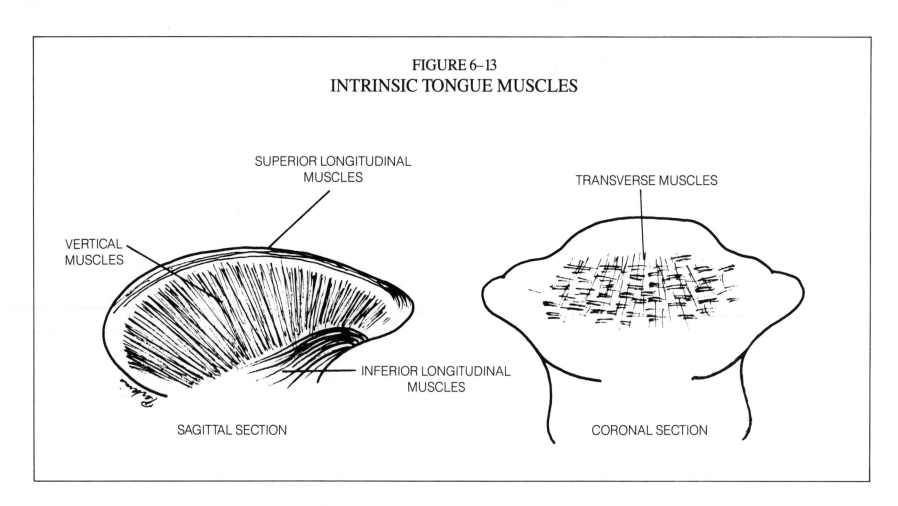

FIGURE 6–13
INTRINSIC TONGUE MUSCLES

SUPERIOR LONGITUDINAL MUSCLES

TRANSVERSE MUSCLES

VERTICAL MUSCLES

INFERIOR LONGITUDINAL MUSCLES

SAGITTAL SECTION

CORONAL SECTION

The four intrinsic lingual muscles are the *superior longitudinal*, *inferior longitudinal*, *vertical*, and *transverse* (Fig. 6–13). The *superior longitudinal muscle* is a thin layer below the dorsum. It can shorten the tongue and curl the tip and sides. The *inferior longitudinal* is a paired bundle of fibers on the sides of the undersurface. It, too, can shorten the tongue, but it pulls the tip downward. The *vertical* fibers are in the sides of the tongue and can flatten it. The *transverse* fibers extend out from the center to the sides and can narrow and elongate it.

Functional Anatomy of Speech, Language, and Hearing

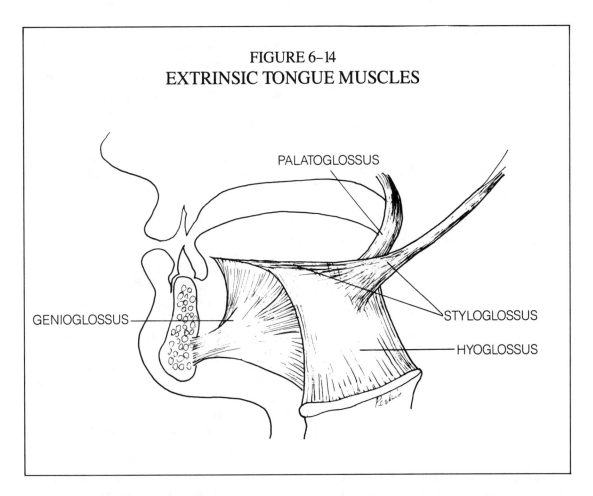

FIGURE 6-14
EXTRINSIC TONGUE MUSCLES

PALATOGLOSSUS

GENIOGLOSSUS

STYLOGLOSSUS

HYOGLOSSUS

The extrinsic lingual muscles are the *genio-glossus, hyoglossus, palatoglossus,* and *stylo-glossus* (Fig. 6–14). The *genioglossus* is the largest muscle of the tongue, forming the stem that extends from front to back. It consists of several bundles that fan out from the inside midline of the jaw. They insert along the center of the tongue all the way from the tip to the hyoid bone, which is the foundation of the tongue. They pull the tongue into a trough.

The *styloglossus* originates from the styloid process just below the ear and inserts into the sides of the dorsum. It is the antagonist of the genioglossus, so its contraction draws the tongue backward and upward.

The *hyoglossus* originates from the hyoid bone and rises in back alongside the genioglossus. Its contraction pulls the sides of the back of the tongue downward. The *palatoglossus* has already been discussed as a muscle that lowers the soft palate. Because it inserts into the back of the tongue from above, it works in opposition to the hyoglossus. The palatoglossus pulls the back sides of the tongue upward to groove it.

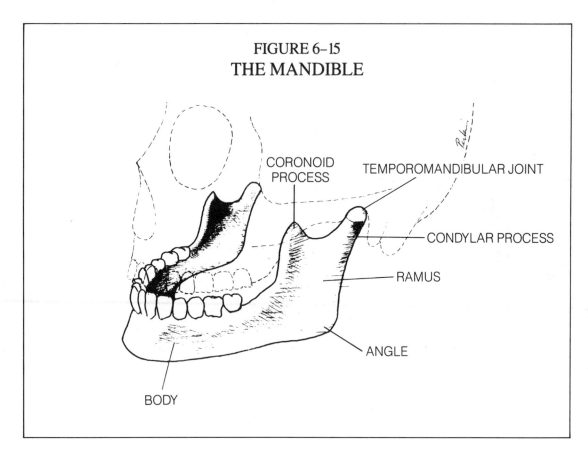

FIGURE 6–15
THE MANDIBLE

CORONOID PROCESS

TEMPOROMANDIBULAR JOINT

CONDYLAR PROCESS

RAMUS

ANGLE

BODY

Jaw

Technically, the jaw is the *mandible*. It has evolved and still functions in humans mainly for chewing. Although it can contribute to speech by adjusting the size of the vocal tract, it normally moves considerably more when singing than when speaking. In fact, if you are a ventriloquist, the trick of your trade is to speak without moving your jaw, or lips, at all. If the mandible does not move during speech, vocal tract adjustments (exclusive of soft palate and some pharyngeal wall movements) are made entirely by the tongue. If the jaw does move, articulation is a collaborative interaction of tongue and mandible.

Mandible. Several mandibular landmarks need to be noted. The *body of the mandible* contains the lower teeth and serves as the skeletal framework for the floor of the mouth (Fig. 6–15). The *ramus* is the vertical portion of the jaw that projects upward almost at a right angle to the *body*. In fact, the point of that right angle is called the *angle*. At the top of the ramus are two projections: the *coronoid process* and the *condylar process*. It is the head of the condyle that hinges the jaw to the skull in the *temporomandibular joint*.

The mandible is suspended from the skull by slings of muscle and tendon. The major ligamentous attachments are the temporomandibular,

sphenomandibular, and stylomandibular. These attachments insert on the mandible at the neck of the condyle, the ramus, and the ramus and angle, respectively. All three attachments are thus on the posterior portion of the mandible, and they effectively surround the temporomandibular joint on each side of the skull.

The actual articulation of the jaw relative to the skull is between the anterior and superior surfaces of the condyle and the articular eminence (projection) of the zygomatic process of the temporal bone. The condyle can move in three ways: (1) a hinging motion of the condylar head within the articular disc, (2) a gliding motion between the articular disc and the articular eminence, which protrudes the mandible, and (3) a translational movement, in which the mandible moves laterally relative to the maxilla. The hinged movement is for biting and is important for speech. The latter two movements are for grinding, so they have little to do with speech.

In the adult the hinge rotation permits a maximal rotation of about 25 mm measured between the upper and lower central incisors. A person standing or sitting upright normally holds the mandible in a slightly open (lowered) position that yields a "freeway space" of 2 to 4 mm between the upper and lower teeth. This slight opening is a balance of two forces — gravity acting in a downward direction and the antigravity pull of the jaw muscles exerting an upward force. When the teeth are clenched in maximal occlusion force, the biting forces between the incisors can be up to 11 to 25 kg and, between the molars, in the range of 29 to 90 kg.

The envelope of mandibular motion has been described as circumductory, meaning that the jaw can move from one extreme position to another without returning to an intermediate neutral position. For example, you should be able to protrude your jaw, then lower it to achieve substantial opening, and finally move it to either side.

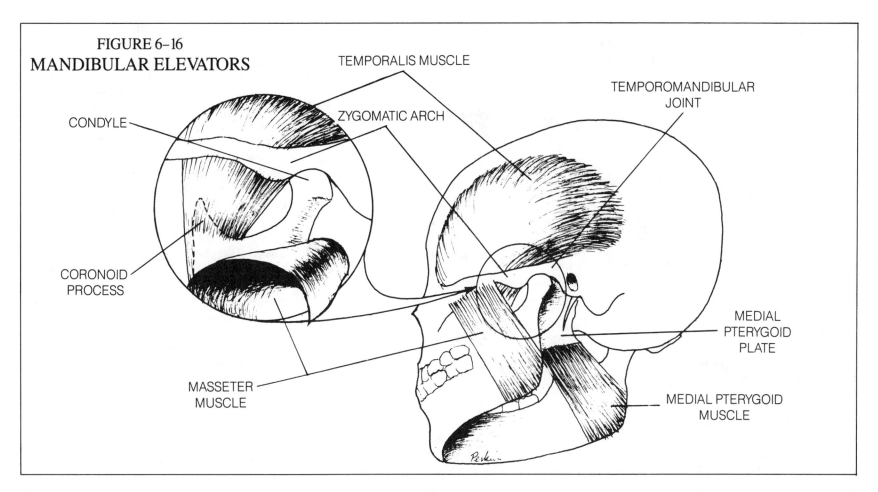

FIGURE 6–16
MANDIBULAR ELEVATORS

CONDYLE

CORONOID
PROCESS

TEMPORALIS MUSCLE

ZYGOMATIC ARCH

TEMPOROMANDIBULAR
JOINT

MEDIAL
PTERYGOID
PLATE

MASSETER
MUSCLE

MEDIAL PTERYGOID
MUSCLE

Mandibular Muscles. Powerful muscles are needed to close the jaw for biting and chewing. Opening the jaw, on the other hand, requires very little effort, so the mandibular depressors are relatively weak. You will probably not want to carry out a rigorous experiment to demonstrate the contrast in power between the elevators and depressors. But, if you have occasion to be attacked by a crocodile, hold its mouth closed and you will survive (or so they say). Thus, as far as speech is concerned, we are grossly overpowered for mandibular closure.

The mandible is also capable of more movements than are needed for speech. The temporomandibular joint permits the jaw to grind from side to side and to protrude for biting. Neither of these actions is essential to speech. Only opening and closing is of concern, but the mandibular muscles that produce protrusion and grinding also contribute to opening, so we cannot ignore them. First, though, we will consider the mandibular elevators (Fig. 6–16).

The *masseter* (the Greek word for chewer) is the most prominent as well as most powerful man-

dibular muscle. It originates from the *zygomatic arch* (the cheek bone) and inserts into the angle and ramus of the mandible. It is adapted for powerful closure by its size, leverage, and angle of insertion.

The *medial pterygoid muscle* is named for its origin, the medial pterygoid plate. It is the counterpart on the inside of the mandible of the masseter on the outside. It, too, inserts into the angle and ramus, but on the inside. Thus, the jaw is cradled in a muscular sling that provides strong closure.

The *temporalis* is a flat, fan-shaped muscle

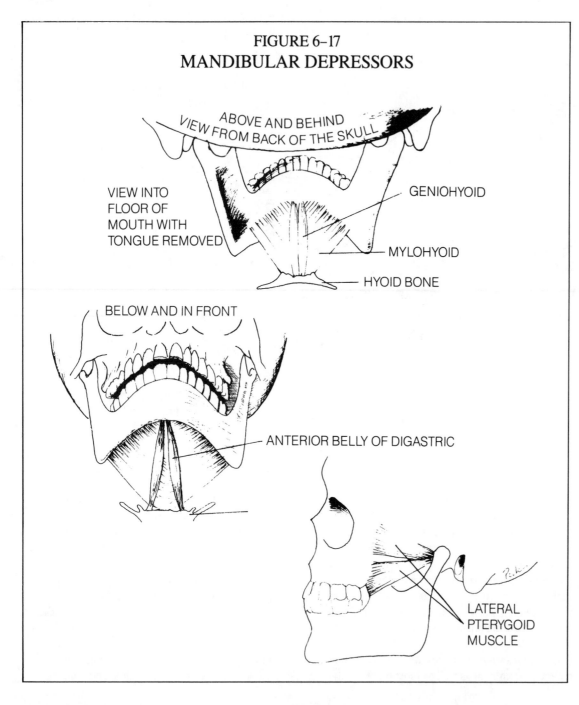

FIGURE 6–17
MANDIBULAR DEPRESSORS

ABOVE AND BEHIND
VIEW FROM BACK OF THE SKULL

VIEW INTO
FLOOR OF
MOUTH WITH
TONGUE REMOVED

GENIOHYOID

MYLOHYOID

HYOID BONE

BELOW AND IN FRONT

ANTERIOR BELLY OF DIGASTRIC

LATERAL
PTERYGOID
MUSCLE

that, as its name suggests, arises from the indentation in the temple, the *temporal fossa*. As it descends and narrows, it passes under the zygomatic arch to insert into the coronoid process. Because the leverage of this insertion provides speed rather than power, the temporalis can raise the jaw quickly.

The *lateral pterygoid muscle* is the first of four mandibular depressors to be discussed. It originates in part from the greater wing of the sphenoid bone as well as from the lateral pterygoid plate. It extends horizontally backward to insert into the neck of the condyle just below the temporomandibular joint. It not only produces grinding and protrusion of the jaw, it also assists in opening it.

The other three mandibular depressors are relatively small muscles that pull on the body of the mandible, thereby opening it as it swings backward around its temporomandibular pivot (Fig. 6–17). The *mylohyoid* forms the muscular floor of the mouth. Its fibers arise from inside the lower edge of the body of the mandible. The *geniohyoid* originates from the center of the jaw just above the mylohyoid. Below it is the *anterior belly of the digastric*. It, too, originates from the center of the jaw. All three of these muscles insert in different ways into the hyoid bone. When the hyoid is fixated, the effect of contracting these three muscles is to pull backward on the jaw, which swings it open.

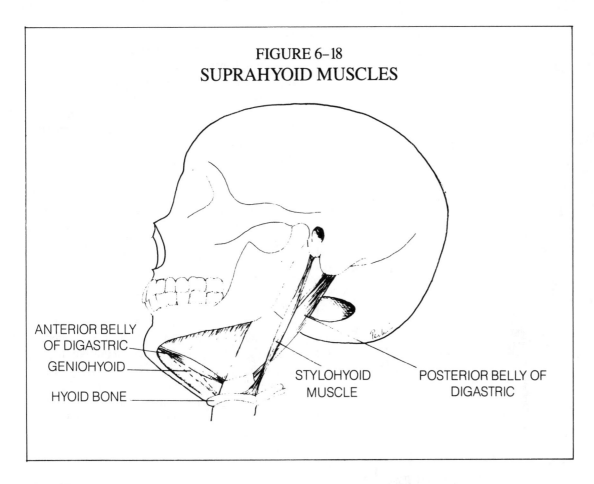

FIGURE 6–18
SUPRAHYOID MUSCLES

ANTERIOR BELLY
OF DIGASTRIC

GENIOHYOID

HYOID BONE

STYLOHYOID
MUSCLE

POSTERIOR BELLY OF
DIGASTRIC

general directions: forward, back and up, and down. The *suprahyoid* muscles suspend it and pull it back and forth, the *infrahyoid* muscles pull it downward.

Suprahyoid Muscles. We have already glimpsed the three suprahyoid muscles that suspend the hyoid bone from the jaw: the *mylohyoid*, *geniohyoid*, and *anterior belly of the digastric* (Fig. 6–18). With the mandible fixated, these muscles pull the hyoid forward and slightly upward — the movement required to protrude the tongue.

Two other suprahyoid muscles suspend the hyoid from the skull: the *stylohyoid* and the *posterior belly of the digastric*. The stylohyoid descends from the styloid process to pull up and back on the hyoid. The posterior belly of the digastric, originating from the *mastoid process* at the base of the ear, also pulls up and back. Its insertion into the hyoid is unusual, however. As you might suspect from the names, the digastric has two muscle bellies. They are attached to each other by a tendon. The tendons of these paired muscles (all hyoid muscles are paired) slip through a fibrous loop, one on each side of the hyoid. These loops, in turn, attach to the hyoid, so both bellies of the digastric pull on the hyoid indirectly rather than by direct insertion.

Hyoid Bone

You may recall from the discussion of the larynx that the topic of extrinsic laryngeal muscles was deferred to this chapter. You may also note that the hyoid is the last topic to be considered in this chapter. The reason is to provide perspective. The hyoid bone is the platform from which the larynx and trachea are suspended. It is the platform from which the jaw is pulled open. It is also the platform to which the tongue is attached. (For those of you who have been puzzled by the paradox of how the tongue can be stuck out when there is obviously no muscle to pull it out, part of the answer is at hand.

The tongue is mounted on the hyoid bone, so one way to protrude the tongue is to pull the hyoid forward.) Thus, the hyoid is crucial not just to the larynx, or just to the mandible, or just to the tongue. It is equally important to all three.

A marvel of the hyoid is that so much can be accomplished with so little. It is a horseshoe-shaped bone that is so small it could almost be covered by a quarter. What's more, it is the only bone in the body not attached to another bone. It "floats" in a muscular sling much as a suspension bridge hangs from its cables. Unlike a bridge, however, the hyoid "cables" can be pulled in three

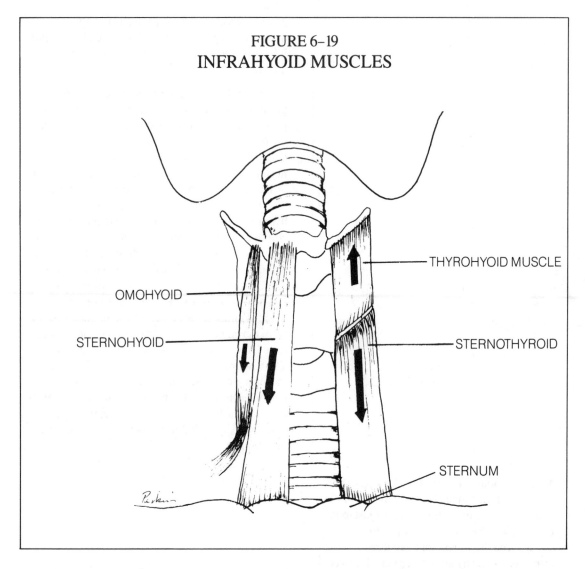

FIGURE 6–19
INFRAHYOID MUSCLES

OMOHYOID

STERNOHYOID

THYROHYOID MUSCLE

STERNOTHYROID

STERNUM

is fixated, however, it pulls the larynx up, a movement you can observe when swallowing.

The other two strap muscles attach directly to the hyoid from their points of origin. The *sternohyoid* is unambiguous in its function. It originates from the sternum, inserts into the hyoid, and pulls down on it. The *omohyoid*, by contrast, also inserts into the hyoid, but it is a double-bellied muscle that originates from the shoulder. Of its several functions, the only one of interest to us is its assistance in lowering the hyoid.

Speech sounds are products of speech equipment movements, which are products of dynamic forces interacting among about 100 speech muscles. A wonderment of speech is how these forces are coordinated at rates upward of a dozen readjustments per second. The tongue and jaw fly through their trajectories, moving from one position to the next. Simultaneously, the vocal folds are being abducted, adducted, and adjusted for pitch, loudness, and quality. At the hub of this blur of activity is the hyoid bone. A change of force, say to position the jaw, requires readjustments of the forces that position the tongue and larynx. Nowhere is the wonderment of speech greater than in how the vectors of forces on the hyoid are coordinated.

Infrahyoid Muscles. The four infrahyoids, the muscles that pull down on the hyoid, are often referred to collectively as the *strap muscles* (Fig. 6–19). Indeed, they resemble straps laid across the larynx as they descend from the hyoid. Only two of these muscles, however, insert into the larynx — the *sternothyroid* and the *thyrohyoid* — so, technically, these are the only ones that qualify as *extrinsic laryngeal muscles*. As their names indicate, the *sternothyroid* originates from the sternum and inserts into the thyroid cartilage to pull the larynx down. The *thyrohyoid* originates from the thyroid cartilage. As a functional extension of the sternothyroid, it pulls the hyoid down. If the hyoid

CHAPTER SIX
Self-Study
Articulatory Anatomy

Review Glossary

Vocal tract: The pharyngeal, oral, and nasal cavities

  Pharynx: The throat

    Laryngopharynx: The lower throat from larynx to base of the tongue

      Inferior constrictor muscle: Encircling the laryngopharynx from the thyroid, this muscle contributes little to speech

      Cricopharyngeus muscle: The sphincter muscle at the top of the esophagus that vibrates in esophageal speech

      Oropharynx: The throat seen in a mirror from base of the tongue to the soft palate

      Middle constrictor muscle: Encircling the oropharynx from the hyoid bone, this muscle is of little functional significance to speech

      Stylopharyngeus muscle: Extending from styloid process into pharyngeal wall, this paired muscle has little to do with speech

    Nasopharynx: The upper throat from soft palate to base of the skull

      Adenoid (pharyngeal tonsil): The tonsil on the base of the skull at the top of the nasopharynx

    Eustachian tube: The tube extending from nasopharynx to middle ear by which pressure in the ear is normalized

    Salpingopharyngeus muscle: A small muscle extending from pharyngeal wall to eustachian tube that helps open it

    Superior constrictor muscle: The muscle encircling the nasopharynx to the pterygomandibular ligament that assists in velopharyngeal closure

    Sphenoid bone: The base of the skull above the nasopharynx

      Pterygoid plates: The medial and lateral vertical bones forming the back walls of the nasal cavity

        Hamulus of the pterygoid: A hook-like projection jutting down from the medial pterygoid plates on both sides of the nasal cavity

  Oral cavity: The mouth extending from the lips to the posterior faucial arch that sweeps up to the soft palate

    Buccal cavity: The space between the cheek and the teeth

    Tonsillar ring: A band of lymphoid tissue encircling the opening of the respiratory and digestive tracts

      Pharyngeal tonsils (adenoids): The lymphoid tissue at the top of the nasopharynx

      Palatine tonsils: The lymphoid tissue at the entrance to the oropharynx

      Lingual tonsils: The lymphoid tissue at the base of the tongue

    Lips: The entrance to the oral cavity with identifying landmarks of vermilion border and prolabium (cupid's bow)

      Orbicularis oris muscle: The sphincter muscle encircling the lips that purses and rounds them

      Risorius muscle: A weak paired muscle extending from corner of the mouth into the cheek that assists in lip spreading

      Buccinator muscle: The major paired cheek muscle extending from the lips to the pterygomandibular ligament that spreads the lips in a smile (it is a functional continuation of the superior constrictor muscle)

    Hard palate: The bony roof of the mouth

      Maxilla: The bone forming the *alveolar ridge* (gum ridge) with its sockets for upper molar, bicuspid, cuspid, and incisor teeth (primary palate), and *palatine process* (secondary palate), which is the anterior hard palate

      Palatine bone: The posterior bone of the hard palate to which the soft palate attaches

        Deciduous teeth: The first set of 20 teeth that are shed between 6 and 12 years

        Permanent teeth: The 32 teeth that erupt between 6 and 17 years

    Soft palate (velum): The movable portion of palate that can open or close the nasal cavity from the oral and pharyngeal cavities

      Levator palatini muscle: The pair of muscles, each extending from a eustachian tube entrance into the velum, that elevates it against the nasopharynx for velopharyngeal closure

      Tensor palatini muscle: The pair of muscles extending from a eustachian tube entrance and ending in a tendon that hooks around a hamulus of the pterygoid to stretch the velum and open the eustachian tube

Palatine aponeurosis: The flattened tendon of the tensor palatini that is the fibrous framework of the soft palate to which the velar muscles attach

Palatopharyngeus muscle: The pair of muscles, extending from velum into pharyngeal wall (forming the posterior faucial arch), that depress the soft palate

Palatoglossus muscle: The pair of muscles, extending from velum to base of the tongue, that depress the soft palate or elevate the back of the tongue

Mandible: The jaw, consisting of body, angle, and ramus

Coronoid process: The anterior upward projection of the ramus to which the temporalis muscle attaches

Condylar process: The posterior upward projection of the ramus that fits into the temporomandibular joint, which is the hinge of the mandible

Masseter muscle: The paired muscle, extending from the zygomatic arch (cheek bone) to the angle and ramus, that elevates the mandible

Temporalis muscle: The paired muscle, extending from temporal fossa to coronoid process, that elevates the mandible

Medial pterygoid muscle: The paired muscle, extending from medial pterygoid plate to the inside angle and ramus, that elevates the mandible

Lateral pterygoid muscle: The paired muscle, extending backward from lateral pterygoid plate to the condyle, that grinds and protrudes the jaw and assists in lowering it

Anterior belly of the digastric muscle: The anterior portion of paired muscle, below the floor of the mouth, extending from center of the jaw to hyoid bone and on to the skull, that assists in lowering the mandible

Geniohyoid muscle: The paired muscle, above the floor of the mouth, extending from center of the jaw to the hyoid bone, that assists in lowering the mandible

Mylohyoid muscle: Muscular floor of the mouth that assists in lowering the mandible

Glossus: The tongue, described from front to back by tip, blade, dorsum, and root

Intrinsic lingual (glossal) muscles: The muscles that originate and insert within the tongue

Superior longitudinal muscle: A thin layer of muscle below the dorsum that shortens the tongue and curls its tip and sides

Inferior longitudinal muscle: A paired muscle on the undersurface that shortens the tongue and pulls the tip downward

Vertical muscle: The vertical fibers found in the sides of the tongue that flatten it

Transverse muscle: The horizontal fibers found from top to bottom of the tongue that narrow and elongate it

Extrinsic lingual (glossal) muscles: The muscles originating outside of the tongue that insert into it

Genioglossus muscle: The muscle extending from centerline of the jaw into the tongue along midline from front to back that pulls it into a trough

Hyoglossus muscle: The paired muscle extending from hyoid bone up into the back of the tongue lateral to the genioglossus to pull the dorsum down

Styloglossus muscle: The paired muscle extending from styloid process near the ear to the side of the tongue that pulls it backward and upward

Palatoglossus muscle: The paired muscle from velum to back of the tongue that pulls the side of the dorsum up

Hyoid bone: The horseshoe-shaped floating bone, suspended by suprahyoid muscles and anchored by infrahyoid muscles, that is the foundation for the tongue and from which the larynx is suspended

Suprahyoid muscles (see *Mandible*): The muscular sling that can pull the hyoid up, forward to protrude the tongue, or backward to retract the tongue

Mylohyoid muscle: The muscular floor of the mouth that helps suspend the hyoid anteriorly

Geniohyoid muscle: The paired muscle above the mylohyoid muscle that, originating from the center of the jaw, suspends and pulls the hyoid anteriorly

Anterior belly of the digastric muscle: The paired muscle below the mylohyoid muscle that, originating from the center of the jaw, suspends and pulls the hyoid anteriorly

Posterior belly of the digastric muscle: The paired continuation of the anterior belly that extends from the hyoid to the mastoid process below the ear to pull the hyoid up and backward

Stylohyoid muscle: The paired muscle that extends from the hyoid to the styloid process near the ear to pull the hyoid up and backward

Infrahyoid muscles: The strap muscles that anchor the hyoid from below and pull it downward

Sternohyoid muscle: The paired muscle that extends from sternum to hyoid to pull it downward

Omohyoid: The paired double-bellied muscle from shoulder to hyoid that assists in lowering the hyoid

Thyrohyoid muscle: The paired extrinsic laryngeal muscle extending from hyoid to thyroid cartilage that pulls the larynx upward

Sternothyroid muscle: The paired extrinsic laryngeal muscle, extending from sternum to thyroid cartilage, that pulls the larynx downward

Nasal cavity: The cavity extending from nasopharynx to nares

 Nasal septum: The cartilaginous-bony partition separating the nasal cavity into two chambers

  Vomer: The bony posterior portion of the nasal septum

 Turbinates (conchae): The mucous membrane covered, scroll-like bones projecting from the lateral walls of the nasal cavity that clean, moisten, and warm inhaled air

Self-Study Drawings

Coloring Instructions

1. Use different primary colors for the oral, nasal, and pharyngeal cavities. Use different shades or tones of the cavity color for structures within that cavity.
2. Fill in *A* through *W* in Drawing 6–I with appropriate anatomical terms (*L* is a review term from Chapter 4).
3. Using colored pencils, draw an identifying line from each term to its approximate anatomical location.
4. Fill in *a* through *j* in Drawing 6–II, *u* through *z* in Drawing 6-III, and *aa* through *hh* in Drawing 6–IV with appropriate muscles.
5. Using different colored pencils color the muscles in the drawings and the matching terms in *a* through *j, u* through *z,* and *aa* through *hh* the same.
6. Color terms in the Glossary with the same colors used for those terms or the drawings.
7. Check your answers in Appendix E.

DRAWING 6–I

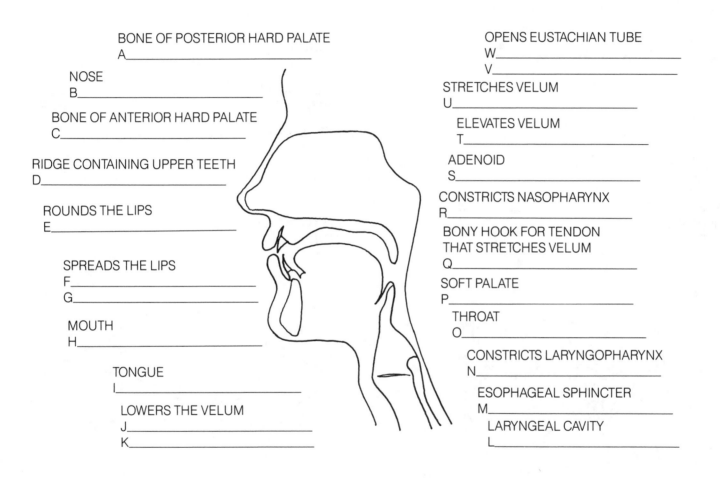

BONE OF POSTERIOR HARD PALATE
A_____

NOSE
B_____

BONE OF ANTERIOR HARD PALATE
C_____

RIDGE CONTAINING UPPER TEETH
D_____

ROUNDS THE LIPS
E_____

SPREADS THE LIPS
F_____
G_____

MOUTH
H_____

TONGUE
I_____

LOWERS THE VELUM
J_____
K_____

OPENS EUSTACHIAN TUBE
W_____
V_____

STRETCHES VELUM
U_____

ELEVATES VELUM
T_____

ADENOID
S_____

CONSTRICTS NASOPHARYNX
R_____

BONY HOOK FOR TENDON
THAT STRETCHES VELUM
Q_____

SOFT PALATE
P_____

THROAT
O_____

CONSTRICTS LARYNGOPHARYNX
N_____

ESOPHAGEAL SPHINCTER
M_____

LARYNGEAL CAVITY
L_____

DRAWING 6–II

SHORTENS TONGUE   a_____

b_____

CURLS TIP DOWN   c_____

CURLS TIP AND
SIDES UP   d_____

DRAWS TONGUE   e_____
BACKWARD AND
UPWARD

FLATTENS TONGUE   f_____

THICKENS TONGUE   g_____
(POINTS)

LOWERS CENTER   h_____
OF TONGUE

PULLS BACK SIDES   i_____
OF TONGUE DOWN

PULLS BACK SIDES   j_____
OF TONGUE UP

SAGITTAL SECTION

CORONAL SECTION

DRAWING 6–III

ELEVATES MANDIBLE

u_____

v_____

w_____

LOWERS MANDIBLE

x_____

y_____

z_____

LOOKING DOWN
FROM
BACK EDGE OF SKULL

DRAWING 6–IV

PROTRUDES TONGUE

aa_____

bb_____

PULLS ENTIRE TONGUE (HYOID)
UPWARD AND BACKWARD

cc_____

dd_____

RAISES ENTIRE TONGUE (HYOID)
UPWARD

ee_____

ff_____

gg_____

hh_____

RAISES LARYNX   ii_____

LOWERS LARYNX   jj_____

LOWERS HYOID   kk_____

ll_____

mm_____

nn_____

Self-Study Test of Terminology

Self-Study Instructions: These questions can be used to help you assess how much you have retained from studying the Review Glossary. Answers are given in Appendix E.

(1) _____ The lower throat from larynx to base of the tongue

(2) _____ The throat seen in a mirror from base of the tongue to the soft palate

(3) _____ The pharyngeal, oral, and nasal cavities

(4) _____ The base of the skull above the nasopharynx

(5) _____ The upper throat from soft palate to the base of the skull

(6) _____ A small muscle extending from pharyngeal wall to eustachian tube that helps open it

(7) _____ The space between the cheek and the teeth

(8) _____ Encircling the oropharynx from the hyoid bone, this muscle is of little functional significance to speech

(9) _____ The muscle encircling the nasopharynx to the pterygomandibular ligament that assists in velopharyngeal closure

(10) _____ The throat

(11) _____ The tube extending from nasopharynx to middle ear by which pressure in the ear is normalized

(12) _____ The sphincter muscle at the top of the esophagus that vibrates in esophageal speech

(13) _____ The mouth, extending from the lips to the posterior faucial arch that sweeps up to the soft palate

(14) _____ Extending from styloid process into pharyngeal wall, this paired muscle has little to do with speech

(15) _____ A hook-like projection jutting down from the medial pterygoid plates on both sides of the nasal cavity

(16) _____ Encircling the laryngopharynx from the thyroid, this muscle contributes little to speech

(17) _____ The medial and lateral vertical bones forming the back walls of the nasal cavity

(18) _____ The pair of muscles, each extending from a eustachian tube entrance and ending in a tendon that hooks around a hamulus of the pterygoid to stretch the velum

(19) _____ The tonsil on the base of the skull at the top of the nasopharynx

(20) _____ The tonsil between the faucial arches

(21) _____ The pair of muscles, extending from velum to base of the tongue, that depress the soft palate or elevate the back of the tongue

(22) _____ The posterior bone of the hard palate to which the soft palate attaches

(23) _____ The anterior upward projection of the ramus to which the temporalis muscle attaches

(24) _____ The sphincter muscle encircling the lips that purses and rounds them

(25) _____ The movable portion of palate that can open or close the nasal cavity from the oral and pharyngeal cavities

(26) _____ The major paired muscle extending from the lips to the pterygomandibular ligament that spreads the lips in a smile

(27) _____ The pair of muscles, each extending from a eustachian tube entrance into the velum, that elevate it against the nasopharynx for velopharyngeal closure

(28) _____ The entrance to the oral cavity with identifying landmarks of vermilion border and prolabium (cupid's bow)

(29) _____ The jaw, consisting of body, angle, and ramus

(30) _____ The bony roof of the mouth

(31) _____ The flattened tendon of the tensor palatini that is the fibrous framework of the soft palate to which the velar muscles attach

(32) _____ Weak paired muscles extending from corner of the mouth into the cheek that assist in lip spreading

(33) _____ The pair of muscles, extending from velum into pharyngeal wall (forming the posterior faucial arch), that depress the soft palate

(34) _____ The bone forming the alveolar ridge (gum ridge) with its sockets for upper molar, bicuspid, cuspid, and incisor teeth (primary palate) and palatine process (secondary palate), which is the anterior hard palate

(35) _____ The paired muscle, extending from the zygomatic arch (cheek bone) to the angle and ramus, that elevates the mandible

(36) _____ A thin layer of muscle below the dorsum that shortens the tongue and curls its tip and sides

(37) _____ The paired muscle, extending from medial pterygoid plate to the inside angle and ramus, that elevates the mandible

(38) _____ Muscular floor of the mouth that assists in lowering the mandible

(39) _____ The paired muscle, extending from center of the jaw to the hyoid bone, that assists in lowering the mandible

(40) _____ The muscles originating outside the tongue that insert into it

(41) _____ The paired muscle, extending backward from the lateral pterygoid plate to the condyle, that grinds and protrudes the jaw and assists in lowering it

(42) _____ The tongue, described from front to back by tip, blade, dorsum, and root

(43) _____ The posterior upward projection of the ramus that fits into the temporomandibular joint, which is the hinge of the mandible

(44) _____ The muscles that originate and insert within the tongue

(45) _____ The paired muscle, extending from temporal fossa to coronoid process, that elevates the mandible

(46) _____ The vertical fibers found in the sides of the tongue that flatten it

(47) _____ The paired muscle above the mylohyoid muscle that suspends and pulls the hyoid anteriorly

(48) _____ The paired muscle extending from styloid process near the ear to side of the tongue that pulls it backward and upward

(49) _____ The paired continuation of the anterior belly that extends from the hyoid to the mastoid process below the ear to pull the hyoid up and backward

(50) _____ The paired extrinsic laryngeal muscle extending from hyoid to thyroid cartilage that pulls the larynx upward

(51) _____ The anterior portion of paired muscle, extending from center of the jaw to hyoid bone and on to the skull, that assists in lowering the mandible

(52) _____ A paired muscle on the undersurface that shortens the tongue and pulls the tip downward

(53) _____ The horseshoe-shaped floating bone suspended by suprahyoid muscles and anchored by infrahyoid muscles, that is the foundation for the tongue and from which the larynx is suspended

(54) _____ The horizontal fibers found from top to bottom of the tongue that narrow and elongate it

(55) _____ The muscular floor of the mouth that helps suspend the hyoid anteriorly

(56) _____ The muscle extending from centerline of the jaw into the tongue along midline from front to back that pulls it into a trough

(57) _____ The paired muscle extending from hyoid bone up into the back of the tongue lateral to the genioglossus to pull the dorsum down

(58) _____ The paired muscle that extends from the hyoid to the styloid process near the ear to pull the hyoid up and backward

(59) _____ The muscular sling that can pull the hyoid up, forward to protrude the tongue, or backward to retract the tongue

(60) _____ The paired muscle that extends from sternum to hyoid to pull it downward

(61) _____ The paired muscle from velum to the back of the tongue that pulls side of the dorsum up

(62) _____ The paired extrinsic laryngeal muscle extending from sternum to thyroid cartilage that pulls it downward

(63) _____ The strap muscles that anchor the hyoid from below and pull it downward

(64) _____ The paired muscle below the mylohyoid muscle that suspends and pulls the hyoid anteriorly

(65) _____ The paired double-bellied muscle from shoulder to hyoid that assists in lowering the hyoid

Speech Functions of Articulatory Muscles

Self-Study Instructions: This test can be used to help you assess how well you understand the speech functions of articulatory muscles. Terms to be filled in are from the Review Glossary. Answers are given in Appendix E.

Speech Function	*Muscles*
Tongue Movements	
Raises sides	(1) _____
Raises back	(2) _____
Lowers midline	(3) _____
Lowers back	(4) _____
Curls tip	(5) _____
Protrudes	(6) _____
	(7) _____
Retracts	(8) _____
	(9) _____
Spreads	(10) _____
Points	(11) _____
Shortens	(12) _____
	(13) _____
Velar Movements	
Raises	(14) _____
Lowers	(15) _____
	(16) _____
Tenses	(17) _____

Lip Movements
    Rounds   (18) _____

    Spreads   (19) _____

                                       (20) _____

Mandibular Movements
    Opens   (21) _____

                                       (22) _____

    Closes   (23) _____

                                       (24) _____

                                       (25) _____

Laryngeal Movements
    Raises   (26) _____

    Lowers   (27) _____

Pharyngeal Movements
    Nasopharyngeal constriction   (28) _____

    Oropharyngeal constriction   (29) _____

    Laryngopharyngeal constriction   (30) _____

CHAPTER SEVEN
Swallowing Articulatory Physiology

This chapter is about the molding of the air stream into speech. This is a relatively straightforward task in one sense and a very complex one in another. Because normal speech is not spoken one sound at a time, but rather at high speeds with low-speed speech equipment, matters are complicated mightily. The fact is that some articulators can only move at about half the rate at which speech sounds are produced. To achieve normally rapid connected speech involves overlapping articulatory movements for one sound with movements for other sounds. The complexities that result are staggering, so we will only glimpse them at the end of the chapter and devote most of our effort to the more manageable task of relating vocal tract movements and adjustments to the production of the various types of speech sounds. Because much of the equipment used for speaking is used primarily for swallowing, it is important to glimpse the physiology of swallowing before launching into speech articulation.

SWALLOWING

Many of the muscles that are used in speech participate in swallowing (also called *deglutition*).

Swallowing involves movements of the lips, tongue, velopharynx, jaw, oropharynx, laryngopharynx, larynx, hyoid bone, and esophagus. That is to say, a simple swallow involves substantial movements of many structures in the head and neck. But before we take a closer look at the physiology of swallowing, let's take a moment to put swallowing into perspective.

Swallowing develops early in life — well before birth, as a matter of fact. The fetus begins to swallow at about 10 to 11 weeks after conception. Adults swallow about 600 to 900 times per day. Frequency of swallowing is least during sleep (2 to 9 swallows per hour) and highest during eating (about 300 swallows per hour). Like many bodily functions, swallowing usually is taken for granted. But it can be impaired. Disorders of swallowing, called *dysphagias*, are a serious consequence of many injuries to the neck or oral cavity and some neurological conditions. These disorders of swallowing are of interest here because speech-language pathologists are becoming increasingly involved in the management of these disorders and because swallowing and chewing may be important forces in the formation of the oral and pharyngeal structures. Concerning this second issue, it has been proposed that the oral and pharyngeal structures should be understood in terms of a "performance anatomy" — an anatomy that comes about through the use of its structures in particular activities. Because chewing (mastication) and swallowing (deglutition) generate strong forces, these actions help to mold the oral anatomy. Speech generates much smaller forces and therefore is not as important a factor as feeding in shaping oral anatomy.

Swallowing can be conceptualized as a process in which the following actions occur: the passage in advance of the bolus (food to be swallowed) is opened as the passage behind the bolus is constricted to move the food along. In addition, secondary passages must be closed to prevent (1) reflux of food into the nasopharynx and (2) entry of food into the larynx. The act of swallowing can be divided into three phases. The first, *oral phase*, collects the bolus within the oral cavity and pushes it backward to the pharynx by a sequential arching of the tongue against the palate. The second is called the *pharyngeal phase* and is marked by the arrival of the bolus at the faucial pillars. With this phase, the neural control switches from voluntary to reflexive and respiration is interrupted. The tongue participates in this phase by flexing backward on the hyoid bone to thrust the bolus into the pharynx. Both the larynx and the pharynx elevate during this phase. The larynx moves upward and forward under the root of the tongue, and the epiglottis tips downward and backward to cover the laryngeal aperture, which is also closed by constrictions of the vocal folds. The pharyngeal tube elevates as if to engulf the bolus, after which a peristaltic wave travels along it to carry the bolus to the esophagus. The pharyngeal phase ends with the reopening of the laryngeal airway and the resumption of respiration, which has been interrupted for an interval of between half a second to 4 seconds. The *esophageal phase* carries the bolus from the pharyngoesophageal sphincter to the cardiac (gastroesophageal) sphincter. This final transport, which takes 3 seconds or so for liquids and up to 11 seconds for solids, is accomplished by peristaltic contractions that progress along the length of the esophagus.

ARTICULATORY PHYSIOLOGY

It is this same mechanism with which we suck, chew, and swallow that is commandeered for speech. The way speech articulation works is described by the *source-filter theory*. The central idea of this theory is that sound is generated at a *source* (the larynx is the source of a voiced sound, for example). It is then *filtered* through the vocal tract, which modifies it into speech. To simplify the organization of this task, we will first examine the source of the noise components of consonants, and then we will reconsider the vocal tract for its filter functions as a resonator.

Noise Generation: Source

With the exception of semivowels, all consonants include an element of noise. If the consonant is voiced, the noise is added to the voice generated at the *glottal source*. If voiceless, the consonant is characterized entirely by noise. You will recall that the air stream for voiceless sounds passes through the open glottis without meeting much resistance, except for the *h* sound in a word like *hat*. Not until the air flows through the larynx and into the vocal tract does it encounter enough resistance in the form of a narrowly constricted channel, or an abrupt opening of an obstruction of the upper airway, to generate a noise. Thus, the source of noise of consonants, whether voiceless or voiced, is at some location in the vocal tract. The two exceptions are the *h*, as in *how,* and the glottal stop (it's like a minicough) that is a characteristic of the

Cockney dialect. The source of both of these sounds is the glottis. It is the distinctive source of noise for a particular consonant that is usually described when identifying how most consonants are produced.

Oral Pressure

As you can see, the vocal tract has two functions: to serve as a filter for all vowels and consonants, and to serve as a source of noise for most consonants. We will turn to the filter function later. A necessary prerequisite for noise generation is the ability to build pressure behind a constriction or occlusion. Technically, this is the ability to impound *intraoral air pressure*. To impound this pressure in the mouth requires *velopharyngeal competence*, the ability to seal off the nasal cavity from the oral cavity. When this seal cannot be accomplished, whether because of a cleft palate, paralyzed velum, or a soft palate too short to reach the upper pharyngeal wall, air leaks through the nose and intraoral pressure is reduced. It is this weakening of intraoral pressure that makes speech so difficult to understand in persons with a cleft palate.

The nasal airway is used for nasal consonants and nasal vowels, but otherwise it remains closed. The mechanism of velopharyngeal closure involves pulling the velum up and back against the adenoids of the posterior pharyngeal wall. (Because the adenoids in some children make velopharyngeal closure possible, surgeons no longer remove adenoids routinely.) At the same time the soft palate is raised, the upper pharyngeal side walls are pulled inward to complete the sphincteric closure. With the nasal cavity sealed off, intraoral pressure can be impounded and noise consonants can be produced along with nonnasal vowels.

Turbulent Noise

The noise element of consonants produced by friction (called fricatives and affricates) is the result of *turbulence*. Sounding much like the hiss of steam, turbulence noise occurs when the air channel is constricted enough to disrupt the smooth flow of the stream, much as a river flows smoothly until it rushes through a narrow channel. Turbulence is one of the two types of noise generated for consonants (the other being bursts), so there are two manners of production. If turbulence is used, the particular friction consonant depends on how "sharp" the noise is and on whether the air stream is voiced or voiceless.

Sharpness increases with the velocity of air movement and the sharpness of the cutting edge across which it is blown. The *s* sound, for instance, is sharper than *sh* because of higher velocity and a sharper cutting edge. The difference is similar to blowing across the stretched sharp edge of a sheet of paper and blowing across a curled edge. With *sh*, the air is driven through a constriction between the blade of the tongue and the hard palate. This makes for a relatively soft, curved constriction. With *s*, the channel is narrower, so the velocity of the air is greater as it is directed across the edge of the center teeth.

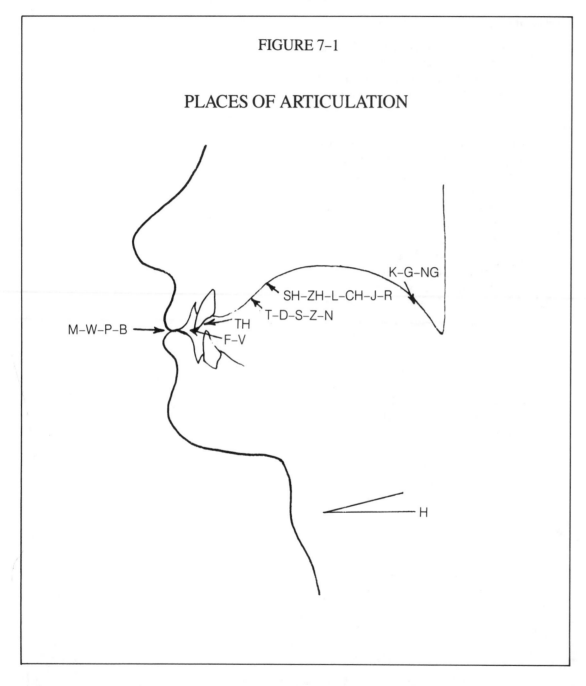

FIGURE 7–1

PLACES OF ARTICULATION

K–G–NG

SH–ZH–L–CH–J–R

T–D–S–Z–N

M–W–P–B

TH

F–V

H

The *place of articulation* (the place in the vocal tract where the constricted airway generates turbulence) is the other feature by which friction consonants are differentiated. Even as small a difference in location as between the places where *f* and *th* are produced is sufficient to make these sounds detectably different. With *f*, the constriction is fairly broad between the lower lip against the upper front teeth. With *th*, the broad constriction is between the tongue and the upper front teeth. Although the places of turbulence for English sounds are mostly in the front of the mouth, a constriction could generate friction any place in the vocal tract as far down as the glottis, where, indeed, *h* is produced (Fig. 7–1).

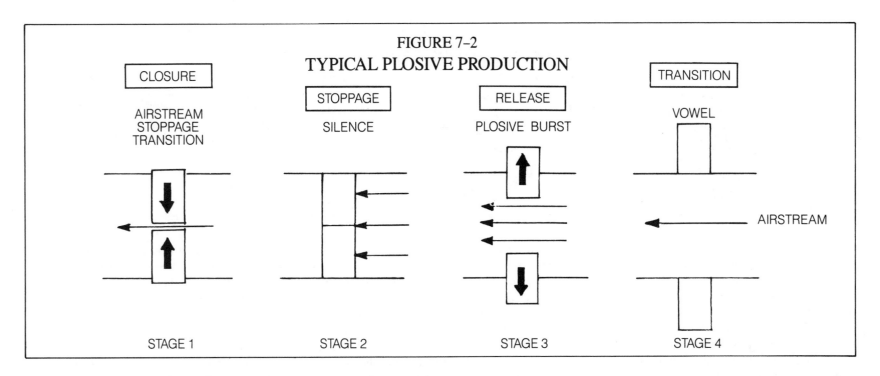

FIGURE 7–2
TYPICAL PLOSIVE PRODUCTION

CLOSURE	STOPPAGE	RELEASE	TRANSITION
AIRSTREAM STOPPAGE TRANSITION	SILENCE	PLOSIVE BURST	VOWEL
			AIRSTREAM
STAGE 1	STAGE 2	STAGE 3	STAGE 4

Bursts of Noise

The other manner of production of a noise element of consonants is to explode a *burst*, a puff of air, as in *p*. To generate a burst, the air stream is stopped by the tongue or lips, so this type of consonant is sometimes called a *stop*. It is also called a *plosive* because of the explosive manner in which it is released.

Plosives, or stops if you prefer, progress through four stages. In the first stage, *closure*, the tongue or lips move into a blockage of the air stream. (Acoustically, this movement can be detected as an articulatory transition.) During the second stage, pressure builds behind this stoppage (Fig. 7–2). (Acoustically, this stage is marked by a brief *gap* of silence if the plosive is voiceless; if voiced, it is relative silence with the only sound behind the buzz of the voice.) The third stage, in

which the stoppage is *released*, varies considerably, as you can discover for yourself if you pronounce the "p" in the words "pin," "spin," and "stop." The release can be *aspirated*, in which a distinct puff of air is released from the vocal folds following the burst, as in "pin." It can be released unaspirated with only a release burst, as in "spin." Or, the release can just not materialize, so the burst itself is not produced. Instead of the pressure being exploded past the stoppage, it dwindles before the occlusion is released, in which case the plosive is *unreleased*, as in "stop." (Acoustically, unreleased plosives merely extend the gap of silence of the stoppage. Released plosives leave an acoustic signature in the form of a burst of noise (the characteristics of the signature depend on the velocity and volume of air released). In the fourth stage, the stoppage is removed. The tongue or lips move

through a *transition* from the occlusion position to the position for the sound that follows. (This transition has a characteristic acoustic signature, which is an important clue for the detection of a particular plosive sound.)

As with friction consonants, production of a particular plosive also depends on two types of articulatory features: whether it is voiced or voiceless and where the occlusion in the vocal tract is placed. If the body of the tongue is pushed up against the velum and the air stream is voiced, the plosive will be *g*; if the air stream is voiceless, it will be *k*. If a voiceless air stream is stopped and released at the alveolar ridge by the blade of the tongue, the sound will be *t*; if voiced, it will be *d*. If air is occluded at the lips; the plosive will be *p* if voiceless, *b* if voiced.

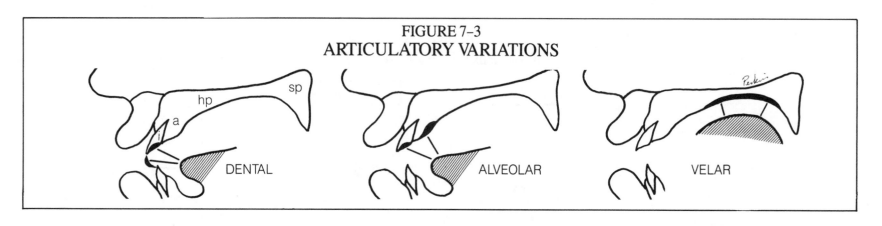

FIGURE 7–3
ARTICULATORY VARIATIONS

DENTAL

ALVEOLAR

VELAR

Articulatory Variations

What we sometimes consider to be the same sound really can be formed in different ways. Figure 7–3 shows some of the variations in production of English sounds. The drawing on the left shows the way in which *dental* sounds (like the first sounds in the words *this* and *thin*) are produced. These sounds are called dental because they are made by touching the tip of the tongue to the front teeth. Either the tongue can be inserted between the upper and lower incisors or it can be placed in a slightly higher position just behind the upper incisors. Some people form the sound in one way and other people make it the other way. Moreover, one individual speaker may use both ways of making the sound, depending on other sounds that precede or follow it.

The middle drawing in Figure 7–3 depicts the production of *alveolar* sounds, which are made by a complete or partial closure between the tongue tip and the alveolar ridge of the maxilla. The alveolar sounds include the first sounds in the following words: *dip, tip, sip, zip, lip, nip*. As you might guess from the large number of sounds made with this articulation, it is very heavily used in English speech. In fact, about half of the consonant sounds used in ordinary conversation are made at the

alveolar place of production. As we already have mentioned briefly, some sounds normally made as alveolars are made with a dental articulation under certain circumstances. Say the following pairs of words and try to tell which of each pair is made with an alveolar articulation and which with a dental articulation: *mid-width*; *nine-ninth*; *well-wealth*. If you are like most speakers, then you should have produced the first word in each pair with an alveolar articulation and the second with a dental articulation.

The drawing on the right in Figure 7–3 applies to the velar place of articulation, in which the dorsum or top of the tongue is raised high in the mouth to touch the undersurface of the hard or soft palate. Because this articulation is made against or close to the velum, these sounds are called *velars*. They include the final sounds in the words *rag*, *rack*, *rang*. The drawing shows two lines to portray velar articulation. To see why this portrayal is necessary, try to tell where your tongue is placed for the initial sounds when you say the following pairs of words: *key-car*; *gate-goat*; *cat-cot*; *guest-ghost*. Most people can feel that the tongue is more toward the front for the initial consonant in the first member of each pair. Why? Because the tongue position for the consonant is adjusted to the posi-

tion for the following vowel. The first word of each pair contains a front vowel (meaning that the tongue is carried toward the front of the oral cavity), whereas the second word contains a back vowel (meaning that the tongue is positioned more toward the back of the oral cavity). The velar consonant is made at a place of articulation that is either front or back, depending on whether the following vowel is front or back. This means that the tongue "knows" where the following vowel will be made even before the vowel itself is produced.

These examples are sufficient to show that speech production is not a simple matter of putting the articulators in one position and one position only for each sound. Speakers are quite versatile in their articulatory patterns and what we hear as "one sound" (like all initial sounds in the words *keep, cape, cap, coon, cope*) really differ in their place of articulation. Another example of this flexibility is to produce speech either with your jaw free to move or with a pencil clenched between your teeth. When the jaw is free to move, it usually assists the articulations of the tongue and lower lip, but when the jaw is fixed, the tongue and lower lip do the work on their own.

Table 7–1. Consonant Production

Place of Articulation

Manner	Lips −	Lips +	Lips-Teeth −	Lips-Teeth +	Teeth-Tongue −	Teeth-Tongue +	Gum-Tongue −	Gum-Tongue +	Palate-Tongue −	Palate-Tongue +	Velum-Tongue −	Velum-Tongue +	Glottis −
Plosive	p pop	b bob					t tot	d dot			k cot	g got	
Fricative			f fine	v vine	th thin	th then	s sing	z zing	sh leash	zh leisure			h how
Affricate									ch chose	j Joe's			

Summing Up: Physiology of Noise Generation

The physiology of producing turbulence and pulse characteristics of consonants could be summed up under *manner of articulation*, *place of articulation*, and whether a *voiced (+) or voiceless (−)* air stream is being modulated (Table 7–1).

The voiced-voiceless feature depends on whether the glottis is open or closed for phonation. As we saw in the chapter on phonation, the posterior cricoarytenoids open the glottis and the interarytenoids are largely responsible for closing it. This much of the physiology is relatively straightforward. But when we consider the physiology of adjusting the pitch, loudness, or quality of the voiced air stream, speculation replaces reasonable capacity. One major reason for uncertainty is because of the complex vectors of laryngeal forces that can interact to produce a given adjustment. These vectors can vary so much from individual to individual, and from one situation to another within the same individual, that an accurate and complete generalized account of the physiology of producing a voiced air stream is all but impossible.

The same reservation holds for the same reason when it comes to describing the physiology of the manner and place of articulation. The effect of contracting a specific vocal tract muscle can be described, as we have done. But an accurate description of the pull of the muscles that move the hyoid bone, or that position the blade of the tongue for a particular sound, would likely differ in some degree from person to person. In fact, it would probably differ in the same person from one speech sound context to another. What could be described would be the physiology of a particular instance of a particular sound. This would go beyond the scope of a primer, so we will be content with a display in Table 7–1 of the articulatory features by which the various noise sounds are produced. We will leave the complexities of how much specific muscles pull for specific sounds to advanced studies.

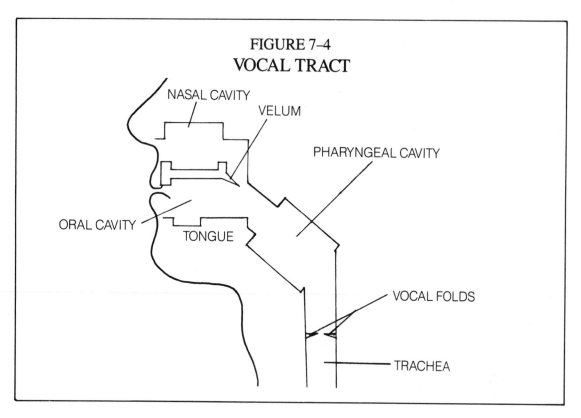

FIGURE 7–4
VOCAL TRACT

NASAL CAVITY

VELUM

PHARYNGEAL CAVITY

ORAL CAVITY

TONGUE

VOCAL FOLDS

TRACHEA

Resonance: Filter

Having examined the vocal tract as a source of noise, we will now consider it as a filter. The vocal tract is essentially a tube, closed at the bottom, the pharyngeal end (for all practical purposes, it is closed at the larynx), and open at the front, the oral-nasal end. (Actually, of course, it can function as a double-barreled tube in front, depending on whether or not the nasal airway is open or closed.) This tube can be constricted or occluded by the lips in front, or by the tongue anywhere along its length, particularly in the mouth (Fig. 7–4). As we have just seen, noise will be generated if the tube is closed enough to create turbulence or bursts. Being a tube, however, it will also function as a *resonator*.

A resonance cavity is not a source of energy; it does not generate sound. Until the air molecules in the cavity are vibrated by wave energy from the glottal source or random noise energy from vocal tract turbulence or pulses, a resonator is silent. Its only function is to respond selectively, as a filter, to those vibratory frequencies to which it is tuned. Were the vocal tract a closed tube like a test tube, it would resonate only one sound, and that sound would resemble *ah*. Obviously, we must be able to tune our resonators to a multitude of frequencies to be able to produce the whole range of sounds of which we are capable.

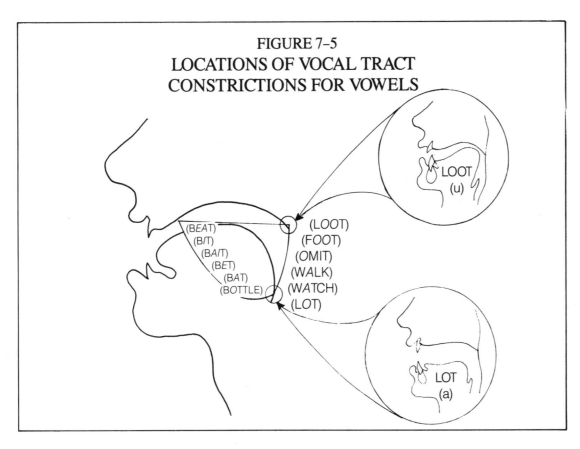

FIGURE 7–5
LOCATIONS OF VOCAL TRACT CONSTRICTIONS FOR VOWELS

LOOT
(u)

(B*EA*T)
(B*I*T)
(BA*I*T)
(B*E*T)
(BAT)
(BOTTLE)

(LOOT)
(FOOT)
(OMIT)
(WALK)
(WATCH)
(LOT)

LOT
(a)

The resonator cavities can be tuned to different frequencies mainly by how much and at what location the vocal tract is constricted. These constrictions can be thought of in terms of how high the arch of the tongue is raised toward the palate, the *vertical place of articulation*. This vertical height determines the degree of constriction. Where the constriction is placed along the palate, however, is equally important to resonance frequencies. This location of the lingual arch is called the *horizontal place of articulation*. Finally, the constriction can occur at the lips, so *lip rounding* plays an important role in tuning vocal tract resonators.

These, then, are the major determinants of vocal tract functions (transfer functions). They are primarily responsible for all of the different vowels and diphthongs we make, and also for the sonorant consonants.* We only need to add a postscript for nasal consonants to complete the broad outline of how the vocal tract functions as a resonance filter. The velopharyngeal valve must be opened and the oral airway closed to direct the air stream through the nose. If the oral airway is occluded at the lips, the sound will be *m*. If it is occluded at the gum ridge, it will be *n*; and if at the velum, it will be *ng*.

Thus, if the air channel is not narrowed so much as to disrupt the smooth flow of the voiced air stream, it will function only as a filter. But constrict this airway a bit more at any place along its length, or run a voiceless air stream at higher velocity through it, and turbulence will result. The vocal tract will then become a source of noise for the fricative and affricate consonants. Constrict it still more until the oral airway is occluded, and plosive pulses will be produced.

This tuning is done by raising or lowering the larynx to change the length of the vocal tract, and by protruding or spreading the lips. The vocal tract can also be altered from a single long cavity, as in the sound *ah*, to a cavity with complex shape variations. The different vowels and semivowels especially will depend on the size and location of the cavities and cavity openings. These resonator size and aperture adjustments are made by changing the degree and place of constriction in the oral airway for vowels, as is shown in Figure 7–5 with a schematic representation on the left and two oral cavity illustrations on the right. For the sonorant semivowels, the air channel is more constricted than for

vowels, but it is still not enough to produce turbulence. Only for nasal sounds is the airway through the nasal cavity opened.

Summing Up: Vocal Tract as Source and Filter

The purpose of this brief summary is to relate the source and filter functions of the vocal tract to each other. The same air stream accomplishes both functions. When the airway through the vocal tract is open enough for smooth laminar flow of the voiced air stream, this tube will function solely as a resonator to filter the sound generated by glottal vibration, the source.

*The articulatory distinction between vowels and consonants is rather arbitrary when they are both produced with a high tongue arch. That is why a sonorant consonant like the *y* in "yes" is called a semivowel, even though it uses the same constriction as the *ee* in "eel," which is classified as a vowel.

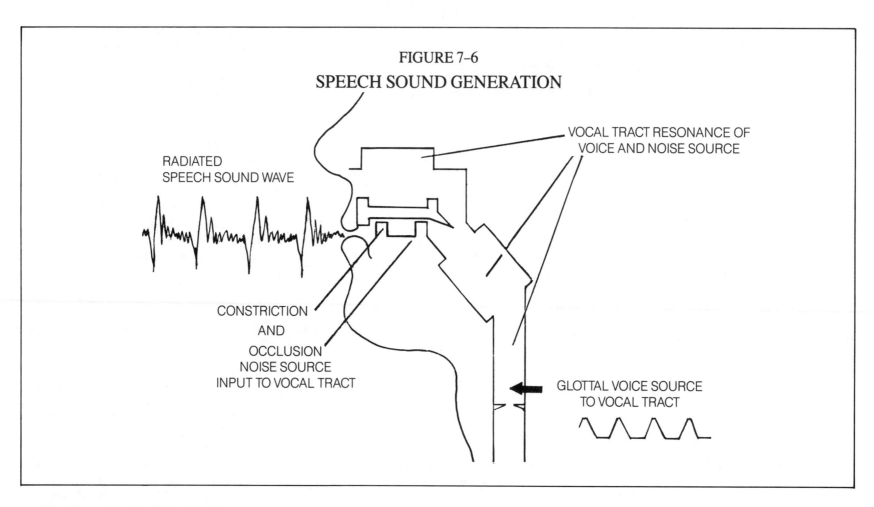

FIGURE 7–6
SPEECH SOUND GENERATION

VOCAL TRACT RESONANCE OF
VOICE AND NOISE SOURCE

RADIATED
SPEECH SOUND WAVE

CONSTRICTION
AND
OCCLUSION
NOISE SOURCE
INPUT TO VOCAL TRACT

GLOTTAL VOICE SOURCE
TO VOCAL TRACT

The air stream with which these turbulence and pulse noises are generated can be voiced or voiceless. With either, the vocal tract will function simultaneously as both source and filter. Even though the airway will be narrowly constricted in places, enough to generate noise, it will still have resonance cavities between these constrictions. Thus, the noise consonants are blends of vocal tract source functions and filter functions. The glottal source of voice and vocal tract sources of noise are shown schematically in Figure 7–6.

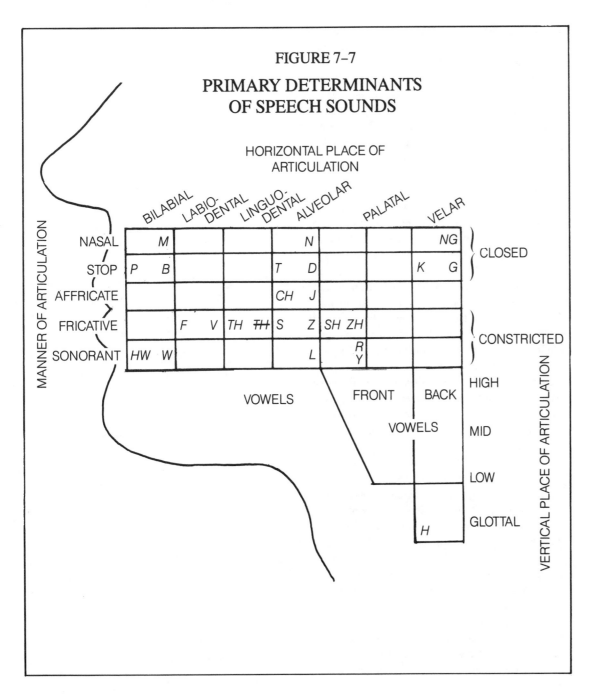

FIGURE 7–7

PRIMARY DETERMINANTS
OF SPEECH SOUNDS

By way of grand summary, Figure 7–7 presents the primary determinants of vowels and consonants. It shows these determinants in relation to the vocal tract. As you can see, one of these determinants is whether the sound is voiced or voiceless. Normally, all vowels are voiced, as are 60 percent of the consonants. A second determinant is the manner of articulation, which mainly describes how the air stream for consonants is managed. Another determinant is vertical place of articulation, which describes the degree of constriction of the airway for vowels. Finally, horizontal place of articulation describes where a constriction is located along the oral airway. It is mainly by controlling these four determinants that we are able to produce all of the sounds of speech even in some instances when vocal tract equipment is defective.

Connected Speech

If you have learned to speak a foreign language, you know that mastering the sounds of that language is no assurance that you will be able to speak it intelligibly, let alone sound like a native. Normally expressive speech flows as a continuous stream of sound, varying in stresses, inflections, and intonations. The fact that we can detect separate words, and can break those words into segments of sound with which they are spoken, is merely a reflection of our knowledge of the language. It is not a characteristic of the way a language is spoken. Try to detect separate words, let alone sounds, of a language you do not know, and all you are likely to identify are changes in pitch and loudness. Or take a word like "Constantinople," which has more syllables in it than many of our sentences. If a foreigner who did not understand English were listening to a conversation in which the answer to a question was "Constantinople," that foreigner would have no idea whether he had heard a short sentence answer or a single long word with many syllables.

Articulatory Physiology

163

As speakers, we do not assemble words with sounds like bricks laid end to end, each brick a separate sound with its own identity, an identity that is unaffected by the sounds on either side of it. As listeners, however, that is essentially how we hear speech. We process the continuous stream of sound generated by a speaker by chopping it into the perceptual elements we recognize as speech sounds of our language. These are the *segmental* elements of speech, as in the three elements of "*c a t*," for example.

Extending across these segments are the *suprasegmental* elements, without which speech would be a monotonous drone. They consist of the *prosodic* features of pitch, loudness, and duration, which are the basis of stress, intonation, and inflection. It is by varying these features that we give expressiveness to speech. They are suprasegmental because they typically apply to more than one segment. For instance, when stress is given to the second syllable in a word like "*abuse*," all of the segments in that syllable are affected by the higher pitch, greater loudness, and longer duration that denote that it is a stressed syllable.

Coarticulation

If humans were by nature slow, pedantic speakers who articulated each sound segment precisely before moving to the next, this section of the text would be unnecessary. Language would be spoken as if we truly were speech-segment bricklayers. Each segment would be laid in place and would be unaffected by those on either side of it. Although syllables of words would receive their usual stress and the inflections and intonations of sentences would still be used, the result would nonetheless sound stilted and peculiar.

Far from being pedantically slow speakers, humans automatically speak at close to the maximum rates they can achieve. We normally utter six or seven syllables per second. Because the average

syllable has over two segments in it, that means we produce 10 to 14 sounds per second. To appreciate how rapid this rate is, try tapping your finger as rapidly as you can. You will be exceptional if you exceed half the rate at which you articulate speech sounds. The relevance of finger tapping is that it can be done about as rapidly as any of the articulators can move. Which raises an intriguing question. How can rapid speech be produced with slow equipment?

The answer turns out to be simple. It is the consequences of the answer that are complex. High-speed speech is achieved the same way skilled typists and pianists perform at high speeds: speakers overlap articulatory movements, typists and pianists overlap finger movements. This means that while one sound is being produced, preparatory movements of the articulators are under way for sounds that are to follow. This is the process of *coarticulation*. It can be observed by comparing the lip adjustments for *h* in the words "*heap*," "*hop*," and "*hoop*." Although all three *h* sounds are linguistically the same, they are very different so far as lip positions are concerned. In preparation for the vowel in "heap" the lips are spread, for "hop" they are neutral, and for "hoop" they are rounded.

Coarticulation is not just an occasional happening, it is a prevailing characteristic of normal speech. Accordingly, we rarely utter "pure" segments of speech. Most segments are "contaminated" to one extent or another by preparatory movements for forthcoming sounds. Thus, to describe the physiology of speech sound production as we actually speak a language would require describing the endless range of coarticulatory interactions. Clearly, this is a task far beyond the scope of this primer.

The fact is that coarticulation has posed a vexing problem for scientists who have attempted to synthesize natural-sounding speech or to automatically recognize speech as it is naturally spoken. If we spoke segment by segment, each segment having a characteristic acoustic signature, then stenographers would undoubtedly have vanished long ago from the employment market. Equipment could easily have been built to recognize each sound as it was spoken. With that problem solved, typewriters could have been hooked up to speech recognizers so that one could literally give dictation to a typewriter rather than to a typist.

Such prospects were on the horizon of speech science several decades ago before the effects of coarticulation were recognized. Despite vast strides, equipment has still not been built that can automatically decode speech as quickly as it is spoken. Deciphering the vast array of acoustical patterns that can result from coarticulatory effects on any sound is still a staggering challenge. Perhaps it would seem unsolvable were it not that a mechanism which can solve this task already exists — the human auditory system.

Production of Sounds in Context

The production of any one speech sound usually requires a number of adjustments of the articulators. For example, let us consider the word *sound*, which consists phonetically of four segments: A noise segment denoted by the letter *s*, a diphthong (a two-element vowel-like sound) represented by the letters *ou,* a nasal consonant symbolized by the letter *n*, and a non-nasal consonant denoted by the letter *d*. The sequence of speech movements for the word *sound* goes about like the following.

First, the sound represented by the *s* requires that a substantial air pressure be developed in the oral cavity to provide the energy of frication noise. The larynx is opened to allow the air pressure in the oral cavity to approximate that in the lungs. The oral constriction is formed by nearly touching the tip of the tongue to the alveolar ridge and by sealing off the sides of the oral cavity with the lateral regions of the tongue. The velopharynx must be closed or the air pressure needed for the frication noise would escape through the nose. A small groove is formed in the midline of the anterior portion of the tongue so that the impounded air escapes through this groove, producing frication noise as it does so. This articulation is held for about 100 to 200 milliseconds (ms) (one tenth to two tenths of a second).

In preparation for the *ou* diphthong, the tongue tip is withdrawn from the alveolar ridge and the entire body of the tongue is retracted in the oral cavity so that the tongue assumes a bulged position that is described as low and back. This movement of the tongue typically is assisted by a lowering of the jaw, which carries the tongue with it as it lowers. The diphthong is a two-part vowel-like sound in which the first vowel is low-back and unrounded and the second vowel is high-back and rounded. Rounded means that the sound is produced with a rounding or protrusion of the lips. Therefore, the diphthong is produced with a changing lip configuration, from unrounded and moderately open to rounded and relatively narrow. Simultaneously with this change in lip configuration, the tongue moves upward (often assisted by a closing movement of the jaw) to satisfy the tongue positioning requirement of the second vowel element. But unless the larynx is vibrating through these diphthong articulations, any sound produced would be whisperlike. So, before the diphthong is articulated, the vocal folds are set into vibration to provide the periodic pulses of air that are heard as voicing. One other articulatory change normally occurs during pronunciation of the diphthong — the velopharyngeal port opens. This opening may seem strange because vowels and diphthongs usually are produced as non-nasal sounds. But we don't have to search far for the reason for this velopharyngeal adjustment. In fact, we need only look to the next sound, the nasal *n*, which requires velopharyngeal opening so that the voicing energy enters the nasal cavity. The speech production system anticipates the requirement for velopharyngeal opening (nasality) during the *ou* diphthong. This means that the diphthong itself becomes somewhat nasalized, but this nasalization does not interfere with pronunciation of the sound. To the contrary, it appears that listeners detect this nasalization during the diphthong and expect the upcoming sound to be a nasal. Of course, anticipation of nasality could not be permitted if the nasal is preceded by a non-nasal sound like *s*, which cannot tolerate velopharyngeal opening.

The total articulation of the diphthong *ou* takes about 150 to 200 ms (two tenths of a second or less). When the diphthong is completed, the tongue tip and tongue body move forward so that the alveolar closure can be formed for the *n* sound. The *n* articulation is held for about 100 ms (another tenth of a second), during which time the velopharynx begins to close because the final sound in the word is a non-nasal consonant. As the velopharynx closes, the sound quality changes from nasal to non-nasal, or from *n* to d. No change in tongue position is required because both *n* and *d* have a requirement for alveolar closure. This explains why *n* and *d* may sound alike when a speaker has nasal congestion from a cold. The *d* articulation is held for about 50 to 100 ms and the word is complete.

The word *sound* can be produced within about half a second (much less if you talk fast). During that half-second, many movements are completed. But this word is relatively simple. Consider what the speech system must do to pronounce a word like *extracurricular*, in which the vibrations of the vocal folds must be turned on and off (on for the *e*, off for the *ks* of "x," kept off for the *t*, back on for the *r* and *a*, off again for the *k* sound of "c," back on for the *urr* vowel, and so forth), the tongue must move nimbly from position to position (first a vowel, then *k*, then *s*, then *t*, then *r*, then another vowel, then to a *k*, and so forth), and the jaw moves up and down to assist the tongue in its articulations. But the word *extracurricular* involves almost entirely tongue sounds, so it doesn't really show the true complexity of speech production.

Consider a word like *upperclassman*, which requires lip sounds (the *p* and *m*) as well as tongue sounds (such as *l*, *s*, and *n*). This word also requires that the vibrations of the vocal folds be turned off and on. And it requires that the velopharynx be opened for the final *man* sequence (two nasal consonants connected by a vowel). Just to see how many adjustments are needed, try to list the sequence of movements and adjustments that must be performed to produce this word. Then, imagine how many movements are needed for a sentence like, "The upperclassman received a low grade point average because he spent too much time on extracurricular activities and too little time on coursework." This sentence can be produced in about 6 to 7 seconds and contains in excess of 100 phonetic segments, each of which is associated with a number of different articulatory movements. Furthermore, the production of this sentence involves many adjustments of the respiratory and phonatory systems, which we have barely hinted at in the discussion so far.

To most of us, speech seems easy, but like so many things we rather take for granted, speech is a remarkably complicated and inadequately understood process. The complexity is only partly appreciated by coming to understand how individual sounds are made. Things become frustratingly involved when sounds are put together to form words within sentences. One thing is very clear from studies of speech articulation: The movements are rapidly sequenced and very often upcoming requirements are anticipated in the sequence of movements. To illustrate this phenomenon, let us examine these words: *The ninth is too soon*. The word *ninth* is composed of the root *nine* and the suffix *th*. Try saying the words *nine* and *ninth* alternately, noticing where the tongue is placed for the second *n* in each words. You should feel a difference. In *nine* the tongue placement for both *n*'s is alveolar but for the second *n* in *ninth* the tongue is fronted, touching the upper central incisors. Why? Because the articulation for *n* in *ninth* is adjusted for the upcoming fricative *th*, which requires that the tongue tip be placed just behind the upper front teeth or even between the upper and lower front teeth. This example demonstrates a pervasive characteristic of speech, namely that no one sound has only one way of being formed.

Next, we shall examine the word *too*. As you might be able to determine for yourself by watching another speaker or by touching your own lips as you say this word, the lip rounding for the rounded vowel *oo* begins during the consonant *t*, even though this consonant produced in isolation is not rounded. That is, the lip rounding for the vowel is anticipated during the consonant. The word *soon* also has features of anticipation. First, lip rounding for the vowel *oo* is anticipated during the *s*. Second, velopharyngeal opening for the *n* is anticipated during the vowel *oo*. Because of these anticipations of upcoming articulatory features, the sounds in the simple utterance *The ninth is too soon* are in effect overlapped or shingled onto one another.

This overlapping, of course, is what has been explained as coarticulation. *Anticipatory coarticulation* is demonstrated by the preceding examples in which a feature of a sound is assumed during an earlier segment in a string of sounds. Sometimes this anticipatory coarticulation can extend over several segments. For example, in the sentence, *Have you eaten stew for breakfast?* the lip rounding for the vowel in *stew* often begins during the *n*

in *eaten*. This example demonstrates that the overlapping of articulations affects not only adjacent sound segments but even segments that occur in different words. A second kind of coarticulation, called *retentive*, occurs when a feature of one sound is carried over onto a following sound. An example is the carryover of velopharyngeal opening for the nasal *n* onto the following vowel *o* in *no*. Most occurrences of this kind of coarticulation can be explained by the fact that the articulators cannot change positions instantaneously, and also by the fact that different articulators are not equally fast. Two of the slower movements are those for velopharyngeal opening and lip rounding, so that these articulations often persist onto a following segment.

The act of speaking is remarkable in its complexity. Even a simple sentence requires a large number of decisions that are made with rapidity to ensure a normal conversational rate of speaking. Ordinary conversation proceeds at a rate of two to three words per second, which translates to about 10 to 14 phonemes per second. Each phoneme, in turn, is the result of many muscular adjustments, to position the tongue, jaw, lips, soft palate, and vocal folds, and to ensure that the respiratory system provides the necessary supply of air to generate sound. The complexity is all the greater in that the speech control system is striving constantly to anticipate upcoming articulatory requirements. To accomplish this, the control system needs to look ahead, to scan the phoneme string to determine future requirements and determine which can be satisfied in advance without destroying the intelligibility of an earlier sound.

CLINICAL POSTSCRIPT

It is surprising to many persons that the loss of a functional palate can have more serious effects on speech intelligibility than a loss of lingual function. Frank B. suffered from oral cancer, for which medical treatment required a surgical removal of virtually all of the tongue, half of the mandible, and other oral tissues. Despite this substantial loss of the articulatory structures, Frank B. was able to produce intelligible speech, even for sentences like *Rabbits were hopping around the room*. An x-ray motion picture of his vocal tract revealed that he made various compensations with his remaining oral structures. For example, his lower lip accomplished articulations that normally are made by the tip of the tongue. This is not to say that his speech was completely normal, as the articulation was not as precise as it is for the talker with an intact articulatory mechanism. His ability to compensate was good enough that he was capable of intelligible speech for the normally redundant transmission of continuous speech. That is, human language — any human language — has a redundancy that hovers around 50 percent, which means that about half of what we say is predictable from the other half. Listeners use this redundancy to cope with noise, with occasional inaudibility of a weak speech signal, or with the articulatory failings of a speaker like Frank B. Without a tongue, Frank B. could speak well enough that most undergraduate students could not guess from recordings of his speech that he had suffered such a severe loss of articulatory tissue.

Jenny W. also had a speech impairment. Her velopharyngeal mechanism was incompetent, meaning that she could not accomplish velopharyngeal closure when it was required for speech sounds. This velopharyngeal incompetence rendered her speech almost unintelligible. Why should this be? Is it because the nasal sounds occur frequently in speech? The three nasal consonants, those in the word *meaning*, make up about 10 percent of the sounds in adult conversational speech, and nasal consonants in English occur at the rate of about twice a second. But then why isn't speech intelligible if the remaining 90 percent of the sounds are normal and if speech is about 50 percent redundant? The answer is that the remaining sounds are not normal. Severe velopharyngeal incompetence affects virtually all of the non-nasal consonants. Some of them will sound like nasal consonants produced at the same place of articulation. For example, *b* will sound like *m*, *d* like *n*, and *g* like *ng*. Thus, *butter* may sound like *munner*, and *dog* may sound like *nong*. Other consonants will be distorted in various ways. The result is that most of the consonants, the sounds most important to intelligibility, are produced inadequately. A speaker with velopharyngeal incompetence cannot compensate for this disorder through the use of another articulator. This kind of problem is corrected by surgery, by prosthetic management (such as a special appliance that the speaker wears to close off the velopharyngeal port), or by speech therapy — either alone or in combination with the other corrective approaches.

Let us close this discussion by mentioning ventriloquism, which is a skill by which a speaker seems to "throw" his or her voice. The word ventriloquism is derived from the combination of two words meaning *stomach* and *speak*, from the belief that ventriloquists spoke from their stomachs. In fact, the ventriloquist does not speak from the stomach anymore than you or I do. Nor do ventriloquists throw their voices, which is physically impossible under normal circumstances. What ventriloquists do is to exploit articulatory compensations (so, for example, their lips are not seen to move for labial sounds like those in the word *bump*), the normal redundancy of speech (so that speech is intelligible even if some sounds are indistinct), and the gullibility of the listener (who believes that the ventriloquist's dummy is in fact doing the talking whenever the dummy's mouth moves).

The third factor relates to a perceptual phenomenon called the McGurk effect, in which a listener (and viewer!) of speech attempts to integrate the acoustic and visual information from a speaker. That is, we expect that we can reconcile what we hear with what we see. If the two sources of information are not in agreement, then one will prevail. This effect was demonstrated in an experiment in which spoken syllables were presented either as an acoustic signal alone or as an acoustic signal paired with a videotape of a talker. When a word like *day* was presented as the acoustic signal but the simultaneously presented videotape was saying *may*, most listener-viewers "heard" *may*.

Both the ventriloquist and the speech-impaired person can take advantage of articulatory compensations and the redundancy of natural languages. There may be a "right" way to talk, but it is certainly not the only way.

CHAPTER SEVEN

Self-Study
Articulatory Physiology

Review Glossary

Vocal tract: The airway extending upward from the vocal folds including throat, mouth, and nasal cavity

Source-filter theory: The theory that the energy for speech sounds is generated at a source in the vocal tract, from the larynx to the lips, and is then filtered through the vocal tract cavities to produce specific vowels and consonants

  Glottal source: The source at the glottis of voiced and whispered sounds

    Voiced sounds: Speech sounds generated with glottal vibration

    Voiceless sounds: Consonants generated without glottal vibration

  Turbulence (source): Noise generated by friction of air flow through constrictions in the vocal tract

  Burst or Pulse (source): A burst of noise generated by explosive release or air flow through an occlusion

  Manner of articulation: The source of sound generation such as plosive (burst), fricative (turbulence), or sonorant and vowel (glottal vibration).

    Plosive (stop): A speech sound generated by a pulse released from an occlusion in the vocal tract

      Closure: Occlusion of the vocal tract as the first phase of plosive production

      Stoppage: Silence resulting from occlusion of the vocal tract

      Released: Abrupt removal of occlusion from the vocal tract with or without aspiration

        Aspiration: The puff of air released during production of plosives as turbulence is generated at the vocal folds

      Unreleased: Production of a plosive in which the occlusion is not abruptly removed

      Transition: The sound produced by movement of the vocal tract from an occluded to an open position

    Fricative: A speech sound generated by turbulence from a constriction in the vocal tract

    Sonorant: A semivowel generated by a voiced sound through a constriction that does not cause turbulence

    Vowel: A voiced sound filtered through an unconstricted vocal tract

    Intraoral pressure: Pressure for speech that builds up in the mouth

    Velopharyngeal competence: The ability to close the nasal cavity from the pharyngeal cavity and thereby generate intraoral pressure

  Place of articulation: The location in the vocal tract of a speech sound determinant

    Horizontal place of articulation: The place along the vocal tract at which a resonator aperture, constriction, or occlusion is located

    Vertical place of articulation: The height of the tongue with respect to the palate that determines occlusion, constriction, and resonator aperture

    Lip position: Lip rounded, neutral, or spread position that determines the front cavity resonator aperture

Connected speech: The flow of speech as it is normally spoken in sentences

  Segmental elements: Individual segments of sound which, when combined, form words

  Suprasegmental elements: The *prosodic features* of pitch, loudness, and duration that are the basis of expressiveness, which apply across two or more speech segments

  Coarticulation: The overlapping of articulatory adjustments for a sound of speech with the adjustments for another sound, which accounts for how high-speed speech is produced with a low-speed mechanism

    Anticipatory coarticulation: The overlapping of articulatory adjustments for a sound of speech with the preparatory adjustments for a subsequent sound

    Retentive coarticulation: The carry-over of articulatory adjustments for one sound onto a following sound

  Prosodic features: The features of pitch, loudness, and duration that are the basis of stress, inflection, and intonation

Dysphagia: Disorder of swallowing

Deglutition: Swallowing

  Oral phase: Collection of the bolus in the oral cavity which is pushed back to the pharynx by sequential arching of the tongue against the palate

  Pharyngeal phase: The switch from voluntary to reflexive control of swallowing when the bolus arrives at the faucial pillars

  Esophageal phase: Peristaltic contractions along the length of the esophagus, which carry the bolus from the pharyngoesophageal sphincter to the gastroesophageal (cardiac) sphincter

Self-Study Test of Terminology

Self-Study Instructions: These questions can be used to help you assess how much you have retained from studying the Review Glossary. Answers are given in Appendix E.

(1) _____ The theory that the energy for speech sounds is generated at a source in the vocal tract, from the larynx to the lips, and is then filtered through the vocal tract cavities to produce specific vowels and consonants

(2) _____ A noise generated by explosive release of air flow through an occlusion

(3) _____ Production of a plosive in which the occlusion is not removed abruptly

(4) _____ A semivowel generated by a voiced sound through a constriction that does not cause turbulence

(5) _____ A speech sound generated by a pulse released from an occlusion in the vocal tract

(6) _____ The source at the glottis of voiced and whispered sounds

(7) _____ The source of sound generation such as plosive (pulse), fricative (turbulence), sonorant, and vowel (both glottal vibration)

(8) _____ Occlusion of the vocal tract as the first phase of plosive production

(9) _____ Speech sounds generated with glottal vibration

(10) _____ The airway extending upwards from the vocal folds including throat, mouth, and nasal cavities

(11) _____ Occlusion of the vocal tract resulting in silence

(12) _____ A voiced sound filtered through an unconstricted vocal tract

(13) _____ Abrupt removal of occlusion from the vocal tract with or without aspiration

(14) _____ Noise generated by friction of air flow through constrictions in the vocal tract

(15) _____ Pressure for speech that builds up in the mouth

(16) _____ The sound produced by movement of the vocal tract from one position to another

(17) _____ The location in the vocal tract of a speech sound determinant

(18) _____ The flow of speech as it is normally spoken in sentences

(19) _____ The ability to close the nasal cavity from the pharyngeal cavity and thereby achieve intraoral pressure

(20) _____ A speech sound generated by turbulence from a constriction in the vocal tract

(21) _____ The height of the tongue with respect to the palate that determines occlusion, constriction, and resonator aperture

(22) _____ The prosodic features of pitch, loudness, and duration that are the basis of expressiveness, which apply across two or more speech segments

(23) _____ The features of pitch, loudness, and duration that are the basis of stress, inflection, and intonation

(24) _____ The overlapping of articulatory movements for a segment of speech with the movements for a subsequent segment, which accounts for how high-speed speech is produced with a low-speed mechanism

(25) _____ Lip rounded, neutral, or spread position that determines the front cavity resonator aperture

(26) _____ Individual segments of sounds, which, when combined, form words

(27) _____ Consonants generated without glottal vibration

(28) _____ The place along the vocal tract at which a resonator aperture, constriction, or occlusion is located

(29) _____ Disorder of swallowing

(30) _____ Swallowing

Self-Study Test of Understanding

Self-Study Instructions: This test can be used to help you assess how well you understand the content of this chapter. Terms to be filled in are from the Review Glossary. Answers are given in Appendix E.

You have been offered a dubious opportunity. When asked for your answer, you said decisively, "It's no." The reason the answer sounded decisive was because of the falling inflection and stress with which the words were spoken; these are (A) _____ features found in normal connected speech. In this utterance, these features underscored the meaning of the words formed with (B) _____ elements of speech.

The first sound segment in the words "it's" was a vowel, which meant the energy for it was generated from a (C) _____ involving vocal cord vibration, so it was a (D) _____ sound. This energy was then transferred through the (E) _____, where it was modulated by articulatory movements into the vowel in "it's."

The sound "t" that followed was a (F) _____ generated by a burst of noise from a (G) _____ air stream that passed through the glottis without vocal cord vibration. The (H) _____ of articulation of this (I) _____ of noise involved four stages of production. First was the (J) _____ of the air stream channel as the vocal tract was occluded by raising the blade of the tongue against the gum ridge. This produced a complete (K) _____ of air flow, during which (L) _____ increased. This increase was made possible by (M) _____, which was your ability to prevent air leakage through the nasal cavity. Next, the occlusion was blown open abruptly as a burst of air was (N) _____ while the tongue moved through the (O) _____ to its position for the next sound, "s."

This transition involved merely lowering and grooving the tongue slightly because "s" used the same (P) _____ of articulation on the gum ridge as was used for "t" and would be used for the next sound "n." However, a (Q) _____ manner of articulation was used to produce the high frequency turbulence of "s."

The next word, "no," began with a (R) _____ semivowel with the same place of articulation as "s" and "t," but with the voiced air stream through the nose. When "n" is produced by itself, the lips assume a neutral position. In the word "no," however, the lips were rounded before "n" began. The reason this happened was because the utterance was spoken at a normally rapid rate, which required (S) _____ that involved moving the lips into a rounded position for "o" before "n" was produced.

The last sound in "no," the vowel "o," sounded different from the vowel in "it's" because the (T) _____ of articulation of "i" involved arching the tongue in the front of the mouth, whereas for "o" it was arched in back. The vowels also differed in (U) _____ of articulation, "i" using a slightly higher arch than "o." They likewise differed in (V) _____, the lips being spread for "i" and rounded for "o."

Clinical Exercises

These exercises allow you to test your knowledge of articulatory physiology as it relates to clinical application. Fill in the blanks with the word or words that best complete the statements.

Megan is a 6 year old girl whose speech was impaired as the result of an automobile accident. Part of the speech testing that was done to evaluate Megan's articulatory impairment was a task called diadochokinetic rate (or diadochokinesis). This task involves the rapid repetition of a specified syllable (e.g., ba ba ba ba ba ba). Usually performance on this task is expressed as the maximum rate of syllable repetition, such as 7 syllables per second. The maximum rate typically is greatest for alveolar articulations. Articulations such as labials and velars tend to be slower.

By choosing different consonants to form the test syllable, the speech-language clinician can evaluate the motor function for different places of articulation, and hence for different groups of muscles. With the syllable *ba*, the clinician can evaluate the (a) _____ place of articulation, whereas *da* could be used to assess the (b) _____ place of articulation, and *ga* could be used to assess the (c) _____ place of articulation.

Different articulatory functions can be evaluated in this simple task by choosing other sounds to form the test syllables. For example, if the clinician suspects that Megan's velopharyngeal function is impaired, a syllable like that for the word *ton* might be used. In this word, the first sound requires velopharyngeal (d) _____ (opening, closure) and the final sound requires velopharyngeal (e) _____ (opening, closure). Describe for each syllable listed below the articulatory feature or features that might be evaluated in a diadochokinetic task.

ha   (f) _____
sha   (q) _____
va   (h) _____
bap   (i) _____

The diadochokinetic task can be increased in difficulty by choosing for complex syllable structures. Many clinicians use the word *buttercup* with young children. The task is the same — simply to say the utterance as many times as possible within a period of time. Note that the word *buttercup* can be used to test for three places of articulation, which are, from left to right in the word, (j) _____, (k) _____, and (l) _____.

Megan's results for this task with a variety of syllables indicated that she had slower than normal rates of production for the syllables *da*, *ta*, *sa*, *za*, *sha*, *ka*, *ga*, *ma*, and *na*. How might these results be summarized in terms of impaired place or manner features of articulation: (m) _____

(you should look for at least four features).

CHAPTER EIGHT
Speech Acoustics

Whatever you hear, whether the cooing of doves or loved ones, the thunder of lightning or an angry voice, all sounds involve vibration, which means movement. What moves in the sounds we normally hear are air molecules (other substances also transmit acoustic vibrations, so you may have heard sound underwater or by putting your ear to a railroad track). If we think about air at all, it is likely to be about how clear, smoggy, cold, hot, or windy it is. What we are not likely to think about is how elastic it is. If air molecules are pushed, they behave like dancers who are jostled on a tightly packed dance floor. They bump against neighboring dancers (molecules), but then bounce back to their original positions (Fig 8–1). No single dancer travels far when hit. What does travel across the dance floor is the disturbance (the sound wave).

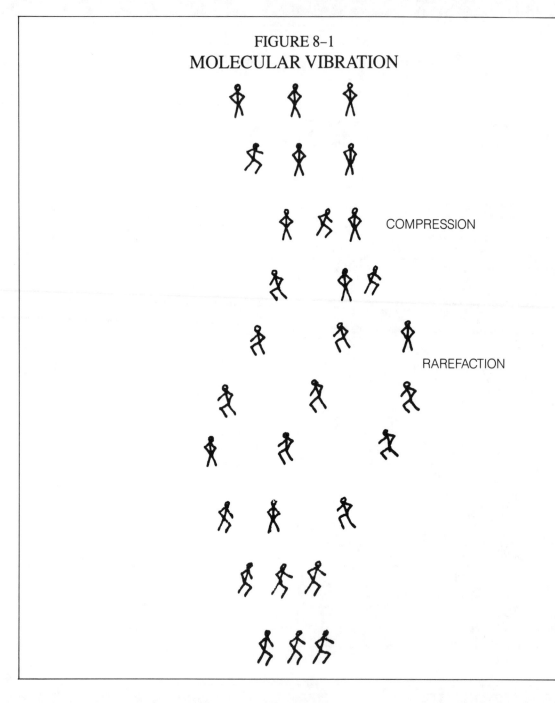

FIGURE 8–1
MOLECULAR VIBRATION

COMPRESSION

RAREFACTION

SOUND WAVE CHARACTERISTICS: TIME DOMAIN

Sound waves are changes in pressure as they occur across time. These waves rise and fall above and below atmospheric pressure. They vary in how much the pressure changes from one time to another (amplitude) and in how rapidly it changes (frequency).

Compression and Rarefaction

When molecules are jostled so that they are pushed together and bump into each other they are said to be *compressed*. Pressure is determined by how close together molecules are, so compressed air is high-pressure air. Conversely, when molecules move apart, this low-pressure condition is called *rarefaction*. These two conditions alternate because the air molecules move toward and away from each other as they swing back and forth, just as two children would if they were in swings, one directly in front of the other (Fig. 8–2). Note in this analogy that the frame of the swing does not move; only the children move to and fro.

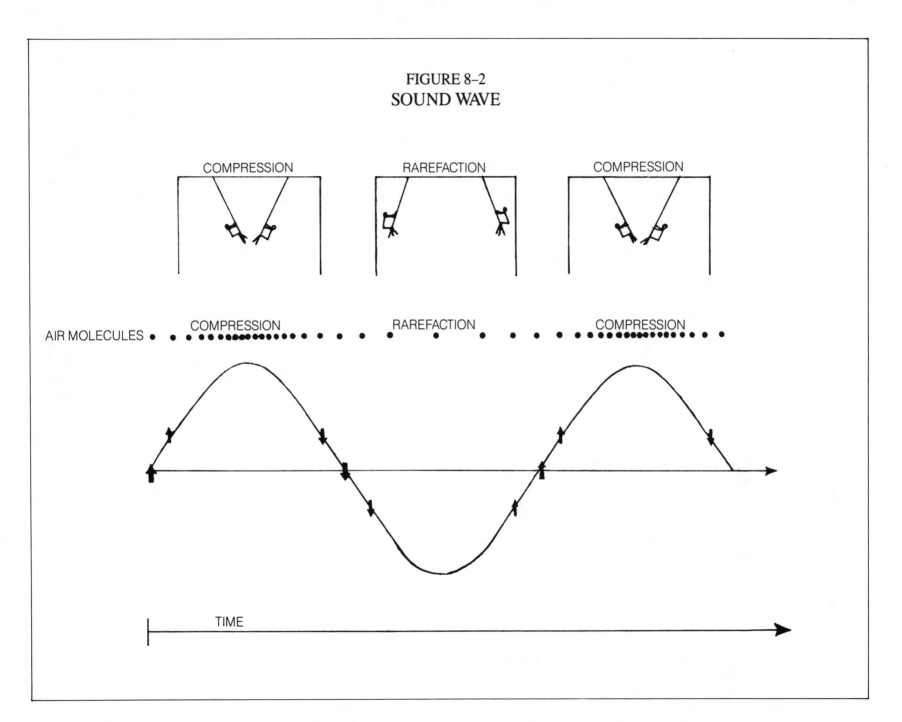

FIGURE 8–2
SOUND WAVE

COMPRESSION   RAREFACTION   COMPRESSION

AIR MOLECULES

COMPRESSION   RAREFACTION   COMPRESSION

TIME

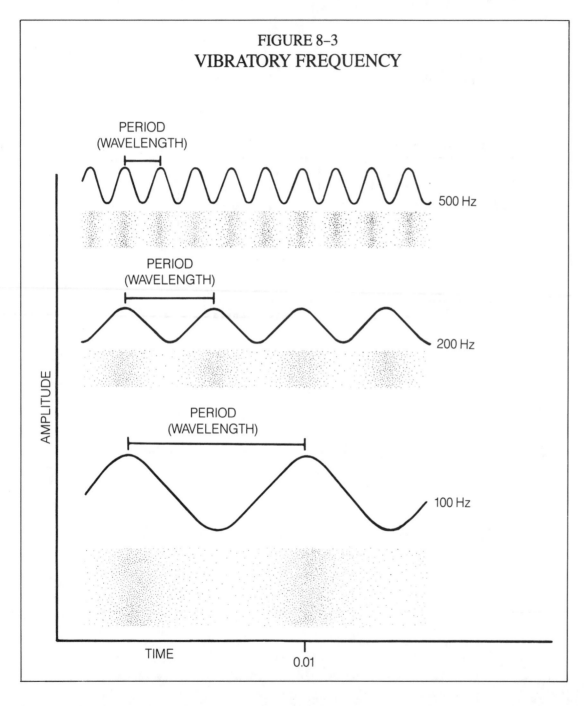

FIGURE 8–3
VIBRATORY FREQUENCY

PERIOD
(WAVELENGTH)

500 Hz

PERIOD
(WAVELENGTH)

200 Hz

PERIOD
(WAVELENGTH)

100 Hz

AMPLITUDE

TIME

0.01

Frequency and Amplitude

Still using this analogy, let's consider a few other characteristics of swinging, which is merely a popular way of talking about *vibration*. One of the characteristics is how high the children swing. This corresponds to *amplitude* of vibration.

Another characteristic is how long it takes to swing through a *cycle*, say from the top of the swing when the children are closest together (compression) to the top of the swing when they're farthest apart (rarefaction) and back to the "compression" top. This is the *period* of vibration, the length of time to complete a cycle. It is measured by *wave length*, the distance over which one cycle is completed when it is graphically recorded. The period determines frequency of vibration. Vibratory cycles are measured in *hertz* (*Hz*), a designation of the number of cycles per second. Thus, air molecules that take $1/100$ of a second (0.01 second) to complete a cycle of vibration (say from compression to rarefaction and back to compression) would be vibrating at 100 Hz (Fig. 8–3). Put another way, 100 cycles of 0.01 second duration would occur in 1 second.

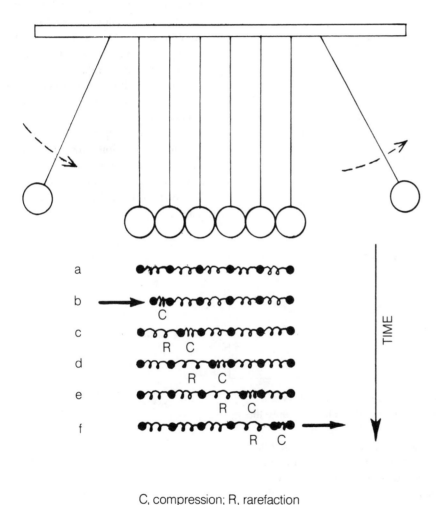

FIGURE 8–4
SOUND TRANSMISSION

a

b →   C

c   R C

d   R C

e   R C

f   R C →

TIME

C, compression; R, rarefaction

Sound Transmission

In preparation for understanding how a sound wave travels, let's distinguish two types of air movement by extending our analogy. Suppose it is New Year's Day and our two children are in their swings that are mounted on a flower-covered trailer in the Rose Parade. The swings are now traveling along the parade route, while at the same time the children swing toward and away from each other. Even if the children were not swinging, they would still be moving as the trailer moves. When this type of movement occurs with air molecules, it is wind. As you might suspect, it is the swinging of molecules, their vibration, that travels through the air as a sound wave.

Some analogies are offered to help you visualize sound transmission. This transmission process was well illustrated several years ago with a popular table-top toy involving a row of steel balls suspended by strings. When a ball on one end was pulled away from the row (equivalent to rarefaction) and released, it collided (compression) with the row of other balls. The only ball observed to move, however, was the one at the opposite end (Fig. 8–4). Obviously, the compression force was transmitted from one ball to the next until it reached the end where the effect of that force swung the last ball into visible vibration. In sound, waves of compression followed by waves of rarefaction move through air at sea level at about 1,100 feet per second.

This transmission is also illustrated schematically in Figure 8–4 as a series of collisions between tiny balls that represent air molecules. It is important first of all to realize that each molecule moves only slightly to and fro in response to sound energy. As the illustration shows, the first molecule is displaced to the right by the sound energy. It collides with the molecule to its right so that in time frame *b* the propagating sound wave has just begun to influence the left-most air molecules.

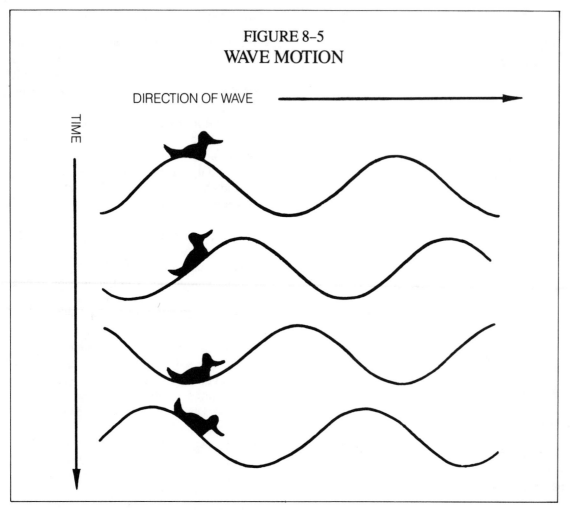

FIGURE 8–5
WAVE MOTION

DIRECTION OF WAVE

TIME

If the source of the sound energy is a tuning fork, each molecule will move to and fro, over and over again, as the tuning fork vibrates. If we replace the tuning fork with one of higher frequency, then the result will be that the air molecules move to and fro at a faster rate (recall that frequency is the number of vibrations per second). If we first tap the tuning fork lightly and then strike it harder, the difference in molecule vibration will be a larger to and fro movement. That is, the displacement of the molecules will increase.

Visible evidence that it is only the wave that moves can be observed by watching ducks riding waves. As the wave passes, the duck rises and falls but does not move with it (Fig. 8–5). To visualize how sound waves spread out in all directions from a source of vibration, drop a rock in the middle of a glassy-smooth pool and watch the waves fan out as sound waves would in Figure 8–6 when a balloon is periodically inflated and deflated by a pump.

Time frame *c* shows that the first molecule has returned to its original position, drawn back by the normal elasticity of air (represented in the drawing by the tiny springs connecting molecules). Because both the first and second particles have vacated the collision zone observed in time frame *b*, we now see a region of rarefaction (or rarefaction front) in time frame *c*. Meanwhile, the second molecule has been driven rightward to collide with the third molecule, creating a region of compression (com-

pression front). In this way, sound travels as a series of compressions and rarefactions until the right-most molecule finally is reached.

Thus, sound travels in a fashion similar to the way in which a row of dominoes will fall, beginning at one end and progressing to the other. We can make the analogy closer if we imagine that each domino is connected to the floor by a spring so that the dominoes return to their upright position after they fall and collide with their neighbors.

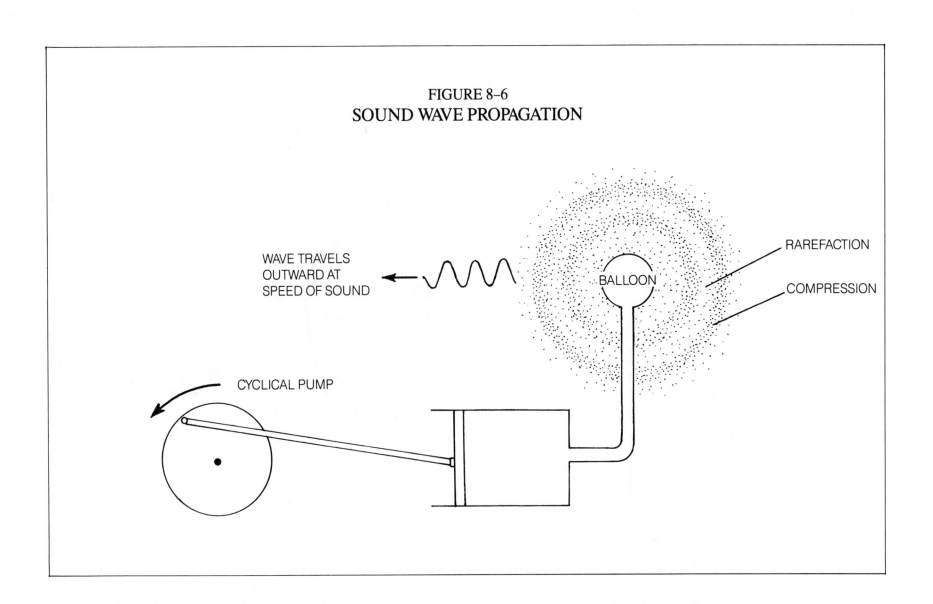

FIGURE 8–6
SOUND WAVE PROPAGATION

WAVE TRAVELS
OUTWARD AT
SPEED OF SOUND

BALLOON

RAREFACTION

COMPRESSION

CYCLICAL PUMP

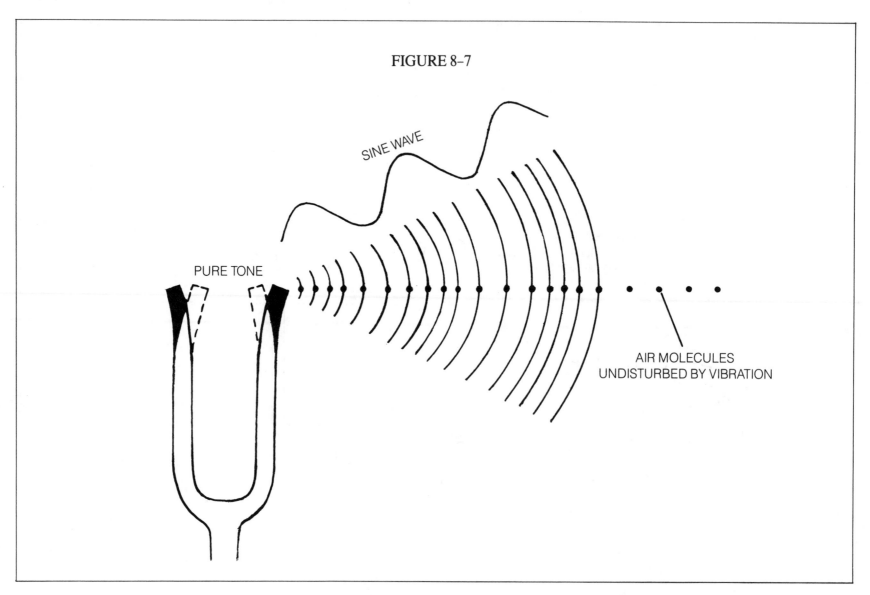

FIGURE 8–7

SINE WAVE

PURE TONE

AIR MOLECULES
UNDISTURBED BY VIBRATION

Wave Forms

Wave forms are graphic displays of sound pressure changes across time. They display a complete record of frequency, amplitude, and time characteristics of sound vibrations.

Sine Wave. The simplest form of vibration can be graphed as a sine wave. It is produced by any swinging object whose vibration can be completely described by frequency and amplitude. For example, these two measures would describe the simple to and fro motion of a child given a smooth push in a swing. When this type of vibration is fast enough to produce a sound, such as when a tuning fork is struck, it is heard as a *pure tone* (Fig. 8–7).

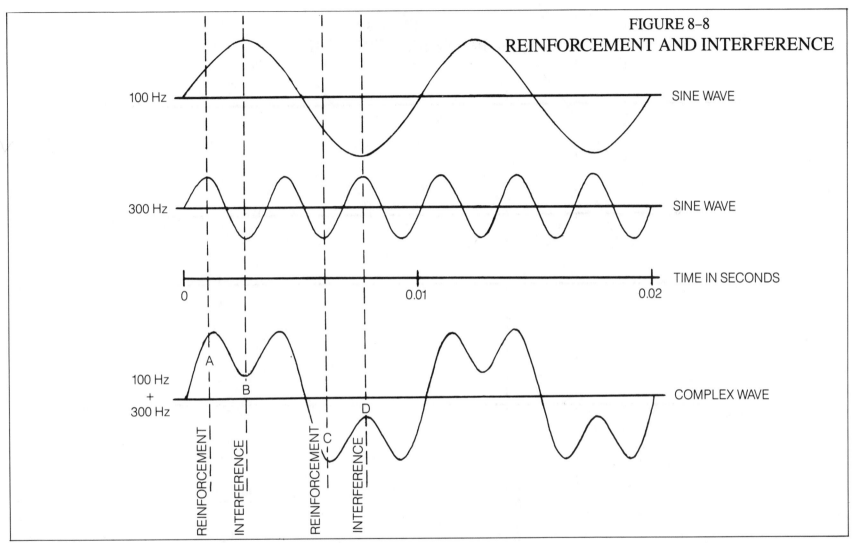

FIGURE 8-8
REINFORCEMENT AND INTERFERENCE

Complex Wave. By contrast to the foregoing example, if the child were given a hard enough push for the swing to be jerky, the jerks would complicate the to and fro motion in ways not completely described by a single frequency or a single amplitude. Because speech typically involves complex vibrations, we must understand how this type of vibration is produced.

A *complex wave* results when two or more sine waves interact with each other. For instance, in Figure 8-8, a 100 Hz sine wave and a 300 Hz sine wave are occurring simultaneously. They both begin with compression waves which *reinforce* each other to produce the peak at *A* in the resultant complex wave. At *B* there is a trough that results from the rarefaction phase of the 300 Hz wave

interfering with the compression of the 100 Hz wave. Then, at *C* and *D*, we again see the results of reinforcement and interference, but this time they occur when two rarefaction conditions reinforce each other, followed by compression and rarefaction phases coinciding.

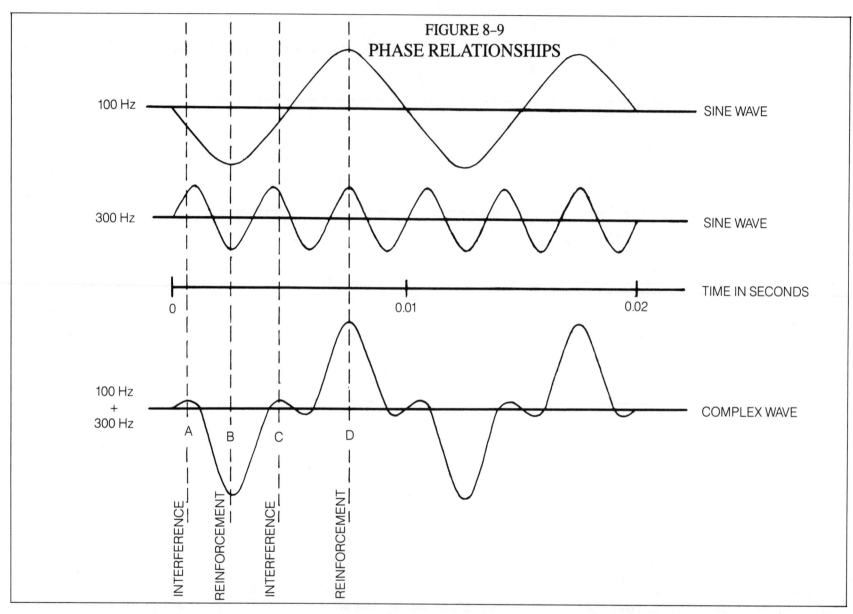

FIGURE 8-9
PHASE RELATIONSHIPS

Now examine the complex wave in Figure 8-9. It appears to be quite different from the complex wave in Figure 8-8. But when the frequencies and amplitudes of the component sine waves are compared, they are identical. How can this be? Closer inspection reveals the difference in complex waves to be a result of the timing of compression and rarefaction phases of the two sine waves. Compare A, B, C, and D in the two figures and you can see that the patterns of reinforcement and interference are different.

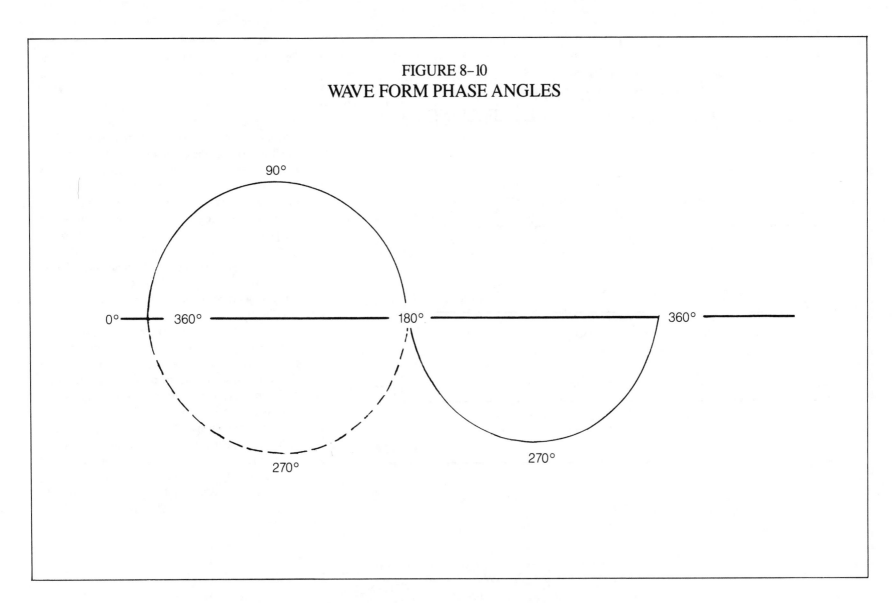

FIGURE 8–10
WAVE FORM PHASE ANGLES

The difference in timing is a difference in *phase angle*. Just as a circle can be described in degrees of arc, from 0° to 360° at which point it begins again, so can a cycle of vibration. To describe the phase of a cycle is equivalent to speaking of the phases of the moon (which has a 28 day cycle). Relative to a new moon (0°), a half moon is at 90°, a full moon is at 180°, and it becomes new again when it reaches 360° (at which time it starts over at 0°). This is the same way in which a vibratory cycle can be described in terms of phase angle, as shown in Figure 8–10.

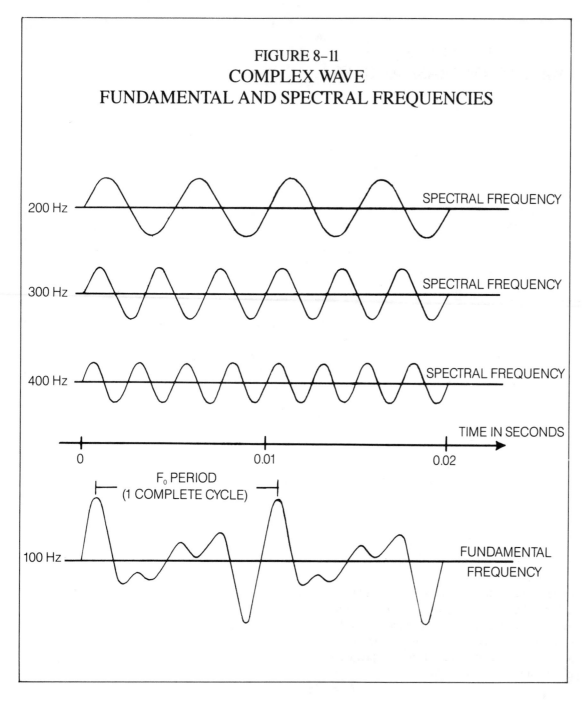

FIGURE 8–11
COMPLEX WAVE
FUNDAMENTAL AND SPECTRAL FREQUENCIES

200 Hz — SPECTRAL FREQUENCY

300 Hz — SPECTRAL FREQUENCY

400 Hz — SPECTRAL FREQUENCY

TIME IN SECONDS

0   0.01   0.02

F_0 PERIOD
(1 COMPLETE CYCLE)

100 Hz — FUNDAMENTAL
FREQUENCY

One more aspect of a complex wave needs to be considered. Inspect the wave in Figure 8–11 and you will see that it is a result of three sine waves of different frequencies, 200 Hz, 300 Hz, and 400 Hz. Just as the sine waves in Figures 8–8 and 8–9 produced complex waves by reinforcement and interference, so would the three sine waves in Figure 8–11 produce the complex wave shown. The point to note in this figure is that this complex wave repeats itself at 100 Hz, a frequency different from the three sine waves that produced it. What we have, then, in a complex wave are the component frequencies that produce the wave, *spectral frequencies*, and the resultant frequency at which the complex wave repeats itself, the *fundamental frequency* (F_0). F_0 can be the lowest spectral frequency, but it need not be, as in this example (Fig. 8–11).

Summing up wave-form properties, what they provide are graphic representations of vibratory pressure changes as they occur from one instant to the next. These include the pressure changes at the ear drum that are basic to normal hearing. Thus, what both sine waves and complex waves show are frequencies (both spectral and fundamental), amplitudes of spectral vibrations, and the effects of phase relationships among the component spectral frequencies. The wave form, then, provides the raw data of acoustic vibration. It contains all of the acoustic information available from the actual vibration.

FIGURE 8-12

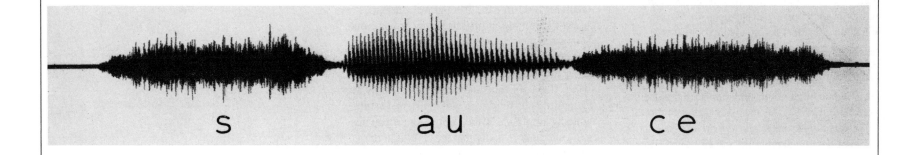

Wave form of the word *sauce*, which illustrates the differences between aperiodic (noise) segments like the initial and final sounds in this word and periodic segments like that represented by the letters *au*.

Tone Versus Noise

How spectral frequencies are organized in relation to each other will determine whether the sound is heard as tone or noise. If they are distributed randomly over a frequency region so that there is no pattern among the frequencies at which vibrations occur, the result will be *noise*. But if there is a pattern which is repeated periodically, the result will be *tone*. The periodicity of this pattern is the fundamental frequency we just dis-cussed. It is the foundation frequency around which a tone is organized (Fig. 8-12).

Any spectral frequency that is a whole number multiple of F_0 is called a *harmonic frequency*. (There are also inharmonic frequencies that are fractional multiples of F_0, which result in dissonance, but we are not much concerned with them.) If F_0 is 100 Hz, then the second harmonic is 200 Hz, the fifth is 500, the eleventh is 1,100, and so forth. Change F_0 to 200 Hz and the second harmonic becomes 400 Hz, the fifth becomes 1,000 and so on.

Knowing this relationship, it is therefore possible to calculate F_0 if only harmonic frequencies are known. F_0 is the highest common denominator which will divide into the harmonic frequencies. For instance, a tone with vibratory energy at frequencies of 1,300, 1,400, 1,700, 2,100, 2,400, and 2,500 Hz would have a fundamental frequency of 100 Hz because no higher number will divide into all of these frequencies. If the harmonics were at 1,200, 2,000, 2,800, 3,200, and 3,600 Hz, F_0 would be 400 Hz.

Repetitive Versus Nonrepetitive Waves

Unlike *repetitive waves* of a tuning fork, which continue as long as the fork continues to vibrate, the way in which speech waves are generated is very different. Recall from Chapter 5 that the source of voice is glottal vibration. Each time the vocal folds blow open and snap shut, a burst of air is released. That glottal pulse sets the air in the vocal tract into vibration. Most of the vibratory energy in each pulse is dissipated (for reasons we will soon consider) before the next pulse is released. The only reason the next burst occurs is because subglottal pressure builds up high enough to blow the folds open again. If there were pressure for only one burst of air, only one glottal pulse would occur. What this means is that each glottal pulse, taken by itself, is *nonrepetitive*. It is only by virtue of continued pressure and glottal resistance that bursts continue to be released. It is the rate at which the vocal folds vibrate which determines the fundamental frequency of the voice. This frequency involves both repetitive (the sequence of glottal pulses) and nonrepetitive (the individual pulse) waves. We can say, then, that voice consists of a repetitive train of periodically released nonrepetitive glottal pulses.

What needs to be understood is how it is possible for a sound vibration to die out in one cycle. Another way to describe a nonrepetitive wave is to say that its F_0 is 0. If it were 1, that would mean the wave repeats itself once each second, so it might have a harmonic spectrum such as 100, 101, 102, 103 Hz, and so forth. If, however, the spectral distribution were 100.00, 100.01, 100.02, 100.03, and so on, the wave would repeat once every hundred seconds. If the decimal point were carried out to 100.0000001, 100.0000002, and so on, the wave would repeat once every million seconds because the spectral frequencies would be only a millionth of a cycle per second apart. Now extend this example so that spectral frequencies are infinitely close

together. Under this condition F_0 would be 0, so the wave would not repeat itself ever, as in Figure 8–13. Clearly, any nonrepetitive wave results from spectral frequencies infinitely close together.

Resonators

A *resonator* is an acoustic filter. Although it functions as a filter, it does not operate like a screen for filtering sand from gravel. Instead, it depends on timing. It operates more as you would if you were pushing a child in a swing. If you time your push to begin just as the child starts the downswing, you will reinforce the amplitude of the swing. If you mistime and push while he is swinging toward you, your push will interfere, thereby reducing amplitude of the swing. And if you mistime your push so badly that the child is at the opposite end of his swing from you, your energy will have been wasted. Just as the timing of your pushes determines your effect on the swing, so does the timing of a resonator's *reflection* of *incidence* waves which enter it determine the frequencies at which it will consume energy by reinforcing or interfering with the sound wave, filtering out frequencies to which it is not tuned, and amplifying, to one extent or another, those to which it is.

Resonator "Tuning." Resonators can be "tuned" to different frequencies. Two major factors that determine the natural frequency at which air molecules in a cavity will vibrate can be observed with two bottles of the same volume, but with different size necks. Blow across the necks until they "ring." You will hear two pitches, the one from the larger-neck bottle being the higher. Now pour water into either bottle and notice how the pitch rises as the volume of remaining air diminishes. This indicates that as the volume of a cavity increases, its frequency decreases, whereas when the aperture increases, so does the frequency to which the resonator is tuned.

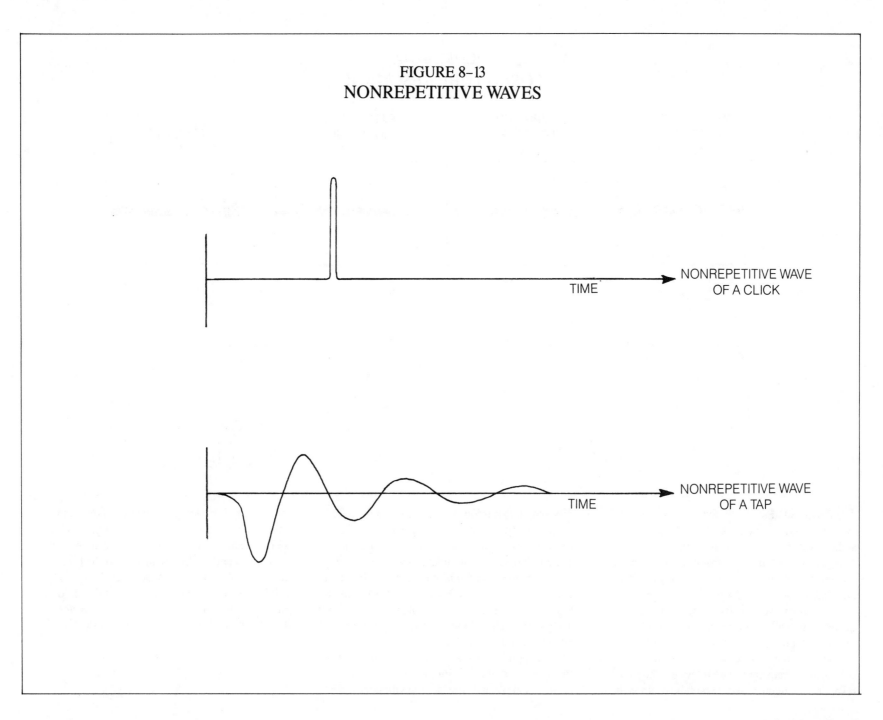

FIGURE 8–13
NONREPETITIVE WAVES

TIME — NONREPETITIVE WAVE OF A CLICK

TIME — NONREPETITIVE WAVE OF A TAP

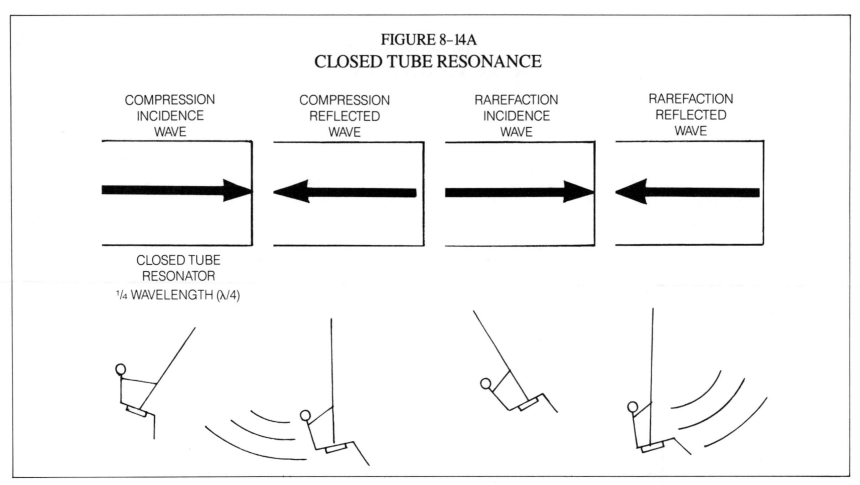

FIGURE 8–14A
CLOSED TUBE RESONANCE

COMPRESSION
INCIDENCE
WAVE

COMPRESSION
REFLECTED
WAVE

RAREFACTION
INCIDENCE
WAVE

RAREFACTION
REFLECTED
WAVE

CLOSED TUBE
RESONATOR
¼ WAVELENGTH (λ/4)

Formants. Especially for the vowel sounds, the vocal tract functions as a tube closed at one end and open at the other, somewhat like a test tube. The typical test tube — that is, one with a uniform diameter along its length — has resonance frequencies that are determined entirely by the length of the tube. For vowel sounds, these resonance frequencies are called *formant frequencies*. A tube like a test tube has an infinite number of resonance frequencies, but in the case of vowels, only the first few formant frequencies are relevant. The first resonance frequency of our test tube example has a

wavelength that is four times as long as the tube. Alternatively, we can state this principle as follows: A tube open at one end and closed at the other will resonate with maximum amplitude a tone whose wavelength is four times the length of the tube. As you saw in Figure 8–3, a wavelength is the distance between identical phase angles on two successive cycles of a wave. The shorter this distance, the higher the frequency of the sound.

To appreciate the significance of the four times the tube length relationship, we will return to an earlier example and consider the vibratory move-

ment of an air molecule as being analogous to a child in a swing. Once set to swinging, the child will come to a stop when direction changes at the top of both ends of the swing arc. At the bottom of the arc, halfway through a swing cycle, velocity will be greatest. Thus, if we think of the child as a molecule, the velocity of this molecule varies during the swing cycle, as in Figure 8–14A and B.

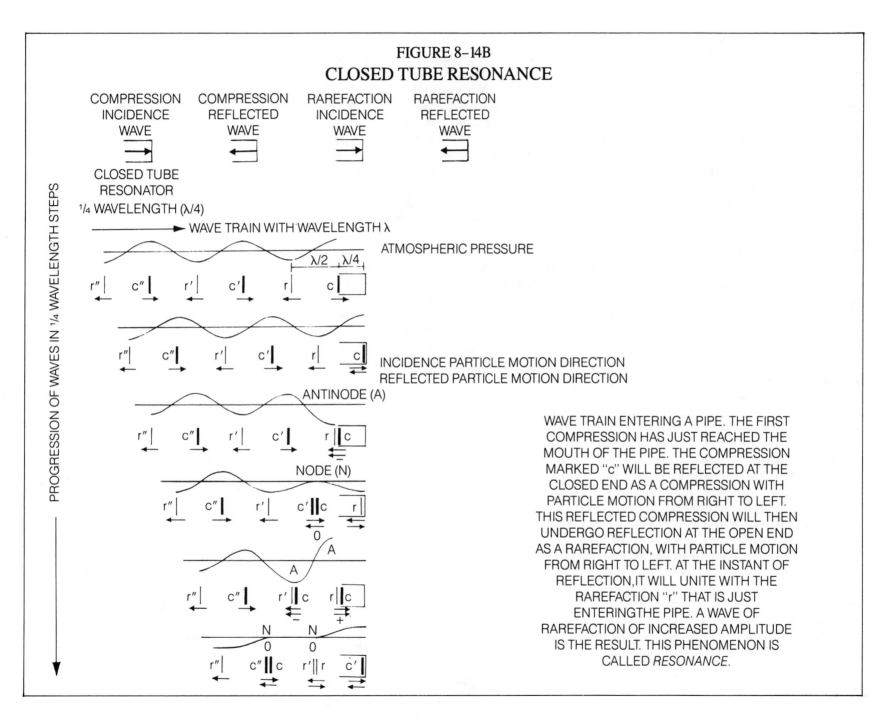

FIGURE 8–14B
CLOSED TUBE RESONANCE

COMPRESSION INCIDENCE WAVE

COMPRESSION REFLECTED WAVE

RAREFACTION INCIDENCE WAVE

RAREFACTION REFLECTED WAVE

CLOSED TUBE RESONATOR
¼ WAVELENGTH (λ/4)

WAVE TRAIN WITH WAVELENGTH λ

ATMOSPHERIC PRESSURE

λ/2   λ/4

r″ c″ r′ c′ r c

INCIDENCE PARTICLE MOTION DIRECTION
REFLECTED PARTICLE MOTION DIRECTION

ANTINODE (A)

NODE (N)

PROGRESSION OF WAVES IN ¼ WAVELENGTH STEPS

WAVE TRAIN ENTERING A PIPE. THE FIRST COMPRESSION HAS JUST REACHED THE MOUTH OF THE PIPE. THE COMPRESSION MARKED "c" WILL BE REFLECTED AT THE CLOSED END AS A COMPRESSION WITH PARTICLE MOTION FROM RIGHT TO LEFT. THIS REFLECTED COMPRESSION WILL THEN UNDERGO REFLECTION AT THE OPEN END AS A RAREFACTION, WITH PARTICLE MOTION FROM RIGHT TO LEFT. AT THE INSTANT OF REFLECTION,IT WILL UNITE WITH THE RAREFACTION "r" THAT IS JUST ENTERINGTHE PIPE. A WAVE OF RAREFACTION OF INCREASED AMPLITUDE IS THE RESULT. THIS PHENOMENON IS CALLED *RESONANCE*.

To understand the resonance of a closed tube, it is convenient to think of a sound that is produced outside the tube and enters it as a wave of compression. This wave may be called the *incidence wave,* and it will return through the tube as a *reflected wave* when it hits the closed end of the tube. Now recall that the compression wave is followed by a rarefaction wave, so that these two waves, the reflected compression wave and the incident rarefaction wave, may meet somewhere within the tube depending on the length of the tube. Furthermore, also depending on the length of the tube, the reflected compression wave may meet with another incident compression wave coming behind it.

The picture we have, then, is of waves meeting within the tube. What happens as a result of these meetings depends on the particle motion of the waves. Consider a compression wave entering the tube with a particle motion from left to right, in the direction of the wave travel. This wave will be reflected as a compression wave, shown in Figure 8–14, with particle motion from right to left. This reflected compression wave will meet with a following rarefaction wave which also has particle motion from right to left. Their meeting results in a rarefaction wave of *increased amplitude* because their particle motions combine and add together. On the other hand, the reflected compression wave will have a particle motion opposite to that of the succeeding incident compression wave, so that their combination will result in no particle motion at all. If the length of the tube relative to the wavelength of the incoming sound is just right, *stationary* or *standing waves* will be created. A stationary wave is produced from the superposition of two oppositely directed similar wave trains. The points on the stationary wave at which no particle motion occurs are called nodes. The points at which maximum particle motion occurs are called antinodes.

All of this is relevant to speech because when you produce a vowel, a stationary wave develops within your vocal tract. You can think of it this way. Imagine pushing a wire slowly back into your mouth as you say a vowel. Imagine further that this wire has on its end a tiny device that can monitor particle motion of the air in front of it. As you push the wire back, it would detect regions of no particle motion (nodes) and other regions of large particle motion (antinodes). Each resonance frequency of a closed tube is associated with a particular pattern of nodes and antinodes which constitute the stationary wave for that resonance. The lowest resonance frequency occurs for a tone that has a wavelength four times the length of the tube. With this tube, the first compression wave will be reflected to combine with an incident rarefaction wave at the mouth of the tube. Because the rarefaction wave follows the compression wave by $\frac{1}{2}$ wavelength, this meeting will occur at the mouth of a tube that is exactly $\frac{1}{4}$ the wavelength of the incoming sound.

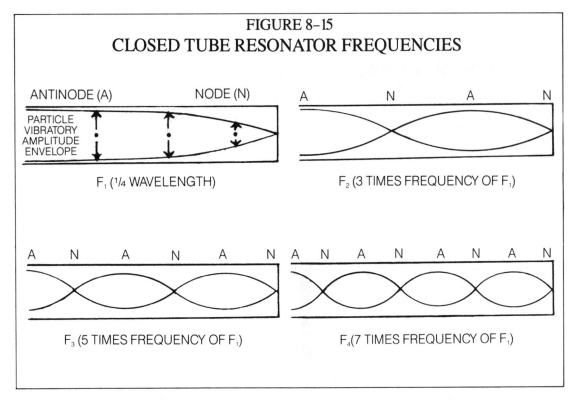

FIGURE 8–15
CLOSED TUBE RESONATOR FREQUENCIES

ANTINODE (A)   NODE (N)

PARTICLE
VIBRATORY
AMPLITUDE
ENVELOPE

F_1 (¼ WAVELENGTH)

A   N   A   N

F_2 (3 TIMES FREQUENCY OF F_1)

A   N   A   N   A   N

F_3 (5 TIMES FREQUENCY OF F_1)

A N A N A N A N

F_4 (7 TIMES FREQUENCY OF F_1)

Stationary wave patterns are shown in Figure 8–15 for the first four resonances of a tube, or in the case of speech, for the first four formants of a vowel. A node is labeled N and an antinode is labeled A. The first formant has one node and one antinode; the second formant has two of each, and so on. For a tube of uniform diameter, all the resonances are related by the quarter-wavelength relationship. That is, the frequency of the first formant (F_1) is determined by the quarter-wavelength relationship explained above. The second formant (F_2) has a frequency three times that of F_1, and the third formant (F_3) has a frequency five times that of F_1. This relationship continues for all formants of interest. We can express this relationship with the formula

$$F_n = 2n - 1 \, (¼ \, l),$$

where F_n is the frequency of formant number n,
n is any integer,
l is the length of the tube, and
$2n - 1$ simply generates the odd number sequence.

If you have followed the discussion so far, you might ask if the stationary waves depicted in Figure 8–15 are of any use except for one vowel, that being the vowel with a uniform diameter of the vocal tract along its length. In fact, they do have a more general application. The full significance of this application goes beyond the scope of an introductory text, but two simple rules should help you to understand how the stationary waves of a simple tube of uniform diameter can be used to predict the formant frequencies of a changeable vocal tract.

The two rules are as follows:

1. When the tube (vocal tract) is squeezed or constricted near a node for any resonance (formant), the resonance frequency (formant frequency) is raised.
2. When the tube (vocal tract) is squeezed or constricted near an antinode for any resonance (formant), the resonance frequency (formant frequency) is lowered.

As a simple example of rule 1, consider the vowel *oo* as in *who*. This vowel involves a constriction at the lips, as you can verify by looking into a mirror as you say *who*. Constriction of the lips is like squeezing the open ends of the tubes shown in Figure 8–15. Squeezing at this point is squeezing near an antinode, which means that all of the formant frequencies should be lowered relative to those of the vowel with uniform diameter. And, indeed, the vowel in *who* has the lowest formant frequencies of all the vowels in English.

We can summarize this discussion as follows. The resonance frequencies of a uniform tube closed at one end and open at the other depend on the length of the tube. For a given tube length, it is possible to describe a stationary wave for each resonance frequency. The stationary wave results from the superposition of reflected and incident waves within the tube. The stationary wave has both nodes (regions of no particle motion) and antinodes (regions of maximum particle motion). Vowels are produced with a vocal tract that acts like a tube closed at one end and open at the other. Therefore, each vowel has a stationary wave pattern for each formant. (For ease of discussion, we considered the resonance of a tube for a sound produced outside the tube, but the same general ideas hold for a sound produced inside the tube. For example, imagine replacing the closed end of the tube in Figure 8–15 with the vibrating vocal folds, which act both as a closed end and a source of sound for the vocal tract.)

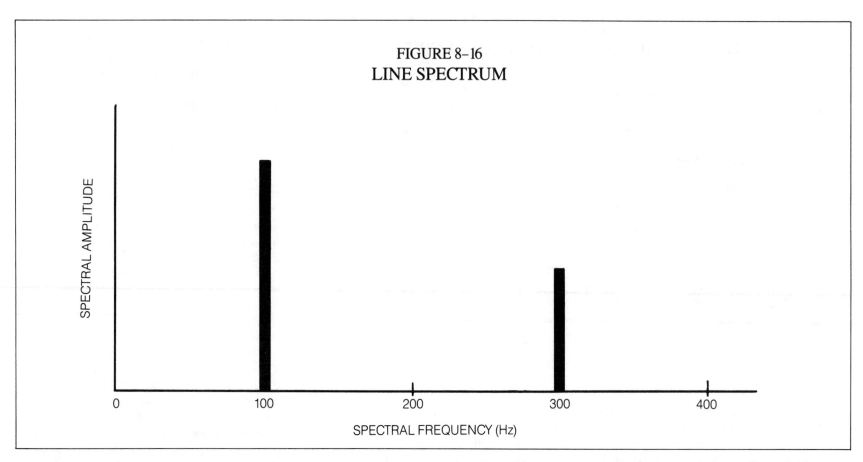

FIGURE 8–16
LINE SPECTRUM

(y-axis) SPECTRAL AMPLITUDE

(x-axis) SPECTRAL FREQUENCY (Hz)

0   100   200   300   400

SOUND SPECTRUM CHARACTERISTICS: FREQUENCY DOMAIN

So far, we have considered acoustics only with wave forms to graphically display vibratory properties of frequency, amplitude, and time. Even though wave forms provide a complete record of vibration, they are of limited value in speech analysis. The two crucial properties are frequency and amplitude. Phase relationships, which reflect the property of time, do not seem of much importance in differentiating speech sounds from each other.

The day may come when phase-angle timing is found to make a difference in some aspect of speech, but it probably will not have much to do with intelligibility; frequency and amplitude seem sufficient to distinguish among all speech sounds. Accordingly, the most efficient and simplest displays of speech acoustics are spectral.

Line Spectrum

Let's go back to Figures 8–8 and 8–9. These were the two complex waves that looked different, but had the same spectral frequencies and amplitudes. You may recall that they looked different

because the phase relationships were different. Since these relationships are not essential, time can be ignored and the two important properties can be displayed more simply. By using a *spectrum*, amplitude can be plotted against frequency. Compare Figure 8–16 with Figure 8–8 and 8–9 and you will see that the same frequency and amplitude information is displayed, but differently. The 100 Hz sine wave with the greater amplitude is plotted as a taller line than the 300 Hz sine wave with less amplitude. Since a single vertical line represents each frequency at which there is vibratory energy, this display is called a *line spectrum*.

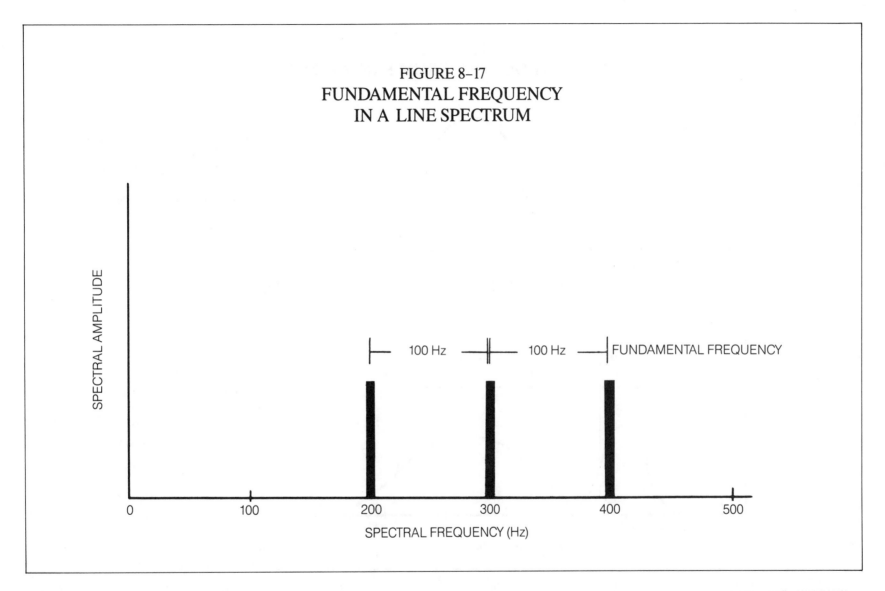

FIGURE 8–17
FUNDAMENTAL FREQUENCY
IN A LINE SPECTRUM

The great advantage of spectral analysis is that it permits simplified representation of the most complex sound. Speech contains infinite numbers of frequencies, each of which in its simplest form is a sine wave that can be completely described by graphing its frequency and amplitude. No matter how complex the wave that results, it can be analyzed into its component pure tones. When that wave is repetitive, it will have a fundamental frequency with whole number multiples as harmonics, which means that the number of frequencies between harmonic frequencies will be equal to F_0. It also means that each harmonic will have a separate line to represent its frequency and amplitude; hence repetitive waves are shown with line spectra such as in Figure 8–17, which presents the complex wave in Figure 8–11 in spectral form.

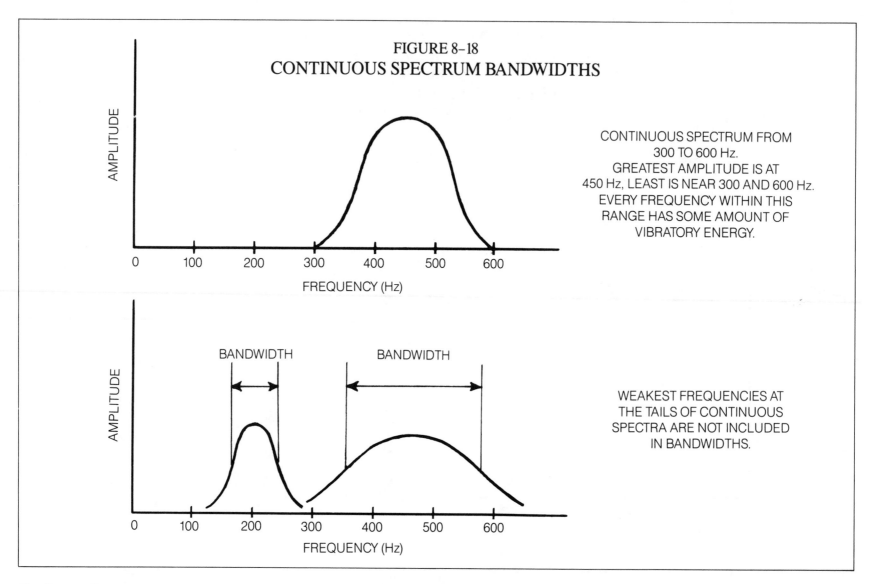

FIGURE 8–18
CONTINUOUS SPECTRUM BANDWIDTHS

CONTINUOUS SPECTRUM FROM 300 TO 600 Hz. GREATEST AMPLITUDE IS AT 450 Hz, LEAST IS NEAR 300 AND 600 Hz. EVERY FREQUENCY WITHIN THIS RANGE HAS SOME AMOUNT OF VIBRATORY ENERGY.

WEAKEST FREQUENCIES AT THE TAILS OF CONTINUOUS SPECTRA ARE NOT INCLUDED IN BANDWIDTHS.

Continuous Spectrum

If we drew a line for each frequency when spectral frequencies are infinitely close to each other, as in a nonrepetitive wave, the result would be a solid mass of lines with no space between them. It would also be a most inefficient way of showing what can be graphed with a *continuous spectrum* quite simply (Fig. 8–18). By drawing a continuous line, the height of which represents the amplitude at any frequency under it, all spectral information is displayed at any of an infinite number of frequencies.

Functional Anatomy of Speech, Language, and Hearing

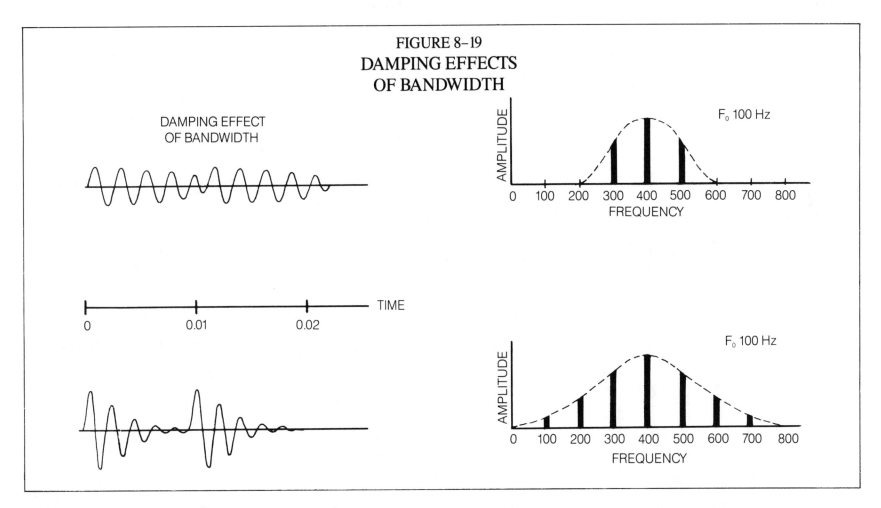

FIGURE 8-19
DAMPING EFFECTS
OF BANDWIDTH

Resonator Bandwidth. Not only is a continuous spectrum used to describe a nonrepetitive glottal pulse, it is also used for resonators. Unlike a tuning fork, which vibrates only at a single frequency, resonators respond to a continuous range of frequencies, the formant frequencies being the ones at which they respond best. The width of this range on each side of this best resonant frequency is the *bandwidth*. It is determined by hardness or softness of the cavity walls. If hard, the bandwidth will be narrow; if soft, it will be wide.

Fortunately for speech, human resonators are soft-walled, so our vocal tract resonator bandwidths are wide. The importance of this for speech is that the vocal tract *damps* the energy in each glottal pulse so that most of it is consumed before the next burst of air is released. The effect of damping can be seen in the rate of decay of sound. This is shown in Figure 8-19. On the left are schematic wave forms of two cycles of a speech wave showing two rates of decay. The peaks of each wave occur when glottal pulses are released. The

rates at which their energy is consumed are determined by the bandwidths of the resonators shown on the right as continuous spectra. Were the phonatory-resonatory system not highly damped, our speech would sound like a piano played with the loud pedal down. All of our sounds would blur into each other. Instead, they can be crisp and sharp because most of the energy for one sound is expended before the next one is produced.

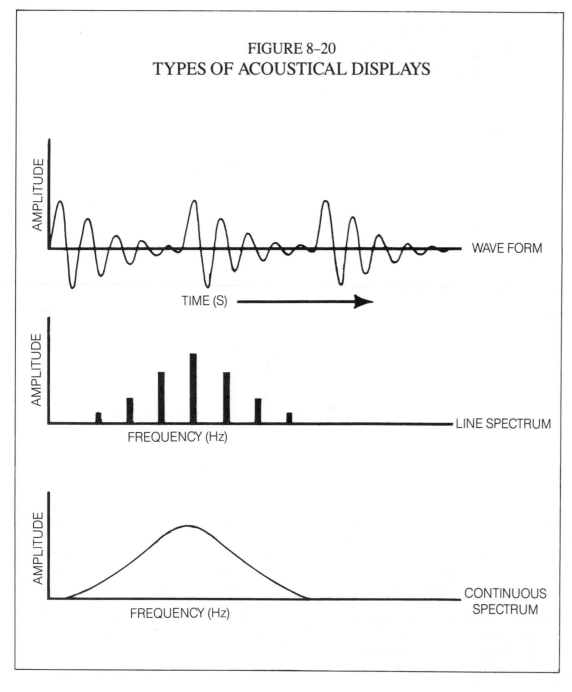

FIGURE 8–20
TYPES OF ACOUSTICAL DISPLAYS

AMPLITUDE

WAVE FORM

TIME (S)

AMPLITUDE

FREQUENCY (Hz)

LINE SPECTRUM

AMPLITUDE

FREQUENCY (Hz)

CONTINUOUS
SPECTRUM

Spectrogram

Everything about speech occurs in the flow of time. Our ideas are arranged and spoken sequentially in temporal order. The word order of sentences is sequential. Within words, the syllables are sequential. Within syllables, the sounds are sequential. And within sounds, the cycles of acoustic vibrations are sequential. Obviously, to visualize speech as it is spoken requires a graphic display that extends across time. A wave form provides such a display, but all of the spectral frequencies and amplitudes are buried in the complexities of the wave vibrations that require a sophisticated *Fourier analysis* to sort them out. Such an analysis provides the spectral information that can be presented in a line spectrum or continuous spectrum. The limitation of these spectra, however, is that they display only spectral vibrations at any given instant. As you can see in Figure 8–20, the horizontal scale for a wave form is time, but for either spectrum the horizontal scale is frequency, with time being omitted.

FIGURE 8–21

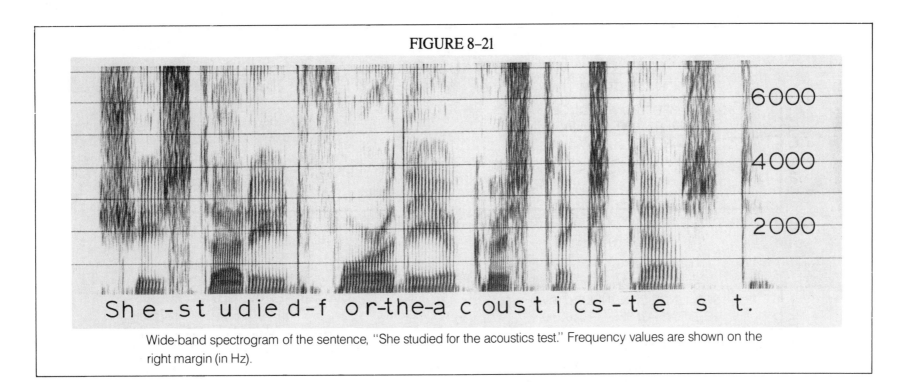

Wide-band spectrogram of the sentence, "She studied for the acoustics test." Frequency values are shown on the right margin (in Hz).

What is needed, obviously, is a running spectral display that extends across time. This is what a *spectrogram* (also called a sonogram) provides. Time is shown along the horizontal scale, frequency on the vertical scale, and intensity is shown by the relative darkness of the pattern at any point in time and frequency. A sonographic display of the brief sentence "She studied for the acoustics test," is presented in Figure 8–21. Theoretically, it would be possible to recognize enough acoustic characteristics to read speech from a sonogram, which is why it was once called "visible speech."

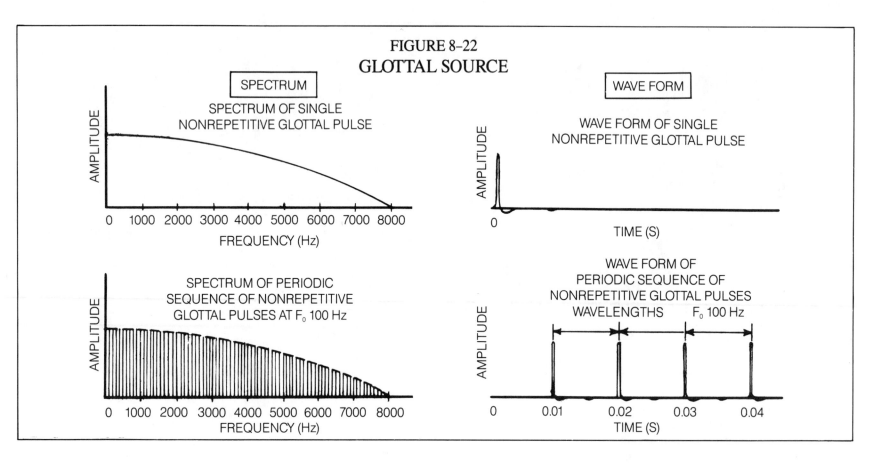

FIGURE 8–22
GLOTTAL SOURCE

SPECTRUM

SPECTRUM OF SINGLE
NONREPETITIVE GLOTTAL PULSE

SPECTRUM OF PERIODIC
SEQUENCE OF NONREPETITIVE
GLOTTAL PULSES AT F_0 100 Hz

WAVE FORM

WAVE FORM OF SINGLE
NONREPETITIVE GLOTTAL PULSE

WAVE FORM OF
PERIODIC SEQUENCE OF
NONREPETITIVE GLOTTAL PULSES
WAVELENGTHS F_0 100 Hz

SPEECH SOUND CHARACTERISTICS

Acoustic Characteristics

Glottal Source Spectrum. As we have seen in earlier chapters, the source of voiced sounds is vocal fold vibration. What that vibration produces is a periodic sequence of glottal pulses. The volume velocity of each burst of air (volume and velocity of air released) sets up compression and rarefaction waves in the air column of the vocal tract. If each pulse, being nonrepetitive, were shown by itself it would be displayed with a continuous spectrum, as it is on the top left diagram of Figure 8–22. Since a periodic sequence of these

pulses is generated for voiced sounds, this is equivalent to the sound being repetitive. As you will recall, this means that it will have a fundamental frequency as well as separate harmonic frequencies, so that a line spectrum display is needed, which is shown on the bottom left of Figure 8–22.

One feature of the wave form of each glottal pulse is worth noting. It is shaped like a spike, which indicates an abrupt increase in pressure when a burst of air is released from the glottis, and then a very rapid drop in pressure as the energy in that burst is quickly consumed (damped). This decay rate is much greater than in the waves in Figure 8–16, which indicates that the bandwidth of

each glottal pulse must be considerably wider than for any of the resonators in that figure. Indeed it is. Instead of bandwidths of hundreds of hertz, the glottal spectrum typically ranges from 0 to 4,000 to 8,000 Hz.

Another feature of this spectrum is that spectral energy diminishes progressively as frequency increases, which accounts for the slope of the spectrum. High-frequency energy is what gives a voice carrying power. A powerful voice, which "projects," is a voice with considerable high-frequency energy. Since the glottal pulse is the source of all energy for voice, this energy is called the *glottal source spectrum*.

FIGURE 8–23

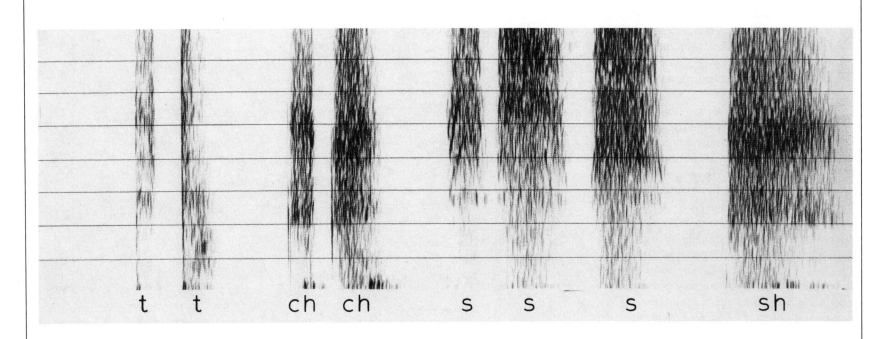

Wide-band spectrogram of noise sounds that are used in English. The sounds were produced in isolation to show different durations and intensities of noise. For example, the *t* sounds at the left are both brief, but the second is longer in duration and more intense than the first. Similarly, the second *ch* is longer and more intense than the first. The three *s* sounds also differ in duration and intensity. This figure shows as well the spectral differences among noise sounds. Compare, for example the *s* sounds with the *ch* and *sh* sounds (the *s* sounds have relatively greater energy in the high frequencies).

Noise Source Spectrum. As you will recall from the preceding chapter, and as shown in Figure 8–23, noise is generated by turbulence of air forced through constrictions or by bursts of air released from occlusions (stoppages) in the vocal tract. Because any noise involves energy randomly scattered within the spectrum, none of it is organized at harmonic frequencies, so noise has no fundamental frequency. What it does have are bandwidths of energy at different frequencies, intensities, and durations. Thus, we can say that the *noise source spectrum* of consonants varies in *spectral frequency*, *spectral intensity*, and *spectral duration*.

Vocal Tract Transfer Function. We are now ready to see what happens when the source spectrum of energy, whether glottal source or noise source, is filtered through the vocal tract resonators, a process called a *transfer function*. What emerges as the output is the *radiated spectrum*, the sound heard by the listener. It includes filtering of the *radiation characteristic*. This is the term for the increase in intensity of the higher frequencies as the sound leaves the resonating cavity at the lips. In addition to the radiation effect, you can see in Figure 8–24 (which illustrates a voiced sound) that the radiated spectrum reflects both the glottal source fundamental with its harmonic frequencies and the vocal tract formant frequencies. Two fundamental frequencies (100 Hz and 300 Hz) are shown to illustrate that the fundamentals and their harmonic frequencies are not altered by the formant frequencies, or vice versa. What is altered sharply is the shape of the glottal source spectrum that emerges as the radiated spectrum. That spectrum has the shape of the vocal tract transfer function and the fundamental frequency of the glottal source. The harmonic frequencies that emerge as output are strongest at the formant frequencies (the frequencies at which the resonators are tuned) and are weakest at frequencies to which the resonators respond least.

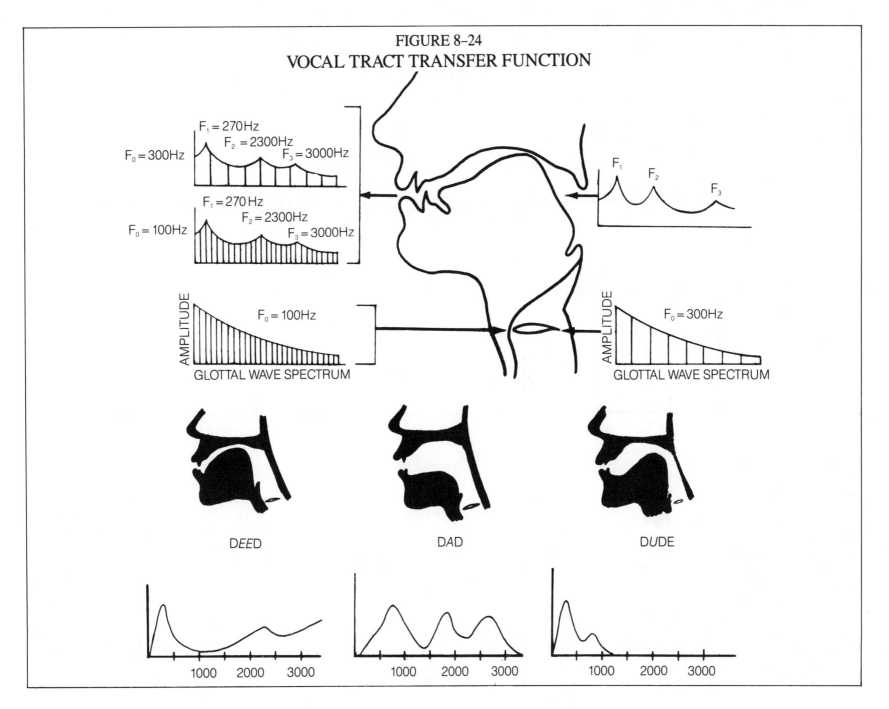

FIGURE 8–24
VOCAL TRACT TRANSFER FUNCTION

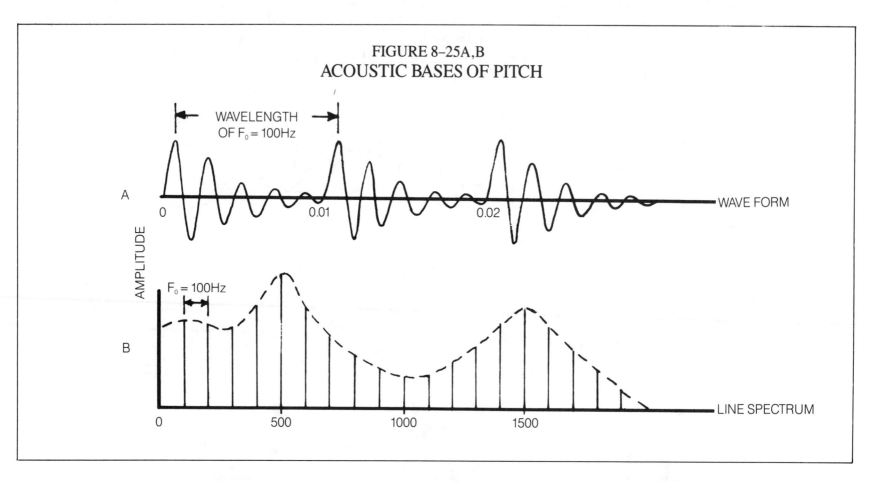

FIGURE 8–25A,B
ACOUSTIC BASES OF PITCH

WAVELENGTH OF $F_0 = 100$Hz

A — WAVE FORM

AMPLITUDE

$F_0 = 100$Hz

B — LINE SPECTRUM

Perceptual Characteristics

The acoustic signal provides the raw data of speech perception, but the sounds we think we hear sometimes aren't really there. Our brains take the acoustic information, analyze it, and interpret it in the context of what we expect to hear. For instance, sounds can be omitted from words, yet listeners, nonetheless, think they hear them. Also, because of the way the brain determines F_0, we often hear pitches at frequencies with no vibratory energy. The result is that there is not necessarily a one-to-one correspondence between the three basic elements of speech perception, *pitch*, *loudness*, and *quality*, and the acoustic bases of these perceptions.

Pitch. The judgment of vocal *pitch* is based mainly, but not entirely, on the fundamental frequency of a voice. The rate at which vocal folds vibrate is, then, the sole determinant of F_0 and the primary determinant of pitch perception.

F_0 can be determined from a wave form by measuring the period of one cycle of a complex wave, as shown in Figure 8–25A. It can also be measured in a line spectrum by determining the spacing between harmonic frequencies (which are multiples of F_0), as in Figure 8–25B. With spectrograms, depending on the type, F_0 can be measured two ways. If it is broad band (wide band) (Fig. 8–25C), the individual glottal pulses show up as vertical striations, so the number which occur per second can be counted. If it is narrow band (Fig. 8–25D), the harmonic frequencies can be seen as horizontal striations and can be measured for F_0 as in a line spectrum.

FIGURE 8–25C,D

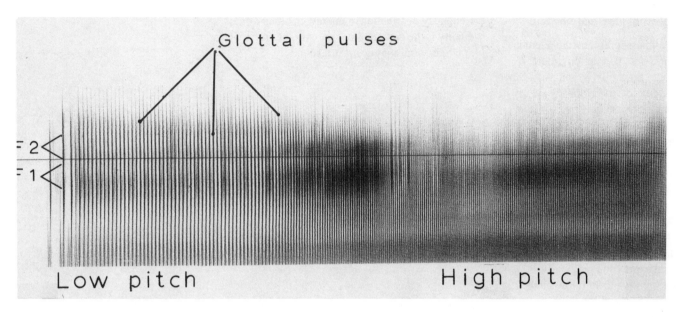

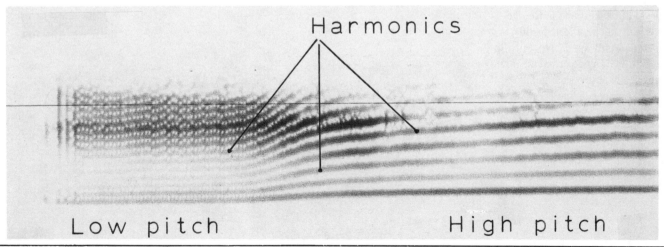

When a voice has no spectral energy at the first harmonic (which is the fundamental), the brain can still deduce F_0 by analyzing the harmonic spectrum for its highest common denominator. Pitch is a suprasegmental element of prosody, and, as such, plays a role in syllable stress, intonation, and inflection. It is through prosody that we achieve expressiveness of ideas and emotions.

Loudness. Another suprasegmental element of prosody is *loudness*. Its perception is determined primarily, but not wholly, by intensity. Since intensity of a sound reflects the vibratory energy in all spectral frequencies, it can only be estimated grossly from the amplitudes of a line spectrum or from the darkness of the spectral tracings on a spectrogram. VU (volume unit) meters, such as on tape recorders, are often used when loudness is to be monitored, but sophisticated electronic equipment is necessary to obtain accurate measures of intensity.

Usually in tandem with pitch, loudness varies from sound to sound. It is also involved in syllable stress and emotional expression ranging from loud, high-pitched shouting to soft, low-pitched sounds of affection. Of course, loudness is also adjusted to fit the size of the room, size of the audience, and the level of background noise. Despite how loud our voices can be, the acoustic energy of speech is remarkably small. Not only do we convert a mere fraction of a percent of air flow into acoustic energy, we also use less than one millionth of the energy for speech that is required to light a 100 watt bulb. At this average energy level for quiet conversation, there is a wide variation in the intensity of the strongest and weakest sounds, the vowel in *law* being about 700 times stronger than the consonant in *th*ink. Of course, with increased loudness when excited, these variations are greater.

Quality: Vowels. The segmental elements of speech (speech sounds) differ from each other only in quality. They are virtually unaffected by pitch or loudness. This is a major reason why spectral analysis is so popular in the study of speech, because quality is determined entirely by the pattern of spectral energy. By definition, *quality* is the frequency distribution of energy. In other words, quality is the pattern of energy over the frequencies at which vibrations occur in a sound.

Spectrographic Features of Vowels. Speech energy ranges roughly from 50 to 10,000 Hz, with the greatest amount clustered between 100 and 600 Hz, the region of the fundamental frequency and first formant. This first formant carries much information about the manner of articulation, that is, about whether the sound is a vowel or a consonant, such as a plosive, fricative, or nasal.

For vowels (diphthongs and semivowels also qualify for this discussion), spectral energy is clustered in formants, the first three or four being of importance to their recognition. The vowel sounds appear on spectrograms as bands of energy that run horizontally, or roughly so. These bands are numbered from bottom (low frequencies) to top (high frequencies) as the first formant, second formant, third formant, and so forth. Almost all of the English vowels can be recognized on the basis of the first two formants, abbreviated as F_1 and F_2. Thus, each vowel can be represented as the relative positions of two formants, as shown on the left in Figure 8–26. F_1 varies in a way that is related fairly closely to the height of the tongue. As the tongue is raised, the F_1 frequency goes down. Thus, low vowels such as those in the words *had* and *hod* have a relatively large F_1 frequency. High vowels such as those in the words *heed* and *who'd* have a relatively low F_1 frequency. F_2 varies in a way that is related to whether the tongue is front or back. Front vowels such as those in *heed* and *had* have a large F_2 frequency, whereas back vowels such as those in *who'd* and *hod* have a small F_2 frequency.

When F_1 and F_2 are plotted as in Figure 8–26, the arrangement of the vowels turns out to be the same as it is when they are plotted by place and manner of articulation (on the right of Figure 8–26, as well as in Figure 7–4 in Chapter 7). This indicates that the first two formants are reasonably good acoustic signatures for the articulatory adjustments of the various vowels. Figure 8–27 shows the spectrograms of vowels and diphthongs as actually spoken.

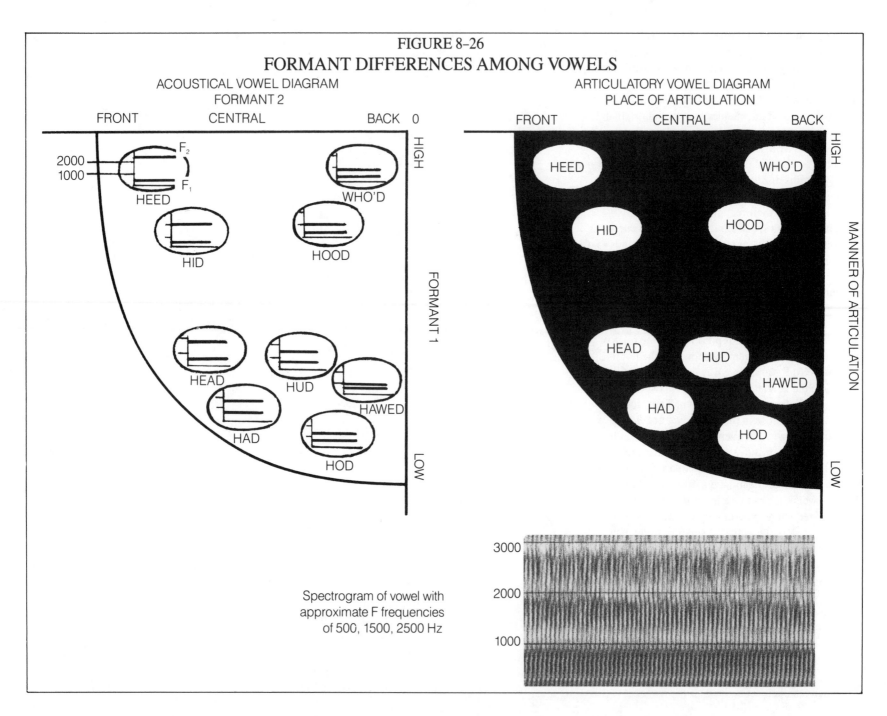

FIGURE 8-26
FORMANT DIFFERENCES AMONG VOWELS

FIGURE 8–27

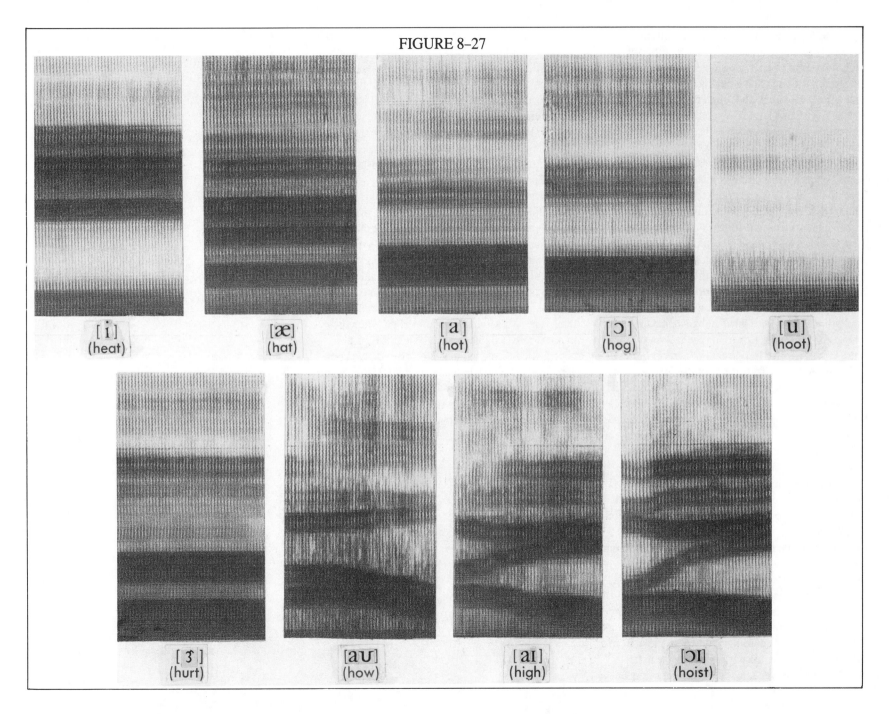

[i]
(heat)

[æ]
(hat)

[ɑ]
(hot)

[ɔ]
(hog)

[u]
(hoot)

[ɝ]
(hurt)

[aʊ]
(how)

[aɪ]
(high)

[ɔɪ]
(hoist)

Quality: Consonants. For recognition of noise consonants, spectral frequency, intensity, and duration serve as cues. For plosive bursts, it is spectral frequency that helps recognition, with *p* being low frequency and *t* high frequency. Spectral frequency is also largely responsible for hearing the difference between sibilants, *s* having spectral energy concentrated above 4,000 Hz, *sh* having energy extending down to 2,000 Hz. The difference between these strong sibilants and the weak fricatives *f* and *th* is spectral intensity. Spectral duration plays a role in distinguishing the brief plosive bursts from the longer noise of fricatives. For instance, when tape recordings of *see* had the *s* segment shortened experimentally from $^{1}/_{10}$ to $^{1}/_{100}$ of a second, the word heard became *tee*.

Not only do *formant transitions* play a major role in distinguishing diphthongs, which you saw in Figure 8–27 where formant bars bend upward or downward from the first to the second vowel, these transitions are also important in the recognition of some consonants. Transitions of the first two formants are of special interest. The first formant shows manner of articulation (because manner depends largely on the extent to which the tongue constricts the vocal tract), whereas the second formant reveals place of articulation, which is particularly important in the recognition of such consonants as plosives. In effect, what the second formant shows acoustically is where in the vocal tract a resonance cavity, constriction, or occlusion is located.

Thus, when the cavity shape changes from one vowel position to another for a diphthong, the second formant reflects this transition. Similarly, the cavity produced by closing the lips for *p* is different from that for *t* which is different from *k*; each has a different frequency (the frequency of its spectral burst). Accordingly, when we move from a vowel to a plosive, the particular plosive to be produced can be recognized by the burst frequency toward which the second formant bends. If it is *p* or *b*, it will bend toward 1,000 Hz; if *t* or *d*, it will be toward 2,000 Hz; if *k* or *g*, toward 3,000 Hz. Recognition of which sound is which in each pair depends on the first formant; it shows which is voiced and which is voiceless. Schematic examples of these transitions can be seen in Figure 8–28.

As we speak, vocal tract shape changes constantly, so that second formant transitions also change constantly. These transitions play a role to some degree in recognition of most sounds. For distinctions such as between *th* and *f*, or among *m*, *n*, and *ng*, in addition to plosives and diphthongs, these transitions are vital. They are also vital to some sounds that, in a sense, are not there. For instance, when *stop* is pronounced without opening the lips for *p*, it is not there in the same way that it is in *put*. Pronounce these two words separately and you will detect a burst of air when the *p* in *put* is released, whereas in stop, it is typically not released, so no burst occurs. How do we know the sound is there, let alone which it is? The reason is because the lips move into position for *p*, so the second formant transition reveals this movement, which is sufficient to recognize that *p* is present even though it is not released.

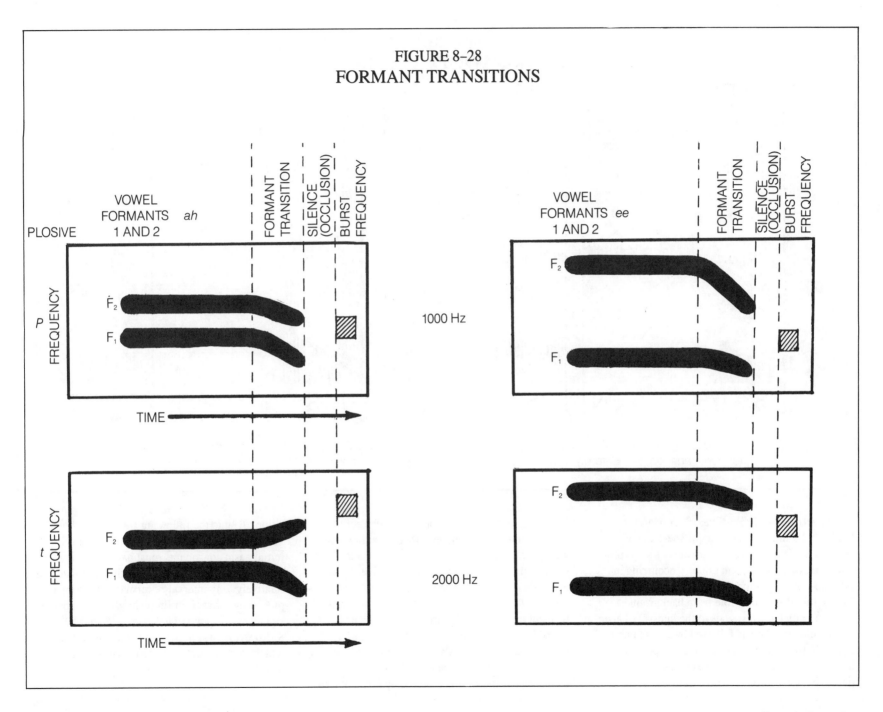

FIGURE 8–28
FORMANT TRANSITIONS

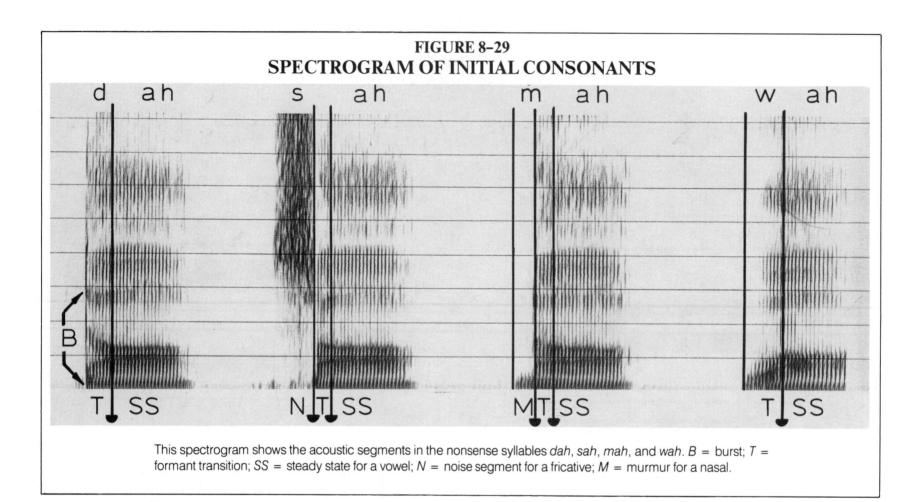

FIGURE 8–29
SPECTROGRAM OF INITIAL CONSONANTS

This spectrogram shows the acoustic segments in the nonsense syllables *dah*, *sah*, *mah*, and *wah*. B = burst; T = formant transition; SS = steady state for a vowel; N = noise segment for a fricative; M = murmur for a nasal.

Spectrographic Features of Consonants. Figure 8–29 illustrates the major spectrographic features for four types of consonants — stop (plosive), fricative, nasal, and glide — occurring in syllable-initial position. The stop begins with a silence (not distinguishable from background silence), which corresponds to the interval of articulatory closure. This is followed by a brief burst of noise (B) that is produced as the air impounded behind the articulatory closure escapes in a quick puff. The noise burst is in turn followed by an interval of formant transition (T), which reflects the articulatory movements into a following vowel steady state (SS). The formant transitions may not occur if the stop is followed by a fricative, a nasal, or another stop. The fricative begins with a noise segment (N) and then may be followed by rapid formant transitions (T) particularly if the next sound is a vowel. The nasal starts with a nasal murmur (M), a low-intensity segment with a very low-frequency band of energy called the nasal formant. The murmur is followed by formant transition (T) into the following sound, which with virtual certainty will be a vowel because syllable-initial nasal consonants must have following vowels to make an English word. The glide consists of a relatively long interval of formant transition (T) preceding a vowel (in English, glides that begin a syllable must immediately precede vowels). Table 8–1 provides a summary of the acoustic cues by which stop, nasal, and fricative consonants are detected.

Table 8–1. Consonant Acoustic Cues

	Bilabial	Labiodental	Linguodental	Linguoalveolar	Linguopalatal	Linguavelar	Glottal
Stop	(bay, pay) F_1 increases F_2 increases Burst has flat or falling (low frequency) spectrum			(dough, toe) F_1 increases F_2 decreases except for high-front vowels Burst has rising (high-frequency) spectrum		(go, key) F_1 increases F_2 increases or decreases depending on following vowel Burst has mid-frequency spectrum	
Nasal	(may) F_1 increases F_2 increases Nasal murmur			(no) F_1 increases F_2 decreases except for high-front vowels Nasal murmur		(king) F_1 increases F_2 increases or decreases depending on following vowel Nasal murmur	
Fricative		(fin) F_1 increases F_2 increases except for some back vowels Noise segment has weak, flat spectrum	(thin) F_1 increases F_2 increases except for some back vowels Noise segment has weak, flat spectrum	(sin) F_1 increases F_2 decreases except for high-front vowels Noise segment has intense, high-frequency spectrum (above 4,000 Hz)	(shin) F_1 increases F_2 increases or decreases depending on following vowel Noise segment has intense, high-frequency spectrum (above 3,000 Hz)		(him) F_1 and F_2 are the same as following vowel Noise segment has weak, flat spectrum

Primary acoustic cues for stop, nasal and fricative consonants produced at different places of articulation. Cues are described for the consonants in syllable-initial, prevocalic position (except for *ng,* which does not occur in this position in English). Formant transitions are indicated for F_1 and F_2 as increasing or decreasing in frequency.

FIGURE 8-30
SPECTROGRAM OF FINAL CONSONANTS

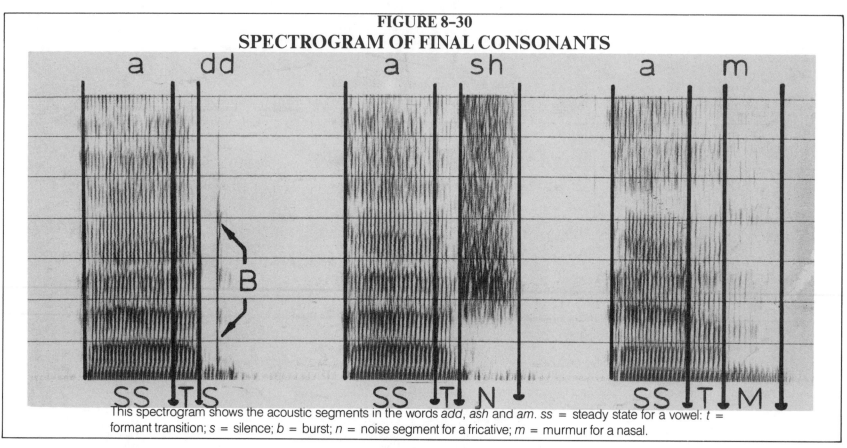

This spectrogram shows the acoustic segments in the words *add*, *ash* and *am*. ss = steady state for a vowel: *t* = formant transition; *s* = silence; *b* = burst; *n* = noise segment for a fricative; *m* = murmur for a nasal.

The spectrographic features for these sounds are not necessarily the same when they occur at the end of a syllable. Figure 8–30 shows the spectrographic appearance of syllable-final stops, fricatives, and nasals (glides are omitted because glides do not occur syllable-finally in English). Depending on the preceding sound, all three classes — stops, fricatives, and nasals — may begin with an interval of formant transitions. As you probably can guess by now, transitions are most likely if the preceding sound is a vowel. For stops, the next segment is a silence (*S*) corresponding to articulatory closure. The silence may be, but is not neces-

sarily, followed by a noise burst (*B*). The burst occurs if the stop is released so that air escapes in an audible puff. For fricatives, the invariant spectrographic feature is a noise segment (*N*). Similarly, nasal consonants have as an invariant feature a nasal murmur (*M*).

The spectrographic features shown in Figures 8–29 and 8–30 can be combined to form the acoustic patterns in more complex syllables. For example, consider the syllable *spins* — a phonetic sequence of fricative, stop, vowel, nasal, and fricative. The syllable would consist of the following acoustic segments:

initial fricative: noise segment
stop: silence; noise burst; formant transition
vowel: formant steady state
nasal: formant transition; nasal murmur
final fricative: noise segment

Let us take as another example the syllable *winced*, a phonetic sequence of glide, vowel, nasal, fricative, and stop:

glide: formant transition
vowel: formant steady state
nasal: formant transition; nasal murmur
fricative: noise segment
stop: silence; noise burst

Reading Spectrograms

The spectrogram is a basic tool of speech analysis. In the hands of an expert, it can reveal a great amount about the speech pattern it represents and even about the speaker who produced it. Some police departments use spectrograms as "voice prints" to identify suspects from whom a voice recording was obtained. For example, recordings may be made of individuals who use the telephone to threaten others. Although the use of "voice prints" as legal evidence is questionable, they have been submitted as evidence in some states. An expert can use spectrograms in ways that we cannot examine in detail here, but we will take some time to show examples of the interpretation of spectrograms.

Spectrograms come in different types, depending on the reason for analysis and the characteristics of the speaker. Two basic types are *wide-band* and *narrow-band* spectrograms. These two types differ in the frequency width of the filter that analyzes the signal. Let's compare these two types of analysis for a sample of phonation of vowel "ah" produced with a continuously increasing fundamental frequency; that is, a vowel with a rising pitch. Figures 8–31 and 8–32 show analyses of such a vowel with a wide-band spectrogram and narrow-band spectrogram, respectively. These spectrograms have been made to show the acoustic energy over a range of only 2,000 Hz, compared with 8,000 Hz for conventional spectrograms. We have selected this small frequency range because our concern is with laryngeal behavior during phonation, specifically, the change in fundamental frequency.

The wide-band spectrogram in Figure 8–31 analyzes the vocal fold vibrations as discrete vertical lines, each of which reflects a puff of air from the glottis that excites the resonances (formants) of the vocal tract. When the fundamental frequency is low, these vertical striations are relatively far apart. As fundamental frequency increases, they become more closely spaced. Although the formants are difficult to visualize on this expanded spectrogram, they can be seen as the relatively darker areas on either side of the horizontal line, which is a 1,000 Hz-frequency marker.

The narrow-band spectrogram in Figure 8–32 applies to exactly the same sound represented in Figure 8–31. But because the narrower analyzing filter offers a better (finer) analysis in frequency rather than time, the vocal fold vibrations appear as harmonics, the roughly horizontal bands of energy running upward from the bottom of the spectrogram. The first, or lowermost, harmonic is the fundamental frequency. The other harmonics occur at integer multiples of the first. As the fundamental frequency increases across the spectrogram, the harmonics become more widely spaced because they are separated by the fundamental frequency. Thus, as the fundamental frequency increases, so does the spacing among the harmonics. The formants are once again visible as relatively darker bands above and below the 1,000 Hz frequency marker that runs horizontally across the spectrogram.

FIGURE 8-31

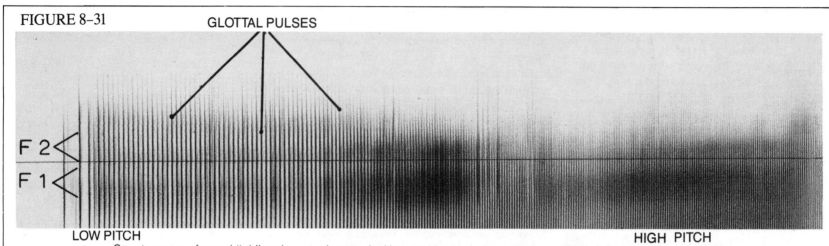

GLOTTAL PULSES

F 2

F 1

LOW PITCH

HIGH PITCH

Spectrogram of vowel "ah" as in *pot*, phonated with a continuously increasing fundamental frequency (perceived as a progressively higher pitch). This kind of spectrogram, called a wide-band spectrogram, analyzes the laryngeal vibrations of voicing as individual glottal pulses, each of which represents a puff of air that escapes as the vocal folds burst apart. At the beginning of phonation, labeled "Low pitch," the glottal pulses are relatively widely spaced. As the fundamental frequency increases, moving toward the end of the spectrogram marked "High pitch," the glottal pulses become more closely spaced. Thus, increasing fundamental frequency is associated with more glottal pulses per unit of time. The horizontal line is a frequency marker at 1000 Hz.

FIGURE 8-32

HARMONICS

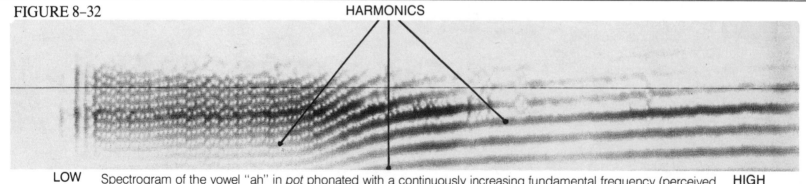

LOW PITCH

HIGH PITCH

Spectrogram of the vowel "ah" in *pot* phonated with a continuously increasing fundamental frequency (perceived as a progressively higher pitch. This kind of spectrogram, called a narrow-band spectrogram, analyzes the vocal fold vibrations as harmonics, that is, spectral components occurring at integer multiples of the fundamental frequency. At the beginning of the vowel, labeled "Low pitch," the harmonics are closely spaced in frequency. As the fundamental frequency increases, moving toward the end of the spectrogram labeled "High pitch," the harmonics become more widely spaced in frequency. Thus, increasing fundamental frequency is associated with a higher first harmonic (which is the fundamental frequency) and a wider spacing of the harmonics. The horizontal line on the spectrogram is a frequency marker at 1000 Hz.

Vowel formants appear on spectrograms as bands of energy, usually oriented approximately horizontally on the pattern. Wide-band spectrograms are shown for four front vowels in Figure 8–33 and for four back vowels in Figure 8–34. Taking Figure 8–33 first, we can see that the F_1 frequency increases across the vowels going from left to right, and that the F_2 frequency decreases as we move in the same direction. The front vowels have one primary acoustic property in common — they all have a relatively high F_2 frequency. However, the F_1 frequency changes from low to high across the four vowels shown. Although the differences in F_1 frequency may not appear especially large compared with the differences for the F_2 frequency, they are perceptually very significant. The high-front vowel in *heed* has the lowest F_1 frequency and the low-front vowel in *had* has the highest F_1 frequency. That is, the F_1 frequency varies primarily with tongue height for the vowel: The higher the tongue, the lower the F_1 frequency.

Figure 8–34 is a wide-band spectrogram of the words *who'd*, *hood*, *hoed*, and *hod*, each of which contains a back vowel. Note first of all that the F_2 frequency of these back vowels is lower than is the F_2 frequency of the front vowels shown in Figure 8–33. As a general rule, front vowels have a high F_2 frequency and back vowels have a low F_2 frequency. Another way of stating the difference between front and back vowels is that the front vowels have a relatively wide separation of F_1 and F_2, whereas the back vowels have an F_1 and F_2 that are close together. Within the four back vowels shown, the frequency of F_1 increases from left to right. This is exactly the same relationship we saw above for the front vowels: As the height of the tongue decreases, the F_1 frequency increases. One final observation to be made about Figure 8–34 pertains to the end of each word. Notice that the second formant sweeps upward just before the vowel ends: This formant frequency change is a transition associated with the articulatory movement from the vowel to the *d* consonant.

So far we have seen spectrograms of vowels contained in simple words. What if vowels are produced one after another in a continuous sequence? A spectrogram of such a sequence is shown in Figure 8–35, which was made of a four-vowel sequence involving the vowels that occur in the words *heed*, *who'd*, *hod*, and *had*. The first vowel (the one in *heed*) ends at the point labeled *a*. It is followed by the vowel in *who'd*. How can we describe the pattern of formant change? Notice that the F_1 frequency hardly changes at all, but the F_2 frequency changes considerably. This result accords with the rules given earlier. Because both of these vowels are high vowels, they both have a low F_1 frequency. Therefore, F_1 frequency does not change much between them. The F_2 frequency, on the other hand, goes from a very high value for the front vowel in *heed* to a very low value for the back vowel in *who'd*. The very low F_2 frequency for the high back vowel is reached just before the point labeled *b*, at which point the articulation changes to the low back vowel in the word *hod*. At this point, the F_1 frequency increases, which corresponds to a lowering of the tongue in the mouth, and the F_2 frequency changes slightly (mostly as the result of a change in lip articulation). Because the vowels in *who'd* and *hod* are back vowels, they both have a relatively low F_2 frequency. The vowel in *hod* ends at the point labeled *c*, at which point the articulation changes to the vowel in *had*. Both the vowel in *hod* and the vowel in *had* are low vowels; therefore, they both have a high F_1 frequency. As expected, the F_1 frequency does not change much at point *c*. However, the F_2 frequency does change, because the vowel in *hod* is a back vowel and the vowel in *had* is a front vowel. Back vowels have low F_2 frequencies and front vowels have high F_2 frequencies.

FIGURE 8-34

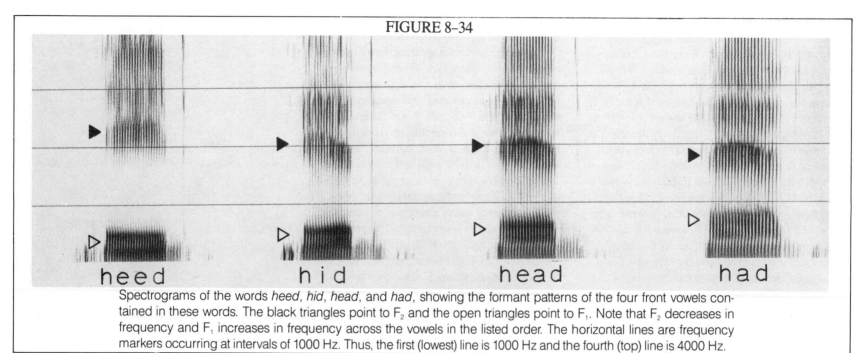

Spectrograms of the words *heed*, *hid*, *head*, and *had*, showing the formant patterns of the four front vowels contained in these words. The black triangles point to F_2 and the open triangles point to F_1. Note that F_2 decreases in frequency and F_1 increases in frequency across the vowels in the listed order. The horizontal lines are frequency markers occurring at intervals of 1000 Hz. Thus, the first (lowest) line is 1000 Hz and the fourth (top) line is 4000 Hz.

FIGURE 8-33

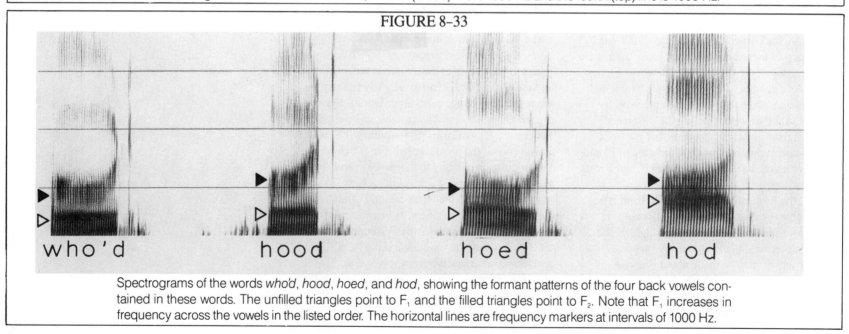

Spectrograms of the words *who'd*, *hood*, *hoed*, and *hod*, showing the formant patterns of the four back vowels contained in these words. The unfilled triangles point to F_1, and the filled triangles point to F_2. Note that F_1 increases in frequency across the vowels in the listed order. The horizontal lines are frequency markers at intervals of 1000 Hz.

FIGURE 8–35

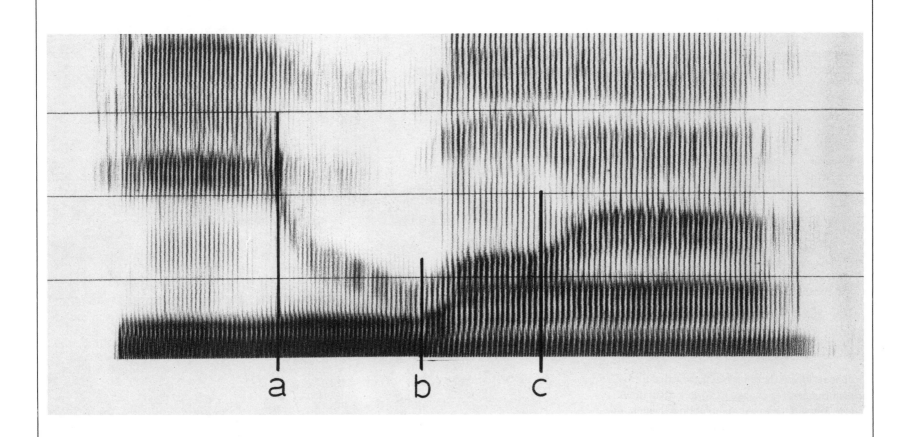

Spectrogram of four vowel sounds produced in succession and without interruption. They are, from left to right, the vowels in *heed*, *who'd*, *hod*, and *had*. The time points *a*, *b*, and *c* indicate transition times described in the text.

FIGURE 8–36

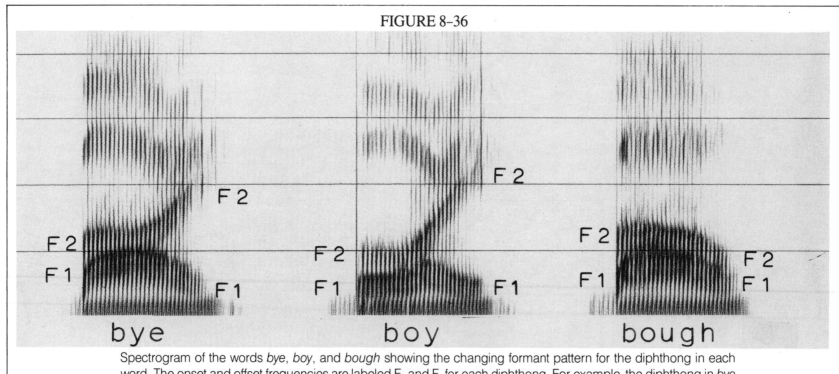

Spectrogram of the words *bye*, *boy*, and *bough* showing the changing formant pattern for the diphthong in each word. The onset and offset frequencies are labeled F_1 and F_2 for each diphthong. For example, the diphthong in *bye* is produced with a falling F_1 frequency and a rising F_2 frequency. Whereas vowels tend to have a stable formant pattern, diphthongs have essentially changing formant patterns that reflect a slow change in the vocal tract shape. The horizontal lines are frequency markers at intervals of 1000 Hz.

The results we have just seen show that the formant frequencies change as vowel articulations change. We will look next at diphthongs, which, as their name suggests, are like two-element vowels (*di* means two and *phthong* means sound). Diphthongs begin with one vowel, the onglide, and end with another, the offglide. Basically, the tongue glides between two vowel positions. Spectrograms of diphthongs are shown in Figure 8–36. Each of the diphthongs shown has a changing pattern of the F_1 and F_2 frequencies. For example, the diphthong in the word *bye* has a falling F_1 frequency and a rising F_2 frequency.

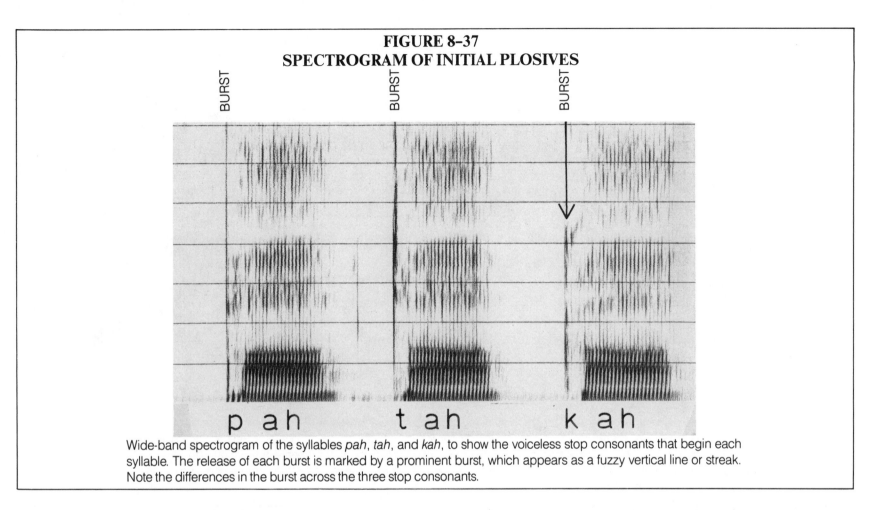

FIGURE 8-37
SPECTROGRAM OF INITIAL PLOSIVES

BURST

BURST

BURST

p ah   t ah   k ah

Wide-band spectrogram of the syllables *pah*, *tah*, and *kah*, to show the voiceless stop consonants that begin each syllable. The release of each burst is marked by a prominent burst, which appears as a fuzzy vertical line or streak. Note the differences in the burst across the three stop consonants.

We have seen that vowels and diphthongs have spectrograms in which the formant patterns are strong and well defined. Now we turn to consonants, first the stop consonants *p*, *t*, and *k*. As can be seen in Figure 8–37, each of these consonants appears on a spectrogram as a sequence of acoustic events. Following a period of silence (which corresponds to the interval of articulatory closure of the stop), the built-up air pressure is released as a brief *burst* of noise. This burst is followed by a segment of weaker noise called aspiration noise,

which is generated as air flows through the adducting vocal folds. When the vocal folds have been adducted for the phonatory state, laryngeal vibrations begin for the vowel that follows the voiceless stop consonant. Thus, for each of the syllables *pah*, *tah*, and *kah*, we see a very brief noise burst, a longer segment of weaker noise, and a following vowel. One last feature should be noted. If you look carefully at the burst for each stop consonant, you should be able to see differences in the frequency regions of the noise energy. The burst for *p*

has almost the same amount of energy over the entire frequency range of the spectrogram, so the burst appears as a fuzzy line of fairly uniform darkness over the frequencies from 0 to 8,000 Hz. In contrast, the burst for *t* has greater energy in the higher frequencies, above 3,000 to 4,000 Hz. Finally, the burst for *k* contains most of its energy in the middle frequencies, between about 1,000 and 4,000 Hz. It has been shown that listeners can distinguish these three stops when only the brief noise bursts are presented for identification.

FIGURE 8–38

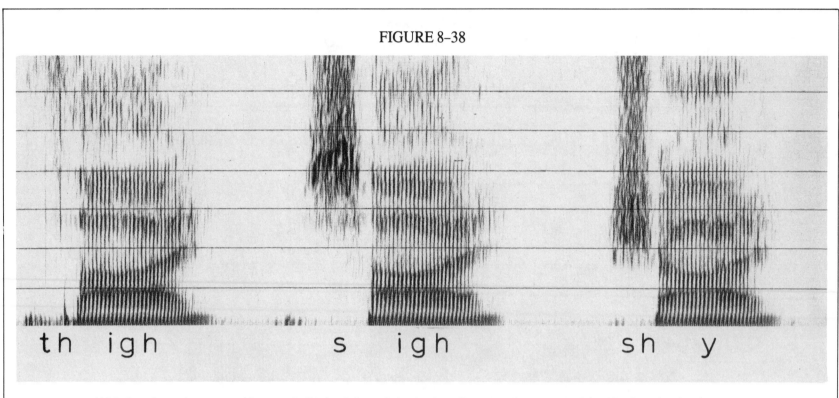

Wide-band spectrograms of the words *thigh*, *sigh*, and *shy*, to show the acoustic patterns of the fricatives that begin each word. Among the differences to be noted is that *th* is weak in total energy and has a fairly uniform distribution of the energy across frequencies; *s* has more energy and the energy is located primarily in the high frequencies (above about 4000 Hz); and, finally, *sh* is intense like *s* but has energy extending to lower frequencies (down to about 2000 Hz). The horizontal lines are frequency markers at intervals of 1000 Hz.

Spectrograms of another group of consonants, the fricatives, are shown in Figure 8–38. The fricatives occur in the words *thigh*, *sigh*, and *shy*. The fricative portion of each word appears as a kind of smear of energy, rather weak for *th* but stronger for *s* and *sh*. The frequency regions of the noise energy differ among the three fricatives. The noise for *th* is so weak that it is difficult to see exactly where the energy lies, but it typically is fairly uniform across frequency. The noise energy for *s* is mostly in the high frequencies, 4,000 Hz and above. The noise energy for *sh* extends to lower frequencies than it does for *s*. Thus, the fricatives differ in total energy and in the frequency regions of the noise energy.

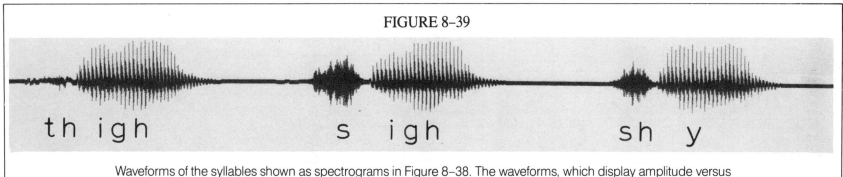

FIGURE 8–39

th igh   s igh   sh y

Waveforms of the syllables shown as spectrograms in Figure 8–38. The waveforms, which display amplitude versus time, are an alternative to spectrograms as a way of visualizing the acoustic pattern. Note that the waveform displays make apparent the differences in amplitude between the weak fricatives *th* and the intense fricatives *s* and *sh*.

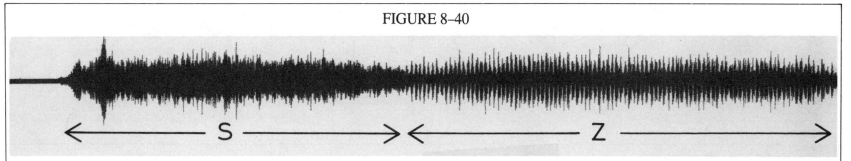

FIGURE 8–40

$\longleftarrow$ s $\longrightarrow$$\longleftarrow$ z $\longrightarrow$

Waveform of the sound produced when a prolonged *s* is changed to a prolonged *z* (that is, a voiceless fricative is immediately followed by a voiced fricative with the same place of articulation). The voicing change occurs at the point marked by the opposing arrowheads in the middle of the waveform.

The difference in amount of energy can be seen in waveforms as well. Figure 8–39 shows the waveforms of the words that appear in the spectrogram of Figure 8–38. The noise for *th* is so weak that it is barely noticeable as a fuzzy thickening of the baseline. But for the *s* and the *sh*, the noise segment is comparatively intense. Notice also how the waveform for the fricative segments differs from that for the following diphthong. The noise waveform is random in its fine structure, but the waveform of the diphthong clearly shows the periodic voicing energy as nearly equally spaced vertical pulses.

But, you might ask, what would voiced fricatives look like? These sounds have noise energy, but they also have the periodic energy of voicing. For the answer to this question, study the waveform in Figure 8–40, which shows a prolonged *s* (a voiceless fricative) that changes at the point marked by the opposing arrowheads into a prolonged *z* (a voiced fricative). What happens is that the noise energy in *z* is shaped (modulated) by the puffs of voicing. As a result, the waveform shows the periodic glottal pulses, but it also shows noise energy mixed with the periodic excitation.

FIGURE 8–41

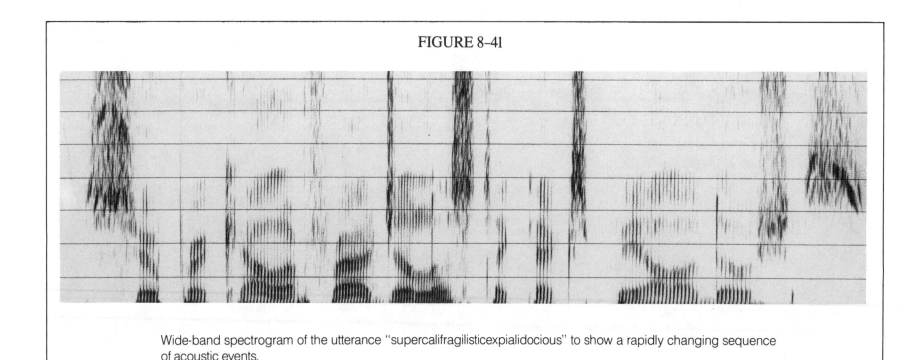

Wide-band spectrogram of the utterance "supercalifragilisticexpialidocious" to show a rapidly changing sequence of acoustic events.

The spectrograms illustrated to this point were made for relatively simple utterances. Things become much more complicated as the utterances become longer and produced at faster speaking rates. Now, for something completely ridiculous (as an old television comedy show used to put it), we turn to a somewhat more complex utterance, the whimsical word from "Mary Poppins": super-califragilisticexpialidocious. This perverse example illustrates the rapid changes in acoustic patterns that a spectrogram can reveal (Fig. 8–41). You might try your hand at guessing what some of the acoustic segments represent. If nothing else, you should be able to identify the fricatives at the beginning, middle, and end of the "word."

Learning to "read" a spectrogram takes considerable practice and even the experts make mis-takes for some segments. One reason for the diffi-culty is that what we think of as the same sound can look quite different in different contexts. The expert has to be aware of these variations. Another source of difficulty is that individual speakers vary somewhat in their acoustic characteristics. As has been discussed earlier, formant frequencies vary with the length of speakers' vocal tracts. Figure 8–42 gives an example of differences in formant frequencies for speakers with vocal tracts of vary-ing lengths. This spectrogram was made for three speakers producing in quick succession the vowel "ee" (as in *heed*). Moving from left to right, the first speaker was a man, the second a 9 year old girl, and the third a 6 year old boy. The F_2 fre-quency increases across the three speakers roughly as follows: about 2,250 Hz for the man, 3,100 Hz for the 9 year old girl, and 3,300 Hz for the 6 year old boy. Despite the acoustic differences among the three productions, they all are heard as vowel "ee." Obviously, then, the phonetic decisions we make in listening to speech do not depend on *abso-lute* acoustic properties. Rather, we make these decisions on the basis of *relative* acoustic proper-ties. One of the challenging problems in program-ming computers to understand human speech is to solve this problem of "speaker normalization," or the ability to understand speakers who vary in their acoustic characteristics. Interestingly, it appears that human infants have this capability even within the first few weeks or months of life. That is, in-fants at this age seem to hear a father's "ee" vowel as somehow being equivalent to the same vowel produced by the mother.

FIGURE 8–42

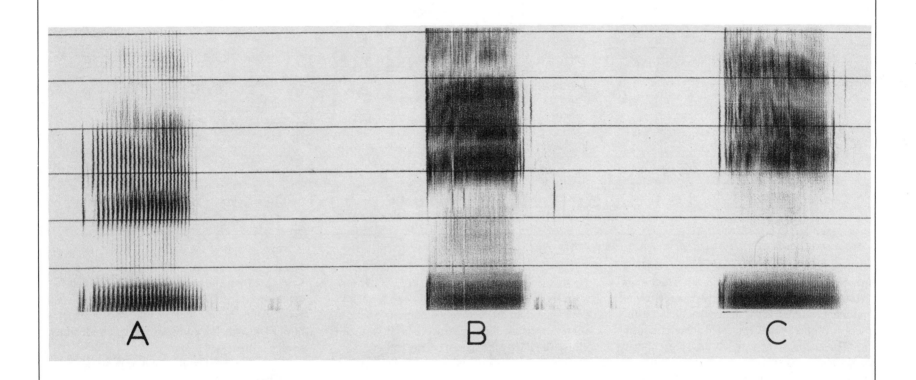

Wide-band spectrogram of the vowel "ee" (as in the word *heed*) produced by three different talkers: *A*, man; *B*, a 9 year old girl; and *C*, a 6 year old boy. Compare the formant patterns in the three productions. The absolute formant frequencies differ but the relative pattern is preserved.

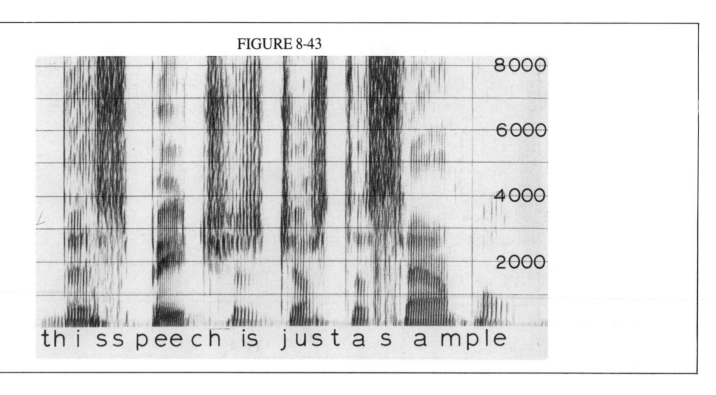

FIGURE 8-43

Spectrogram of Sentences. If we examine a spectrogram like that in Figure 8–43, which shows a complex sequence of sounds, we can see several important features. First, notice that the acoustic energy of some sounds is located at high frequencies. For example, the *s* sounds have most of their energy above 4,000 Hz. It is these higher frequencies that are most difficult to hear in hearing impairments caused by nerve damage (sensorineural hearing loss). Persons with this kind of hearing loss often cannot discriminate sounds like *s* that have mostly high-frequency energy.

This spectrogram also shows that speech sounds differ in their durations. The vowel in *speech* is longer than the vowel for *a*. The noise segment for *s* is longer than the noise burst for *t*, although they are similar in their frequencies of noise energy.

The first two formants, F_1 and F_2, stay within the frequency range of about 200 to 2,000 Hz for most sounds. Recall that only these two formants are required for the recognition of most vowels. It is not surprising, then, that speech is fairly intelligible even if only the speech energy below 2,000 Hz is available to listeners. In fact, ordinary telephones transmit the frequencies between about 500 to 3,500 Hz, yet speech is usually quite intelligible.

Word boundaries are not necessarily clearly marked on spectrograms. Where is the word boundary between *this* and *speech*? Notice that there is only one noise segment for *s* in the first two words. Is this the final *s* in *this* or the initial *s* in *speech*? Of course, it is both, which means that the listener must assign the word boundary. One of the difficulties in reading a spectrogram is that

boundaries between phonetic segments or between words are frequently hard to identify. A highly experienced spectrogram reader can do quite well given sufficient time, but even the best expert in this task seems slow compared to the rate at which speech is processed by ear.

It might seem that it should be possible to describe each speech sound with respect to an unchanging acoustic feature, or at least some combination of acoustic features. But such is not the case. The unfeasibility of this idea became apparent early on in the modern era of speech research. In the 1950s considerable effort was expended to develop a reading machine for the blind. Much of this research proceeded on the assumption that the sounds of speech are put together like beads on a string to make words, phrases, or sentences. Careful productions of words were recorded on mag-

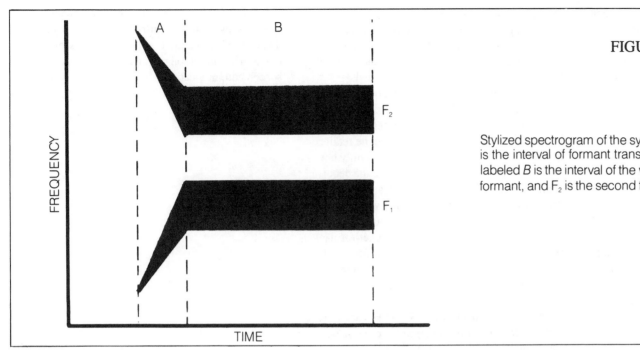

FIGURE 8–44

Stylized spectrogram of the syllable "doo." The portion labeled *A* is the interval of formant transitions. The portion labeled *B* is the interval of the vowel steady state. F$_1$ is the first formant, and F$_2$ is the second formant.

netic tape. Then, individual sounds were extracted from the recorded words and stored in a machine which could combine them to form different words. The result was dismal. Much of the recomposed speech was unintelligible and some of the recorded segments were perceived as entirely different sounds (for example a *p* might sound like a *k* in the recomposed speech).

The failure of this enterprise points up a key issue in the acoustic study of speech — the *lack of acoustic invariance* of phonetic segments. Individual phonemes often take on a different acoustic appearance in different words. That is, speech sounds show *contextual variation*. The *d* in *deep* has different acoustic features than does the *d* in *dupe*. For this reason we cannot simply splice the *d* segment from *deep*, replace it for the *d* segment in *dupe* and expect to hear something that sounds like *dupe*.

It is not even a straightforward matter to identify the acoustic segment of speech that corresponds to a given speech sound. The formant pattern shown in Figure 8–44 is basically the combination of formant-frequency change in the syllable *doo*. The first part of the pattern consists of a bending of the formants; this is called the *formant transition*. The second part of the formant pattern is flat; this is the vowel steady-state. When only the second portion is presented to listeners, a vowel sound — in this case *oo* — is heard. When the entire pattern — transition plus steady state — is presented, listeners hear the syllable *doo*. Logically, then, we might expect that the isolated formant transition would be heard as the consonant *d*. But it isn't. In fact, many listeners don't even hear this segment as a speech sound. Instead, they hear it as a chirp or bleep. This transitional segment is perceived as a consonant *d* only when it is com-

bined with a following steady-state formant segment for a vowel. Some researchers have taken this result to mean that speech is optionally perceived in syllables, that is, the syllable is the unit of speech perception.

A sentence consists of a sequence of phonemes and each phoneme consists of one or more acoustic segments. To understand speech, a listener must recognize the segments and retain their order to decide which words were intended by the speaker. Sometimes even a brief alteration in the sound pattern can make a difference in linguistic interpretation. For example, if a brief silence interrupts the *s* and *l* segments in the word *slit*, the pattern is then heard as *split*.

Finally, in Figure 8–45, you can see the same sentence displayed in a wave form, a wide-band spectrogram, and a narrow-band spectrogram. Each is suited to certain types of measurement and to visualization of certain types of acoustic features.

Clinical Postscript

One of the authors saw some very bad movies in his youth. But perhaps we can put these questionable cinema experiences to good use in testing our understanding of speech acoustics. In one of these very bad movies, a person who was accused of lying was punished by having her tongue cut out. As the result of this punishment, she was left mute — unable to say a single sound. Does this make sense? Or was the author of this story mistaken about the role of the tongue? The answer is that it doesn't make sense. Removal of the tongue does not make a person mute, so long as the larynx can still function.

A person with aglossia (i.e., without a tongue) can make sounds, although they may not have the intelligibility or quality of normal speech. Interestingly, some persons with aglossia fare quite well in spite of this remarkable defect of the oral anatomy. One man lost his tongue almost entirely (along with part of his mandible or lower jaw) to oral cancer, yet his speech was sufficiently intelligible that he could be understood by almost anyone. Not every aglossic individual is able to retrain his residual speech apparatus as well as this man did, but the success of this one person is testimony to the capacity that many persons have to compensate for severe injuries or abnormalities of the speech apparatus. This successful compensation also emphasizes the point that speech sounds can be produced with more than one vocal tract shape. When the tongue is removed, the vocal tract can be shaped by the remaining articulators, such as the jaw, lips, and walls of the vocal tract. The aglossic man used these remaining structures to create vocal tract shapes appropriate to the sounds of English. In the final analysis, adequacy of articulatory adjustments, compensatory or normal, is determined by how close the acoustic result is to normal.

But getting back to those bad movies, another one was about a shrinking man. He shrank so much that he eventually was no larger than an insect. But despite this change in size, he retained his normal voice. Sensible or not? Certainly not, because as this chapter has explained, the acoustic characteristics of a person's speech are determined primarily by the length of his or her vocal tract. Longer vocal tracts have lower formant frequencies, and shorter vocal tracts have higher formant frequencies. In addition, the vocal fundamental frequency, or what we hear as the pitch of the voice, depends on the mass and length of the vocal folds. It is for this reason that a man has a lower pitched voice than a woman. So, a real shrinking man would not retain his normal voice as he became smaller. To the contrary, his voice would change, first sounding like that of a woman, then that of a child, and finally like nothing else we have ever heard.

A good example to illustrate how our impressions of a speaker's age and size depend on the acoustic characteristics of his or her voice is given by the situation in which a record or tape is played back at a faster speed than that at which it was recorded. The faster playback speed shifts all the frequency components of the recorded voice upward, giving it a higher pitch overall. Because of this upward shift, an original recording of a deep male voice may sound childlike, even chipmunklike, at a faster playback speed. A similar phenomenon occurs in so-called "helium speech," or the speech of deep-sea divers who breathe air with a large proportion of helium. Helium is lighter than ordinary air (hence a helium-filled balloon rises when placed in the air) and this changes its acoustic properties such that propagated sounds have higher frequency components. When speaking in helium-rich air, a deep-voiced diver sounds diminutive, rather like a talking chipmunk. This alteration of voice quality impairs speech communication, so efforts have been made to correct for the unusual voice quality.

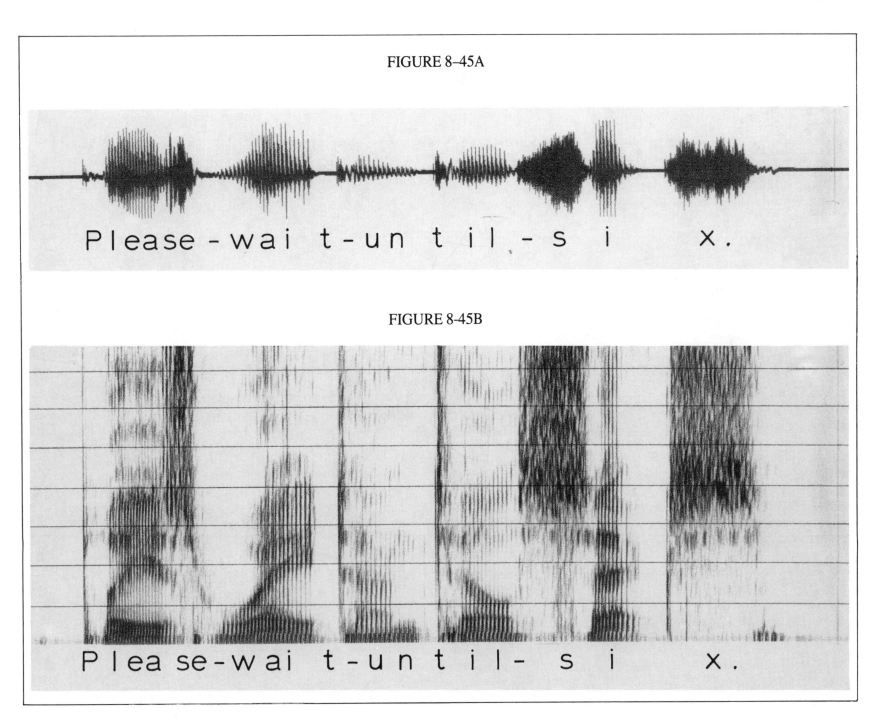

FIGURE 8–45A

Please - wai t - un t il - s i   x.

FIGURE 8-45B

P lea se - w a i t - u n t il - s i   x.

FIGURE 8-45C

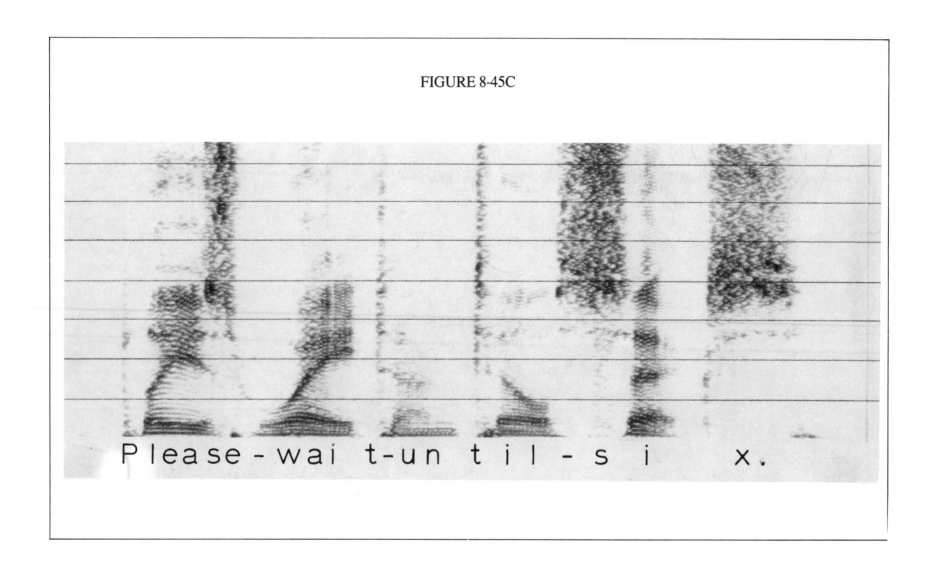

CHAPTER EIGHT
Self-Study
Speech Acoustics

Review Glossary

Sound characteristics: Characteristics of any acoustical vibration

    Compression phase: The phase of a sound wave in which molecules are compressed and raise pressure above atmospheric pressure

    Rarefaction phase: The phase of a sound wave in which molecules separate and lower pressure below atmospheric pressure

    Vibration: Oscillatory pressure changes between compression and rarefaction

        Cycle: A complete vibration through a compression phase and a rarefaction phase

            Period: The duration of a cycle

            Wavelength: The distance over which a period extends when vibration is recorded graphically

        Frequency: The number of periods of vibration per second

            Hertz (Hz): One period of vibration; the measure of frequency

        Amplitude: The amount of pressure change in a vibratory cycle

Time-domain characteristics: Characteristics of sound-pressure changes across time

    Wave form: Graphic representation of sound-pressure changes across time

    Sine wave: The wave form of a *pure tone*, the simplest form of vibration, which can be described completely by a single frequency and amplitude

    Complex wave: The wave form resulting from the interaction of two or more pure tones occurring simultaneously

        Reinforcement: The additive effect of compression conditions or rarefaction conditions coinciding

        Interference: The subtractive effect of compression conditions coinciding with rarefaction conditions

        Phase angle: The measurement of a cycle (equivalent to a circle) in degrees with 0° being the beginning of a compression phase

        Repetitive wave: A wave composed of a finite number of frequencies and amplitudes that repeats itself periodically

        Nonrepetitive wave: A complex wave composed of an infinite number of frequencies that does not repeat itself

Frequency-domain characteristics: Characteristics of sound that vary in frequency

    Spectrum: Graphic representation of frequencies and amplitudes of vibration

        Line spectrum: A spectrum in which the amplitude of a signal at a particular frequency is represented by the height of a vertical line; it is used to display a finite number of frequencies and amplitudes, on the horizontal and vertical axes, respectively

        Continuous spectrum: A spectrum in which the height of a continuous line represents the amplitude at any frequency beneath that line; it is used to display an infinite number of frequencies and amplitudes

    Spectrogram (sonogram): A spectrum of frequency and intensity recorded across time: it is used to display speech signals across time

    Spectral frequency: A frequency at which there is vibratory energy (amplitude)

    Fundamental frequency (f_o): The frequency at which a complex wave pattern repeats itself

    Harmonic frequency: A frequency that is a whole-number multiple of the fundamental frequency, which is the 1st harmonic

    Tone: A sound that results from periodic vibrations that have spectral energy at harmonic frequencies

    Noise: A sound that results from aperiodic vibrations

    Fourier analysis: The analysis by which the spectral frequencies composing the complex wave are determined

    Resonator characteristics: Characteristics that determine the filter function of resonators

Transfer function (filter function): The frequency distribution of the filters (resonators) of the vocal tract that shape the vowel and consonant energy

Radiated spectrum: The frequency distribution of energy of speech sounds that emerge from the vocal tract

Radiation characteristic: Increase in intensity of higher frequencies as sound leaves the vocal tract resonator at the lips

Resonator (filter): A cavity that selectively filters out energy at frequencies to which it is not "tuned" and amplifies at frequencies to which it is tuned

Bandwidth: The range of frequencies to which a resonator is tuned

Damping: The speed with which a resonator consumes energy

Closed-Tube resonator: A resonator open at one end and closed at the other

Incidence wave: The compression or rarefaction wave that enters a closed-tube resonator

Reflected wave: The compression or rarefaction wave that is reflected off the end of a closed-tube resonator

Formant frequency: The frequency that designates a peak of vocal tract resonance

Speech-perception characteristics: Characteristics by which segmental and suprasegmental elements of speech are perceived

Pitch: Perception of the frequency of a sound; vocal pitch is perception of the fundamental frequency

Loudness: Perception of the intensity of a sound

Quality: Perception of the frequency distribution of energy (the aspect of a sound that is independent of pitch and loudness), the characteristic by which speech sounds differ from each other

Steady-State: A continuous segment of speech that does not change in quality

Vowel: Perceptual category of a steady-state segment that forms a syllable nucleus

Diphthong: Perceptual category of two vowels blended together in the same syllable

Sonorant: Perceptual category of vowel-like consonants

Fricative: Perceptual category of a steady-state noise consonant

Stop or plosive: Perceptual category of a noise consonant involving stoppage of the air stream

Voiceless consonant: Perceptual category of a consonant produced without vibration of the vocal folds

Voiced consonant: Perceptual category of a consonant produced with vibration of the vocal folds

Stress: Perception of a syllable as stressed or unstressed, which is determined by the suprasegmental elements of pitch, loudness, and duration

Speech-acoustic characteristics: Acoustic characteristics by which speech-sound segments differ

Glottal-source spectrum: Spectrum of energy generated for voiced sounds

Noise-source spectrum: Spectrum of energy generated for noise components of consonants

Spectral frequencies: The frequency range within which noise energy is greatest

Spectral intensity: The intensity of noise

Spectral duration: The duration of a segment of noise

Noise segment: A steady-state consonant segment, varying in spectral frequency and intensity, produced by turbulence

Noise burst: A brief noise, varying in spectral frequency, produced by the release of a stop consonant

Silence segment: The period of silence produced by closure of the vocal tract while articulating a stop consonant

First formant: The lowest frequency peak of vocal-tract energy, which decreases as height of the tongue increases

Second formant: The second-lowest frequency peak of vocal-tract energy, which is high with front vowels and low with back vowels

Formant transition: The change in a formant frequency as one voiced sound blends into another

Nasal murmur: A very low frequency and low-intensity band of energy that is the nasal formant

Acoustic noninvariance: Variability of the acoustic basis for the perception of a speech sound

Contextual variation: Variations in the acoustic appearance of a sound as it occurs in different contexts from word to word

Self-Study Test of Terminology

Self-Study Instructions: These questions can be used to help you assess how much you have retained from studying the Review Glossary. Answers are given in Appendix E.

(1) _____ The phase of a sound wave in which molecules separate and lower pressure below atmospheric pressure

(2) _____ The distance over which a period extends when vibration is recorded graphically

(3) _____ Graphic representation of sound-pressure changes across time

(4) _____ The additive effect of compression conditions or rarefaction conditions coinciding

(5) _____ A complex wave composed of an infinite number of frequencies that does not repeat itself

(6) _____ The wave form of a pure tone, the simplest form of vibration, which can be described completely by a single frequency and amplitude

(7) _____ A spectrum of frequency and intensity recorded across time; it is used to display speech signals across time

(8) _____ A frequency that is a whole-number multiple of the fundamental frequency which is the first harmonic

(9) _____ The analysis by which the spectral frequencies composing the complex wave are determined

(10) _____ The phase of a sound wave in which molecules are compressed and raise pressure above atmospheric pressure

(11) _____ The number of periods of vibration per second

(12) _____ The measurement of a cycle (equivalent to a circle) in degrees with 0° being the beginning of a compression phase

(13) _____ The wave form resulting from the interaction of two or more pure tones occurring simultaneously

(14) _____ One period of vibration; the measure of frequency

(15) _____ A sound that results from periodic vibrations that have spectral energy at harmonic frequencies

(16) _____ A spectrum in which the height of a continuous line represents the amplitude at any frequency beneath that line; it is used to display an infinite number of frequencies and amplitudes

(17) _____ The subtractive effect of compression conditions coinciding with rarefaction conditions

(18) _____ A complete vibration through a compression phase and a rarefaction phase

(19) _____ A wave composed of a finite number of frequencies that does repeat itself

(20) _____ A frequency at which there is vibratory energy (amplitude)

(21) _____ Graphic representation of frequencies and amplitudes of vibration

(22) _____ A sound that results from aperiodic vibrations

(23) _____ Oscillatory pressure changes between compression and rarefaction

(24) _____ The duration of a cycle

(25) _____ The range of frequencies to which a resonator is tuned

(26) _____ The frequency at which a complex wave pattern repeats itself

(27) _____ A spectrum in which the amplitude of a frequency is represented by the height of a vertical line; it is used to display a finite number of frequencies and amplitudes

(28) _____ The frequency distribution of energy of the filters (resonators) of the vocal tract that shape the vowel and consonant energy

(29) _____ Perception of a steady-state segment that forms a syllable nucleus

(30) _____ The compression or rarefaction wave that is reflected off the bottom of a closed-tube resonator

(31) _____ Increase in intensity of higher frequencies as sound leaves the vocal tract resonator at the lips

(32) _____ Perception of a consonant produced without vibration of the vocal folds

(33) _____ A resonator open at one end and closed at the other

(34) _____ The frequency range within which noise energy is greatest

(35) _____ Perception of a syllable as stressed or unstressed, which is determined by the suprasegmental elements of pitch, loudness, and duration

(36) _____ The frequency distribution of energy of speech sounds that emerge from the vocal tract

(37) _____ The frequency that designates a peak of vocal-tract resonance

(38) _____ A cavity that selectively filters out energy at frequencies to which it is not "tuned" and amplifies at frequencies to which it is tuned

(39) _____ The compression or rarefaction wave that enters a closed-tube resonator

(40) _____ Perception of a steady-state noise consonant

(41) _____ Perception of the intensity of a sound

(42) _____ Perception of a noise consonant involving stoppage of the air stream

(43) _____ Perception of the frequency distribution of energy (the aspect of a sound that is independent of pitch and loudness), and is the characteristic in which speech sounds differ from each other

(44) _____ The speed with which a resonator consumes energy

(45) _____ Perception of two vowels blended together in the same syllable

(46) _____ A steady-state consonant, varying in spectral frequency and intensity, produced by turbulence

(47) _____ Spectrum of energy generated for voiced sounds

(48) _____ A continuous segment of speech that does not change in quality

(49) _____ Perception of the fundamental frequency of a sound

(50) _____ Variability of the acoustic basis for the perception of a speech sound

(51) _____ The lowest-frequency peak of vocal-tract energy, which decreases as height of the tongue increases

(52) _____ Spectrum of energy generated for noise components of consonants

(53) _____ The change in a formant frequency as one voiced sound blends into another

(54) _____ The intensity of noise

(55) _____ A brief noise, varying in spectral frequency, produced by the aspirated release of a stop consonant

(56) _____ Variations in the acoustic appearance of a sound as it occurs in different contexts from word to word

(57) _____ The duration of a segment of noise

(58) _____ The second-lowest frequency peak of vocal-tract energy, which is high with front vowels and low with back vowels

(59) _____ Perception of a consonant produced with vibration of the vocal folds

(60) _____ A very low frequency and low-intensity band of energy that is the nasal formant

(61) _____ The period of silence produced by closure of the vocal tract while articulating a stop consonant

(62) _____ Perception of vowel-like consonants

Self-Study Test of Speech Applications of Acoustics

Self-Study Instructions: The formant frequency graph for vowels shown in Figure 8–26 is convenient for showing the relationships between vowel formants and articulatory features of vowels, but it is not the standard plot of formant frequencies. The standard graph, which we will call an F_1/F_2 chart, shows the F_1 frequency on the horizontal axis and the F_2 frequency on the vertical axis. Each vowel can be represented as a single point on the F_1/F_2 chart. All of the different vowels within a language, or several languages for that matter, can be shown as points on the chart. Thus, the F_1/F_2 chart is a convenient and useful way to describe the acoustic structure of the vowels. However, for some purposes, it is not sufficient to know only the frequencies of the first two formants; in these cases, it may be necessary to specify also the frequency of the third formant, or the fourth, and so on. In the exercises that follow, you will use the F_1/F_2 chart. Be sure to note that this chart is oriented differently than the one first introduced in this chapter.

Acoustic Application Question 1

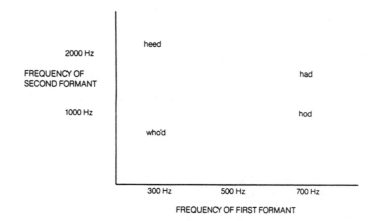

Formant chart: The words written on the chart are located in the relative positions of their first and second formant frequencies when spoken by an adult male. For example, the vowel in *heed* has a low first formant frequency and a high second formant frequency, so this word is written in the upper left corner. Refer to this chart as you answer questions for the charts on the following pages.

Acoustic Application Question 2

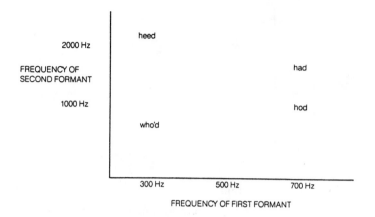

Formant chart: Write on the chart the approximate locations of the vowels in the words *hate*, *heard*, and *hoed*. *Hate* has a first formant and second formant frequency intermediate to those for the vowels in *heed* and *had*. *Heard* has a midcentral vowel, so that its first and second formant frequencies are in the center of the graph. *Hoed* has a first formant and second formant frequency intermediate to those for the vowels in *who'd* and *hod*. Check your answers in Appendix E.

Acoustic Application Question 3

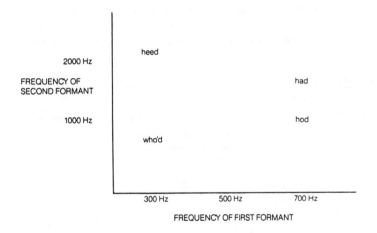

Formant chart: Recall that the formant frequencies for a given speaker depend on the length of the vocal tract. Because men have a longer vocal tract than women, the formant frequencies of a man's vowels are lower than those for a woman. Write on the chart in capital letters the approximate locations for the vowels in the words *heed*, *had*, *hod*, and *who'd* for a woman speaker. Check your answers in Appendix E.

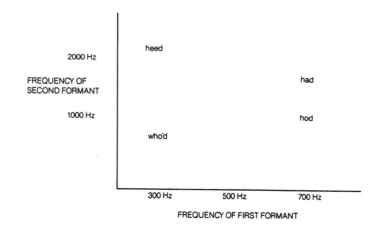

Formant chart: Recall that the frequency of the second formant varies primarily with the position of the tongue in the front-back dimension of vowel articulation. The more fronted the tongue, the higher the second-formant frequency. Imagine that a speaker suffered from a problem that prevented him from moving the tongue to the frontmost vowel positions. Write in capital letters on the formant chart the approximate positions of the vowels in the words *heed* and *had* for this speaker. Check your answers in Appendix E.

Acoustic Segments in Words: Write in the blanks for each word the acoustic segment that correctly completes the sentence. The first three words are completed for examples. Fill in the blanks for the remaining items. Segments in parentheses are optional (may or may not occur, depending on how the word is produced). Silence is used to indicate a stop closure period, but it should be noted that not all stop closures are completely silent, as some contain voicing energy. Check your answers in Appendix E.

seed   Noise + formant transition + vowel steady state + formant transition + silence + (release burst)

moose   nasal murmur + formant transition + vowel steady state + formant transition + noise

sand   noise + formant transition + vowel steady state + formant transition + nasal murmur + silence + (release burst)

stab   noise + _____ + release burst + formant transition + _____ + silence + (release burst)

bass   release burst + _____ + vowel steady state + formant transitions + _____

west   long formant transition + vowel steady state + formant transition + noise + _____ +

_____

wish   long formant transition + vowel steady state + _____ + _____

sheep   _____ + _____ + vowel steady state + formant transition + silence +

_____

bob   _____ + formant transition + _____ + formant transition +

_____ + (release burst)

meets   nasal murmur + formant transition + _____ + _____ + silence +

_____

mast   _____ + _____ + vowel steady state + formant transition + noise + silence + (release

burst)

A Whimsical Exercise for the Curious and Brave

(Your own satisfaction determines the right answer; if you perform it publicly, give yourself an "A.")

The text for composer Milton Babbitt's "Phonemena" is an assemblage of English phonemes, 24 consonants, and 12 vowels. The sounds were selected for such acoustic properties as formant frequencies, envelopes, and durations. The first version of this composition was written for soprano and piano; a later version was written for soprano and synthesized tape. Critics have described the result as sounding like poetry — a lively, expressive language that one cannot understand.

Create your own composition of noises, silences, and sonorant segments (sonorant sounds have well-defined formant patterns; thus, vowels, nasal consonants, and glides are examples of sonorants). Note how the sounds are grouped below in terms of major acoustic properties. Study each grouping and explain why they belong in the category shown. Then select sounds to make patterns, such as *Noise burst*, *sonorant*, *long noise*, *silence*, *sonorant*, *sonorant*.

NOISE BURST

The sounds ordinarily associated with the alphabet letters
b, d, g, p, t, k

SILENCE

Same as above: a brief silence precedes the noise burst; or simply use a silent segment.

LONG NOISE

Any fricative will do here. The intense fricatives are those ordinarily associated with the alphabet letters *s*, *z*, *sh*. Less intense fricatives are those typically represented by the letters *th*, *f*, and *v*.

SONORANT

Sonorants have a pronounced resonant quality, meaning that they are typically voiced and are made with a relatively open vocal tract. They include the vowels, the nasal consonants, the glides, and the liquids. As we have seen, vowels have a well-defined formant pattern which is the acoustic product of the vocal tract resonances. Vowels vary in duration, with some vowels being long and others short. Compare the following pairs of words and try to determine which member of each pair contains the longer vowel: *peek*-pick, *cooed*-could, head-*had*, put-*pot* (the italicized word contains the longer vowel). By alternating long and short vowels, you can create a simple rhythm. A different kind of sonorant quality can be achieved with nasal consonants, which we associate with the alphabet letters *m*, *n*, and *ng*. These sounds are weaker overall than vowels, but they have a strong, low-frequency resonance (the nasal formant). Thus, alternating vowels with nasal consonants will produce an intensity envelope that waxes and wanes. Glides, which typically occur as the alphabet letters *w* and *y*, are similar to vowels except that they possess gradually changing formant patterns rather than steady-state formant patterns. The liquids are the sounds we think of for the alphabet letters *r* and *l*. They are similar to glides in having a more rapid rate of change. Thus, the sequence *la la la* will have a faster rate of acoustic change than the sequence *ya ya ya*.

Some sounds are complex 't they are formed of more than one acoustic segment. As discussed in this chapter, stops like *b* or *d*, when produced in syllable-initial position, usually have both a noise burst and a rapid formant transition into the following vowel. Sounds called affricates also are acoustically complex as they contain both a silent segment and a noise segment. Listen for these two segments as you say the final sounds in the words *rich* and *ridge*. Affricates differ from fricatives in that they tend to have a more abrupt onset of the noise and a somewhat shorter noise duration. Can you hear these differences as you alternately say *shoe-chew*? Thus, you could use the fricatives when you want an easy-onset noise segment in your composition, and the affricates when you want a more abrupt and shorter noise. Compare *sha sha sha* with *cha cha cha*.

You are now ready to produce your own composition. For example, you might compose a sequence of noises that vary in their pitch, duration, intensity, and onset: s–f–sh–th–ch–ch–sh. Or you might create a melodious pattern of vowels, glides, and liquids. Finally, you might try to listen to samples of different languages and characterize them in terms of their acoustic sequences. For example, why is German often described as guttural and harsh, whereas French is described as romantic and smooth? Or why does the English word *skunk* sound rough and sharp whereas the word *Alabama* sounds relatively smooth and rhythmic?

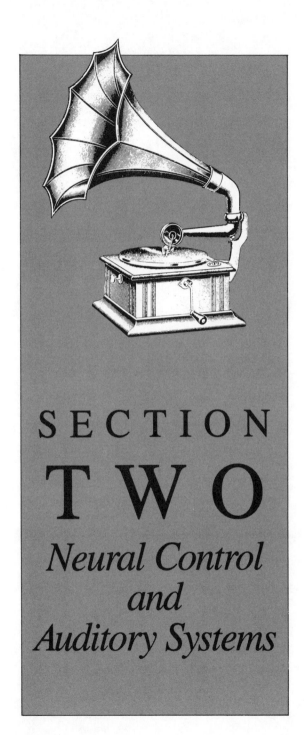

S E C T I O N
T W O
Neural Control and Auditory Systems

CHAPTER NINE
Hearing Anatomy

Considering its puny size, the ear is a prodigious instrument. With equipment that could almost be packaged in a sugar cube, we can distinguish all of the sounds of speech, along with nearly a half million other sounds. We can locate the direction from which they come, even to the extent of listening in on juicy gossip we are not supposed to hear at a noisy cocktail party. We can detect a sound so weak that it moves the ear drum only one tenth the diameter of a molecule. And fortunately for rock concert lovers, we can withstand sounds that are ten trillion times stronger — but not for long if you value your ears. How can so much be accomplished with so little?

Man's auditory equipment has been inherited from our aquatic ancestors. Its human form reflects its evolutionary lineage. In ancient form, it began as a fluid-filled balance organ. That form still exists. It is the *inner ear* that now contains sensitive detectors not only of balance but also of sound. Not until amphibians moved from oceans to land as their major habitat did acute hearing develop. Because pressure waves which reached the fluid-filled inner ear were now transmitted by air rather than water, an *impedance mismatch* had to be resolved. This mismatch results from the fact that compressible air can barely move incompres-

OUTLINE

ANATOMY OF THE EAR
Outer Ear: Acoustic System
Middle Ear: Mechanical System
  Eustachian Tube
  Ear Drum
  Auditory Ossicles
  Amplifying Sound
  Ear Protection
Inner Ear: Hydraulic System
  Cochlea
Inner Ear: Neural System
  Basilar Membrane
  Organ of Corti
  Hair-Cell Supports
Hair Cells

SELF-STUDY
Review Glossary
Self-Study Coloring Instructions
Self-Study Test of Terminology
Speech Reception Function of the Ear

sible fluid. Air vibrations had to be amplified. This need was met by evolution of the *middle ear*, which provides amplification in the form of mechanical linkage. Finally, sound gathering equipment evolved as the *outer ear*. At least in the case of humans, it serves to amplify those sounds they need to hear best, the sounds of speech.

What has evolved as the human ear is an energy transformation system. Sound waves reach the outer ear as acoustic energy. They are transformed at the ear drum into mechanical energy for amplification to overcome the impedance mismatch, and for transmission across the middle ear cavity to the fluid-filled inner ear. There they are again transformed, this time to hydraulic energy. Hydraulic waves then activate neural sensory equipment. With this transformation into bioelectric energy, the auditory signal is ready for transmission and processing in the auditory system of the brain.

ANATOMY OF THE EAR

We will undertake our exploration of the structure of the ear in the same order that it transforms environmental sounds into neural signals: the outer ear through the middle ear to the inner ear (Fig. 9–1).

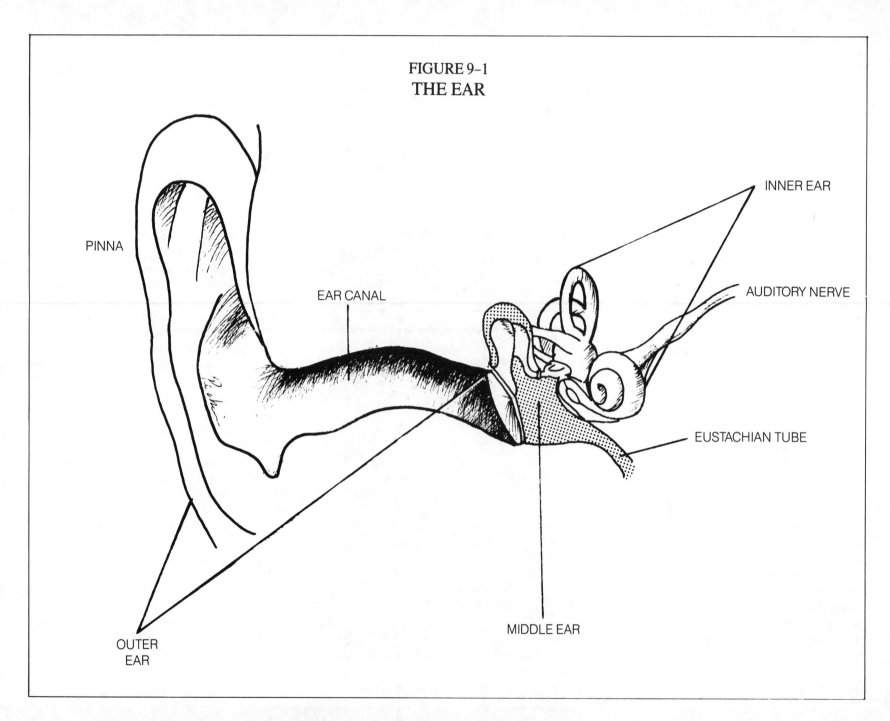

FIGURE 9–1
THE EAR

INNER EAR

AUDITORY NERVE

PINNA

EAR CANAL

EUSTACHIAN TUBE

MIDDLE EAR

OUTER
EAR

Outer Ear: Acoustic System

The *outer ear* consists of two parts. The visible sound-gathering part, which includes the lobe we tug on in contemplative thought, has either of two names: *auricle* or *pinna*. If you are given to saber duels and lose your auricles, do not despair; they may have had cosmetic value but they were of little use for hearing. The part of the outer ear that is important is the *ear canal*, which also has other names: *external auditory canal* and *external auditory meatus* (meaning opening).

The canal is important because it is the tube that conveys sound waves to the ear drum. It secretes *cerumen* (ear wax), which prevents the canal from drying out and discourages insects from feeling at home. It is also lined with *cilia* (small hairs) that filter out dust. Compulsive ear-cleaners deprive themselves of this natural protection. Of considerably more importance is the fact that this tube is about an inch long and has the *tympanic membrane* (the ear drum) stretched across the end, separating the external canal from the middle ear cavity.

Being air-filled, the canal functions as a closed tube resonator. This means that it will amplify waves near its resonant frequency, which will be waves four times its length (the reasons were discussed in Chapter 8). These resonant frequencies are in the neighborhood of 2,500 to 4,000 Hz, which, interestingly, are of particular importance in the perception of speech. At these frequencies, the sound pressure at the ear drum will be two to four times greater than the pressure at the entrance to the canal.

One other feature of the outer ears worth noting is that there are two of them. Why not just one? Auditory acuity would not suffer much, if at all. What would suffer considerably would be the ability to localize sound. That ability depends on having an ear on opposite sides of the head with which to detect differences in time of arrival of a sound in one ear in comparison with the other. Without this ability, detection of where a sound is coming from is impaired, especially in a noisy environment.

Middle Ear: Mechanical System

The *middle ear* is an air-filled cavity within the temporal bone, the hardest bone in the body. It has evolved as the primary solution to the impedance mismatch of having to generate waves of hydraulic pressure with waves of air pressure. The reason it is an air-filled cavity is because it is where acoustic energy of air pressure waves are converted to mechanical vibrations.

This conversion occurs at the tympanic membrane, which vibrates in response to the changes in air pressure that travel down the ear canal. For this tightly stretched membrane to vibrate properly, the air pressure inside the middle ear must be the same as the atmospheric pressure outside. On the other hand, if the acoustic pressure wave that travels down the ear canal also traveled into the middle ear, the two waves would cancel each other and the ear drum would not vibrate. What is required is a mechanism that closes the middle ear cavity to vibratory pressure changes, but that permits it to open and adjust to changes in atmospheric pressure.

Eustachian Tube

When your ears have popped during flying or mountain climbing, you have experienced the middle ear pressure-equalization mechanism in operation. A small channel, the *eustachian tube* (Figs. 9–1 and 9–2), runs from the middle ear to the nasopharynx. Normally, this tube is closed at its nasal entrance, which is fortunate as its closure prevents the direct transmission of breathing and speech sounds to the middle ear. It can be opened for pressure adjustments by a muscle involved in swallowing. This is why swallowing and yawning are useful methods of making the ears pop; both involve contraction of a velopharyngeal muscle.

A large number of children have repeated middle ear infections. If such infections are severe enough and occur frequently enough, they can damage the auditory apparatus and interfere with the child's language development and progress in school. One reason for the high frequency of occurrence of middle ear infections in young children is that the child's eustachian tube is short and nearly horizontal compared with that of the adult (Fig. 9–2). This orientation of the eustachian tube makes it quite easy for infections from the sinuses, throat, or upper respiratory tract to spread to the middle ear by way of the eustachian tube. The spread of infection is assisted by the enlarged adenoids and other lymphoid tissues typical in young children. The lymphoid tissues swell even more during infection, and this additional swelling can block completely the opening of the eustachian tube into the middle ear. The blockage prevents drainage of the fluids from the middle ear and worsens the infection. Chronic, or repeated, middle ear infections are the major cause of hearing loss in children.

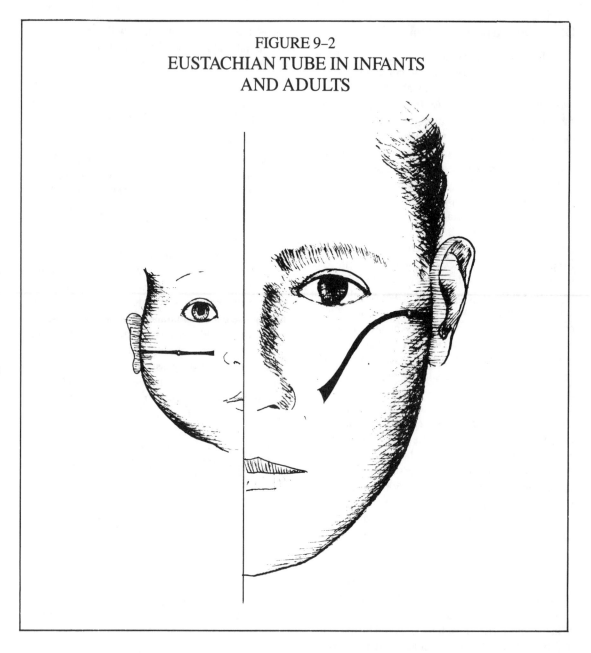

FIGURE 9–2
EUSTACHIAN TUBE IN INFANTS
AND ADULTS

Ear Drum

The ear drum (the tympanic membrane) is a thin, tough fibrous membrane that attaches to the bony wall of the ear canal by a cartilaginous ring called the *annulus*. This membrane seals the canal from the middle ear cavity. It is cone-shaped, much like a tiny loudspeaker, so it is well suited to its task of responding to pressure waves with mechanical movements. Like the tympani (kettle drums) in an orchestra, tension of the tympanic membrane can be adjusted. At low frequencies, it vibrates as a whole, but at high frequencies, different portions of the membrane respond to different frequencies.

Auditory Ossicles

Bridging the gap across the middle ear, thereby connecting the outer ear to the inner ear, is a linkage of three tiny bones, the *auditory ossicles*, also called the *ossicular chain*. The *malleus* is shaped like a primitive club or mallet, the *incus* (the middle bone) vaguely resembles an anvil, and the *stapes* strongly resembles a stirrup (Fig. 9–3). They are often called the hammer, anvil, and stirrup. Together, they transmit ear drum vibrations to the fluid in the middle ear, and in the process, may increase pressure on the fluid slightly.

This amplification, such as it may be, is accomplished by a leverage arrangement, with the incus functioning as the fulcrum for the lever. The "handle" of the malleus attaches to a slope of the cone-shaped ear drum. Because the amplitude of vibration is greatest at the center of the cone, this maximum movement is transmitted to the handle. The head of the incus is attached firmly to the head of the malleus, so these two bones vibrate as a single unit around the fulcrum, much as a clothespin hanging loosely on a line swings back and forth. The incus also has a handle. It attaches to and pushes on the stapes. Because the handle of the incus is shorter than that of the malleus, it works as a lever by trading amplitude of vibratory movement of the malleus for vibratory force against the stapes. (The claw of a hammer for pulling nails uses the same principle. Whatever force is used to pull the handle a large distance is multiplied by the claw that pulls the nail a short distance.)

The auditory ossicles are suspended by ligaments in the middle ear. Fortunately, they are suspended in such a delicate balance that they abruptly cease to vibrate when sound vibrations cease. Were their suspension otherwise, so that they continued to vibrate after the sound ended, our ears would be filled with overlapping vibrations that would jumble our reception of the sounds we were trying to hear.

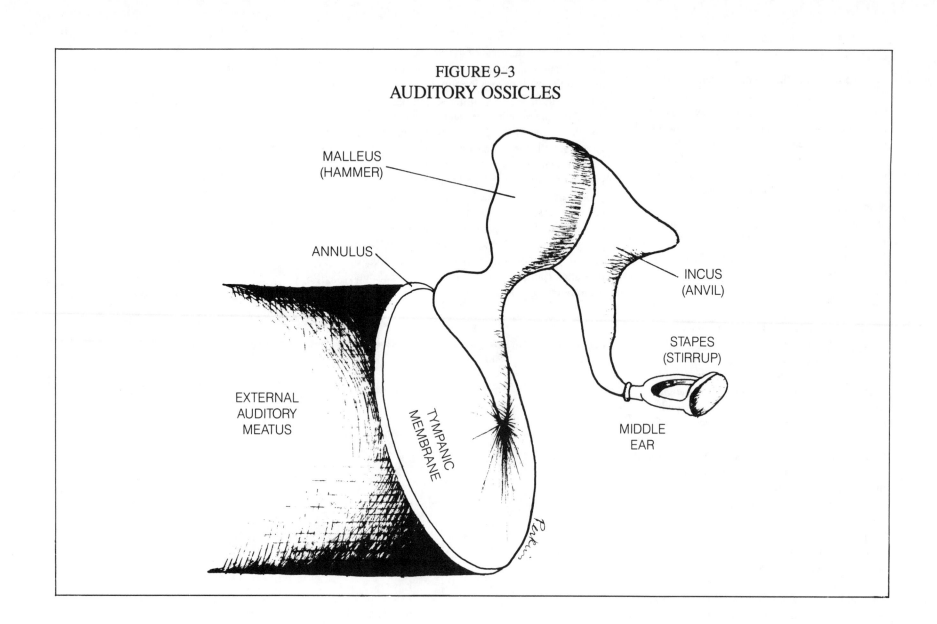

FIGURE 9–3
AUDITORY OSSICLES

MALLEUS
(HAMMER)

INCUS
(ANVIL)

ANNULUS

STAPES
(STIRRUP)

EXTERNAL
AUDITORY
MEATUS

TYMPANIC
MEMBRANE

MIDDLE
EAR

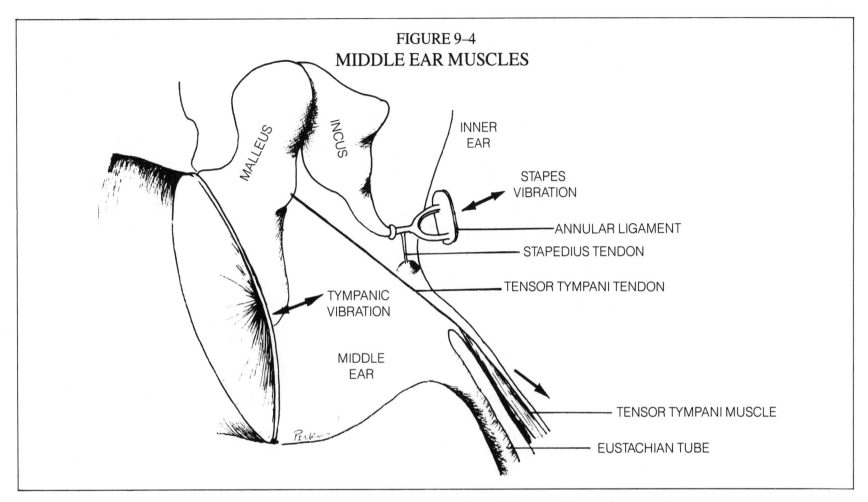

FIGURE 9–4
MIDDLE EAR MUSCLES

MALLEUS

INCUS

INNER EAR

STAPES VIBRATION

ANNULAR LIGAMENT

STAPEDIUS TENDON

TENSOR TYMPANI TENDON

TYMPANIC VIBRATION

MIDDLE EAR

TENSOR TYMPANI MUSCLE

EUSTACHIAN TUBE

Amplifying Sound

The biggest source of amplification of acoustic pressure comes from the difference in size of the ear drum and the stapes. The *footplate of the stapes* (the bottom part of the stirrup) fits into the *oval window* (a hole in the bone of the inner ear). It is attached to the oval window by the *annular ligament* (Fig. 9–4), which seals the fluids of the inner ear from the air of the middle ear. This flexible attachment permits the footplate to swing back and forth, thereby converting mechanical ear drum vibrations into hydraulic waves. Occasionally, the annular ligament ossifies, which is equivalent to the footplate developing a bony attachment to the oval window. When this happens, the footplate can no longer move. With the footplate fixed, vibrations cannot be conducted across the middle ear, so this type of hearing impairment is called a conductive loss. The vibrations are still transmitted through the bones of the head, however, which means that this loss is not complete. You can simulate it by plugging your ears and observing how much of the world about you can still be heard.

Because the area of the footplate is about 14 times smaller than the area of the ear drum, the "garden-party effect" operates. For the same reason that ladies' high heels sink into the watered lawn (their entire weight, dainty as they may be, is concentrated on two small spiked heels), all of the force of air pressure waves against the relatively large tympanic membrane is concentrated on the tiny footplate.

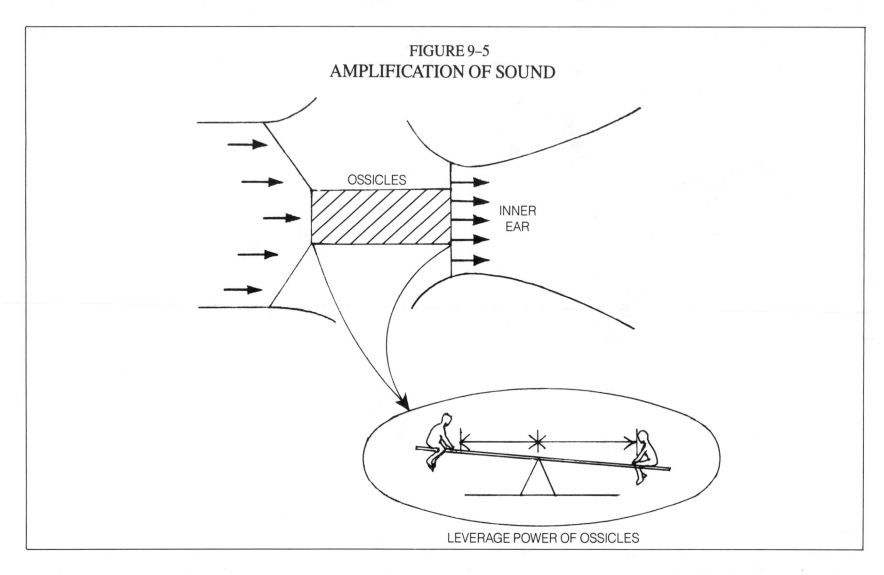

FIGURE 9–5
AMPLIFICATION OF SOUND

OSSICLES

INNER
EAR

LEVERAGE POWER OF OSSICLES

The impedance mismatch that must be overcome to transfer acoustic vibrations into hydraulic waves is, therefore, solved three ways. First, some important speech frequencies (2,500 to 4,000 Hz) are amplified two to four times by the resonance frequencies of the ear canal. Second, the leverage of the ossicular chain multiplies the tympanic vibration slightly, if at all (Fig. 9–5). Third, the larger ear drum area working against the smaller stirrup multiples the mechanical force 14 times. Thus, the pressure at the footplate of the stapes is probably a bit more than 14 times greater than at the tympanic membrane. But for the speech frequencies (2,500 to 4,000 Hz) that the ear canal resonates, the pressure at the entrance to the canal is multiplied two to four times before it reaches the ear drum, so by the time it reaches the stapes it is multiplied about 28 to 56 times (2 × 14 up to 4 × 14). Thanks to this amplification, we can hear sounds that are about 1,000 times weaker than we could otherwise hear.

Ear Protection

The middle ear contains the two smallest striated muscles in the body: the *tensor tympani* and the *stapedius*. Together their contraction is the basis of the *acoustic reflex*, presumably a reflex that has evolved to protect the delicate hearing equipment from damaging loud sounds, and possibly to tune the ear to respond selectively to high speech frequencies. It may also have a role in protecting us from our own voices when they are too loud. If you can "deafen" people by yelling in their ears with air-conducted sound, think of what you could do to your own ears with bone conduction added. The fact that neural innervation of the acoustic reflex is associated with laryngeal innervation, and that it is triggered by similar frequencies to those that have the most intensity in the voice, suggests that this reflex does indeed help to protect us from ourselves.

The manner in which this protection is provided pits these two auditory muscles against each other. They pull on opposite ends of the ossicular chain, thereby reducing its responsiveness, especially to low frequencies under 1,000 Hz. The *tensor tympani*, which does just what its name suggests, stiffens the ear drum. Only its tendon can be seen in the middle ear cavity. The muscle itself is contained in a bony canal that runs parallel to the eustachian tube. The tendon makes a sharp bend as it emerges from the bony socket to stretch across the middle ear and insert into the malleus. By pulling on this ossicle, the tympanic membrane is stretched tighter, making it more resistant to the large vibrations of loud sound.

The muscle of the *stapedius* is also contained in a bony tube. Only the tendon is visible as it emerges from the back wall of the middle ear cavity to insert into the head of the stapes (Fig. 9–4). The stapedius has two actions. One draws the stapes away from the oval window. In this respect it is antagonistic to the tensor tympani and acts to stiffen the ossicular chain against transmission of loud sounds. At extremely loud sounds, the other stapedial action occurs. It changes the axis around which the stapes vibrates. Up to moderately loud sounds, the footplate works much like a tiny bellows hinged at one end. Because the annular ligament is more rigid at the posterior end, the anterior end can swing through a relatively large arc as it vibrates against the fluid in the inner ear (Fig. 9–6).

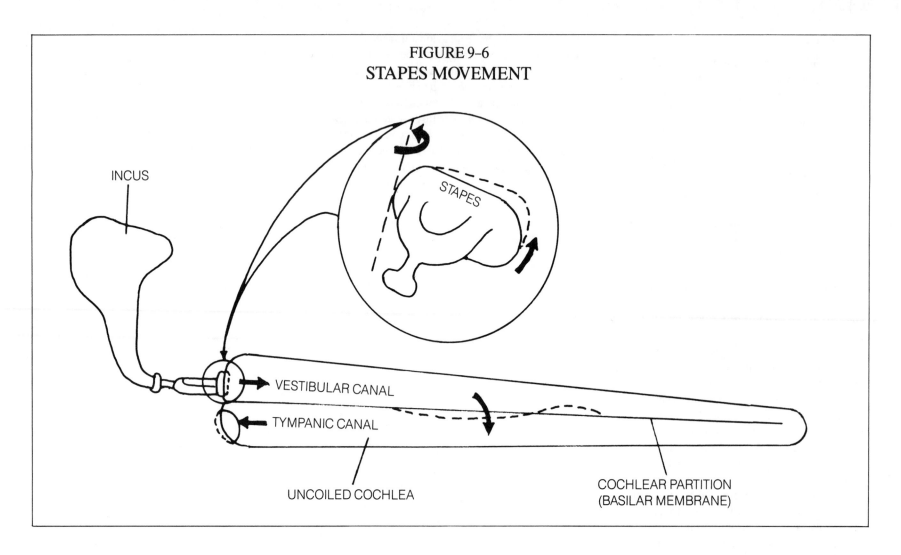

FIGURE 9–6
STAPES MOVEMENT

INCUS

STAPES

VESTIBULAR CANAL

TYMPANIC CANAL

UNCOILED COCHLEA

COCHLEAR PARTITION
(BASILAR MEMBRANE)

With high intensity sound, the axis shifts from the end of the footplate toward the midline. To appreciate the effect of this shift in axis, stretch your imagination. (This will be good exercise. It will soon be stretched again even more.) Imagine an aquarium with three doors. Two are hinged on the side like swinging doors (this is the arrangement in our bellows analogy). The other is hinged in the middle like a revolving door. Imagine fur-

ther that the doors have a flexible seal that permits them to swing in or out of the aquarium without its springing a leak. Now, if you push one of the swinging doors into the tank, the incompressible liquid will push the other swinging door out an equal amount. On the other hand, if you push on the revolving door, the distance you push in on one side will be equal to the distance the other side of the door moves out. Neither of the swinging doors

would move because all of the fluid compression on one side of the revolving door would be relieved on the other side. For the same reason, shifting the vibratory axis of the stapes toward the midline reduces the pressure applied to the fluid in the inner ear, thereby reducing, but not eliminating, the damaging effects of very loud sounds.

FIGURE 9–7
INNER EAR: BONY LABYRINTH

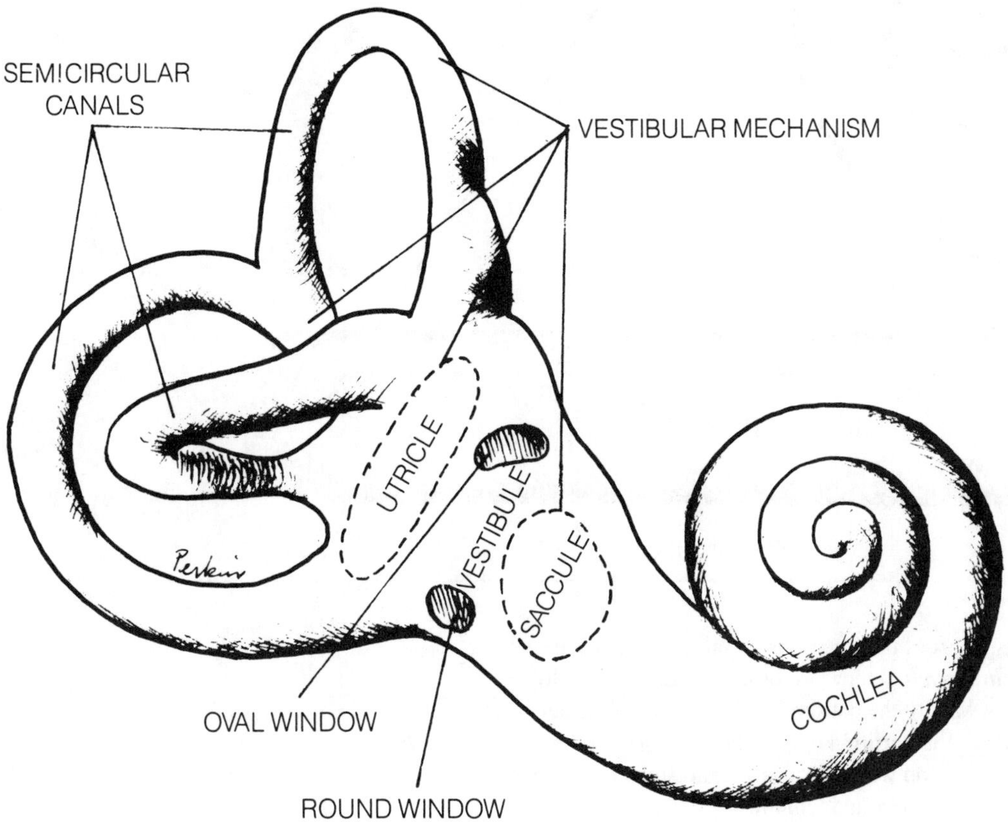

SEMICIRCULAR CANALS

VESTIBULAR MECHANISM

SEMICIRCULAR CANALS

UTRICLE

VESTIBULE

SACCULE

COCHLEA

Perkein

OVAL WINDOW

ROUND WINDOW

Inner Ear: Hydraulic System

In preparation for our trip through the inner ear, stretch your imagination again. Visualize a cavern with two exits close together. One is oval and is sealed with a movable door (the footplate of the stapes). The other is round and is sealed with a flexible membrane (the *round window*). Extending off to one side is a passageway that spirals upward for 2½ turns before it ends (this is the *cochlea*, the organ of hearing, which, if uncoiled, would measure about 1½ inches in length). Off in the other direction is a narrow passage leading into a small room (the *saccule*, and continuing into another small room (the *utricle*). From this room extend three semicircular tunnels (*the semicircular canals*), one going up, one going out, and one going sideways. In the inner ear, this cavern that we have casually inspected from one end to the other has bony walls, hence its name: the *bony labyrinth* (Fig. 9–7).

The end of the cavern we have just reached (the *vestibular mechanism*) is the organ with which we maintain balance and detect bodily movement. Because it has little relevance to our interest in hearing, we will return to the central room of the cavern, the *vestibule*.

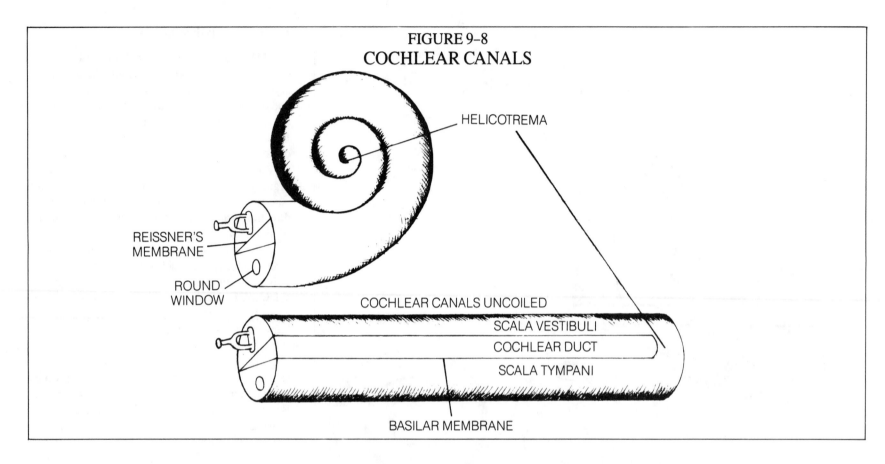

FIGURE 9–8
COCHLEAR CANALS

HELICOTREMA

REISSNER'S
MEMBRANE

ROUND
WINDOW

COCHLEAR CANALS UNCOILED

SCALA VESTIBULI

COCHLEAR DUCT

SCALA TYMPANI

BASILAR MEMBRANE

Cochlea

Imagine now that you have stretched a plastic sheet from the floor to the roof of the vestibule, so that the round window is sealed off from the vestibule, but the oval window opens into it. Further, imagine that this sheet stretches almost, but not quite, the entire length of the spiral passageway. What this would give you would be two channels separated by the plastic partition (the *cochlear partition*). Beginning in the vestibule, you would be able to walk up the spiral ramp on one side of the partition (the *scala vestibuli*). After 2½ turns, near the top of the ramp, the partition would end

just short of the top of the spiral, leaving space (the *helicotrema* to move to the other side. You could now walk to the bottom of the spiral on the other side of the partition (the *scala tympani*). At the bottom, you would dead-end against the membrane that seals the round window.

This is an imaginary exercise, so assume that you have attached a much tougher sheet of plastic to the existing partition at the floor, but at the roof the new sheet has been spread out over the tympanic canal to form a sealed tube (the *cochlear duct*) between the two passageways. The thin original partition is *Reissner's membrane*; the new, tougher one is the *basilar membrane* (Fig. 9–8).

FIGURE 9–9
MEMBRANOUS LABYRINTH

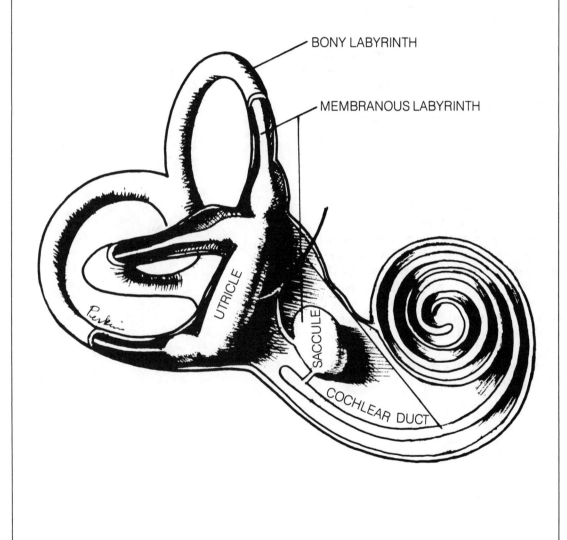

BONY LABYRINTH

MEMBRANOUS LABYRINTH

UTRICLE

SACCULE

COCHLEAR DUCT

Assume, too, that you have extended this tube the length of the spiral passageway from the helicotrema to the vestibule. There, you have connected it to another tube that you have extended into the saccule and utricle, and through all of the semicircular canals. With this vestibular extension added on to the cochlear duct, the entire tube that runs the length of the bony labyrinth is called the *membranous labyrinth* (Fig. 9–9).

What remains to complete the anatomy of the hydraulic part of the ear is to fill the membranous labyrinth with a fluid called *endolymph*, which is quite viscous, almost like jelly. Remember that the membranous labyrinth is the sealed tube extending from one end of the inner ear to the other, so this means that the cochlear duct is also filled with endolymph. This leaves the bony labyrinth, which is filled with *perilymph*. Perilymph is about twice as viscous as water. Reminiscent of its ancestral origins, it resembles ocean water in its various properties. Perilymph has the same properties as cerebrospinal fluid, which fills certain spaces within and around the brain and spinal cord. Apparently, perilymph is cerebrospinal fluid that reaches the inner ear by a tiny passage called the cochlear aqueduct. The cochlea is so tiny that only a fraction of a drop of perilymph is needed to fill the labyrinth.

As the footplate of the stapes pushes in and out against the perilymph in the vestibule, the mechanically transmitted vibrations are transformed into hydraulic waves. Because fluid is incompressible, the footplate would not generate hydraulic waves at all were it not for the round window, which is the sole exit for pressure applied at the oval window. It is the neural equipment for responding to these waves that is our next topic.

Inner Ear: Neural System

Mounted on the basilar membrane for its entire length is the *organ of Corti*, the neural equipment for converting hydraulic energy into bioelectric energy. The organ of Corti is immersed in the endolymph that fills the cochlear duct. Above it is Reissner's membrane separating the sealed duct from the perilymph-filled vestibular canal. Below the basilar membrane is the perilymph-filled tympanic canal, which terminates at the round window.

Basilar Membrane

The basilar membrane is especially important to the functioning of the neural equipment of hearing. This membrane is stretched between the outer wall of the bony labyrinth and the bony core, the *modiolus*, around which the cochlear channels spiral for $2^1/_2$ turns (Fig. 9–10). (It is through this core that the neural fibers from the organ of Corti are gathered together to form the auditory nerve.)

The basilar membrane is attached to the outer wall by the *spiral ligament*. Along the inner wall, it attaches to a spiral bony shelf, the *spiral lamina*, that extends out from the modiolus like the threads of a screw. Near the end of the cochlear duct, closest to the vestibule with its oval window, this bony shelf extends far out toward the outer wall. Accordingly, the basilar membrane is very narrow at this basal end. The farther toward the apex of the cochlea the spiral lamina goes, the narrower it becomes. Thus, at the apical end, the basilar membrane must extend farther to reach the bony shelf, so it is widest near the helicotrema. It is also lax and massive at this end, whereas near the oval window it is 100 times stiffer.

Organ of Corti

Between 15,000 and 20,000 auditory nerve receptors are contained in the organ of Corti as it is coiled along the basilar membrane. These receptors, each with its own *hair cell*, are arranged in four rows: one row of *inner hair cells* and three rows of *outer hair cells*. The outer hair cells number about 12,000 and the inner hair cells about 3,000. Resting on the outer, but not the inner, rows of these *cilia* (the hairs of these cells) is a gelatinous mass, the *tectorial membrane*. It is a roof-like flap with a slim attachment to the *limbus*. The limbus is mounted on the spiral lamina and anchors the tectorial membrane to the modiolus.

Hair Cell Supports. Because any movement of the cilia generates a neural auditory signal, it is vital that the hair cells be firmly buttressed. Were the cilia to move accidentally rather than in response to vibration, our ears would generate signals without benefit of sounds. The inner row of hair cells is supported by the *border cells of Held*, the outer three rows by *cells of Claudius* and *cells of Hensen*. Between the inner and outer rows are the *pillars of Corti*, forming a triangular brace through which runs the *tunnel of Corti*. Alongside each row are rather rigid *phalangeal processes*, which are connected at their tops by the *reticular lamina* to the pillars of Corti and the support cells on both sides. The cilia project up through the reticular lamina and are held firmly in place by it.

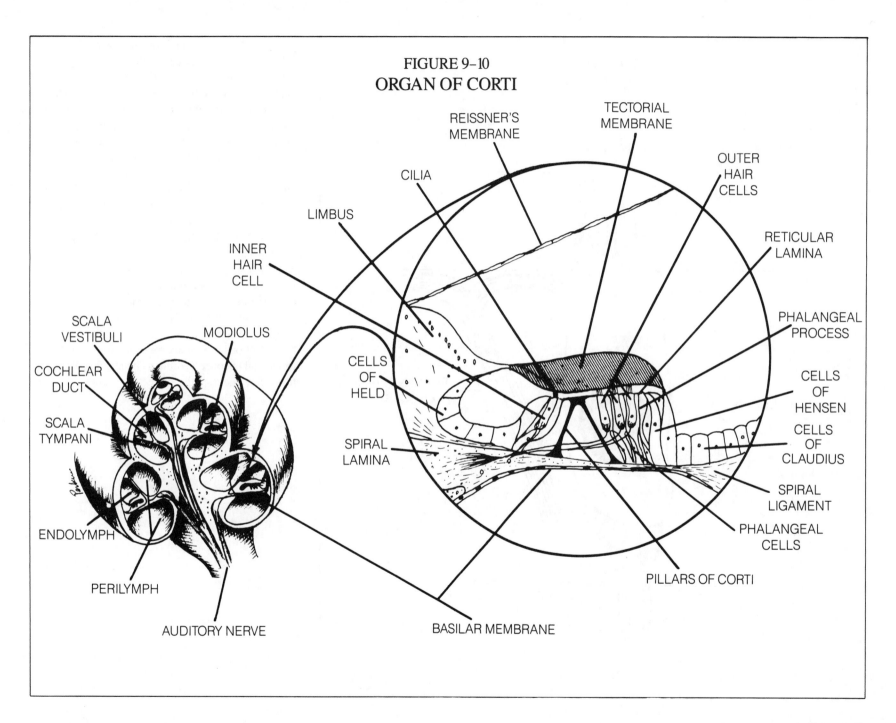

FIGURE 9–10
ORGAN OF CORTI

REISSNER'S MEMBRANE

TECTORIAL MEMBRANE

CILIA

OUTER HAIR CELLS

LIMBUS

RETICULAR LAMINA

INNER HAIR CELL

PHALANGEAL PROCESS

SCALA VESTIBULI

MODIOLUS

CELLS OF HELD

CELLS OF HENSEN

COCHLEAR DUCT

CELLS OF CLAUDIUS

SCALA TYMPANI

SPIRAL LAMINA

SPIRAL LIGAMENT

ENDOLYMPH

PHALANGEAL CELLS

PERILYMPH

PILLARS OF CORTI

AUDITORY NERVE

BASILAR MEMBRANE

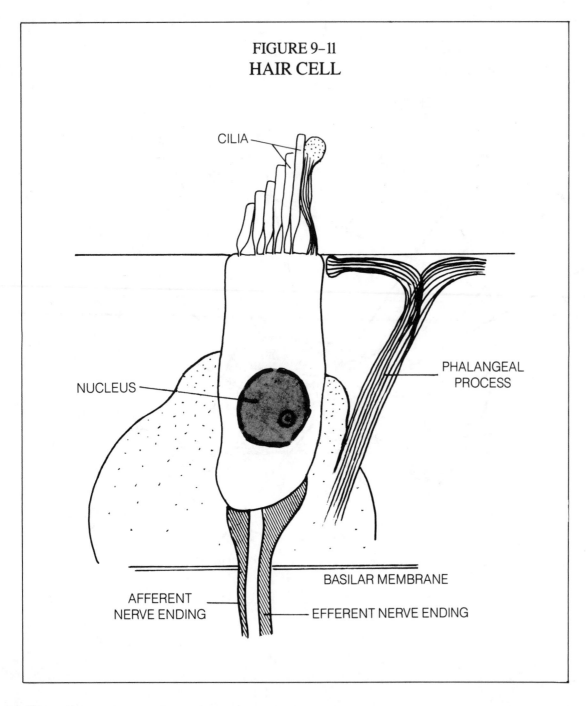

FIGURE 9–11
HAIR CELL

CILIA

NUCLEUS

PHALANGEAL
PROCESS

BASILAR MEMBRANE

AFFERENT
NERVE ENDING

EFFERENT NERVE ENDING

Hair Cells. The hair cells rest on phalangeal cells (it is from phalangeal cells that phalangeal processes extend upward). Each hair cell has a phalangeal cell, so there are an inner row and three outer rows of phalangeal cells. The outer cells are also called *Deiters' cells*. The nerve fibers end at the top of these phalangeal cells, so the hair cells are in contact with nerve ends, but do not contain them. This means that the cilia of the hair cells are not nerve ends. The movement of these cells, however, is what generates a neural response. Each inner hair cell has 30 to 60 cilia and each outer hair cell has 75 to 100. Thus, the organ of Corti may contain a million or more cilia attached to the hair cells. The cilia have a characteristic arrangement, much as is shown in Figure 9–11, which permits each hair cell to respond maximally to movement in only one direction. By having hair cells arranged to respond in different directions, the various directions of vibratory movement can be detected and encoded neurally. The physiology of these movements is the subject of Chapter 10.

CHAPTER NINE
Self-Study
Hearing Anatomy

Review Glossary

Outer ear: The portion of the ear that receives sound waves
  Auricle (pinna): The visible shell of the ear
  External auditory canal: The tube leading sound waves to the ear drum that resonates speech frequencies
    Cerumen: Wax in the ear canal
    Cilia: Dust-filtering fine hairs in the ear canal
Middle ear: The air-filled cavity in which air vibrations are transmitted and amplified mechanically to overcome impedance mismatch with inner ear fluid
  Tympanic membrane: The ear drum separating ear canal from middle ear that converts acoustic to mechanical vibrations
    Annulus: The cartilaginous ring attaching the tympanic membrane to the bony wall
  Auditory ossicles: The three-bone ossicular chain that transmits and amplifies mechanical vibrations across the middle ear
    Malleus (hammer): The bone attached to the ear drum
    Incus (anvil): The middle bone of the ossicular chain
    Stapes (stirrup): The bone that converts mechanical to hydraulic energy in the inner ear
      Oval window: The opening in the inner ear into which the stapes fits
      Footplate of the stapes: The portion of the stapes that fits into the oval window and presses against fluid in the inner ear
      Annular ligament: The attachment of the footplate of the stapes to the oval window
  Acoustic reflex: The muscular reflex that protects the inner ear against damaging loud sound
    Tensor tympani muscle: The muscle attached to the tympanic membrane that stiffens it
    Stapedius muscle: The muscle attached to the stapes that alters its vibration and stiffens the ossicular chain
  Eustachian tube: The canal from nasopharynx to middle ear that permits maintenance of atmospheric pressure in that cavity
Inner ear: The fluid-filled bony labyrinth containing sound, balance, and movement detectors
  Vestibular mechanism: The equilibrium and acceleration detection mechanism
    Semicircular canals: The three fluid-filled canals by which turning movements of the head are detected
    Saccule: The membranous cavity in the vestibule that detects forward and sideways movements
    Utricle: The membranous cavity that opens into the semicircular canals and detects forward and sideways movements
  Vestibule: The central room into which the oval window opens that connects to both vestibular mechanism and auditory receptors
    Perilymph: The fluid filling the vestibule and all areas of the bony labyrinth of the inner ear connected to it
  Membranous labyrinth: The membranous tube, extending throughout the bony labyrinth that contains the sound, position, and movement detectors
    Endolymph: The fluid that fills the membranous labyrinth
  Cochlea: The spiral-shaped organ of hearing within the inner ear
    Scala vestibuli: The perilymph-filled canal extending from the vestibule to the apex of the cochlear spiral
    Scala tympani: The perilymph-filled canal extending from apex of the cochlea to the round window
    Helicotrema: The isthmus at the apex of the cochlea through which perilymph can flow from scala vestibuli to scala tympani
    Round window: A membrane-sealed opening in the inner ear that relieves pressure applied to incompressible fluid at the oval window by vibratory movement of stapes
    Cochlear duct: The portion of the membranous labyrinth, containing the auditory sensory receptors, that forms the partition between scala vestibuli and scala tympani
      Basilar membrane: The partition tuned to different frequencies along its length, on which the organ of Corti rests, that separates cochlear duct from scala tympani
      Reissner's membrane: The thin partition separating the cochlear duct from the scala vestibuli

Modiolus: The bony core of the cochlea through which the auditory nerve reaches the organ of Corti

Spiral lamina: The bony shelf that extends out from the modiolus, like threads of a screw, to which the basilar membrane attaches

Spiral ligament: The attachment of the basilar membrane to the outer wall of the cochlea

Organ of Corti: The auditory receptor, coiled along the length of the basilar membrane, that contains auditory nerve ends

Hair cells: The cells, arranged in four rows, with cilia extending up from the top which, when bent, generate an auditory neural signal

Tectorial membrane: The gelatinous rooflike flap resting on the cilia that bends them when sound waves deflect the basilar membrane

Limbus: The slim attachment of the tectorial membrane to the spiral lamina

Phalangeal cells: The cells, containing auditory nerve ends, on which hair cells rest

Hair cell supports: The cells of Held that buttress inner hair cells; the cells of Claudius and of Hansen that buttress outer rows of hair cells; the pillars of Corti that brace inner and outer rows; and the phalangeal processes that connect to the reticular lamina that holds the hair cells firmly in place

Self-Study Coloring Instructions

1. Fill in the terms for *B*, *H*, and *L* in Drawing 9–I.
2. Using different primary-colored felt-tip pens, color in *B*, *H*, *L*, and accompanying terms.
3. Fill in the remaining terms for *A* through *X*, in Drawings 9–I and 9–II, and *a* through *t* in Drawing 9–III.
4. Using different colored pencils for remaining terms, color in *A* through *X* and *a* through *t*, and accompanying terms. Use darker shades or tones of the colors in *B*, *H*, or *L* for structures within each of these areas.
5. Color terms in the Glossary with the same colors used for those terms on the drawings.
6. Check your answers in Appendix E.

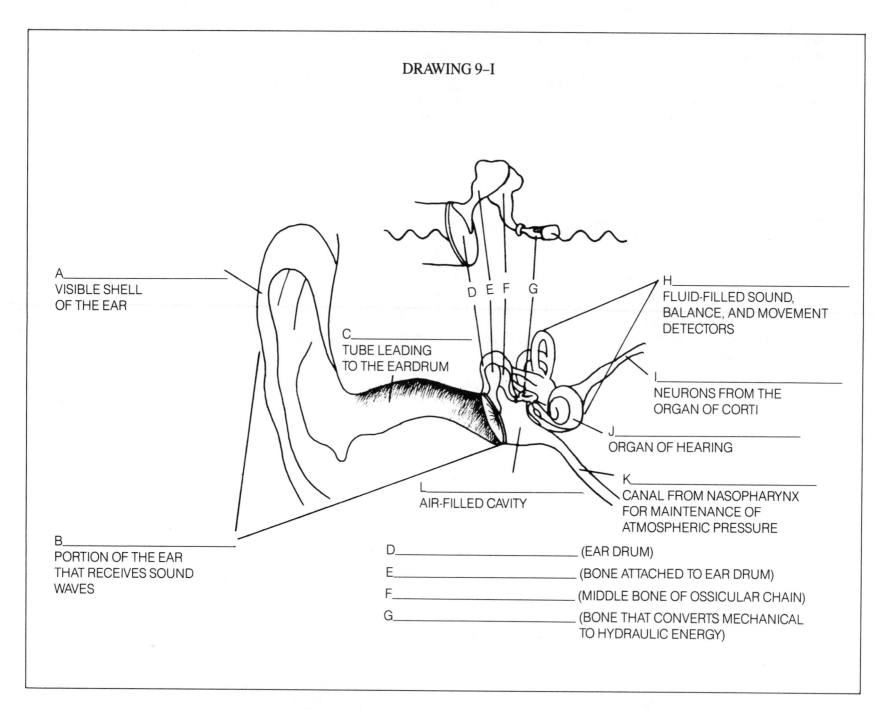

DRAWING 9–1

A_____
VISIBLE SHELL
OF THE EAR

C_____
TUBE LEADING
TO THE EARDRUM

D E F G

H_____
FLUID-FILLED SOUND,
BALANCE, AND MOVEMENT
DETECTORS

I_____
NEURONS FROM THE
ORGAN OF CORTI

J_____
ORGAN OF HEARING

L_____
AIR-FILLED CAVITY

K_____
CANAL FROM NASOPHARYNX
FOR MAINTENANCE OF
ATMOSPHERIC PRESSURE

B_____
PORTION OF THE EAR
THAT RECEIVES SOUND
WAVES

D_____ (EAR DRUM)

E_____ (BONE ATTACHED TO EAR DRUM)

F_____ (MIDDLE BONE OF OSSICULAR CHAIN)

G_____ (BONE THAT CONVERTS MECHANICAL
TO HYDRAULIC ENERGY)

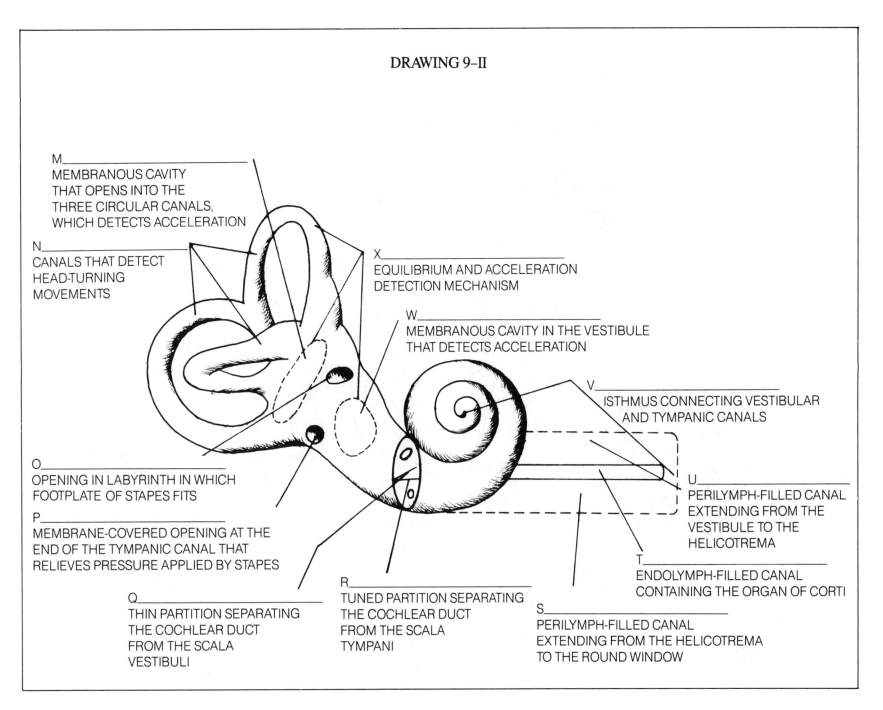

M_____
MEMBRANOUS CAVITY
THAT OPENS INTO THE
THREE CIRCULAR CANALS,
WHICH DETECTS ACCELERATION

N_____
CANALS THAT DETECT
HEAD-TURNING
MOVEMENTS

X_____
EQUILIBRIUM AND ACCELERATION
DETECTION MECHANISM

W_____
MEMBRANOUS CAVITY IN THE VESTIBULE
THAT DETECTS ACCELERATION

V_____
ISTHMUS CONNECTING VESTIBULAR
AND TYMPANIC CANALS

O_____
OPENING IN LABYRINTH IN WHICH
FOOTPLATE OF STAPES FITS

P_____
MEMBRANE-COVERED OPENING AT THE
END OF THE TYMPANIC CANAL THAT
RELIEVES PRESSURE APPLIED BY STAPES

U_____
PERILYMPH-FILLED CANAL
EXTENDING FROM THE
VESTIBULE TO THE
HELICOTREMA

T_____
ENDOLYMPH-FILLED CANAL
CONTAINING THE ORGAN OF CORTI

Q_____
THIN PARTITION SEPARATING
THE COCHLEAR DUCT
FROM THE SCALA
VESTIBULI

R_____
TUNED PARTITION SEPARATING
THE COCHLEAR DUCT
FROM THE SCALA
TYMPANI

S_____
PERILYMPH-FILLED CANAL
EXTENDING FROM THE HELICOTREMA
TO THE ROUND WINDOW

DRAWING 9–III

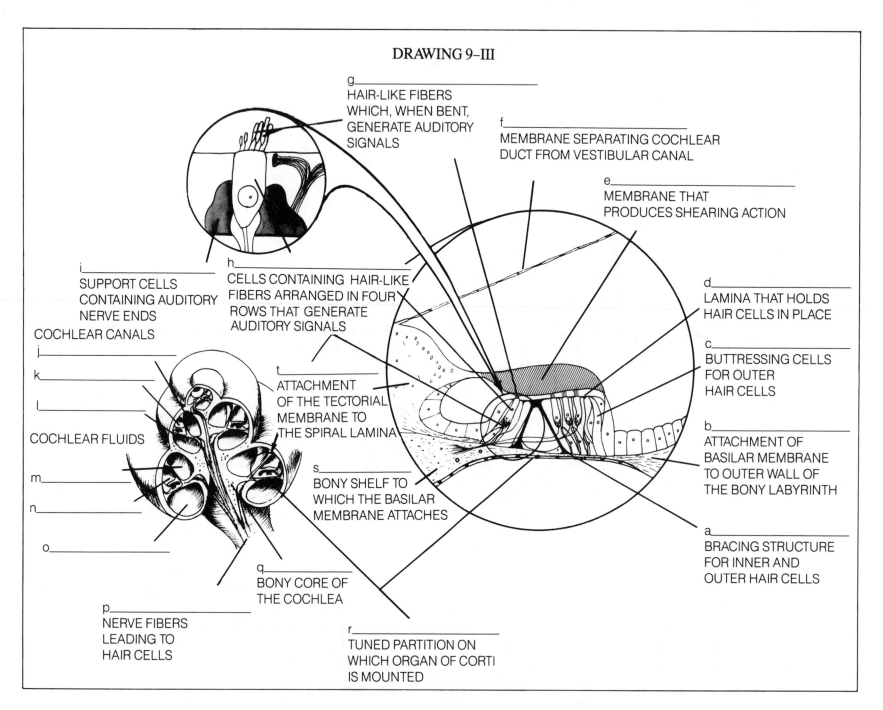

g_____
HAIR-LIKE FIBERS
WHICH, WHEN BENT,
GENERATE AUDITORY
SIGNALS

f_____
MEMBRANE SEPARATING COCHLEAR
DUCT FROM VESTIBULAR CANAL

e_____
MEMBRANE THAT
PRODUCES SHEARING ACTION

i_____
SUPPORT CELLS
CONTAINING AUDITORY
NERVE ENDS
COCHLEAR CANALS

h_____
CELLS CONTAINING HAIR-LIKE
FIBERS ARRANGED IN FOUR
ROWS THAT GENERATE
AUDITORY SIGNALS

d_____
LAMINA THAT HOLDS
HAIR CELLS IN PLACE

c_____
BUTTRESSING CELLS
FOR OUTER
HAIR CELLS

j_____

k_____

l_____

COCHLEAR FLUIDS

t_____
ATTACHMENT
OF THE TECTORIAL
MEMBRANE TO
THE SPIRAL LAMINA

b_____
ATTACHMENT OF
BASILAR MEMBRANE
TO OUTER WALL OF
THE BONY LABYRINTH

m_____

s_____
BONY SHELF TO
WHICH THE BASILAR
MEMBRANE ATTACHES

n_____

o_____

a_____
BRACING STRUCTURE
FOR INNER AND
OUTER HAIR CELLS

q_____
BONY CORE OF
THE COCHLEA

p_____
NERVE FIBERS
LEADING TO
HAIR CELLS

r_____
TUNED PARTITION ON
WHICH ORGAN OF CORTI
IS MOUNTED

Functional Anatomy of Speech, Language, and Hearing

Self-Study Test of Terminology

Self-Study Instructions: These questions can be used to help you assess how much you have retained from studying the Review Glossary. Answers are given in Appendix E.

(1) _____ The air-filled cavity in which air vibrations are transmitted and amplified mechanically to overcome impedance mismatch with inner ear fluid

(2) _____ The attachment of the footplate of the stapes to the oval window

(3) _____ The central room into which the oval window opens that connects to both vestibular mechanism and auditory receptors

(4) _____ The portion of the ear that receives sound waves

(5) _____ The membranous cavity in the vestibule that detects forward and sideways movements

(6) _____ The muscle attached to the stapes that alters its vibration and stiffens the ossicular chain

(7) _____ The membranous tube, extending throughout the bony labyrinth, that contains the sound, position, and movement detectors

(8) _____ The middle bone of the ossicular chain

(9) _____ The visible shell of the ear

(10) _____ The fluid-filled bony labyrinth containing sound, balance, and movement detectors

(11) _____ The spiral-shaped organ of hearing within the inner ear

(12) _____ The muscle attached to the tympanic membrane that stiffens it

(13) _____ The equilibrium and acceleration detection mechanism

(14) _____ The opening in the inner ear into which the stapes fits

(15) _____ Wax in the ear canal

(16) _____ The bone that converts mechanical to hydraulic energy in the inner ear

(17) _____ The cartilaginous ring attaching the tympanic membrane to the bony wall

(18) _____ The bone attached to the ear drum

(19) _____ The canal from nasopharynx to middle ear that permits maintenance of atmospheric pressure in that cavity

(20) _____ Dust-filtering fine hairs in the ear canal

(21) _____ The tube leading sound waves to the ear drum that resonates speech frequencies

(22) _____ The portion of the stapes that fits into the oval window and presses against fluid in the inner ear

(23) _____ The fluid filling the vestibule and all areas of the bony labyrinth of the inner ear connected to it

(24) _____ The membranous cavity that opens into the semicircular canals and detects forward and sideways movements

(25) _____ The three fluid-filled canals by which turning movements of the head are detected

(26) _____ The muscular reflex that protects the inner ear against damaging loud sound

(27) _____ The three-bone ossicular chain that transmits and amplifies mechanical vibrations across the middle ear

(28) _____ The ear drum, separating ear canal from middle ear, that converts acoustic to mechanical vibrations

(29) _____ The fluid that fills the membranous labyrinth

(30) _____ The perilymph-filled canal extending from apex of the cochlea to the round window

(31) _____ The portion of the membranous labyrinth containing the auditory sensory receptors that forms the partition between scala vestibuli and scala tympani

(32) _____ The perilymph-filled canal extending from the vestibule to the top of the cochlear spiral

(33) _____ The cells, arranged in four rows, with cilia extending up from the top which, when bent, generate an auditory neural signal

(34) _____ The cells of Held that buttress inner hair cells; the cells of Claudius and of Hansen that buttress outer rows of hair cells; the pillars of Corti that brace inner and outer rows, and the phalangeal processes that connect to the reticular lamina that holds the hair cells firmly in place

(35) _____ The bony core of the cochlea through which the auditory nerve reaches the organ of Corti

(36) _____ The slim attachment of the tectorial membrane to the spiral lamina

(37) _____ A membrane-sealed opening in the inner ear that relieves pressure applied to incompressible fluid at the oval window by vibratory movement of stapes

(38) _____ The auditory receptor, coiled along the length of the basilar membrane, that contains auditory nerve ends

(39) _____ The thin partition separating the cochlear duct from the scala vestibuli

(40) _____ The isthmus at the apex of the cochlea through which perilymph can flow from scala vestibuli to scala tympani

(41) _____ The gelatinous roof-like flap resting on the cilia that bends them when sound waves deflect the basilar membrane

(42) _____ The partition tuned to different frequencies along its length, on which the organ of Corti rests, that separates cochlear duct from scala tympani

(43) _____ The attachment of the basilar membrane to the outer wall of the cochlea

(44) _____ The cells, containing auditory nerve ends, on which hair cells rest

Speech Reception Function of the Ear

Self-Study Instructions: This test can be used to help you assess how well you understand the speech reception function of the ear. Terms to be filled in are from the Review Glossary. Answers are given in Appendix E.

Speech Reception Functions

Amplifies speech frequencies
    Acoustically
    Mechanically
    Hydraulically

Converts vibratory energy
    Acoustic to mechanical
    Mechanical to hydraulic
    Hydraulic to bioelectric (neural)
Analyzes vibratory frequencies
Neurally encodes vibratory information

Ear Anatomy

(1) _____

(2) _____

(3) _____

(4) Large _____

    acting on small _____

_____

(5) _____

(6) _____

(7) _____

(8) _____

(9) _____
(shearing force of tectorial membrance bending hair cell cilia)

CHAPTER TEN
Physiology of the Ear

AUDITORY PHYSIOLOGY

Georg von Békésy, who received the Nobel Prize for his ingenious research on hearing, marveled at the capabilities of the ear. He remarked that if the ear were just a bit more sensitive than it is, we would hear the random movements of molecules in the air. Fortunately we are spared such an incessant cacophony. Instead, we possess a sense organ that can respond to sound vibrations over a frequency range of about 16 to 20,000 Hz and over a range of intensities of about 1 to 10 trillion.

The outer and middle ear are supplements to our auditory equipment. The middle ear, particularly with its mechanical amplification apparatus, adds considerably to hearing; how else would we hear pins drop or soft, loving sounds? Without the middle or outer ear, however, we could still hear, albeit not as well. Little more need be said about how these aspects of hearing operate than was presented in Chapter 9.

What has only been hinted is how the hydrau-

lic and neural systems of the inner ear function. These are the processes that are fundamental to hearing. We will consider them in relation to how they send a coded version of the original sound to the brain. It is from this encoding of frequencies and intensities that the brain assembles our perceptions of the elements of sound (pitch, loudness, and quality) and through which we can detect who is on the phone when hardly more than a word has been spoken.

Hydraulic Processes

Both frequency and intensity characteristics arrive at the oval window of the inner ear as mechanical vibrations of the stapes that closely mirror the acoustic vibrations of the original sound. Within the cochlea, the hydraulic waves that result also correspond to these vibrations. This means that frequency is reflected in the number of waves of compression generated per second, and intensity is reflected in their amplitudes.

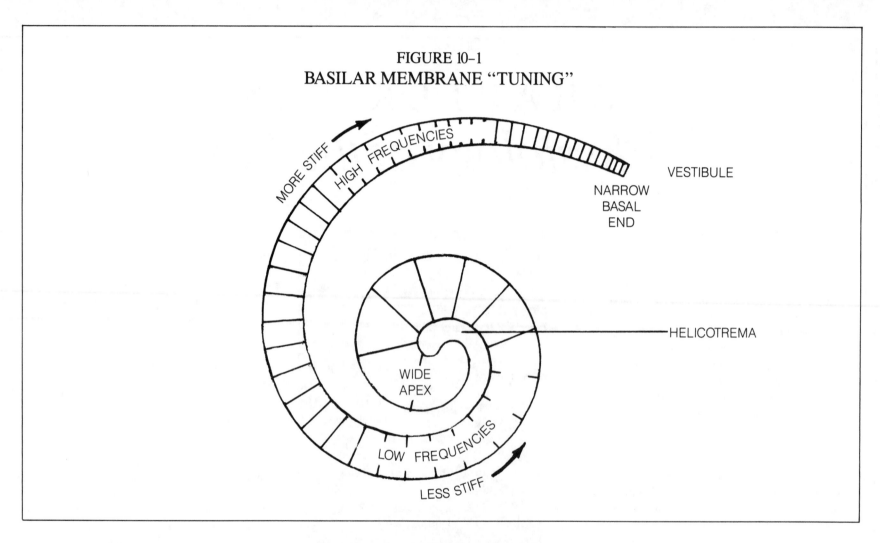

FIGURE 10-1
BASILAR MEMBRANE "TUNING"

MORE STIFF

HIGH FREQUENCIES

VESTIBULE

NARROW
BASAL
END

HELICOTREMA

WIDE
APEX

LOW FREQUENCIES

LESS STIFF

The question now is how the cochlea responds to waves. The answer has been sought for well over a century. Although not complete, the explanation that has gained acceptance earned von Békésy a Nobel award. The basilar membrane was long suspected of holding the key. It somewhat resembles a harp with its short, tense strings at one end and long, lax strings at the other. Although the basilar membrane does not have strings, it is none-theless short and stiff at the basal end near the oval window and wide and lax at the other end near the helicotrema (Fig. 10-1). Thus, it can be viewed as a "tuned" membrane that responds selectively to different frequencies — high frequencies at the narrow end near the oval window extending pro-gressively to low frequencies at the wide end near the apex.

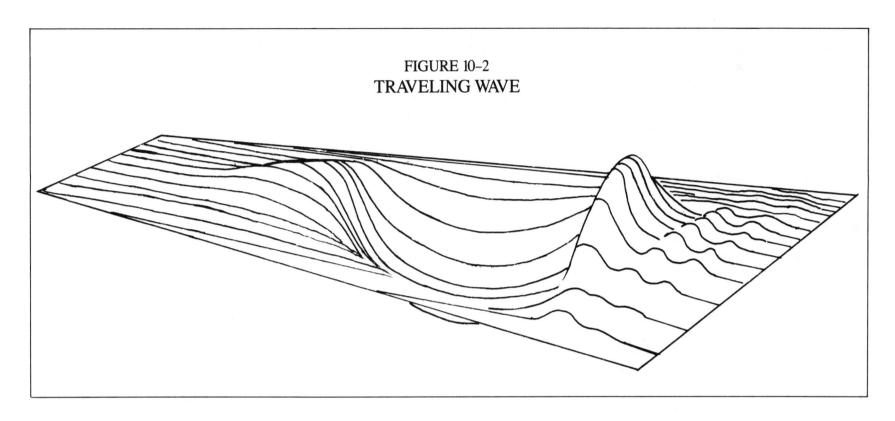

FIGURE 10–2
TRAVELING WAVE

Traveling Waves

von Békésy's discovery was that the vibration is transmitted along the basilar membrane as a *traveling wave*. Superficially, this appears to be the type of wave you would see if you cracked a whip or shook a bedsheet. Actually, it is quite different because, once generated, the hydraulic wave is not free to travel on its own. The fluid in the cochlea can, for the most part, only move in phase with movements of the stapes and round window. The timing of the wave is dictated by the stapes, the pattern largely by the basilar membrane. The wave builds to a peak and then ends abruptly. Its energy is largely spent at the crest, so once maximum displacement is reached, the wave decays rapidly. The place on the basilar membrane at which it crests is the place at which the membrane is tuned to a particular frequency. The extent of movement of the basilar membrane in response to hydraulic waves is a mere fraction of the movement of the ear drum. In fact, it is about the diameter of a hydrogen atom, so to illustrate it requires that it be portrayed as a grossly exaggerated movement.

Whereas a sound wave moves through air at a relatively constant velocity, this is not the case with a traveling wave. Its velocity diminishes; hence, its wavelength gets longer the farther the wave travels from the stapes (Fig. 10–2). This is why the distance between frequencies on the basilar membrane becomes longer the farther away from the stapes they are located, as you saw in Figure 10–1.

Frequency Analysis. For the sake of simplicity, assume that the sound generating the traveling wave is that of a tuning fork held near the ear. A tuning fork is used because it vibrates at a single frequency, the simplest of all vibrations. Through using tuning forks of different frequencies, the effects of different frequencies on traveling waves can be described more easily.

The air-conducted acoustic energy from the tuning fork will be delivered to the stapes, which will rock in and out against the perilymph in the vestibule; the more intense the sound, the greater the amplitude of movement. As it rocks in, the compression wave will move toward the only exit through which it can be equalized, the round window. (Without the round window, the incompressible cochlear fluid would make stapes vibration impossible.) Because the round window is located at the end of the tympanic canal on the opposite side of the cochlear partition from the oval window, the inward movement of the stapes will attempt to displace the cochlear partition, including the basilar membrane, into the tympanic canal (Fig. 10–3). When the rarefaction portion of the wave follows and the footplate is drawn away from the oval window, the vibratory movement reverses and the cochlear partition will tend to bulge into the vestibular canal. These are the movements with which all air-conducted vibrations begin. As far as responding to various frequencies is concerned, the difference is in what happens to the wave after it is generated.

The cochlea follows the line of least resistance in equalizing pressure differences. The cochlear partition offers resistance mainly by the mass and stiffness of the basilar membrane. Like pushing children in swings, the stapes pushes waves of pressure down the vestibular canal. If the children were in swings of different lengths, you would have to slow the timing of your pushes for long swings and speed it up for short ones. For the same rea-son, pressure from stapes pushes for low frequencies is shunted through the basilar membrane where the membrane is wide and thick (hence it is timed to slow pushes), and for high frequencies pressure is shunted through where the membrane is light and taut (hence it is timed to fast pushes).

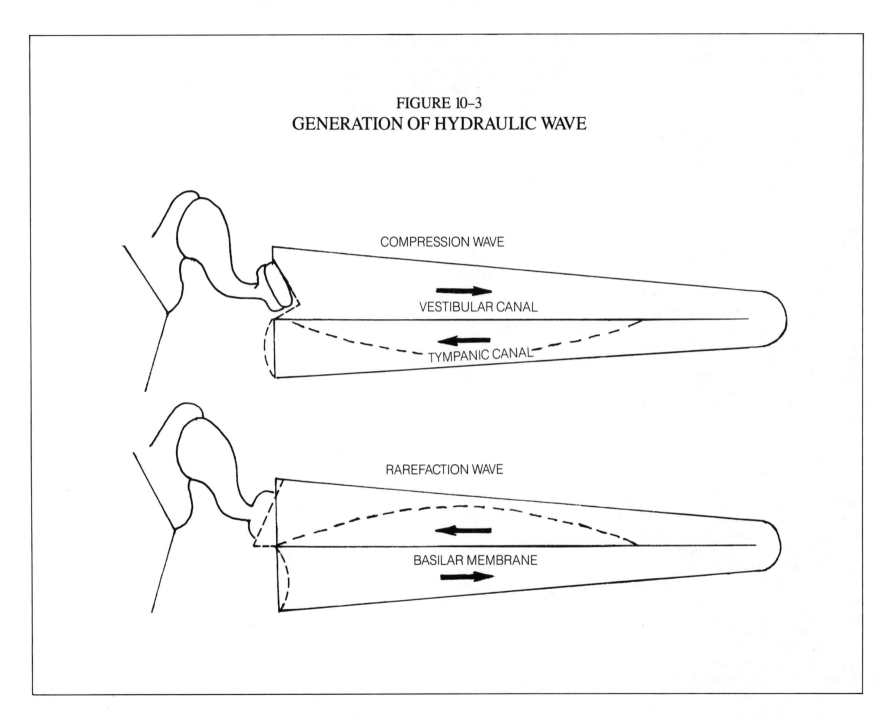

FIGURE 10–3
GENERATION OF HYDRAULIC WAVE

COMPRESSION WAVE

VESTIBULAR CANAL

TYMPANIC CANAL

RAREFACTION WAVE

BASILAR MEMBRANE

To illustrate, we will begin with a tuning fork that vibrates at a very low frequency, let us say 50 Hz. The displacement will travel to the far end of the basilar membrane near the apex before it peaks. This is the place at which the membrane will shunt the pressure through to the round window most efficiently. At low frequencies of up to 100 Hz, the whole membrane follows the in-out movements of the stapes with simple up-down movements. Below 25 Hz, the stapes pushes the perilymph so slowly that it encounters less resistance by flowing through the helicotrema, en route to the round window, than if the pressure of the pushes were shunted through the cochlear partition. Accordingly, the ear does not respond well to frequencies much below 50 Hz.

With a midfrequency tuning fork, say 1,000 Hz, the wave will grow to maximum amplitude about half-way along the basilar membrane (Fig. 10–4). The higher the frequency, the shorter the distance the wave travels. At the highest frequencies, the wave is as short as it can be; it crests as close to the basal end as is possible. Moreover, the higher the frequency, the more resistance the perilymph offers to being moved by the stapes. Therefore, at best, our hearing extends only to about 20,000 Hz.

Unlike tuning fork sounds, speech sounds are complex, as are most sounds in life. This means that they contain two or more (usually more) frequencies. Speech, for example, contains a number of formant frequencies, to say nothing of a multitude of other frequencies. Our ability to detect the pitch and quality of a sound depends on the ability of the ear to respond to these different frequencies at the same time.

We have seen the response to one frequency at a time. How does the basilar membrane respond to many frequencies at the same instant? The answer is by functioning as a frequency analyzer. Because the membrane is tuned to respond selectively to any frequency within the hearing range, crests in the traveling waves as one follows another can occur at any location along the membrane at any instant, much as rocks dropped one after another into still water produce complex, overlapping traveling wave patterns.

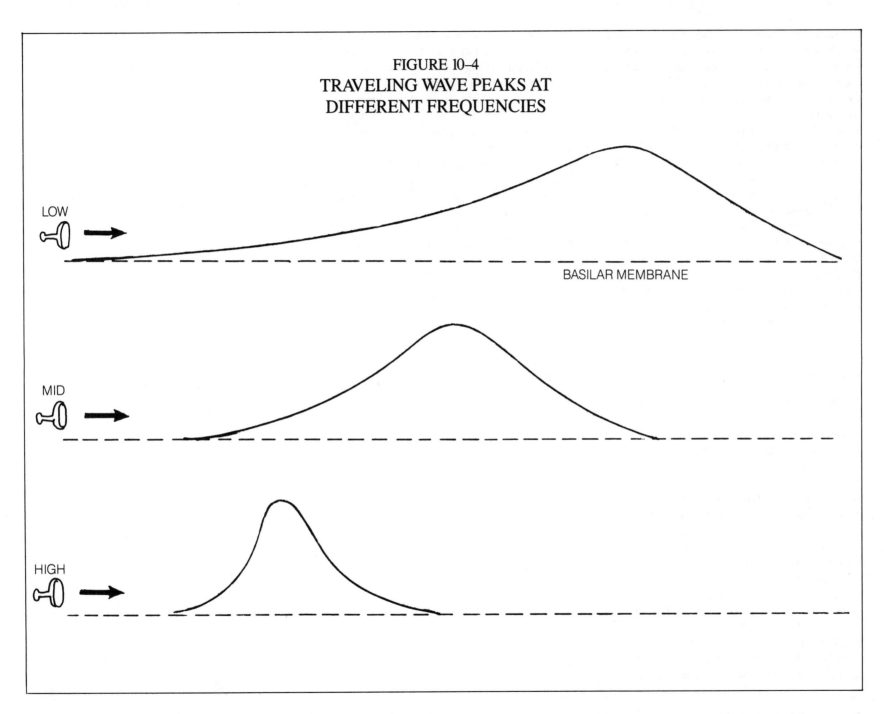

FIGURE 10–4
TRAVELING WAVE PEAKS AT
DIFFERENT FREQUENCIES

LOW

BASILAR MEMBRANE

MID

HIGH

Bone Conduction. The fact that the traveling wave begins at the oval window suggests that the reason for this location is because this is where the stapes applies the pressure. Not so. When sound is conducted to the inner ear by bone rather than by air and the stapes is immobilized, the hydraulic waves still begin at the basal end of the cochlea and travel toward its apex until they crest and decay. For bone conduction to be possible, an exit must be available with which to vent the pressure. Otherwise, no traveling wave could occur.

The reason the location of the source of pressure is immaterial is that compression of fluid in a solid container, such as the inner ear, is transmitted instantly and equally to all parts of the cavity. Because both exits — the round window and the oval window — are at the basal end of the cochlea, that is where the pressure if relieved. As a consequence, that is where the cochlear partition is displaced and the traveling wave initiated.

Neural Processes

What remains in this chapter is how the mechanical motion of the basilar membrane is encoded into neural auditory signals that the brain can interpret. This is accomplished in the organ of Corti mounted along the length of the basilar membrane. More to the point, it is accomplished by bending the cilia of the hair cells. The key to this bending action is in the manner of attachment of the basilar and tectorial membranes.

Recall from the last chapter that the basilar membrane is attached to the spiral ligament that coils upward along the outside wall of the cochlea. Along the inner core of the modiolus, the membrane attaches to the bony spiral lamina. This bony shelf is rigid, whereas the spiral ligament is flexible. Therefore, displacement of the membrane by a traveling wave will be greater along the outer wall than along the inner wall. This would appear to explain why the inner row of hair cells near the bony shelf has fewer than one fourth the number of hair cells than the outer three rows: The outer rows have more movement to which to respond.

Recall, too, that the tectorial membrane is a hinged flap of gelatinous tissue that rests on the outer rows of cilia. The point to note is that its attachment to the limbus is not directly above the attachment of the basilar membrane to the bony shelf. By virtue of the hinges of these two membranes being offset from each other, any displacement will drag the tectorial membrane across the top of the organ of Corti with a *shearing force* (Fig. 10–5). The result will be to bend the cilia.

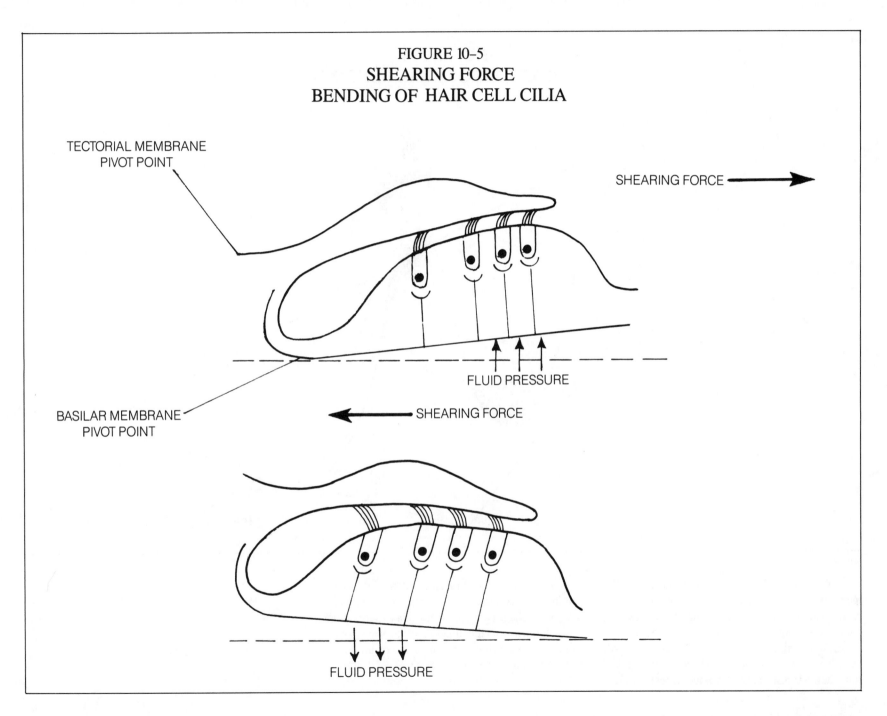

FIGURE 10–5
SHEARING FORCE
BENDING OF HAIR CELL CILIA

TECTORIAL MEMBRANE
PIVOT POINT

SHEARING FORCE

FLUID PRESSURE

BASILAR MEMBRANE
PIVOT POINT

SHEARING FORCE

FLUID PRESSURE

FIGURE 10-6
DIRECTIONS OF CILIA BENDING

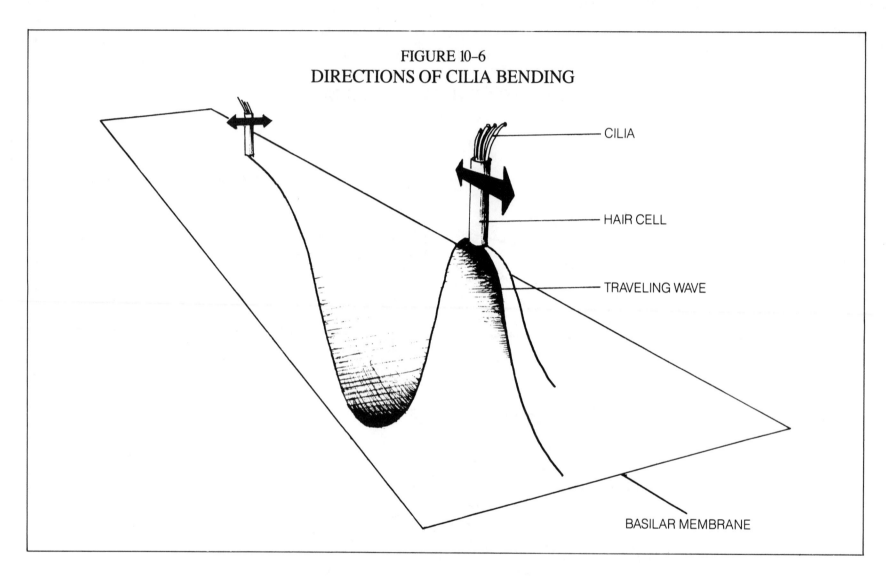

CILIA

HAIR CELL

TRAVELING WAVE

BASILAR MEMBRANE

If a traveling wave is sent up the cochlea, all parts of the cochlear partition will vibrate in phase with each other (at least up to high intensities). When the tectorial membrane is displaced downward, the basilar membrane will move downward. Similarly, these two membranes will move upward together. Even slight up-down movements of the cochlear partition will magnify lateral movements of the cilia, so sensitivity to sound is increased. Also, the shearing force operates in two directions: longitudinal from the direction of the wave, and radial from the lateral shearing. The result is complex bending of the cilia (Fig. 10-6).

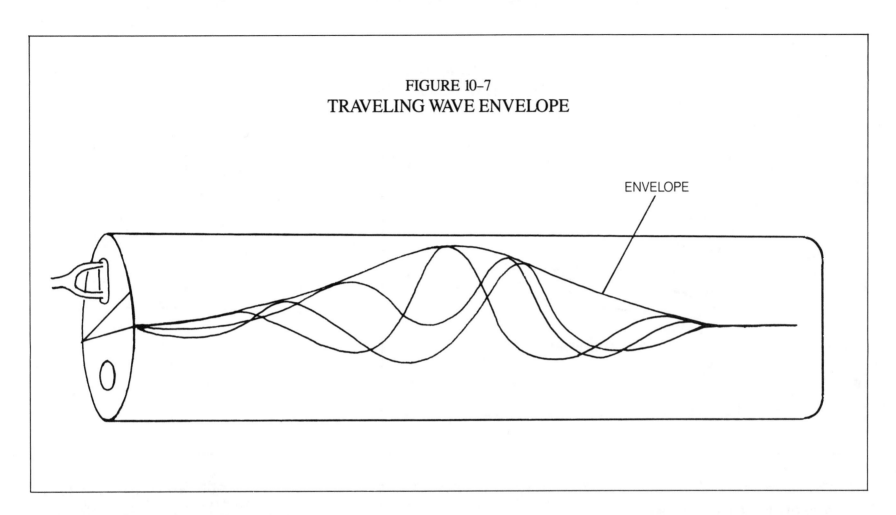

FIGURE 10–7
TRAVELING WAVE ENVELOPE

ENVELOPE

Another aspect of the complex motion is that the traveling wave is far more complex than the *wave envelope* reveals. That envelope merely summarizes the amplitudes of the vibration. In point of fact, the displacement pattern that is summarized in a wave envelope involves movements that barely resemble the envelope. As you can see in Figure 10–7, which shows a single 1,000 Hz wave at different stages of its crest, the movements have only one feature in common — they peak at about the same frequency.

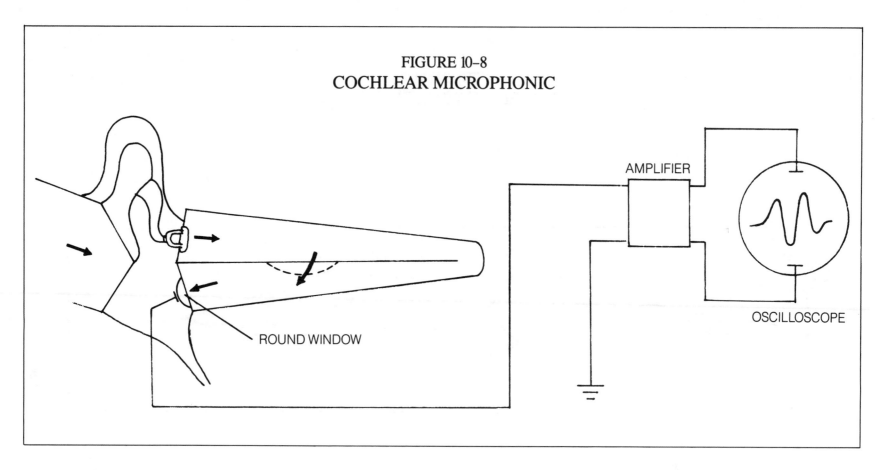

FIGURE 10–8
COCHLEAR MICROPHONIC

AMPLIFIER

OSCILLOSCOPE

ROUND WINDOW

Generating the Auditory Signal

Exactly how movement of cilia produces neural auditory signals has only recently been discovered. What had been known is that the base of the hair cell is in direct contact with the auditory nerve end. Also known was the fact that the outer hair cells are primarily responsive to lateral shear. The inner hair cells, which do not drag against the tectorial membrane, probably have a different function because they are activated by velocity of basilar membrane movement rather than by shearing force. What is now known is that the hair cell functions like a neuron. The base of the hair cell

makes synaptic contact with the auditory nerve ends. Even though the hair cell does not have an axon, as do neurons, it nonetheless generates a neural response when its cilia move as little as a trillionth of a meter. This neural response is transmitted across the synapse to the auditory nerve in a fashion to be described in Chapter 11.

Cochlear Microphonic. The best evidence that cilia movement generates the auditory signal is the *cochlear microphonic* (Fig. 10–8). This is the name given to the electrical activity in the auditory nerve that mirrors the waveform of the sound that produced it. This bioelectric response, which can

also be recorded inside and outside the cochlea, mirrors the sound so closely that when played through a loudspeaker, it is all but indistinguishable from the original sound. From such evidence, it seems probable that the cochlear microphonic results from the hair cells somehow stimulating the auditory nerve.

Auditory Pathways to the Brain

More than 30,000 nerve fibers from the organ of Corti join together to form the *auditory nerve*. They extend about an inch from the cochlea through the skull before they enter the brain. Once the auditory pathway from each ear reaches the brain, it is organized much like two parallel railway systems running between the same cities with each having its own passenger terminals. Neural traffic can transfer from one line to the other at several terminals. The auditory nerve feeds into the *cochlear nucleus*, the first terminal in the auditory pathway, much as a bus line brings passengers from the suburbs to a city's railway stations. The end of the line for the auditory nerve is the cochlear nucleus, so at this level, low in the brainstem, all neural auditory impulses "transfer" to the *ascending auditory pathway*. (The transfer point between one nerve cell and another is called a *synapse*.)

The ascending auditory pathway extends to the *auditory cortex*, one in each *temporal lobe* of the brain (the lobe inside the temple of the skull). Between the cochlear nucleus and the auditory cortex are three sets of terminals, one on each side of the brain stem (Fig. 10–9). The lowest and smallest set is the *superior olive*. Here auditory information from one ear can be matched with information from the other. The auditory pathway extending from the level of the cochlear nucleus, and also the superior olive, to the next highest terminal is called the *lateral lemniscus*. At this level, each of the two terminals is called an *inferior colliculus*. Here combined information from both ears provides a basis for the kind of quick reflexive response you make to a loud unexpected noise (the startle reflex). The last terminal in the brainstem, where all auditory impulses transfer to *auditory projection fibers* if they are to reach the auditory cortex, is the *medial geniculate body*.

This arrangement provides for the transfer of auditory neural impulses from one side of the brainstem to the other at three levels: cochlear nucleus, superior olive, and inferior colliculus. With right-left interconnections at these levels, an auditory signal can ascend all the way to the medial geniculate body and auditory cortex on the same side (*ipsilateral*), or cross over to the opposite side (*contralateral*) at the cochlear nucleus, superior olive, or inferior colliculus. Although the "main line" is a contralateral route from the ear on one side to the brain on the other, this can be a misleading impression of how the auditory system is "wired." In reality, inputs from both ears are well represented on both sides of the brain. This permits comparisons of information about frequency, intensity, and time of arrival of the acoustic signal at the two ears. Were it not for these comparisons, we would be seriously hampered in ability to detect direction of a sound and to focus attention in a noisy environment. Nevertheless, the "main line" contralateral auditory pathway does make it slightly easier to understand speech better with the right ear than with the left; the main line from the right ear is to the left temporal lobe, where the speech center is usually located.

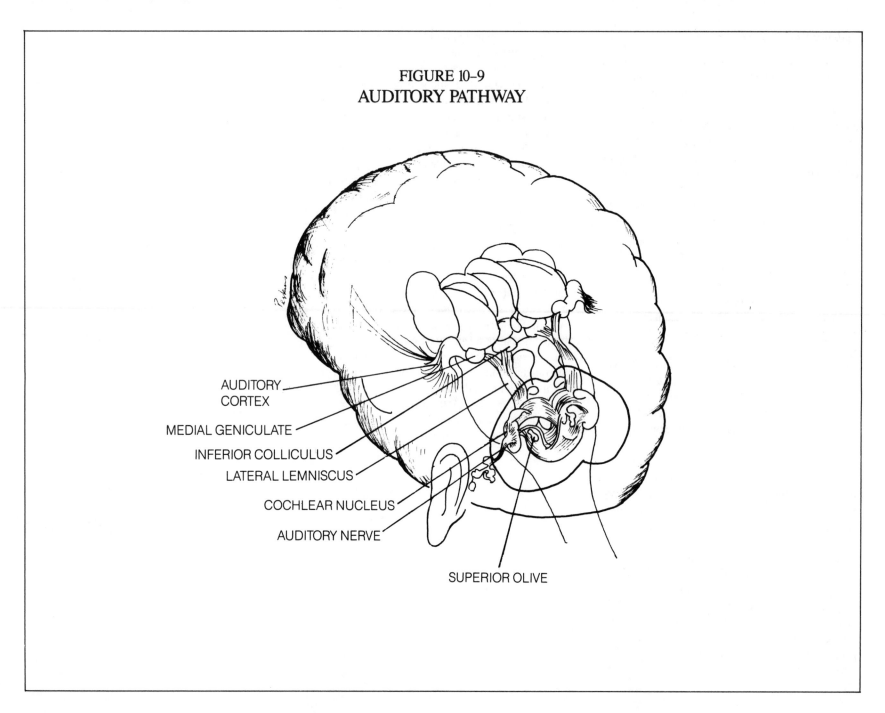

FIGURE 10-9
AUDITORY PATHWAY

AUDITORY CORTEX

MEDIAL GENICULATE

INFERIOR COLLICULUS

LATERAL LEMNISCUS

COCHLEAR NUCLEUS

AUDITORY NERVE

SUPERIOR OLIVE

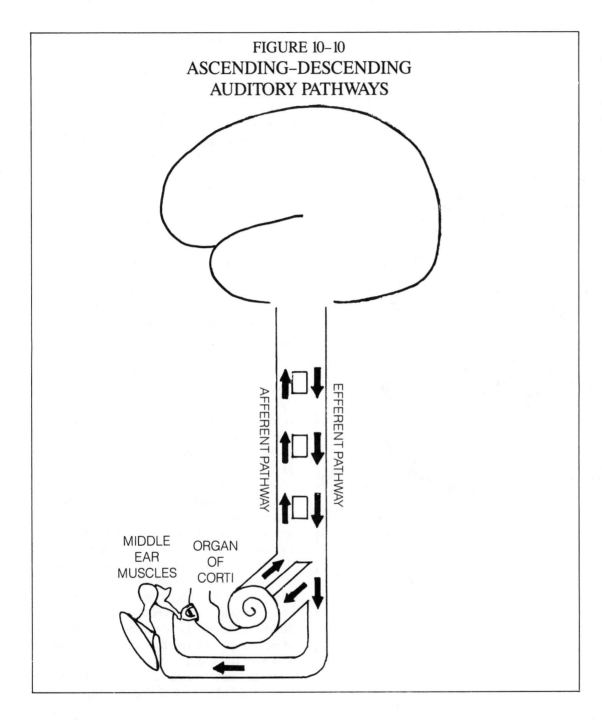

FIGURE 10–10
ASCENDING–DESCENDING
AUDITORY PATHWAYS

AFFERENT PATHWAY

EFFERENT PATHWAY

MIDDLE
EAR
MUSCLES

ORGAN
OF
CORTI

Descending Pathways. The auditory nerve is generally thought of as a sensory nerve. Certainly for its primary function, it is. About 98 percent of its fibers carry *afferent* information from the cochlea to the brain. About 500 nerve fibers, however, carry *efferent* neural impulses from the brain to the ear (Fig. 10–10). This information is used to control the operation of the ear. Some of it goes to the middle ear muscles, which help protect against dangerously loud sounds and tune the ossicular chain to respond to soft sounds. Much of this efferent information, though, goes to or near the hair cells of the cochlea. There the sensitivity of auditory sensory fibers is regulated, mainly by inhibiting their response. This auditory control can be directed from various levels ranging from the cortex to the cochlear nucleus. By means of this cochlear regulation, response to unimportant sounds can be inhibited. This helps to screen out irrelevant background noise and improve attention to important sounds.

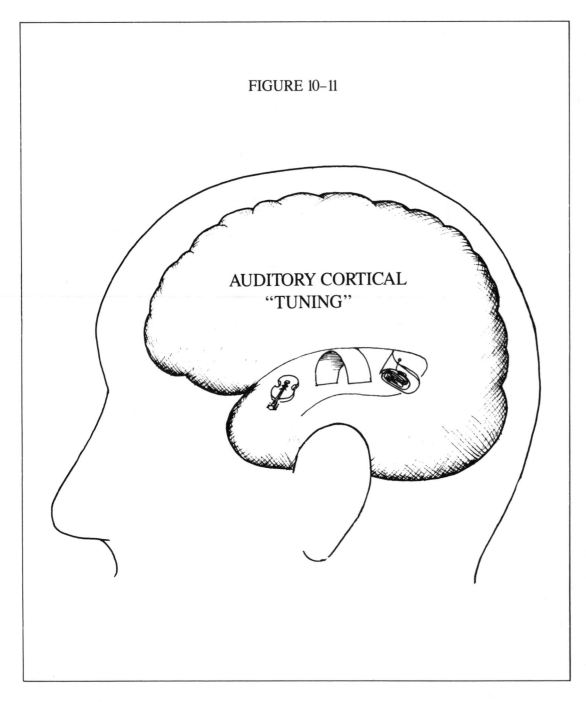

FIGURE 10–11

AUDITORY CORTICAL "TUNING"

Encoding Frequency and Intensity

Our ability to perceive pitch, loudness, and quality characteristics that differentiate all sounds ranging from a cannon's roar to a baby's whimper depends on decoding frequency and intensity. Information about the frequencies at which sound waves vibrate provides the major basis for perceiving pitch and quality. The other half of quality comes from intensity, which also provides the major basis for perception of loudness. All of our auditory experience, then, derives from neurally encoded information about frequency and intensity of the acoustic signal.

Frequency. The auditory system encodes frequency by *place of excitation* and by *frequency of excitation*. A basis for place-of-excitation encoding exists throughout the entire system. From tuning of the basilar membrane, to neural response in the organ of Corti, to auditory fiber arrangement at every level of the brain, frequency response is spatially organized. This is called *tonotopic organization*.

Each nerve cell at every level of the auditory system has best frequencies at which it will respond. In the organ of Corti, frequency selectivity is sharpened by inhibition of response of cells surrounding the place on the basilar membrane at which the traveling wave crests. In fact, cells are tuned so sharply that each one, whether in the organ of Corti or the auditory cortex, is described by a *tuning curve* that reveals the frequencies at which it responds best. But the tuning is much sharper at the lower neural levels than the higher ones; cells in the cortex are tuned to a relatively wide range of frequencies. Still, a rough point-for-point representation of the cochlea can be found in the auditory cortex: Low frequencies near the apex of the cochlea are arranged in the outside upper portion of the cortical auditory center; high frequencies from the base of the cochlea are on the inside of the temporal lobe (Fig. 10–11).

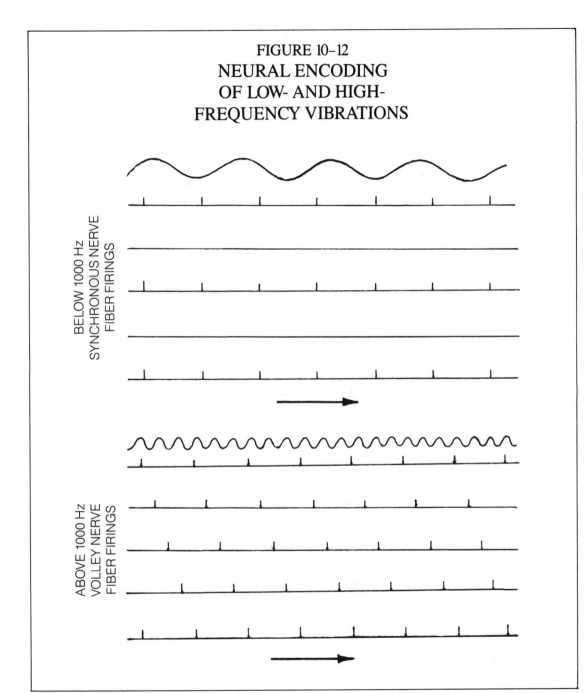

FIGURE 10–12
NEURAL ENCODING OF LOW- AND HIGH- FREQUENCY VIBRATIONS

BELOW 1000 Hz SYNCHRONOUS NERVE FIBER FIRINGS

ABOVE 1000 Hz VOLLEY NERVE FIBER FIRINGS

In addition to place of excitation, frequency of excitation — the rate at which auditory nerve fibers respond to sound — also provides a basis for encoding the frequencies in the signal. This basis for encoding is also more apparent at lower than higher levels of the auditory system. At the cochlear-nucleus level, for example, neural firing rate clearly reflects the frequency of vibration, but the medial-geniculate level rarely follows rates above a few hundred hertz.

Encoding by frequency of excitation is more straightforward below 1,000 Hz than above. Single nerve cells cannot fire much faster than this rate, but below it, individual fibers can fire in synchrony with each cycle of vibration (Fig. 10–12). Above 1,000 Hz, however, they apparently fire in volleys, hence this encoding explanation is called the *volley theory*. At higher frequencies, the cells are organized into groups. Groups may fire every other cycle, or every third or fourth cycle, depending on how high the frequency and how long they need to recover before they can fire again.

Intensity. A basis for encoding intensity is much more apparent in the cochlea than it is in the brain. In the cochlea, amplitude of the traveling wave increases as intensity of the sound increases. In addition, the cochlear microphonic, which is linked to neural response in the organ of Corti, grows in direct proportion to signal intensity. Seemingly, therefore, as intensity increases, single nerve fibers respond more frequently, or for longer durations before they fatigue, or more fibers are recruited in the firing, or some distinctive pattern of response occurs.

Summing Up

The auditory system preserves the form of the acoustic signal as long as the response is in the ear. The auditory canal provides some amplification of important speech frequencies, and the ossicular chain amplifies all frequencies enough to produce traveling waves in the fluid-filled cochlea. These waves in turn generate neural signals in the organ of Corti that directly reflect the frequency and intensity of the original sound.

As the neurally encoded signal is examined at higher levels of the auditory system, and as the complexity of the signal increases, the manner in which it is represented in the brain becomes less obvious. For signals as complex as speech, the cortical level seems to be essential to its representation. Thus, even though the higher levels of the brain receive neurally encoded information about the frequencies and intensities of speech, it is apparently the ability to recognize patterns in this encoded information that enables us to understand what we hear.

CLINICAL POSTSCRIPT

Some years ago, deaf individuals often were called deaf-mutes because it was assumed that the deaf could not learn to talk. Fortunately, this is a more enlightened time and the term *deaf-mutism* has fallen into disfavor. Many deaf individuals do in fact learn to speak, although the path to successful oral communication is by no means an easy one. Learning to speak without adequate hearing is a challenging task. In fact, it can be difficult even for persons who acquire hearing losses after they learn speech to maintain precise articulation, particularly for high-frequency sounds like the *s* and *sh* in the word *sunshine*. High-frequency sounds often are most affected by a hearing loss that results from nerve damage (called sensorineural hearing loss).

It has not been clear to scientists who study speech development in children just how early in development a hearing loss can affect an infant's vocalizations. In fact, diametrically opposed views

have been published on this issue. Some writers have maintained that deaf infants simply do not babble. Other writers have reported that deaf infants babble in pretty much the same way that infants with normal hearing do.

A recent opportunity to answer this question arose when it was learned from a routine hearing test given to newborns that one boy had a severe hearing loss while his identical twin brother had normal hearing. Arrangements were made to follow the vocal development of the twins. This study provided an unusual opportunity to study the effect of a hearing loss in two infants who were matched both genetically and with respect to their environment.

This study showed that the boy with the hearing loss did in fact babble but that the phonetic and acoustic characteristics of his babbling differed from those of his normally hearing twin. A major difference was in the production of sounds with high-frequency energy. The boy with a hearing loss (let's call him Hal) rarely produced consonant-like sounds such as fricatives and trills. His normal-hearing brother (Ned) produced these kinds of sounds a great deal. There were even differences in the kinds of vowel sounds that were produced. Ned produced a wide range of vowels that sounded on the whole like most of the vowels in English. Hal produced primarily low-front vowels or central vowels. He rarely produced vowels that were judged to be high-front vowels, like those in the words *heed* and *hid*. Recall from Chapter 8 (Speech Acoustics) that high-front vowels have a relatively high F_2 frequency. Apparently, a high F_2 frequency, like the high-frequency noise energy of fricatives and trills, was beyond the effective frequency range of hearing for Hal. Hal's production of predominantly low-front and central vowels and few consonants indicates that his babbling vocalizations reflected his hearing loss. Sounds with primarily low-frequency energy were in the major-

ity, whereas sounds with significant energy in the high frequencies (for which Hal had very little usable hearing) were in a slim minority.

This study tells us that what an infant hears is important even in babbling. Hearing loss can have an effect on vocalization well before the infant is judged to be producing words. This means that babbling may be important to later speech development because it gives the infant an opportunity to link his or her articulations with a resulting sound pattern. By this view, babbling is a learning experience that predates speech. What the infant learns from this experience may be helpful in the development of speech itself.

It is interesting that the word *infant* literally means "not speaking." If we take this definition strictly, then infancy extends into the second year of life, until such time as the child has a sufficient vocabulary that adults consider him or her to be a speaker. But even before the infant speaks, he or she makes sounds. The ability to produce and to hear these sounds is an early step toward the faculty of speech.

CHAPTER TEN

Self-Study

Physiology of the Ear

Review Glossary

Traveling wave: The hydraulic wave, propagated by the stapes, that travels along the basilar membrane

   Basilar membrane tuning: The differences in width and stiffness of the basilar membrane along its length that determine the frequencies to which it will respond at any point

     Frequency analysis: The selective response of different points along the basilar membrane to different frequencies

     Complex wave analysis: The response of the basilar membrane to more than one frequency at the same time

   Bone conduction: Generation of traveling waves by vibrations transmitted by bone rather than by air with the stapes

   Wave envelope: The envelope that summarizes the complex vibrations of the traveling wave

Auditory signal generation: The process by which hydraulic waves are translated into neural signals

   Shearing force: The force that bends the cilia of hair cells to generate a neural signal when the tectorial and basilar membranes vibrate in response to traveling waves

   Cochlear microphonic: Bioelectrical response in the auditory nerve that mirrors the wave form of the sound producing it

Frequency encoding: Encoding of vibratory frequency by place and frequency of excitation

   Place of excitation: The place of neural response to different frequencies throughout the auditory system

     Tonotopic organization: Spatial response to different frequencies in the nervous system as well as in the organ of Corti

     Tuning curve: Frequencies to which neurons in the auditory system are tuned

   Frequency of excitation: Firing of auditory neurons in synchrony with cycles of vibration

     Volley theory: The firing of auditory neurons in volleys at frequencies above 1,000 Hz

Intensity encoding: Increased amplitude of the traveling wave and cochlear microphonic as sound intensity is increased, which is somehow also encoded in neurons in the auditory pathway

Ascending auditory pathway: The neural pathway from the cochlea to the primary auditory cortex with synapses at the cochlear nucleus, superior olive, inferior colliculi, and medial geniculate body

   Contralateral path: The path that connects the cochlea on one side to the cortex on the opposite side

   Ipsilateral path: The path that connects the cochlea and cortex on the same side

Descending auditory pathway: The pathway from the brain to the ear used to control auditory reflexes and cochlear responses

Self-Study Test of Terminology

Self-Study Instructions: These questions can be used to help you assess how much you have retained from studying the Review Glossary. Answers are given in Appendix E.

(1) _____ Generation of traveling waves by vibrations transmitted by bone rather than by air with the stapes

(2) _____ Frequencies to which neurons in the auditory system are tuned

(3) _____ The differences in width and stiffness of the basilar membrane along its length that determine the frequencies to which it will respond at any point

(4) _____ The path that connects the cochlea on one side to the cortex on the opposite side

(5) _____ Encoding of vibratory frequency by place and frequency of excitation

(6) _____ The process by which hydraulic waves are translated into neural signals

(7) _____ Increased amplitude of the traveling wave and cochlear microphonic as sound intensity is increased that is somehow also encoded in neurons in the auditory pathway

(8) _____ The selective response of different points along the basilar membrane to different frequencies

(9) _____ The place of neural response to different frequencies throughout the auditory system

(10) _____ The pathway from the brain to the ear used to control auditory reflexes and cochlear responses

(11) _____ The firing of auditory neurons in volleys at frequencies above 1,000 Hz

(12) _____ The force that bends the cilia of hair cells to generate a neural signal when the tectorial and basilar membranes vibrate in response to traveling waves

(13) _____ The hydraulic wave, propagated by the stapes, that travels along the basilar membrane

(14) _____ Bioelectrical response in the auditory nerve that mirrors the wave form of the sound producing it

(15) _____ The path that connects the cochlea and cortex on the same side

(16) _____ Firing of auditory neurons in synchrony with cycles of vibration

(17) _____ The envelope that summarizes the complex vibrations of the traveling wave

(18) _____ Spatial response to different frequencies in the nervous system as well as in the organ of Corti

(19) _____ The response of the basilar membrane to more than one frequency at the same time

(20) _____ The neural pathway from the cochlea to the primary auditory cortex with synapses at the cochlear nucleus, superior olive, inferior colliculi, and medial geniculate body

Self-Study Test of Understanding

Self-Study Instructions: This test can be used to help you assess how well you understand the content of this chapter. Terms to be filled in are from the Review Glossary. Answers are given in Appendix E.

They were parked beside the highway. She whispered "yes," which was not what he wanted to hear. She said it with a rising inflection, indicating she had asked him a question, not given him an answer. Still, softly as she had spoken, the acoustic waves she generated were sufficient to vibrate his tympanic membrane, which transmitted the mechanical movements across the air-filled middle ear to the fluid-filled inner ear. There, the vibratory movements of the footplate of the stapes propagated (A) _____ of hydraulic pressure along the (B) _____. This membrane is "tuned" by differences in width and (C) _____ to respond selectively to different wave frequencies.

His detection that she had asked a question began with his (D) _____ analysis of the rise in pitch as she said "yes." The low-pitch wave peaked toward the apex (at the helicotrema end of the basilar membrane) as her utterance began and then moved toward the base (the vestibular end) as the pitch rose. Not only did her pitch change but so did the spectral frequencies of the different sounds in the word. Thus, the basilar membrane was engaged in (E) _____ wave analysis, in which the ear responded simultaneously to different spectral frequencies as well as to the fundamental frequency of her voice. All of these frequencies were reflected in the (F) _____ that summarized the complex vibrations at any instant.

It was the (G) _____ of the (H) _____ membrane as it bent the (I) _____ of the hair cells in the organ of Corti that translated the hydraulic waves into (J) _____ generation of neural pulses. This neural response, called the (K) _____ (which can be measured in the cochlea), mirrors the wave form of the acoustic vibration at the tympanic membrane.

Pitch and speech-sound quality information are (L) _____ encoded for transmission up the (M) _____ to the various auditory centers in the brain. The lowest center is the (N) _____, where all the neurons of the auditory nerve synapse. From there, the signals may be transmitted ipsilaterally or (O) _____ via the superior olive, lateral lemniscus, and inferior colliculi to the (P) _____ of the thalamus, where they all synapse before being sent to the (Q) _____ in the cortex.

Frequency encoding is accomplished by (R) _____, which involves the location of neural response to different frequencies at the various centers of the auditory system, and by (S) _____, which involves the firing of neurons in synchrony with vibratory cycles. When that firing rate exceeds 1,000 Hz, auditory neurons fire in (T) _____. Evidence of frequency information being preserved throughout the auditory system is seen in (U) _____, the spatial response to different frequencies in the brain as well as in the organ of Corti, and in the (V) _____, which are the frequencies at which various neurons in the auditory system respond.

Not only frequency encoding but also (W) _____ encoding is somehow accomplished by the auditory system. As loudness increases, so do (X) _____ of traveling waves and (Y) _____ (the electrical signal measured at the round window), but how this intensity information is transmitted up the auditory pathway is not well understood. What is understood is why the background drone of traffic noise did not drown out the message, "yes." That drone had continued so relentlessly that it had lost its novel stimulus value, so the (Z) _____ had carried instructions to the cochlea to shut down its response to this drone until some interesting auditory event happened. "Yes" was interesting, but it could have been more interesting.

CHAPTER ELEVEN
The Nervous System

Our exploration of the nervous system will be akin to an extraterrestrial encounter. Were you an alien from another planet, not wishing to land among us, yet seeking to investigate the possibility of intelligent life on earth, you might hover at a distance. What you would be able to learn about us would be roughly comparable to what we will be able to reveal about the brain in this primer on how speech is understood and used.

From your spaceship, the most visible features of our civilization would be cities, towns, and highways. You could also probably detect traffic and measure some of its characteristics. What you could not observe is why the traffic moves as it does, or why things operate as they do.

Similarly, we can describe neural equivalents of cities (large communication networks located in the brain), towns (small communication networks inside and outside the brain), and streets and highways (communication lines extending from one center to another). We can also describe neural traffic through this network. We even have a fair notion of which parts of this network are used for speech, language, and hearing. But we are still far from understanding how the brain operates for an activity as complicated as speech. Even being able to explain such a seemingly simple occurrence as is reflected in a statement like "I have an idea" is beyond us.

Not only is the answer beyond us, but for the purpose of this text, so also is the sophistication needed for the attempts to find it. The task is formidable. Understanding the design of a mechanism with an estimated 20 to 100 billion *neurons* (nerve cells) interconnected billions and billions of ways is challenging enough. The problem is magnified when this mechanism is packaged in a container smaller than a football (our brains weigh about 1,500 grams). The problem is even more immense when we try to study how it coordinates about 140,000 electrical signals per second during speech. And now it has been discovered that these electrical signals are generated by biochemical processes which neuroscientists are only beginning to explore.

DIVISIONS OF THE NERVOUS SYSTEM

To keep our "bites" to manageable size, we will devote two chapters to mapping the anatomical structures of the nervous system and three to studying its functions for speech, language, and hearing. These functions will include how sensory input is processed, how central processes coordinate and integrate all neural activity, and how motor output to the musculature is controlled. The first of the anatomy chapters will be concerned with all parts of the nervous system not protected by the skull or vertebral column. These parts consist largely of transmission lines, like back roads, that carry signals to the muscles and from the sense organs. Being peripheral to (away from the center of) the main parts of the nervous system, which are protected by bones, this anatomical division is called the *peripheral nervous system* (Fig. 11–1). The name of the central anatomical division, contained within the bony housing that consists of the brain and spinal cord, is, appropriately, the *central nervous system* (*CNS*). It will be the subject of the other anatomical chapter.

In addition to being divided by anatomy, the nervous system is also divided by function. Its overall task is to determine aspects of the environment worthy of response and to cope with the environment according to the individual's needs. There are, however, two environments. The one of which we are most aware, at least if we are healthy, is external. It is the one for which all animals evolve species-specific coping strategies. It is also the one for which humans have acquired speech. And it is the one to which the central nervous system is devoted.

The other environment is internal. You are not likely to be aware of it unless illness strikes. Then it may preoccupy your attention, but to little purpose. The internal processes of the body are conducted automatically, hence the name of the functional division which controls them, the *autonomic nervous system* (*ANS*). Fortunately, we have been freed from the need to regulate breathing, digestion, how the heart pumps, how the arteries contract, how the glands secrete. We arrive at birth with the ANS programmed to conduct these functions automatically. Because anatomically most of the ANS is located in the peripheral nervous system, it is in connection with this system that we will explore the ANS briefly.

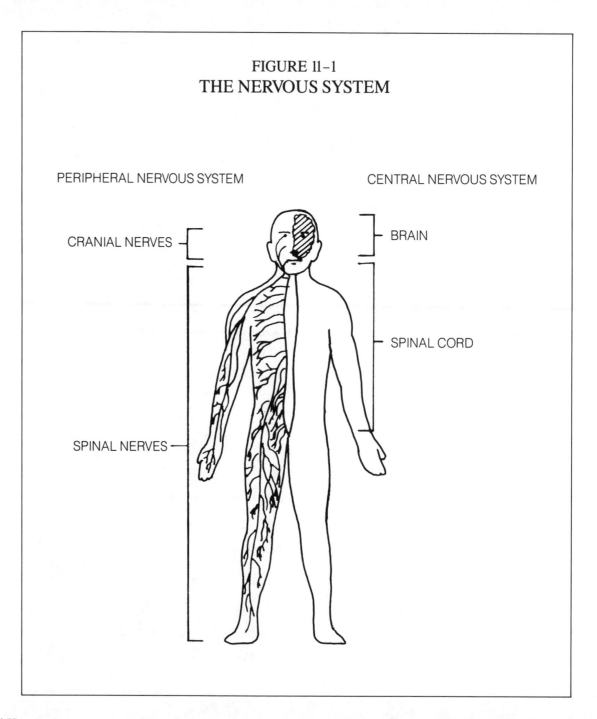

FIGURE 11–1
THE NERVOUS SYSTEM

PERIPHERAL NERVOUS SYSTEM

CENTRAL NERVOUS SYSTEM

CRANIAL NERVES

BRAIN

SPINAL CORD

SPINAL NERVES

GROWTH OF THE BRAIN

The infant has proportionately more neural tissue than the adult: The newborn has a nervous system that is one fourth of its adult weight but a body that is only 5 percent of the adult value. Brain growth proceeds in three major phases. From conception until birth, the brain grows primarily as the result of an increase in the number of cells (cell division). (Fetal neural and auditory development are summarized in Appendix C.) From birth to 10 or 12 months of age, the brain grows by two factors: first, a continued increase in the number of cells, and second, increases in cell size. Finally, from 10 to 12 months of age until maturity, increases in cell size contribute to further brain growth.

As shown in Figure 11-2, the brain increases in weight dramatically from about 3 months of gestational age to about 5 years of age. A slight sex difference appears after brain weight reaches about 1,000 grams, after which the male brain outweighs the female brain by about 125 to 150 grams. The adult brain weighs about 1,500 grams, or between 3 and 4 pounds. About 70 to 80 percent of this weight is water, followed by lipids (10 to 12 percent) and proteins (8 percent). The surface of the cerebral cortex wrinkles as it grows, so that the cortical surface area eventually equals about 1,650 sq cm.

Of course, increasing size is not the only dimension of brain maturation. Another important index of maturation is the process of myelination, the covering of axons with a fatty insulating sheath (myelin). Myelin first appears in the motor roots of the spinal cord, shortly followed by its appearance in the sensory roots. Myelination continues at least until puberty, with the association areas of the cortex being some of the last fibers to complete myelination. There is evidence that the order or sequence of myelination is associated with the

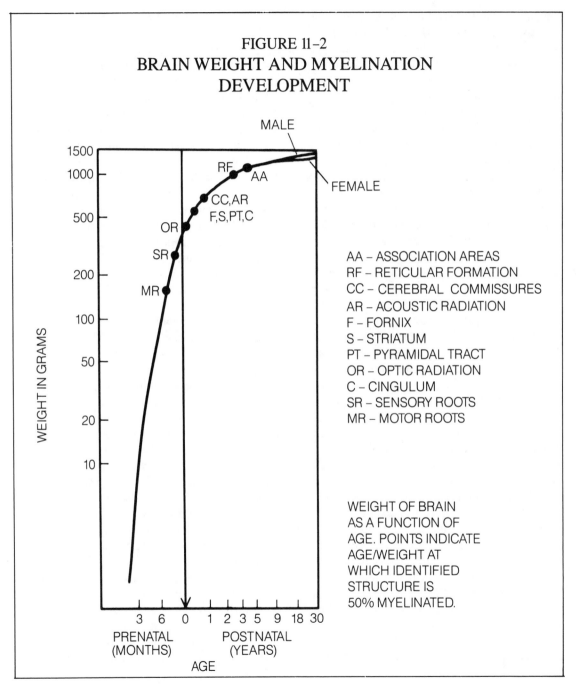

FIGURE 11-2
BRAIN WEIGHT AND MYELINATION
DEVELOPMENT

AA – ASSOCIATION AREAS
RF – RETICULAR FORMATION
CC – CEREBRAL COMMISSURES
AR – ACOUSTIC RADIATION
F – FORNIX
S – STRIATUM
PT – PYRAMIDAL TRACT
OR – OPTIC RADIATION
C – CINGULUM
SR – SENSORY ROOTS
MR – MOTOR ROOTS

WEIGHT OF BRAIN
AS A FUNCTION OF
AGE. POINTS INDICATE
AGE/WEIGHT AT
WHICH IDENTIFIED
STRUCTURE IS
50% MYELINATED.

eventual thickness of myelin, such that fibers with thick covering were the earliest to begin the process. Figure 11-2 indicates the age and brain weight at which various brain structures have completed about 50 percent of their myelination. Clearly, myelination is a gradual process extending into middle and even late childhood.

We already have discussed the idea of a "performance anatomy" of the vocal tract. Basically, a performance anatomy is an anatomy that is determined in part by the uses to which it is put. We can say that structure permits function, but function can shape structure. The anatomy of the vocal tract appears to be shaped to some degree by the actions of this system, particularly chewing and swallowing, which deliver fairly large forces to the structures that give shape to the oral cavity. Is there also a performance anatomy of the brain? That is, is the structure and development of the brain determined in part by the use of the brain?

Consider Laura Bridgeman, who was born in 1829 and lost all visual and auditory capacities at the age of 2 years as the result of scarlet fever. She went on to acquire sign language and became noted for her mental abilities. (Incidentally, she was taught to communicate at the Perkins School for the Blind in Boston, the same institution at which Helen Keller's famed teacher, Anne Sullivan, received her training.) Laura Bridgeman was sufficiently well known that Charles Dickens visited her in Boston in 1842. He wrote as follows about her: "There she was before me; built up, as it were, in a marble cell, impervious to any ray of light, or particle of sound; with her poor white hand peeking through a chink in the wall, beckoning to some good man for help, that an immortal soul might be awakened" (from Charles Dickens, *American Notes*, Boston, Cassino Press, 1842, p. 44). Dickens' reference to the "poor white hand" probably refers to the fact that Laura Bridgeman used sign language to express herself and received messages by touching the hands of others as they signed to her.

Upon her death, Laura Bridgeman's brain was carefully removed and preserved. At the suggestion of a prominent psychologist, G. Stanley Hall, a professor of neurology at Clark University, H. H. Donaldson, studied her brain for two years, in what has been described as one of the most thorough studies of a single human brain. What Donaldson discovered was that Laura Bridgeman's brain had marked anatomical abnormalities in the auditory and visual areas. This work apparently inspired H. Berger, who discovered the electroencephalogram, to conduct experiments on the effects of sensory deprivation on brain development. Berger sutured shut the eyelids of young cats and dogs and then studied their brain development. Research along this line continues today, and several researchers have concluded that deprivation of normal functional experience can arrest or otherwise disturb the development of the brain.

Thus, it appears that the brain develops, in part, in response to sensory information that it receives. It may also be influenced in its development by its own manipulation of the world about it, as through the arms and legs and hands. It is interesting to note here the phenomenon of the "phantom limb." Persons who have an amputated limb often report sensations of the presence of the missing body part, such as its position in space. Even more remarkable is the fact that this experience also has been reported to occur for persons with congenitally missing limbs.

For our purposes it is sufficient to note that the brain develops in a way that is influenced by function. This idea may be relevant to the so-called "wild" or "feral" children who have been isolated from normal social contact during their formative years. Generally, it appears that once the normal period of language acquisition has passed, these children have very little capacity to develop language. Have they lost this capacity because their brains failed to receive the timely stimulation that results in the capacity to acquire language?

Aging of the Brain

The growth of the brain ceases in young adulthood, and by age 40 a reverse process begins. The brain loses weight and pigments accumulate in nerve cells. The loss of weight is due to the following factors: reduction in size of brain cells, reduction in the number of cells, a relative increase in supporting tissue over preexisting tissues, shrinkage and condensation of the material outside the brain cells, and increased deposits of intracellular metabolic products. (The brain is not the only part of the body to decline in size, weight, or volume with age. Stature also tends to become smaller and the vital capacity of the lungs is reduced.) By one estimate, the loss of weight of the brain in a 90 year old person would leave a brain the size of a 3 year old child's. Claims have been made that the brain loses up to 150,000 nerve cells per day. Such figures are open to question, but it is interesting to ponder statistical attrition of the brain given this rate of loss from an original 20 billion neurons: It would take about 400 years for total depletion.

Normal aging of the brain is dismal enough to contemplate, but these changes are small compared to the ravages of Alzheimer's disease. This disease can leave people severely demented within 3 to 10 years after its onset. No cure is known at this time. Several theories have been proposed to account for the development of Alzheimer's disease, but it is too early to pick one that is totally satisfactory. The victim of Alzheimer's disease suffers a loss of neurons, may have a reduction in neurotransmitters (especially acetylcholine), possesses neurons with abnormal structures, and seems to have abnormal deposits of protein and cellular debris. As if this list is not long enough, there is also evidence of high concentrations of aluminum in the brain tissues of persons with Alzheimer's disease. What all this means in human terms is a progressive deterioration in mental ability: failing memory, language disorders, and emotional disturbances, to mention only three effects.

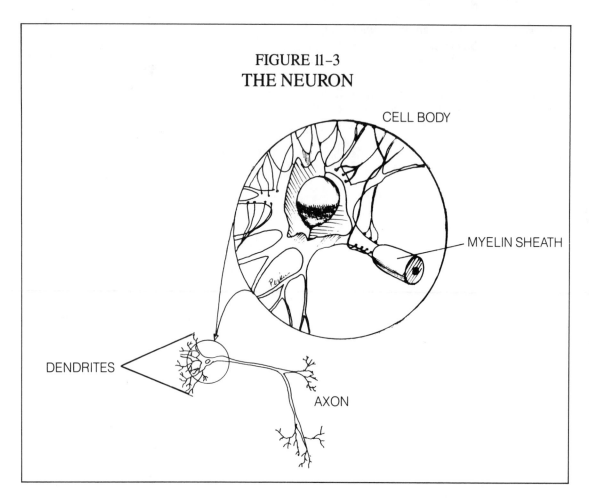

FIGURE 11–3
THE NEURON

CELL BODY

MYELIN SHEATH

DENDRITES

AXON

develop from its rudimentary origins. Like another specialized type of cell, muscle, neurons differ from other cells. They respond to electrical stimulation by discharging *neural pulses* (neurons transmit the discharge as a pulsed signal; muscles contract). Neurons also have been thought to differ from all but muscle cells in another respect: they usually do not regenerate — you are born with almost all you will have (judging from recent evidence, however, this may not be true).

Considering the nature of the neuron, the question that troubles some neurosurgeons who have removed a portion of the brain is a baffling one. With an excised chunk of brain lying in a pan, their question is, "Where is the mind?" It certainly does not seem to be in a single neuron or even in an aggregation of many neurons. Apparently, mind is an example of the whole being greater than the sum of the parts, in this case the parts being neurons.

NEURONS

Having considered the nervous system in broad scope, we will now turn to its smallest unit, the *neuron*. Like the basic building block of all living matter, a neuron is a cell. As such, it has a *cell body* surrounded by a membrane through which nutrients can enter and wastes can be shed (Fig. 11–3). Within the cell body is a *nucleus*. With increased complexity, as organisms have evolved from single cells to humans with billions of cells, the cells have become specialized in their function. One such function is communication. Neurons have met this need by developing extensions or processes (generally two) from the cell body. The extensions that collect and transmit electrical impulses toward the cell body are *dendrites*. The extension that transmits impulses away from the cell body is an *axon*.

The neuron has taken 400 million years to

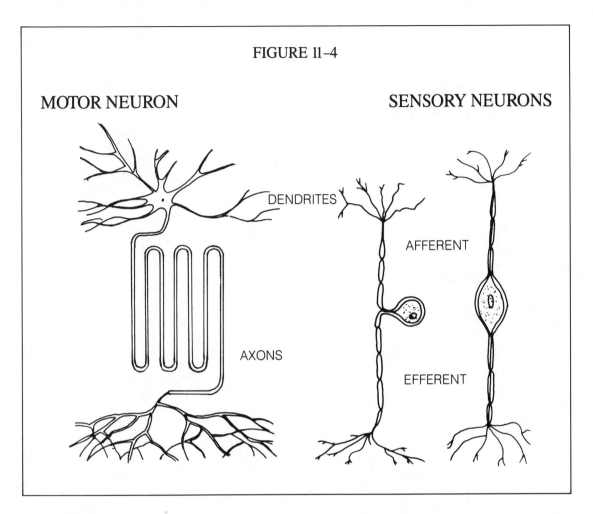

FIGURE 11-4

MOTOR NEURON

SENSORY NEURONS

DENDRITES

AFFERENT

AXONS

EFFERENT

Types of Neurons

Although all nerve cells are specialized to transmit electrical signals, they can vary considerably in their design. A typical motor neuron has multiple dendrites extending from the cell body (these are *afferent* processes, which conduct neural activity toward the cell body), and a single axon (an *efferent* process, which conducts neural pulses away from the cell body), sometimes several feet long (Fig. 11-4). Some sensory neurons, however, have afferent processes that are more like axons than dendrites. In some, the afferent and efferent extensions are almost like a single axon connected to a cell body off to the side. In others, the cell body has axon-like extensions in both directions. Beyond these more common types of neurons are a variety of others, found mostly in the brain (Fig. 11-5). No matter which variety, neurons have afferent and efferent processes that depend on the cell body for survival. A process severed from its cell body will usually die.

FIGURE 11–5
CORTICAL NEURONS

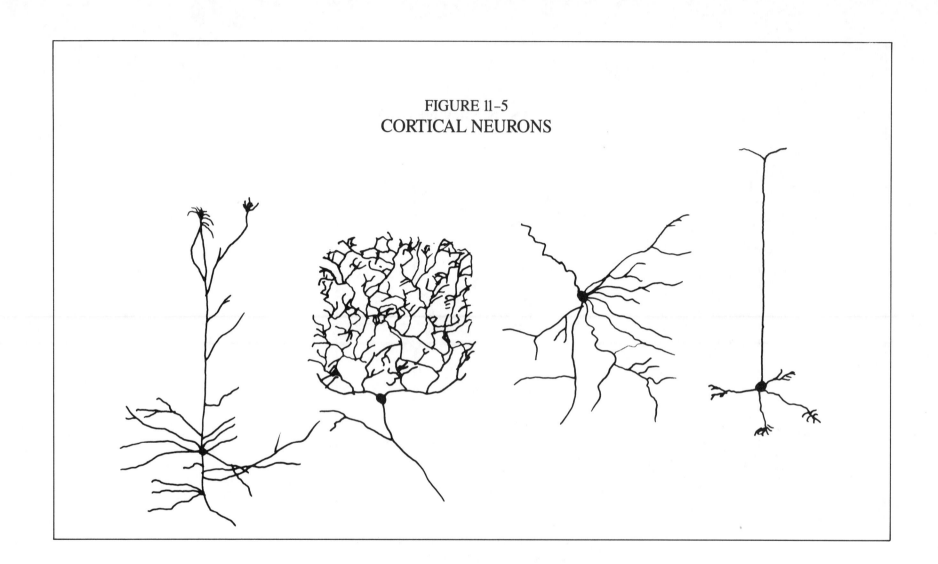

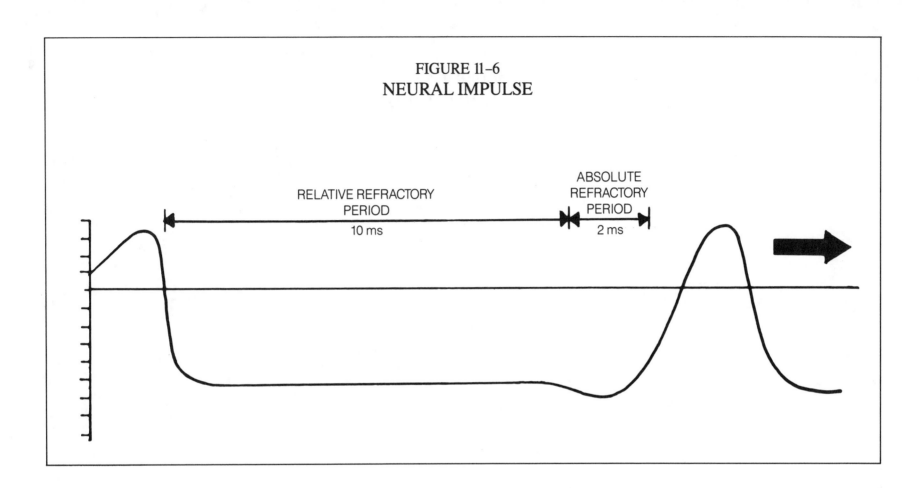

FIGURE 11–6
NEURAL IMPULSE

RELATIVE REFRACTORY
PERIOD
10 ms

ABSOLUTE
REFRACTORY
PERIOD
2 ms

Neural Conduction

Each nerve cell marches to its own drummer; if left to its own devices, it will eventually fire an electrical discharge spontaneously. Being a biological unit, it is cyclical in its readiness for firing. Immediately after firing, it has an *absolute refractory period* of 1 millisecond (ms) or two when no amount of stimulation can trigger it. Then it enters a relative refractory period of about 10 ms during which it progressively recovers its ability to fire (Fig. 11–6). Early in this period, only intense stimulation will force it to fire again.

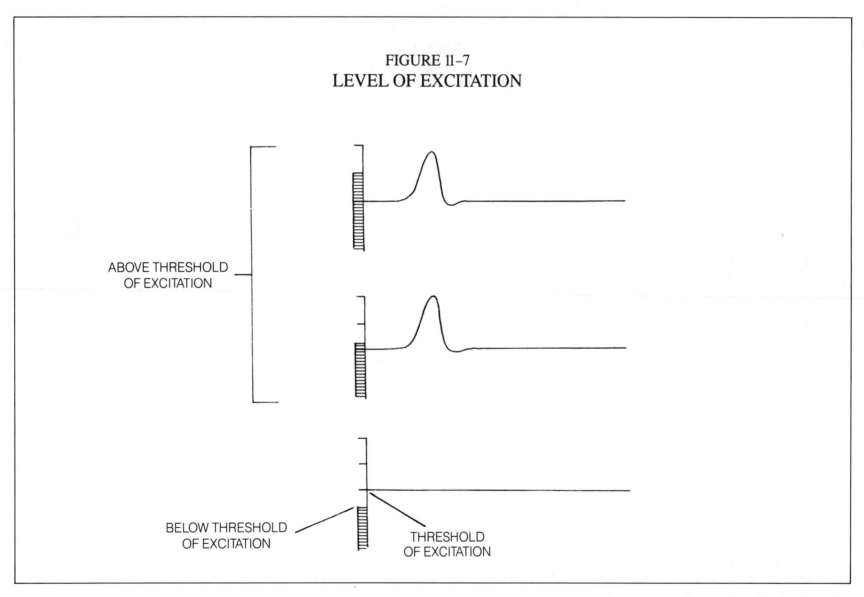

FIGURE 11–7
LEVEL OF EXCITATION

ABOVE THRESHOLD
OF EXCITATION

BELOW THRESHOLD
OF EXCITATION

THRESHOLD
OF EXCITATION

When it comes to firing, a neuron operates on an all-or-nothing principle, just as does a fuse, which, once ignited by sufficient heat, burns just as rapidly when lit by a match as when lit by a blow torch. Similarly, as long as stimulation is insufficient to reach the neuron's threshold (which varies depending on where it is in its refractory period), it will not fire at all. When its *threshold of excitation* is exceeded, however, it will discharge at full capacity (Fig. 11–7). The amplitude of the discharge is independent of the intensity of the stimulus.

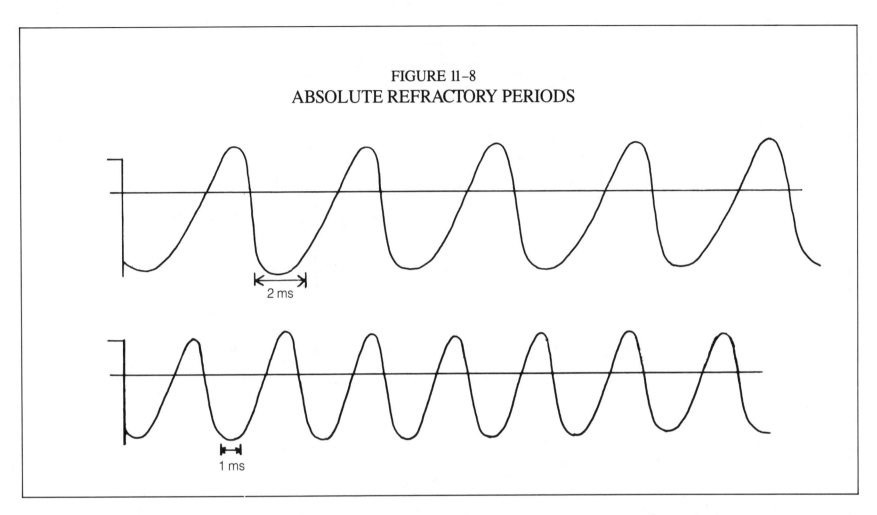

FIGURE 11-8
ABSOLUTE REFRACTORY PERIODS

2 ms

1 ms

What intensity does affect is the rate at which neurons fire. As intensity increases, so does the number of neural pulses per second. Some nerve fibers can fire as many as 1,000 times per second. The upper limit of a neuron's firing rate is the duration of its absolute refractory period, during which it cannot be forced to fire. If that duration were 2 ms rather than 1 ms, it would take longer before it could possible fire, so the upper firing limit would be closer to 500 than to 1,000 per second (Fig. 11-8).

Compared with the speed of electricity through wires, the velocity of a neural pulse is incredibly slow. Instead of being near the speed of light, as is electricity, it is even slower than the speed of sound. Depending on the neuron's diameter and insulation, its pulse velocity will range from a few feet per second to a few hundred feet per second. Velocity increases not only with increases in diameter but also with the insulation. Large neurons are covered with a white fatty insulation, a *myelin sheath*. When there are gaps in this

sheath, called *nodes of Ranvier*, the highest neural velocities are obtained as the pulse skips rapidly from one node to the next. The effect of speeding up transmission rate is to increase the number of pulses that can travel along a neuron at any one time. Aside from the nodes of Ranvier, which are a relatively recent evolutionary development, the neuron has not changed much in the last 100 million years. In this respect, the nerve cell stands in stark contrast to the extraordinary evolution of the nervous system.

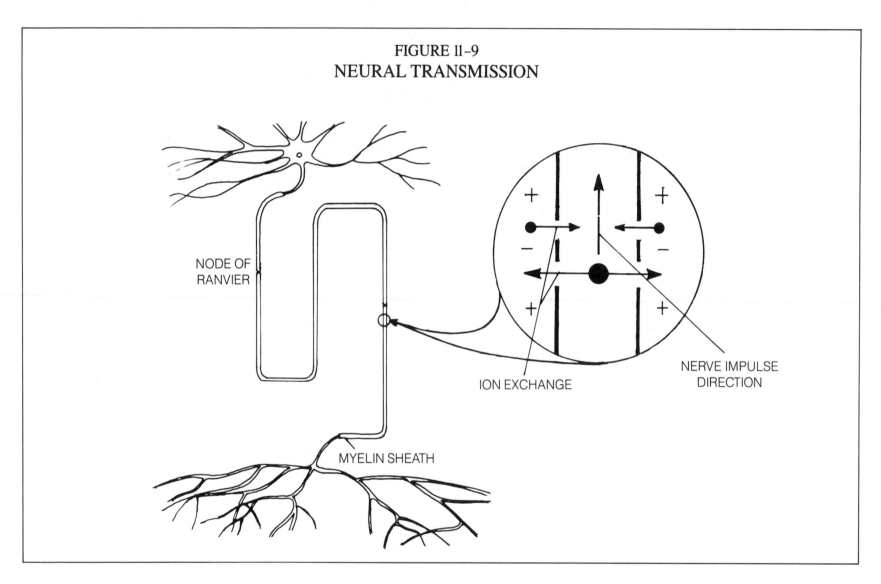

FIGURE 11-9
NEURAL TRANSMISSION

NODE OF
RANVIER

ION EXCHANGE

NERVE IMPULSE
DIRECTION

MYELIN SHEATH

Neural Pulse. Why, when a neuron fires, is the electrical pulse transmitted so slowly? The answer requires an explanatory detour. Each neuron generates its own electrical activity. When the afferent processes (dendrites) provide sufficient stimulation to exceed the threshold of excitation of the cell body, a neural pulse is discharged that travels in an efferent direction along the axon (the efferent process).

How that pulse is transmitted depends on the *surface membrane* of the axon, which is normally an insulator. It maintains the chemical difference between potassium ions inside and the sodium ions outside the cell. The axon is like a battery. In its resting state, a voltage difference exists between the inside and outside of the membrane, but no current flows. When the neuron discharges, the membrane at the cell body suddenly becomes permeable. Sodium ions now enter and current flows through the membrane to discharge the inside voltage difference (Fig. 11-9).

Functional Anatomy of Speech, Language, and Hearing

The speed of transmission depends on how rapidly the permeability of the membrane travels down the axon — again, much in the fashion of an ignited fuse (Fig. 11–10). Immediately after the membrane discharges at any given point, it becomes absolutely refractive for 1 ms or so, and then it becomes progressively less refractive as the chemical difference inside and outside the cell restores its readiness to fire again. Thus, the neuron is not a wire that conducts an electrical charge that has been generated elsewhere. Instead, it generates its own charge, which, when fired, travels the length of the axon perpendicular to the direction of ion movement through the membrane (Fig. 11–11). This is the "language" used within the neuron to communicate. It is an all-or-nothing language.

To understand the electrical activity of the nervous system, we should begin with the realization that neurons are bathed in a saltwater solution. Mixed within this solution are atoms of sodium (Na), potassium (K), and chloride (Cl). By their nature sodium and potassium atoms tend to lose one of their electrons. Because electrons carry a negative charge, the loss of an electron leaves the sodium and potassium atoms as positively charged ions (designated Na^+ and K^+). The nature of the chloride atom is to pick up an extra electron, giving it a negative charge (and hence it becomes a negatively charged ion, Cl^-). Now, so long as these ions are uniformly mixed in a salt solution, the mixture maintains electrical neutrality. But if positively charged ions were separated from the negatively charged ions, a voltage (a difference in electrical potential) is created. Neural cells of the body perform exactly this function, causing ions to be unequally represented across the cell membrane. Each neuron is a kind of physiological battery.

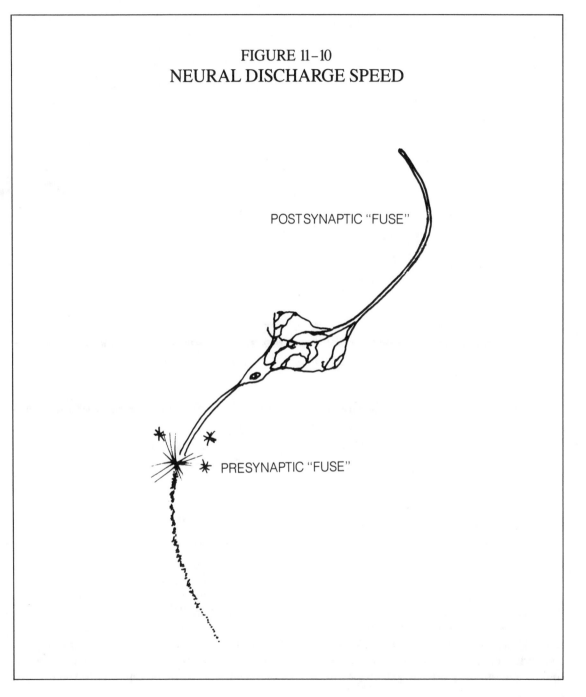

FIGURE 11–10
NEURAL DISCHARGE SPEED

POSTSYNAPTIC "FUSE"

PRESYNAPTIC "FUSE"

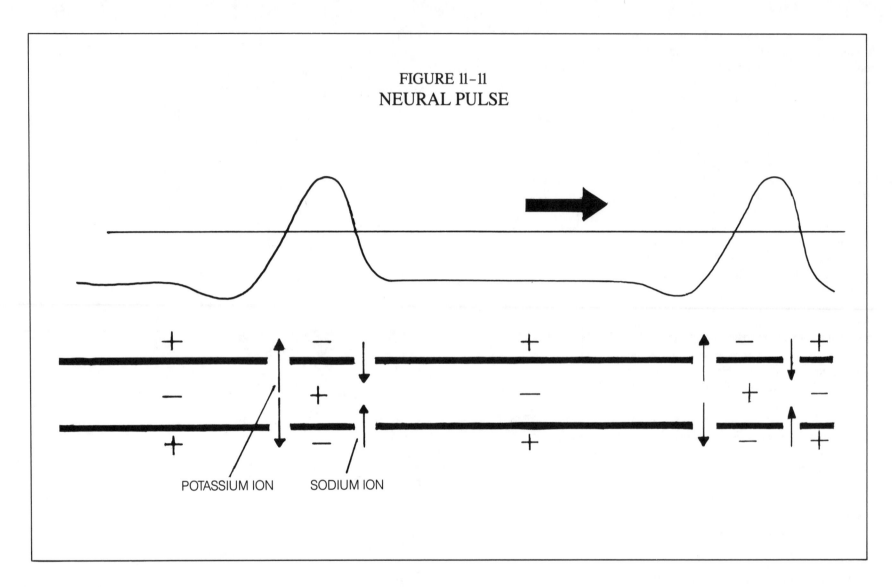

FIGURE 11–11
NEURAL PULSE

POTASSIUM ION   SODIUM ION

It is said that nature abhors a vacuum. If so, it also must abhor inequalities of any sort, including the inequality of ions across a cell membrane. Positive ions attract negative ions, so that ions tend to "leak" across the cell membrane, seeking an equilibrium of the charged atoms. A resting neuron contains one tenth as many sodium ions as the extracellular fluid, and, at the same time, it has 10 times as many potassium ions. How is this imbalance maintained? The answer is that every neuron contains about 1 million tiny pumps, each of which can expel 200 sodium ions and bring in 130 potassium ions every second. This imbalance of sodium and potassium maintains the voltage within the neuron at –70 millivolts (a millivolt is one thousandth of a volt; an ordinary flashlight battery, "D" size, is rated at 1.5 volt.) Maintaining this voltage takes work and oxygen — which explains the brain's continuous demand for oxygen.

Functional Anatomy of Speech, Language, and Hearing

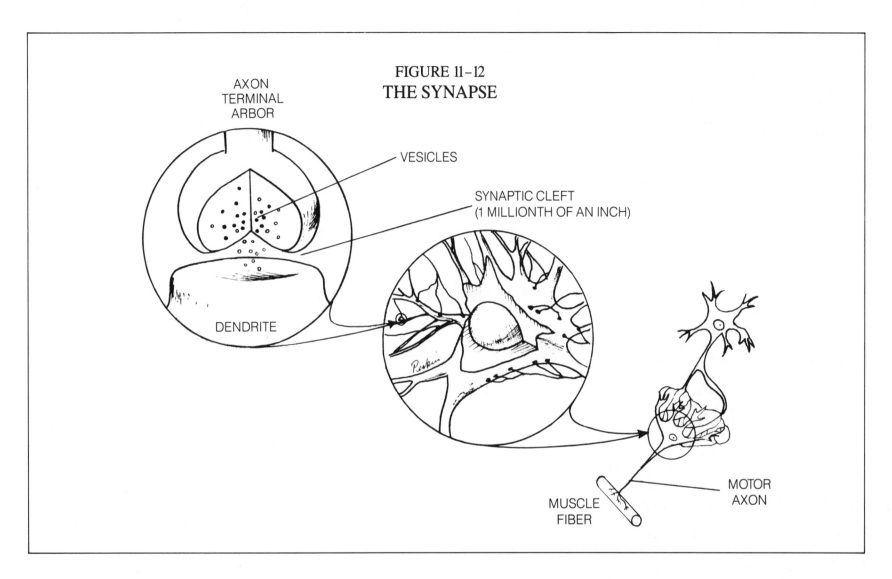

FIGURE 11–12
THE SYNAPSE

AXON
TERMINAL
ARBOR

VESICLES

SYNAPTIC CLEFT
(1 MILLIONTH OF AN INCH)

DENDRITE

MUSCLE
FIBER

MOTOR
AXON

The Synapse

The "language" used to communicate between neurons is quite different from all-or-nothing; it is a *graded* biochemical response. The junction at which neural pulses transfer from one neuron to another is a *synapse* (Fig. 11–12). If the human brain has 100 billion neurons, then it has at least 100 trillion synapses. There are several types of synapses. In one of the most common, the tip of an axon branch (the *terminal arbor*) of one neuron makes close contact with a dendrite of another (Fig. 11–12). In other types, the terminal arbor makes direct contact with the cell body, or with a sensory cell (such as a hair cell in the organ of Corti where acoustic vibrations are encoded into neural pulses), or a muscle cell (which contracts when stimulated electrically). No matter what type, it is at the synapses that bioelectric activity in one neuron initiates bioelectric activity in another. It is how this activity is initiated in a synapse that is different.

To think of a synaptic contact as being like touching a "live" wire to another wire is misleading. The contact of neurons at synapses is fundamentally different. For one thing, the transmission of the pulse across the synapse is biochemical, not electrical. For another, some chemicals facilitate firing of the next cell, others inhibit it. For still another, direct physical contact at the synapse does not occur. Admittedly, the synaptic gap is only a millionth of an inch, but it would be a "loose connection" if the synapse resembled connected wires.

Basically, an impulse begins as ion channels are opened. Upon sensory stimulation (by light, sound, touch, smell), the appropriate *transducer neuron* (sensory receptor) opens its sodium channels so that the voltage inside the neuron becomes positive. For other nontransducer neurons, the impulse is created as channels in the membrane are opened by a neurotransmitter chemical released from another neuron. The neurotransmitter enters the synaptic cleft, combines with receptor molecules, and opens the ion channels in the next neuron along the path of impulse transmission. Different transmitters open different channels (sodium, potassium, or chloride). Synaptic inputs producing positive voltages are called excitatory; those producing negative voltages are called inhibitory. The balance of these voltages is the deciding factor in impulse transmission. If the voltage is large enough, the impulse is propagated. In this way, the impulse travels like flame along a fuse. The impulse is about one thousandth of a second in duration and can reach a speed of 300 miles per hour, much slower than the speed of electric current (which is almost the speed of light), but fast enough to travel from a person's big toe to the brain in about one fiftieth of a second.

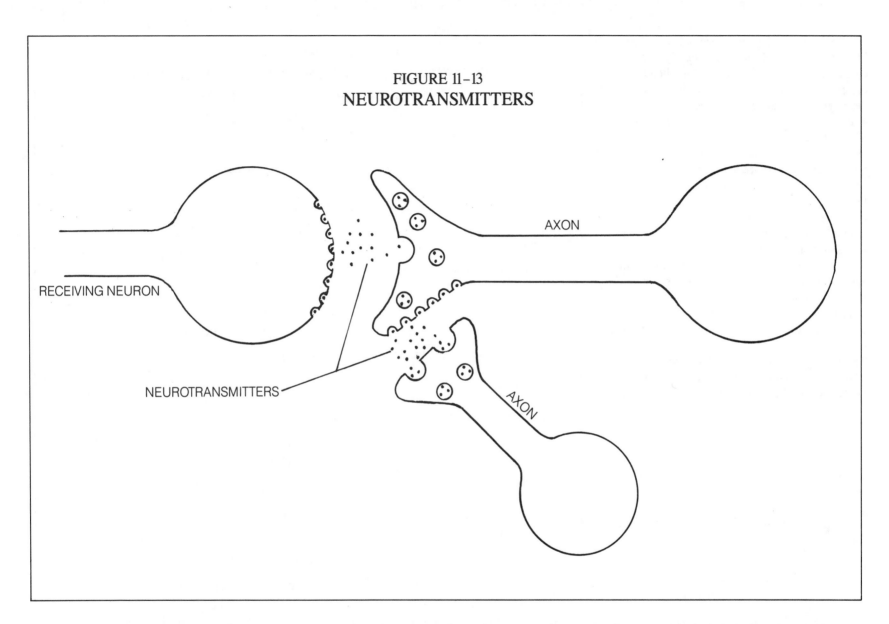

FIGURE 11–13
NEUROTRANSMITTERS

AXON

RECEIVING NEURON

NEUROTRANSMITTERS

AXON

Neurotransmitters. When a neural pulse reaches the end of an axon, it releases tiny quantities of *neurotransmitters*, chemicals that pass across the synaptic gap to receptors that change the electrical activity in the next cell (Fig. 11–13).

Neurotransmitters are proving to be a communication system within a communication system. Some 30 types have already been discovered, and many more are suspected to exist. Deficiencies of neurotransmitters have been linked to mental illness as well as to neurological diseases such as parkinsonism and myasthenia gravis. Hallucinogenic drugs, as well as opiates that suppress pain, seem to act on the brain by mimicking the action of natural neurotransmitters.

The Nervous System

The creation of neurotransmitters is a tale in itself. Each neuron is an extraordinarily elaborate chemical factory. It manufactures the chemical components in the cell body and transports them the length of the axon (in a manner much like a snake swallowing a rat), to its tip end, an *axon terminal*. Each terminal is a chemical assembly plant where the components for a particular neurotransmitter are packaged and stored in tiny oval-shaped membranous sacs called *synaptic vesicles* (Fig. 11–14).

When a nerve impulse arrives at the axon terminal, a large number of these stored vesicles are released into the synaptic space. The number can vary. The vesicles travel quickly to a postsynaptic receptor on a dendrite or on the cell body of the next neuron. The receptor is tailored to receive a particular neurotransmitter with the precision of a key fitting a lock. Thus, the *neuroreceptor* is able to decode the biochemical message it receives. That message will tell a neuron to become excited or inhibited, a muscle cell to contract, or a gland cell to secrete a hormone.

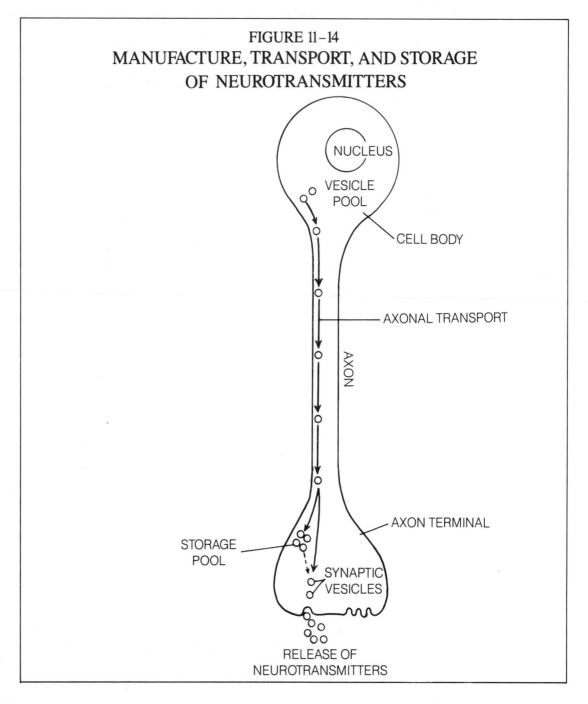

FIGURE 11–14

MANUFACTURE, TRANSPORT, AND STORAGE OF NEUROTRANSMITTERS

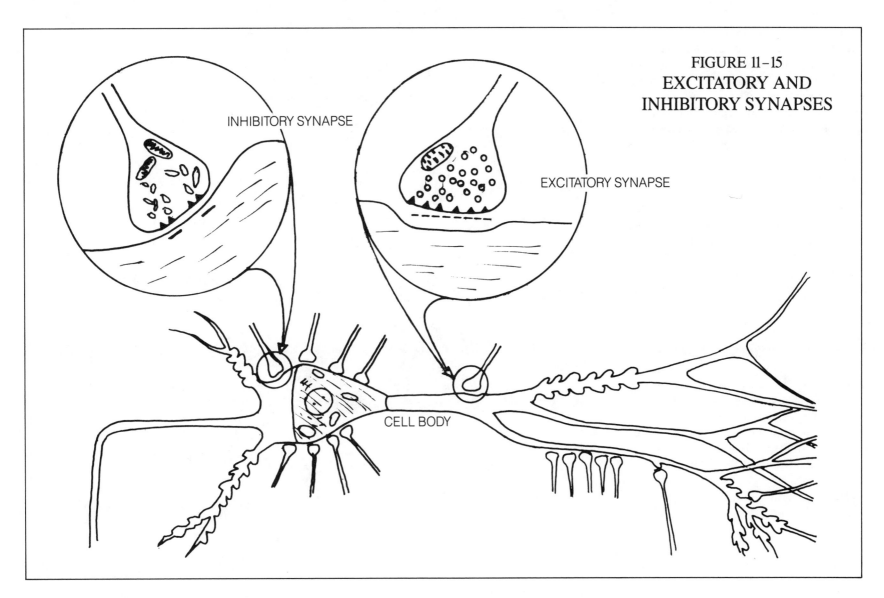

FIGURE 11-15
EXCITATORY AND
INHIBITORY SYNAPSES

INHIBITORY SYNAPSE

EXCITATORY SYNAPSE

CELL BODY

Each neuron has anywhere from 1,000 to 10,000 synapses from which it receives information from something like 1,000 other neurons. This means that even though a nerve cell may manufacture only one kind of neurotransmitter, still, with information coming from about 1,000 other neurons, any given neuron is likely to be under the influence of a variety of neurotransmitters. The net effect of these competing stimuli — to inhibit or excite — is that the neuron exists in a state of poised instability. Whether it will fire or not will depend on a kind of chemical vote at each of its thousands of synapses (Fig. 11–15). If the inhibitory transmitters win, it will remain quiescent. If the excitatory group predominates, it will fire. Moreover, each neuron can cast up to 1,000 votes per second.

The sum of the matter is that the neuron provides the brain with two systems for encoding information. One involves patterns of electrical activity which reverberate through the network of billions of nerve cells. The nervous system is estimated to hum with trillions and trillions of neural pulses per hour. This system is staggeringly complex when each cell is viewed as either activated or not activated. Our major task will be to glimpse how this vast network is organized to make purposeful behavior possible.

But over and above this network is the chemical network of neurotransmitters which has only been discovered in recent years. These are the neurotransmitters that inhibit or excite neurons to discharge electrical pulses. Each of the 30 known or suspected neurotransmitters has a chemically coded message of its own (such as is involved in sexual arousal, pain, and pleasure), which is also transmitted along with its "vote" to fire or not to fire. The various transmitters are not scattered randomly throughout the brain. Instead, they are localized in specific clusters of neurons whose axons project to other highly specific brain regions, such as the dopamine pathways shown in Figure 11–16. How this coding system operates, especially as it has any bearing on speech, is only now becoming apparent. We will not explore it further, beyond noting that it may increase the apparent complexity of the nervous system by several magnitudes.

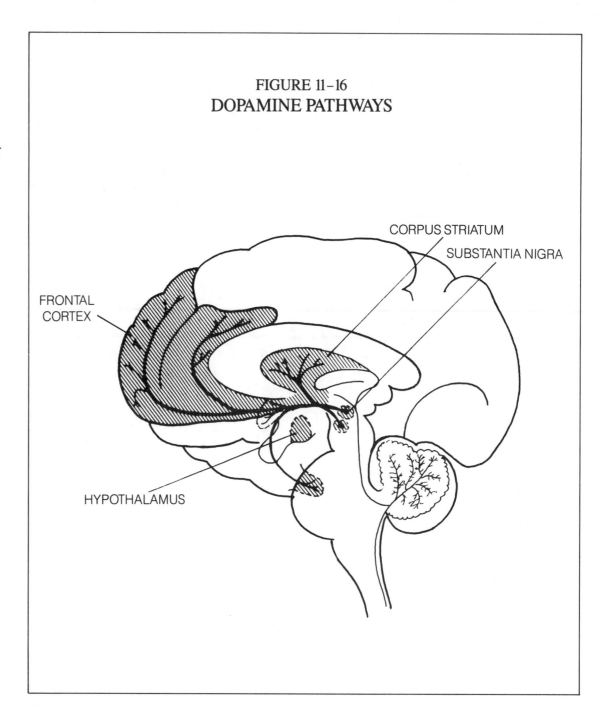

FIGURE 11–16
DOPAMINE PATHWAYS

CORPUS STRIATUM

SUBSTANTIA NIGRA

FRONTAL CORTEX

HYPOTHALAMUS

CHAPTER ELEVEN

Self-Study

The Nervous System

Review Glossary

Central nervous system (CNS): Anatomically, the division of the nervous system contained within the skull and vertebral column. Functionally, the division of the nervous system that mediates adjustments to the external environment

Peripheral nervous system: The anatomical division of the nervous system located outside of the skull and vertebral column

Autonomic nervous system (ANS): Anatomically located mostly in the peripheral nervous system; functionally it controls the internal environment

Neuron: The nerve cell, which contains *dendrites* (afferent processes) carrying pulses toward the *cell body* with its *nucleus*, and an *axon* (efferent process) carrying pulses away from it

  Myelin sheath: The fatty insulation on axons of large neurons

  Nodes of Ranvier: Gaps in the myelin sheath that speed up neural transmission

  Surface membrane: The axon membrane through which current flows during the neural pulse

Neural pulse: The bioelectric discharge of a neuron

  Absolute refractory period: The brief period after a neuron fires during which no amount of stimulation can trigger another discharge

  Threshold of excitation: The level of stimulation above which a neuron will discharge

Synapse: The junction at which neural pulses transfer from the axon of one neuron to the dendrite of another

  Terminal arbor or axon terminal: The tip of a branch of an axon

  Presynaptic neuron: A neuron whose axon leads to a synapse

  Postsynaptic neuron: A neuron whose dendrite receives pulses from a synapse

  Neurotransmitters: The chemicals that pass across a *synaptic gap* that change the electrical activity in the *receptor neuron* (postsynaptic neuron)

   Synaptic vesicles: Membranous sacs in which neurotransmitters are stored until release into a synaptic gap

  Excitatory synapse: A synapse that transmits neurotransmitters that *facilitate* discharge in a postsynaptic neuron

  Inhibitory synapse: A synapse that transmits neurotransmitters that *inhibit* discharge in a postsynaptic neuron

  Neuroreceptor: A dendrite receptor keyed to receive a particular neurotransmitter

Self-Study Coloring Instructions

1. Fill in the terms for *A* through *V* in Drawings 11–I through 11–IV.
2. Using different pencils, color in *A* through *V* and the accompanying terms.
3. Color terms in the Glossary with the same colors used for those terms on the drawings.
4. Check your answers in Appendix E.

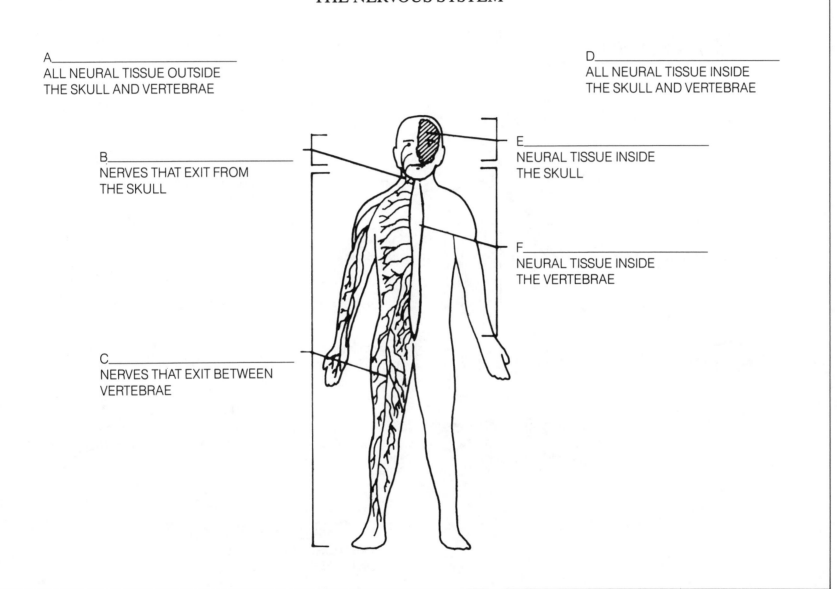

DRAWING 11–I
THE NERVOUS SYSTEM

A_____
ALL NEURAL TISSUE OUTSIDE
THE SKULL AND VERTEBRAE

B_____
NERVES THAT EXIT FROM
THE SKULL

C_____
NERVES THAT EXIT BETWEEN
VERTEBRAE

D_____
ALL NEURAL TISSUE INSIDE
THE SKULL AND VERTEBRAE

E_____
NEURAL TISSUE INSIDE
THE SKULL

F_____
NEURAL TISSUE INSIDE
THE VERTEBRAE

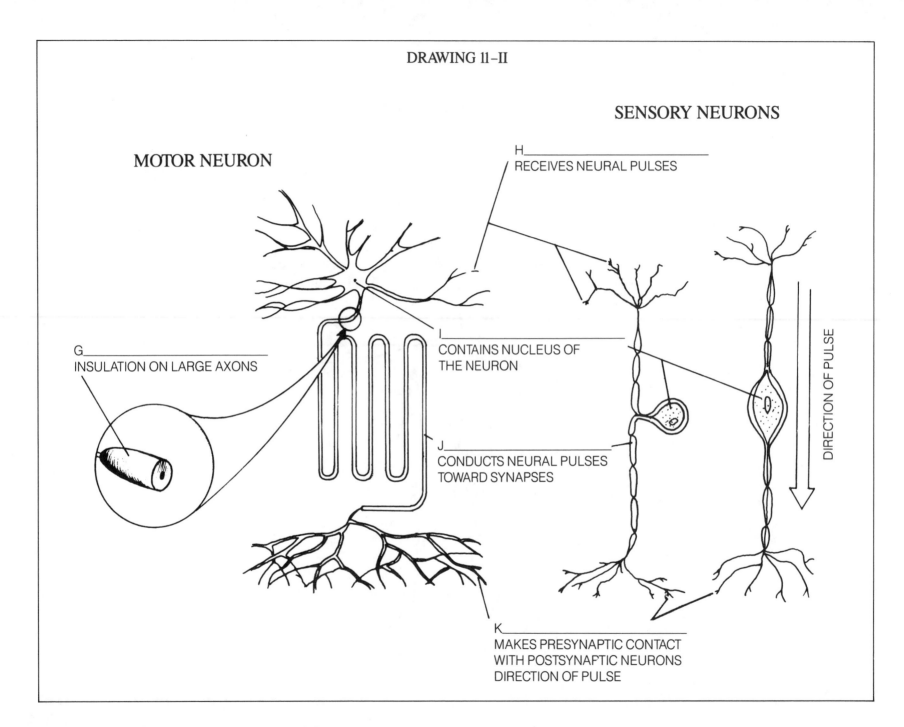

DRAWING 11–II

SENSORY NEURONS

MOTOR NEURON

H_____
RECEIVES NEURAL PULSES

G_____
INSULATION ON LARGE AXONS

I_____
CONTAINS NUCLEUS OF
THE NEURON

J_____
CONDUCTS NEURAL PULSES
TOWARD SYNAPSES

DIRECTION OF PULSE

K_____
MAKES PRESYNAPTIC CONTACT
WITH POSTSYNAPTIC NEURONS
DIRECTION OF PULSE

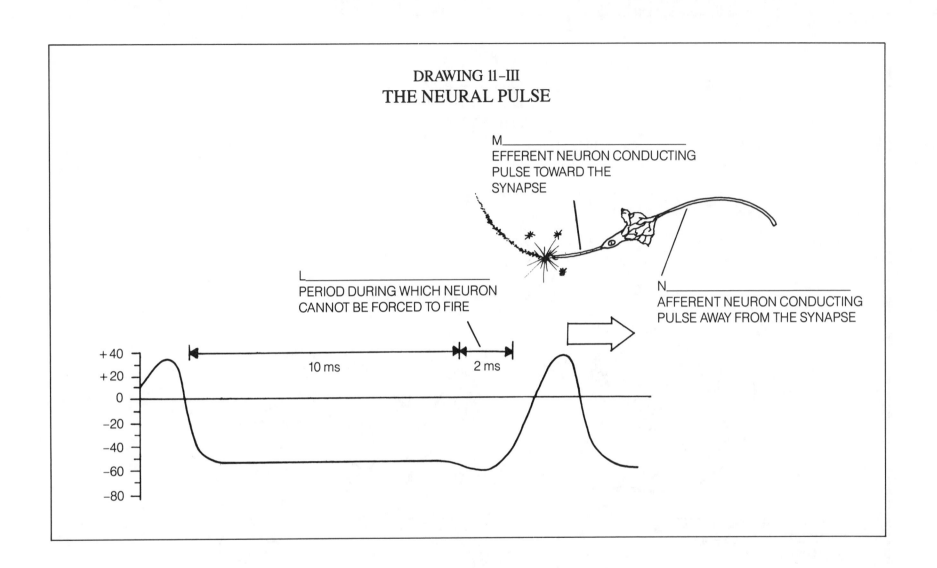

DRAWING 11–III
THE NEURAL PULSE

M_____
EFFERENT NEURON CONDUCTING
PULSE TOWARD THE
SYNAPSE

L_____
PERIOD DURING WHICH NEURON
CANNOT BE FORCED TO FIRE

N_____
AFFERENT NEURON CONDUCTING
PULSE AWAY FROM THE SYNAPSE

10 ms

2 ms

+40
+20
0
−20
−40
−60
−80

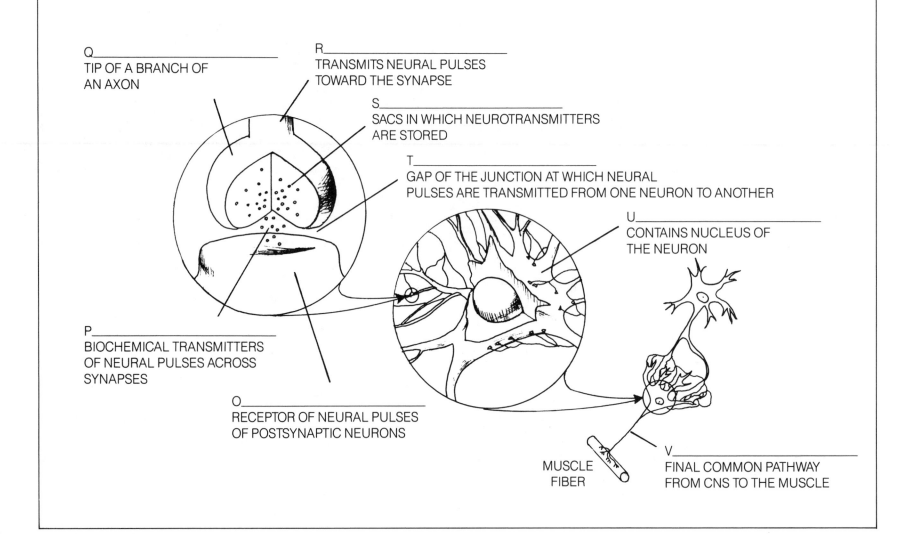

DRAWING 11–IV
THE SYNAPSE

Q_____
TIP OF A BRANCH OF
AN AXON

R_____
TRANSMITS NEURAL PULSES
TOWARD THE SYNAPSE

S_____
SACS IN WHICH NEUROTRANSMITTERS
ARE STORED

T_____
GAP OF THE JUNCTION AT WHICH NEURAL
PULSES ARE TRANSMITTED FROM ONE NEURON TO ANOTHER

U_____
CONTAINS NUCLEUS OF
THE NEURON

P_____
BIOCHEMICAL TRANSMITTERS
OF NEURAL PULSES ACROSS
SYNAPSES

O_____
RECEPTOR OF NEURAL PULSES
OF POSTSYNAPTIC NEURONS

MUSCLE
FIBER

V_____
FINAL COMMON PATHWAY
FROM CNS TO THE MUSCLE

Self-Study Test of Terminology

Self-Study Instructions: These questions can be used to help you assess how much you have retained from studying the Review Glossary. Answers are given in Appendix E.

(1) _____ Anatomically located mostly in the peripheral nervous system, functionally it controls the internal environment

(2) _____ The tip of a branch of an axon

(3) _____ The bioelectric discharge of a neuron

(4) _____ The fatty insulation on axons of large neurons

(5) _____ Membranous sacs in which neurotransmitters are stored until release into a synaptic gap

(6) _____ Anatomically, the division of the nervous system contained within the skull and vertebral column. Functionally, the division of the nervous system that mediates adjustments to the external environment

(7) _____ The level of stimulation above which a neuron will discharge

(8) _____ The nerve cell, all types of which contain dendrites, afferent processes, carrying pulses toward the cell body with its nucleus, and an axon, an efferent process, carrying pulses away from it

(9) _____ The junction at which neural pulses transfer from the axon of one neuron to the dendrite of another

(10) _____ The anatomical division of the nervous system located outside of the skull and vertebral column

(11) _____ The axon membrane through which current flows during the neural pulse

(12) _____ A synapse that transmits neurotransmitters that facilitate discharge in a postsynaptic neuron

(13) _____ Gaps in the myelin that speed up neural transmission

(14) _____ The brief period after a neuron fires during which no amount of stimulation can trigger another discharge

(15) _____ The chemicals that pass across a synaptic gap that change the electrical activity in the receptor

(16) _____ A neuron whose axon leads to a synapse

(17) _____ A synapse that transmits neurotransmitters that inhibit discharge in a postsynaptic neuron

(18) _____ A neuron whose dendrite receives pulses from a synapse

(19) _____ A dendrite receptor keyed to receive a particular neurotransmitter

Neural Transmission Functions

Self-Study Instructions: This test can be used to help you assess how well you understand the neural transmission functions. Terms to be filled in are from the Review Glossary. Answers are given in Appendix E.

Neural Function	*Neuroanatomy*
Generates neural pulse	(1) _____ of neuron (will eventually discharge spontaneously if not fired earlier under influence of other neurons)
Transmits neural pulse	
Within neuron	(2) From _____ toward
	(3) _____ of neuron
	to axon (4) _____
Across neurons	(5) _____ released
	from (6) _____
	across (7) _____
	to (8) _____
	of (9) _____
	neuron to (10) _____
	or (11) _____ its discharge
To musculature and from sense organs	(12) _____
To viscera for control of internal environment	(13) _____
	(14) _____
To higher brain centers for adaptation to external environment	(15) _____

CHAPTER TWELVE

Peripheral Nervous System Anatomy

The *peripheral nervous system* consists primarily of transmission lines carrying neural signals back and forth between the body and the portions of the nervous system protected by a bony cage (which are the main portions). Any neural tissue located outside of the skull or spinal column is, by definition, in the peripheral nervous system. This means that nerves that serve arms, toes, hands, lungs, heart, sense organs, and so forth, enter the peripheral nervous system as soon as they exit from the bony housing. This term is only an anatomical classification, which has no more to do with neural processes than crossing statelines has to do with the process of traveling through various states. Why bother with it, then? The reason is because it contains important neural structures that are less confusing to discuss separately in small chunks than as integral parts of one huge communication network. We will worry about integration in the final chapters.

PERIPHERAL NERVES

By all rights, we could cover the peripheral nervous system under two headings, spinal nerves and cranial nerves. These terms identify the two

general locations from which all nerves leave the bony housing: *spinal nerves* exit through the spinal column, *cranial nerves* exit from the base of the skull (Fig. 12–1).

In the adult, the peripheral nervous system has a total mass that is equal to about three quarters of the central nervous system. It has been estimated that the peripheral nervous system contains about 2.5 million fibers that carry messages to and from each side of the central nervous system. Approximately 2 million fibers are sensory, with the remaining number of slightly more than 0.5 million being motor. These estimates are difficult to derive and should be regarded with caution. As would be expected from the larger number of sensory than motor fibers, the sensory divisions of the nerves are larger than the motor ones. The average diameter of the cranial and spinal nerves ranges from a low of about 0.5 mm (motor component of the smallest spinal nerve) to a largest size of about 5mm (sensory component of the fifth cranial nerve).

The sensory components of the cranial and spinal nerves are the transmission pathways for millions of sensory receptors that inform the central nervous system about events both inside and outside the body. For example, the olfactory

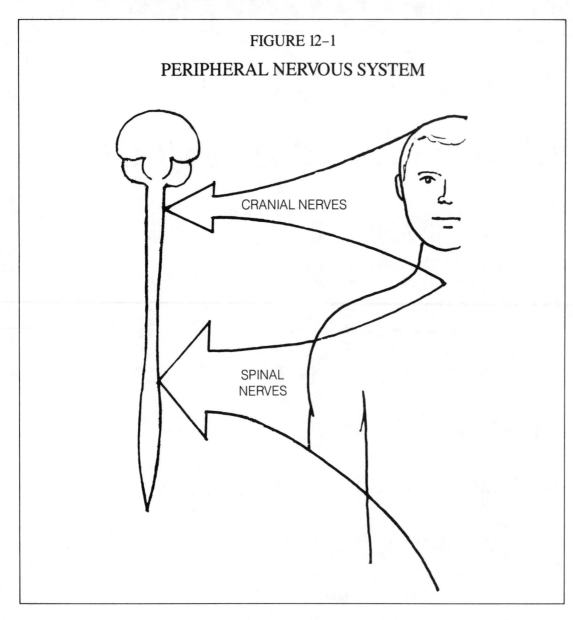

FIGURE 12-1

PERIPHERAL NERVOUS SYSTEM

CRANIAL NERVES

SPINAL
NERVES

(smell) receptors number about 200 million. With respect to vision, each eye possesses about 4 to 7 million cones and 75 to 175 million rods. Cranial Nerve V, about which we will say more later, contains about 140,000 sensory fibers on each side (like all peripheral nerves it is paired). The auditory nerve, Cranial Nerve VIII, receives sensory information on each side from about 30,000 receptors (called hair cells) within the organ of hearing.

The cranial nerves on each side are made up of an estimated 1,300,000 *sensory fibers* and 72,000 *motor fibers.* If the optic (vision) and olfactory (smell) fibers are removed from this number, the remainder totals about 300,000 sensory and 72,000 motor fibers, or a ratio of about 4:1 between sensory and motor. The spinal nerves on each side contain about 1 million sensory fibers in their posterior roots and about 210,000 fibers in their anterior roots. By summing the 1,372,000 cranial nerve fibers and the 1,210,000 spinal nerve fibers, we see a total nerve fiber population on each side of about 2.5 million, as mentioned earlier.

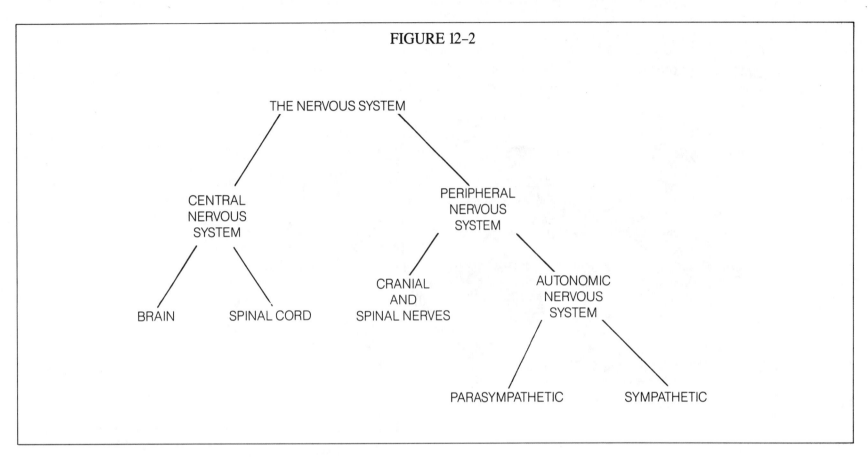

FIGURE 12-2

THE NERVOUS SYSTEM

CENTRAL NERVOUS SYSTEM

PERIPHERAL NERVOUS SYSTEM

BRAIN

SPINAL CORD

CRANIAL AND SPINAL NERVES

AUTONOMIC NERVOUS SYSTEM

PARASYMPATHETIC

SYMPATHETIC

We will take two liberties with our organization scheme (Fig. 12–2). One is that we will discuss the connections of peripheral nerves within the spinal cord and brainstem. In this way, we can preserve a sense of where sensory information is received, and where signals are loaded aboard motor nerves for transmission to muscles and glands. The other is that we will discuss connections of the autonomic nervous system, in so far as we are concerned with them. They are mainly outside of the skull and spinal column, so this affords the opportunity to clear the deck further for consideration of the central nervous system in the next chapter.

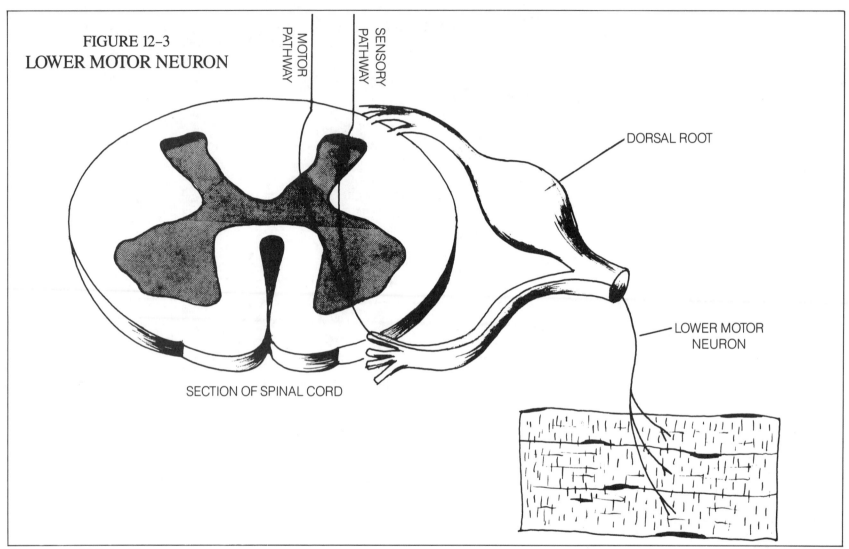

FIGURE 12–3
LOWER MOTOR NEURON

MOTOR PATHWAY

SENSORY PATHWAY

DORSAL ROOT

LOWER MOTOR NEURON

SECTION OF SPINAL CORD

Sensory and Motor Nerves

A preliminary word is in order about the difference between sensory and motor nerves in the peripheral nervous system. The cell bodies of sensory nerves are located outside the brain or spinal cord. Thus, neurons that receive sensory signals in the brain or spinal cord are separated by at least one synapse from the sensory nerve that picks up and transmits the signal from the receptor, such as a cochlear hair cell. Cell bodies of motor nerves, however, are located within the brainstem or spinal cord. The axons that extend from these cell bodies go directly to muscle fibers. Accordingly, a motor nerve in the peripheral nervous system is sometimes called *the final common pathway,* because it is the only connection a muscle fiber has with the nervous system. This nerve is also called the *lower motor neuron* because it is the lowest level at which higher motor centers can exert control of the body's musculature (Fig. 12–3).

Table 12–1. Cranial Nerves

On	Olfactory (I)	Sense of smell (olfaction)—S
Old	Optic (II)	Sense of sight (vision)—S
Olympus's	Oculomotor (III)	Eye movement—M
Towering	Trochlear (IV)	Eye movement—M
Top	Trigeminal (V)	Sensory to face and head; motor for mastication—S/M
A	Abducens (VI)	Eye movement—M
Finn	Facial (VII)	Sensory to tongue; motor for facial expression—S/M
And	Acoustic (VIII)	Sensory for audition and balance; small efferent component—S(E)
German	Glossopharyngeal (IX)	Sensory to tongue and pharynx; motor to pharynx—S/M
Vended	Vagus (X)	Complex nerve with sensory or motor fibers, or both, to larynx, respiratory system, gastrointestinal system. cardiac system—S/M
At	Accessory (XI)	Motor to shoulder, arm and throat—M
Hops	Hypoglossal (XII)	Motor to tongue, possible position (proprioception) sense—M(S)

A summary table for the cranial nerves based on the mnemonic *On old Olympus's towering top a Finn and German vended at hops* (other variants used by struggling anatomy students include "On old Olympus's towering top a fat auld German viewed a hop" and "On old Olympus topmost top a fat-eared German viewed a hop"). The cranial nerve number is shown in parentheses after the name of the nerve; function is summarized at the far right; and type of function is abbreviated S for sensory, M for motor, S/M for mixed, S(E) for sensory with possible efferent component, and M(S) for motor with possible sensory component.

CRANIAL NERVES OF SPEECH

Twelve pairs of cranial nerves emerge from the base of the skull through holes called *foramina* (singular, *foramen) (*Table 12–1). Each cranial nerve has a Roman numeral and a name. They are numbered, not in order of importance, but according to the height in the brain of their point of exit. The highest (closest to the top of the brain), the *olfactory nerve* (cranial nerve I) has to do with smell, followed by four nerves dealing with vision and eye muscles, the *optic* (II), *oculomotor* (III), *trochlear* (IV), and *abducens* (VI) (Fig. 12–4). Actually, the olfactory and optic nerves are extensions of the brain. They only emerge into the peripheral nervous system to the extent that the eyes are in sockets outside of the skull, and the olfactory receptors in the nasal mucosa just below the skull. None of these are of direct relevance to speech, so we will not elaborate on them.

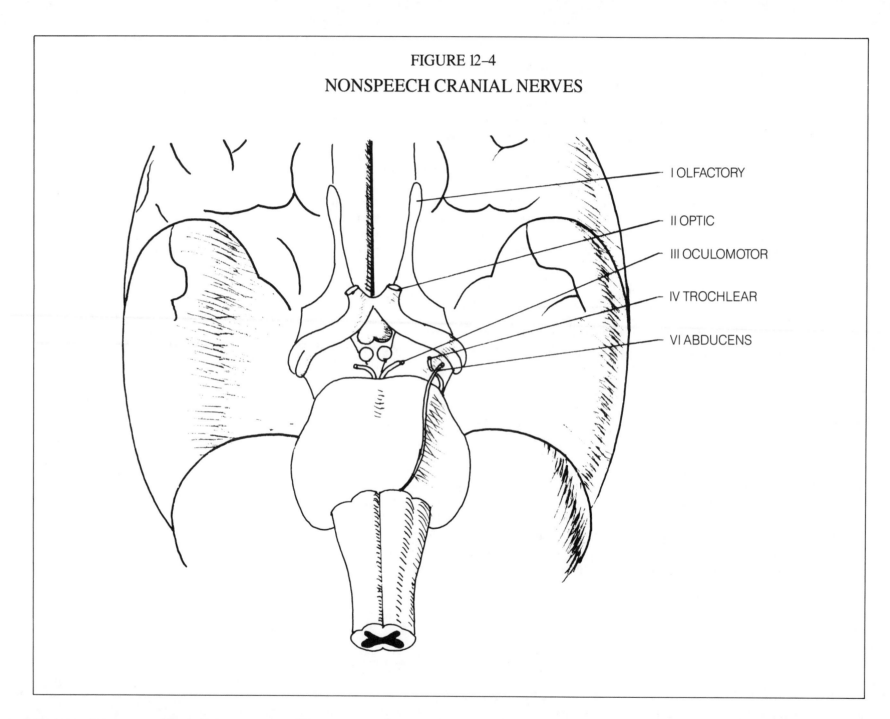

FIGURE 12–4
NONSPEECH CRANIAL NERVES

I OLFACTORY

II OPTIC

III OCULOMOTOR

IV TROCHLEAR

VI ABDUCENS

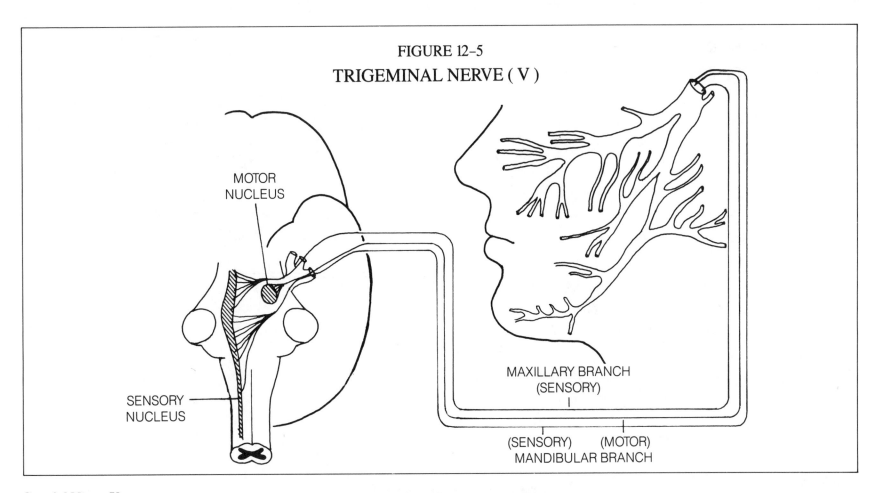

FIGURE 12-5

TRIGEMINAL NERVE (V)

MOTOR
NUCLEUS

SENSORY
NUCLEUS

MAXILLARY BRANCH
(SENSORY)

(SENSORY)   (MOTOR)
MANDIBULAR BRANCH

Cranial Nerve V

The *trigeminal nerve (V)* is the largest of the cranial nerves. It is named for the three branches of sensory and motor fibers that fan out from it. The upper branch carries sensations from around the eyes and nose, so we will not pursue it. The middle branch, the *maxillary branch,* is also sensory, but some of the sensations come from such speech structures as the mucous membranes lining portions of the mouth and throat. The lowest branch, the *mandibular branch,* carries a mixture of sensory and motor fibers. The sensory compo-

nents are from portions of the jaw and tongue. The motor fibers, however, are what make the trigeminal nerve important to speech; they serve mandibular and tongue muscles (Fig. 12–5).

The sensory nuclei that receive the input from all sensory fibers of the trigeminal nerve extend almost the length of the brainstem. (This is probably not surprising, considering the variety of sensory functions served by this nerve.) The motor nucleus, however, containing the cell bodies of the motor axons of nerve V, is located in a single clump about halfway up the brainstem.

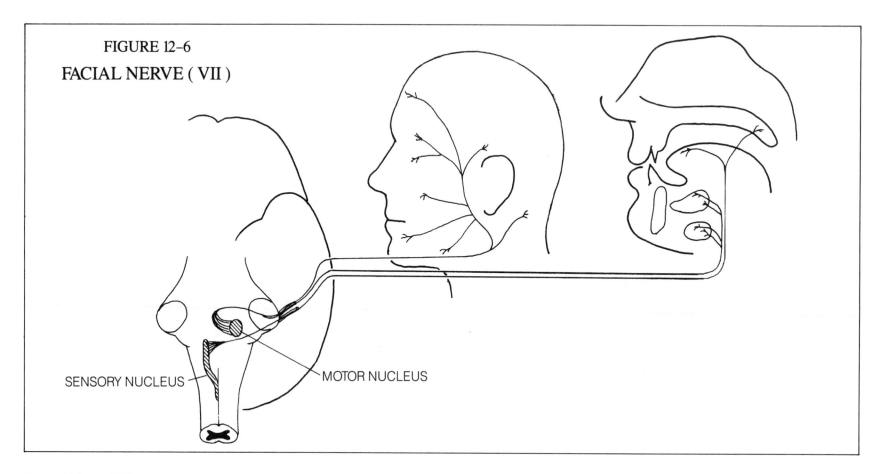

FIGURE 12-6

FACIAL NERVE (VII)

SENSORY NUCLEUS   MOTOR NUCLEUS

Cranial Nerve VII

The *facial nerve (VII),* like the trigeminal, contains both sensory and motor fibers. Its major significance for speech and hearing is that it supplies muscles of the face and the stapedius muscle in the middle ear. As for its sensory function, it serves the mucosa of the soft palate and provides taste from the front of the tongue. Without an intact facial nerve, facial expression and lip movements of speech, as well as taste, would be impaired. Depending on the damage, the effects can be grotesque, ranging from an immobile mask if the nerves on both sides were paralyzed, to one side of the face being normally expressive while the paralyzed side seems frozen.

Because structures in the mouth, nose, and throat evolved originally for eating and breathing, they have connections with the autonomic nervous system. Some of these connections are found in the facial nerve, which serves glands and mucous membranes in the vocal tract.

The motor nucleus, which sends axons to the facial muscles, is located below the motor nucleus of the trigeminal nerve (Fig. 12-6). (Actually, the nucleus of cranial nerve VI, with which we are not involved, is sandwiched between them.)

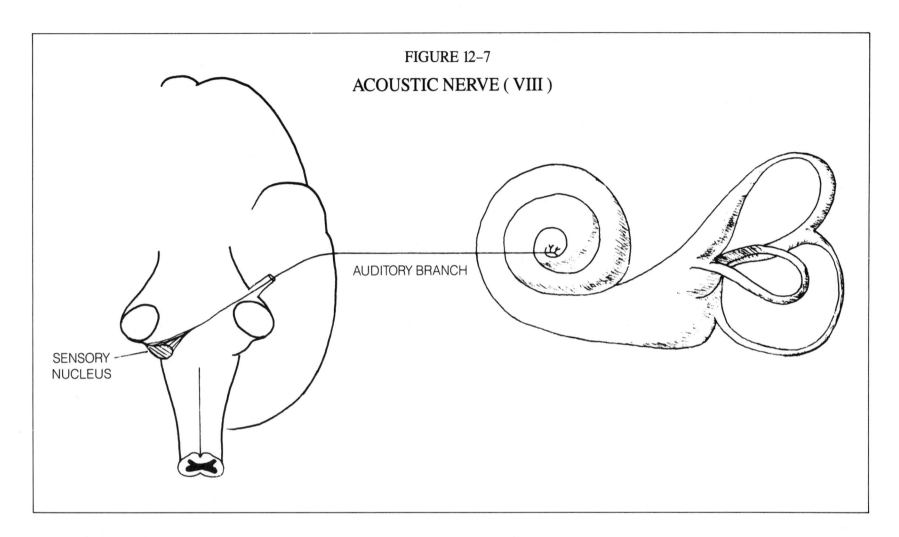

FIGURE 12-7

ACOUSTIC NERVE (VIII)

AUDITORY BRANCH

SENSORY
NUCLEUS

Cranial Nerve VIII

The *acoustic nerve (VIII)* is primarily sensory, but it carries nerves for two types of sensation: hearing and balance. For the same reasons we did not study the mechanism in the inner ear by which we maintain balance and perceive acceleration — the vestibular mechanism — we will not study the *vestibular branch* of the acoustic nerve. Obviously, the *auditory branch* is of vital interest (Fig. 12-7). Because we traced it from the hair cells in the organ of Corti to the cochlear nucleus in the lower part of the brainstem (where all fibers of the auditory branch synapse), we will not elaborate beyond the discussion in Chapter 10.

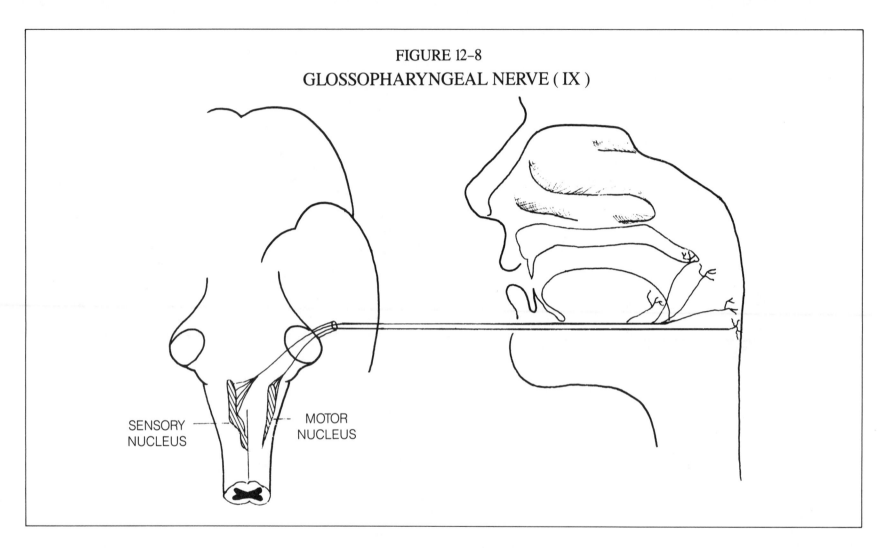

FIGURE 12–8

GLOSSOPHARYNGEAL NERVE (IX)

SENSORY NUCLEUS

MOTOR NUCLEUS

Cranial Nerve IX

The *glossopharyngeal nerve (IX)* somewhat like nerve VII, contains autonomic as well as sensory and motor fibers. Whereas nerve VII serves the face, the glossopharyngeal nerve, as its name implies, serves the tongue (glossus) and pharynx. It carries taste from the back of the tongue as well as supplying the pharyngeal mucosa and some glands. Most of its importance for speech is in its motor supply to some of the pharyngeal muscles (Fig. 12–8).

Both the motor and sensory nuclei of the glossopharyngeal nerve lie below the cochlear nucleus in the lowest level of the brainstem. The nuclei of this nerve also serve other cranial nerves.

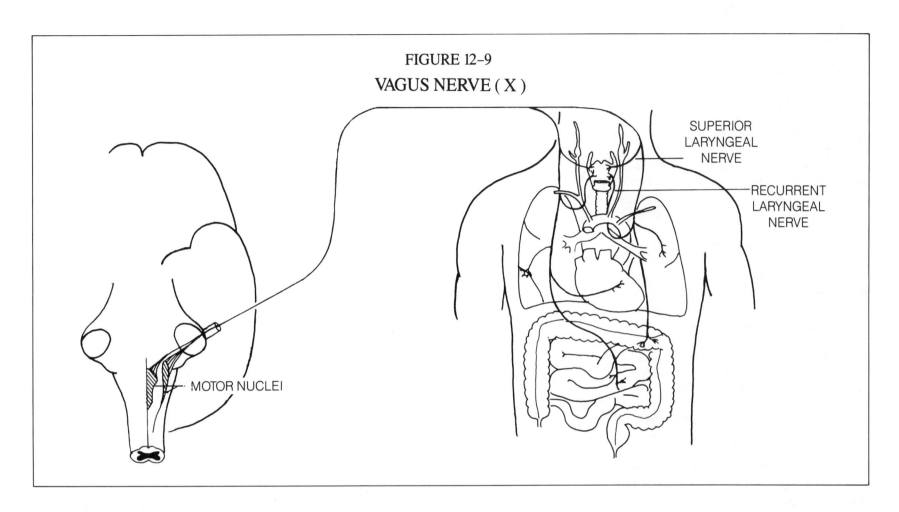

FIGURE 12–9
VAGUS NERVE (X)

SUPERIOR
LARYNGEAL
NERVE

RECURRENT
LARYNGEAL
NERVE

MOTOR NUCLEI

Cranial Nerve X

The *vagus nerve (X)* is named for the wandering course it follows ("vagus" means wanderer) all the way down through the chest and into the abdomen (Fig. 12-9). It, too, contains a mixture of autonomic, sensory, and motor fibers. It supplies more visceral structures (as you might suspect from its course) than any other cranial nerve. One of its speech functions is to supply some of the muscles and mucosa of the pharynx and soft palate.

The vagus has numerous branches, two of which are essential to speech. One of these main branches is the *superior laryngeal nerve,* which in turn, has two branches: the *external* and *internal branches.* The external branch carries motor axons to the cricothyroid muscle, which is largely responsible for lengthening the vocal cords for pitch adjustment. The internal branch is sensory and supplies the region from the base of the tongue and the mucosa of the supraglottal cavity (the laryngeal inlet).

The main branch that is most famous — or infamous, because of its vulnerability to damage — is the *recurrent laryngeal nerve*. Without it, voice would be impossible. Both the right and left recurrent nerves branch from the vagus below the level of the larynx. Accordingly, they have to double back on themselves (hence the name "recurrent") to supply all of the intrinsic laryngeal muscles — except the cricothyroid — and the subglottal laryngeal mucosa. The left recurrent nerve is longer than the right, and it loops under the aorta artery before ascending to the larynx. Because these nerves pass beneath the thyroid glands in their ascent, they are vulnerable to damage during thyroid surgery.

The effects of damage to laryngeal nerves can range from minor to major disaster. If one of the recurrent nerves were injured, one side of the larynx would be paralyzed, but a hoarse voice would usually be possible. If both sides were injured, the vocal cords frequently would be paralyzed in a closed position, which would make breathing exceedingly difficult. If they happened to be paralyzed in an open position, voice would then be impossible. The greatest risk would be from anesthetization of the internal branch of the superior laryngeal nerve (the likelihood of injury to this branch is slight). This branch provides the sensation for the gag reflex. Were this reflex anesthetized, the chance of choking on a piece of food would be considerable.

The motor and sensory nuclei of the cranial nerve X, some of which are shared with nerve IX, are located near the bottom of the brainstem. The fact that these nuclei are at such low levels bespeaks their importance for preservation of life. The more essential a function, such as breathing, the more primitive it is. This means that it evolved early. The neural centers that dispatch and receive signals for that function are in the oldest and lowest levels of the brain.

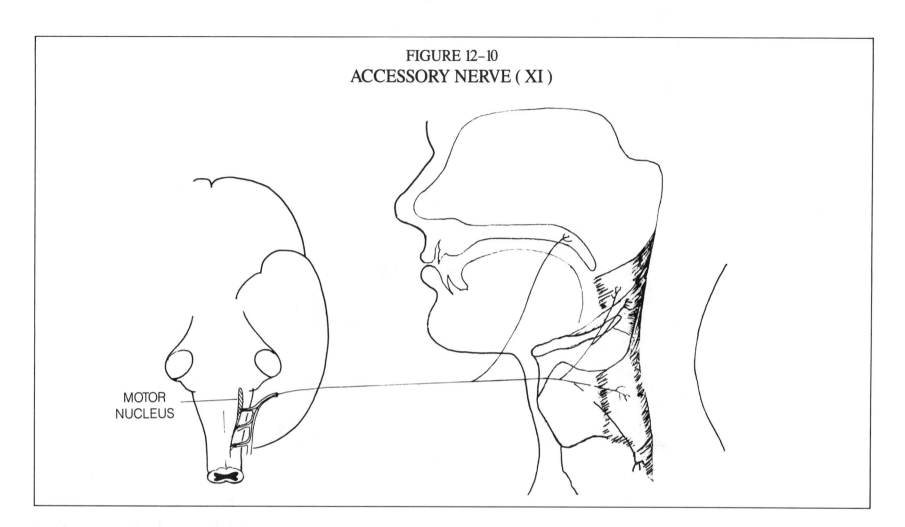

FIGURE 12-10
ACCESSORY NERVE (XI)

MOTOR
NUCLEUS

Cranial Nerve XI

The *accessory nerve* contains only motor fibers. It serves muscles of the pharynx, soft palate, and neck (Fig. 12–10). It is different from other cranial nerves in two respects. One is that it originates from motor nuclei in both the brainstem and the spinal cord. The other is that some of its branches join another nerve, the vagus, for distribution to the pharynx and velum.

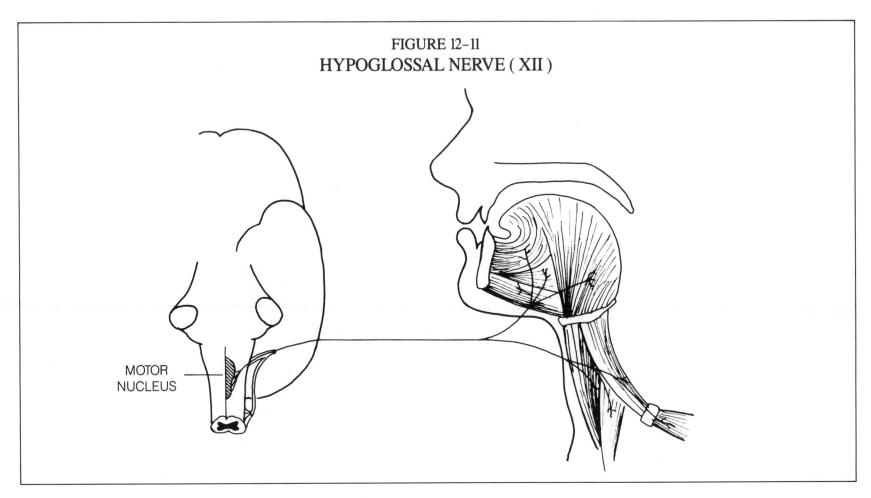

FIGURE 12-11
HYPOGLOSSAL NERVE (XII)

MOTOR
NUCLEUS

Cranial Nerve XII

The *hypoglossal nerve* is named for the structure it mainly serves, the tongue (Fig. 12–11). It is a motor nerve that supplies all of the intrinsic lingual muscles, most of the extrinsic muscles, and the infrahyoid muscles. Its nucleus is at the bottom of the brainstem, which bespeaks the importance of the tongue to swallowing, and the importance of swallowing to survival.

Summary

The innervation pattern of the cranial nerves most important for speech can be summarized according to the following verbal formula:

1. The extrinsic and intrinsic tongue muscles are innervated by the hypoglossal (XII) nerve, except the palatoglossus, which is grouped with (2) below.
2. Muscles of the palate, pharynx, and larynx are supplied by the vagal group (IX, X, XI), except the tensor palatini, which is grouped with (3) below.
3. The muscles of mastication are innervated by the trigeminal (V) nerve, except the posterior belly of the digastric, which is grouped with (4) below.
4. The muscles of facial expression are innervated by the facial (VII) nerve, which also supplies the stapedius muscle of the middle ear. The other middle ear muscle, the tensor tympani, is innervated by the trigeminal (V) nerve.

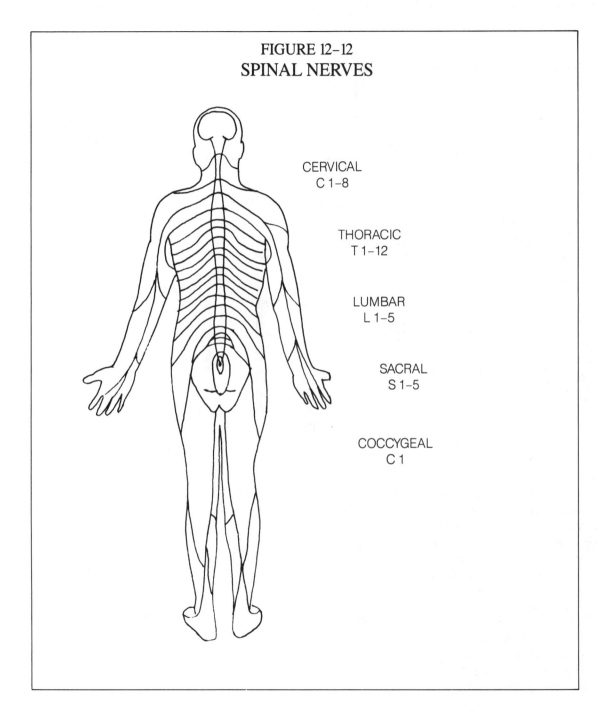

FIGURE 12–12
SPINAL NERVES

CERVICAL
C 1–8

THORACIC
T 1–12

LUMBAR
L 1–5

SACRAL
S 1–5

COCCYGEAL
C 1

SPINAL NERVES

Spinal nerves are of concern to us because they serve the respiratory apparatus. They also have a large role in control of the autonomic nervous system. This system is of some interest because much of our speech equipment (such as the mouth, throat, and larynx) evolved originally to serve basic biological needs, hence it is intimately connected to the ANS.

Thirty-one pairs of *spinal nerves* emerge from between the vertebrae. They are identified by the level of the spinal column from which they exit: *cervical, thoracic, lumbar, sacral,* and *coccygeal* (Fig. 12–12). The thoracic nerves are of special interest because they serve respiration by innervating muscles of the chest wall. Unlike cranial nerves, which differ considerably from one to another, spinal nerves are quite similar.

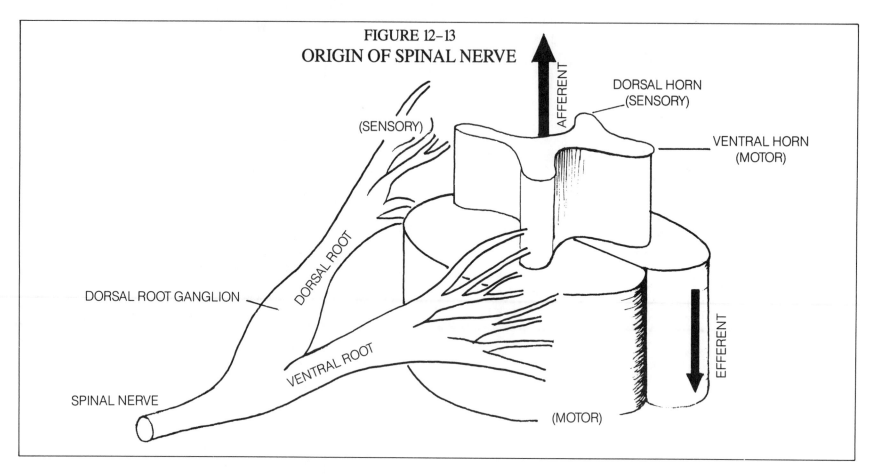

FIGURE 12–13
ORIGIN OF SPINAL NERVE

AFFERENT

DORSAL HORN
(SENSORY)

VENTRAL HORN
(MOTOR)

(SENSORY)

DORSAL ROOT

DORSAL ROOT GANGLION

VENTRAL ROOT

EFFERENT

SPINAL NERVE

(MOTOR)

Each spinal nerve is connected to the spinal cord by a *dorsal root* and a *ventral root* (Fig. 12–13). The ventral root contains efferent fibers carrying motor signals. The bulk of these fibers are lower motor neurons going directly to skeletal muscles. Cell bodies of the motor fibers are located in the *ventral,* or *anterior, horns* of the core of the spinal cord. Cell bodies constitute the *gray matter* of the nervous system, and transmission fibers between cell bodies form the *white matter.* In the spinal cord, cell bodies are organized in columns resembling an "H" on the inside of the cord, as can be seen in Figure 12–13. The anterior (ventral) horns contain cell bodies of motor nerves; the posterior (dorsal) horns contain sensory cell bodies. Surrounding this gray matter is the white matter of afferent and efferent pathways connecting the spinal cord to the brain. The dorsal root contains afferent fibers carrying sensory information from the body to the nervous system. Unlike the ventral root, cell bodies of the dorsal root are in the *dorsal root ganglion* ("ganglion" is another name for a collection of cell bodies) outside, rather than inside, the spinal cord. The dorsal and ventral roots join together in a single bundle before leaving the vertebra as a spinal nerve.

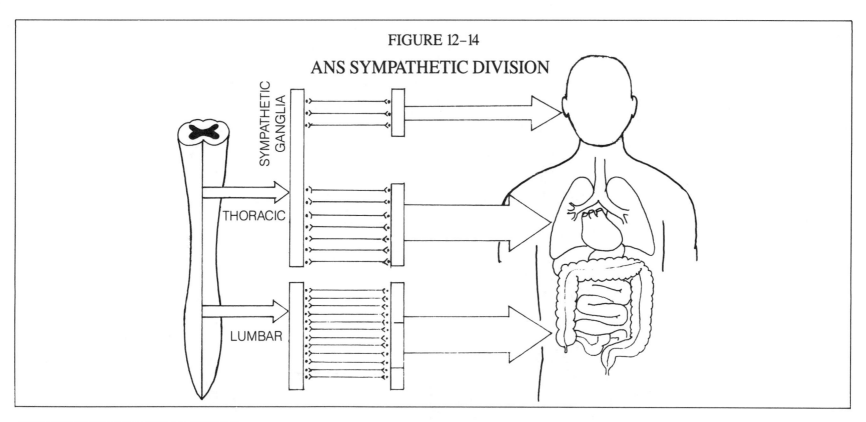

FIGURE 12-14

ANS SYMPATHETIC DIVISION

SYMPATHETIC GANGLIA

THORACIC

LUMBAR

AUTONOMIC NERVOUS SYSTEM

The *autonomic nervous system* (ANS) is a functional system for controlling the internal environment. Its master control center is deep in the brain (the hypothalamus). We will encounter it in the next chapter. In this chapter, we will look briefly at how the ANS is constructed in the peripheral nervous system to control the internal organs of the body.

The ANS has two divisions that work in opposition to each other. The *sympathetic division* (sometimes called the *thoracolumbar division* because these are the levels of the spinal cord that serve this division) prepares the body for "flight or fight." It activates the internal environment to cope

with emergency. The *parasympathetic division* (also called the *craniosacral division* because it is supplied by cranial nerves and sacral level spinal nerves) is responsible for calming the viscera after an emergency has passed. Thus, if you turned a corner in your hometown and came face to face with a lion, your heart would pump faster, you would breathe deeper, you would perspire, and your digestion would slow. These would be among the expected reactions produced by your sympathetic division. If you discovered the lion was merely stuffed and on display, then your parasympathetic division would reverse these visceral reactions and restore you to your normally unjangled condition.

Because the sympathetic division must act quickly in preparing the body for emergency, it is "wired" to sound a general alarm. As you can see in Figure 12-14, no direct connection exists between the spinal cord and visceral organs. Unlike skeletal muscle fibers, each of which has its own private lower motor neuron to innervate it, the sympathetic division supplies innervation more or less by broadcast. The ventral roots of thoracic and lumbar spinal nerves contain sympathetic motor fibers that all go to an interconnected chain of *sympathetic ganglia,* which extends along the outside of the spinal column. From there, connections may go to other ganglia before reaching the organ to be innervated.

Peripheral Nervous System Anatomy

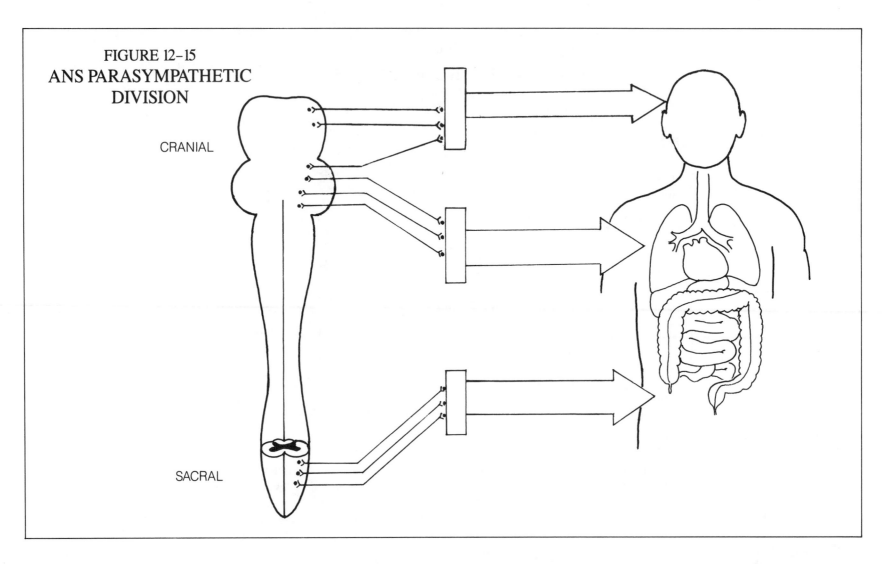

FIGURE 12–15
ANS PARASYMPATHETIC
DIVISION

CRANIAL

SACRAL

Virtually all of the organs served by the sympathetic division are also served by cranial and sacral motor fibers of the parasympathetic division (Fig. 12–15). They, too, synapse in ganglia before reaching the organ served. These ganglia are not as interconnected as in the sympathetic chain.

This chapter on the peripheral nervous system has been concerned with cranial and spinal nerves that carry sensory information about the body and external world to the spinal cord and brain, and motor information to the skeletal muscles and visceral organs. We concentrated on the cranial nerves that are important to speech and language, yet touched on spinal nerves enough to show how chest wall muscles receive innervation for respiration. Finally, we concluded with a glimpse of the autonomic nervous system, which is of little direct concern to speech and language. In fact, the most direct concerns — the ANS nerves to the mouth, throat, and larynx — were skirted intentionally. The gain in understanding would not have warranted the cost of sorting out the complex intricacies of these connections.

CHAPTER TWELVE

Self-Study

Peripheral Nervous System Anatomy

Review Glossary

Gray matter: The characteristic appearance of collections of cell bodies in the nervous system

White matter: The characteristic appearance of bundles of axons in transmission pathways of the nervous system

Sensory fiber: The component of a nerve that carries information from a peripheral sense organ

Motor fiber: The component of a nerve that carries information to muscles and glands

Spinal nerves: Nerves emerging from cervical, thoracic, lumbar, sacral, or coccygeal vertebrae that carry motor and sensory information to and from the body

   Ventral horn (anterior horn): The cluster of cell bodies of motor neurons in the spinal cord

   Ventral root: The motor axons that emerge from the spinal cord to join a spinal nerve

   Lower motor neuron: The neuron that is the final common pathway over which any motor signal must travel to reach a muscle

   Dorsal horn (posterior horn): The cluster of sensory neuron synapses in the spinal cord

   Dorsal root: The sensory axons that enter the spinal cord from the spinal nerve

   Dorsal root ganglion: The cluster of cell bodies of sensory neurons near their entrance to the spinal cord

Cranial nerves: The 12 pairs of nerves that emerge from the brainstem through foramina in the base of the skull

   I   Olfactory (sense of smell): Unrelated to speech

   II   Optic nerve (sense of sight): Unrelated to speech

   III   Oculomotor nerve (eye muscles): Unrelated to speech

   IV   Trochlear nerve (eye muscle): Unrelated to speech

   V   Trigeminal nerve: Sensory fibers to face, motor fibers to jaw and tongue muscles

   VI   Abducens nerve (eye muscle): Unrelated to speech

   VII   Facial nerve: Motor fibers to facial muscles; sensory fibers unrelated to speech

   VIII   Acoustic nerve: Sensory fibers of hearing and balance from cochlear and vestibular mechanisms

   IX   Glossopharyngeal nerve: Motor fibers to pharyngeal muscles, sensory fibers unrelated to speech

   X   Vagus nerve: Branches of this nerve serve pharynx and larynx; superior laryngeal nerve subdivides into external branch with motor fibers to the cricothyroid muscle and internal branch with sensory fibers from the larynx; recurrent laryngeal nerve carries motor fibers to remaining intrinsic laryngeal muscles

   XI   Accessory nerve: Motor fibers to muscles of neck, pharynx, and velum

   XII   Hypoglossal nerve: Motor fibers to muscles of the tongue and infrahyoid strap muscles

Autonomic Nervous System (ANS): The nervous system that regulates the internal environment

   Sympathetic division: The division of the ANS connected to the spinal cord through thoracic and lumbar vertebrae, that arouses internal organs for fight or flight

     Sympathetic ganglia: The chain of synapse clusters connecting the sympathetic axons as they emerge from the spinal cord to neurons leading to internal organs

   Parasympathetic division: The division of the ANS connected to the brain by cranial nerves and to the spinal cord by sacral nerves, that calms the viscera after an emergency

Self-Study Coloring Instructions

1. Fill in the appropriate terms in blanks *A* through *Y* and *a* through *m* in Drawings 12–I through 12–IV.
2. Using felt-tip pens, draw a line through *A* with yellow and *B* with light red; *C* through *D* should be shades of yellow; *E* through *F* dark shades of red; and *G* through *I* shades of purple.
3. Using colored pencils match the colors for *J* through *P, Q* through *Y,* and *a* through *m* to the appropriate colors for *C* through *D, E* through *F,* and *H* through *I*.
4. Color terms in the Glossary with the same colors used for those terms in the drawings.
5. Check your answers in Appendix E.

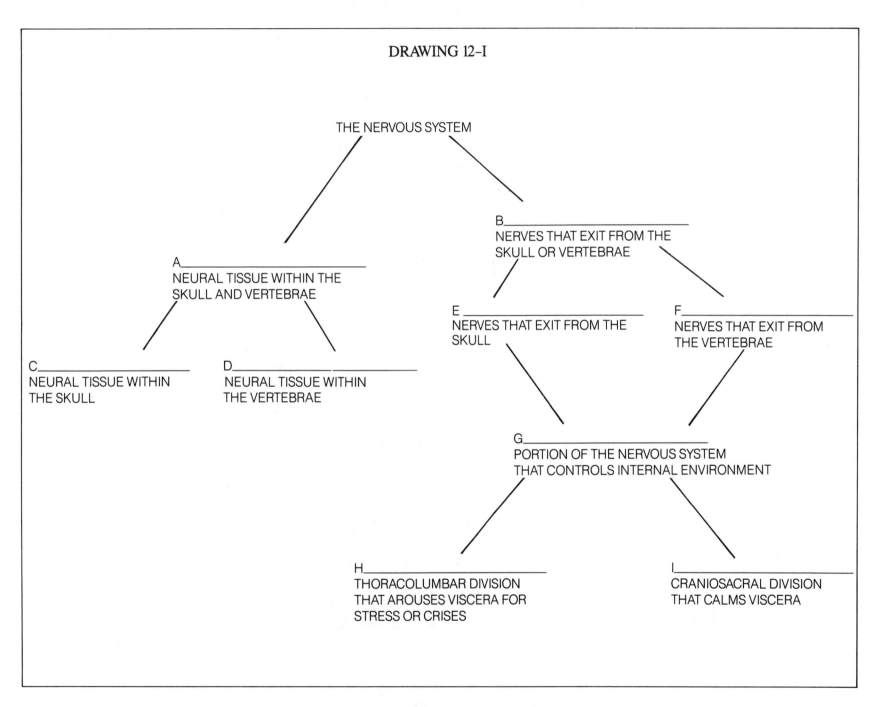

DRAWING 12–I

THE NERVOUS SYSTEM

A_____
NEURAL TISSUE WITHIN THE
SKULL AND VERTEBRAE

B_____
NERVES THAT EXIT FROM THE
SKULL OR VERTEBRAE

C_____
NEURAL TISSUE WITHIN
THE SKULL

D_____
NEURAL TISSUE WITHIN
THE VERTEBRAE

E_____
NERVES THAT EXIT FROM THE
SKULL

F_____
NERVES THAT EXIT FROM
THE VERTEBRAE

G_____
PORTION OF THE NERVOUS SYSTEM
THAT CONTROLS INTERNAL ENVIRONMENT

H_____
THORACOLUMBAR DIVISION
THAT AROUSES VISCERA FOR
STRESS OR CRISES

I_____
CRANIOSACRAL DIVISION
THAT CALMS VISCERA

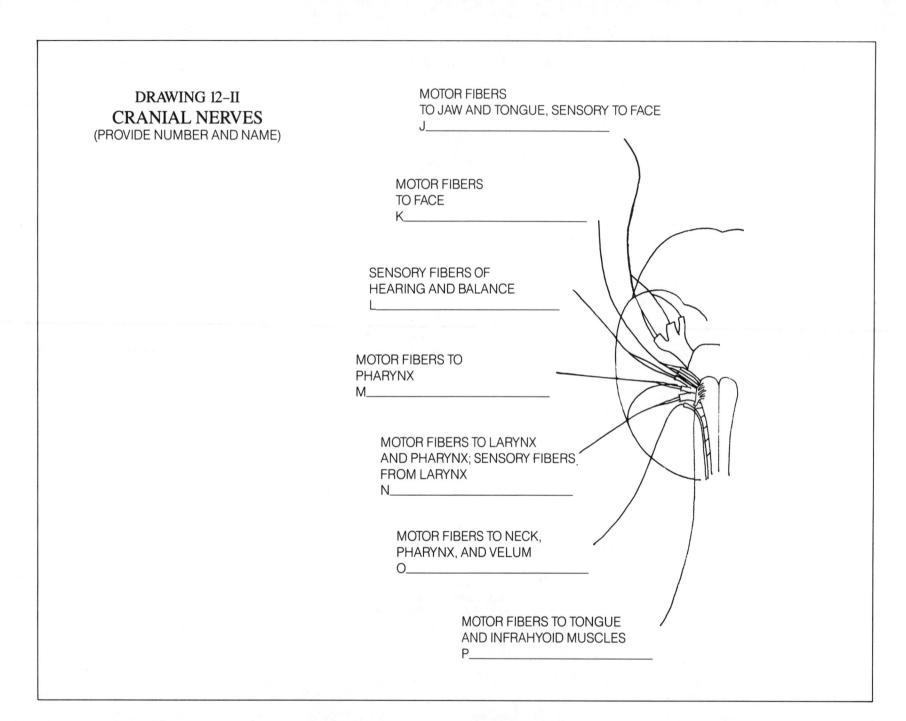

DRAWING 12–II
CRANIAL NERVES
(PROVIDE NUMBER AND NAME)

MOTOR FIBERS
TO JAW AND TONGUE, SENSORY TO FACE
J_____

MOTOR FIBERS
TO FACE
K_____

SENSORY FIBERS OF
HEARING AND BALANCE
L_____

MOTOR FIBERS TO
PHARYNX
M_____

MOTOR FIBERS TO LARYNX
AND PHARYNX; SENSORY FIBERS
FROM LARYNX
N_____

MOTOR FIBERS TO NECK,
PHARYNX, AND VELUM
O_____

MOTOR FIBERS TO TONGUE
AND INFRAHYOID MUSCLES
P_____

DRAWING 12–III
SPINAL CORD SECTION

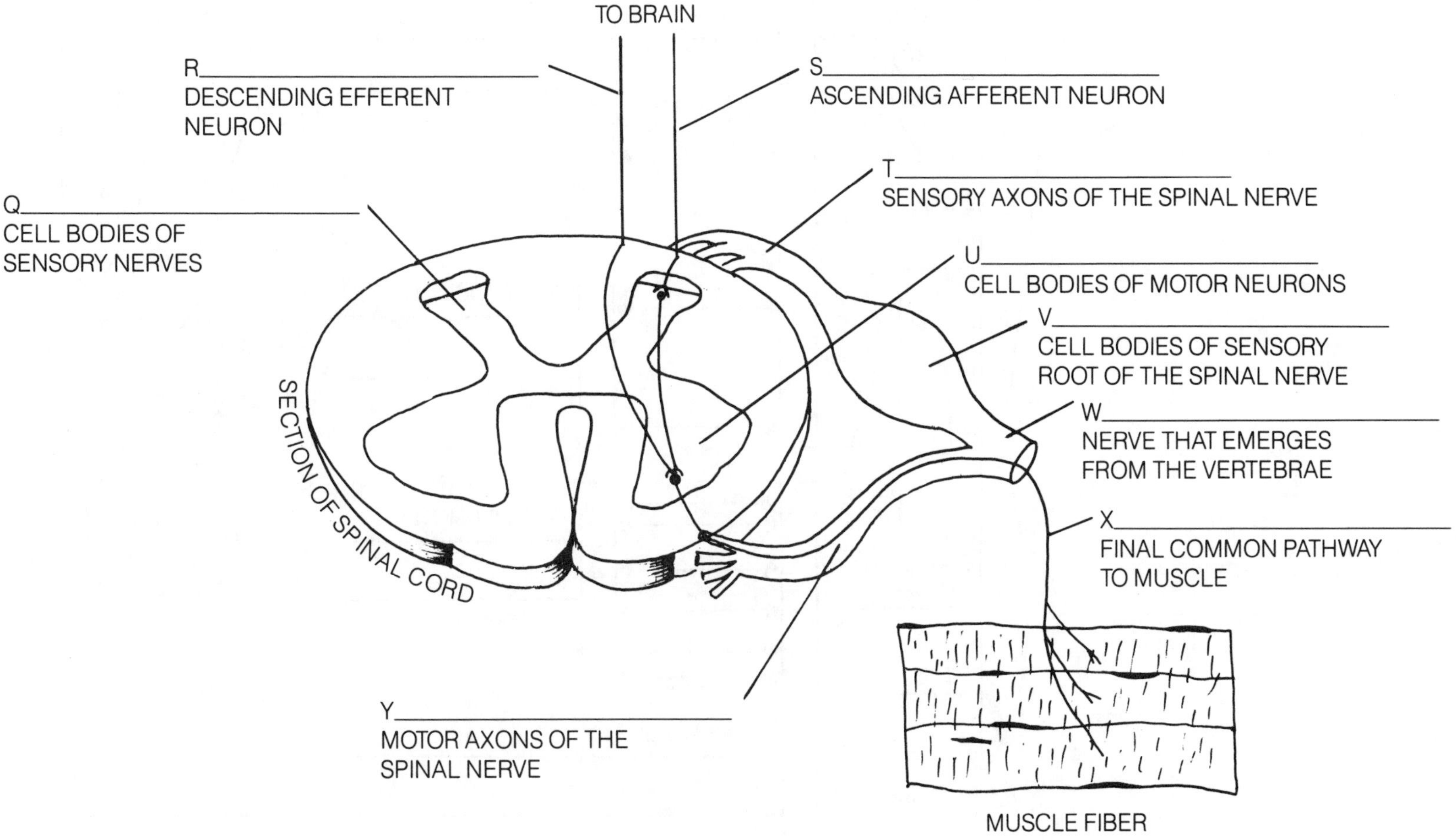

TO BRAIN

R_____
DESCENDING EFFERENT
NEURON

S_____
ASCENDING AFFERENT NEURON

T_____
SENSORY AXONS OF THE SPINAL NERVE

Q_____
CELL BODIES OF
SENSORY NERVES

U_____
CELL BODIES OF MOTOR NEURONS

V_____
CELL BODIES OF SENSORY
ROOT OF THE SPINAL NERVE

SECTION OF SPINAL CORD

W_____
NERVE THAT EMERGES
FROM THE VERTEBRAE

X_____
FINAL COMMON PATHWAY
TO MUSCLE

Y_____
MOTOR AXONS OF THE
SPINAL NERVE

MUSCLE FIBER

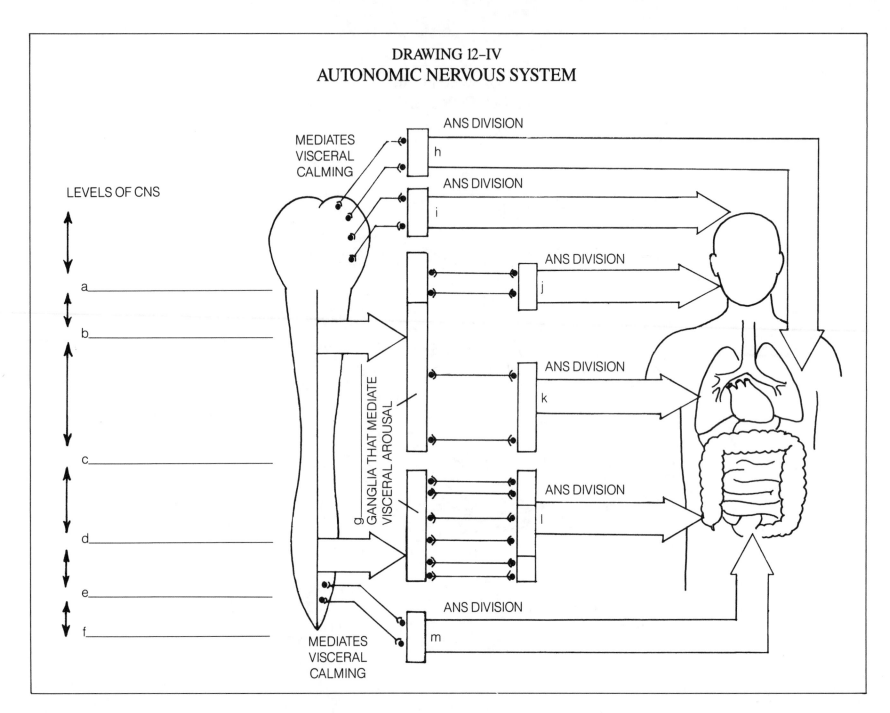

DRAWING 12–IV
AUTONOMIC NERVOUS SYSTEM

LEVELS OF CNS

a _____

b _____

c _____

d _____

e _____

f _____

MEDIATES
VISCERAL
CALMING

MEDIATES
VISCERAL
CALMING

GANGLIA THAT MEDIATE VISCERAL AROUSAL

g

ANS DIVISION

h

ANS DIVISION

i

ANS DIVISION

j

ANS DIVISION

k

ANS DIVISION

l

ANS DIVISION

m

Functional Anatomy of Speech, Language, and Hearing

Self-Study Test of Terminology

Self-Study Instructions: These questions can be used to help you assess how much you have retained from studying the Review Glossary. Answers are given in Appendix E.

(1) _____ The cluster of sensory neuron synapses in the spinal cord

(2) _____ Nerves emerging from cervical, thoracic, lumbar, sacral, or coccygeal vertebrae that carry motor and sensory information to and from the body

(3) _____ The cluster of cell bodies of sensory neurons near their entrance to the spinal cord

(4) _____ The cluster of cell bodies of motor neurons in the spinal cord

(5) _____ The neuron that is the final common pathway over which any motor signal must travel to reach a muscle

(6) _____ The sensory axons that enter the spinal cord from the spinal nerve

(7) _____ The motor axons that emerge from the spinal cord to join a spinal nerve

(8) _____ The 12 pairs of nerves* that emerge from the brainstem through foramina in the base of the skull

(*9) _____ Unrelated to speech

(*10) _____ Unrelated to speech

(*11) _____ Unrelated to speech

(*12) _____ Unrelated to speech

(*13) _____ Unrelated to speech

(*14) _____ Branches of this nerve serve pharynx and larynx; superior laryngeal nerve subdivides into external branch with motor fibers to the cricothyroid muscle and internal branch with sensory fibers from the larynx; recurrent laryngeal nerve carries motor fibers to remaining intrinsic laryngeal muscles

(*15) _____ Motor fibers to pharyngeal muscles, sensory fibers unrelated to speech

(*16) _____ Motor fibers to facial muscles, sensory fibers unrelated to speech

(*17) _____ Motor fibers to muscles of the tongue and infrahyoid strap muscles

(*18) _____ Sensory fibers to face, motor fibers to jaw and tongue muscles

(*19) _____ Sensory fibers of hearing and balance from cochlear and vestibular mechanisms

(*20) _____ Motor fibers to muscles of neck, pharynx, and velum

(21) _____ The division of the autonomic nervous system, connected to the brain by cranial nerves and to the spinal cord sacral nerves, that calms the viscera after an emergency

(22) _____ The division of the autonomic nervous system, connected to the spinal cord through thoracic and lumbar vertebrae, that arouses internal organs for fight or flight

(23) _____ The nervous system that regulates the internal environment

(24) _____ The chain of synapse clusters connecting the sympathetic axons as they emerge from the spinal cord to neurons leading to internal organs

(25) _____ The characteristic appearance of bundles of axons in transmission pathways

(26) _____ The component of a nerve that carries information from a peripheral sense organ

(27) _____ The characteristic appearance of collections of cell bodies

(28) _____ The component of a nerve that carries information to muscles and glands

Speech Functions of the Peripheral Nervous System

Self-Study Instructions: This test can be used to help you assess how well you understand the speech functions of the peripheral nervous system. Terms to be filled in are from the Review Glossary. Answers are given in Appendix E.

Speech Function	Neuroanatomy
Motor signals to	
Respiratory muscles of	
the chest wall	(1) _____ _____
	_____ spinal nerves
Intrinsic phonatory muscles	
of the larynx	(2) _____
Abduct vocal cords	(3) _____
Adduct vocal cords	(4) _____
Stiffen vocal cords	(5) _____
Lengthen vocal cords	(6) _____
Raise and lower larynx	(7) _____
Pharyngeal constrictors	(8) _____
	(9) _____
Raise and lower velum	(10) _____
Articulatory muscles of tongue	(11) _____
Raise and lower jaw	(12) _____
Round and spread lips	(13) _____
Sensory signals from ear	(14) _____

CHAPTER THIRTEEN
Central Nervous System Anatomy

Ancient Greeks thought the function of the brain was to cool the blood, like a radiator. A few decades ago, the brain was compared to a switchboard. More recently we thought of it as a giant computer. In reality, it is much more than any of these.

It is becoming increasingly clear as more and more different types of neurotransmitters and neurohormones are discovered that the brain is a glandular communication system as well as an electrical transmission network. That we are only beginning to understand its complexity is reflected in neuron counts that have risen from estimates of 10 billion a decade or so ago to as high as a trillion. When we asked a neurosurgeon friend the reason for such wildly different estimates, he replied, not entirely facetiously, "The fellow who does the counting hasn't finished yet."

Recognizing that each neuron can involve thousands of synapses where communication goes on with untold numbers of neurotransmitters, our neurosurgeon went on to say that he now views the brain as providing an infinite number of interconnections, which suggests to him a neurological basis for the philosophic concept of free will, which opens the prospect that mind and brain interact. On one hand, there is no doubt that the

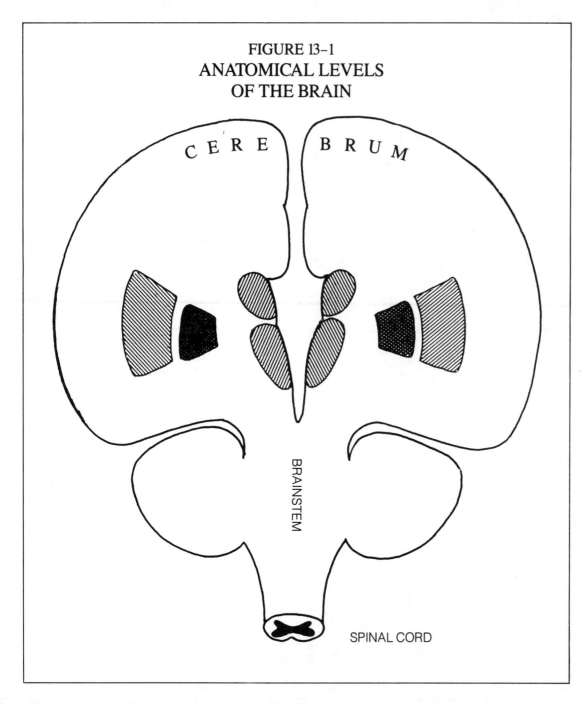

FIGURE 13–1
ANATOMICAL LEVELS
OF THE BRAIN

CEREBRUM

BRAINSTEM

SPINAL CORD

brain is the organ with which we think and feel. Possibly, however, the way we think and feel is also a determinant of how the brain functions.

This is a heady prospect, but our concerns are more immediate. The brain has evolved much as an ancient building that has been lived in by untold generations. Modifications and improvements have been added on, but little has been torn out. New structures have been attached to old structures with the result that some of the functions of those old structures have changed.

These structural changes are reflected in the organization of the *central nervous system* (CNS), which is contained within the skull and spinal column. The brain is in the skull, specifically in the cranium. The spinal cord extends down from it (Fig. 13–1) through a tunnel in the vertebrae. Whereas the spinal cord is organized similarly at all levels, so that a section of it at the tip will resemble sections at, say, chest levels, the brain becomes increasingly different in its anatomical organization at progressively higher levels.

The reason for this difference is that the spinal cord is mainly a cable for transmitting afferent and efferent signals back and forth between the brain and the peripheral nervous system. Accordingly, these transmission lines have a consistent arrangement within the spinal cord. Although important synaptic connections within the gray matter of the cord are responsible for basic reflexes, they, too, are organized similarly from one level to another.

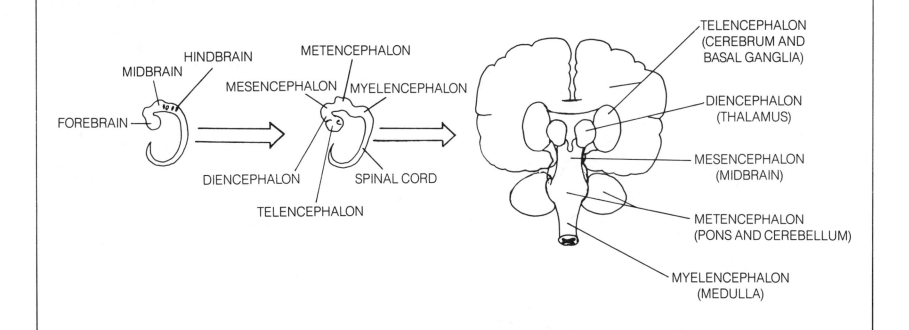

FIGURE 13–2
DEVELOPMENTAL STAGES
OF THE BRAIN

With the brain, however, the major function is synaptic transfer of neural signals. The brain is a gigantic miniaturized switching mechanism that processes inputs from all of the senses, integrates them with memory and thought processes, and organizes them for purposive action. At the lowest levels of the brain, these operations are reflexive. At the highest levels they involve abstract thought. Accordingly, the neural equipment for these functions changes from one level of the brain to another.

In this chapter, we will inspect the various major structures of the brain that are important for speech, language, and hearing. These structures begin developing in the embryo, first as the forebrain, midbrain, and hindbrain; later during fetal development they subdivide into the embryological levels of the completed brain with which the child is born. The *hindbrain* subdivides into the *myelencephalon* and *metencephalon*. The *midbrain* does not subdivide, but remains as the *mesencephalon*. The *forebrain* subdivides into the *diencephalon*

and *telencephalon*.

It is from these embryological divisions that the anatomical structures of the brain emerge. Thus, as shown in Figure 13–2, the telencephalon gives rise to the *cerebrum* and *basal ganglia*, the diencephalon to the *thalamus* and *hypothalamus*, the mesencephalon remains the *midbrain*, the metencephalon gives rise to the *pons* and *cerebellum*, and the myelencephalon to the *medulla*. These are the anatomical levels that will be considered.

FIGURE 13–3
BRAINSTEM STRUCTURES

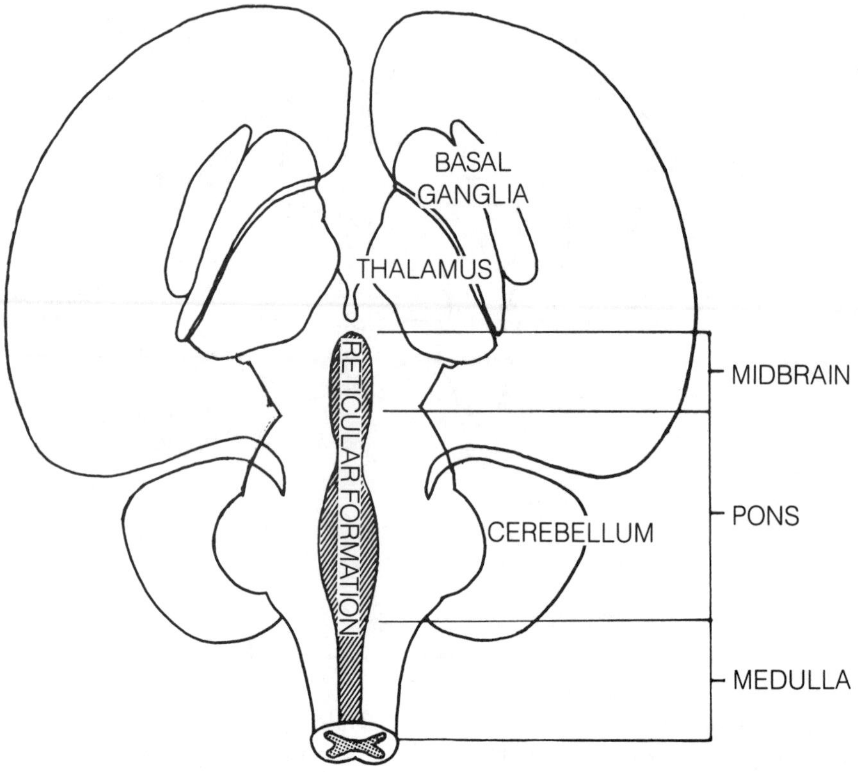

BASAL GANGLIA

THALAMUS

RETICULAR FORMATION

MIDBRAIN

PONS

CEREBELLUM

MEDULLA

BRAINSTEM

Enough has been said about the spinal cord for our purposes, so we will begin the discussion in this chapter at the bottom of the brainstem, which consists of the trunk of the brain up to the level at which it branches into two stalks, leading to two hemispheres. This stem is, in effect, the continuation of the transmission pathways from the spinal cord to the base of the cerebrum. Thus, the structures of the brainstem that we will examine are the medulla, pons, midbrain, and reticular formation (Fig. 13–3). Above them are the thalamus, basal ganglia, and cerebrum.

The brainstem is the primitive brain dating back half a billion years. It is virtually the entire brain of a cold-blooded reptile, hence its designation as the reptilian brain. It was, and is, mainly concerned with survival, controlling such bodily functions as breathing and heart rate. It also controls alertness for incoming information of importance to life. Much as we may choose to think of ourselves as rational humans, our evolutionary roots are still with us. Emotions were here long before thinking.

FIGURE 13-4

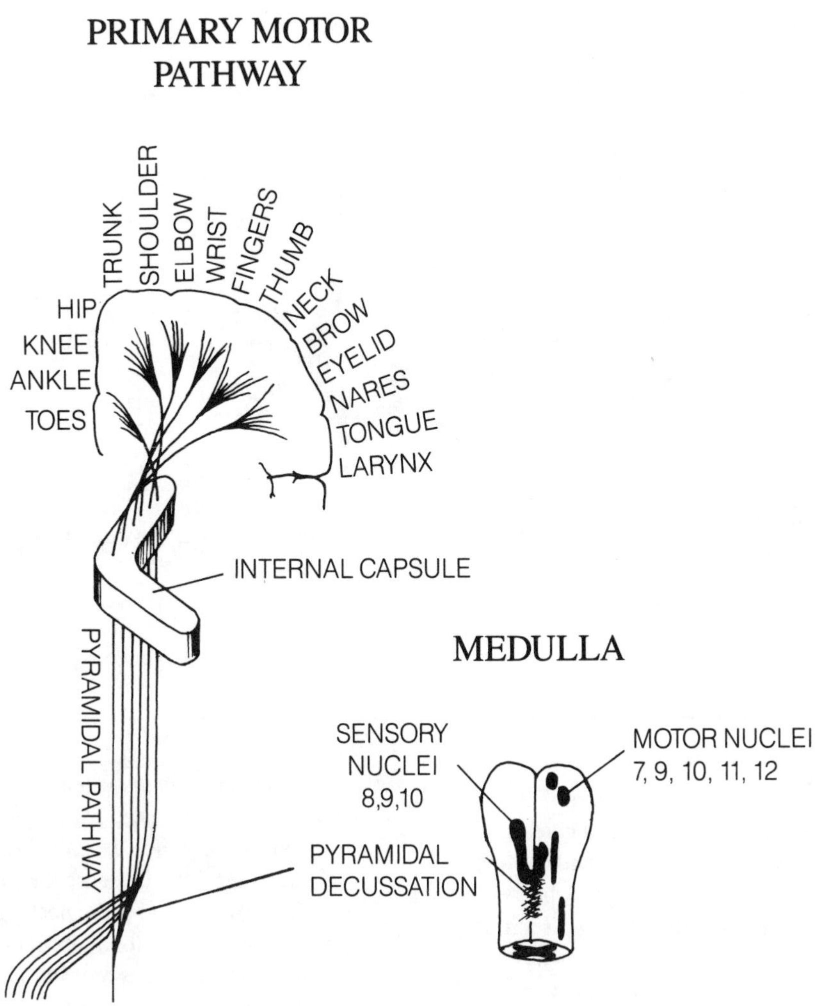

PRIMARY MOTOR
PATHWAY

Labels (left to right, curving over): HIP, KNEE, ANKLE, TOES, TRUNK, SHOULDER, ELBOW, WRIST, FINGERS, THUMB, NECK, BROW, EYELID, NARES, TONGUE, LARYNX

INTERNAL CAPSULE

PYRAMIDAL PATHWAY

MEDULLA

SENSORY NUCLEI 8,9,10

MOTOR NUCLEI 7, 9, 10, 11, 12

PYRAMIDAL DECUSSATION

Medulla

After the spinal cord passes through the relatively large hole in the skull called the *foramen magnum,* it becomes the *medulla* (Fig. 13–4). This lowest level of the brainstem most closely resembles the spinal cord because it consists primarily of transmission pathways. One of these is the major pathway for signals to muscles from the motor centers in the cerebral cortex. This pathway is called the *pyramidal tract.* Because much of this tract from the right cerebral hemisphere and the tract from the left hemisphere cross over each other in the medulla, the left side of the brain controls the right side of the body and vice versa. This crossover is known as the *pyramidal decussation.* It is the heavy myelin insulation, particularly on pyramidal fibers, from which the medulla gets its embryological name: myelencephalon (meaning myelinated brain).

Also within the medulla are nuclei (nuclei being clumps of cell bodies where synapses occur) of several cranial nerves that serve speech and hearing. Most notable of these, along with motor nuclei of cranial nerves IX through XII, are the cochlear and olivary nuclei of the auditory pathway.

Another feature of the medulla that must be noted is the *restiform body (inferior cerebellar peduncle),* which connects the sensory feedback channels from muscles, tendons, and joints to the cerebellum. (We will consider the significance of this information when we discuss the cerebellum.) *Peduncles* are stalks or arms, sometimes called *brachia,* of transmission fibers. In this case, the inferior cerebellar peduncles are stalks of fibers that pass through the medulla en route to the cerebellum from the body.

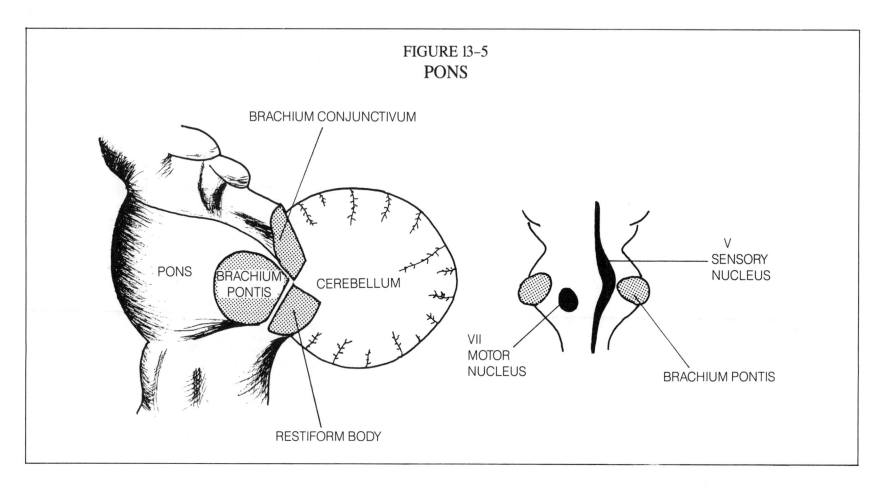

FIGURE 13–5
PONS

BRACHIUM CONJUNCTIVUM

PONS

BRACHIUM PONTIS

CEREBELLUM

RESTIFORM BODY

V
SENSORY
NUCLEUS

VII
MOTOR
NUCLEUS

BRACHIUM PONTIS

Pons

Pons means bridge, which is the basis for the name of the segment of brainstem just above the medulla (Fig. 13–5). The most distinguishing characteristic of the pons is the *brachium pontis* (the *middle cerebellar peduncle*) that bridges across the brainstem to join the two cerebellar hemispheres, as shown in Figure 13–5. Like an arm wrapped around the pons, it connects the motor planning centers of the brain to the cerebellum. The pons also contains nuclei for cranial nerves V and VII.

Midbrain

The *midbrain,* as its name suggests, is in the middle, between the hindbrain and the forebrain (Fig. 13–6). It is a connecting link between lower and higher centers of the brain. As such, it contains the massive *brachium conjunctivum (superior cerebellar peduncle)* by which the cerebellum is connected to the motor centers of the cerebrum and basal ganglia. These latter connections are in the *red nucleus,* also located in the midbrain. So, too, is the *substantia nigra,* an important motor center that has been implicated in Parkinson's disease.

The midbrain also contains relay stations in the auditory and visual pathways. There are four stations, each a nucleus, called *colliculi.* The pair of nuclei serving vision are the superior colliculi; the inferior colliculi serve hearing and mediate startle responses to loud, abrupt sounds. Together these nuclei appear as four bumps on the back side of the midbrain. They are referred to collectively as the *quadrigeminal bodies.*

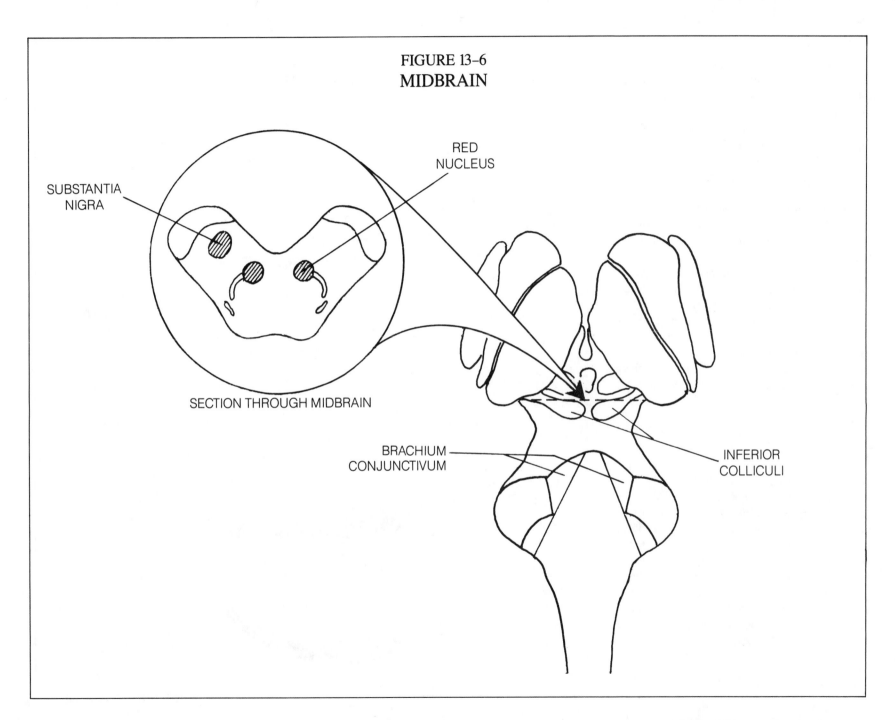

FIGURE 13-6
MIDBRAIN

RED
NUCLEUS

SUBSTANTIA
NIGRA

SECTION THROUGH MIDBRAIN

BRACHIUM
CONJUNCTIVUM

INFERIOR
COLLICULI

Thalamus

Above the midbrain, the brainstem divides into two stalks from which the two cerebral hemispheres sprout. Below these hemispheres are the thalamic bodies, one in each stalk, generally known as the *thalamus*. It is the head end of the old sensory system from which the cerebrum evolved. Accordingly, all sensory pathways (with the exception of olfaction, which is the oldest, most primitive sense) terminate in the thalamus. From there, sensory information is relayed to the cerebrum. In the case of hearing, the auditory relay nucleus is called the *medial geniculate body* (both thalamic bodies have one).

The thalamus is far more than a relay station, however. It is perhaps the most essential subcortical integrating mechanism of the brain. It stitches together information from all of the senses, except olfaction, and from all parts of the brain. As might be expected, therefore, the thalamus is more than a single nucleus, it is a large aggregation of nuclei about the size of a small egg. As can be seen in Figure 13–7, most of the cerebral cortex is connected to it.

Closely associated with the thalamus are several other nuclei, only one of which we will discuss. The *hypothalamus*, as its name suggests, is situated below the thalamus at the base of the brain. In fact, the tip end of the hypothalamus attaches to the *pituitary gland*, the body's master gland, which sits in a well-protected bony saddle in the skull. Because the hypothalamus is a part of the central nervous system, hence responsive to the external environment, and because it is connected to the autonomic as well as the *endocrine system*, it serves to control the internal environment so that the organism responds appropriately to the demands of the outside world.

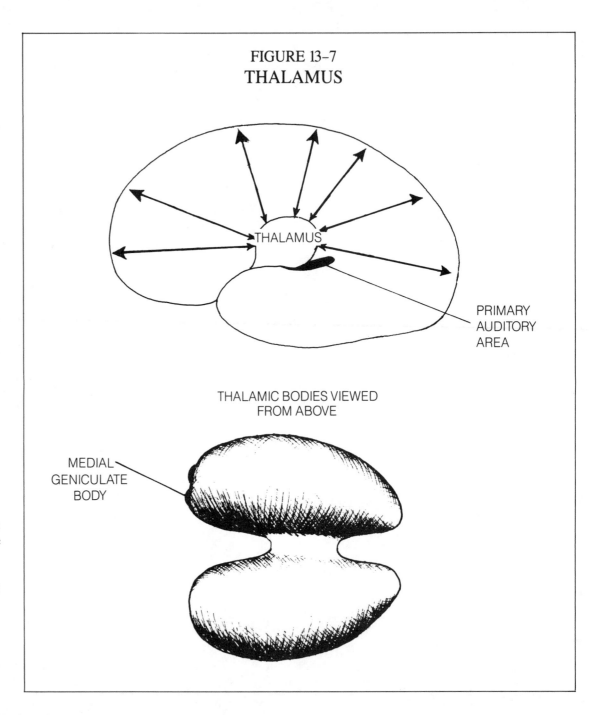

FIGURE 13–7
THALAMUS

THALAMUS

PRIMARY
AUDITORY
AREA

THALAMIC BODIES VIEWED
FROM ABOVE

MEDIAL
GENICULATE
BODY

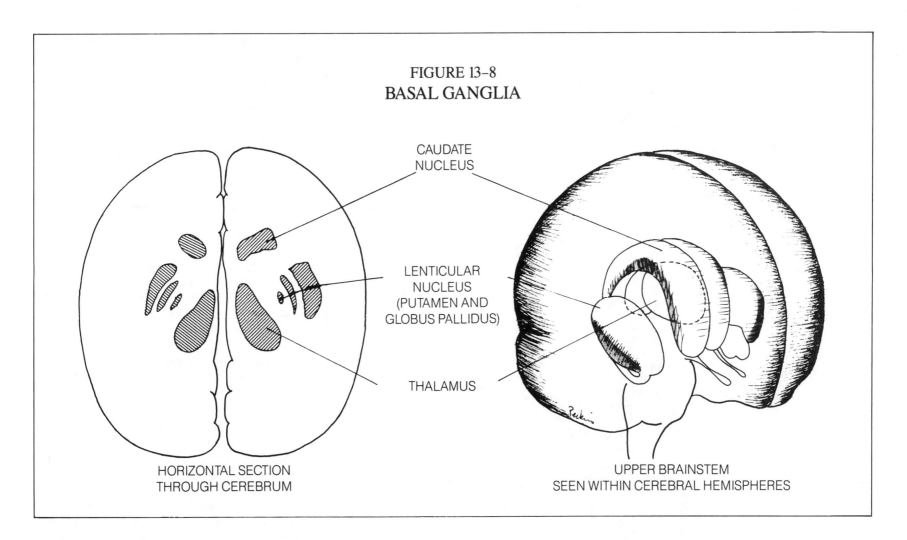

FIGURE 13-8
BASAL GANGLIA

CAUDATE
NUCLEUS

LENTICULAR
NUCLEUS
(PUTAMEN AND
GLOBUS PALLIDUS)

THALAMUS

HORIZONTAL SECTION
THROUGH CEREBRUM

UPPER BRAINSTEM
SEEN WITHIN CEREBRAL HEMISPHERES

Basal Ganglia

Just as the thalamus is at the top of the old sensory system from which the cerebrum evolved, so is the *basal ganglia* at the head end of the old motor system. In man, it now functions as a motor relay and integrating center. Although some disagreement exists as to which nuclei belong in it, all agree that it has two major nuclei, the *caudate nucleus* and the *lenticular nucleus*.

The lenticular nucleus, named for its resemblance to a lens, is lateral to the thalamus and consists of two nuclei, the *putamen* and *globus pallidus*. The caudate (the term means having a tail) gets its name from its shape. The head of the caudate attaches to the lenticular nucleus and, as can be seen in Figure 13-8, the tail wraps around the thalamus.

FIGURE 13-9
INTERNAL CAPSULE

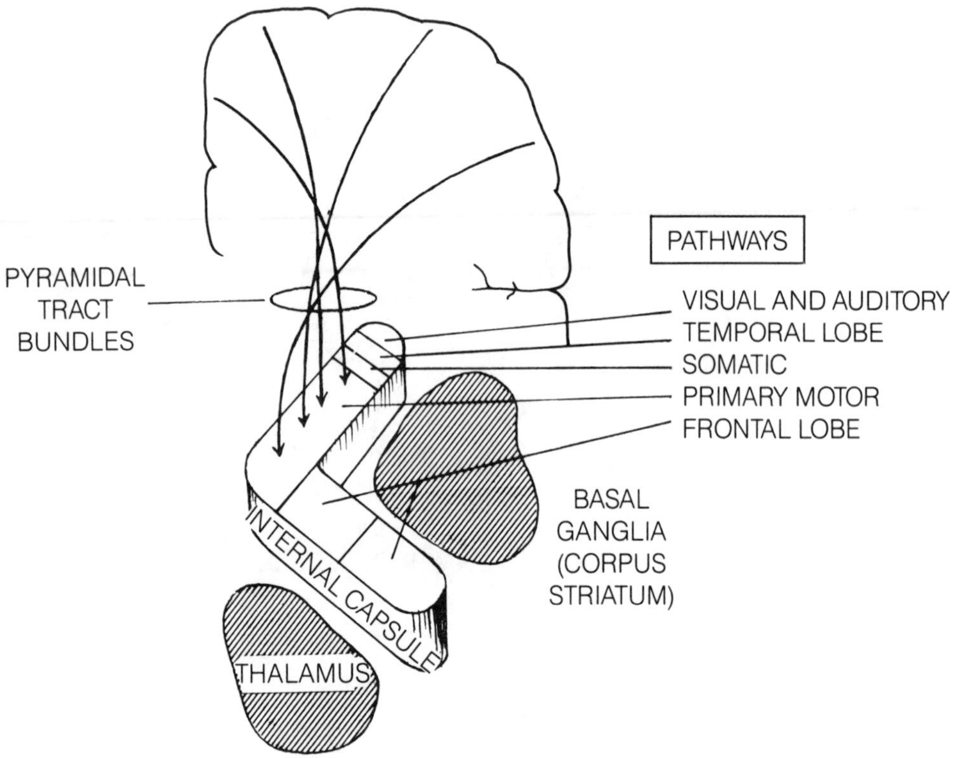

PYRAMIDAL
TRACT
BUNDLES

PATHWAYS

VISUAL AND AUDITORY
TEMPORAL LOBE
SOMATIC
PRIMARY MOTOR
FRONTAL LOBE

BASAL
GANGLIA
(CORPUS
STRIATUM)

INTERNAL CAPSULE

THALAMUS

Separating the caudate from the lenticular nucleus is a massive pathway connecting the cerebral cortex with the brainstem and spinal cord. Called the *internal capsule* (Fig. 13–9), its fibers are insulated with white myelin. The visual effect of these fibers passing through the basal ganglia is to create a striated appearance. Hence, the basal ganglia are also called the *striate bodies* or *corpus striatum*.

Reticular Formation

Neuroanatomists have long known that the *reticular formation* extends from the thalamus down through the brainstem into the upper spinal cord (Fig. 13–10). They named it for its netlike appearance, formed by a mixture of gray and white matter. Recall that gray matter (cell bodies) is arranged as a continuous column in the spinal cord and as clumps (nuclei and ganglia) in the brainstem. The white matter (transmission fibers) surrounds and is discrete from the gray matter. Why this standard arrangement in the nervous system is different in the reticular formation was not understood until little more than a few decades ago.

With understanding of how the reticular system functions has come an enlarged conception of how the entire nervous system is organized functionally (Fig. 13–10). Early attempts to stimulate this system electrically produced just about any response, all of them frustratingly inconsistent. We now know that the reticular system is an integrative mechanism for both sensory input and motor output. As such, it is essential to consciousness and attention.

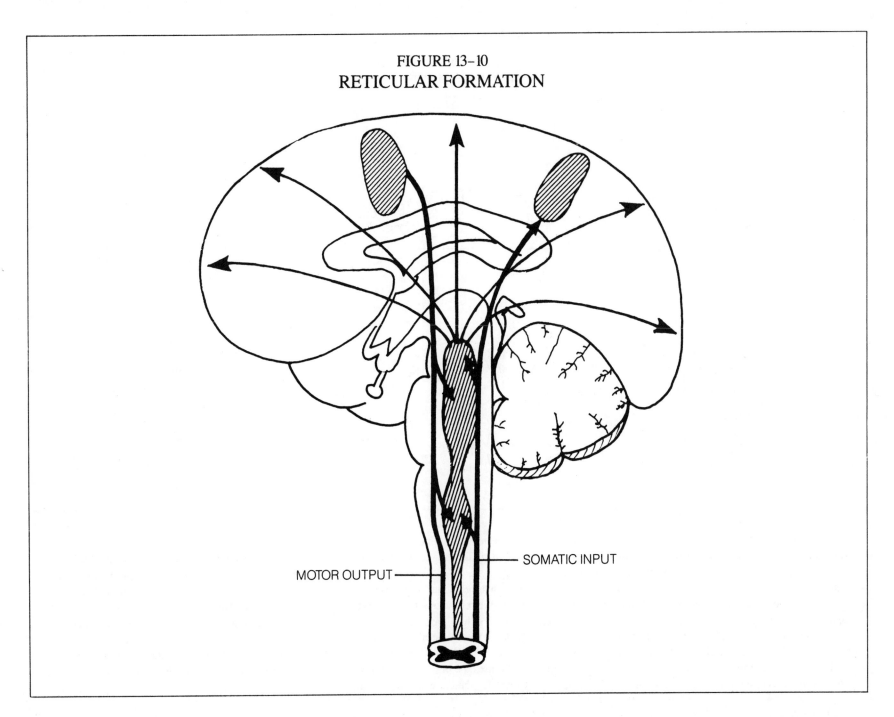

FIGURE 13–10
RETICULAR FORMATION

MOTOR OUTPUT

SOMATIC INPUT

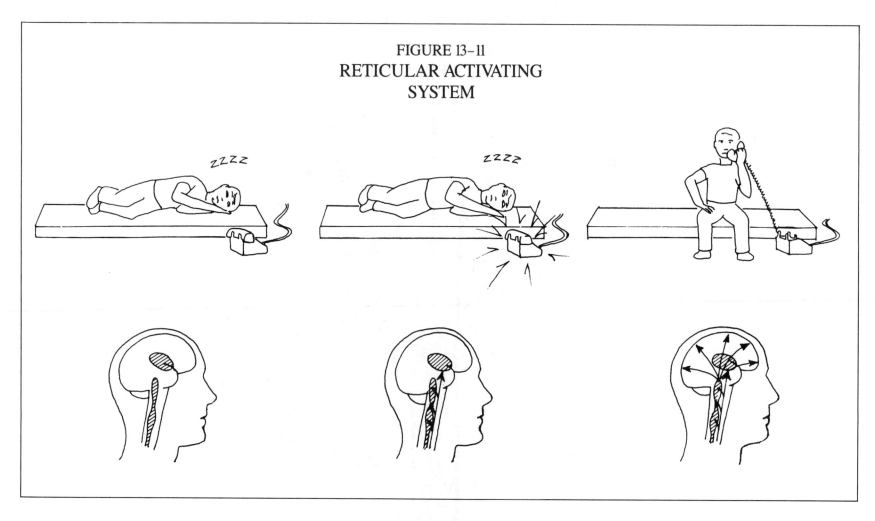

FIGURE 13–11
RETICULAR ACTIVATING SYSTEM

For sensory channels, it is a nonspecific activating system. For this sensory function is is called the *reticular activating system (RAS)*. As can be seen in Figure 13–11, all sensory paths send collateral fibers into the reticular system so that it can make a preliminary determination of whether or not a stimulus is worthy of attention. This is done by testing stimuli for what has been dubbed "*novelty.*" By novelty, neuroscientists mean the extent to which a signal is unanticipated, the assumption

being that unexpected stimuli need special attention — they could signal danger or some unplanned delight.

Thus, when a novel signal is received in any sensory channel, the reticular activating system receives a "copy" of the signal via collateral connections. Being the "general alarm" for the nervous system, the RAS, with connections to the entire cortex, arouses the brain, even from sleep, and prepares it to respond to what may be impor-

tant information (Fig. 13–11).

Just as the RAS directs sensory traffic by amplifying or inhibiting it, depending on novelty of the stimulus, so does the reticular formation direct motor traffic. It can amplify or inhibit motor activity, ranging from voluntary movement at the cortical level to the lowly "knee-jerk" reflex at the spinal level. It is a system that must function properly for movements to be smooth and polished.

CEREBRUM

The cerebral hemispheres evolved out of the two stalks at the top of the brainstem. The oldest, most primitive parts have long been known to serve the most basic sense of all, olfaction. Some dubbed it the "smell brain"; formally it was known as the *rhinencephalon*. More recently, it has been found to be intimately involved in emotion, memory, and learning, as well as with associated autonomic and endocrine functions. It is now called the *limbic system*.

The newer parts of the cerebrum, by far the most massive components of the brain, have evolved to provide man with highly differentiated responses to his environment. Because vision and hearing are so vital to adaptive responses, especially elaborate brain mechanisms have emerged to handle them. Also elaborate are the mechanisms for processing body feedback by which appropriate responses are controlled. Most recently acquired are the mechanisms for thought, language, and speech, which use information from the older-developed senses and motor-control apparatus for the unique functions of human cognition and communication.

We will now look at these cerebral structures beginning with those of the limbic system, moving on to the lobes of the cerebral hemispheres, and then to the connections within and between hemispheres, and the connections of the cerebrum with the brainstem. Our objective is to locate and identify these structures so that you can visualize them when we discuss their functions.

Limbic System

The limbic structures evolved 300 to 200 million years ago. Dominated by smell, this system became the highest level of the reptilian brain. But this primitive function has given way to higher

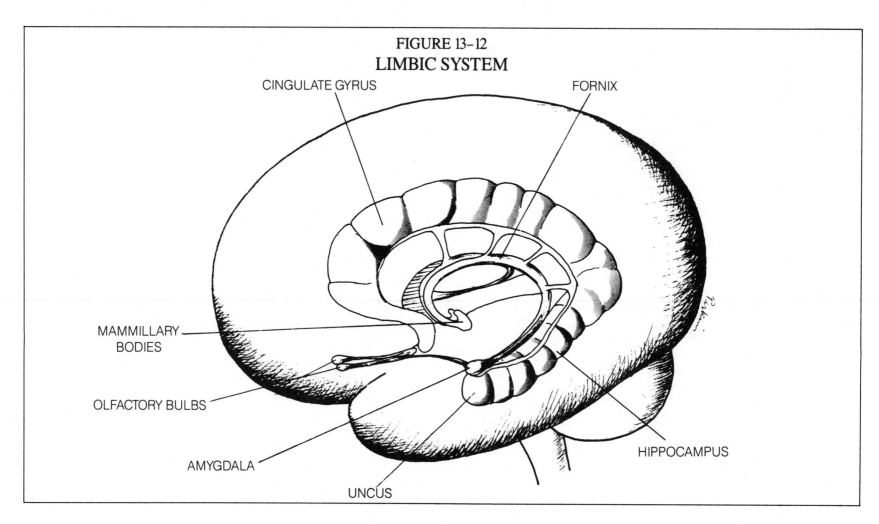

FIGURE 13-12
LIMBIC SYSTEM

CINGULATE GYRUS

FORNIX

MAMMILLARY BODIES

OLFACTORY BULBS

AMYGDALA

UNCUS

HIPPOCAMPUS

functions in mammals, which, being warm-blooded, rely on it for temperature regulation, along with feeding, fighting, fleeing, and sexual reproduction. The limbic system is thought of as the mammalian brain because it is so highly developed in mammals. Man's brain, however, has evolved so far beyond that of lower animals that cerebral structures dwarf the limbic system.

The major components of the limbic system, shown in Figure 13-12, consist of the *hippocam-pus, fornix, cingulate gyrus, mammillary bodies, amygdala, uncus,* and the *olfactory bulbs.* These components are located along the bottom of the cerebrum in an arrangement that loops around the top of the brainstem near the medial surface of each hemisphere. In addition to receiving the primary input and delivering output to the reticular formation, the limbic system also is connected with the frontal lobes, as well as with the hypothalamus. Reticular connections apparently operate to define the potentiality of a novel stimulus for reward or punishment. Frontal lobe connections mediate our awareness of such sensations and emotions as smell, taste, hunger, thirst, sexual excitement, anger, and fear. Hypothalamic connections enable our visceral responses to fit appropriately with our feelings — when fearful, for instance, the gut response should prepare us for "flight or fight."

Cerebral Cortex

The cerebral hemispheres dominate the brain, both in size and function. They make possible our "unique" human attributes. They began evolving about 200 million years ago. It took most of that time to reach 400 cc in size. But once the human's distinctive evolution began, the brain quadrupled to 1,500 cc in 4 million years, the fastest any organ has evolved in history.

Above the level of the brainstem, in the cerebrum, the organization of gray and white matter is reversed, as can be seen in Figure 13-13. Instead of gray matter being on the inside, as it is in the spinal cord and brainstem, in the cerebrum it is located on the outside. There it is called *cerebral cortex.* The cortex (meaning bark, in this case the bark on the cerebral hemispheres) is about an eighth of an inch thick and consists of the six layers of different types of cells, shown in Figure 13-14. These layers vary in thickness and arrangement throughout the cortex. Because billions of them must be accommodated within the relatively small space of the skull, the cortex has folded in on itself to form ridges, shallow depressions, and deep depressions (a ridge is a *gyrus,* a shallow depression a *sulcus,* and a deep depression a *fissure*). Only about one third of the cortex is visible on the surface.

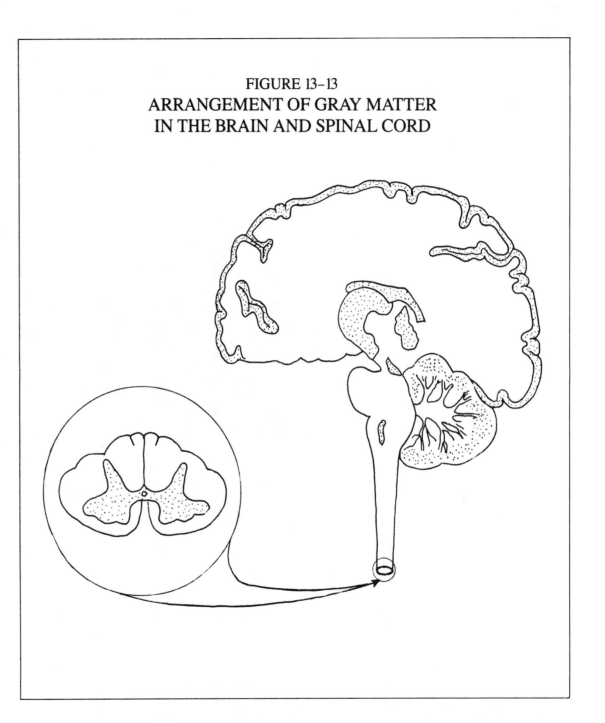

FIGURE 13-13
ARRANGEMENT OF GRAY MATTER
IN THE BRAIN AND SPINAL CORD

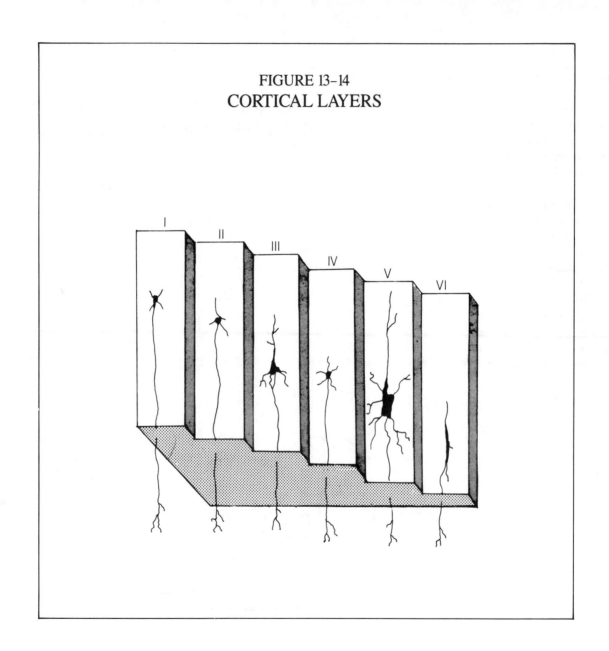

FIGURE 13-14
CORTICAL LAYERS

FIGURE 13–15
CEREBRAL FISSURES

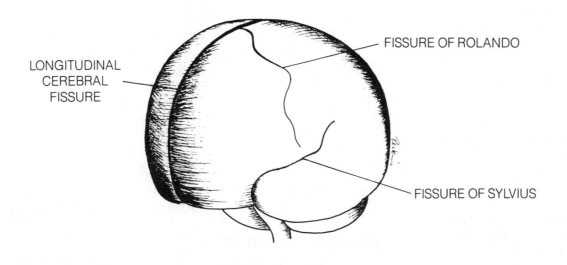

LONGITUDINAL
CEREBRAL
FISSURE

FISSURE OF ROLANDO

FISSURE OF SYLVIUS

Three cerebral fissures are landmarks of note (Fig. 13–15). The *longitudinal cerebral fissure* separates the two hemispheres. The *fissure of Rolando (central fissure)* separates the frontal part of its hemisphere, which serves mostly motor functions, from the remainder which contain the sensory lobes. One of these, the temporal lobe, is separated from its hemisphere by the *fissure of Sylvius (lateral fissure)*, like a thumb on a mitten. Now let us turn to the lobes themselves, with the exception of the occipital lobe. Located farthest back in the cerebrum, the occipital lobe is not of direct concern to us.

Frontal Lobe

Anatomically, the *frontal lobe* is the portion of the cerebrum anterior to the fissure of Rolando. In general, the farther away from (forward of) the fissure, the more abstract the motor planning function that is served. Far from mediating abstractions, the *primary motor cortex,* immediately anterior to the central fissure in the *precentral gyrus,* contains a preponderance of pyramidal motor cells that connect to the body in such a topographical arrangement as to form the *homunculus* in Figure 13–16. This is the point for point representation of muscles of the body in the motor cortex. As you can see, the mouth and fingers are grossly enlarged because they have so much more motor representation than, say, the chest wall. There is nothing abstract about the result of electrically stimulating a point on the motor cortex — it produces a discrete isolated movement, whereas stimulation of the frontal-most regions will likely result in no discernible response.

The vast majority of the cortex, particularly the frontal lobe, is "silent." That is, points on it do not have a specific function as do the *projection areas* which connect the cortex to the muscles and sense organs. These silent regions are *association areas* in which neural signals are integrated and organized for purposeful plans. One planning center of particular interest is *Broca's area* in the *inferior frontal gyrus* of the left hemisphere (in most people). This area is just forward of the motor cortex for the speech mechanism; it is where the plans are assembled for motor speech production. Assisting in motor planning of propositional speech is the *supplementary motor cortex* in the upper left frontal lobe of the dominant hemisphere.

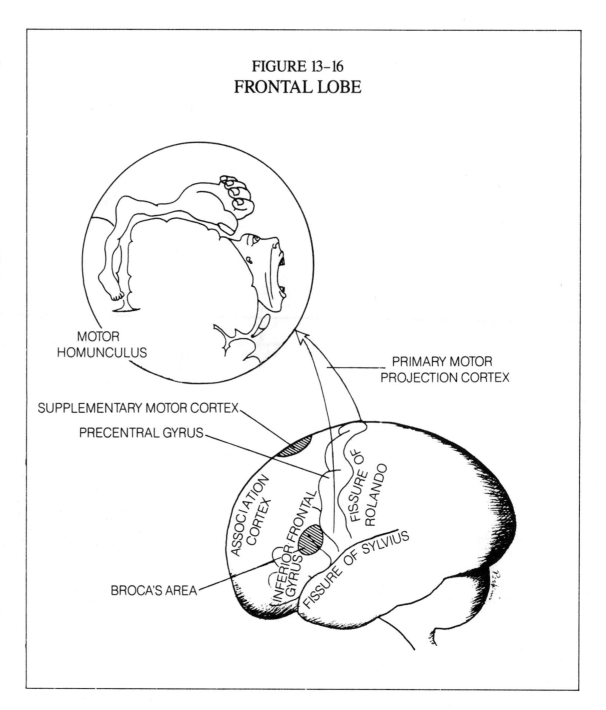

FIGURE 13–16
FRONTAL LOBE

MOTOR HOMUNCULUS

PRIMARY MOTOR PROJECTION CORTEX

SUPPLEMENTARY MOTOR CORTEX

PRECENTRAL GYRUS

ASSOCIATION CORTEX

INFERIOR FRONTAL GYRUS

FISSURE OF ROLANDO

FISSURE OF SYLVIUS

BROCA'S AREA

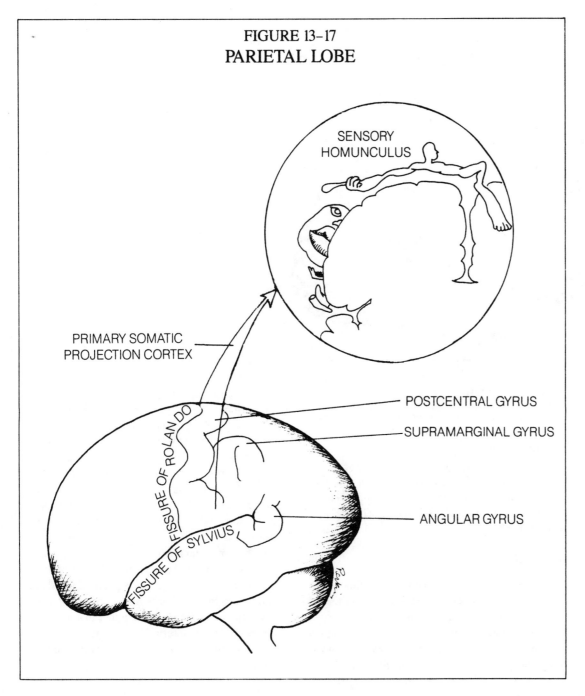

FIGURE 13–17
PARIETAL LOBE

SENSORY HOMUNCULUS

PRIMARY SOMATIC PROJECTION CORTEX

FISSURE OF ROLANDO

FISSURE OF SYLVIUS

POSTCENTRAL GYRUS

SUPRAMARGINAL GYRUS

ANGULAR GYRUS

Parietal Lobe

Immediately posterior to the fissure of Rolando is the *postcentral gyrus*, which can be seen in Figure 13–17. It is the *primary somatic sensory cortex*, in which feedback from the body is represented in the sensory homunculus. The sensory homunculus matches the motor homunculus closely. In view of the importance of feedback to motor control, this close match is not surprising. Two other areas of some importance to speech are the *supramarginal gyrus* and *angular gyrus*.

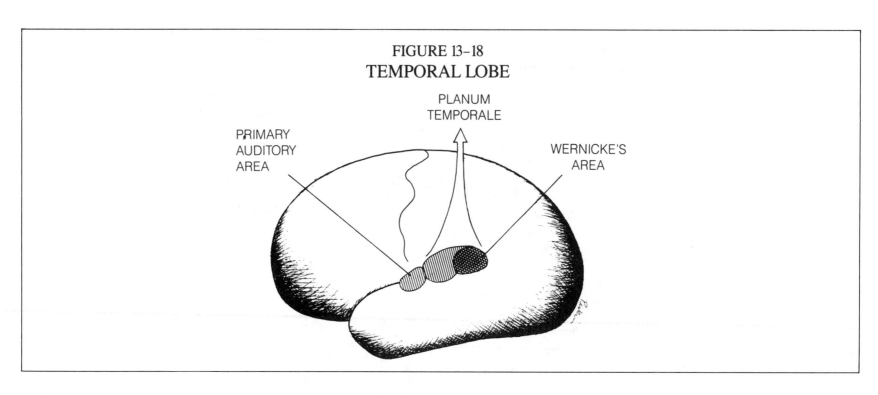

FIGURE 13–18
TEMPORAL LOBE

PLANUM
TEMPORALE

PRIMARY
AUDITORY
AREA

WERNICKE'S
AREA

Temporal Lobe

The *temporal lobe,* like a thumb tucked under and separated from each cerebral hemisphere by the fissure of Sylvius, is of special importance to us in two ways: it contains the *primary auditory cortex* and, in the dominant hemisphere, the major language formation center called *Wernicke's area* (Fig. 13–18). A possible anatomical basis for this language formulation center being in the dominant temporal lobe, usually the left, is the fact that it is located in the *planum temporale,* on the upper surface of the lobe inside the sylvian fissure, which is typically larger in the left lobe than the right. The location of Wernicke's area near the intersection of the temporal, parietal, and occipital lobes may also be significant for language. This location would seem to facilitate coordination of auditory, visual, and bodily senses.

Cerebral Pathways

The cerebrum contains three types of fibers: projection, association, and commissural. *Projection fibers* form the pathways to and from the brainstem and spinal cord to the primary sensory and motor areas of the cortex. *Association fibers* interconnect various cortical areas within each hemisphere. *Commissural fibers* interconnect the two hemispheres.

Projection Pathways

All senses, with the exception of olfaction, which connects directly to the limbic system, send afferent signals to the thalamus for relay to the various primary sensory areas of the cortex. For audition, the thalamic center from which auditory projection fibers extend is the *medial geniculate body.* These fibers terminate in the *transverse gyrus of Heschl,* the primary auditory cortex of both temporal lobes. The *tactile* and *kinesthetic* senses are carried by projection fibers from the thalamus to the primary somatic cortex in the postcentral gyrus of both parietal lobes. The tactile fibers carry information about touch; the kinesthetic fibers, with nerve endings in muscles, tendons, and joints, provide the basis for awareness of movement. The cortical motor fibers, connecting with motor centers in the brainstem and spinal cord, are also projection fibers. They form the *pyramidal tract* (named for its pyramidally shaped cell bodies in the primary motor cortex). All cortical projection fibers come together in a massive bundle called the internal capsule which, as we have seen in Figure 13–9, descends through the basal ganglia.

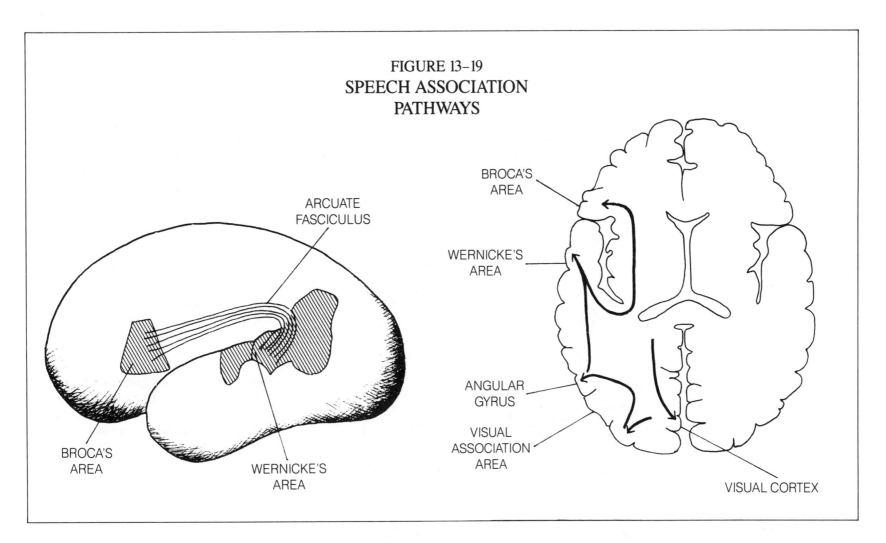

FIGURE 13-19
SPEECH ASSOCIATION
PATHWAYS

ARCUATE
FASCICULUS

BROCA'S
AREA

WERNICKE'S
AREA

BROCA'S
AREA

WERNICKE'S
AREA

ANGULAR
GYRUS

VISUAL
ASSOCIATION
AREA

VISUAL CORTEX

Association Pathways

Both long and short association fibers interconnect the various areas of the cortex in each hemisphere. The long bundle of fibers of special interest to us is the *arcuate fasciculus,* extending from the region where language is comprehended (Wernicke's area) to the region where speech movements are organized (Broca's area). Short association fibers connect the primary sensory areas — particularly the auditory cortex to Wernicke's area, and Broca's area to the motor cortex — where the organized signals are transmitted to the speech muscles.

Another feature of association pathways that is characteristic of humans, and may be important to language, is that they interconnect the different sensory areas (Fig. 13–19). This is apparently not the case in animals, in which one sense does not help another sense much when recognizing objects. But with humans, information is shared among the sensory modalities. The sound of a familiar girl's voice, for example, may lead you to expect to see a specific face, smell a particular perfume, and anticipate a special touch.

Central Nervous System Anatomy

367

FIGURE 13–20
CORPUS CALLOSUM

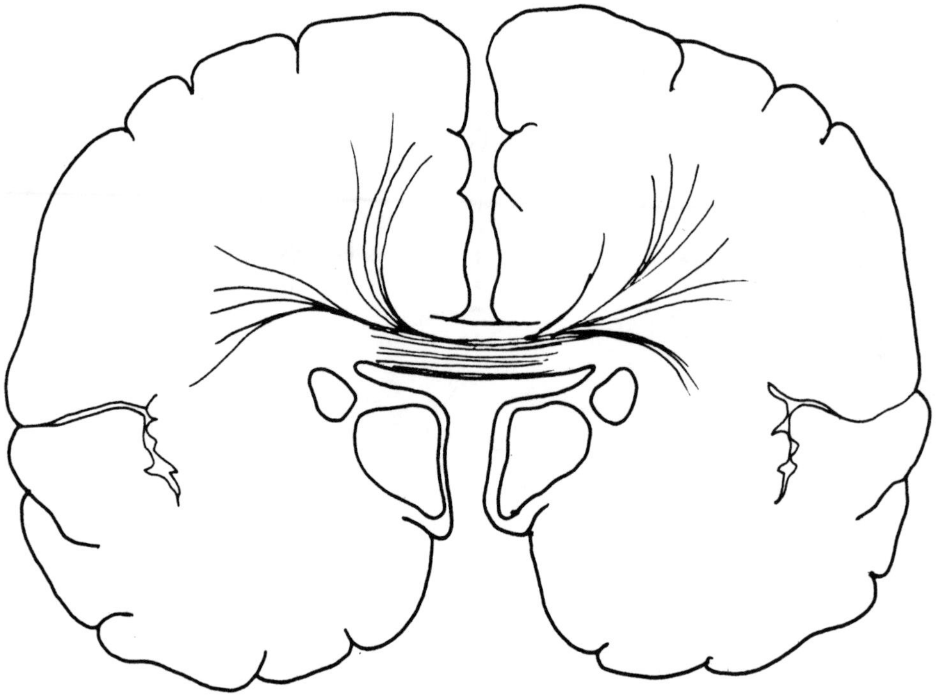

Commissural Pathways

Along with four small commissural pathways interconnecting the hemispheres is the great central commissure, the *corpus callosum* (Fig. 13–20), with its 300 million commissural fibers. We will limit our discussion to this commissure. Only in recent years, with studies of effects of severing this massive bundle (for the purpose of surgical control of seizures, not for the sake of experimentation) has the importance of the corpus callosum begun to emerge. In many ways, the two hemispheres can function independently, so that effects of disconnecting them need not be apparent. But if the task requires that the right hand should know what the left hand is doing, a conflict can arise if the two hemispheres are not in agreement as to what the two hands should be doing. In one experiment in which the two disconnected hemispheres learned different answers to the same problem, the left hand pointed to the correct answer, and the right hand to another. The subject confirmed verbally that the right hand was correct, but this was merely evidence that the speech mechanism and the right hand were controlled by the left hemisphere, which had no knowledge of what the right hemisphere knew to be accurate.

CEREBELLUM

The *cerebellum* is an automatic motor coordinating center situated at the base of the brain behind the brainstem (Fig. 13–21). It has evolved along with the rest of the brain, so it has a primitive portion, the *archicerebellum*; an old portion, the *paleocerebellum*; and a new portion, the *neocerebellum*. The archicerebellum maintains equilibrium, the paleocerebellum adjusts musculature to resist gravity, and the neocerebellum controls the synergy of voluntary movement.

The neocerebellum, like the cerebrum, has become a massive structure involving two hemispheres. The connection between these hemispheres is the archicerebellum and paleocerebellum. Also like the cerebrum, the cell bodies are on the outside in the wrinkled cerebellar cortex; unlike the cerebrum, the right side of the body is connected to the right side of the cerebellum and the left side to the left.

So far as voluntary movements are concerned, the cerebellum functions more or less as a subcontractor to cerebral motor centers. Accordingly, it must receive plans for upcoming voluntary motor movements from the cerebrum and for reflexive action from the brainstem. These are transmitted to the pons, where they synapse and are relayed to the neocerebellum via the middle cerebellar peduncle. With these plans, the cerebellum has information about the target movement to be achieved.

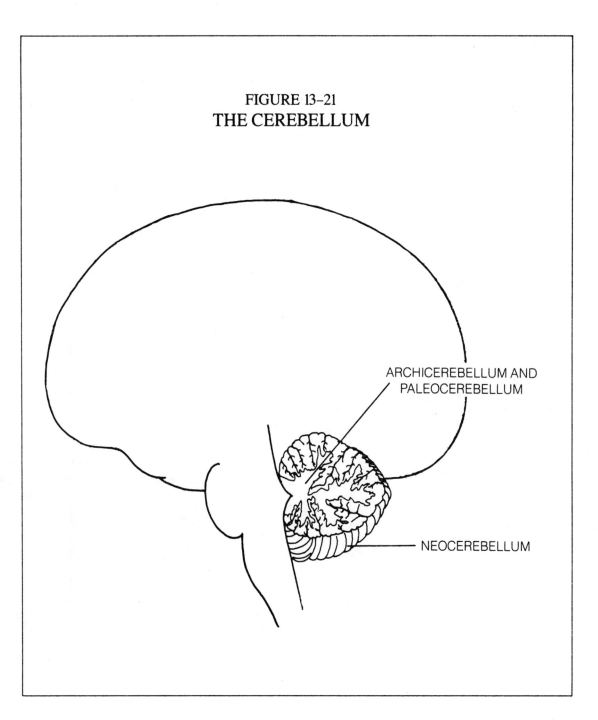

FIGURE 13–21
THE CEREBELLUM

ARCHICEREBELLUM AND
PALEOCEREBELLUM

NEOCEREBELLUM

What it now needs to coordinate synergic speech movements is mainly *proprioceptive* information from muscles, tendons, and joints (Fig. 13–22) (it also receives auditory feedback, and, of less direct concern, visual and vestibular feedback). Proprioceptive information arrives from the body via the inferior cerebellar peduncle. This is the same information from the same sensory receptors that provide kinesthetic signals to the somatic cortex. Whereas the cortex uses the information for awareness of movement, the cerebellum uses it for automatic coordination, more specifically, for regulation of muscle force and timing of movement.

What the cerebellum must do is compare the intended target position of the movement with the current location of the structure to be moved. The difference in these positions is the basis for the signal that will move the structure smoothly from where it is to where it is intended to go. This cerebellar signal is then transmitted by way of the superior cerebellar peduncle and the red nucleus in the midbrain to the thalamus, and then to cortical motor areas. There, the cerebellar input is coordinated with motor plans preparatory to transmission of motor signals to the musculature.

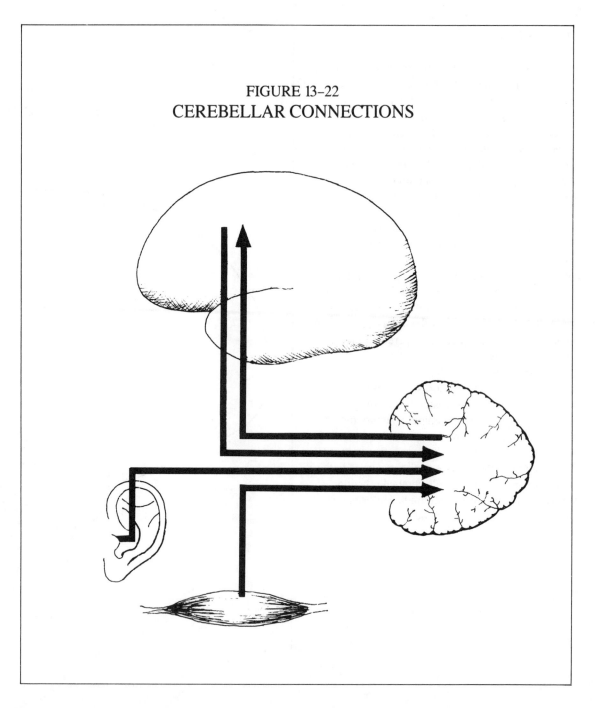

FIGURE 13–22
CEREBELLAR CONNECTIONS

Summary

This has been a brief exploration of the anatomical structures of the central nervous system. We have attempted to give you a visual impression of what these structures look like, where they are located, and how they are interconnected. So that you can have a preliminary sense of their significance for us, a glimpse is offered of their functions that have relevance for speech, language, or hearing.

We began at the bottom of the brainstem with the medulla, which contains the nuclei of several cranial nerves and is the upward continuation of the spinal cord. Above it is the pons, also with cranial nerve nuclei to speech structures, but most notably with the bridge-like pathway to the cerebellum. The midbrain, poised between hindbrain and forebrain, is a relay mechanism. Above it, the brainstem branches into two large trunks, on top of which are the cerebral hemispheres. Connecting the sensory apparatus to these hemispheres is the thalamus; connecting the cortical motor mechanisms is the basal ganglia. These are massive brainstem nuclei that relay and integrate neural traffic. Running the length of the brainstem from the upper spinal cord is the reticular formation, which activates the brain for sensory processing and directs motor traffic for smooth movement.

At the base of the cerebrum is the limbic system, which mediates such vital functions as emotion and memory, with its main connections to the reticular formation, the frontal lobes, and the hypothalamus. Each cerebral hemisphere, with cell bodies in the convoluted cortex, has a frontal lobe devoted mainly to motor functions, a parietal lobe for receiving and processing tactile and kinesthetic information from the body, an occipital lobe for vision, and a temporal lobe for audition. It is the temporal lobe that plays a critical role in hearing and language, particularly in the dominant hemisphere.

Connecting the cerebrum to the brainstem and spinal cord are projection fibers, interconnecting cortical areas are association fibers, and interconnecting hemispheres are commissural fibers. Connected to the motor centers of the cerebrum and brainstem, and drawing on movement information from the body, the cerebellum serves as an automatic motor coordinating center. Situated at the base of the brain, the cerebellar hemispheres have evolved along with the cerebral hemispheres to provide automatic coordination for a sophisticated repertoire of responses, with speech being the prime example.

PROTECTION AND NOURISHMENT

Meninges

The brain, precious organ that it is, is carefully protected by layers of bone and tissue. An important point in understanding these coverings is that the brain has the consistency of thick jelly. Deprived of its coverings, the brain slumps and oozes. If they have seen a brain at all, most people have seen only preserved brains, which differ from living brains in color (preserved brains are gray or a brownish yellow, whereas the fresh brain is pinkish) and in overall form (preserved brains usually hold the shape of a cranium; fresh brains fill the cranium as jello might fill a jello mold).

To appreciate the care with which the brain is protected in the skull, you might imagine preparing a package for a delicate object that is to be sent across the country. You probably would choose a package that is hard and tough on the outside to protect against blows, falls, and punctures, and cushioned on the inside to absorb potentially damaging forces. The brain is packaged in essentially the same way.

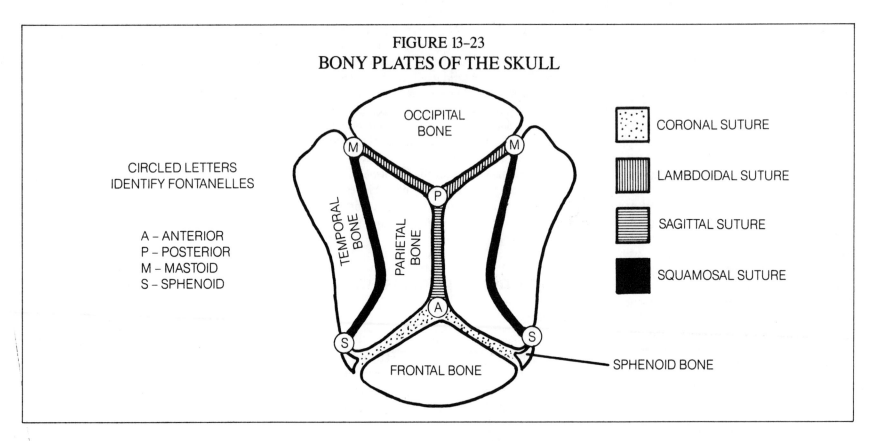

FIGURE 13–23
BONY PLATES OF THE SKULL

OCCIPITAL BONE

CIRCLED LETTERS
IDENTIFY FONTANELLES

A – ANTERIOR
P – POSTERIOR
M – MASTOID
S – SPHENOID

TEMPORAL BONE

PARIETAL BONE

FRONTAL BONE

CORONAL SUTURE

LAMBDOIDAL SUTURE

SAGITTAL SUTURE

SQUAMOSAL SUTURE

SPHENOID BONE

The hard outer covering (underneath the scalp, that is) is bone — actually three layers of bone. The first layer is hard bone called the *outer table.* The second layer is a softer, more absorbent layer of cancellous bone called the *diploë.* Under the diploë is another layer of hard bone, the *inner table.* Thus, the skull is really a sandwich of bone: a collapsible filler surrounded by hard protective layers.

Removing the bone does not yet expose the brain itself, which lies under three more layers that are collectively called the *meninges* (plural of meninx, which is Greek for membrane). The outermost of the meninges is the *dura mater.* This membrane is thick, tough, and fibrous. It gives essential form to the brain and also is the site of much intracranial sensation. Headaches, for example, arise from sensory receptors in the dura mater. The word mater refers to mother, which word was attributed to the meninges because the Arabs thought that these membranes were the source of all other bodily membranes. Lying under the dura mater is the *arachnoid membrane,* which is closely applied to the dura mater and is connected by thin filaments to the innermost meninx, the *pia mater.* The filaments, called arachnoid trabeculae, create a spider's web (arachnoid means spider) of connections between the arachnoid and the pia mater. The space formed by these filaments is the subarachnoid space, which connects with the ventricular cavities and, like them, is filled with cerebrospinal fluid. This fluid-filled space is still another feature of the brain's careful packaging. The myriad of filaments that traverse this space are like tiny ropes that moor the brain within a liquid moat. Just as a boat moored to a dock can survive a fierce storm without being damaged or washed away, so can the brain survive much physical insult within its liquid cushion. The pia mater is a thin membrane closely applied to the brain, following its contours even into the depths of its sulci. So it is that the brain is packaged in bone, liquid, and membrane. Like the brain, the spinal cord is also wrapped in essentially the same meningeal layers within the protection provided by the vertebrae.

FIGURE 13-24
SKULL GROWTH

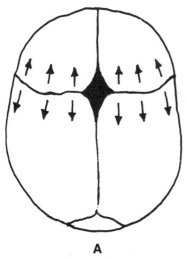

A

HEAD GROWTH ALONG
CORONAL SUTURE INCREASES
HEAD SIZE FROM FRONT
TO BACK

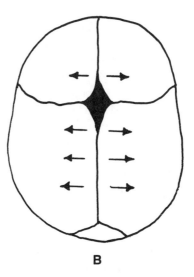

B

HEAD GROWTH ALONG
SAGITTAL SUTURE INCREASES
HEAD SIZE FROM SIDE TO SIDE

Sutures and Fontanelles

The skull of the infant is really a number of bony plates that fit loosely together (Fig. 13–23). The skull does not become a single structure until the nonossified (nonbony) connecting tissues between the skull plates have been replaced by bone. The lines of juncture are called *sutures*. At certain places the sutures are widened to form conspicuous openings called *fontanelles* (meaning little fountains). The fontanelles are the "soft spots in baby's head," the places where the cranial bones do not meet to give the impression of continuous bone. The bones of the newborn's skull are flexible enough in their arrangement to be misshapen and distorted by the forces exerted on them by the birth canal. Many parents have had to be reassured by their doctors that their baby's oddly shaped head is not a permanent feature. Indeed, the ossification of the sutures can take several years for completion, and the most notable of the fontanelles, the anterior fontanelle at the junction of the frontal and parietal bones, usually closes between 7 and 24 months of age (Fig. 13–24).

With maturation, the child has a central nervous system that is encased in the three meninges and an outer protective layer of bone. Of course, these coverings are not without openings, as blood vessels, nerves and other substances must enter and exit the bony cavity to which the central nervous system is entrusted for safekeeping.

Ventricles

The *ventricles* (from the Latin for "little belly") are fluid-filled spaces within the brain. The ancients thought that the ventricles were the essential site of brain functions. St. Augustine, in the fourth century A.D., attributed different mental functions to each ventricle, of which there are four (if the paired lateral ventricles are counted as two). The lateral ventricles are situated within each cerebral hemisphere and connect via a narrow duct with the third ventricle, which is no more than a narrow slit within the thalamus (Fig. 13–25). The third ventricle communicates with the larger fourth ventricle, which is located in front of the cerebellum and behind the pons.

The chief importance of the ventricles is that they produce and contain a watery, colorless substance called *cerebrospinal fluid* (CSF). This fluid is produced primarily by a region of the ventricle called the choroid plexus. From its reservoirs within the ventricles, CSF flows over the surfaces of the brain until it eventually enters the bloodstream. Thus, CSF is continually produced and reabsorbed within the brain. Although this fluid does contain some nutrients, its primary function is protective in that it forms a liquid moat within which the brain is moored. As already mentioned, the liquid space that surrounds the brain is a major protection against injury. Cerebrospinal fluid can be understood as filtered blood, very much like plasma, the part of the blood that remains after red and white corpuscles and platelets are removed.

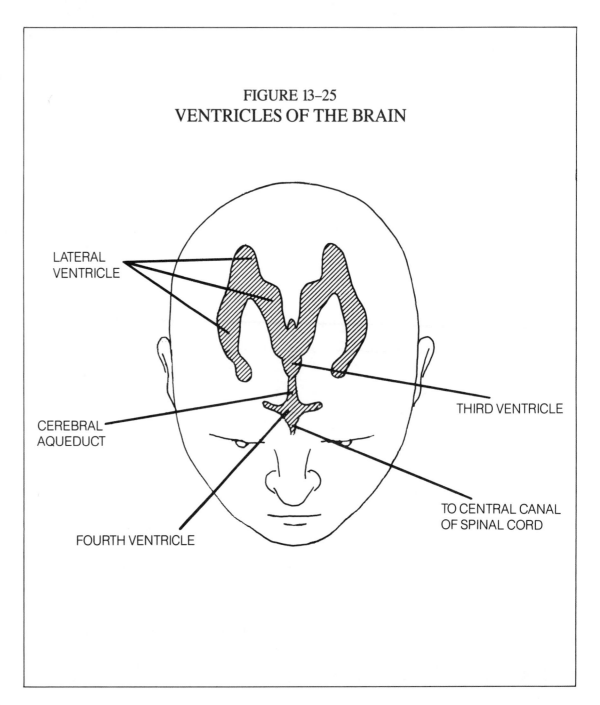

FIGURE 13–25
VENTRICLES OF THE BRAIN

LATERAL VENTRICLE

THIRD VENTRICLE

CEREBRAL AQUEDUCT

TO CENTRAL CANAL OF SPINAL CORD

FOURTH VENTRICLE

Blood Circulation

The brain requires large amounts of blood. Even a brief interference with circulation can result in serious damage. The brain's appetite for blood can be appreciated by the fact that the brain constitutes only 2 percent of the body's weight but demands 25 percent of the blood that leaves the heart under resting conditions. Roughly, the brain receives its own weight in blood every minute. Blood flow to the brain diminishes by about one fourth between the ages of 30 and 60 years. However, the brain normally compensates for such reduced flow by taking a larger proportion of oxygen from the blood. Four blood vessels supply the brain — two *vertebral arteries* and two *carotid arteries* (with internal and external branches) (Fig. 13–26). The vertebral arteries gain access to the cranium through the foramen magnum (literally "large hole") through which the spinal cord runs. The internal carotids penetrate through the foramen lacerum (literally "lacerated hole") and then follow a circuitous route before branching into smaller vessels. The carotid and vertebral arteries feed into an arterial complex at the base of the brain called the *circle of Willis*. This circle, which is the source of all significant direct blood supply to the brain, is an *anastomosis* (meaning connection of blood vessels by collateral channels). The most direct continuation of the internal carotid is the *middle cerebral artery,* a very important artery for speech and language. This artery supplies a large part of the brain, including the insular cortex, the cortex on the brain's lateral surface, major regions of the frontal lobe and temporal pole, and the basal ganglia and thalamus. Damage to this artery — a stroke — can severely impair speech and language function.

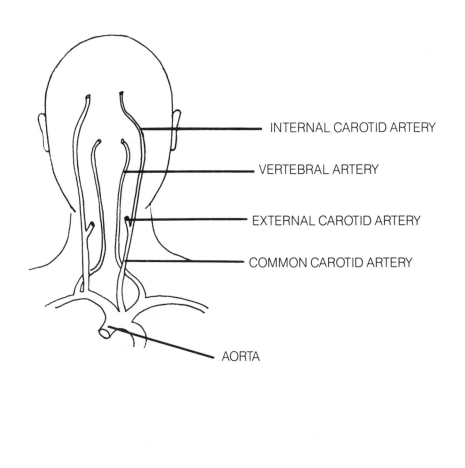

FIGURE 13–26
ARTERIES TO THE BRAIN

INTERNAL CAROTID ARTERY

VERTEBRAL ARTERY

EXTERNAL CAROTID ARTERY

COMMON CAROTID ARTERY

AORTA

FIGURE 13–27
CEREBRAL ARTERIES

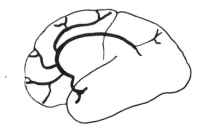

CIRCULATION AREA
OF ANTERIOR CEREBRAL
ARTERY, VIEWED ON
MEDIAL ASPECT OF
RIGHT HEMISPHERE

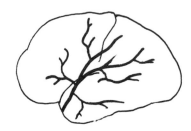

CIRCULATION AREA
OF MIDDLE CEREBRAL
ARTERY, VIEWED ON
LATERAL ASPECT OF
LEFT HEMISPHERE

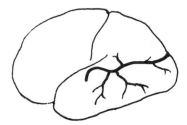

CIRCULATION AREA
OF POSTERIOR CEREBRAL
ARTERY, VIEWED ON
MEDIAL ASPECT OF
RIGHT HEMISPHERE

One means of studying brain activity in relation to behavior is to monitor regional blood flow in the brain. Blood flow increases to regions of the brain where neurons are highly active. So, if the blood flow increases in a certain part of the brain when a particular behavior is performed (like speaking, reading, listening), it is a reasonable assumption that the region of increased blood flow is an important part of the brain in controlling that activity (Fig. 13–27). But how is it possible to measure blood flow in the intact brain? The answer lies in the use of x-rays. A radioactive tracer is introduced into the blood and the concentration of this tracer is monitored by an array of radioactivity counters placed over the scalp. Each counter is sensitive to the radioactivity just below it. Blood flow is proportional to the rate at which the tracer is cleared from the given region of the brain.

A major cause of injury to the brain is a *stroke,* or a sudden and severe disruption of blood supply, also known by the term cerebrovascular accident (CVA). There are several kinds of strokes. *Hemorrhages* are leakages of blood or uncontrolled bleeding that damage brain tissue both by causing injurious pressure and by reducing the oxygen supply to neurons. *Thrombosis* refers to a blood clot that clogs a vessel, thereby intervening with circulation. An *embolus* means plugging of a vessel either by a clot or other object (such as an atherosclerotic plaque) which has travelled through the bloodstream. An *aneurysm* is a bulging of the blood vessel, usually caused by a weak spot in the wall of the vessel. The word *lesion* refers to an area of damage. One kind of lesion is an *infarct,* which is destruction of tissue caused by a vascular accident.

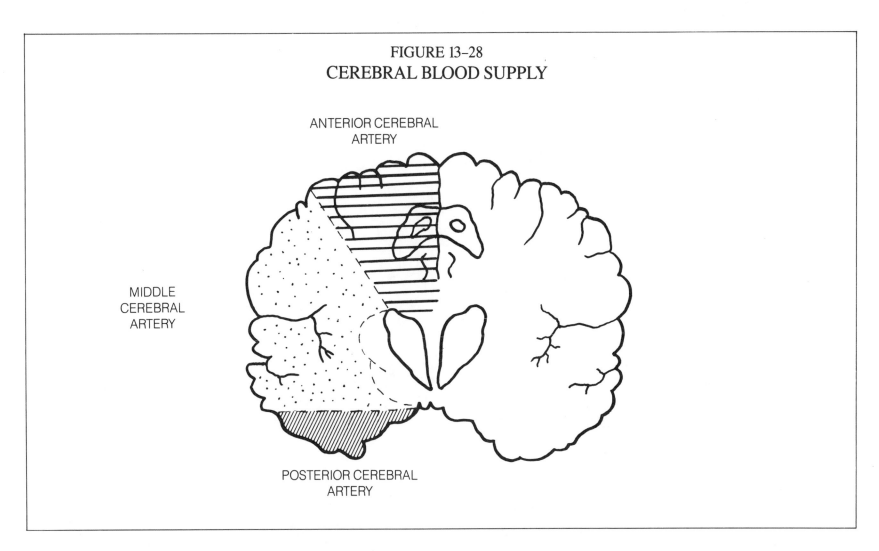

FIGURE 13–28
CEREBRAL BLOOD SUPPLY

ANTERIOR CEREBRAL
ARTERY

MIDDLE
CEREBRAL
ARTERY

POSTERIOR CEREBRAL
ARTERY

An infarct in certain areas of the brain is likely to result in language disorders called aphasias. Once such area is Broca's area (Fig. 13–19) and another is Wernicke's area (Fig. 13–18). Although these areas are traditionally associated with language disorders, more recent evidence indicates that these disorders can result also from damage to other areas of the brain, including subcortical structures such as the thalamus. As mentioned earlier, the middle cerebral artery, which is essentially an extension of the internal carotid, is especially important in supplying blood to parts of the brain most directly involved in speech and language (Fig. 13–28). Damage to this artery in the form of hemorrhage, thrombosis, embolus, or aneurysm can result in a stroke that impairs language.

CHAPTER THIRTEEN
Self-Study
Central Nervous System Anatomy

Review Glossary

Spinal cord: The portion of the CNS contained within the vertebral column

Brain: The portion of the CNS contained within the skull

   Cerebrum: The largest and newest part of the brain, developed from the tops of the two stalks of the brainstem, that makes discriminative behavior possible

   Brainstem: The portion of the brain from the entrance of the spinal cord into the skull, through the foramen magnum to the level of the midbrain; it contains the major transmission parts of the brain, including the pyramidal tract.

   Embryological levels of brain development: The five major divisions of the fetal brain

   Myelencephalon: The lowest level of the brainstem that develops from the hindbrain to become the medulla

   Metencephalon: The upper portion of the hindbrain that becomes the pons and cerebellum

   Mesencephalon: The midbrain, both embryologically and anatomically

   Diencephalon: The highest subcortical level of the brain (where it divides into two stalks), develops from the forebrain to become the thalamus and hypothalamus

   Telencephalon: The end brain, developed from the forebrain, that becomes the cerebrum

  Anatomical subcortical levels of the brain

   Medulla: The level of the brainstem immediately above the foramen magnum that most resembles the spinal cord with its transmission pathways, although containing cranial nerve nuclei and the pyramidal decussation

    Restiform body: The inferior cerebellar peduncle connecting sensory feedback from the body to the cerebellum

   Pons: The level of the brainstem with input connections to the cerebellum and with nuclei of cranial nerves

    Brachium pontis: The middle cerebellar peduncle connecting the cerebrum to the cerebellum

   Midbrain: The level of the brainstem with output connections from the cerebellum and with important reflex centers

    Brachium conjunctivum: The superior cerebellar peduncle connecting the cerebellum to motor centers in the brainstem and cerebrum

    Red nucleus: The motor center that receives information from the cerebellum

    Substantia nigra: The neurotransmitter center of importance to motor control

    Quadrigeminal bodies: Reflex centers for hearing and vision

     Inferior colliculi: The pair of auditory reflex centers mediating the startle reflex to loud sounds

   Thalamus: The head end of the old sensory system, where all sensory input (except olfaction) is received and integrated for transfer to the cerebrum

    Medial geniculate body: The paired auditory reflex center that connects the thalamus to the cortical auditory centers

    Hypothalamus: The visceral control center, located below the thalamus, that connects the CNS with the ANS and with the endocrine system through the pituitary gland

   Reticular formation: The integrating mechanism extending through the brainstem from spinal cord to cerebrum that amplifies or inhibits both sensory and motor traffic and is the seat of consciousness

    Reticular activating system (RAS): The name of the reticular sensory mechanism

    Novelty: The unexpectedness of a signal that is the basis for RAS activation

  Anatomical levels of the cerebrum

   Basal ganglia: The old motor centers at the base of the cerebrum that consist of the caudate nucleus and the globus pallidus and putamen, which together form the lenticular nucleus

   Internal capsule: The bundle of transmission fibers, connecting cerebral cortex with brainstem, that pass through the basal ganglia, giving it a striated appearance and the name "corpus striatum"

   Limbic system: The olfactory bulbs, hippocampus, fornix, cingulate gyrus, mammillary bodies, amygdala, and uncus, which evolved to mediate the sense of smell (hence the embryological name rhinencephalon) and emotion, and which is critical for learning

Cerebral cortex: The "bark" on the surface of the cerebrum containing gray matter (cell bodies)

    Projection fibers: The fibers contained in the internal capsule that form the pathways between primary cortical sensory and motor areas and the brainstem and spinal cord

    Association fibers: The fibers interconnecting different cortical areas within the same hemisphere

        Arcuate fasciculus: The associational pathway between the two major speech areas, Wernicke's area and Broca's area

    Commissural fibers: The neurons interconnecting the cerebral hemispheres

        Corpus callosum: The major commissural pathway between hemispheres

    Longitudinal cerebral fissure: The deep crevice that separates the cerebral hemispheres

    Fissure of Rolando: The crevice separating the frontal lobe from the parietal lobe in each hemisphere

    Fissure of Sylvius: The crevice separating the temporal lobe from the frontal and parietal lobes in each hemisphere

    Frontal lobe: The lobe that mediates planning and motor control

        Broca's area: Anatomically in the inferior frontal gyrus, it is the motor speech control area

        Supplementary motor area: The area in the upper left frontal lobe that assists in motor speech planning

        Primary motor cortex: Anatomically the precentral gyrus, it contains point-for-point muscle representation which can be drawn schematically as the motor homunculus

    Temporal lobe: The lobe that mediates hearing, and in the dominant hemisphere mediates language

        Primary auditory cortex: Anatomically the transverse gyrus of Heschl, it receives auditory projection fibers in both hemispheres

        Wernicke's area: The language-formulation area in the dominant hemisphere located in the planum temporale

    Parietal lobe: The lobe that mediates the tactile (touch) and kinesthetic (movement) senses

        Primary somatic sensory cortex: Anatomically the postcentral gyrus, it contains point-for-point sensory representation of the body forming a sensory homunculus that resembles the motor homunculus

        Angular gyrus: The area at the intersection of parietal, temporal, and occipital lobes that is of importance in oral reading in the dominant hemisphere

    Supramarginal gyrus: The area behind the postcentral gyrus of some importance to speech in the dominant hemisphere

    Occipital lobe: The lobe that mediates vision

    Cerebellum: The automatic motor coordinating center at the base of the cerebrum that has evolved from archicerebellum and paleocerebellum (for equilibrium) to neocerebellum (which has enlarged into two hemispheres along with the cerebrum) that controls synergy of voluntary movement

        Proprioception: Feedback information to the cerebellum from muscles, tendons, and joints

Brain protection and nourishment

    Skull: The three layers of bone (*outer table, diploë,* and *inner table*) encasing the brain

      Sutures: The junctures where bony plates join together

        Fontanelle (soft spot): Opening in the skull between sutures

    Meninges: The three layers of membrane (*dura mater, arachnoid membrane,* and *pia mater*) in which the brain is wrapped

    Ventricles: Spaces in the brain filled with *cerebrospinal fluid*

    Cerebral arteries: The four arteries that supply the brain

      Vertebral arteries: The two arteries entering the cranium through the foramen magnum

      Carotid arteries (internal and external branches): The two arteries entering the cranium through the foramen lacerum

      Circle of Willis: An *anastomosis* of arteries at the base of the brain connecting vertebral and carotid arteries to *anterior, middle,* and *posterior cerebral arteries*

    Stroke or cerebrovascular accident (CVA): Damage to an artery causing brain injury

      Hemorrhage: Leaking or uncontrolled bleeding from a blood vessel

      Thrombosis: Blood clot that clogs a vessel

      Embolus: Any obstruction in a vessel

Aneurysm: Bulging of a vessel at a weak spot
Lesion: The area of damage
Infarct: Damage caused by CVA
Middle cerebral artery: The artery that, when injured, can impair speech or language

Self-Study Coloring Instructions

1. Fill in the appropriate terms *A* through *W* in Drawings 13–I and 13–II.
2. Using pencils for Drawing 13–I, color *A* through *C* red, yellow, and blue. Use different shades of these primary colors for the embryological structures *D* through *H* that develop from *A* through *C*. Then use shades of the *D* through *H* colors for the anatomical structures *J* through *P* into which they develop.
3. Fill in the appropriate terms *Q* through *W* and *a* through *n* in Drawings 13–III and 13–IV.
4. Use shades of the colors for *J* through *P* for those same structures and parts of those structures in *Q* through *W* and *a* through *n*.
5. Fill in the term for *o* and the terms for *p* through *v* for which *w* is the collective name in Drawing 13–V.
6. Color *o* the same color as was used for *B*. Color *p* through *w* with different shades of the same color as was used for *A*.
7. Fill in the terms for *aa* through *uu* in Drawing 13–VI. Use the anatomical names for terms in parentheses.
8. Color *aa* through *uu* with different shades of the same color as was used for *A*.
9. Color terms in the Glossary with the same colors used for those terms on the drawings.
10. Check your answers in Appendix *B*.

DRAWING 13–I

EMBRYOLOGICAL LEVELS OF BRAIN

ANATOMICAL LEVELS OF BRAIN

EARLY

LATE

A_____

B_____

C_____

E_____
EVOLVES FROM "A"

D_____
EVOLVES FROM "A"

F_____
EVOLVES FROM "B"

G_____
EVOLVES FROM "C"

H_____
EVOLVES FROM "C"

I_____
EVOLVES FROM "C"

EVOLVES FROM

P_____ "D"

O_____ "D"

N_____ "E"

M_____ "F"

L_____ "G"

K_____ "G"

J_____ "H"

Central Nervous System Anatomy

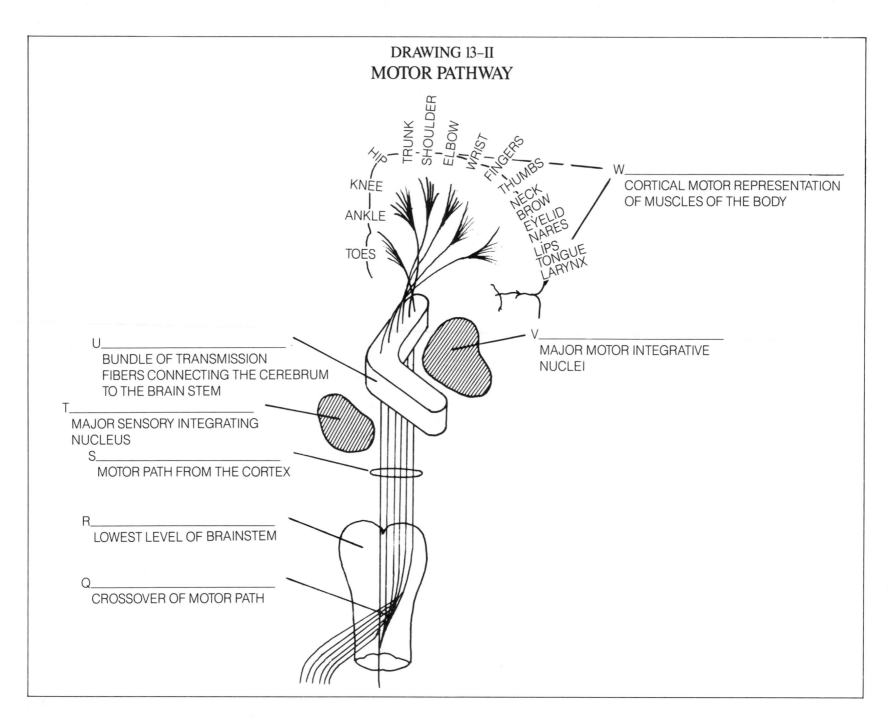

DRAWING 13–II
MOTOR PATHWAY

HIP
KNEE
ANKLE
TOES
TRUNK
SHOULDER
ELBOW
WRIST
FINGERS
THUMBS
NECK
BROW
EYELID
NARES
LIPS
TONGUE
LARYNX

W_____
CORTICAL MOTOR REPRESENTATION
OF MUSCLES OF THE BODY

V_____
MAJOR MOTOR INTEGRATIVE
NUCLEI

U_____
BUNDLE OF TRANSMISSION
FIBERS CONNECTING THE CEREBRUM
TO THE BRAIN STEM

T_____
MAJOR SENSORY INTEGRATING
NUCLEUS

S_____
MOTOR PATH FROM THE CORTEX

R_____
LOWEST LEVEL OF BRAINSTEM

Q_____
CROSSOVER OF MOTOR PATH

DRAWING 13–III

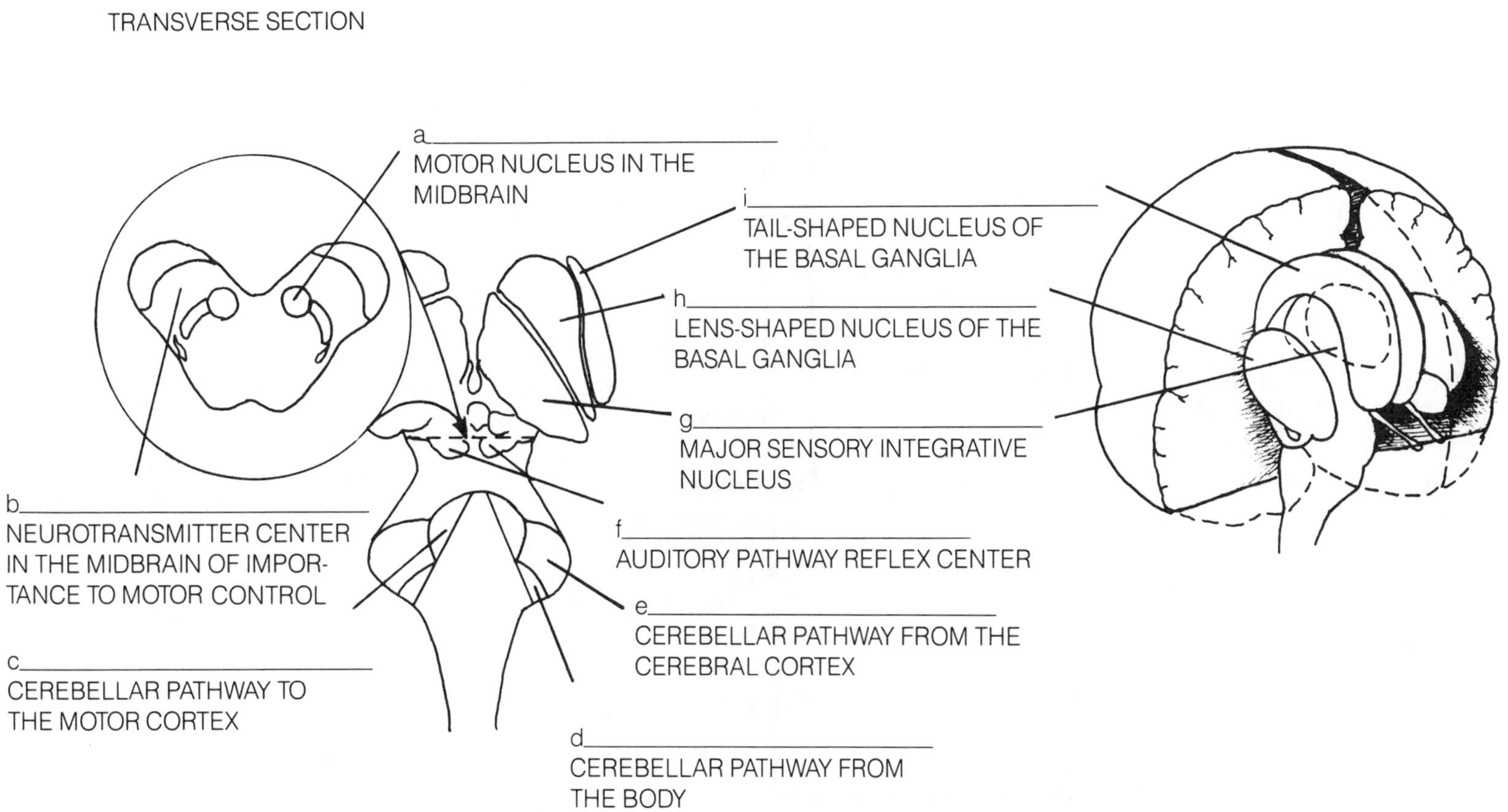

TRANSVERSE SECTION

a_____
MOTOR NUCLEUS IN THE
MIDBRAIN

i_____
TAIL-SHAPED NUCLEUS OF
THE BASAL GANGLIA

h_____
LENS-SHAPED NUCLEUS OF THE
BASAL GANGLIA

g_____
MAJOR SENSORY INTEGRATIVE
NUCLEUS

b_____
NEUROTRANSMITTER CENTER
IN THE MIDBRAIN OF IMPOR-
TANCE TO MOTOR CONTROL

f_____
AUDITORY PATHWAY REFLEX CENTER

c_____
CEREBELLAR PATHWAY TO
THE MOTOR CORTEX

e_____
CEREBELLAR PATHWAY FROM THE
CEREBRAL CORTEX

d_____
CEREBELLAR PATHWAY FROM
THE BODY

DRAWING 13–IV

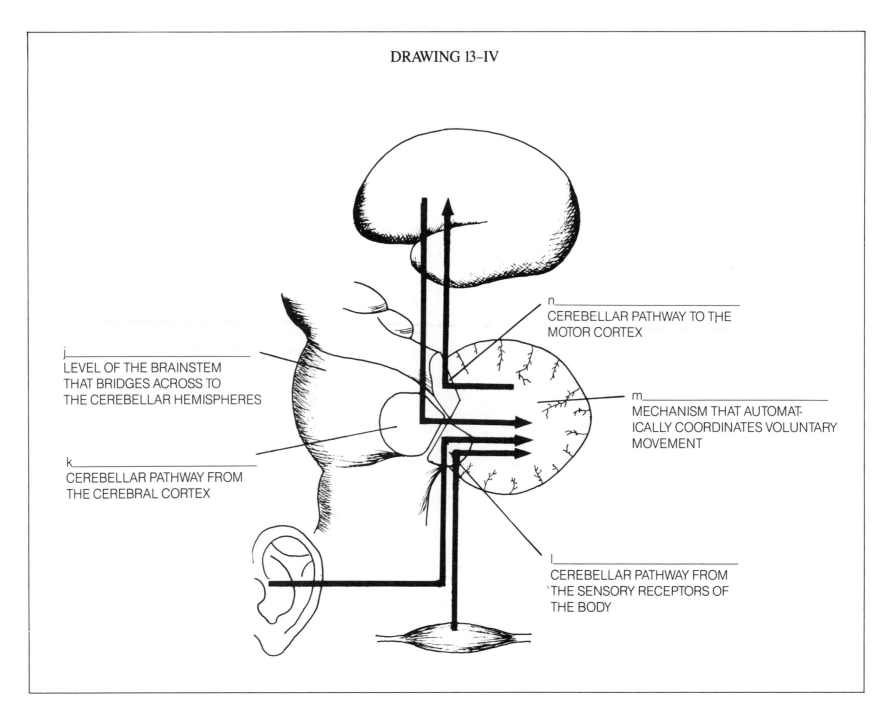

n_____

CEREBELLAR PATHWAY TO THE
MOTOR CORTEX

j_____

LEVEL OF THE BRAINSTEM
THAT BRIDGES ACROSS TO
THE CEREBELLAR HEMISPHERES

m_____

MECHANISM THAT AUTOMAT-
ICALLY COORDINATES VOLUNTARY
MOVEMENT

k_____

CEREBELLAR PATHWAY FROM
THE CEREBRAL CORTEX

l_____

CEREBELLAR PATHWAY FROM
THE SENSORY RECEPTORS OF
THE BODY

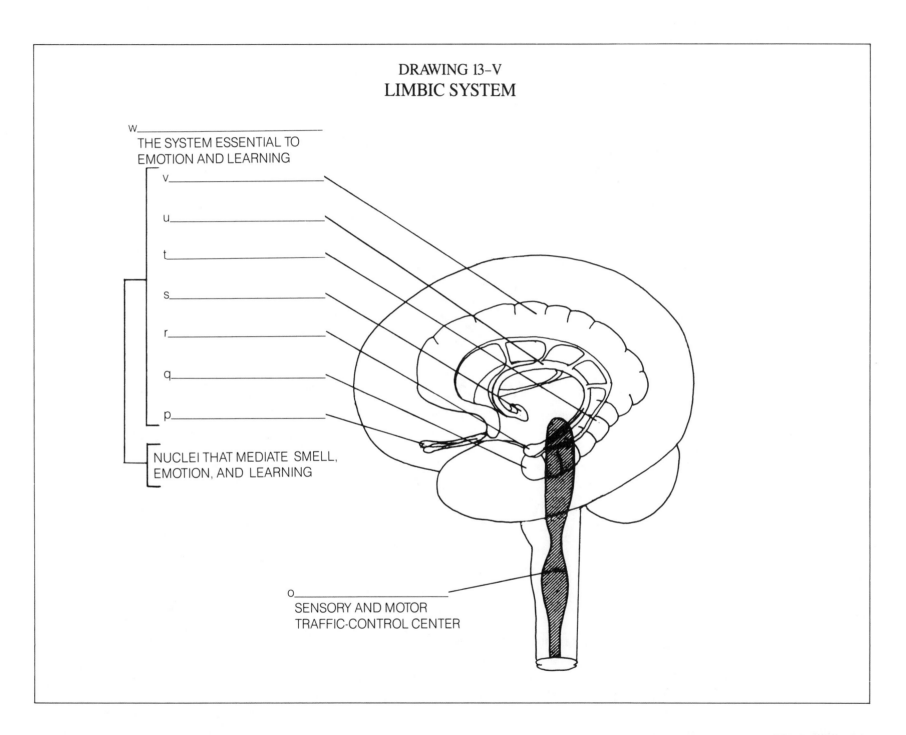

DRAWING 13–V
LIMBIC SYSTEM

w_____
THE SYSTEM ESSENTIAL TO
EMOTION AND LEARNING

v_____

u_____

t_____

s_____

r_____

q_____

p_____

NUCLEI THAT MEDIATE SMELL,
EMOTION, AND LEARNING

o_____
SENSORY AND MOTOR
TRAFFIC-CONTROL CENTER

DRAWING 13–VI

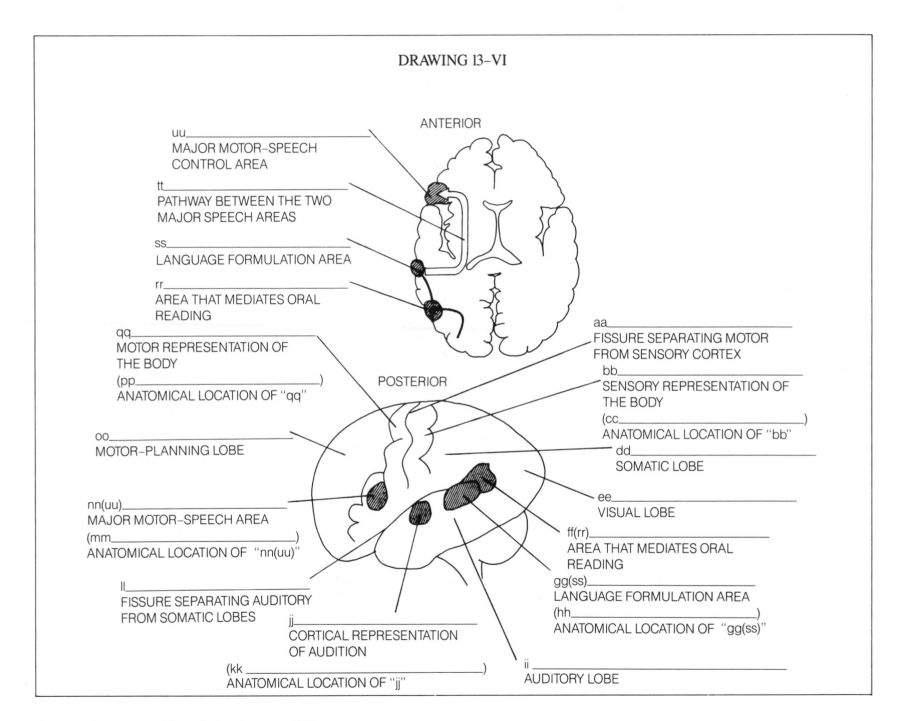

ANTERIOR

uu_____
MAJOR MOTOR–SPEECH
CONTROL AREA

tt_____
PATHWAY BETWEEN THE TWO
MAJOR SPEECH AREAS

ss_____
LANGUAGE FORMULATION AREA

rr_____
AREA THAT MEDIATES ORAL
READING

aa_____
FISSURE SEPARATING MOTOR
FROM SENSORY CORTEX

bb_____
SENSORY REPRESENTATION OF
THE BODY
(cc_____)
ANATOMICAL LOCATION OF "bb"

dd_____
SOMATIC LOBE

qq_____
MOTOR REPRESENTATION OF
THE BODY
(pp_____)
ANATOMICAL LOCATION OF "qq"

POSTERIOR

oo_____
MOTOR–PLANNING LOBE

ee_____
VISUAL LOBE

nn(uu)_____
MAJOR MOTOR–SPEECH AREA
(mm_____)
ANATOMICAL LOCATION OF "nn(uu)"

ff(rr)_____
AREA THAT MEDIATES ORAL
READING

gg(ss)_____
LANGUAGE FORMULATION AREA
(hh_____)
ANATOMICAL LOCATION OF "gg(ss)"

ll_____
FISSURE SEPARATING AUDITORY
FROM SOMATIC LOBES

jj_____
CORTICAL REPRESENTATION
OF AUDITION

(kk_____)
ANATOMICAL LOCATION OF "jj"

ii_____
AUDITORY LOBE

Functional Anatomy of Speech, Language, and Hearing

Self-Study Test of Terminology

Self-Study Instructions: These questions can be used to help you assess how much you have retained from studying the Review Glossary. Answers are given in Appendix E.

(1) _____ The portion of the brain from the entrance of the spinal cord into the skull, through the foramen magnum, to the level of the midbrain; it contains the major transmission parts of the brain, including the pyramidal tract

(2) _____ The level of the brainstem with input connections to the cerebellum and with nuclei of cranial nerves

(3) _____ The midbrain, embryologically

(4) _____ The superior cerebellar peduncle connecting the cerebellum to motor centers in the brainstem and cerebrum

(5) _____ The lowest level of the brainstem that develops from the hindbrain to become the medulla

(6) _____ The end brain, developed from the forebrain, that becomes the cerebrum

(7) _____ The portion of the CNS contained within the vertebral column

(8) _____ The unexpectedness of a signal that is the basis for RAS activation

(9) _____ The upper portion of the hindbrain that becomes the pons and cerebellum

(10) _____ Reflex centers for hearing and vision

(11) _____ The portion of the CNS contained within the skull

(12) _____ The motor center in the midbrain that receives information from the cerebellum

(13) _____ The level of the brainstem with output connections from the cerebellum and with important reflex centers

(14) _____ The largest and newest part of the brain, evolved out of the tops of the two stalks of the brainstem, that makes discriminative behavior possible

(15) _____ The highest level of the brainstem (where it divides into two stalks) that develops from the forebrain to become the thalamus and hypothalamus

(16) _____ The middle cerebellar peduncle connecting the cerebrum to the cerebellum

(17) _____ The inferior cerebellar peduncle connecting sensory feedback from the body to the cerebellum

(18) _____ The neurotransmitter center of importance to motor control

(19) _____ The paired auditory reflex center that connects the thalamus to the cortical auditory center

(20) _____ The bundle of transmission fibers, connecting cerebral cortex with brainstem, that pass through the basal ganglia giving it a striated appearance and the name "corpus striatum"

(21) _____ The area in the upper left frontal lobe that assists in motor speech planning

(22) _____ The head end of the old sensory system where all sensory input (except olfaction) is received and integrated for transfer to the cerebrum

(23) _____ The fibers contained in the internal capsule that form the pathways between primary cortical sensory and motor areas and the brainstem and spinal cord

(24) _____ The integrating mechanism extending through the brainstem from spinal cord to cerebrum that amplifies or inhibits both sensory and motor traffic and is the seat of consciousness

Central Nervous System Anatomy

(25) _____ The old motor centers at the base of the cerebrum that consist of the caudate nucleus and the globus pallidus and putamen, which together form the lenticular nucleus

(26) _____ The language-formulation area in the dominant hemisphere located in the planum temporale

(27) _____ The area behind the postcentral gyrus of some importance to speech in the dominant hemisphere

(28) _____ The neurons interconnecting the cerebral hemispheres

(29) _____ The visceral control center, located below the thalamus, that connects the CNS with the ANS and with the endocrine system through the pituitary gland

(30) _____ Anatomically the transverse gyrus of Heschl, it receives auditory projection fibers in both hemispheres

(31) _____ The name of the reticular sensory mechanism

(32) _____ The "bark" on the surface of the cerebrum containing gray matter (cell bodies)

(33) _____ The area at the intersection of parietal, temporal, and occipital lobes that is of importance in oral reading in the dominant hemisphere

(34) _____ The olfactory bulbs, hippocampus, fornix, cingulate gyrus, mammillary bodies, amygdala, and uncus, which evolved to mediate the sense of smell (hence the embryological name rhinencephalon) and emotion, and which is critical for learning

(35) _____ The lobe that mediates hearing, and in the dominant hemisphere, that mediates language

(36) _____ The fibers interconnecting different cortical areas within the same hemisphere

(37) _____ The crevice separating the temporal lobe from the frontal and parietal lobes in each hemisphere

(38) _____ Feedback information to the cerebellum from muscles, tendons, and joints

(39) _____ Anatomically the precentral gyrus, it contains point-for-point muscle representation, which can be drawn schematically as the motor homunculus

(40) _____ Anatomically the postcentral gyrus, it contains point-for-point sensory representation of the body forming a sensory homunculus that resembles the motor homunculus

(41) _____ The crevice separating the frontal lobe from the parietal lobe in each hemisphere

(42) _____ The associational pathway between the two major speech areas, Wernicke's area and Broca's area

(43) _____ The automatic motor coordinating center at the base of the cerebrum that has evolved from archicerebellum and paleocerebellum (for equilibrium) to neocerebellum (which has enlarged into two hemispheres along with the cerebrum), that controls synergy of voluntary movement

(44) _____ The deep crevice that separates the cerebral hemispheres

(45) _____ The lobe that mediates vision

(46) _____ Anatomically in the inferior frontal gyrus, it is the motor speech control area

(47) _____ The lobe that mediates the tactile (touch) and kinesthetic (movement) senses

(48) _____ The lobe that mediates planning and motor control

(49) _____ The pair of reflex centers mediating the startle reflex to loud sounds

(50) _____ Brain lesion caused by arterial aneurysm, embolus, thrombosis, or hemorrhage

(51) _____ An anastomosis of arteries connecting vertebral and carotid arteries to anterior, middle, and posterior cerebral arteries

(52) _____ The blood vessel that, when injured, can impair speech or language

(53) _____ The middle layer of bone in the skull

(54) _____ Spaces in the brain filled with cerebrospinal fluid

(55) _____ An opening in the skull between sutures

(56) _____ The membrane composed of dura mater, arachoid membrane, and pia mater

Speech Functions of the Central Nervous System

Self-Study Instructions: This test can be used to help you assess how well you understand the speech functions of the central nervous system. Terms to be filled in are from the Review Glossary. Answers are given in Appendix E.

Speech Function

Sensory feedback to guide speech

Auditory system
    Contains cochlear and olivary nuclei of auditory
        pathway

Mediates auditory loudness reflexes

Integrates and relays all auditory input to the
    cortex for speech analysis

Receives collateral sensory input which is tested
    for novelty to determine if cerebrum should
    be aroused to make discriminative judgments

Neuroanatomy

(1) _____ system

(2) _____ system

(3) _____, which
    derives phylogenetically from the

(4) _____

(5) _____, located
    at the (6) _____
    level of the brainstem, which
    derives phylogenetically from the

(7) _____

(8) _____,
    which are portions of the

(9) _____, which
    derives phylogenetically from the

(10) _____

(11) _____
    system extending from upper

(12) _____
    through all levels of the

(13) _____

Receives auditory input from both ears and tests
for speech characteristics

(14) _____ area,

anatomically in (15) _____

in each (16) _____

lobe of the (17) _____,
which evolved from the

(18) _____ and

receives input from the
thalamus over auditory

(19) _____ fibers

Analyzes phonetic components of speech

(20) _____ area in the

(21) _____ gyrus of

the frontal lobe of the

(22) _____ hemisphere

receives input from the
nondominant auditory area via

the (23) _____,
which is composed of

(24) _____ fibers

Decodes linguistic structure of speech for
meaning of propositional message

(25) _____ area,

anatomically in the

(26) _____ of

the (27) _____

lobe in the (28) _____
hemisphere

Tests auditory input to determine worthiness for
short-term memory storage preparatory to
learning

(29) _____ system,

which is connected to the

(30) _____ system,

determines potential for reward
or punishment of input to the

(31) _____ lobes

to mediate awareness of emotion,

and to the (32) _____
to provide appropriate visceral response

Proprioceptive system
    Provides somatic feedback for automatic
       coordination of speech movements

(33) _____,
    which is the inferior

(34) _____ peduncle
    connecting sensory feedback
    from the speech mechanism to the

(35) _____, which
    evolved from the

(36) _____

    Provides awareness of touch and movements of
       the speech mechanism

(37) _____ area
    located in the

(38) _____ gyrus

    of each (39) _____ lobe

Motor speech formulation
    Maps ideas into language

(40) _____

    Converts linguistic formulation of ideas into
       motor speech

(41) _____

    Connects the language area with the speech area

(42) _____
    which is composed of

(43) _____ fibers

    Assists in processing of propositional speech

(44) _____
    located in the upper left
    frontal lobe, and the

(45) _____ in

    the left (46) _____
    lobe above the fissure of

(47) _____

    Connects reading mechanism to speech mechanism
       for oral reading

(48) _____ gyrus
    located at the intersection of
    temporal, parietal, and

(49) _____ lobes
    in the dominant hemisphere

    Controls discrete movements of speech muscles

(50) _____

located in the

(51) _____ gyrus
anterior to the fissure of

(52) _____ in each
(53) _____ lobe

Generates reflexive movements that provide
background adjustments for discrete speech
movements

(54) _____

consisting of (55) _____

nucleus and (56) _____
nucleus located at the base of each
cerebral hemisphere

Connects the input and output systems with the
integrative systems for language and speech

(57) _____
is the bundle of ascending
and descending transmission fibers
passing through the basal ganglia
that connect the

(58) _____
with the brainstem

Connects speech-motor planning centers with
automatic movement coordination
mechanism

(59) _____,

which is the (60) _____
cerebellar peduncle, connects
the cortex with the

(61) _____

Connects automatic movement output from the
cerebellum to cortical and brainstem speech-
motor control centers

(62) The _____

(the (63) _____
cerebellar peduncle) connects
cerebellar output to the

(64) _____ in the
midbrain and to cortical motor centers

Generates neurotransmitters of importance to
fluent speech-motor control

(65) _____,

located in the midbrain

CHAPTER FOURTEEN
Neurology of Speech: Input Processing

INPUT PROCESSING

We stand as biological heirs of a highly sophisticated apparatus developed to permit goal-seeking behaviors. The most sophisticated legacy of all is the equipment for language and speech. It is the culmination of successful biological mechanisms that have survived compelling tests for survival. It is an inheritance with parts that date back beyond the most ancient kingdom, beyond civilization, beyond the time when our ancestors slithered from the primeval sea. The mechanisms we now utilize for speech have been safeguarded across these billions of years at molecular, cellular, and behavioral levels of organization. Clearly, we are launched for our journey through life with much of our neurological organization for speech provided as a legacy of evolution (Fig. 14–1).

We know that our capacity to learn to speak is innate, but that the skills of the specific language we master are acquired. We must, therefore, conclude that our innate capacity for language has been encoded for genetic transmission across the ages, and, in all normal human infants, is mani-

fested at birth in their neural organization. That even a single protein molecule can store many times this much information is apparent when we realize that if all of its possible DNA code combinations were synthesized, the resulting mass of amino acids would exceed the weight of the universe.

We must, likewise, conclude that the speaking skills infants acquire are manifested in patterns of neural organization that develop as they live out their lives, and with their passing, cease, not to be replicated in their children. Whereas the molecular code is more than adequate for storing genetic information, the cellular code of neuronal circuits would, by itself, far exceed any conceivable demands for storing learned experience.

The molecular story of speech is yet to be written. What is known, in broad outline and with reasonable certainty, is its neural organization. Much of this knowledge comes from speech effects of violent injuries inflicted on the brain both by nature and man: head wounds, as well as strokes and disease. Some knowledge comes indirectly from seizures that require neurosurgery: with the

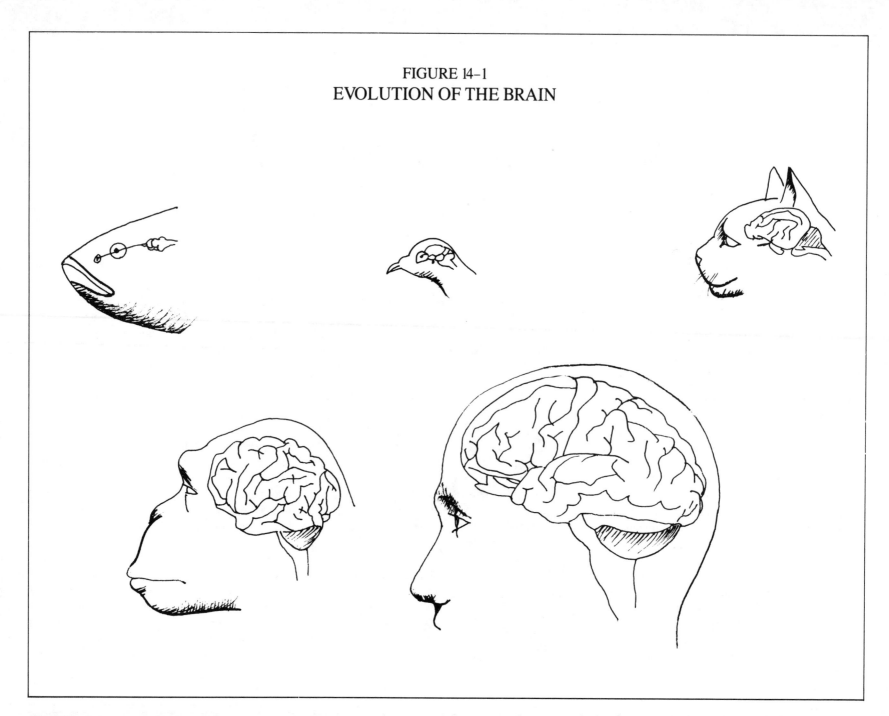

FIGURE 14–1
EVOLUTION OF THE BRAIN

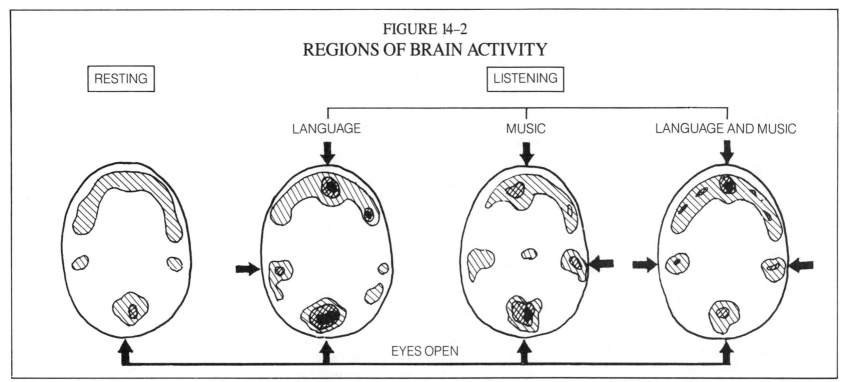

FIGURE 14–2
REGIONS OF BRAIN ACTIVITY

RESTING

LISTENING

LANGUAGE   MUSIC   LANGUAGE AND MUSIC

EYES OPEN

brain exposed, speech areas can be mapped by stimulation with electrodes. Some information comes from anesthetizing one or the other cerebral hemisphere, or by disconnecting the hemispheres surgically. Some data come from studies of regional cerebral blood flow, which increases in those areas that actively process neural information for a task such as speech. Samples of how different regions of the brain are active when resting, listening to both language and music, listening to language alone, and listening to music alone are shown in Figure 14–2. Finally, some knowledge comes from electroencephalographic recordings taken from electrodes on the skull.

Viewed broadly, the brain is organized into *transmission systems* and *integrative systems.* The transmission systems process *input* information from sensory equipment and carry motor *output*

information to the muscular system in an interactive arrangement that is best described as the *neuromuscular system.*

The function of the integrative system is implied in the term: It integrates new input information with previously stored information to permit selection of output information. But, the more that is learned about the nervous system, the more the function of the integrative system blurs into that of the transmission systems. Which system deciphers speech, for instance? The input system does more than transmit sensory information, so the answer probably is that both systems are involved in the integrative processes that make decoding (understanding) possible. Which system organizes the neuromuscular patterns for smoothly coordinated speech? The output system does more than passively transmit prepackaged bundles of patterned

motor information to the muscles of speech — the neuromuscular system participates in the packaging.

The operations that the nervous system performs are easier to delineate with certainty than are the neural systems by which these operations are performed. There is no doubt that information is received and analyzed, so this is called *input processing* (not to be confused with the *input system,* which undoubtedly participates in the processing). There is no doubt that information from the various sensory sources is integrated and elaborated centrally, so this is called *central processing.* There is likewise no doubt that motor information is patterned and coordinated for movement, so it is called *output processing* or *patterning.*

Neurology of Speech: Input Processing

Sensory Pathways

Not many years ago, the transmission pathways of the nervous system were thought to be essentially one-way streets: presumably, the afferent sensory paths carried information about the environment to the brainstem and cortex. There, it was integrated and analyzed by means of associational neural circuitry; the efferent motor paths then carried appropriate signals to the muscles to effect the organism's response. That the brain was designed along the lines of a telephone switchboard was a tempting analogy.

Auditory Pathways

While this classic concept of neural organization prevailed, the *auditory pathway* with its many synaptic relay stations — to take an example of special interest to us — was viewed in terms of the value of auditory information to the various neural structures that received it. Neuroanatomists have long known that the auditory paths that lead from the organ of Corti in the inner ear to the cerebral cortex are bilateral (interconnect with both ears) and have synaptic connections en route with the *cochlear nucleus,* the *superior olivary nucleus,* the *lateral lemniscus,* the *inferior colliculus,* and, in the *thalamus,* the *medial geniculate body* (Fig. 14–3). From the medial geniculate body, the fibers fan out to the *auditory projection area* of the cortex.

The value of auditory information has been more apparent at some of these levels than at others. At the cortical level, traditionally conceived as supreme in the hierarchical organization of the nervous system, auditory sense data were considered necessary for integration with other sensory information and for participation in higher psychological functions, such as perception, attention, discrimination, and the like. At the thalamic level, emotional responses to sound could be mediated. At lower levels in the brainstem, reflexive responses, such as startle reactions to loud sounds, could be accomplished. The value of auditory data for the *cerebellum* (anatomists discovered that it, too, is connected with the auditory path in the brainstem) was not clear. Nor was it clear originally, in the classic conception, why the reticular formation received auditory information. The reason has since become apparent, as we will soon see.

Loopholes in the Classic Concept. The classic conception of sensory transmission is one that common sense supported. When neuroanatomists described fiber tracts leading from sensory receptors to various centers in the brain, what more sensible conclusion should be reached than that these fibers carried sensory information along a one-way path to these centers? And when neurophysiologists, using anesthetized animals, found that the classic sensory paths carry high-amplitude signals to the cortex with great reliability and consistency, and that these signals are confined to the classic sensory receiving area where they are greatly amplified, what better confirmation could there have been of the fixed transmission function of the sensory pathways?

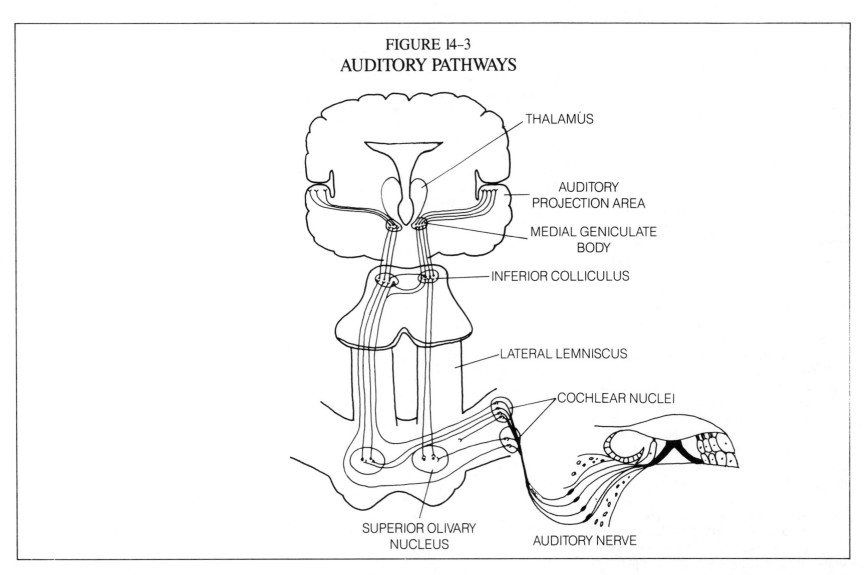

FIGURE 14–3
AUDITORY PATHWAYS

THALAMUS

AUDITORY
PROJECTION AREA

MEDIAL GENICULATE
BODY

INFERIOR COLLICULUS

LATERAL LEMNISCUS

COCHLEAR NUCLEI

SUPERIOR OLIVARY
NUCLEUS

AUDITORY NERVE

But, when the waking brain was investigated in animals without central anesthesia, quite a different picture appeared. The idea of variable transmission of sensory signals replaced that of stable transmission. The size of evoked neural responses to a given stimulus varied. Widespread cortical and subcortical responses were found instead of responses limited to the classic sensory areas. What did all of this apparent confusion in the waking brain mean? Neuroscientists are now just about convinced of the meaning: The entire brain, sensory and motor transmission systems as well as integrative system, is organized to accomplish one's purpose of the moment. This means that neural traffic in the transmission paths travels both ways. It means that the sensory system is plastic rather than fixed in its response to a stimulus — that more is required for perception than the receipt of sensory data in the cortex.

Behavioral Purpose and Neurophysiology

To ascribe reasons to nature's design of the nervous system is to lapse into teleology. It is a lapse that we will permit ourselves, however, because it will help to clarify a principle that seems to underlie all operations of the brain. The principle is this: The nervous system appears to be designed to maintain the status quo; it works to convert novel stimuli to familiar stimuli. It is as if nature decided that the brain need busy itself vigorously only when the unexpected occurs. So long as the world is behaving according to one's expectations, then, presumably, one can cope safely; minimal neural activity is needed. The neural apparatus seems to have been created on the assumption that the world will continue today the way we experienced it in all of our yesterdays. Accordingly, the nervous system is not prepared to deal with a world of unlimited variety. Instead, it works in terms of experiences limited by past successes and failures, especially those of infancy and childhood.

Novelty is determined by comparison of new events with past experience; to the extent that they are dissimilar, to that extent the new event is novel. Look at Figure 14-4 and what you will probably see on the right is a Maltese cross (normally lighted from above). Turn the page upside down, though, and the light pattern you have learned to expect will be on the left, which is where the Maltese cross will likely be seen. Our nervous systems are so conservative that we are poorly prepared to recognize or react appropriately to new or different stimuli. We deal with novel events either of two ways: distort them to conform to our past experiences, or respond to them with arousal and alertness.

The first course is the more conservative, and the more typical — in fact, neurological design makes this alternative virtually inevitable; we are built to discover similarity in events and to ignore dissimilarity. The sense of comfort we find in the familiar is a subjective manifestation of this method of coping. Of course, reality is distorted by fitting it to our expectations rather than by fitting our perceptions to stimuli as we actually receive them. This, though, is a price that we pay for the economy of perceiving just those features that permit us to classify objects rather than perceive the rich detail that would make each perception unique. Only when details become familiar can we deal with them easily, which is probably why Asians look alike to Westerners, and, no doubt, vice versa.

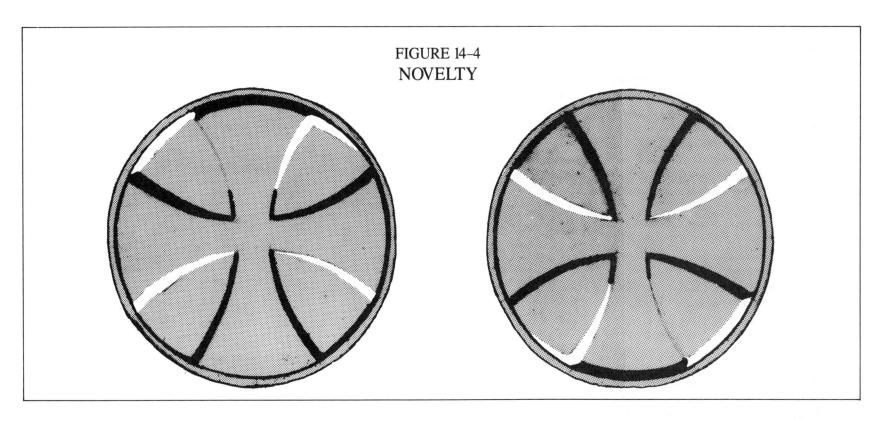

FIGURE 14-4
NOVELTY

The second method of coping with novelty — to respond to it — is the stuff of which alertness, learning, and arousal are made. Apparently, learning occurs when, confronted with a novel situation, the nervous system is unable to force the unexpected stimuli to conform to past experiences and present purposes.

Whether or not we will respond to novelty is, it seems, a matter about which we are not able to make rational, conscious judgments. Acceptance or rejection of unanticipated stimuli evidently occurs early during the process of perception. The determination seems to be made, prior to awareness, on the basis of some unconscious determination of purpose at the moment. If it fits this purpose to respond to unpredicted stimuli, we will suddenly be jerked alert and oriented toward the

novelty. We will experience an abrupt arousal as, for instance, when a chance remark catches our attention during an otherwise boring discussion. And this determination to respond or not respond may very well take place during the early input stages of sensory transmission — which brings us back to the necessity of viewing input processing as an integral manifestation of purposeful functioning of the entire organism.

Neurophysiology of Input Processing

How does the sensory system operate to permit us to accept or reject a stimulus? Only fragments of the complete answer are available, but the overall scheme is apparent. In brief, the higher neural centers must be activated and involved in

controlling the sensory input. The senses utilize dual afferent routes in their influence on cortical activity. One route entails the classic sensory paths, such as the one we discussed for audition. It transmits and processes specific information that is used for discrimination and analysis. The other afferent route is that of the nonspecific *reticular activating system*. This system provides general arousal of the brain for response to specific signals coming in over classic sensory paths. Then, so that higher centers can unify all systems in accomplishing a purpose, a downstream *sensory control mechanism* adjusts input so that it is integrated with all other neural operations. So much for the skeleton of the answer. Now, let us add flesh to these bones.

Specific Sensory Input System for Speech.
A major question that awaits an answer, ultimately, is how a listener manages to analyze the stream of speech into a structure of phonemes, morphemes, and sentences that will yield meaning. Three things are obvious: (1) this is a problem of input, (2) this input problem requires considerable auditory discrimination and analysis, and (3) the classic auditory transmission pathways that carry the specific information with which we make discriminative judgments about what we hear are involved. Not so obvious, however, are the neural mechanisms by which these operations are accomplished. How does the sensory system provide answers to such questions as the following: "Has anything happened?" (A question of detecting a signal against a background of neural activity.) "What is it?" (A question of identifying quality.) "How much of it is there?" (A problem of quantity.) "Is this stronger than that?" (Discrimination between stimuli is required.) "Where is it?" "Is it moving or changing in time?" "What pitch is it?" (These last questions all involve time, a dimension especially crucial to perception of speech.)

How much of the acoustical analysis of speech is performed in the ear? One way or another, all of the auditory data that the brain will need to answer such questions as were just posed must be encoded as neural signals in the cochlea. We will save elaboration of what the ear accomplishes for the next chapter. It is sufficient here to offer four observations about what that accomplishment will prove to be.

The first reflects empirical evidence; the ear, of all sensory receptors, is uniquely equipped to respond to the dimension of time. Additionally, it is designed to respond selectively to stimuli of different frequencies as well as of different intensities.

The second observation could point to an achievement of the auditory transmission pathway just as well as to a cochlear accomplishment. From the preceding discussion, we saw that the determination must be made at some level in the sensory system of whether to force a stimulus pattern to conform to our expectation, or to respond with arousal to its novelty. Clearly, this determination requires some sort of unconscious decision-making process. But this process could transpire somewhere along the auditory path as well as in the cochlea.

The third observation appears to settle any ambiguity about where the decision is carried out, at least for nonspeech sounds. Evidence indicates that the brain deals in a linear manner with the information it receives in neurally encoded form from the sensory receptors; the central nervous system apparently does not make nonlinear transformations of sensory inputs. In other words, both subjective sensory experience of, say, pitch, and behavioral response are directly proportional, not to the stimulus received by the sensory receptor but to the neurally encoded response of the receptor. This means that whatever distortion our image of the real world may suffer, we must do our twisting of reality in the initial stage at which the impinging stimuli are transduced into neural impulses. Acceptance or rejection of stimulus novelty would appear to be an operation performed by the sensory receptor.

The fourth observation is based on the proposal that speech perception is accomplished by a special mechanism. When the unique acoustic patterns of speech are detected, their frequency and intensity changes (any instant of speech has many frequencies and intensities) occur almost simultaneously, yet they are not heard as changes in pitch and loudness (as they would be otherwise), but as changes in the whole speech sound, not just its components. How much the ear is directly involved in carrying out speech detection remains to be determined. In all likelihood, speech is not decoded sound by sound until a sentence is finally perceived, but, rather, the other way round — it is decoded from the top down. Until you understand what you've heard, you're not likely to be certain of the sounds in the words you heard. To add to the complexity of this special mechanism for perceiving speech, it seems especially sensitive to detection of sounds produced by movements of the speech mechanism.

Experiments indicate that auditory abilities by which infants discriminate differences in sound that can make differences in the meaning of words are apparently inherited. For instance, whether you hear *pin* or *bin,* when spoken, depends on whether you hear *p* or *b* at the beginning of each word. If the time it takes the vocal folds to start vibrating is less than 30 ms, you will hear *bin*; if longer than 30 ms, you will hear *pin*. This ability to discriminate between *p* and *b* has been found in infants soon after birth. It seems that if these abilities are not heard and practiced during earliest years of life, they will disappear rapidly. When infants born into three different language cultures were compared, they were equally able to hear distinctions among consonants used in all three languages. A year later, their abilities to make distinctions used in their native language had improved, but they were no longer able to hear distinctions used in the other languages.

Nonspecific Reticular Activating System.
The portion of the *reticular formation* that is concerned with input processing is, as we saw in the preceding chapter, the *reticular activating system*. It is considered a nonspecific input system because it serves all sensory channels. As can be seen in Figure 14–5, the classic sensory paths (the cross-hatched arrow) give off collateral fibers into the reticular formation (solid black arrows). Within this structure is a network of paths to the *limbic system, hypothalamus,* and *thalamus* from which fibers are distributed diffusely throughout all regions of the cortex. These anatomical connections are suggestive of how the reticular activating system functions. By virtue of inputs from all sensory systems and connections with the entire cortex, this system is able to arouse the brain and maintain its readiness to respond to incoming sensory signals. Were it not for this activation, the brain would literally sleep through even the heaviest bombardment of stimulation.

Not only can the cortex be awakened by the reticular activating system's response to environmental stimuli, it can also be awakened by its own activity. All of us, doubtlessly, have had the experience of jerking awake with recollection of a forgotten appointment or a "brilliant" solution to a plaguing problem. We accomplish this self-awakening, presumably, by signals to the reticular formation from some cortical area that projects fibers down into it; in turn, the reticular formation responds over its diffuse projections into the cortex to arouse the whole forebrain.

The neuroanatomical fact that the reticular formation is intimately and extensively connected with the *limbic system* is of particular importance. To ignore these connections would be a bit like ignoring a missing engine in a sports car. These connections are vital to our emotional life and awareness. Limbic connections with the reticular formation apparently operate to define the potentiality of a novel stimulus for reward or punishment.

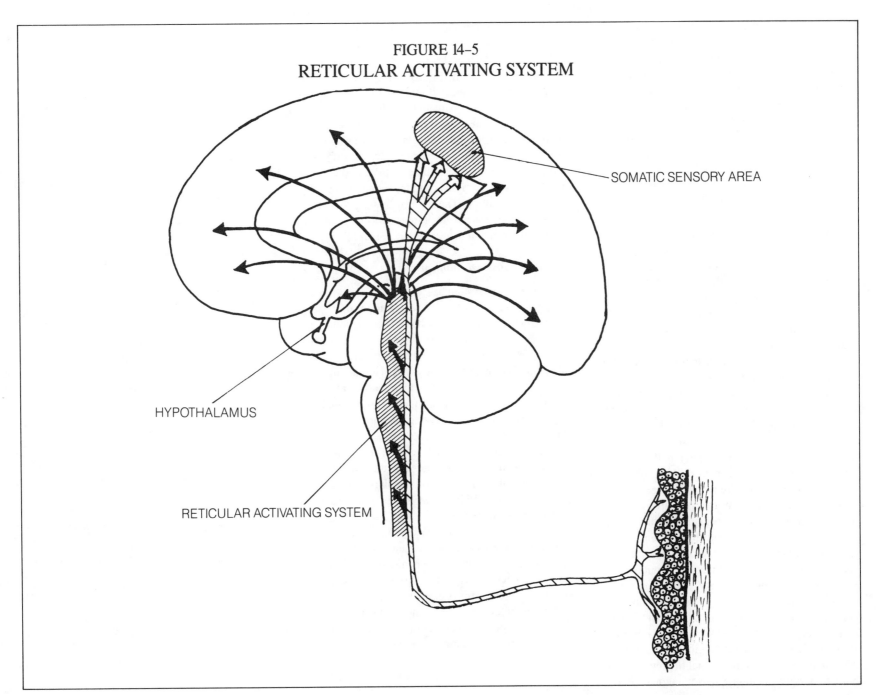

FIGURE 14–5
RETICULAR ACTIVATING SYSTEM

SOMATIC SENSORY AREA

HYPOTHALAMUS

RETICULAR ACTIVATING SYSTEM

In effect, the reticular system submits unexpected events to the limbic system to determine their potential biological significance (Fig. 14–6). If the limbic system determines that this novel situation holds threat of punishment, it notifies the reticular system to sound the alarm and prepare all systems to fight or flee. If the novelty holds prospects of pleasure, the reticular system is notified to prepare all systems to go forth and seek more of the same. If the novel stimulus is judged as having little or no importance, the reticular formation is told to forget it; as far as this stimulus is concerned, the brain can sleep.

What is the significance of this neurological arrangement for input processing of sensory information? Just this: The brain will be receptive to sensory signals so long as they are novel or have motivational significance. Stimuli devoid of novelty or motivational value are stimuli for which the reticular activating system will not arouse the brain. Without arousal, neither perception nor learning is possible. A change in any parameter of a stimulus is the basis for detecting novelty. With hearing, for example, changes in frequency, intensity, or patterns of energy in an acoustic signal could elicit an arousal response from the reticular activating system. Modern urban society provides ample evidence of this auditory example in operation. We are continuously immersed in high-intensity noise to which we normally are oblivious, except when it changes: Witness the effect of a new noise that suddenly appears in our favorite car, or the paralyzing effect of the abrupt silence of a jet engine failure on take-off, or the attentive response of hearing your own name leap out of the noisy babble of a cocktail party.

If you have followed the line of reasoning being developed here, you should be about ready to point up an apparent discrepancy in this argument. We have discussed at some length the reticular activating system as being crucial to preparing the brain to perceive incoming sensory signals. Ear-lier, however, we saw the strong probability that the extent of response to a stimulus is determined in the sensory receptor. Using hearing as an example, this means that any limitation to be imposed on an auditory response will probably occur in the cochlea, a structure upstream from the reticular formation. The dilemma, then, is how to account for the importance of the reticular activating system on sensory input to the cortex when the effects of this system will be carried out in the ear, the structure that feeds signals into the reticular formation in the first place. The solution to this problem brings us to the last aspect of input processing of sensory information that we will consider.

Sensory Control Mechanism

The sensory system has, classically, been considered a channel for one-way neural traffic into the brain. Only recently has it become abundantly evident that the sensory system handles two-way traffic — and therein lies the solution to our dilemma. The central nervous system has an important upstream pathway by which sensory response to stimuli can be controlled. This descending pathway parallels, in reverse direction, the classic input transmission route with all of its synaptic relay stations. Just as the classic ascending pathways sends collateral fibers into the reticular formation in the brainstem, and similarly, just as cerebral and cerebellar pathways send collaterals into the reticular formation, so, too, does the *descending sensory control pathway* that you saw in Figure 10–10. This arrangement suggests that the upstream sensory control mechanism obtains information from throughout the brain that is processed by the reticular system. The notable inhibition or facilitation of sensory-input transmission that results from stimulation of the reticular formation lends credence to this possibility.

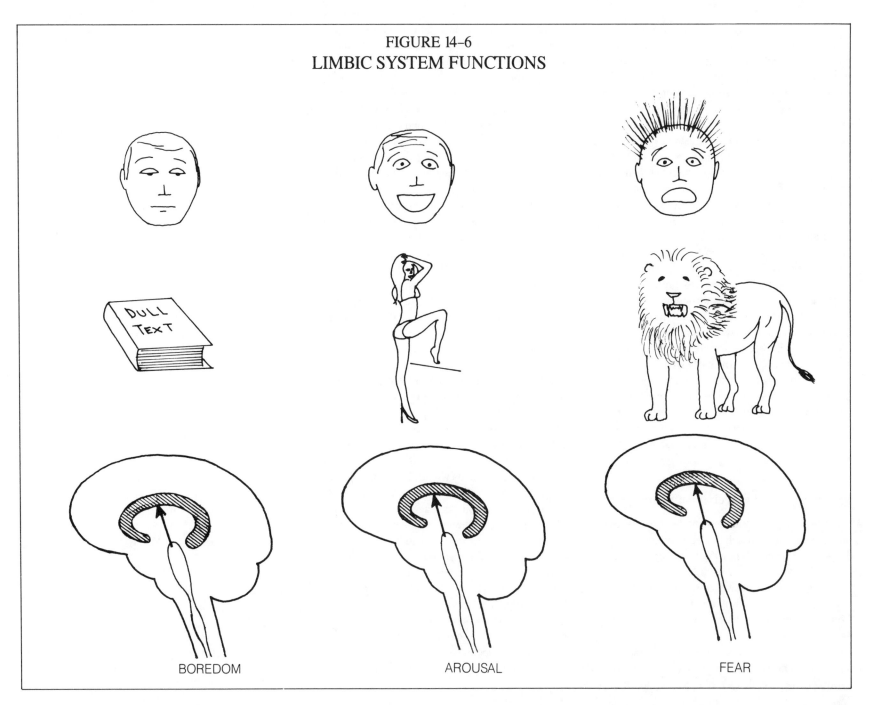

FIGURE 14–6
LIMBIC SYSTEM FUNCTIONS

BOREDOM

AROUSAL

FEAR

What is pointed up by discovery of reticular and sensory control mechanisms is that the old physiological boundaries between central sensory processes and central motor processes are invalid. The brain is not organized like a telephone switch-board, but instead, operates as a transactional mechanism. It seems to be composed less of inde-pendent linear pathways for nonstop express traffic from receptors to higher centers than of mutually interdependent loop circuits that stitch together the various parts of the network into a functional whole. The classic ascending sensory pathways, the classic "pyramidal" and "extrapyramidal" descending motor pathways, and the newly discov-ered descending sensory control pathways are all knit together by the reticular system. The net result is an intermingling of widely distributed sensory impulses with other signals throughout the brain, a modifying of sensory input (usually inhibiting it unless the signal is novel or has motivational sig-nificance) — in short, a selecting and modulating of sensory messages in the early stages of trans-mission. The sensory control system, in effect, provides perceptual processes with a purpose against which incoming signals are tested. Only those deemed novel or of motivational value seem worthy of being passed along for analysis in the higher neural centers.

Speech as Input: Perceiving a Sentence

What we have discussed are the input process-ing mechanisms available for perceiving and un-derstanding speech. Knowing how they operate for this task, however, is quite another matter.

There is no one theory of speech perception; rather there are competing theories which differ from one another in several ways. Each theory is an attempt to explain certain characteristics of speech perception. Our discussion is biased toward a theoretical perspective called *active.* In contrast to other theories called *passive,* active theories assert that listeners use various kinds of informa-tion available to them to make hypotheses about an incoming speech message. Passive theories assume that the speech signal is interpreted automatically as acoustic cues are discerned by the listener.

Another basic dichotomy by which theories of speech perception are classified is *bottom-up* ver-sus *top-down.* The directions of processing sug-gested by these terms derive from a model of sig-nal analysis in which the lowest level is the purely auditory (recognition of acoustic cues) and the highest level is purely linguistic (semantic-syntactic). A bottom-up theory holds that percep-tual decisions are made solely with reference to the incoming acoustic signal. Such models are data-driven in the sense that the acoustic signal is the basic source of data from which perception arises. A top-down model proposes that perception is guided by hypotheses or hunches that take form in the listener's appreciation of context (knowledge of the situation and the speaker) and cognitive or linguistic information.

Why would there be any reason not to assume that speech perception is not entirely passive and bottom-up? After all, isn't speech just a sequence of acoustic segments, the perception of which determines the phonetic segments, syllables, words, and sentences produced by a talker? Let us consider some reasons why this view is dubious.

First, consider the following experiment. A recording of a simple sentence, such as *Tom missed class yesterday,* is altered by removing the noise segment associated with the *s* in *class* and replac-ing it with some other sound — a cough, an elec-tronic noise, or even a belch. The altered sentence is then presented to listeners who are asked to identify any missing or unusual sounds. Typically, listeners detect no abnormality, except that they might hear a kind of noisy background. But they hear the intact sentence, with no speech sound missing. Now if speech perception were completely a passive, bottom-up process, this distortion of the signal should be readily apparent. The perception of the intact sentence indicates that the speech perception process has "restored" the replaced sound (hence this perceptual phenomenon is called *phonemic restoration*). How can it be restored? Apparently, because the system of speech perception seeks to know the meaning of a sentence and in so doing, determines words that best fit the acoustic pattern, even in the face of some discrepancies. That is, the system ignores the altered *s* because this one deviant segment is not critical to the recognition of the overall message.

In another kind of experiment, a word is presented repeatedly to listeners on a tape loop. The listeners are asked to say when the stimulus changes (though in fact it never does change, as the same item is simply presented over and over again). Most listeners hear a change after a few repetitions of the stimulus. For example, the word *dress* might be heard as *address* or *stress* or *stressed*. If speech perception were simply a bottom-up process, why should listeners hear different words when in fact only the same word is repetitively presented? This phenomenon, called *verbal transformation*, indicates that speech perception is not governed by the acoustic speech signal in a simple one-to-one fashion.

It is clear from a variety of experiments that listeners can fill in or predict missing information in a speech message. Part of this ability derives from the redundancy of language. Because many linguistic units are predictable from the context in which they *occr it is not ncssary that every unit in fact be prsnt for lnguage to be undrstood* (notice the missing letters in this sentence — can you guess what they are?)

An active model of speech perception is based on the idea that the perceptual system uses more than the acoustic signal of speech to reach an interpretation of the listener's message. The basic acoustic information is the bottom-up aspect of speech perception, which is complemented by top-down information, such as semantic and syntactic information.

Such a view of speech perception explains why it has been extremely difficult to program computers to understand speech. A computer with the full facility of speech understanding like that in humans probably would have to possess about the same linguistic knowledge that humans have. This point also reveals the complexity of the brain's operations in understanding a speech message.

Understanding Meaning

The immediate and overriding goal of ordinary speech perception is to comprehend a speaker's meaning. This turns out not to be a simple matter. First, the relation between a word's meaning and its pronunciation or spelling is almost always arbitrary. The learner of a language has to learn idioms, or word combinations whose meaning is not directly derived from the meanings of the component words. Completely defining the meaning of a word is nearly impossible, as there is no known limit to the extent of information which could be associated with a word. Even large dictionaries define words incompletely. Many words come to have meanings which must be defined with respect to the culture of the language's speakers. And individual speakers vary markedly in the way in which their vocabularies relate to particular areas of experience, as well as in the size of their vocabularies. Meaning can be literal, that is, determined by the words used and their syntactic relations, or it can be determined by the context in which the utterance appears. Finally, meaning is negotiable between speakers. Words may be defined de novo, or established meanings can be modified as desired. Linguistic subcultures often are marked by special vocabularies. Beatniks of the 1960s were known to, like man, dig it. Valley girls may regard it as grody to the max.

Beyond these considerations, understanding sentences can be complicated in other ways. Occasionally we have difficulty in grasping the sense of a sentence. Two examples of sentences that may be difficult for you to interpret are shown below.

1. The horse raced past the barn fell.
2. The man who hunts ducks out on weekends.

Do these sentences make sense to you? Do they seem like grammatical sentences at all? If you cannot make sense out of them, then examine the rephrasing of each sentence below.

1a. The horse that was raced past the barn fell.
2a. The man who hunts likes to duck out on weekends.

Why are sentences 1 and 2 troublesome? The reason is that each involves a sequence of words that tends to trigger a misleading interpretation. In sentence 1 it is natural to think of the word *horse* as subject of the verb *raced*. This interpretation doesn't work because the sentence contains a hidden passive verb, as shown in sentence 1a. In sentence 2 we are led into a faulty interpretation because it is natural to think of *ducks* as the object of the verb *hunts*. But as the rephrasing in sentence 2a shows, *ducks* is the verb of the subject *man*.

What these examples demonstrate is that linguistic inference is sometimes difficult. On occasion, we must reanalyze sentences to make sense out of them. Sentences that force us to reanalyze are called "garden-path sentences" because they lead us down the garden path. Another example of such a sentence is created by homophonous words (words that sound the same but have different meanings). Consider the fragment in sentence 3 versus that in sentence 4.

3. Rapid writing with his left hand. . . .
4. Rapid righting with his left hand. . . .

Choosing whether sentence 3 or 4 is the correct interpretation from a spoken production has to wait until the sentence offers clarifying information, such as in sentence 5.

5. Rapid righting with his left hand saved from loss the contents of the canoe.

The complete sentence makes the choice clear: *writing* and *canoe* do not fit together but *righting* and *canoe* do. When listeners hear the phrases in sentences 3 and 4, which sound the same, they do not know whether *writing* or *righting* is correct until the entire sentence is heard.

What do listeners do when the linguistic interpretation of a sentence is ambiguous? To some extent they hold off or delay linguistic inference, but the more common reaction is to draw inferences according to the contextual information that is available. Indeed, the opinion of some scientists who study language comprehension is that inferences are at work everywhere. It is conceivable that when we listen to sentences, we generate and reject many unwanted or inappropriate inferences. Occasionally, we are aware of this process. One author was engaged in a conversation at a cocktail party in which a speaker said something like, "That's how it is with (syntax/sin tax)," with the words in parentheses indicating the choices that came to mind upon hearing the remark. The word *syntax* sounds like *sin tax,* and for some reason the word *syntax* was the first alternative to be considered. When this word did not fit with the context of the conversation, it was discarded in favor of *sin tax.*

Listening even to everyday conversation probably engages complex inferential processing, which draws upon a wide range of human experience. This conclusion points up another reason why it has been difficult to program computers to understand spoken language. The computer needs to know more than the rules of language; it also needs to know something of human experience.

For all this, speech perception normally proceeds so effortlessly as to deny interference. Indeed, it is nearly impossible for us not to perceive another's speech — short of occluding our ears or falling asleep. When someone speaks, there is an almost obligatory comprehension — not necessarily a full and accurate understanding, to be sure — but an undeniable processing of the words spoken. This remarkable faculty fails in certain aphasias. Persons with this kind of language disorder cannot comprehend words spoken to them. This receptive language disorder is traditionally associated with damage to Wernicke's area and is sometimes known as Wernicke's aphasia (or receptive aphasia). Some persons with damage to this general area of the brain produce jargon, "speech" that they seem to use sincerely in communication, but which is incomprehensible to normal listeners.

CLINICAL POSTSCRIPT

Our discussion of the input processing of speech has focused on speech as an acoustic signal. The brain gains access to this signal by means of the auditory system, which transduces the physical energy of sound into nervous impulses that travel along systems of nerves. Of course, this is the usual means of perceiving speech. But it is not the only way.

A small number of deaf-blind individuals have been taught to perceive speech through tactile cues obtained by placing their hands on a speaker's face. Appropriate positioning of the fingers allows them to sense lip and jaw movements, air flow through the nostrils (as for nasal sounds), and laryngeal vibrations. These tactile cues are sufficient that an individual trained in this method, called *Tadoma* after two early users named Tad and Oma, can understand conversational speech. Thus, a person born without the senses of sight and hearing can learn not only to produce speech but also to understand another speaker by virtue of tactile cues. Research has shown that normal individuals temporarily deprived of visual and auditory cues

for speech can learn to use the tactile cues of the Tadoma method.

Although few people use the Tadoma method today, its successful use by a number of deaf-blind persons holds implications for the development of tactile aids for the sensory impaired and for theories of speech perception. It is a remarkable fact that speech can be understood as a series of tactile cues by the Tadoma user, as a series of visual cues by a proficient lip reader (also called a speech reader), or as a series of acoustic cues by the majority of people. Whatever cues form the sensory message of speech, the information that eventually reaches the brain is interpreted according to the rules of the language.

One of the authors had a conversation with a deaf-blind man who communicated with an electronic aid that converted keyboard strokes to tactile signals (for incoming messages) and keyboard strokes to visual display (for outgoing messages). When this man wanted to send a message, he typed it on a keyboard and the message was displayed visually for the other person to read. When the other person responded, he or she simply typed a message on another keyboard and the communication device converted the keyboard strokes to tactile signals that the deaf-blind man sensed with his fingers. The topics of conversation ranged from the man's career plans (he was studying for a Ph.D. degree in computer science), to his grief over the death of a close family member, to his relationship with God. Even abstract spiritual and philosophical ideas could be communicated to this man through the sensory channels of his fingers placed on vibrating buttons. The man was eminently thoughtful and sensitive to the finest of human emotions. He was a most interesting conversational partner. The human brain understands the world and even the unworldly through any sensory modality open to it.

CHAPTER FOURTEEN
Self-Study
Neurology of Speech: Input Processing

Review Glossary

Transmission system: A system that processes input signals from sensory equipment, or that carries motor output signals to the muscular system

    Input system: A neural system that transmits signals from sensory receptors to the brain

      Auditory pathway: The transmission pathway that carries auditory signals from the cochlea over the auditory nerve to the cochlear nucleus, on to the superior olivary nucleus, up the lateral lemniscus to the inferior colliculi, and on to the medial geniculate body in the thalamus for relay over projection fibers to the primary auditory cortex

      Descending sensory control pathway: The pathway that carries efferent signals to sensory receptors with which receptor input is regulated

    Input processing: The transmission, analysis, and integration of sensory signals

    Neuromuscular system: An output system that transmits motor signals from the brain to the muscles

Integrative system: A central processing system that integrates input information with stored information to permit selection of appropriate output information

    Reticular activating system (RAS): The nonspecific system that arouses the brain when input information from a specific sensory pathway is determined to be novel

      Novelty: The extent to which input information is dissimilar from information stored from past experience

    Limbic system: A central processing system of importance to emotion and memory that determines the biological significance of input information

Speech perception: The detection, recognition, and understanding of the spoken message

    Active theory: The type of theory in which listeners hypothesize what they think they have heard spoken

      Top-down theory: The type of theory in which speech perception is guided by contextual, linguistic, and cognitive knowledge

    Passive theory: The type of theory in which listeners automatically discern speech from the acoustic signal

      Bottom-up theory: The type of theory in which perceptual decisions are built up solely from incoming acoustic data

    Phonemic restoration: Perception of an intact sentence in which speech sounds are actually missing

    Verbal transformation: Change in the word perceived when a word is presented repeatedly

Self-Study Test of Terminology

Self-Study Instructions: These questions can be used to help you assess how much you have retained from studying the Review Glossary. Answers are given in Appendix E.

(1) _____ The transmission pathway that carries auditory signals from the cochlea over the auditory nerve to the cochlear nucleus, on to the superior olivary nucleus, up the lateral lemniscus to the inferior colliculi, and on to the medial geniculate body in the thalamus for relay over projection fibers to the primary auditory cortex

(2) _____ An output system that transmits motor signals from the brain to the muscles

(3) _____ A system that processes input signals from sensory equipment, or that carries motor output signals to the muscular system

(4) _____ A central processing system of importance to emotion and memory that determines the biological significance of input information

(5) _____ The nonspecific system that arouses the brain when input information from a specific sensory pathway is determined to be novel

(6) _____ The pathway that carries efferent signals to sensory receptors with which receptor input is regulated

(7) _____ A neural system that transmits signals from sensory receptors to the brain

(8) _____ The extent to which input information is dissimilar from information stored from past experience

(9) _____ The transmission, analysis, and integration of sensory signals

(10) _____ A central processing system that integrates input information with stored information to permit selection of appropriate output information

(11) _____ Change in the word perceived when a word is presented repeatedly

(12) _____ Detection, recognition, and understanding of the spoken message

(13) _____ Guidance of speech perception by contextual, linguistic, and cognitive knowledge

(14) _____ Perception of an intact sentence in which speech sounds are actually missing

(15) _____ Speech perception in which listeners automatically discern speech from the acoustic signal

Self-Study Test of Understanding

Self-Study Instructions: This test can be used to help you assess how well you understand the content of this chapter. Terms to be filled in are from the Review Glossary. Answers are given in Appendix E.

A father and mother and their infant son are in their beds during a rainstorm. They live under the landing path of a major airport. The husband is attempting to fall asleep, but is frustrated by three noises: airplanes landing, peals of thunder, and, most irritating of all, the deep breathing of his wife as she sleeps soundly. At one point, amid the crashing thunder, the noise of an especially low airplane shakes the house. The wife's breathing alters not one bit. A few minutes later, during a lull in the storm and while he is yet wide awake, his wife, who is still breathing heavily, suddenly leaps from the bed for no apparent reason and rushes to their son's room. Most fathers, who undoubtedly can duplicate this tale, know what has happened. While the father was preoccupied with the big acoustic events of the evening, the mother ignored them and slept deeply until the faint sound of crying galvanized her into action.

This instance is prosaic in the annals of parenthood, but it provides a good illustration of how an (A) _____ system can cope with an apparently paradoxical situation, and of the probable neurophysiology of the wife's peculiar auditory behavior.

As she slept peacefully through the rumble of thunder and the whine of jets, large acoustic waves swept into her ears, which promptly inhibited the transformation of much of this mechanical energy into neural signals. What information was processed in the sensory (B) _____ system, specifically in the classic ascending (C) _____, was also submitted along the way by collateral fibers to the (D) _____ for a test of its (E) _____. This system, with information from its connections with the cortex, determined that thunder and airplanes landing were neither unexpected, a threat of harm, or of importance to anything she needed to do; from connections with the (F) _____ system it was determined that thunder and airplanes held no promise of biological significance; from connections with the motor system and the cerebellum, it was determined that no movements were planned (and thunder and airplanes wouldn't help much if they were). The (G) _____, by discounting the importance of these thunder and airplane noises, declined to arouse her brain to receive them. Instead, the (H) _____ was given orders to continue inhibiting their reception and transmission. Those impulses that did reach the (I) _____ receiving area in the temporal lobes were greeted with very little neural integrative activity — sleep prevailed.

Against this thunderous background, a wee infant sound intruded. The acoustical energy in this barely perceptible cry was neurally encoded, along with the other noises, and transmitted up the classic (J) _____. When it was submitted to the (K) _____ en route, however, for the test of its significance, it was immediately judged as novel. It was a change, albeit slight, from the thunder and airplane sounds. Then, the cortex with its reticular connections came back with the probable message: "A mother's duty is to tend to her child. Hop to it!" The (L) _____ connections came back with the possible message; "Maternal instincts will be gratified if you tend to your child." The motor and cerebellar connections came back with the information that she was flat on her back and would have to get coordinated by activation of her (M) _____ system, to move in the direction of the sound. All of this (N) _____ processing occurred, presumably, without benefit of consciousness. The reticular activating system then alerted the entire brain (she awakened), and instructed the (O) _____ mechanism to facilitate reception and transmission of the cry so as to provide maximal information to the (P) _____ system about her infant's distress. The signals that arrived in her aroused brain via the classic auditory pathway were not only facilitated, but were greeted by widespread neural excitation. She was now alert, knew why she was awake, and knew what she had to do.

CHAPTER FIFTEEN
Neurology of Speech: Central Processing

CENTRAL PROCESSING

Where should we look in the human brain for the linguistic blueprint? The answer will probably have to possess certain general characteristics when it is complete. First of all, the blueprint contains vast quantities of information, so it must be stored in some large memory bank. Second, both nature and nurture must have access to the bank; nature must be able to store that portion of the blueprint that will be the genetic inheritance of how to learn language; nurture must be able to store that portion that involves the specific rules of the specific language that each normal child learns. Third, nature and nurture must store their blueprints in different parts of the bank; nature's storage must be subject to genetic transmission, nurture's to expiration with death. Fourth, the bank must have varying degrees of security. For each normal child born since man acquired speech to know innately how to acquire the mother tongue means that nature's storage must be incredibly secure. The security of nurture's storage, on the other hand, must vary: the syntactic, morphemic, and phonemic blueprints are generally not affected equally by neurological disability; different brain injuries affect different aspects of language differently.

To place the issue within the scope of current information we must ask a smaller, but no less significant, question. What processes in the brain underlie acquisition and use of speech? Whatever these processes may be, they must mediate our knowledge of the rules of language by which speech is decoded and encoded. Because rules are abstractions, they cannot be observed directly; only their effects are observable. Some major effects of these rules for which neurological correlates could be sought are the following:

1. The acoustic speech signal is decoded for pitch, loudness, quality, and temporal information.
2. The stream of auditory information about speech is discriminated for phonemic, morphemic, syntactic, and semantic units and their sequence.
3. The various meanings of linguistic symbols and associated emotions are elaborated.
4. The idea to be expressed is selected.
5. The semantic, syntactic, morphemic, and phonemic units are chosen and organized sequentially for expression of the propositional message and its emotional overtones.
6. The phonetic flow of sound is coordinated for rate, rhythm, duration, fluency, pitch, loudness, and quality.

7. The feel of speech production as well as the sound of speech produced is utilized to guide the speaking performance.

In all likelihood, the brain has not the vaguest notion (to put the matter anthropomorphically) of what a phoneme, morpheme, word, or sentence is. To search the nervous system for where these linguistic units are stored would probably be futile. More likely, these units are represented as different patterns of neural operations which, when assembled in a particular sequence, are experienced as sounds, syllables, words, and sentences.

The process may not be too dissimilar from the manufacture of automobiles (or any other manufactured product). Once the car is designed, orders are sent out for thousands of different parts: nuts, bolts, gears, pistons, valves, pumps, and so forth, which are produced by various plants, sometimes all over the world. From these parts, carburetors, transmissions, engines, and the like are assembled. They, in turn, are shipped to assembly plants where they are put together to make a car. Not until all of the parts are assembled are they identified as an automobile.

The analogy seems applicable to the neurology of speech. After the intended statement has been designed, the linguistic parts must be manufactured and assembled, all the way from grammatical structures to sound segments. Each sound is an assembly of distinctive physiological features, such as where the tongue is placed, whether the air stream is voiced or voiceless, whether it is directed through an open cavity adjusted for resonance, is directed through a constriction for turbulence, or is stopped for an explosive burst of pressure. Change any one of these features, and the speech sound changes.

More to the point, each of these features involves distinctive positions and movements of speech structures, which means that in this form, these features are the direct result of neural activity. That the nervous system may go about processing speech in some such fashion is suggested by the fact the entire brain is active during speech (as if a multitude of widely scattered subcontractors were manufacturing the component parts), but the greatest activity is localized in discrete areas of the brain, most of which are in the dominant hemisphere (as if these were the plants in which the component parts are assembled).

Central Elaboration of Speech

The two primary speech centers in the dominant hemisphere that neurologists have known for about a century are *Broca's area* and *Wernicke's area* (Fig. 15–1). More recently, the angular gyrus, supramarginal gyrus, and supplementary motor cortex of the dominant hemisphere, along with the nondominant hemisphere, and subcortical structures have been found to be important. Although boundaries of these speech centers are disputed — often because of disagreement as to which language functions they serve — they are widely acknowledged as being major areas of speech and language processing.

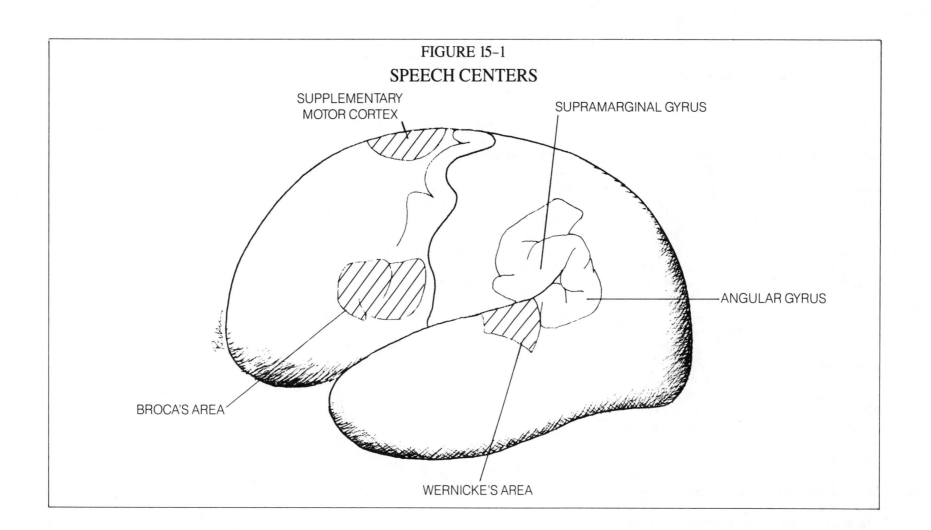

FIGURE 15–1

SPEECH CENTERS

SUPPLEMENTARY
MOTOR CORTEX

SUPRAMARGINAL GYRUS

ANGULAR GYRUS

BROCA'S AREA

WERNICKE'S AREA

Historically, a source of evidence for these boundaries is the aphasias, which are impairments of language resulting from damage to the brain — especially, but not necessarily, to the cerebral cortex. At least to a certain degree, it is possible to link major types of aphasia with damage to specific regions of the cortex. However, these relations are by no means inviolate, and it is better to think of these relations as probabilistic rather than deterministic. Figure 15–2 shows the regions of brain damage (blackened areas) that are classically associated with four major types of aphasia — Wernicke's aphasia, Broca's aphasia, global aphasia, and anomia.

Wernicke's aphasia is characterized by spontaneous speech that is often fluent but lacking in meaning. In extreme cases, it may sound like jargon — sound patterns that are fluently uttered but which are virtually incomprehensible to the listener. Auditory comprehension also is impaired in persons with this type of aphasia. Not surprisingly, then, repetition also is impaired. Spontaneous writing sometimes shows well-formed letters, but reading comprehension tends to be poor. As shown in Figure 15–2, the area of brain damage is principally the posterior-superior part of the temporal lobe. This aphasia also is called *posterior* or *fluent*.

In *Broca's aphasia*, spontaneous speech typically is nonfluent and agrammatical. It may sound slow, labored, and telegraphic, with function words like articles, conjunctions, and prepositions missing. Auditory comprehension is relatively spared. Spontaneous writing is usually poor, but reading comprehension is somewhat better. Simple repetition of words is less impaired than spontaneous speech. Figure 15–2 shows that the brain damage for this aphasia is in the posterior and inferior part of the frontal lobe, or what is sometimes called the foot of the third frontal convolution. (Broca's aphasia is also called *anterior* or *nonfluent* aphasia.)

Global aphasia usually is a severe impairment, affecting nearly all aspects of language function. Frequently, spontaneous speech is reduced to a severely limited telegraphic style. Most functions tend to be poor, including spontaneous speech, auditory comprehension, repetition, reading comprehension, and spontaneous writing. The damage often is extensive and may include the regions described for Wernicke's and Broca's aphasia.

Anomia, or *anomic aphasia,* usually has a spontaneous speech pattern that is fluent. Both comprehension and repetition tend to be intact, but naming is specifically impaired. Persons with this type of aphasia perform very poorly on tasks of confrontation naming, in which they must say as quickly as possible the name of an object or picture presented to them. The area of damage is the angular gyrus.

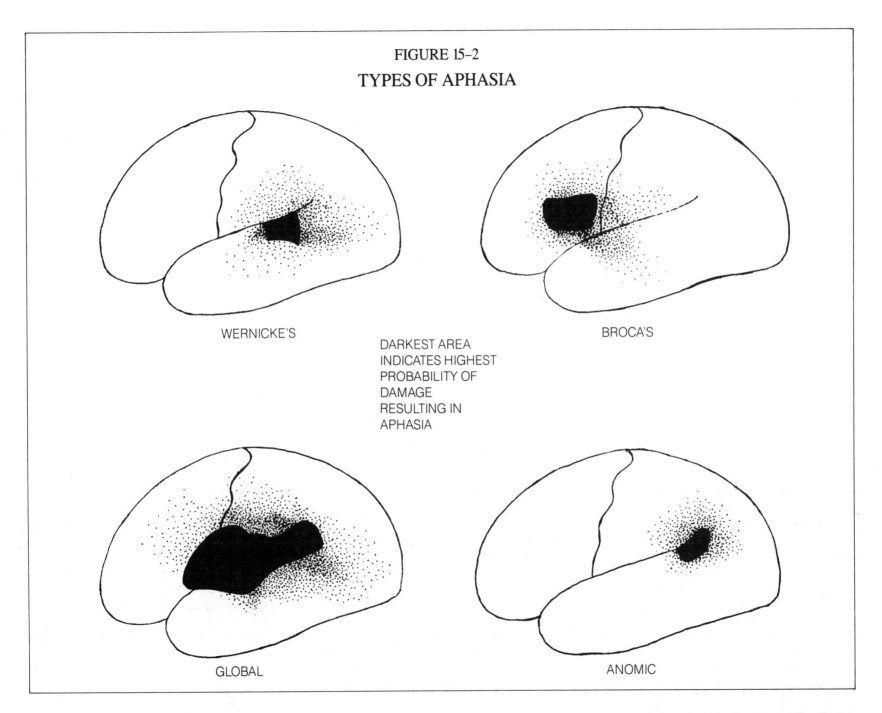

FIGURE 15–2

TYPES OF APHASIA

WERNICKE'S

BROCA'S

DARKEST AREA
INDICATES HIGHEST
PROBABILITY OF
DAMAGE
RESULTING IN
APHASIA

GLOBAL

ANOMIC

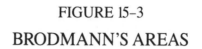

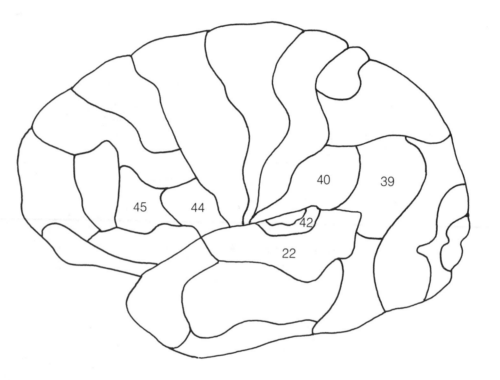

FIGURE 15–3

BRODMANN'S AREAS

Why do some parts of the brain seem to be better suited for speech processing than others? The answer may be that different parts of the brain have neural equipment better suited to processing special features of the speech signal than others. Neuroanatomists have long known that the six layers of cells in the cortex vary in number, type, density, and development from one area to another. These variations were plotted by Brodmann years ago, and were numbered as shown in Figure 15–3.

What makes these numbers interesting for us is the fact that the different speech centers can be located by them. Compare Figures 15–1 and 15–3 and you will see that Broca's area correlates with Brodmann's areas 44 and 45; Wernicke's area with area 42 and parts of 22, the angular gyrus with area 39; the supramarginal gyrus with areas 22 and 40. These different cellular arrangements are found in all human brains, but a given arrangement is not necessarily in the same location in all people. Yet, wherever the cellular arrangement of a particular speech area is located is where the functions of that speech center seem to be found.

That such a correlation exists between neural equipment and speech requirements is not surprising. Some aspects of the speech signal, notably the rapid transitions from one sound to another, require high-speed processing. Other aspects, such as the pitch, loudness, and durational components of syllable stress, are slower and, apparently, are processed by different equipment in different locations. Equally important for matching neural equipment to speech requirement is the extent to which speech characteristics are structured. Highly structured features, such as phonologic and grammatical rules, seem to require left-hemisphere processing.

Cerebral Dominance

As a speech scientist has said, "We do not have a wedge driven between two anatomically and functionally separate hemispheres." The left and right sides have been contrasted in various ways: propositional-emotional, verbal-nonverbal, analytic-holistic, serial-parallel, and algebraic-geometric are examples. None of these contrasts is without exception. Both hemispheres are capable of at least rudimentary functions normally served by the other. They work together as an integrated unit, with one side or the other assuming control of a particular activity (presumably, the side that is dominant for an activity controls it). By implication, this means that a major reason for having the hemispheres connected is so that the dominant hemisphere can suppress the nondominant hemisphere for a given activity.

Although the two hemispheres, when surgically disconnected from each other, can perform as if we had two independent brains in our heads, normally they are yoked together, mainly by the *corpus callosum*. This large bundle of fibers interconnecting them apparently also has a major function of keeping activity in a particular area on one side in phase with the activity in that area on the other side. Presumably, were activities of the hemispheres not temporally linked, the propositional and emotional components of speech, along with the stream of sounds and their matching melodies, could get out of synchrony.

The Label on Time's Arrow. The key to a prominent function of the dominant hemisphere involves time. For the biological world, at least, the arrow of time flies in only one direction; it cannot be reversed. Time is so basic to all living matter that even humans, who can contemplate their temporal (and temporary) existence, rarely appreciate how deeply embedded they are in time's flight. Every aspect of living carries a "time la-bel." We live our lives by calendars and clocks. If we wish to know what we did on a given date at a given time, we can consult a man-made, time-labeled record such as a diary. If we wish to know where we are on the biological time-labeled sequence, we check the aging process. If we wish to remember which of two events occurred first, we recall the events with their time labels from our memory.

Nowhere are time labels more important than for speech. A word is a sequence of linguistic events: for speech, a sequence of phonemes; for writing, a sequence of letters. The place in the sequence is the time label. Just as history would be a jumble of fragmentary events if their sequence were randomized, so language would be a meaningless shamble of sounds and letters were the speech and writing sequences distorted. Were we to lose the capacity for identifying the correct order of phonemes, we might hear "radiator" as 'i tor a rad," or "tor i rad a." Even if one's capacity to time label phonemes were not eliminated but merely reduced, the disruption of meaning would still be profound; we must be able to decode and encode the phonetic sequence at the average rate of about 14 phonemes per second if we are to function as normal listeners and speakers. Those who cannot decipher the sequence at this rate will be flooded with a confusion of hissings, buzzings, and boomings; they will be unable to separate the speech signals from the noise.

The temporal lobe of the dominant hemisphere, including Wernicke's area and the angular gyrus, appears to function as the time-labeling mechanism of the brain. When subjects are asked to determine whether two somatic events occur simultaneously or to identify the sequence in which they occur, their decisions consistently take a few thousandths of a second (2 to 6 ms) longer when the sensation comes in from the left rather than the right side of the body. This is the delay that would be expected if the sensory information received in the right hemisphere had to be transferred to the dominant left hemisphere for temporal analysis. As would be expected for auditory sensation, however, no delay occurs because, unlike other sensory receptors, both ears are connected to the major as well as to the minor hemispheres.

It is interesting to note that we apparently become conscious of sensation only when we time label it in the dominant hemisphere. To be conscious of something is to be conscious of it *now.* Our sense of "now" seems to be determined by the moment of arrival of a signal for time labeling in the dominant temporal lobe. Again, here is evidence that a person's conscious life (verbal aspects more, probably, than emotional or perceptual experiences) may be run by the major hemisphere.

Perhaps language functions appear to reside in the dominant temporal area because it is this region that is better equipped to analyze input and output speech signals for simultaneity, interval, and sequence. Whether the time-labeling ability of the dominant temporal lobe is sufficient to explain all of the central linguistic elaboration processes is open to question. Logically, we must be able to determine the sequence of sounds in a word before comparing the sequence heard with the memory of the sequence to determine the meaning of the word. All of us, doubtlessly, have parroted some statement we have heard without benefit of assigning it meaning. Thus, the auditory sequencing mechanism can be intact, but an individual still may not comprehend the meaning of what is heard or said.

Speech Structures

Dominant Hemisphere

Wernicke's Area. Located as it is adjacent to the primary auditory area in the dominant temporal lobe, and being a specialized auditory association area, *Wernicke's area* is the pivotal language center. It is essential to comprehension and formulation of both spoken and written language. If it is damaged, the resultant speech will sound as if sentences are being spoken fluently and with normal inflections. The words, however, are often inappropriate, if not sheer nonsense. Ideas are still mapped by language, but erratically. The direct connection between meaning and language that normally exists is impaired, not only in the production of what is spoken but also in the understanding of what is heard.

The traditional explanation of why Wernicke's area is in the dominant temporal lobe is because it is a part of the *planum temporale.* This is the portion of the upper surface of the lobe that, as you saw in Figure 13–17, is strikingly larger in the left hemisphere than in the right. Moreover, the enlarged region includes Wernicke's area.

Broca's Area. Whereas Wernicke's area, in close proximity to the primary auditory area, is essential to speech comprehension, Broca's area, in close proximity to the primary motor area for the mouth, is essential to speech production. If this area is injured, speech becomes slow and labored, but comprehension is not seriously affected. Articulation is slurred and sentences are grammatically incomplete, giving speech a telegraphic quality, but the responses generally make sense.

Some have claimed that the frontal cortex of Broca's area is larger and thicker in the left hemisphere, but these claims have been disputed. An anatomical reason why this speech center is in the dominant hemisphere may exist, but if it does, it is not yet clearly apparent. Still, some think that a region in the vicinity of Broca's area shows characteristics of being a mechanism that decodes speech as efficiently as it is encoded.

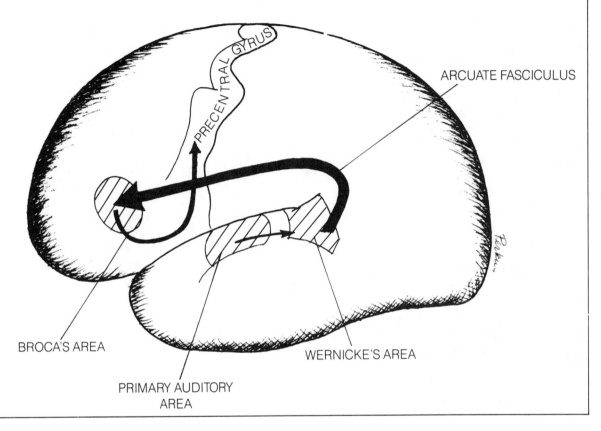

FIGURE 15–4
**REPEATING WORDS
HEARD**

ARCUATE FASCICULUS

PRECENTRAL GYRUS

BROCA'S AREA

WERNICKE'S AREA

PRIMARY AUDITORY
AREA

The argument has been offered that the listener must decode speech in much the same way that it is encoded, namely, by recovering the articulatory events by which the sounds were produced in the first place. If listening to speech required recognizing each separate sound at the rate at which it occurs in normal speech, all that could be heard would probably be an unintelligible blur of noise. The ear does not seem able to distinguish one sound from the next at such a fast rate. The major concept of the *motor theory of speech perception* is that the same mechanism is used to determine the high-speed sound sequence for listening as is used for speaking.

An anatomical feature that clearly is apparent is the *arcuate fasciculus,* the large pathway interconnecting Broca's area with Wernicke's area (Fig. 15–4). A lesion in this pathway impairs the ability to repeat words accurately; wrong sounds are combined in wrong sequences: "stop" may come out "pots," "tops," "post," or even less likely combinations. Hearing the word repeated correctly does not improve performance, even though the speaker is aware of the error. Peculiarly, neither the ability to comprehend speech nor the ability to generate spontaneous statements fluently is impaired.

What this strange combination of symptoms reveals is how speech is processed in the dominant hemisphere. When heard, the primary auditory area transmits the signals to Wernicke's area for decoding. If what is heard is to be repeated, Wernicke's area is thought to send a representation to Broca's area, where articulatory details for speaking the message are formulated. This articulatory blueprint is supplied to the motor cortex to drive muscles of the speech mechanism to produce the necessary sounds in the necessary sequence.

Angular Gyrus. As was seen in Figure 15–1, the *angular gyrus*, positioned equidistant from the primary auditory, visual, and somatic areas, may be responsible for the fact that language symbols are *supramodal,* that is, they transcend divisions among the senses in some sort of *cross-modal* (each sensory area is connected to other sensory areas) integrative arrangement. This is to say that the meaning of the word "bird," as distinct from perception of the bird itself, does not require that, sequentially, we conjure up an image of its distinctive plumage, remember the sounds of its mourning song, recall the fragrance of the new-mowed field in which it sang, and then, after sufficient integration of these remembered sensations, conclude: "Aha! Bird." Fortunately for bird-watchers (and possibly for watched birds) the word links together all of these sensory parts.

Each sensory modality seems to be connected to a supramodal system that evokes the name of an object. The name can, then, serve as a bridge among discriminations learned in different senses. You might, for instance, become embroiled in an angry exchange with a stranger on the telephone, learn his name, later see a picture of an impressive-looking man, discover from his name that he is the man with whom you were angry, and subsequently find yourself much less impressed with his appearance. The effect of the auditory impression is transferred by means of the name to the visual impression.

The angular gyrus would seem to be optimally situated for this supramodal function, but without doubt it connects the spoken language system with the visual language system. When the angular gyrus is damaged, the visual cortex is disconnected from Wernicke's area, which interferes with reading and writing. The reason is apparent in Figure 15–5. If a written word is to be spoken, the primary visual cortex is thought to relay the visual form to the angular gyrus, where it is associated with the corresponding auditory pattern in Wernicke's area. Speaking, then, proceeds as if the word had been heard. Conversely, if the spoken name of an object is to be understood and visualized, the auditory signal is transferred to Wernicke's area, and then on to the angular gyrus and visual association cortex for visualization, another supramodal response.

Supramarginal Gyrus. As a rule of thumb, the farther removed an association area is from a primary area, the more abstract its function. Accordingly, effects of impairing such areas are less obvious and predictable. Also, the areas closest to the fissure of Sylvius (which separates temporal from parietal lobes) are more critical to the use of phonemes, whereas more remote marginal regions are vital to use of words as meaningful units. Thus, the *supramarginal gyrus,* shown in Figure 15–1, is thought to be a part of a central language system, which also includes the angular gyrus and auditory association areas.

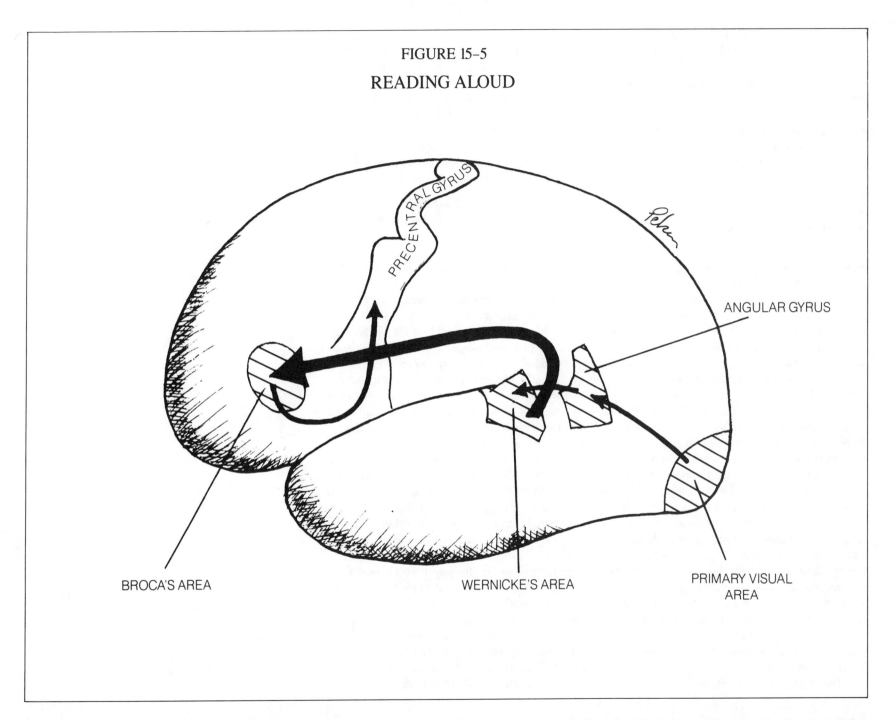

FIGURE 15–5

READING ALOUD

PRECENTRAL GYRUS

ANGULAR GYRUS

BROCA'S AREA

WERNICKE'S AREA

PRIMARY VISUAL
AREA

Supplementary Motor Cortex. Although controversial as a speech and language region, the *supplementary motor cortex* is thought to play a role in word finding, rhythm, phonation, articulation, and facilitation of propositional speech, while suppressing "automatic" nonpropositional speech. Located on the upper inside surface of the dominant frontal lobe anterior to the motor strip, as shown in Figure 15–1, its speech functions seem notably similar to those of the thalamus, with which it is closely connected.

Nondominant Hemisphere

Bear in mind that with speech we express not only ideas but also emotions. Both can be expressed simultaneously. We need not state such feelings as elation, depression, joy, sorrow, or anger explicitly. They can be communicated while reading from a phone book. What spouse who has disappointed a mate cannot detect the frustration and anger revealed by tone of voice and inflections in that mate's most superficially innocuous statements?

The dominant hemisphere for these functions is the *nondominant hemisphere.* This anomalous, if not contradictory, labeling merely reflects how recently emotion has been recognized as having a major role in speech. Although emotion and the affective and intonational components of communication seem to be predominantly right-hemisphere functions, the fact of the matter is that both hemispheres contribute to the other's primary function. The left hemisphere seems to participate in positive emotions and the right hemisphere contributes to propositional communication by keeping it related to the larger global context. It is as if the left hemisphere plays the individual notes of speech while the right hemisphere preserves the melody — the right side sketches the outline, the left fills in the details.

The idea that language functions are split between the left and right hemispheres is intriguing, especially because this idea runs against the traditional view that language processing (both production and comprehension) is located in the left hemisphere. The newer view is that language is processed in both hemispheres and that the hemispheres have complementary advantages in language processing. To discover what these respective advantages are, we need to take a moment to describe the organization of language.

Colorless Green Ideas Sleep Furiously. With this now famous sentence, the linguist Noam Chomsky sought to point out the nature of syntax. Syntax has to do with the ordering of words in a sentence (or other unit of language organization). Notice that the odd sentence that opens this paragraph is not entirely odd. The ordering of the words *does* meet certain expectations we have about what sentences should look like. To see this, we simply have to replace each word with a more plausible word, such as *Large fat felines sleep contentedly.* The selection of words is a matter of semantics; the ordering of the words is a matter of syntax. Both semantics and syntax are relatively abstract levels of linguistic organization — that is, these levels are far removed from the output level of phonemes or sound segments. The notion of abstractness also applies to semantics. Some words denote abstract concepts, as in *Complicated mixed metaphors stream endlessly.* Other words are more concrete, as in the example *Small efficient cars travel economically,* and — getting even more concrete — *Large heavy cars go fast.* Words are composed of sounds; the way in which sounds are arranged to form words is called phonology. The study of speech sounds is called phonetics. Ideas are communicated through speech by the proper sequences of sounds, which allows the listener to understand the words intended by the speaker.

Yet speech is more than just a sequence of phonetic segments. It also has a rate or tempo, stress pattern, intonation, and an emotional color. These are grouped together under the term prosody. Prosodic features are also called suprasegmental features because they affect stretches of speech larger than a phonetic segment. We can say that speech is made up of two kinds of information, segmental and prosodic. Generally, segmental information is more finely structured in time and usually is embedded in the more slowly changing prosodic information.

It has been known for a long time that damage to certain regions of the left hemisphere is associated with impaired language. Depending on its site, the damage can produce impairments in language production, language comprehension, or both. These language disorders (aphasias) are thought to result from damage to the centers of language that process language or to the pathways that connect these centers. There is evidence that aphasias are not truly "losses" of language, for aphasic persons are inconsistent in their language usage, sometimes being successful and sometimes not. This inconsistency is suggestive of a problem in accessing language information, which itself may be fundamentally intact.

But after hundreds of pages have been written in scientific journals about thousands of patients with aphasia and left-hemisphere damage, there is a growing recognition that damage to certain regions of the right hemisphere also can impair communication. Some persons with right-hemisphere damage fail to perceive or comprehend patterns of intonation in speech correctly. They may have difficulty even in understanding the emotion conveyed by a speaker's voice, that is, whether the speaker is happy, angry, or sad. Other persons with right-hemisphere damage may have difficulty in producing intended patterns of stress or intonation reliably. Some cannot produce an intended emotion effectively. All of these difficulties can be labeled as problems with prosody. The hypothesis

arises that the left hemisphere normally processes primarily the segmental content of speech while the right hemisphere processes primarily the prosodic components. Some evidence from experiments on normal subjects substantiates this view. It has been concluded that the two hemispheres process their preferred forms of information extracted from the speech signal simultaneously. It appears, then, that the speech message, which can be split conceptually into segmental and prosodic components, is split by the brain into corresponding divisions.

If the hemispheres do, in fact, simultaneously process different information from the speech message, how does this cerebrally separated information come together to give the listener (or speaker) a unified concept of the message? A likely candidate is the corpus callosum, the band of fibers that connects the cerebral hemispheres. A number of interesting studies have been conducted on a small but intriguing population, persons who for medical reasons have had the fibers of the corpus callosum cut. In these individuals, the two hemispheres are largely disconnected (other pathways of connection may exist). Tests of vocabulary in these persons have shown that the right hemisphere does possess language although its verbal store is not as rich as that of the left hemisphere. The vocabulary of the right hemisphere tends to be more concrete (recall the abstract-concrete distinction of semantics) and also more emotional.

Subcortical Mechanisms

Thalamus. The thalamus is undoubtedly involved in the central elaboration of speech, but its role is fuzzy, at best. One reason is that this is a relatively new area of inquiry. It was not until 1959 that two pioneer neurosurgeons, Penfield and Roberts, first reported effects on speech by electrical stimulation of the thalamus. They concluded that activity of the cortical speech areas is coordinated through the thalamus. Evidence to confirm or reject their conclusion has not yet been produced.

Subsequent investigations have not shown impairment of comprehension by thalamic surgery or electrical stimulation. What is typically impaired is speech production. Rate accelerates with decreased volume, or the converse — rate decelerates with increased volume. Speech is blocked and becomes dysfluent. Compulsive yelling is sometimes observed.

In any event, language functions are lateralized in the thalamus, as they are in the cortex, presumably because the left thalamic nuclei are connected to the left cerebral hemisphere. Because they constitute a tightly coupled neural system, the thalamus seems to be integrally involved in communication and emotion, as well as in arousal and attention.

The view is growing that the idea of "speech centers" — the thalamus being such a center — is inappropriate. Instead, speech with its propositional and emotional aspects goes through several stages of processing within integrated cortical-subcortical networks. This is a departure from the classic notion that speech is processed by being shipped from one center to another for encoding or decoding.

Limbic System. A man known simply as H.M. is well known in the study of neurology. His story is very important in the current understanding of the function of the hippocampus. H.M. has a short-term memory dysfunction. He can read a book or magazine and then, upon picking up the same reading material a short time later, fail to realize that he has already read it. His next-door neighbors remain strangers to him, and if people H.M. has just met leave the room for a few minutes and then return, H.M. does not recognize them. However, H.M. can recall events of his childhood

or events that preceded the brain surgery that apparently impaired his memory.

H.M., although forgetting events after short periods of time, still might remember a teacher from his grade-school years. The disorder of short-term memory prevents him from entering information in long-term memory.

Short-term memory is distinguished from two other types of memory. *Immediate memory* usually involves full attention to a task, such as remembering a phone number. Recall is tested shortly after the information was presented. *Short-term memory* (or postdistractional memory) refers to memory tasks for which the subject does not devote full attention. A distracting task often is used to test this memory process. Finally, *long-term memory* applies to information that is retained for lengthy periods, such as remembrances of one's childhood, the name of a professor from whom a course was taken five years ago, or the answer to a trivia question. Short-term memory is the doorway to long-term memory, as new information is held in short-term memory before it is gradually stored in long-term memory.

H.M. has had his memory disorder since undergoing surgery for relief of epilepsy. One treatment for epilepsy is to destroy surgically the brain tissue that is the focus for the epileptic condition. Frequently, destruction of this "trigger zone" provides relief from seizures. H.M. had epileptic foci in both the right and left hippocampi in the limbic system, which were destroyed by the neurosurgeon. H.M.'s memory deficit is taken to mean that the hippocampus is vital to short-term memory. Given the severity of H.M.'s memory disorder, neurosurgeons now avoid bilateral destruction of the hippocampus. Destruction of only one side, however, results in relatively minor memory disturbance.

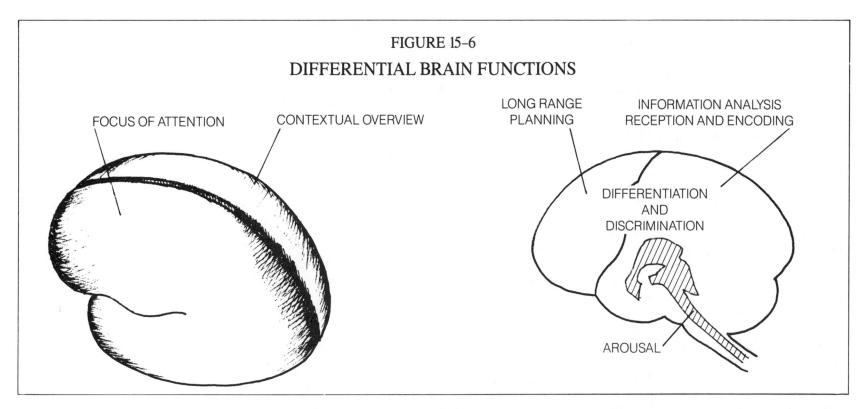

FIGURE 15–6

DIFFERENTIAL BRAIN FUNCTIONS

FOCUS OF ATTENTION

CONTEXTUAL OVERVIEW

LONG RANGE PLANNING

INFORMATION ANALYSIS RECEPTION AND ENCODING

DIFFERENTIATION AND DISCRIMINATION

AROUSAL

Why Brain Specialization?

The idea that the brain has specialized areas for specialized functions is misleading. The nervous system has no isolated areas or channels devoted exclusively to single functions. It is a gigantic neural network in which every neuron is ultimately interconnected with every other neuron. Stimulate one area of the brain and within 10 ms, the entire network would have received the neural effects of that stimulation. Specialized areas are merely local networks interconnected with the larger network. We have no "smart cells" that make independent decisions.

For this network to function optimally, any given portion of it can only process one activity at a time. If adjacent areas must cope with two or more acts concurrently, they interfere with each other, and performance suffers. Just as two cooks need separate spaces to prepare different dishes to be served at the same time, so does increasing distance of functional cerebral space enhance performance.

Marcel Kinsbourne, a noted neuropsychologist, has used this *principle of functional cerebral distance* to account for the evolution of laterality and specialization of brain function. Kinsbourne points out that two very different concurrent functions are required for any animal to cope with its world. One function is to preserve the context in which an activity occurs, the other is to focus on that activity. Without focus, attention to an activity is missing. But a hungry animal, intent on feeding, for instance, would jeopardize its survival if its attention to food excluded peripheral awareness of lurking dangers, such as a stalking cat waiting to pounce on a less than vigilant bird. (One of the authors saw this happen while writing this paragraph, he notes with a twinge of guilt, as a finch was too busy for its own good pecking at seed on the deck that had fallen from his bird feeder. The author didn't see the cat until it was too late, and more to the point, neither did the finch.)

The principle of functional cerebral distance is manifested in the brain in several major ways: between hemispheres, between frontal and posterior regions of the hemispheres, and between cerebrum and brainstem. With respect to the hemispheres, the right one is specialized in maintaining a contextual overview of what is going on, particularly in perceiving relationships (Fig. 15–6). The left hemisphere is devoted to sequential analysis of specific features that are the focus of attention. Between frontal and posterior cerebral regions, the frontal lobes specialize in complex and long-range planning. The posterior areas receive, analyze, and code information. If disconnected, we could perceive, but not act, or act without relation to what was happening. Finally, between cerebrum and brainstem, the cerebrum differentiates and discriminates. The brainstem, including particularly the reticular and limbic systems, energizes the cerebrum. Without it, we would be in a perpetual coma.

The important consideration in these contrasting functions of widely separated regions is that they are not alternative functions; they are complementary. Each must go on simultaneously with the others. The cerebrum would not function at all without brainstem systems to activate it. Similarly, perception does not shut down while future plans are being formulated. Nor does peripheral awareness of the context in which one is acting stop while attention is focused on the act of the moment (except for golfer Jack Nicklaus, who has claimed that a cannon could be shot off while he was putting and he would not hear it). An act that has more than one component before it can be performed will require that those components be processed in separate parts of the brain if they are not to interfere with each other.

Dreaming

A little understood phenomenon of brain activity is dreaming. Virtually everyone dreams, although most dreams are quickly forgotten so that the awake person is hardly aware of the richness of dreams. Dreaming is associated primarily with a stage of sleep called REM (rapid eye movement) sleep. During this stage the eyes move rapidly in their sockets. Thus, this eye movement, which can be detected by the electrical activity in the eye

muscles, is an indication that the sleeping individual is dreaming. In experiments on sleep and dreaming, scientists have awakened persons who are just entering the REM stage, thus supposedly preventing the occurrence, or at least normal completion, of dreams. The subjects in these experiments become highly irritable, which suggests that dreams are an important brain activity.

It remains a puzzle why we apparently need to dream. One possibility that has been suggested is that dreams are the means by which the mind sorts out and rids itself of experiences that are not to be committed to long-term memory and "unlearn" useless or even disturbing information. Another thought on the matter is that dreams not only dispel the unwanted experiences but also analyze, file, and, possibly, elaborate on experiences that are to be represented in memory. Dreams, then, are a sort of mental clearinghouse, a way to separate the truly significant from the less significant. Dreaming perhaps helps us to interpret and organize experiences at a time when the brain is not occupied with the affairs of waking life. This could explain why people become irritable if they are prevented from dreaming. Maybe the brain needs to dream as a way of maintaining its smooth and effective functioning, somewhat in the way that a computer and its programs can be checked out and corrected when it is "off-line." It has been estimated that about 90 percent of dreams relate to activities of the previous day. Thus, waking activities are the fuel for dreaming, and dreams, in turn, are the brain's summary of one day and the preparation for another day.

Before we leave this area of speculation it is worth taking a moment to consider an experiment on sleeping cats done by a scientist named Michel Jouvet. He cut the nerve fibers that ordinarily inhibit muscular response during sleep (this inhibition keeps the dreamer from injury that might result from "acting out" dreams — running, striking out, and so forth). The cats then were observed during REM sleep. They arose, stalked nonexistent mice, and pounced on the imaginary prey — all of this while asleep. These observations are consistent with the idea that dreams are the brain's way of testing, refining, and exercising "programs" that are useful in waking life. Thus, Shakespeare's words "to sleep, perchance to dream" might underestimate the deliberateness of the brain seeking to dream. Is the brain at rest a brain at work?

Summary

What can we conclude about central elaboration of speech from a chapter that begins by describing localized areas of the brain that perform specialized speech functions and concludes by arguing that the brain is a huge network which contains no regions devoted exclusively to special functions? Tempted as you may be to answer, "not much," in reality, the answer is, "a considerable amount."

Two concurrent messages must be formulated in every utterance: The *propositional component* is organized according to semantic, grammatical, and phonologic rules. It is the component that can be translated from spoken to written word without impairment of meaning. It is organized sequentially at every linguistic level. Ideas must follow each other in proper paragraph and sentence order. Phrases, words, and syllables within the phrase must be organized sequentially. Similarly, the *speech-sound segment* arrangement will determine, to a large extent, the meaning of the word spoken: the four letters of "rise," when rearranged, for example, become "sire."

On the other hand, some word meanings, such as the difference between "pro*ceeds*" and "*pro*ceeds," will depend on *prosody*: the stress and intonational patterns of speech. These patterns are *suprasegmental*; they cut across sound segments.

The same is true of the intent of the message. It, too, is revealed by paralinguistic features that involve the same suprasegmental elements as used in prosody. "Come here," spoken longingly has an entirely different intent than when spoken in anger. The words are the same, but patterns of pitch, loudness, and duration reveal the difference in intent.

The *intent of the message* provides the context. It is the framework onto which the propositional message is woven. As such, it is typically processed in the right hemisphere. Concurrent with it, and dependent on it, are the propositional components, which must obey the sequential rules of language. Phonologic rules, especially, are highly structured and require high-speed processing, so they are encoded and decoded in the hemisphere that seems best equipped to handle them, the left hemisphere.

The presence of specialized speech areas in the left hemisphere may simply reflect the principle of functional cerebral distance. By having the two major speech networks — Broca's area and Wernicke's area — widely separated, their concurrent activities in semantic-grammatical formulation and phonologic formulation presumably do not interfere with each other. Even more widely separated are the simultaneous activities required for processing the background intent with its emotional overtones in the right hemisphere, while linguistic details of the propositional message are being processed in the left hemisphere. By virtue of coordination of the neural networks in these two hemispheres and of the specialized networks within them, all of the components of speech can be combined in the marvel of a fluent utterance.

CLINICAL POSTSCRIPT

While he was President of the United States in 1919, Woodrow Wilson suffered a stroke, paralyzing his left side. He denied his illness and went so far as to dismiss his Secretary of State for discussing the President's condition with the Cabinet. Many commentators feel that Wilson's performance as a leader was greatly diminished after the stroke. Indeed, some believe that his administration came to a virtual standstill. But the President continued to deny that his judgment or performance was affected by his condition.

Recalling that one side of the brain essentially controls the other side of the body, you might have guessed that President Wilson suffered a right-hemisphere stroke. This stroke did not significantly impair his speech or language, but it may have impaired other functions. In 1919 relatively little was known about the effects of right-brain damage. But within the last decade or so, a syndrome of right-hemisphere brain damage has increasingly been recognized. One of the features of this syndrome is denial of illness. In fact, some persons with right-brain damage are actually euphoric and have an ill-founded sense of capability and well-being. Some individuals with right-brain damage have difficulties in accurately recognizing emotions that are expressed by others, or in appropriately expressing emotions themselves. It has been reported that the speech of these persons often is colorless and flat, as though the normal emotion and prosody were stripped away. Right-brain damage has also been linked to a syndrome of neglect or apathy, as though the affected person does not really care about responsibilities or social conduct. In a few instances in which surgical removal of the right hemisphere was necessary because of severe brain damage, the patient — who is now exclusively left-brained — retains apparently normal speech and language but conversational interactions become quite unusual. The patient reacts to jocular comments in an inappropriately serious manner, and language becomes highly direct. For example, if asked, "Would you pass the salt?" the patient might respond, "Yes, I will pass the salt."

Some writers have made much — perhaps too much — of the differences between the right and left hemisphere. Books have been written on how you can develop your right-hemisphere talents. Whether or not these books overstate the functional differences between the left and right hemispheres, they are based on an intriguing set of discoveries about the human brain. To some degree, the hemispheres appear to complement one another. That is, the left and right hemispheres process information or gain knowledge in different ways. One way we can characterize these differences is to list contrasting attributes or descriptors for each side of the brain. The following list of contrasts was compiled from the literature on hemispheric specialization (although specialization probably is too strong a word; hemispheric advantage is better).

Left Brain	*Right Brain*
Verbal	Nonverbal
Intellect	Intuition
Analytic	Holistic
Convergent	Divergent
Intellectual	Sensuous
Serial	Parallel
Focal	Diffuse
Deductive	Imaginative
Active	Receptive
Discrete	Continuous
Abstract	Concrete
Algebraic	Geometric
Propositional	Oppositional
Propositional	Affective
Realistic	Impulsive
Transformational	Associative
Lineal	Nonlineal
Historical	Timeless
Explicit	Tacit
Objective	Subjective
Activation	Arousal

The list could be extended, but perhaps these terms suffice to give you an idea about how contemporary psychology and neurology have come to view the two sides of our brains. If nothing else, the list may give you a good excuse if someone accuses you of being double-minded.

Self-Study

Neurology of Speech: Central Processing

Review Glossary

Central processing: The integration of input information with stored information for selection and elaboration of appropriate output information

Cerebral dominance: The dominance of one hemisphere over the other, particularly in the control of speech and handedness

    Functional cerebral distance: The separation of functions that compete for cerebral processing into distant areas of the brain

    Dominant hemisphere: The hemisphere with primary control of language

      Broca's area: The area in the prefrontal cortex essential for motor speech formulation

        Motor theory of speech perception: The theory that the same mechanism is used to determine the high-speed sound sequence for listening as is used for talking

      Wernicke's area: The area in the planum temporale of the temporal lobe essential to language comprehension and formulation

        Sensory modality: A specific sensory system

        Cross-modal: A sensory area that is connected to other sensory areas

        Supramodal: The characteristic of language symbols by which they transcend sensory modalities

      Supplementary motor cortex: The area in the superior prefrontal cortex thought to be important in propositional speech

      Angular gyrus: The area near the intersection of temporal, occipital, and parietal lobes thought to connect written language mechanisms with spoken language mechanisms

      Supramarginal gyrus: The area in the parietal lobe above the fissure of Sylvius thought to be important in speech-sound formulation

      Arcuate fasciculus: The large pathway interconnecting Wernicke's area with Broca's area

      Time label: The property that identifies where in the flow of speech each linguistic unit (sound, syllable, word, and so forth) fits

      Propositional message: The message as encoded in language

    Nondominant hemisphere: The hemisphere thought to be mainly responsible for emotional and intonational components of speech

      Message intent: The underlying meaning of a message

Subcortical speech mechanisms: Subcortical centers, especially the thalamus, of importance in mapping cognition with language

Brodmann areas: A system for classifying areas of the cortex according to cellular arrangement

Memory: The storage of information in the nervous system

    Immediate memory: The brief memory requiring full attention to a task

    Short-term memory: The brief memory for which full attention is not required, and which is essential to long-term memory

    Long-term memory: The relatively permanent memory that is resistant to shock and sometimes to head injury

Self-Study Test of Terminology

Self-Study Instructions: These questions can be used to help you assess how much you have retained from studying the Review Glossary. Answers are given in Appendix E.

(1) _____ The area in the parietal lobe above the fissure of Sylvius thought to be important in speech-sound formation

(2) _____ The dominance of one hemisphere over the other, particularly in the control of speech and handedness

(3) _____ The area in the planum temporale of the temporal lobe essential to language comprehension and formulation

(4) _____ The hemisphere thought to be mainly responsible for emotional and intonational components of speech

(5) _____ A sense that is connected to other senses

(6) _____ Subcortical centers, especially the thalamus, of importance in mapping cognition with language

(7) _____ The area in the superior prefrontal lobe thought to be important in propositional speech

(8) _____ The integration of input information with stored information for selection and elaboration of appropriate output information

(9) _____ The large pathway interconnecting Wernicke's area with Broca's area

(10) _____ The hemisphere with primary control of language

(11) _____ A specific sensory system

(12) _____ The underlying meaning of a message

(13) _____ The area in the prefrontal cortex essential for motor speech formulation

(14) _____ The characteristic of language symbols that they transcend sensory modalities

(15) _____ The property that identifies where in the flow of speech each linguistic unit (sound, syllable, word, and so forth) fits

(16) _____ The theory that the same mechanism is used to determine the high-speed sound sequence for listening as is used for speaking

(17) _____ The message as encoded in language

(18) _____ The area near the intersection of temporal, occipital, and parietal lobes thought to connect written language mechanisms with spoken language mechanisms

(19) _____ The separation of functions that compete for cerebral processing into distant areas of the brain

(20) _____ A system for classifying areas of the cortex according to cellular arrangement

(21) _____ Storage of information in the nervous system

(22) _____ Brief memory, for which full attention is not required

Self-Study Test of Understanding

Self-Study Instructions: This test can be used to help you assess how well you understand the content of this chapter. Terms to be filled in are from the Review Glossary. Answers are given in Appendix E.

You are hurrying to class when you hear a familiar voice call your name. This information reaches your brain via the (A) _____ of audition. This is a (B) _____ sense in that it is a modality associated with other senses, so that, without looking, you have a visual image of the friend who called you. She asks if you would be interested in studying for finals with her and Lotta Rhinakshus, a mutual acquaintance.

This inquiry is received in both ears and is transmitted over contralateral and ipsilateral pathways to the primary auditory areas in both hemispheres. Once it is recognized as a speech signal, the auditory input of the (C) _____ message to the (D) _____ right hemisphere is transferred to the (E) _____ left hemisphere where it is decoded in a manner that seems at least partially described by the (F) _____. To decode speech requires the (G) _____ ability, among others, to (H) _____ the sequence of sounds, syllables, and words.

Hearing Lotta's name, a (I) _____ symbol, you not only have an image of what she looks like and how she sounds, but you also remember that she wears musk, a scent you dislike, which seems to epitomize your dislike of Lotta generally. Accordingly, your (J) _____ is that you can't stand the thought of studying with Lotta, but what you actually say in your (K) _____ is that you'd love to join them, but you can't.

The meaning of this response has its origin in (L) _____, which begin the mapping of this idea into language. As this mapping progresses and becomes more explicit, the emotional and intonational components are processed mainly in the (M) _____, whereas the linguistic elements are processed in the (N) _____. Presumably, this division of labor has evolved to maintain (O) _____, which reduces competition for cortical processing space, and which has been proposed as an explanation of (P) _____.

The cortical areas for linguistic planning are usually found in the (Q) _____. Their specific locations may have to do with the cytoarchitecture of certain (R) _____ areas that seem conducive to speech and language processing. The area essential to language comprehension and formulation, (S) _____ area, is located in the (T) _____ of the dominant (U) _____ lobe. This area is connected to (V) _____ area for motor-speech planning by a major pathway, the (W) _____. Assisting in motor-speech formulation of propositional speech is the (X) _____ in the dominant superior prefrontal cortex, and the (Y) _____ in the dominant parietal lobe, which helps in speech-sound formulation.

With a feeling of relief, mediated by the limbic system and inadvertently revealed in your voice by (Z) _____ hemisphere processing, you take leave of your friend as you again say, insincerely, how sorry you are you can't study with them.

CHAPTER SIXTEEN

Neurology of Speech: Processing Output

OUTPUT PROCESSING

How is an idea, once selected for expression, converted into speech? How are words arranged in sequence to form a grammatical sentence? How are the sounds of each word arranged in proper order? How can these sounds be produced at a faster rate (10 to 15 per second) than the neuromuscular system can function; that is, how can high-speed speech performance be achieved with low-speed neuromuscular machinery?

Speech Formulation Characteristics

The answers to such questions will round out this discussion of how the nervous system functions for speech. You can observe many of the characteristics of speech formulation in yourself. Note, for example, how you produce a sentence. You may, if it is short enough, work it out completely in your mind before you speak it. You may work it out a phrase at a time. More likely, you may take it a few words at a time, letting the grammatical form of what follows be dictated by what you have already said (a process that often yields convoluted sentences that wander through an idea so as to render the intended meaning utterly opaque). All of these tactics require that you hold in mind the words of the sentence already spoken; this is the minimal memory requirement for ensuring that the next word chosen will fit grammatically.

Observe that these word selection and pronunciation processes tend to operate unconsciously and automatically except at points of indecision, or when self-corrections occur. Spontaneous speech is filled, typically, with backing and filling or groping for the right word to express your meaning, of rephrasing to remove yourself from a grammatical dead end, and of correcting a mispronunciation or a slurred sound. Corrections can be made all the way from changing production of a single sound to restating an entire sentence.

Memory Mechanisms for Speech

Several neurological operations can be inferred from this commonplace ability. A *working-memory mechanism* must be available for holding words in mind while all of the linguistic rules are being applied. This mechanism must be capable of storing information in varying amounts from sentences to sounds. Moreover, it must be capable of being quickly erased and replaced with the next message to be spoken. Presumably, semantic, syntactic, and morphemic rules must be applied before the phonemes to be uttered are selected. With the phonemes in order, the motor signals to the speech muscles must be assembled and timed so that the articulators move smoothly from the formation of one sound to the next. The load placed on working memory will be determined considerably by the extent to which application of these linguistic rules is automatic or under volitional direction. To be able to concentrate on saying what you mean requires that you not have to attend to grammatical and phonologic rules, as you would if you were learning to speak a foreign language.

The Efficient Speech-Encoding System

By virtue of *coarticulation,* speech movements can occur at fast rates because the nervous system uses a highly efficient encoding system; motor commands for successive phonemes are processed simultaneously. In other words, motor plans are laid in advance for moving the articulators from one position to the next. Thus, while one sound is being uttered, neural signals are already on the way to move the necessary speech muscles to the next position. Speech movements are overlapped in similar fashion to the way finger movements are overlapped when typing.

If this conception is true, it means that we organize our neural apparatus to understand speech by the movements used to produce speech. Support for this possibility is seen in evidence that the human auditory system is specially tuned to respond to vocal-tract movements. This also means that distinctions in speech that can be heard are linked closely to distinctions that can be produced. It will not be surprising if this is so. Visual perception, for example, is almost certainly organized this way. We detect one type of movement from another by learning to look while actively moving. As an example, subjects who were given prismatic glasses that made straight lines look curved, and vice versa, were able to adapt within an hour when they walked about actively; when they were pushed in a wheelchair over the same route for the same time, their visual perception remained distorted. Apparently the sensory apparatus must know what the motor apparatus is doing if our image of the world is to be normal.

Emotional Expression

We are inclined to think of speech as consisting of those sounds that a secretary could transcribe and then type in a letter. Suppose, however, that you were dictating a letter to someone you

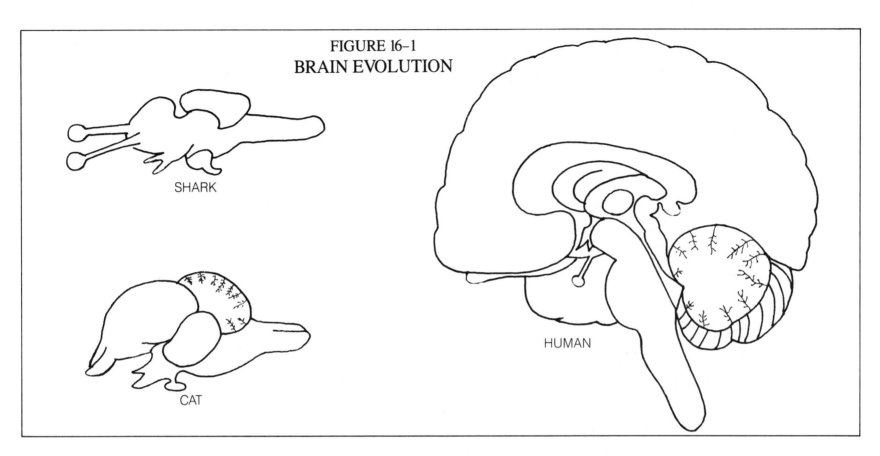

FIGURE 16–1
BRAIN EVOLUTION

SHARK

CAT

HUMAN

detested, but, for whatever reason, felt obligated to congratulate, so the tone of the dictation dripped with sarcasm. No one reading the letter, other than your secretary and you, would know that it was an exercise in insincerity. This is a prosaic example of an aspect of speech — the aspect of emotion — about which little is known. When emotion has been studied, it has usually been in its stronger forms, such as anger or depression. Still, even a subtle tone of voice can announce a speaker's intent so loudly that this aspect is probably a part of every utterance.

Emotion is expressed through paralinguistic elements. Whereas speech sounds depend largely on vocal-tract adjustments, paralinguistics depends mainly on laryngeal and respiratory adjustments of pitch, loudness, and duration. Because prosodic elements of syllable stress, which also are composed of pitch, loudness, and duration, are an integral part of highly structured linguistic operations, they can apparently be processed either in the left hemisphere, along with speech sounds, or in the right hemisphere. Emotions and attitudes, on the other hand, are reflected in intonation patterns that are relatively unstructured and change relatively slowly, so they appear to be processed in the right hemisphere. The differences in structure and processing speed seem to be the major determinants of which hemisphere is used.

Control of emotional expression is reflected in the evolutionary history of the brain (Fig. 16–1). The reptilian brain consisted of reticular system, midbrain, and basal ganglia. With the paleomammalian brain, found in lower mammals, the limbic system evolved. It is an important basis of emotional expression. In humans, the neomammalian brain permits generation of ideas. Thus, whereas reptiles and fish presumably experience only sensation, and animals with a limbic system can also express emotions, humans alone can think with a neomammalian brain, feel with the limbic components of that brain, and experience sensation with reptilian vestiges found in the oldest parts of that brain.

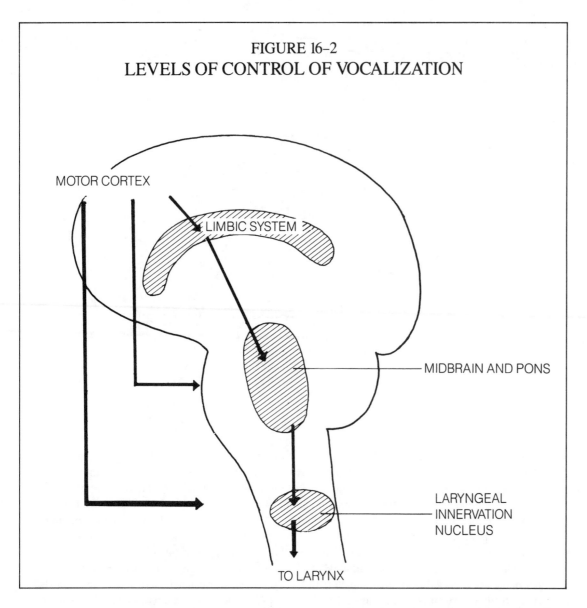

FIGURE 16–2
LEVELS OF CONTROL OF VOCALIZATION

MOTOR CORTEX

LIMBIC SYSTEM

MIDBRAIN AND PONS

LARYNGEAL
INNERVATION
NUCLEUS

TO LARYNX

Thus, humans, in whom meaning and emotion are interwoven, seem to have a cortically organized speech system overlaid on a primitive vocal regulatory system. Nonhuman vocalization and human emotional expressions, such as laughing and cry-ing, are controlled by the limbic system with little cortical involvement. Speech, on the other hand, while not excluding limbic participation, relies mainly on cortical, thalamic, and cerebellar processing (Fig. 16–2).

Functional Anatomy of Speech, Language, and Hearing

Neural Mechanisms for Motor Patterning

Separation of patterning of neuromuscular signals to produce a speech act from the patterning for linguistic planning to transform an idea into a meaningful sequence of words and phonemes is as arbitrary as separating twilight from darkness. Still, there is an essential difference between these activities, so there must also be a neurological difference. All of linguistic planning entails cognitive application of abstract rules. It involves decisions about how ideas are organized into sentences; about how sentences are organized grammatically; about choices of words that express exact meaning; about sequences of sounds for accurate pronunciation of words.

Neuromuscular patterning for converting these linguistic rules into tangible acts of speech entails, by contrast, ordering muscular contractions for specific overt acts of speech. For example, the word "go" has two phonemes (/g/ and /o/) that must be recognized if an individual is to understand the meaning of the word. Phonetically, however, these two phonemes (which are linguistic abstractions) can be produced an indefinite number of slightly different ways and still be heard as the word "go." Theoretically, each sound spoken is like a snowflake; it never occurs exactly the same way twice. So, even at the level of sound selection and production, the difference exists between abstract linguistic planning and overt speech movement signals.

Linguistic planning was, basically, the subject of the preceding section on central neural elaborative processes. In this section, the focus will be on the neural mechanisms for planning specific muscular contractions for production of specific speech sounds. We will begin by considering the component mechanisms involved and will conclude by integrating these mechanisms into the functional network that is thought to be the basis of motor speech.

Cortical Mechanisms

Although speech is typically thought of as being controlled in localized areas of the left hemisphere, there are exceptions. When attention to speech is required, extensive regions of the brain are activated. Harry Whitaker, a neurolinguist, has hypothesized that less cortex is required for processing of skills as they become automatic. He has proposed that after speech is learned (a task presumably requiring the entire brain), less neural processing is needed. Once automatized, control becomes localized in the specialized speech areas. There, with less brain being used, speech can be produced rapidly and with little attention, thus leaving cortical space available for thinking about what is being said rather than how to go about saying it.

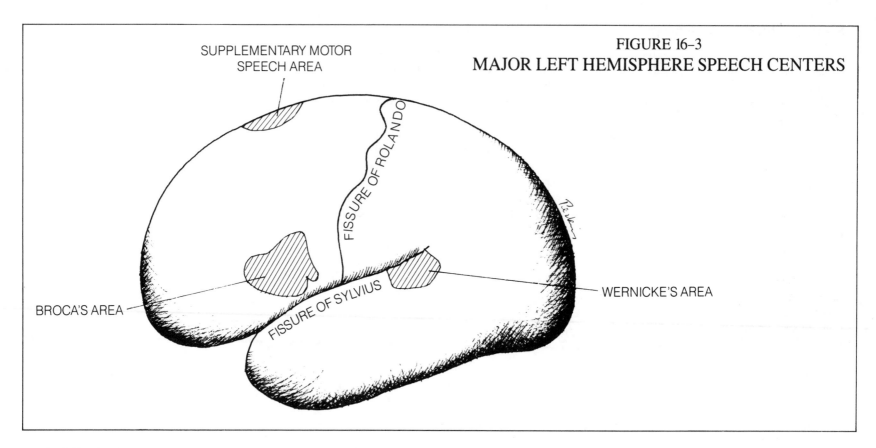

FIGURE 16–3

MAJOR LEFT HEMISPHERE SPEECH CENTERS

SUPPLEMENTARY MOTOR
SPEECH AREA

FISSURE OF ROLANDO

BROCA'S AREA

FISSURE OF SYLVIUS

WERNICKE'S AREA

Left Hemisphere. More than any other location in the brain, *Broca's area,* typically found in the lower frontal lobe of the dominant hemisphere (Fig. 16–3), is consistently associated with planning and execution of spoken language. When damaged, articulation becomes labored and ability to generate grammatical sentences is impaired. Comprehension is generally not much affected. Occasionally, though, when this area has been injured, speech has not been disturbed. Thus, even the most certain center of speech function is not that certain.

Although *Wernicke's area,* in the posterior left temporal lobe (Fig. 16–3), does not participate in the motor organization of speech, it is essential to meaningful speech. When impaired, not only is comprehension affected, but in addition the speech produced, while being well articulated and fluent, is likely to be meaningless and full of jargon. So, there would be no speech to organize motorically without the contribution made by Wernicke's area.

Facilitating propositional over automatic speech, the *supplementary motor speech area,* in the upper left frontal lobe (Fig. 16–3), is also thought to play a role in control of rhythm, phonation, and articulation. These are much the same functions as are assigned to the dominant side of the thalamus, with which the supplementary motor region is thought to be closely connected. Some think that this region can substitute for Broca's area in planning volitional motor speech. The *supramarginal gyrus,* behind the postcentral gyrus, is also thought to play a role in this task. Overall, the picture that emerges for the dominant left hemisphere is that certain regions are relatively frequently involved in speech and language processes, but none are always involved in a particular function. The areas bordering the fissure of Sylvius have been found to be mainly concerned with articulatory processing. Language-processing functions of semantics, syntax, and word-finding seem to be accomplished largely in front and in back of the articulatory area. The supplementary motor area is involved in both speech and language functions.

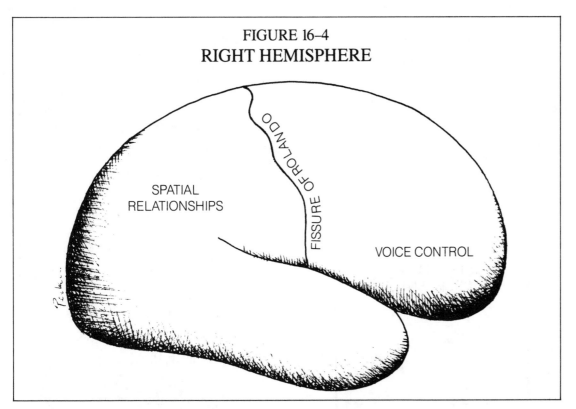

FIGURE 16–4
RIGHT HEMISPHERE

SPATIAL RELATIONSHIPS

FISSURE OF ROLANDO

VOICE CONTROL

Right Hemisphere. There apparently are no distinct areas in the right hemisphere for speech production comparable to Broca's or Wernicke's areas. The regions of the right hemisphere involved in speech processing do not seem to be as delineated as are those in the dominant hemisphere (Fig. 16–4). Nonetheless, the right hemisphere is now coming to be recognized as a mechanism for processing components of speech. What these components are is still a matter of some conjecture. It is generally thought to process melodic elements, but pitch contrasts involved in word stress, for instance, may be managed by either hemisphere. That the right hemisphere processes the prosodic expressions of attitude and emotion seems more certain, presumably because these expressions are less structured. The right hemisphere is also thought to organize motor mechanisms of emotional expression, but it appears to be better at managing negative emotional states; positive emotions seem to be controlled in the left hemisphere.

With the less structured affective aspects of speech organized in the right hemisphere, and the highly structured linguistic aspects organized in the left, the question arises as to how these separated components are integrated into any given moment of speech. Higher level coordination of propositional and prosodic components seems to be mainly through the corpus callosum. Integration of subcortical motor components is thought to be accomplished in the brainstem, particularly in the reticular formation.

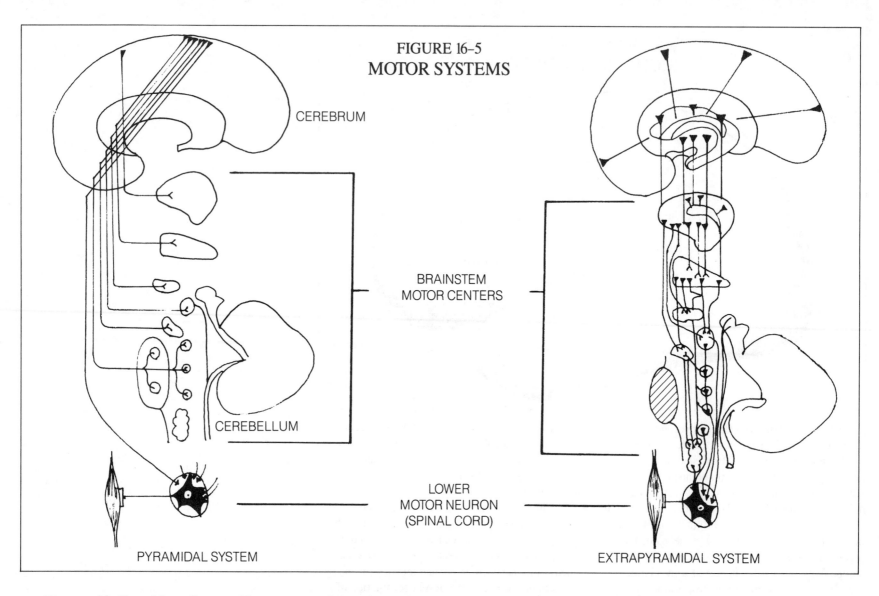

FIGURE 16–5
MOTOR SYSTEMS

CEREBRUM

BRAINSTEM
MOTOR CENTERS

CEREBELLUM

LOWER
MOTOR NEURON
(SPINAL CORD)

PYRAMIDAL SYSTEM

EXTRAPYRAMIDAL SYSTEM

Direct and Indirect Motor Systems. The *pyramidal* and *extrapyramidal motor systems* are the two motor systems that deliver signals to cranial and spinal nerves for innervation of skeletal muscles, including speech muscles. As you can see in Figure 16–5, the pyramidal system is "wired in parallel," unlike the extrapyramidal system, which is "wired in series." This permits the more recently evolved pyramidal system, which is mainly excitatory and mediates purposeful volitional movement, to dominate the older extrapyramidal system, which is both inhibitory and excitatory and mediates various reflexive responses, as in postural adjustments and emotional expression. As we discussed in Chapter 13, the reticular system directs traffic of these motor systems, amplifying or inhibiting signals to produce smooth movements.

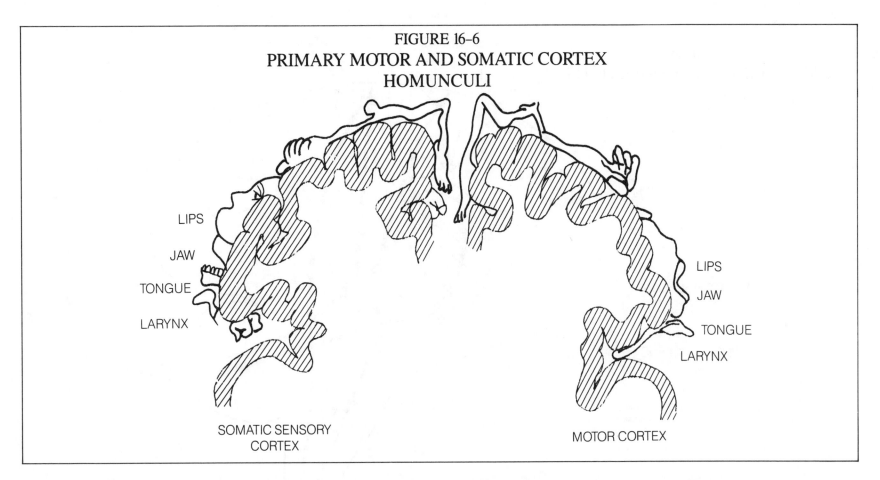

FIGURE 16-6
PRIMARY MOTOR AND SOMATIC CORTEX
HOMUNCULI

LIPS

JAW

TONGUE

LARYNX

LIPS

JAW

TONGUE

LARYNX

SOMATIC SENSORY
CORTEX

MOTOR CORTEX

The pyramidal system is designed to provide discrete control for skilled movement. Its topography in the primary motor cortex is arranged so clearly that stimulation of specific cortical motor areas consistently produces movements in specific muscles. Actually, only a fraction of the pyramidal system originates from the primary motor cortex. Most of this system begins in the premotor areas of the frontal cortex and in the postcentral regions of the parietal lobe. Those parts of the body that require finest control, such as tongue, lips, and fingers, have the largest supply of pyramidal motor neurons, and incidentally, of sensory neurons to

feed back information about muscle contraction and movement. As can be seen in Figure 16–6, the speech structures have rich cortical innervation, which is the basis for the precision with which speech movements are controlled.

Speech can occur under any condition in which humans survive; whether en route to the moon, swimming, parachuting, jumping, eating, or in an emotional state of ecstasy, man still talks. Obviously, we are built to coordinate the motor activities of speech with just about any reflexive activity of which we are capable. The pyramidal system, with its nonstop motor traffic from cortex

to lower motor neuron, is an express route for fine coordination of speech. But alone, the pyramidal system produces only isolated segments of movement. For these movements to be smoothly integrated, pyramidal activity must be harmonized with that of the extrapyramidal system, which, like the mail train, stops at every motor station from the cortex to the spinal cord to pick up neural information for reflexive adjustment. Where the extrapyramidal system provides indirect connections of the motor cortex to lower motor neurons, the pyramidal system, like a nonstop flight, connects the cortex to these neurons directly.

Neurology of Speech: Output Processing

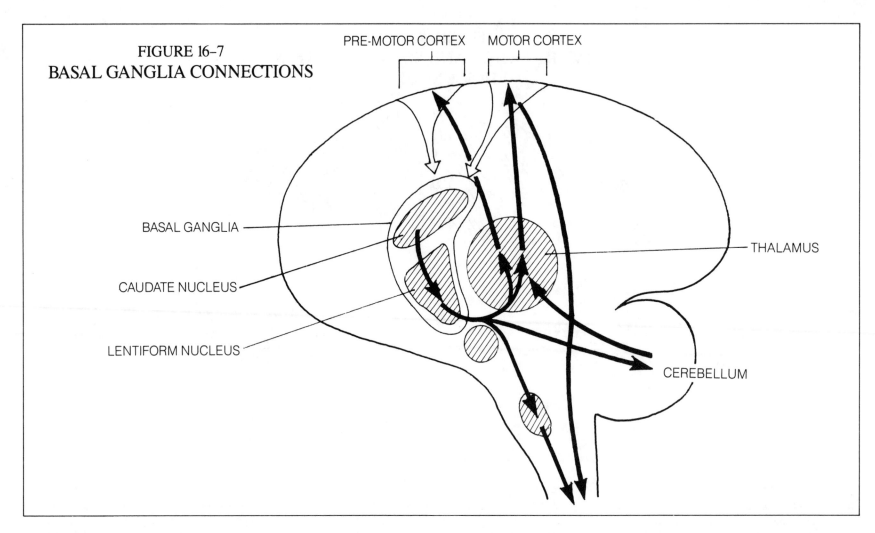

FIGURE 16-7
BASAL GANGLIA CONNECTIONS

PRE-MOTOR CORTEX   MOTOR CORTEX

BASAL GANGLIA

CAUDATE NUCLEUS

LENTIFORM NUCLEUS

THALAMUS

CEREBELLUM

Subcortical Mechanisms

Like cortical centers, the subcortical centers involved in motor-speech processing should not be thought of as isolated structures that carry out independent operations on the speech signal. Instead, they are regional networks within larger neural networks that are connected together in loops. For the sake of discussion, we will look briefly at the components of these loops before reassembling them into an integrated whole.

Basal Ganglia. Located at the top of the brainstem, the basal ganglia are the largest of the subcortical motor centers in the extrapyramidal system. As shown in Figure 16-7, they receive information primarily from motor and premotor areas, connected back to the motor cortex by way of the thalamus. The basal ganglia are thought to be important in generating motor programs. In fact, the basal ganglia, in conjunction with the cerebellum, may be more responsible for speech production than is the motor cortex. This possibility is supported by the profound motor problems, such as cerebral palsy, that result from damage to the basal ganglia and cerebellum. Such damage causes more impairment of speech control than does injury to the motor cortex.

Cerebellum. In any servosystem, and the nervous system is a supreme example of a self-regulating mechanism, the intended performance is compared with actual performance to improve accuracy. At target practice, for instance, if we miss the bull's eye, we check to determine which way to correct our aim for the next shot. The correction depends on detecting a discrepancy between intent and *feedback* information about the performance. In such self-adjusting mechanisms as computers, detection of performance error and correction for it is accomplished in devices called *comparators*.

The cerebellum has been described as the comparator of the nervous system. It is informed in advance of the movement intended. This plan is sent ahead several milliseconds before beginning the act, presumably to prepare the cerebellum for a check on adequacy of the performance when proprioceptive feedback about the movement arrives from muscles, tendons, and joints. As you can see from the diagrams in Figure 16–8, the cerebellum is supplied abundantly with feedback from ears, eyes, and body to keep well informed of the movements and sounds that are actually produced. With extensive connections from the entire cortex, such as those shown in Figure 16–8, the cerebellum is apprised of plans for consciously directed volitional action; with brainstem circuits, it is apprised of plans for unconscious reflexive action. With these inputs, and with outputs mainly back to the motor cortex for speech, the cerebellum checks response against command, sends modified impulses back to the motor centers, and sends these impulses, indirectly, out to the muscles. This corrective modification serves to smooth the response by coordinating contraction of the agonistic muscles producing the desired movement as well as of the antagonistic muscles opposing it.

How the cerebellum carries out these functions is still open to conjecture. It is more wrinkled and tightly packed than the cerebrum, having 75 percent of the surface area of either of the much larger hemispheres, but only 10 percent of the total brain mass. As homunculi can be drawn for cerebral representation of the body, so too can homunculi represent localized functions of the cerebellar cortex; specific cerebellar areas are devoted to monitoring muscle behavior from specific parts of the body. The cerebellum performs its tasks mainly by inhibiting rather than facilitating excitability of neurons. It generates high-frequency electrical waves that are more than 10 times as fast as those of the cerebral cortex, but the voltage is 10 times weaker than cerebral voltage. Large areas of cerebellar hemispheres, which constitute nearly 90 percent of the cerebellum, can be removed with no enduring effect. Cerebellar sensory areas can even be destroyed with no measurable sensory loss. Yet, removal of the entire cerebellum produces severe disturbance in muscular coordination. These are some of the pieces that are known to fit into the puzzle, which will have to be explained when the puzzle is solved.

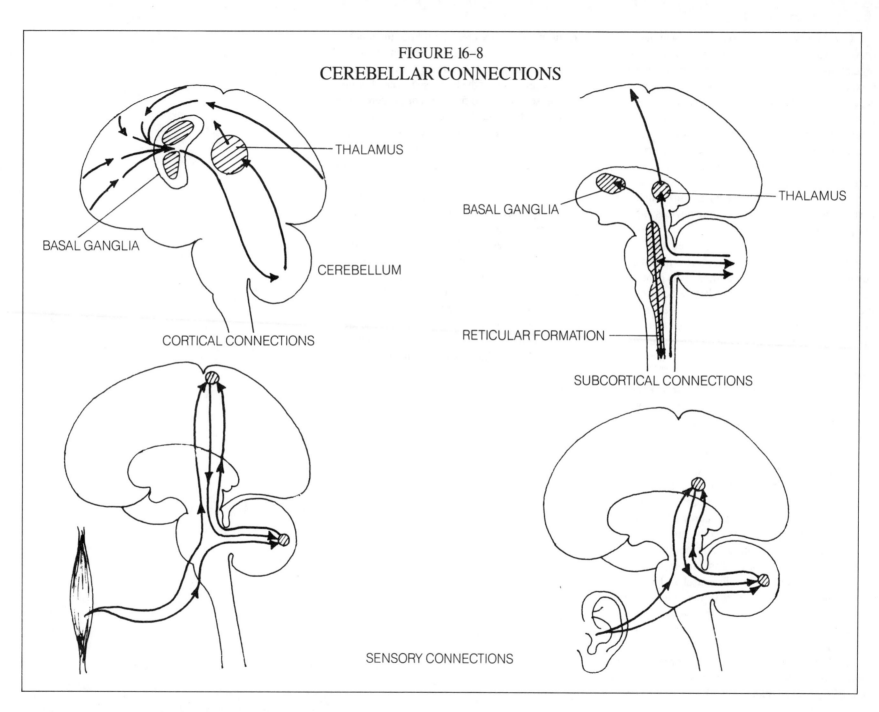

FIGURE 16–8
CEREBELLAR CONNECTIONS

THALAMUS

BASAL GANGLIA

CEREBELLUM

CORTICAL CONNECTIONS

BASAL GANGLIA

THALAMUS

RETICULAR FORMATION

SUBCORTICAL CONNECTIONS

SENSORY CONNECTIONS

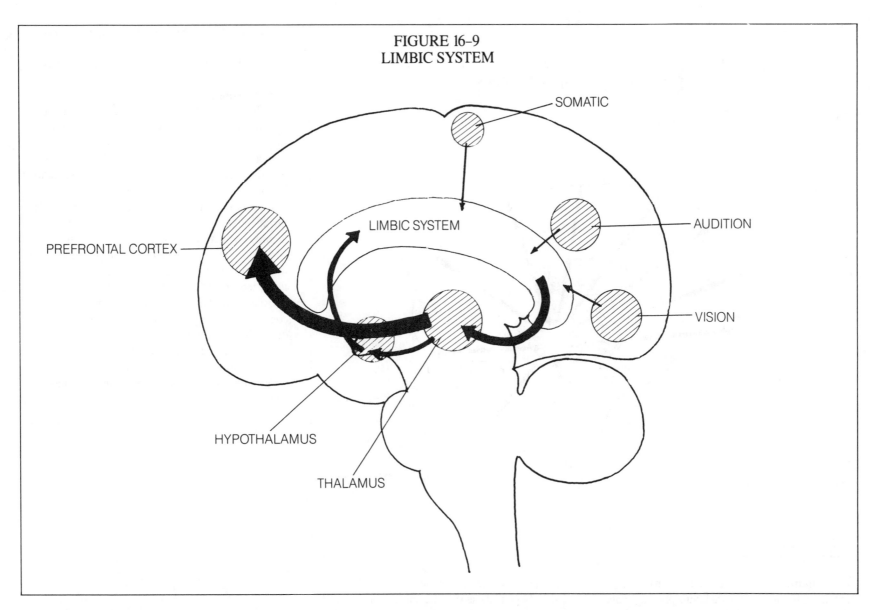

**FIGURE 16–9
LIMBIC SYSTEM**

SOMATIC

LIMBIC SYSTEM

PREFRONTAL CORTEX

AUDITION

VISION

HYPOTHALAMUS

THALAMUS

Limbic System. More or less encircling the basal ganglia, and with connections to the hypothalamus (the control center of the autonomic nervous system), the limbic system mediates information about internal states such as thirst, hunger, fear, rage, pleasure, and sex (Fig. 16–9). It also receives information from the prefrontal cortex as well as from primary sensory areas and their related association areas; it can, thereby, color perceptions emotionally. In turn, the limbic system is connected back to the prefrontal cortex via the thalamus. By virtue of this reciprocal relationship, the prefrontal cortex exerts control over emotions — and emotional expression — arising from the limbic system.

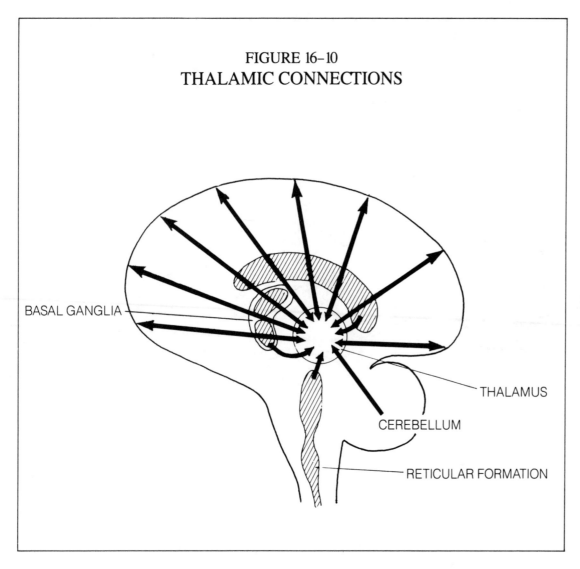

FIGURE 16-10
THALAMIC CONNECTIONS

BASAL GANGLIA

THALAMUS

CEREBELLUM

RETICULAR FORMATION

Lower Motor Neuron. Like a grand piano, the neuromuscular system can be used for performance ranging from exquisite precision to gross clumsiness. The *lower motor neuron* (with its synaptic connections in the spinal cord and brainstem from the pyramidal and extrapyramidal motor systems) corresponds to the piano key. The muscle fiber, to which the lower motor neuron attaches via cranial or spinal nerves, corresponds to the hammer that strikes the piano string. Just as the piano key and hammer form a functional unit, so do the lower motor neuron and muscle fiber (Fig. 16-11). Strike the piano key with sufficient force and the hammer will strike the string; the harder the key is struck, the louder will be the sound. Fire the lower motor neuron and the muscle will contract; the faster the firing to a fiber and the more fibers innervated simultaneously, the stronger the muscle contraction. Whether or not firing will occur is determined by whether the sum of facilitatory influences from higher motor centers is greater than the sum of inhibitory influences. These influences are weighed at the synapses of lower motor neurons.

Thalamus. As could be inferred from the preceding discussion, the thalamus plays a pivotal role in motor-speech processing. Having extensive connections to the right hemisphere, as well as being the relay station between the cortex and the limbic system, basal ganglia, and cerebellum, it is the key structure in the integration of the proposi-tional and emotional components of speech (Fig. 16-10). Beyond these specific speech functions, it plays a major role in arousal, attention, and short-term memory. Virtually all parts of the cortex are so extensively connected to the thalamus as to make cortical and thalamic functions all but inseparable.

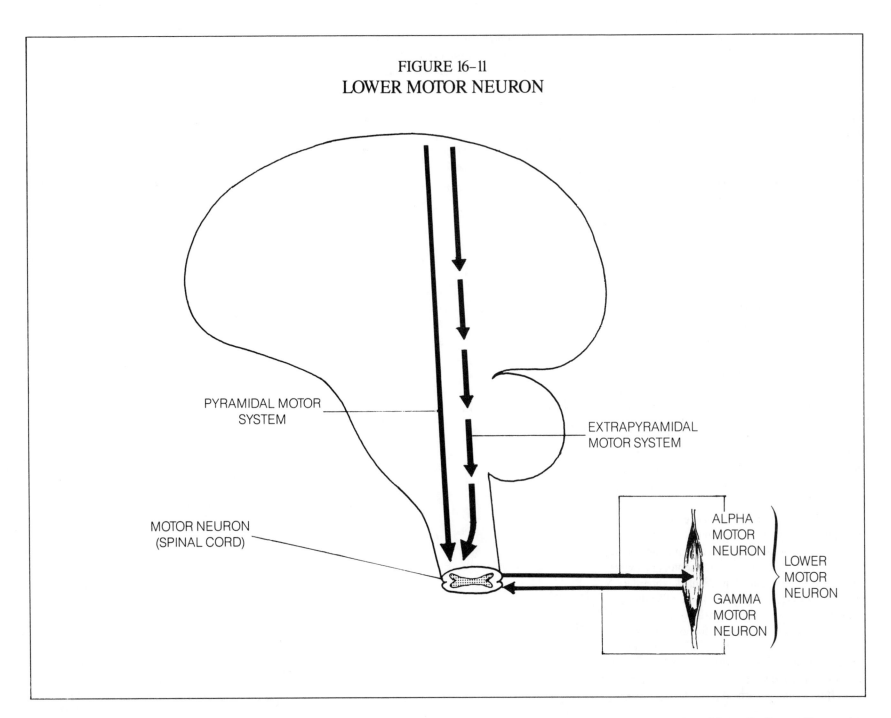

FIGURE 16–11
LOWER MOTOR NEURON

PYRAMIDAL MOTOR
SYSTEM

EXTRAPYRAMIDAL
MOTOR SYSTEM

MOTOR NEURON
(SPINAL CORD)

ALPHA
MOTOR
NEURON

LOWER
MOTOR
NEURON

GAMMA
MOTOR
NEURON

The neuromuscular system, like the grand piano, permits skilled performance only when property tuned. The piano is tuned by adjusting tension in the strings, the neuromuscular system by adjusting tension in the muscles. Muscle tone is maintained by the balance of tension between opposing muscles. When the biceps, say, contracts to flex the arm, it is opposed by the triceps (the biceps as the prime mover is the *agonist,* the triceps the *antagonist*). The more the antagonist resists relaxing as the agonist contracts, the greater the muscle tone — the less slack in the system. Muscles are tuned reflexively by the *gamma system.* This system, which provides high-speed feedback, a particularly important requirement for the control of high-speed speech movements, regulates the background of muscle tone against which all movements, innervated by the *alpha system,* are made. Tone is low when relaxed, high when alert. This arrangement permits fitting quickness of response to estimation of the situation. If a quick response is needed, as in most skilled performances, slack must be minimal; therefore, muscle tone must be high. Similarly, if a situation holds threat, quickness is of the essence. For an easy demonstration of the effect of different levels of muscle tone in an animal, clap your hands behind the back of a cat lazing drowsily before a fire, and then behind the back of that same cat arched face to face with a dog.

The lower motor neuron "keyboard," like its musical counterpart, has no control over the uses to which it is put. As a novice can bang dissonance from the piano, so can old motor centers in lower levels of the brain control the spinal keyboard to produce gross reflexive responses. Unlike the grand piano, however, which usually sits idle awaiting the touch of an artist, the lower motor neuron keyboard is in constant use. The higher the neural level, the more priority it has for control of this keyboard, and the more skillful the performance. But, when the cortical level, for example, relinquishes control (as in sleep, intoxication, an emotional outburst, or injury), the next level down that is ready to function then gains control. So long as an organism remains alive, some level will be ready to function — the lower that level, the cruder will be its function. From this discussion, it should be apparent that higher centers must inhibit lower ones in order to control the spinal keyboard and produce skilled responses.

Reticular Formation. By its connections with cortical motor centers, thalamus, basal ganglia and other brainstem motor centers, cerebellar centers, and sensory pathways — in brief, by its connections with the pyramidal, extrapyramidal, and sensory systems — the reticular system is centrally located to stitch all of the separate activities of the nervous system into an integrated whole (Fig. 16–12). It awakens the brain and keeps it alert; it monitors the stimuli that flood our senses, accepting those of importance to us and rejecting the rest; it directs neural traffic, focusing and refining our motor responses to the problem at hand; in fact, it is probably basic to thinking, to attention, to selection of ideas, and to reasoning about them. The reticular system, then, seems to be at the neurological hub of speech, especially the integration of its emotional and propositional components.

Organizing Principle of Rhythm. The nervous system is like a gigantic orchestra with billions of instruments; each neuron is, potentially, capable of playing its own tune. Were neurons free to function alone, our heads would be filled with bioelectrical noise. An orchestra's activity is organized around a musical beat, and the conductor ensures that each instrument plays the proper note at the proper time. Timing is the essence of musical success. It is also, undoubtedly, the essence of the brain's success. Timing of the impulses that play on the lower motor neuron keyboard from all of the neural centers in the brainstem and cerebrum is crucial for coordinated movement. When movements occur as rapidly as they must at normal speech rates, neural timing can make the difference between tongues that tumble over sounds and tongues that produce a smooth flow of speech.

The rhythm of speech seems to be in the neighborhood of 6 beats per second. The rate of syllable production is in this vicinity, and it is also a rate that seems to coincide with the rate at which

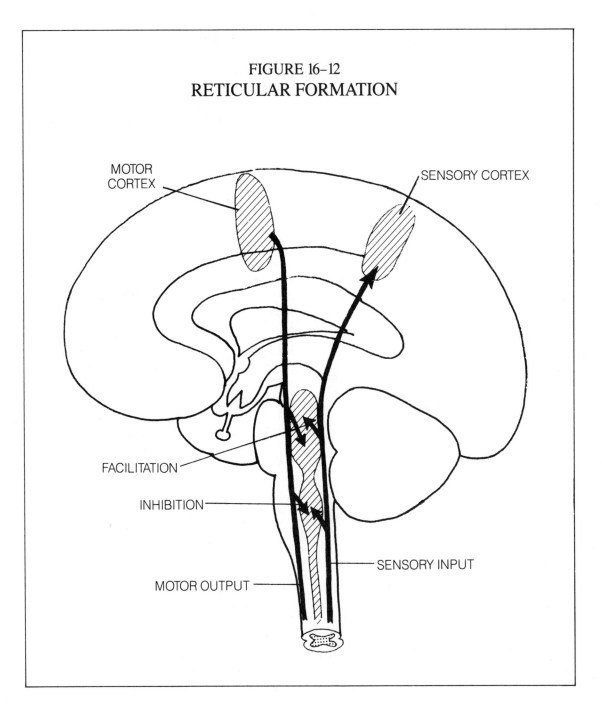

FIGURE 16–12
RETICULAR FORMATION

MOTOR CORTEX

SENSORY CORTEX

FACILITATION

INHIBITION

SENSORY INPUT

MOTOR OUTPUT

we think, as well as the rate at which a finger can be tapped. Considering that over 100 muscles are involved in speech production and that these muscles must accommodate transitions for an average of 2 to 4 phonemes per syllabic beat (this works out to about 14 phonemes per second), clearly some organizing principle must operate to coordinate the immensely complex neural activity of speech production.

Rhythmic activity is a fundamental property of the brain. Brain waves vary widely; in a normal adult, they can range from 3 to 40 cycles per second (cps), depending mainly on wakefulness and attention. Electroencephalographic recordings made over different regions of the brain reveal different frequencies. Over the occipital area, primarily concerned with vision, the dominant frequency is 9 to 10 cps, a rhythm that does not seem relevant to speech. Over the temporoparietal region (the posterior speech area), though, the frequency is about 7 cps, a rate that does appear closely related to speech. Moreover, it is not until the dominant rhythm of a child's brain reaches 7 cps or faster, around 2 years of age, that he is ready to develop speech. Whether or not rhythm is the organizing principle of the brain that keeps billions of neurons firing in proper order is, however, still a matter of conjecture.

Integration and Summary of Motor-Speech Processing

Volitional Versus Automatic Control

Processing of motor activity for automatic movements is different from the processing for voluntary behavior. Accordingly, we will begin our synthesis of motor-speech formulation by addressing this important difference. It is a difference that hinges on the extent to which a volitional goal of action is being pursued. This applies as much to

speech as it does to riding a bicycle, driving a car, or walking. Any of these activities can be performed automatically, but they can also be volitionally directed under conscious control.

Take walking, for example. Who pays attention to how he walks? But walk along a narrow ledge around the top of a tall building and the level of conscious control of each step is likely to be so high that you may be unable to move — one of the authors still has vivid memory of crawling across the old mile-high wooden bridge as it swayed in the wind over the Royal Gorge. Similarly, speech can be mindless chatter filled with clichés and platitudes, with little evidence of volitional purpose. But if you are giving an important report extemporaneously, which requires that you weigh your words carefully and speak distinctly, then your goals of action will be highly volitional.

Automatic Movement Mechanisms. Automatic movement can be mediated by motor mechanisms ranging from the simplest spinal cord reflexes to brainstem reflexes to cortical control loops between sensory and motor cortex. The principles of reflexive action, on which current understanding is based, were described early in this century by Charles Sherrington, a British physiologist.

The task of any muscle contraction is to produce an intended movement, whether automatic or voluntary. If automatic, the program for initiating that movement is prearranged. If it is reflexively controlled in the spinal cord, such as the knee-jerk, or in the brainstem, such as the respiratory reflex, then the motor-control program is prearranged by being inherited. At the cortical level of control, it is prearranged by having been learned. The lower the level of control, the simpler the preprogrammed movement.

A *reflex* is an unlearned, automatic behavior. Whenever the stimulus that elicits the reflex occurs, the reflex response immediately follows.

Much of the behavior in the infant is reflexive, and this is true of the oral structures as well as other parts of the body. Three reflexes are important to early feeding. The *rooting reflex* is a turn of the infant's head in the direction of an object that touches the cheek. It usually is accompanied by movements of the lips and tongue. Obviously, this reflex is useful in nursing. The *sucking reflex* is a sucking response to nearly anything that touches the infant's lips. The *swallowing reflex* is a swallow in response to liquid or solid food in the back of the infant's mouth. Taken together, these three reflexes provide an efficient sequence of unlearned behavior. The rooting reflex enables the infant to seek the source of nourishment, such as a nipple. After the lips have been positioned so as to contact the nipple, the additional stimulation elicits the sucking reflex, which can extract milk. Finally, the milk enters the infant's mouth where it triggers the swallowing reflex. Many early reflexes disappear with maturation, but swallowing remains partly reflexive, even in the adult. The early phases of swallowing, when food is in the mouth, are under voluntary control, but the later phases, when the food is in the pharynx or esophagus, are under involuntary, reflexive control.

Other reflexes commonly observed in infants are the following.

1. Blink reflex: The infant blinks in response to bright light, a loud sound, or physical stimulation near the eyes.
2. Doll's eye response: In response to a slow turning of the infant's head, the eyes rotate in the direction of the head turn after a short delay.
3. Stepping reflex: When the infant is held erect so that the soles of the feet touch a flat surface, the legs move alternately in a stepping fashion.
4. Head-straightening reflex: When the infant is pulled up by his or her hands into a sitting position, he or she tries to bring the head into an upright posture.
5. Moro (startle) reflex: After a sudden jolt or loss of support of the head, the infant extends the arms and legs, then flexes them, and finally moves the arms in an embracing gesture.
6. Grasp reflex: When a rod is placed in the infant's palm, the fingers close — sometimes tightly enough that infants can support their entire weight while grasping a rod.
7. Babinski (plantar) reflex: A stroking pressure against the sole of the foot brings about a spreading of the toes.

Thus, low-level reflexes are integrated into higher level reflexes, which are integrated to provide the background adjustments for cortically controlled automatic movements. It is the *alpha motor neuron* that innervates the muscle to produce the bodily movement. This innervation is supplied to the lower motor neuron directly from the primary motor cortex in both hemispheres by the pyramidal motor system and indirectly via brainstem and spinal cord reflex centers by the extrapyramidal system.

The other aspect of automatic control is the role of feedback. The motor-control program is designed to initiate an intended movement, but accomplishing the intention requires what Sherrington called proprioceptive feedback, which means feedback from elongation and tension receptors in muscles.

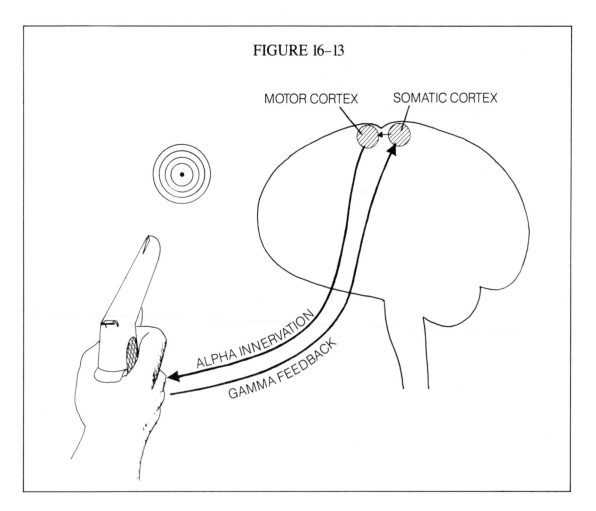

FIGURE 16-13

MOTOR CORTEX   SOMATIC CORTEX

ALPHA INNERVATION

GAMMA FEEDBACK

Suppose your intention was, with your arm extended, to hold your hand steady. This would be accomplished by opposing muscles maintaining just the right balance of force between them. This is done by counteracting lengthening with increased contraction (which increases tension) and counteracting increased tension with relaxation (which results in increased length). This self-regulation of muscle tension is handled by *gamma motor neurons* that use feedback to regulate sensitivity of muscle length receptors.

For small, precise movements, such as are involved in speaking, the pyramidal motor system plays the primary role. Much of the self-corrective feedback to these pyramidal motor cells in the primary motor cortex comes from the sensory area directly behind the motor cortex (the primary somatic cortex). This relationship is shown in Figure 16-13.

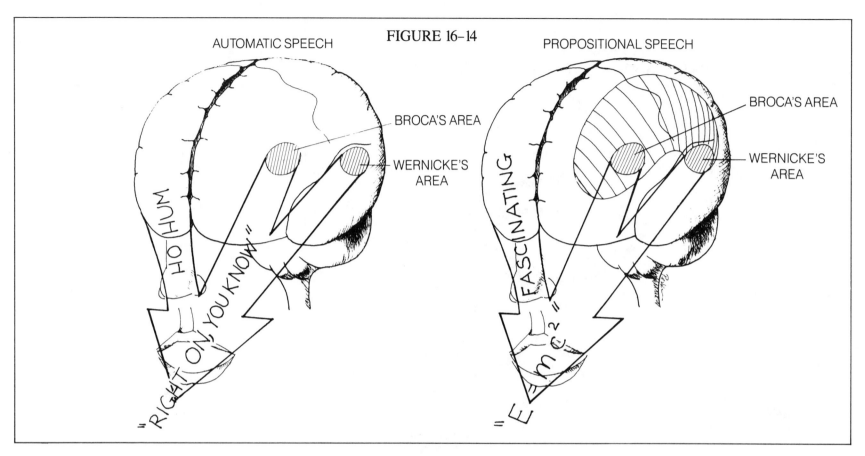

FIGURE 16-14

AUTOMATIC SPEECH

PROPOSITIONAL SPEECH

BROCA'S AREA

WERNICKE'S AREA

BROCA'S AREA

WERNICKE'S AREA

Volitional Movement Mechanisms. Just as automatic movements require a program of motor control and a feedback arrangement for stabilizing them, so do volitional movements. The difference between automatic and voluntary control is the way in which the motor program is prepared. Whereas automatic movement uses an efficiently organized program prearranged either genetically or by learning, voluntary movement programs are tailored to meet a specific goal at a specific moment. In effect, they are ad hoc programs contrived to meet a particular purpose. As with all motor learning, a *motor schema* is established by which movements are coordinated, corrected, and stabilized.

Such a schema is a mental image of the goal to be achieved by the movements. In the case of speech, it can be an auditory image of the phrase to be used, the precision of articulation, the fluency of the utterance, or the tone of voice.

With voluntary control, such as for propositional speech, the goal to be achieved (the statement to be made) is formulated in cortical association areas, presumably through speech centers in the dominant hemisphere (most notably Wernicke's and Broca's areas, with possible involvement of such other areas as the supramarginal gyrus and the supplementary motor cortex), and through the right hemisphere for planning of emotional expres-

sion (Fig. 16-14). All speech, once learned, is built on automatized skills. (If rules of grammar and articulation were not automatic, we would not have room in our heads to think of the meaning of what we say.) These are the skills that Whitaker has proposed are handled efficiently in the speech centers. If mindless chit-chat is going on with little thought given to what is being said, then little speech activity outside of the speech centers would be expected. If thought is being given to the message, or if the grammar of word selection must be corrected to say what is meant, then extensive brain activity would be directing the automatic linguistic operations of the speech centers.

Neurology of Speech: Output Processing

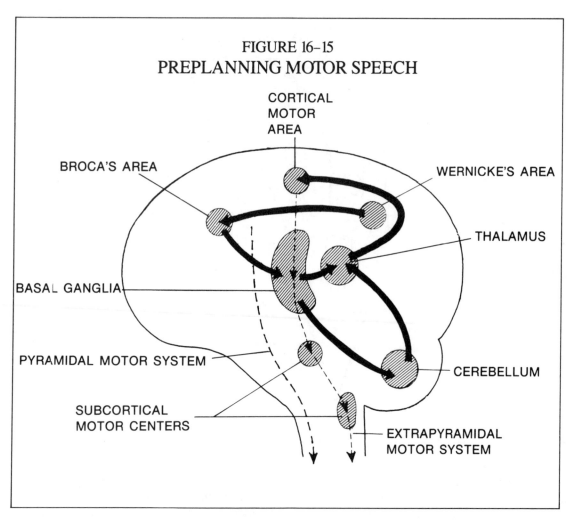

FIGURE 16–15
PREPLANNING MOTOR SPEECH

CORTICAL
MOTOR
AREA

BROCA'S AREA

WERNICKE'S AREA

THALAMUS

BASAL GANGLIA

PYRAMIDAL MOTOR SYSTEM

CEREBELLUM

SUBCORTICAL
MOTOR CENTERS

EXTRAPYRAMIDAL
MOTOR SYSTEM

A fraction of a second before a speech movement is to occur, these cortical plans are apparently transmitted to the basal ganglia and cerebellum where, working together, the motor program to initiate movement is generated. Output from this processing is then relayed back through the thalamus to the motor cortex in both hemispheres, where appropriate motor signals are then sent to the speech muscles to produce the intended movements. This information for initiating a voluntary behavior also is returned to the association cortex, where the planning began, to complete the circuitry for programming speech (Fig. 16–15). As with automatic movement, this volitional program is executed by way of the pyramidal and extrapyramidal motor systems (which transmit their signals to lower-motor neurons for innervation of muscles), and is corrected for any errors by feedback from such centers as the primary somatic sensory cortex.

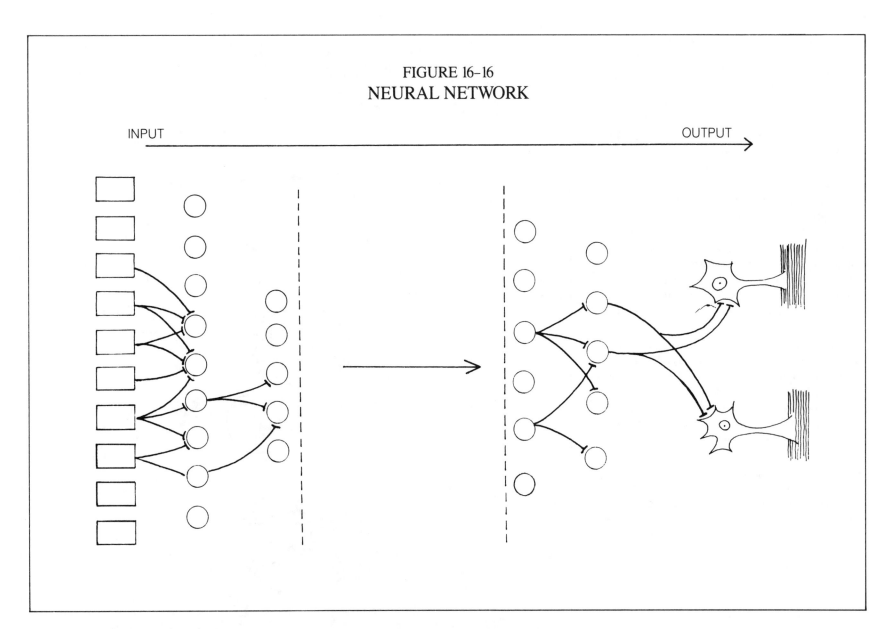

FIGURE 16-16
NEURAL NETWORK

INPUT

OUTPUT

Stages of Processing

The foregoing accounts of automatic and voluntary control mechanisms need to be refined in an important respect. As we have discussed in earlier chapters, speech centers are not separate "shops" that operate in isolation. They are local neural networks that are integral parts of the whole network which constitutes the nervous system.

More is known about what goes on at input and output ends of networks (illustrated schematically in Figure 16-16) than is known about the network regions in between.

Neurology of Speech: Output Processing

461

A more realistic view of how these networks function is to think of them as subsystems with overlapping circuits in which speech processing proceeds in stages. Thus, as shown in Figure 16–17, it has been proposed that an early stage of an utterance is the formulation in the limbic network of a diffuse feeling of what is to be said. This formulation then extends out through linguistic planning networks until it is ready for motor implementation. At this stage, the action to be taken is accomplished by the networks involving cortical association areas, basal ganglia, and cerebellum. At the next stage, cerebellar processing is incorporated through thalamic networks with precentral motor networks for the construction of motor speech programs. This culminates in the final stage reaching from motor cortex through the motor system networks to lower motor neurons for execution of movement (Fig. 16–17).

In this conception, cognitive and emotional components of an utterance are integrated from the beginning of the formulation of a statement. One is not superimposed on the other at a later stage of processing. Thus, what begins as a vague sense of what one wants to say gains specificity as it progresses through stages of processing. At each stage, various neural structures add their contributions to the evolving statement, so that it goes through a series of transformations as it is refined through the interrelated cortical and subcortical structures in the speech network.

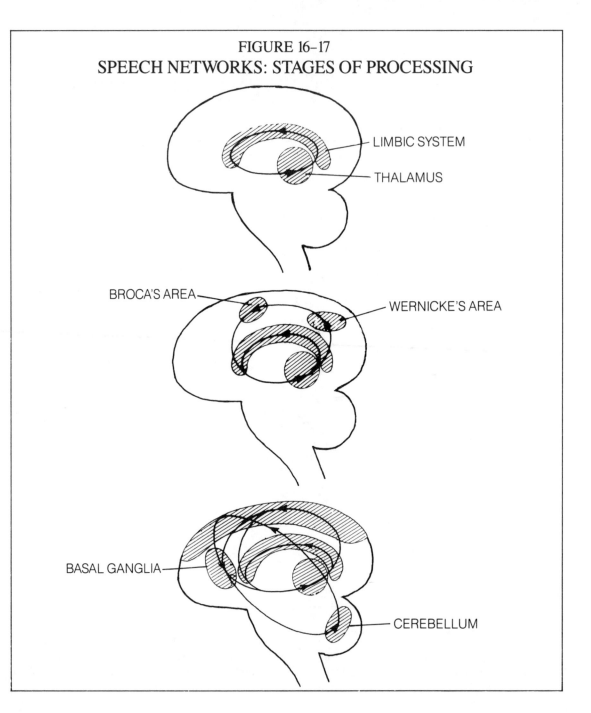

FIGURE 16–17
SPEECH NETWORKS: STAGES OF PROCESSING

LIMBIC SYSTEM
THALAMUS
BROCA'S AREA
WERNICKE'S AREA
BASAL GANGLIA
CEREBELLUM

Speech as Output: How We Produce a Sentence

We now attempt an admittedly simplified summary of a highly complicated and only partially understood process — how we produce a sentence. The process apparently begins at a pre-linguistic level, which we shall term the *general cognitive level*. Here thought is formulated as propositions or relations that precede verbal expression. These nonlinguistic propositions or relations are translated into a form that is accessible by the linguistic system. One theory of this translation is that *plan schema* are formed to represent the components of goal-directed events. The schema might specify the goal of some actor, perhaps together with a sequence of subgoals that specify actions that help to achieve the main goal. For example, imagine noting that a book you borrowed from the library is due today, but that you don't have time to return it. This situation immediately identifies the main goal: to get the book to the library. Let's assume further that you realize that your friend planned to go to the library to research a term paper. The weather is cold and rainy, the library is several miles away, your friend has no car, but you do. The subgoals now fall in line: You will ask your friend (actor) to return the book for you (main goal), offering the use of your car (subgoal). But wait — you just remembered that your friend will not be back until just after you leave for class. More subgoals: Leave your car keys and the book on the table, and ask your roommate to ask your friend to return the book using your car.

These last steps in the process constitute something called *framing*, or the selection of participants and the assignment of roles to these participants. You have selected your friend, your roommate, and the car as participants, and each has been assigned a role.

As your roommate enters the room, you make your request. This means formulating a sentence (or two), which might go like, "Would you please ask Jill to return this book to the library when she goes today. She can use my car." Or you could have said, "I don't have time to return this library book, which is due today, but Jill plans to go to the library and I thought that she could take my car and return the book for me. Would you ask her, please?" Whatever you say, a number of decisions have to be made about the words to use, the way they will be ordered to form a sentence, and how you want to state your request (imploringly, casually, urgently, and so forth). The choice of words is the level of semantics; the ordering of words in a sentence is syntactics (or syntax); and the accompanying emotion is a matter of affect, a paralinguistic aspect (the prefix *para* means "along with" or "beyond").

Research on sentence formulation has shown that we typically do not plan our sentences completely before we begin to speak them. Rather, we begin to talk after only a few words are selected. The remainder of the utterance is formulated "on line" (while we talk). Another feature of verbal formulation is that semantic and syntactic decisions are highly interactive. Our choice of words limits the way we assemble them into sentences, and our choice of sentence structure (for example, word order) determines our possible word selections.

Semantic choices give us the words for an utterance. Recent studies of this process of word selection indicate that it has two stages. The first stage is abstract in that it selects not a word per se but rather a kind of concept of a word. The second stage yields the actual phonological form of a word — its sound pattern. Perhaps it is between these two stages of semantics and phonologic pattern that the "tip of the tongue" phenomenon occurs. This refers to the situation in which a speaker cannot retrieve the desired word but knows that the word is "there," and may even know the first sound of the word. When the word concept is fully clothed in its phonologic dress, we can say that word selection (lexicalization) is completed.

But the utterance is not complete. Each word identified in the processes described so far now must be articulated. Here again, there are at least two stages and maybe even several more. Most writers agree that a stage of phonetic coding is required. This stage specifies the detailed speech pattern, providing sufficient information that the articulators can be controlled to produce the indicated sound segments. Perhaps the segments are translated into phonetic features, such as voicing, nasal, fricative, or velar. Whether by segments or features (or something else), the speech control system issues instructions to the muscles of the speech apparatus. There are reasons to believe that the instructions are grouped into syllabic units. Syllabic organization may account for a large portion of coarticulation. For example, when a speaker says *bee*, the tongue is already in position for the vowel *ee* while the lips close for the consonant *b*. A syllabic grouping of articulatory instructions could explain this outcome in which vowel and consonant features are produced simultaneously.

After phonetic coding, the utterance is given observable form as a pattern of articulation and audible form as a pattern of sound. But the speaker's task is not done. Still required is a stage of self-monitoring, either to confirm correct production or to generate error information from which a corrected utterance can be prepared. Speaking is a process vulnerable to error even in the most articulate among us. Announcers occasionally stumble over words or commit slips of the tongue. In trying to say, "My book is due at the library," a speaker might say, "My dook is bue at the library." We detect these errors by listening to our own speech. Probably all of us have been surprised at the things we hear ourselves say — often to our embarrassment. Many of these errors arise in stages of verbal formulation to which we do not have ready

access during the planning process, so the error is apparent only when it has been articulated for all to hear, as in the case of the radio announcer who introduced the pianist Eddy Peabody with the unfortunate words, "And now Eddy Playbody will pea for you."

CLINICAL POSTSCRIPT

On February 8, Wendell G. lay in a hospital bed, unable to speak and paralyzed on the right side of his body. He had suffered a stroke 24 hours earlier. The attending neurologist concluded from her tests that Wendell G. had an infarct affecting the left cerebral hemisphere in the region supplied by the middle cerebral artery.

The clinical pattern presented by Wendell G. is the classic outcome of a left-hemisphere stroke that disturbs the circulation of the middle cerebral artery. In most right-handed persons, the left hemisphere is dominant for language. Accordingly, language is particularly vulnerable when damage occurs to this hemisphere. The right-sided body paralysis also is consistent with left cerebral damage. Because one side of the brain controls motor functions on the opposite, or contralateral, side of the body, damage to the left hemisphere often leads to impaired motor functions on the right side of the body.

By August, about 6 months following his stroke, Wendell G. had recovered much of this language. His speech was somewhat slurred and labored but was generally intelligible. He continued to have occasional word-finding problems. The paralysis was largely relieved, but Wendell G. experienced numbness in his extremities on the right side.

Wendell G.'s recovery of language and motor function was greatly encouraging to him and his family. Not all stroke victims are as fortunate. Several weeks after his stroke, Wendell G. began to work with a speech-language therapist. In addition to the therapy sessions, Wendell G. worked on home exercises and drills that the therapist had given him.

Recovery of function following a stroke is poorly understood. Some recovery may be spontaneous, perhaps because swelling and other temporary effects of the stroke diminish. Recovery also may come about because other parts of the brain take over the functions that had been originally served by the damaged tissue. It may even be the case that the intact right hemisphere takes over functions that the damaged left hemisphere can no longer perform. This explanation has been suggested as one means of recovery from aphasia (loss of language resulting from brain damage). Because the language ability of the right hemisphere is not as complete as that in the left, language function may not be thoroughly restored by the increased involvement of the right hemisphere. Continued research into brain function and brain disorders should eventually tell us what the mechanisms of recovery of function are. For the present, ignorance overshadows knowledge. But the tremendous growth of neuroscience research in the last decade augurs well for knowledge gains in the future. Exciting discoveries in neuroscience laboratories around the world have opened new possibilities for the understanding of brain functions. One obstacle in the understanding of language functions of the brain is that humans alone possess language (although nonhuman primates and dolphins arguably are capable of something that is language-like). Scientists therefore have had to rely on the "experiments of nature" (naturally occurring disorders) to discover how the complex circuitry of the brain relates to the complex facility of language.

Aphasia is one type of communication disorder resulting from damage to the nervous system. Another disorder is dysarthria, which is a neurological impairment of speech production. The person with dysarthria may have unimpaired language comprehension and formulation but cannot control the speech production system accurately. Dysarthria may result from causes such as traumatic injury to the nervous system, congenital brain damage, neurological disorders such as Parkinson's disease, or stroke.

Most dysarthria speech is slow and labored. Although different dysarthria speakers may sound rather alike to the layman, the expert clinician can recognize different types of dysarthria and can sometimes guess the type of neurological damage from the speech abnormalities. The following brief descriptions of dysarthric individuals give you some idea of the variety of these disorders.

J.P. is a 35 year old man with cerebral palsy of the athetoid type. Muscular contractions called spasms occasionally bring speech to a virtual halt. J.P.'s articulators, especially the tongue, undergo a constant slow, writhing movement. His speech is slow and difficult and frequently nasal. The nasality apparently results from abrupt inappropriate openings of the velopharynx during speech.

M.T. is a 22 year old woman who suffered diffuse brain damage in a motorcycle accident. Her speech is weak, often nearly inaudible, and has a slow, ineffective articulation. She is incapable of sustaining speech of normal loudness.

B.L., 32 years old, has been diagnosed as having a degenerative disease of the cerebellum. His speech has a slow, singsong rhythm, and his articulation is frequently inaccurate and groping. At times his speech sounds as though he is inebriated. The pitch and loudness change abruptly, and speech sounds are both distorted and lengthened.

K.E. is a 57 year old man with a 16 year history of Parkinson's disease. This speech pattern is a striking exception to the general rule that dysarthric speech is slow. In fact, K.E. often sounds as if he speaks too fast, producing words in short rushes of speech characterized by monotone and monoloudness. The individual speech sounds are indistinct and seem to blur together. His loudness tends to trail off the end of sentences.

C.M. is another person with Parkinson's disease. This 62 year old woman has a slow rate of speech with frequent misarticulations, especially for obstruents. In addition to monotone and monoloudness, her voice has an unpleasant, harsh quality. However, under certain highly emotional circumstances, her speech articulation improves markedly, so much so as to sound normal temporarily. Such emotional facilitation of speech production is a little understood phenomenon, but it has been reported to occur in a number of dysarthric individuals.

CHAPTER SIXTEEN
Self-Study
Output Processing

Review Glossary

Linguistic speech planning: The grammatical and semantic operations by which an idea is automatically organized for spoken expression

   Propositional speech: Speech that expresses thinking

   Left hemisphere: The hemisphere that mediates language

     Wernicke's area: The language planning area in the planum temporale of the left temporal lobe

     Broca's area: The motor speech planning area in the lower frontal lobe of the dominant hemisphere

     Supplementary motor cortex: The area in the upper left frontal lobe that facilitates propositional speech

     Supramarginal gyrus: The area behind the postcentral gyrus and above the fissure of Sylvius that may assist in speech-sound formulation

   Working memory: The memory available for holding linguistic elements in mind while the necessary linguistic-motor processes operate in the production of a statement

Emotional expression

   Paralinguistic elements: Prosodic elements of pitch, loudness, and duration by which emotion is expressed

   Limbic system: The primitive cerebral system that mediates emotional expression

   Right (non-dominant) hemisphere: The hemisphere that organizes paralinguistic expressions of attitude and emotion

Motor-speech patterning: The patterning of neuromuscular signals that produce speech movements and adjustments

   Coarticulation: The overlapping of motor-speech commands for successive sounds that permits simultaneous, hence rapid, processing

   Automatic speech: Expressions produced without thought

   Automatic movement: Movements mediated by spinal cord and brainstem reflexes, and prearranged cortical control loops between sensory and motor cortex that do not require working memory

     Reflex: Unlearned automatic behavior

     Rooting reflex: Turning of an infant's head in the direction of an object that touches the cheek

     Sucking reflex: Sucking response to anything touching an infant's lips

     Swallowing reflex: Swallowing in response to food or liquid in the back of an infant's mouth

   Volitional movement: Movements prepared to meet a particular purpose that require use of working memory

     Plan schema: A mental plan that specifies goals and subgoals for achieving an objective

      Framing: Selection of participants and assignments of roles to these participants in a plan schema

     Motor schema: A mental image of a goal to be achieved by a movement

Stages of speech processing: Subsystems of neural networks that expand in stages from a diffuse idea in the limbic stage, to linguistic formulation in the language-planning network stage, to motor speech in the motor implementation stage

Motor mechanisms: The brain and spinal mechanisms by which movements are controlled

   Reticular formation: A brainstem integrative mechanism that coordinates input and output traffic, facilitating and inhibiting motor responses to fit the problem at hand

   Neural rhythms: Patterns of neural firing which, for speech, are about 7 per second

   Pyramidal motor system: The dominant motor system that directly connects the cortex to the neurons supplying the muscles to be used for discrete control of skilled movement

   Extrapyramidal motor system: The indirect motor system that connects cortical and subcortical motor mechanisms for reflexive adjustments

     Basal ganglia: The major brainstem motor center thought to generate motor programs

     Cerebellum: The self-regulation mechanism that compares intended movement targets with proprioceptive feedback to facilitate coordinated movement

     Thalamus: The major brainstem mechanism for integrating emotional and propositional components of speech

Lower motor neuron: The final common pathway over which pyramidal and extrapyramidal signals reach muscles over alpha neurons

Muscle tone: The tuning of resistance between agonistic and antagonistic muscles by gamma neurons that determines the state of background relaxation or tension

Self-Study Test of Terminology

Self-Study Instructions: These questions can be used to help you assess how much you have retained from studying the Review Glossary. Answers are given in Appendix E.

(1) _____ The hemisphere that mediates language

(2) _____ The area in the upper left frontal lobe that facilitates propositional speech

(3) _____ The grammatical and semantic operations by which an idea is automatically organized for spoken expression

(4) _____ The patterning of neuromuscular signals that produce speech movements and adjustments

(5) _____ Movements mediated by spinal cord and brainstem reflexes, and prearranged cortical control loops between sensory and motor cortex that do not require working memory

(6) _____ The tuning of resistance between agonistic and antagonistic muscles by gamma neurons that determines the state of background relaxation or tension

(7) _____ The short-term memory available for holding linguistic elements in mind while the necessary linguistic-motor processes operate in the production of a statement

(8) _____ Speech that expresses thinking

(9) _____ The self-regulation mechanism that compares intended movement targets with proprioceptive feedback to facilitate coordinated movement

(10) _____ Movements prepared to meet a particular purpose that require use of working memory

(11) _____ The primitive cerebral system that mediates emotional expression

(12) _____ Subsystems of neural networks that expand in stages from a diffuse idea in the limbic stage, to linguistic formulation in the language-planning network stage, to motor speech in the motor-implementation stage

(13) _____ The major brainstem mechanism for integrating emotional and propositional components of speech

(14) _____ The hemisphere that organizes paralinguistic expressions of attitude and emotion

(15) _____ The final common pathway over which pyramidal and extrapyramidal signals reach muscles over alpha neurons

(16) _____ The motor speech planning area in the lower frontal lobe of the dominant hemisphere

(17) _____ Expressions produced without thought

(18) _____ A mental image of a goal to be achieved by a movement

(19) _____ The area behind the postcentral gyrus and above the fissure of Sylvius that may assist in speech-sound formulation

(20) _____ Patterns of neural firing which, for speech, are about 7 per second

(21) _____ The indirect motor system that connects cortical and subcortical motor mechanisms for reflexive adjustments

(22) _____ The language planning area in the planum temporale of the left temporal lobe

(23) _____ The brain and spinal mechanisms by which movements are controlled

(24) _____ The overlapping of motor-speech commands for successive sounds that permits simultaneous, hence rapid, processing

(25) _____ The dominant motor system that directly connects the cortex to the neurons supplying the muscles to be used for discrete control of skilled movement

(26) _____ A brainstem integrative mechanism that coordinates input and output traffic, facilitating and inhibiting motor responses to fit the problem at hand

(27) _____ Unlearned automatic behavior

(28) _____ A mental plan that specifies goals and subgoals for achieving an objective

(29) _____ Sucking response to anything touching an infant's lips

Self-Study Test of Understanding

Self-Study Instructions: This test can be used to help you assess how well you understand the content of this chapter. Terms to be filled in are from the Review Glossary. Answers are given in Appendix E.

To speak, an idea is selected in the association areas of the brain and is held in (A) _____ while linguistic and motor processing for speech is performed. By virtue of (B) _____, high-speed speech can be produced by processing successive phonemes simultaneously.

An utterance expresses emotion as well as thought. Emotion is mediated by the (C) _____ and the right hemisphere. It is expressed through the (D) _____ elements of pitch, loudness, and duration. Unlike primitive forms, such as laughing and crying, speech relies heavily on a (E) _____ speech system overlaid on a primitive vocal regulatory system.

Motor-speech patterning is normally (F) _____, which means it is produced without having to rely on working memory for semantic, grammatical, or phonologic planning. We literally do not know how we are going to express an idea, when speaking normally, until we have said it. This requires use of (G) _____, which are built on spinal cord and brainstem reflexes, and on prearranged (H) _____ between sensory and motor cortex. Presumably, once thoroughly learned, speech requires only specialized areas rather than large areas of cortical space. Thus, an idea once formulated linguistically in (I) _____, in the planum temporale of the dominant (J) _____, is then expanded through the speech network, mainly by way of the (K) _____. The feedback by which well-learned precise speech movements are directed is provided mainly by the (L) _____.

If a new speech skill is being learned, (M) _____ will be involved, which will require use of a motor schema and working memory. Conversion of an idea into speech begins in the (N) _____ as a diffuse feeling of what is to be said. It is then processed in stages through linguistic planning and emotional expression networks until it is ready for motor implementation. This involves processing these plans through the (O) _____ (the major motor center at the top of the brainstem), the (P) _____ (the mechanism for automatic coordination of cortical plans with proprioceptive and auditory feedback for guidance of voluntarily controlled movement), and the (Q) _____ (the key center in the brainstem for integrating propositional and emotional components of speech) before they are relayed back to the precentral motor cortex networks in both hemispheres.

The statement to be made is now ready for the final stage of processing through the motor system networks that deliver neural signals to the speech muscles to produce intended movements. This will involve the (R) _____ (the direct motor system from the cortex that provides discrete control of skilled movement), the (S) _____ (the indirect motor system connecting with motor stations throughout the nervous system to provide a background of reflexive adjustments necessary for purposeful movement), and the reticular formation that directs neural traffic, focusing and refining motor responses to fit the needs of the speech to be uttered. These motor networks inhibit or facilitate firing of (T) _____, which are the final common pathways from the brainstem or spinal cord to the musculature.

APPENDIX
A
Selected
Readings

SPEECH AND HEARING ANATOMY

Bateman, H., and Mason, R.: *Applied Anatomy and Physiology of the Speech and Hearing Mechanism.* Springfield, Illinois, Charles C Thomas, 1984. With emphasis on anatomy, a well-written, well-illustrated comprehensive text with clinical applications.

Dickson, D., and Maue-Dickson, W.: *Anatomical and Physiological Bases of Speech.* Boston, Little, Brown and Co., 1982. A well-illustrated presentation of speech anatomy.

Kahane, J., and Folkins, J.: *Atlas of Speech and Hearing Anatomy.* Columbus, Ohio, Charles E. Merrill, 1984. This is a superbly illustrated definitive reference on speech and hearing anatomy.

Kapit, W., and Elson, L.: *The Anatomy Coloring Book.* New York, Harper & Row, 1977. For the beginning student interested in the entire scope of human anatomy, this coloring book offers easy access.

Palmer, J.: *Anatomy for Speech and Hearing.* New York, Harper & Row, 1984. This text has excellent drawings of the speech mechanism.

Schneiderman, C.: *Basic Anatomy and Physiology in Speech and Hearing.* San Diego, College-Hill Press, 1984. Stronger in anatomy than physiology, this text has fine drawings and clinical applications.

Zemlin, W.: *Speech and Hearing Science: Anatomy and Physiology.* Englewood Cliffs, New Jersey, Prentice-Hall, 1981. A virtual encyclopedia of anatomical detail, this is the classic text for speech anatomy.

NEUROANATOMY

Calvin, W. H., and Ojemann, G. Q.: *Inside the Brain.* New York, New American Library, 1980. This account of the structure and function of the brain is a welcome contrast to the typically dry book on neuroscience. The book is informative on a variety of matters relating to the human brain, but it carries the reader along easily and naturally. Case studies and dialogue spice the book. Highly recommended for the beginning student.

DeMyer, W.: *Technique of the Neurologic Examination,* 2nd Ed. New York, McGraw-Hill, 1974. This programmed text is intended for medical students but much of its is approachable even for those without substantial background in neuroanatomy and neurophysiology. It reviews anatomy and physiology, teaches how to conduct a neurologic examination, and describes laboratory tests used by the specialist.

Lemire, R. J., Loeser, J. D., Leech, R. W., and Alvord, E. C., Jr.: *Normal and Abnormal Development of the Human Nervous System.* Hagerstown, Maryland, Harper and Row, 1975. This book for the specialist describes the embryonic and fetal development of the normal and abnormal nervous system. Not recommended for the beginner as general reading, but it contains excellent graphs and photographs.

Minckler, J.: *Introduction to Neuroscience.* St. Louis, C. V., Mosby, 1972. Although this book is somewhat dated, the discussions of neuroanatomy are clearly and effectively presented. It is recommended for the reader who wants a broad coverage of neuroscience. Included are seven chapters on gross anatomy, four on microanatomy, four on functional neuroscience, seven on neural pathways, and two on integrated functions.

Netter, F.: *The Ciba Collection of Medical Illustrations. Volume I, Nervous System; Part I, Anatomy and Physiology.* West Caldwell, New Jersey, Ciba, 1983.

Restak, R. M.: *The Brain: The Last Frontier.* New York, Warner Books, 1979. This book, written for a popular audience, covers a large territory and does so in a generally engaging manner. It conveys much of the excitement of the neurosciences. Any book as expansive as this one runs a risk of inaccuracies in certain areas, and this one commits some unfortunate errors in its discussions of speech. For example, the *pharynx* is given as another name for the *voice box,* and the author writes that vowels, in contrast to consonants, "are not formed by the lips, but depend on the rate of movement of the vocal cords" (p. 410). The reader is warned to be skeptical of any information given on speech.

Smith, A.: *The Mind.* New York, Viking Press, 1984. This capable author, who wrote a best-selling book, *The Body,* describes many fascinating features of the human brain in this book intended for a general audience. The topics range from evolution to anatomy to hemispheric dominance to abnormal ability to the damaged brain. The author relies solely on verbal descriptions to present his material; not a single illustration is included.

BRAIN FUNCTION*

Field, J., Magoun, H., and Hall, V. (Eds.): *Handbook of Physiology, Section I: Neurophysiology, Vol. II.* Washington, D.C., American Physiological Society, 1960. Not specifically concerned with speech, this text contains background information on neural mechanisms basic to speech processing.

Kent, R.: Brain mechanisms of speech and language with special reference to emotional interactions. *In* R. Naremore (Ed.), *Language Science: Recent Advances.* San Diego, College-Hill Press, 1984. A concise state-of-the-art review of the neurology of speech processing.

Millikan, C., and Darley, F.: *Brain Mechanisms Underlying Speech and Language.* New York, Grune & Stratton, 1967. This book is addressed specifically to neural mechanisms of speech.

Ornstein, R., and Thompson, R. *The Amazing Brain.* Boston, Houghton Mifflin, 1984. Written for laymen by two distinguished professors of biology, and illustrated by David Macaulay, this is a remarkably lucid and fascinating account of the origin and functions of the brain.

---

*See also Smith, 1984, and Restak, 1979, under *Neuroanatomy.*

Penfield, W., and Roberts, L.: *Speech and Brain Mechanisms.* Princeton, New Jersey, Princeton University Press, 1959. A readable account of the pioneering electrical stimulation experiments on human brains.

Quarton, G., Melnechuk, T., and Schmitt, F. (Eds.): *The Neuro-Sciences.* New York, Rockefeller University Press, 1967. Information about basic neural processes.

Scientific American, September, 1979, Volume 241. This entire issue is devoted to readable reports on a wide range of brain functions from chemistry of the neuron to neural organization of speech.

SPEECH AND HEARING SCIENCE

Borden, G., and Harris, K.: *Speech Science Primer.* Baltimore, Williams & Wilkins Co., 1980. A readable introduction to the acoustics, physiology, and perception of speech, especially useful for beginning students seeking more information on acoustics and speech perception.

Daniloff, R., Schuckers, G., and Feth, L.: *The Physiology of Speech and Hearing.* Englewood Cliffs, New Jersey, Prentice-Hall, 1980. A particularly useful analysis of the acoustics of phonation and articulation.

Denes, P., and Pinson, E.: *The Speech Chain.* New York, Doubleday, 1973. Now back in print, it remains the classic introductory text to the physics and biology of speech, mainly because it successfully combines scholarship with readability.

Eagle, E. (Ed.): *The Nervous System, Volume 3: Human Communication and Its Disorders.* New York, Raven Press, 1975. This volume is strongest in its extensive coverage of state-of-the-art work in hearing.

Fry, D. B.: *The Physics of Speech.* London, Cambridge University Press, 1979. General acoustics and speech acoustics are discussed in a fairly detailed, yet mostly nonmathematical, fashion. This is a good text for the reader who wants a general introduction to the acoustic aspects of speech. Especially recommended are Chapters 9 (Acoustic analysis: The sound spectrograph), 10 (Acoustic features of English sounds), and 11 (Acoustic cues for the recognition of speech sounds).

Hudspeth, A.: The hair cells of the inner ear. *Scientific American, 248,* 54–64, 1983. A readable account of the recently discovered mechanism by which the neural signal is generated in the inner ear.

Minifie, R., Hixon, T., and Williams, F.: *Normal Aspects of Speech, Language and Hearing.* Englewood Cliffs, New Jersey, Prentice-Hall, 1973. This first edition established it as the classic introduction to speech physiology. It is now in its second edition.

Strong, W., and Plitnik, G.: *Music, Speech, High-Fidelity.* Soundprint, Liberty Press, 1983. Thorough coverage of basic issues related to practical acoustics. Very good chapters on fundamental acoustics, listening environments, speech acoustics, and musical acoustics.

LANGUAGE PRODUCTION AND COMPREHENSION

Fodor, J. A.: *The Modularity of Mind.* Cambridge, Massachusetts, MIT Press, 1983. For the more intrepid reader who likes philosophical argument and is not hindered by terms such as *mutatis mutandis, in rerum naturae,* and *ceteris paribus.* The author presents a theory of mind based on information from the various fields of cognitive science. Whether his theory is correct or not, his arguments are mind challengers. Speech and language figure centrally in many discussions.

Fry, D.: *Homo Loquens.* Cambridge, England, Cambridge University Press, 1977. A scholarly, yet introductory, discussion of humans as the "talking animal" of the title. The book briskly ranges over the topics of language, articulation, acoustics, neural control, development, and disorders.

Liberman, A.: On finding that speech is special. *American Psychologist, 37;* 148–167, 1982. The current version of the motor theory of speech perception that speech is perceived in a phonetic mode, not an auditory, mode.

Matthei, E., and Roeper, T.: *Understanding and Producing Speech.* Suffolk, England, Bungay, 1983. This introductory text opens to the reader the wonder and challenge of psycholinguistics. In nine chapters the authors offer insightful perspectives on the basic question: How is it that human beings can understand and produce a potentially infinite number of novel utterances?

Williams, F.: *Language and Speech: Introductory Perspectives.* Englewood Cliffs, New Jersey, Prentice-Hall, 1972. The perspectives are acoustic, phonological, linguistic, psychological, and sociological. The author give a readable broad overview of speech and language behavior.

APPENDIX

B

Anatomical Terms

ROOTS, PREFIXES, AND SUFFIXES

a- without
ab- away from
ad- toward
antero- in front
anti- against
anthrop- man
arch- first
brachy- abnormally short
capit- head (Latin)
cardio- heart
cephalo- head (Greek)
contra- against
corp- body
dent- tooth
derm- skin
di- twice
dic- say
dis- apart
dys- bad, ill
-ectomy surgical removal
extero- outside
gen- origin
glosso- tongue
-gnosis knowing
-gram drawn or written
graph- writing
hemi- half
hetero- different
histo- tissue
homo- same, similar
hydro- water
hyper- excess
hypo- less; under
idio- distinct, personal
infra- below, lower
inter- between
intra- within
intro- directed inward
-ism state; condition
iso- equal
-itis inflammation
juxta- close to
kine- movement

labio- lip
lalia- speech
loc- place
log- reasoning
macro- large
mal- defect
man- hand
mega- powerful
meningo- membrane
meso- in the middle
meta- change
micro- small
mis- wrong
morph- a specific form
myo- muscle
neo- new
-nomy system of laws
non- absence
-oid resembling
oma- tumor
omni- all (Latin)
onto- existing
-onym name
ortho- straight, correct
-osis diseased condition
oto- ear
pan- all
para- subsidiary
path- disease
ped- foot
pedo- child
phon- sound (Greek)
poly- many
post- after
pre- before
proto- original
pseudo- false
rect- straight
retro- backward, situated behind
rhino- nose
sect- cut, divided
son- sound (Latin)
sphygmo- pulse

sub- beneath
super- of high order
supra- above in position
syn- together
tachy- swift
tele- distant, end
thyro- shield
-tomy a cutting
trachy- rough
trans- across
zo- animal

GENERAL TERMINOLOGY

abduction to draw from the original position (i.e., when the vocal folds move apart)

ablation excision of a structure from the body by mechanical means, as by surgery

adduction to draw toward the main axis (i.e., when the vocal cords approximate)

afferent bringing to or leading toward a central organ

agonist an actively contracting muscle considered in relation to its opposing muscle

amniocentesis examination of amniotic fluid via fluid withdrawn from amniotic cavity; a tool in assessing potential disease in fetus

anatomic position standing erect with arms at the sides and palms of the hands turned forward

antagonist muscle which acts in opposition to another (i.e., the thyroarytenoid is antagonistic to the cricothyroid)

anterior placed before, or situated more toward the front

aperta a type of nasality caused by the nasal orifice being in a patent position

aponeurosis a whitish fibrous membrane that is an expanded tendon (i.e., the central tendon is an aponeurosis of the diaphragm)

articulation connection between bones

atrophy to waste away from disuse or defective nutrition

axial pertaining to or forming an axis, or a central or principal structure about which something turns or is arranged

belly fleshy part of a muscle

bifurcate to divide or fork into two branches (i.e., the trachea bifurcates into two branches)

brachium (plural, brachia) an armlike part or process

buccal pertaining to the sides of the mouth, the cheek, or the mouth as a whole (i.e., the tongue is located in the buccal cavity)

cartilage substance from which some bone ossifies; gristle

caudal located toward the tail

cephalic located toward the head

clausa used in reference to the denasal speech caused by anterior nasal occlusion which creates a cul-de-sac type of resonator

clavicular pertaining to a bone of the pectoral arch; either of two slender bones articulating with the sternum and a scapula and forming the anterior part of a shoulder

clonus a rapid succession of flexion and extension of a group of muscles, usually signifying an affection of the brain or spinal cord

condyle polished articular surface, usually rounded

conceptus products of conception

contralateral fibers that cross over at a decussation in the brain

coronal taken parallel to the long axis of the body in the lateral plane

costal pertaining to the ribs or the side of the body

crest ridge or border

crown-rump length the "sitting" height measurement, used to determine length of embryo

crown-heel length the "standing" height, used to measure length of fetus (after seven weeks)

cul de sac a sac-like cavity or tube open only at one end

decussation crossing over or intersection

deep farther from the surface (in a solid form)

depressor that which lowers

dextral on the right-hand side

diaphysis the shaft of a long cylindrical bone

distal situated away from the point of origin or attachment

dorsal pertaining to, or situated on the back, as of an organ

dystrophy if innervation is insufficient muscles will weaken from disuse or from nutritional deprivation

efferent carrying impulses away from

eminence a low projection or prominence

erector that which draws upward

extension straightening

extensor muscles that extend structures

external outside (refers to wall of cavity or hollow form)

extrinsic a muscle that originates outside of a structure such as the tongue but inserts into it as well

facet small articular area, often a pit

fasciculus a small bundle of fibers within a nerve or central nervous system

fertilization age the reference point of 13 ± 1 days, deducted from the menstrual age, to obtain the actual age of an embryo

fissure a deep depression or natural division or groove between adjoining parts of like substance

flaccid due to inadequate innervation, structures that have become limp and unfirm, usually muscles

flexion bending or angulation

flexors muscles that bend structures at a joint

foramen (plural, foramina) openings in the skull through which cranial nerves or the spinal cord emerge

fossa the depression in the skull from which the temporal muscle originates

frontal vertical; at right angles to sagittal; divides body into anterior and posterior parts

ganglion a collection of cell bodies in the peripheral nervous system

genes the biological unit of heredity, located on a chromosome and transmitted from one generation to another

glossal pertaining to the tongue

glottis the opening at the upper part of the larynx, between the vocal folds

gyrus the outermost portion of a cerebral convolution

head enlarged round end of a long bone; knob

inferior lower in place or position

insertion   relatively movable part of muscle attachment

intrinisic   belonging to or lying within a given part

internuncial   neurons that interconnect one side of the CNS with the other at any level

ipsilateral   fibers that connect on the same side of the brain

joint   connection between bones

lateral   pertaining to the side

lemniscus   small bundle of sensory nerve fibers that ascend through the brainstem

levators   muscles that elevate structures

ligament   fibrous tissue binding bones together, or holding tendons and muscles in place

medial   nearer to midline (or center plane)

median   noting or pertaining to a plane dividing something into two equal halves

midline   divides body into a right and left side

mitosis   the division of a cell

motor   efferent neurons that go from the CNS to muscles

neck   constriction of a bone near its head

oblique   slanting

occlude   to shut or close against each other, as the opposing teeth of the upper and lower jaws

ontogeny   the development of an individual organism

organ   two or more tissues grouped together to perform a highly specialized function

orifice   a mouthlike opening or hole

origin   relatively fixed part of a muscle attachment

patent   open in various degrees to the passage of the breath stream

peduncle   a stalk-like structure composed of white matter connecting various regions of the brain

peripheral   toward the periphery or outer area

phylogeny   the development or evolution of a kind or type of animal

placenta   an organ attached to the uterus to join the mother and offspring during the embryological and fetal periods

posterior   situated behind

process   the bony projection to which a muscle attaches

pronation   the act that turns structures downward

protuberance   a swelling (can be felt under fingers)

proximal   toward the center

ramus   a branch of a nerve in the peripheral nervous system

raphe   a seam-like union between two parts or halves of an organ

rostral   located toward the nose

sagittal   taken parallel to the long axis of the body in the anteroposterior plane

sensorium   the supposed seat of sensation in the brain, usually taken as the cortex or gray matter

sensory   a structure that conveys an impulse that results or tends to result in sensation, as a nerve

shaft   body of a long bone

sheath   protective covering

sinistral   pertaining to the left side of the body

somatic   body structures that relate an organism to its external environment

sphincter   a circular band of voluntary or involuntary muscle which encircles an orifice of the body or one of its hollow organs

spine   pointed projection, or sharp ridge

sulcus   a shallow fissure between two convolutions of the brain

superficial   nearer to surface (refers to solid form)

superior   above

supination   the act which turns structures upward

symphysis   union of right and left sides in the midline

synapse   the region of contact between processes of two or more nerve cells, across which an impulse passes

tendon   fibrous tissue securing a muscle to its attachment

tensor   that which draws tight

thoracic   often referred to as lower chest breathing due to the primary expansion in the chest

tonic   if muscles receive too much innervation they will have extreme muscle tonus or will become hypertonic

tonus   normal state of slight continuous tension in muscle tissue which facilitates its response to stimulation

transverse   anatomical sections which are taken crosswise

tubercle   small bump (can be felt under fingers)

tuberosity   large and conspicuous bump

ventral   toward the belly

visceral   body structures that are involved in the internal environment

APPENDIX

C

Fetal Development

GENERAL FETAL DEVELOPMENT

GESTATIONAL AGE (DAYS)

10

20   Beginnings of foregut and hindgut; heart begins to pump

30   Arm and leg buds appear; stomach takes form; nostrils formed; eyes appear as dark spots

40   Eyelids are formed; cornea is detectable; nose tip appears; head nearly erect; stomach achieves final form

60   Head about half the length of the body; swallowing begins; sex gland differentiation

80   External sex organs visible

END OF FIRST TRIMESTER

100   Fingernails apparent; gastric and intestinal glands form

120   Sucking reflex evident

140   Fingerprints sufficiently developed to permit identification; fetal hiccoughs may occur

160   Lanugo hair covers much of body

180   Eyelids can open and close

END OF SECOND TRIMESTER

200   Retinal layers of eye completed; grasp reflex and Moro reflex are present

240   Strong sucking and Moro reflexes present

270   BIRTH

DEVELOPMENT OF FETAL BRAIN

GESTATIONAL AGE (DAYS)

10   Faint line forms to mark location of spinal cord; neural tube is formed

20   Cerebellar plate formed; cephalic flexure (angle) appears; internal carotid arteries begin to take form from aortic arch

30   Thalamus separates from hypothalamus; frontal and parietal lobe areas are evident; spinal nerve is formed by uniting of motor and sensory root fibers

40   Internal capsule appears; pia mater is formed; putamen is identifiable; dura mater begins formation

60   Brain is about $\frac{1}{2}$ inch long from front to back; cortical gray matter is evident

80

END OF FIRST TRIMESTER (brain weighs about 10 grams)

100   Sylvian fissure appears; myelination of spinal tracts has begun

120   Major spinal nuclei are defined

140   Myelin observed in cranial nerves V and VII; central and parieto-occipital fissures appear

160   Brain is about 2 inches long from front to back; myelin observed in cranial nerves VIII and XII

180

END OF SECOND TRIMESTER

200   Brain weighs 200 grams; myelin observed in cerebellar hemispheres

240   Myelin observed in afferent (sensory) tracts to thalamus and cerebral cortex; all primary sulci are formed

270   BIRTH

DEVELOPMENT OF FETAL AIRWAY

GESTATIONAL AGE (DAYS)

10

20 Beginning of respiratory organs identifiable; primary bronchi take form

30 Oral cavity and mandibular arch are formed; tongue is outlined; location of larynx is visible; trachea detaches from esophagus

40 Cricoid and arytenoid cartilage begin to take form; palate shelves (folds of tissue on each side of head) are present and are beginning to fuse (eventual joining at midline); ossification of mandible begins

60 Fusion of lips is complete (tissues join at midline); lips separate from jaw; shelves of palate are nearly fused

80 Palatal fusion is complete, except perhaps for uvula; thus, oral and nasal passages are distinctly formed

END OF FIRST TRIMESTER

100 Nostrils open; continuous passage exists from nose to lungs

120 Hard tissue formation begins for incisors; hard and soft palates are well differentiated

140

160

180

END OF SECOND TRIMESTER

200 Lip epithelium is well developed; larynx has dropped to level of 6th vertebra, its neonatal position

240

270 BIRTH

DEVELOPMENT OF FETAL AUDITORY SYSTEM

GESTATIONAL AGE (DAYS)

10

20 Auditory ganglion formed, otic plate appears

30 Spiral ganglion begins to differentiate; external ears take shape

40 Spiral ganglion is C-shaped; spiral ganglion has $1\frac{1}{4}$ turns

60

80

END OF FIRST TRIMESTER

100 Ossification of ossicles begins

120

140 Ear is essentially structurally complete

160 Myelin observed in cranial nerve VIII

180

END OF SECOND TRIMESTER

200

240

270 BIRTH

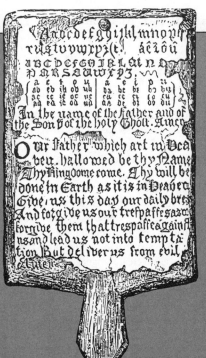

APPENDIX
D
Audiovisual Materials

AUDIOVISUAL MATERIALS — LANGUAGE AND ITS DEVELOPMENT

Films

Sounds of Language (29 min; Bloomington, Indiana University, 1957)
Explains how linguists analyze and classify significant sounds of language. Discusses phonetics and phonemics, the science of sounds; shows and demonstrates the organs of speech.

Language Development (20 min; Del Mar, California, CRM-McGraw Films, 1973)
Covers the infant's early formation of sounds and shows how they are the forerunners of word formation. Indicates that all children experience similar stages in word development. Demonstrates that overgeneralization in language use is common to all language communities, including the sign language of the deaf. Presents the theory that the human mind is preprogrammed to process the information needed to create language. (Developmental Psychology Today Series)

Language Development (22 min; New York, Harper and Row, 1972)
Views the processes of language acquisition in the first four years, examining development of phonemes, syntax, and semantics. Looks at the process by which language is acquired and how the process may be influenced. (Development of the Child Series)

Early Words (22 min; New York, Educational Services Department, John Wiley and Sons, 1972)
Follows the language development of a 22 month old boy whose speech consists largely of one-word utterances. The richness and variety of these utterances reflect a step-by-step development over a 2 year period in which an inherent semantic function in grammar helps the child to decode adult language and achieve mastery of a linguistic system. Produced at the Center for Cognitive Studies, Harvard University.

AUDIOVISUAL MATERIALS — THE RESPIRATORY SYSTEM

Film

Human Body: Respiratory System (14 min: Chicago, Coronet, 1961)
Locates and describes the organs of the respiratory system. Shows in animation and live demonstrations the mechanics of ventilation and the physics of diffusion between alveoli and capillaries. Demonstrates the effect on the respiratory system of varying needs for oxygen and eliminating carbon dioxide.

AUDIOVISUAL MATERIALS — THE LARYNX

Films

Voice Production: The Vibrating Larynx (42 min; Stichting Film en Wetenschap, 1964; also available from the School of Cinema, University of Southern California)
Shows the anatomy, physiology, and functional behavior of the normal human larynx. Observes the vibrations in slow motion. Explains the behavior during chest and falsetto voice, as well as intermediate adjustments. Produced in the physiological laboratory of Groningen University in the Netherlands.

Communication by Voice and Action (14 min; Lawrence, Kansas, Centron, 1979)
Examines how nonverbal aspects of communication — tone of voice, volume, tempo, intonation, facial expressions, gestures, and posture — contribute to the meaning of the message. Analyzes the demonstration and makes the viewer aware of what role nonverbal factors play in communication. (Art of Communication Series)

Tapes

The Human Voice . . . and the Computer (IEEE Soundings Tape 70-S-04). The Institute of Electrical and Electronics Engineers, Inc., 345 E. 47th Street, New York, NY 10017.

Prosodic Features in Speech (G. R. Plitnik, Rt. 1, Box 100A, Mt. Savage, MD 21545; Descriptive Acoustics Demonstration Tape)

AUDIOVISUAL MATERIALS — SPEECH PRODUCTION (SPEECH PHYSIOLOGY)

Films

Speech Chain (20 min; Bell Telephone Laboratories, Murray Hill, New Jersey, 1963)
Traces the so-called speech chain from the conception of an idea in a listener's brain to its reception in a listener's brain. Includes a description of the vocal folds, the articulators and their methods of producing sounds, the outer ear, the inner ear, the action of the nerves as they transmit impulses to the brain of a listener, and research on speech and hearing.

Normal Speech Articulation (25 min; University of Iowa, Iowa City, 1965)
Demonstrates some of the characteristics of speech sounds articulation in normal speakers. Discusses and demonstrates the variation in articulatory characteristics of sounds in connected speech and the effect of such factors as phonetic context, durational aspects of speech, and coarticulation of speech sounds. (Speech, Physiological Aspects Series)

Velopharyngeal Function in Normal Speakers (12 min; University of Iowa, Iowa City, 1967)

Includes animated drawings and x-ray sound motion pictures to study the operation of the velopharyngeal mechanism in normal speech. Identifies anatomical structures and emphasizes the importance of correct velopharyngeal function in normal speech. (Speech, Physiological Aspects Series)

Vocalization and Speech in Chimpanzees (11 min; College Park, Pennsylvania State University, 1950)

Presents the work of Keith J. Hayes and Cathy Hayes, Yerkes Laboratory of Primate Biology, Orange Park, Florida, with speech training of chimpanzees. Shows animals doing normal vocalizing and, after many months of training, speaking on command three words, "mama," "papa," and "cup."

Tapes

The Human Voice . . . and the Computer (IEEE Soundings Tape 70-S-04). The Institute of Electrical and Electronics Engineers, Inc., 345 E. 47th Street, New York, NY 10017.

Synthetic Vowels from Vocal Model (G. R. Plitnik, Rt. 1, Box 100A, Mt. Savage, MD 21545; Descriptive Acoustics Demonstration Tape)

AUDIOVISUAL MATERIALS — ACOUSTICS

Film

Sound Waves and Their Sources (10 min; Chicago, Encyclopaedia Britannica Films, 1950)

Includes a high-speed camera and oscilloscope to describe several types of sound sources, including the vocal organs. Visualizes the transmission of sound waves through the air and explains such characteristics as frequency, amplitude, wave lengths, fundamentals, and harmonics.

Tapes

Interference; Beats; Standing Sound Waves; Standing Waves in a String; Standing Waves in Air Columns; Resonance Curves; Fourier Analysis; Fourier Synthesis (Richard E. Berg, Physics Department, University of Maryland, College Park, MD 20742; set of video tapes)

AUDIOVISUAL MATERIALS — THE AUDITORY SYSTEM

Film

Ears and Hearing (22 min; Chicago, Encyclopaedia Britannica Films, 1969)

Uses animation, graphics, models, and live photography to explain how the ear transforms sound waves into nerve impulses for the brain to interpret as sound. Demonstrates vibration variations and the effects of stimuli. Follows an ear operation correcting a case of conduction hearing loss.

Tapes

Frequency, Amplitude and Tone Quality (Richard E. Berg, Physics Department, University of Maryland, College Park, MD 20742; set of video tapes)

Auditory Illusions and Experiments (Cassette 72232, Edmund Scientific Co., 101 East Gloucester Pike, Barrington, NJ 08007)

Auditory Demonstration Tapes — Harvard University (Laboratory of Psychophysics, Harvard University, Cambridge, MA)

AUDIOVISUAL MATERIALS — THE NERVOUS SYSTEM

Films

Human Body: The Brain (16 min; Chicago, Coronet, 1967)

Employs x-ray photographs, specimens, and animation to visualize the basic functions of the brain, clarify what is known about this organ, and explore some of its mysteries as the central organ of the nervous system and regulator of all voluntary and involuntary actions in the body.

Fundamentals of the Nervous System (16 min; Chicago, Encyclopaedia Britannica Films, 1962)

Uses animation and live-action photography to illustrate the fundamentals of the nervous system. Describes the structure and function of the central, peripheral, and autonomic systems. Shows several rare experiments.

Nervous System of Man (18 min; Bloomington, Indiana University, 1965)

Demonstrates the processes by which the human nervous system controls body movement and functions. Traces the workings of the peripheral nerves and the central and autonomic nervous system through animated digrams. Shows the linkage of all parts of the body to the central nervous system. Discusses the function of the various parts of the brain.

Brain and Behavior (Bloomington, Indiana University-NET, 1963)

Identifies the mechanisms of the brain the control our behavior and demonstrates the way in which the electrical activity in the brain gives us information about human behavior. (Brain and the Nervous System; Focus on Behavior Series)

APPENDIX
E
Self-Study
Answers

CHAPTER 1 and PREFACE

Self-Study Illustrations

(A) Sagittal
(B) Coronal
(C) Transverse
(D) Dorsal, posterior
(E) Medial
(F) Ventral, anterior
(G) Lateral
(H) Caudal, inferior
(I) Cephalic, superior
(J) Nervous system
(K) Respiratory system
(L) Phonatory system
(M) Articulatory system
(N) Auditory system
(a) Nervous system
(b) Output, central processing
(c) Formulation encoder
(d) Lungs
(e) Respiration
(f) Power supply, air compressor
(g) Larynx
(h) Phonation
(i) Sound generation, vibrator
(j) Vocal tract
(k) Articulation
(l) Speech-sound molding, resonator
(m) Ear
(n) Audition
(o) Speech reception detector
(p) Input, central processing
(q) Comprehension decoder

Self-Study Test of Terminology

Preface
(1) Anterior (ventral)
(2) Coronal
(3) Medial
(4) Superior (cephalic)
(5) Transverse
(6) Lateral
(7) Posterior (dorsal)
(8) Sagittal
(9) Inferior (caudal)

Chapter 1
(1) Output processing
(2) Phonatory system
(3) Auditory system for reception of speech
(4) Input processing
(5) Central processing
(6) Central processing
(7) Articulatory system
(8) Audition
(9) Nervous system for speaking
(10) Nervous system for speech comprehension
(11) Respiratory system for speaking
(12) Articulation
(13) Respiration
(14) Phonation

CHAPTER 2

Self-Study Illustrations

(A) Chest wall
(B) Rib cage
(C) Abdominal wall
(D) Viscera
(E) Diaphragm
(F) Mediastinum
(G) Lungs
(H) Pleural membrane, cavity
(I) Diaphragm
(J) Sternocleidomastoid
(K) Scalene
(L) Subclavius
(M) Pectoralis major
(N) Pectoralis minor
(O) Serratus anterior
(P) Serratus posterior superior
(Q) Levatores costarum
(R) External intercostals
(S) Internal intercostals
(T) Transversus thoracis
(U) Subcostals

(V) Serratus posterior inferior
(W) Quadratus lumborum
(X) Rectus abdominis
(Y) External oblique
(Z) Internal oblique

(a) Rectus abdominis
(b) External oblique
(c) Interna oblique
(d) Transversus
(e) Elastic recoil
(f) Untorquing
(g) Gravity

Self-Study Test of Terminology

(1) Rib Cage
(2) Abdominal wall
(3) Rectus abdominis muscle
(4) Internal oblique muscle
(5) Quadratus lumborum muscle
(6) Latissimus dorsi muscle
(7) Internal intercostal muscles
(8) Chest wall
(9) Diaphragm
(10) Abdominal viscera
(11) External oblique muscle
(12) Untorquing of ribs
(13) Transversus muscle
(14) External intercostal muscles
(15) Serratus posterior inferior muscle
(16) Subcostal muscle
(17) Serratus anterior muscle
(18) Pectoralis minor muscle
(19) Sternocleidomastoid muscle
(20) Clavicle
(21) Thorax
(22) Bronchi
(23) Alveolar air sacs
(24) Relaxation pressure
(25) Pulmonary system
(26) Gravity
(27) Pectoralis major muscle
(28) Transversus thoracis muscle
(29) Subclavius muscle
(30) Scalene (anterior, medial, posterior) muscles

(31) Sternum
(32) Lungs
(33) Mediastinum
(34) Scapula
(35) Trachea
(36) Alveolar pressure
(37) Pleural membranes
(38) Elastic recoil
(39) Levatores costarum muscle
(40) Serratus posterior superior muscle
(41) Diaphragmatic aponeurosis

Speech Functions of Respiratory Muscles

(1) Sternocleidomastoid
(2) Scalene
(3) Pectoralis major
(4) Pectoralis minor
(5) Serratus anterior
(6) Levatores costarum
(7) Serratus posterior superior
(8) External intercostals
(9) Diaphragm
(10) Serratus posterior inferior
(11) Quadratus lumborum
(12) Subcostal
(13) Transversus thoracis
(14) Internal intercostals
(15) Rectus abdominis
(16) External oblique
(17) Internal oblique
(18) Transversus

CHAPTER 3

Self-Study Test of Terminology

(1) Overlaid function
(2) Pressure
(3) Alveolar pressure
(4) Volume requirements
(5) Duration requirements
(6) Volume
(7) Expiratory reserve
(8) Forced respiration

(9)   Relaxation pressure
(10) Exhalation (expiration)
(11) Respiration
(12) Subglottal (tracheal) pressure
(13) Pressure requirements
(14) Vital capacity
(15) Frequency requirements
(16) Tidal volume
(17) Residual volume
(18) Inspiratory reserve
(19) Inhalation (inspiration)
(20) Quiet respiration
(21) Resting tidal volume
(22) Active process
(23) Volume solution
(24) Pulsatile solution

(c)   3.5 to 4.0 liters
(d)   Less than
(e)   Shorter than
(f)   Inspiratory capacity or inspiratory reserve volume
(g)   Tidal volume
(h)   3–2
(i)   12 to 20
(j)   Volume
(k)   Inspiratory reserve volume
(l)   Tidal volume
(m)   Expiratory reserve volume
(n)   Residual volume
(o)   Inspiratory reserve volume
(p)   Tidal volume

Self-Study Test of Understanding

(A)   Quiet respiration
(B)   Respiration
(C)   Inhalation, inspiration
(D)   Exhalation, expiration
(E)   Resting tidal volume
(F)   Volume
(G)   Vital capacity
(H)   Overlaid function
(I)   Duration requirements
(J)   Frequency requirements
(K)   Volume requirements
(L)   Forced respiration, inspiration
(M)   Tidal volume
(N)   Inspiratory reserve
(O)   Subglottal pressure
(P)   Pressure
(Q)   Alveolar pressure
(R)   Relaxation pressure
(S)   Pressure requirements
(T)   Expiratory reserve
(U)   Residual volume

Clinical Exercises

(a)   Vital capacity
(b)   3–1

CHAPTER 4

Self-Study Illustrations

(A)   Thyroid
(B)   Cricoid
(C)   Arytenoid
(D)   Muscular process
(E)   Vocal process
(F)   Lateral cricoarytenoid
(G)   External thyroarytenoid
(H)   Adduction with medial compression
(I)   Abduction
(J)   Cricothyroids
(K)   Posterior cricoarytenoid
(L)   Glottis
(M)   Vocal ligament
(N)   Interarytenoids
(O)   Transverse arytenoid
(P)   Oblique arytenoid
(Q)   Internal thyroarytenoid, vocalis
(R)   Adduction for phonation
(S)   Cricoid
(T)   Thyroid
(U)   Thyroepiglottics
(V)   Epiglottis
(W)   Aditus

(X) Aryepiglottics
(Y) Apex (of arytenoid)

Self-Study Test of Terminology

(1) Thyroid
(2) Vocal process
(3) Apex
(4) Laryngeal cartilages
(5) Arytenoid
(6) Extrinsic laryngeal muscles
(7) Interarytenoid muscle
(8) Abduction
(9) Aryepiglottis muscle
(10) Epiglottis
(11) Muscular process
(12) Cricoid
(13) Adduction
(14) Posterior cricoarytenoid muscle
(15) Medial compression
(16) Intrinsic laryngeal muscles
(17) Lamina propria
(18) Cricothyroid muscle
(19) External thyroarytenoid muscle
(20) Thyroepiglottis muscle
(21) Conus elasticus
(22) False vocal folds (ventricular folds)
(23) Internal thyroarytenoid (vocalis) muscle
(24) Lateral cricoarytenoid muscle
(25) Vocal ligament
(26) Thyroarytenoid muscle
(27) Glottal vibration
(28) Aditus (laryngeal collar, laryngeal cavity, supraglottal cavity)
(29) Glottis
(30) Laryngeal ventricle (ventricle of Morgagni)

Vocal Functions of Phonatory Muscles

(1) Posterior cricoarytenoids
(2) Interarytenoids
(3) Oblique arytenoids
(4) Transverse arytenoid
(5) Thyroartenoids

(6) Internal (vocalis)
(7) External
(8) Lateral cricoarytenoids
(9) Vocalis
(10) Cricothyroids
(11) Cricothyroids
(12) Thyroepiglottics
(13) Aryepiglottics

CHAPTER 5

Self-Study Test of Terminology

(1) Aerodynamic-myoelastic theory
(2) Voice adjustments
(3) Laryngeal adjustments
(4) Bernoulli (venturi) effect
(5) Mechanical coupling stiffness
(6) Damped vibration
(7) Subglottal pressure
(8) Biological adjustments
(9) Whisper adjustment
(10) Aerodynamic factors
(11) Vertical phase difference
(12) Mass
(13) Supraglottal pressure
(14) Open phase
(15) Phonatory adjustment
(16) Compliance
(17) Vibratory (glottal) cycle
(18) Closed phase
(19) Open quotient (OQ)
(20) Stiffness (longitudinal tension)
(21) Speed quotient (SQ)
(22) Length
(23) Opening phase
(24) Myoelastic factors (glottal resistance)
(25) Viscosity
(26) Quality
(27) Intraglottal pressure
(28) Pitch
(29) Volume velocity
(30) Closing phase
(31) Loudness

(32) Glottal area

(33) Glottal pulse

(34) Shimmer

(35) Jitter

Self-Study Test of Understanding

(A) Cartilaginous

(B) Phonatory

(C) Pitch

(D) Volume velocity

(E) Glottal pulses

(F) Vibratory cycle

(G) Jitter

(H) Open

(I) Closed

(J) Subglottal, intraglottal

(K) Open quotient (OQ)

(L) Opening

(M) Glottal area

(N) Speed quotient

(O) Aerodynamic-myoelastic

(P) Aerodynamic

(Q) Myoelastic, glottal

(R) Supraglottal

(S) Intraglottal pressure

(T) Bernoulli effect

(U) Vertical phase of difference

(V) Mechanical coupling stiffness

(W) Compliance

(X) Length

(Y) Mass

(Z) Stiffness, longitudinal tension

Clinical Exercises

(a) Lower than normal

(b) Smaller than normal

(c) Harshness

(d) Breathiness

(e) Amplitudes or intensities

(f) Glottal cycles

(g) Adducted

(h) Your sketch should resemble the vocal fold positions shown in Figure 5-3

CHAPTER 6

Self-Study Illustrations

(A) Palatine

(B) Nasal cavity

(C) Maxilla

(D) Alveolar ridge

(E) Orbicularis oris

(F) Buccinator

(G) Risorius

(H) Oral cavity

(I) Glossus

(J) Palatopharyngeus

(K) Palatoglossus

(L) Aditus

(M) Cricopharyngeus

(N) Inferior constrictor

(O) Pharyngeal cavity

(P) Velum

(Q) Hamulus of the pterygoid

(R) Superior constrictor

(S) Pharyngeal tonsil

(T) Levator palatini

(U) Tensor palatine

(V) Tensor palatini

(W) Salpingopharyngeus

(a) Superior longitudinal

(b) Inferior longitudinal

(c) Inferior longitudinal

(d) Superior longitudinal

(e) Styloglossus

(f) Vertical

(g) Transverse

(h) Genioglossus

(i) Hyoglossus

(j) Palatoglossus

(u) Temporalis

(v) Masseter

(w) Medial pterygoid

(x) Lateral pterygoid

(y) Geniohyoid

(z) Anterior belly of digastric

(aa) Geniohoid

(bb) Anterior belly of digastric

(cc)	Posterior belly of digastric
(dd)	Styloglossus
(ee)	Posterior belly of digastric
(ff)	Styloglossus
(gg)	Anterior belly of digastric
(hh)	Genioglossus
(ii)	Thyrohyoid
(jj)	Sternothyroid
(kk)	Thyrohyoid
(ll)	Sternothyroid
(mm)	Sternohyoid
(nn)	Omohyoid

Self-Study Test of Terminology

(1) Laryngopharynx
(2) Oropharynx
(3) Vocal tract
(4) Sphenoid bone
(5) Nasopharynx
(6) Salpingopharyngeus muscle
(7) Buccal cavity
(8) Middle constrictor muscle
(9) Superior constrictor muscle
(10) Pharynx
(11) Eustachian tube
(12) Cricopharyngeus muscle
(13) Oral cavity
(14) Stylopharyngeus muscle
(15) Hamulus of the pterygoid
(16) Inferior constrictor muscle
(17) Pterygoid plates
(18) Tensor palatini muscle
(19) Adenoid (pharyngeal tonsil)
(20) Palatine tonsil
(21) Palatoglossus muscle
(22) Palatine bone
(23) Coronoid process
(24) Orbicularis oris muscle
(25) Soft palate (velum)
(26) Buccinator muscle
(27) Levator palatini muscle
(28) Lips
(29) Mandible
(30) Hard palate

(31) Palatine aponeurosis
(32) Risorius muscle
(33) Palatopharyngeus muscle
(34) Maxilla
(35) Masseter muscle
(36) Superior longitudinal muscle
(37) Medial pterygoid muscle
(38) Mylohyoid muscle
(39) Geniohyoid muscle
(40) Extrinsic lingual (glossal) muscles
(41) Lateral pterygoid muscle
(42) Glossus
(43) Condylar process
(44) Intrinsic lingual (glossal) muscles
(45) Temporalis muscle
(46) Vertical muscle
(47) Geniohyoid muscle
(48) Styloglossus muscle
(49) Posterior belly of the digastric muscle
(50) Thyrohyoid muscle
(51) Anterior belly of the digastric muscle
(52) Inferior longitudinal muscle
(53) Hyoid bone
(54) Transverse muscle
(55) Mylohyoid muscle
(56) Genioglossus muscle
(57) Hyoglossus muscle
(58) Stylohyoid muscle
(59) Suprahyoid muscles
(60) Sternohyoid muscle
(61) Palatoglossus muscle
(62) Sternothyroid muscle
(63) Infrahyoid muscles
(64) Anterior belly of the digastric muscle
(65) Omohyoid
(66) Nasal cavity
(67) Turbinates
(68) Nasal septum
(69) Vomer

Speech Functions of Articulatory Muscles

(1) Styloglossus
(2) Palatoglossus
(3) Genioglossus

(4)   Hyoglossus
(5)   Styloglossus, superior longitudinal
(6)   Geniohyoid
(7)   Anterior belly of digastric
(8)   Posterior belly of digastric
(9)   Styloglossus
(10)   Verticalis
(11)   Transversus
(12)   Superior longitudinalis
(13)   Inferior longitudinalis
(14)   Levator palatini
(15)   Palatopharyngeus
(16)   Palatoglossus
(17)   Tensor palatini
(18)   Orbicularis oris
(19)   Buccinator
(20)   Risorius
(21)   Geniohyoid
(22)   Anterior belly of digastric
(23)   Masseter
(24)   Temporalis
(25)   Medial pterygoid
(26)   Thyrohyoid
(27)   Sternothyroid
(28)   Superior constrictor
(29)   Middle constrictor
(30)   Inferior constrictor

CHAPTER 7

Self-Study Test of Terminology

(1)   Source-filter theory
(2)   Pulse, burst
(3)   Unreleased
(4)   Sonorant
(5)   Plosive (stop)
(6)   Glottal source
(7)   Manner of articulation
(8)   Closure
(9)   Voiced sounds
(10)   Vocal tract
(11)   Stoppage
(12)   Vowel
(13)   Released

(14)   Turbulence (source)
(15)   Intraoral pressure
(16)   Transition
(17)   Place of articulation
(18)   Connected speech
(19)   Velopharyngeal competence
(20)   Fricative
(21)   Vertical place of articulation
(22)   Suprasegmental elements
(23)   Prosodic features
(24)   Coarticulation
(25)   Lip position
(26)   Segmental elements
(27)   Voiceless sounds
(28)   Horizontal place of articulation
(29)   Dysphagia
(30)   Deglutition

Self Study Test of Understanding

(A)   Suprasegmental features
(B)   Segmental elements
(C)   Glottal source
(D)   Voiced sound
(E)   Vocal tract
(F)   Plosive
(G)   Voiceless
(H)   Manner
(I)   Pulse, burst
(J)   Closure
(K)   Stoppage
(L)   Intraoral pressure
(M)   Velopharyngeal competence
(N)   Released
(O)   Transition
(P)   Place
(Q)   Fricative
(R)   Sonorant
(S)   Coarticulation
(T)   Horizontal place
(U)   Vertical place
(V)   Lip position

Clinical Exercises

(a) Bilabial

(b) Linguo-alveolar (or alveolar)

(c) Linguovelar (or velar)

(d) Closure

(e) Opening

(f) Voicing (the *h* is voiceless and the vowel is voiced)

(g) Linguopalatal place of articulation, fricative manner of articulation, change in voicing feature from *sh* to *a*

(h) Labiodental place of articulation, fricative manner of articulation

(i) Bilabial place of articulation, stop manner of articulation, voicing change from *b + a* (both voiced) to *p* (voiceless)

(j) Bilabial

(k) Lingo-alveolar (or alveolar)

(l) Linguovelar (or velar)

(m) Impairments would be suspected for alveolar place of articulation *(d, t, s, z, l)*, palatal place of articulation *(sh)*, velar place of articulation *(ka, ga)*, and the nasal manner of articulation, *(m, n)*.

CHAPTER 8

Self-Study Test of Terminology

(1) Rarefaction phase

(2) Wave length

(3) Wave form

(4) Reinforcement

(5) Nonrepetitive wave

(6) Sine wave

(7) Spectrogram (sonogram)

(8) Harmonic frequency

(9) Fourier analysis

(10) Compression phase

(11) Frequency

(12) Phase angle

(13) Complex wave

(14) Hertz (Hz)

(15) Tone

(16) Continuous spectrum

(17) Interference

(18) Cycle

(19) Repetitive wave

(20) Spectral frequency

(21) Spectrum

(22) Noise

(23) Vibration

(24) Period

(25) Bandwidth

(26) Fundamental frequency

(27) Line spectrum

(28) Transfer function (filter function)

(29) Vowel

(30) Reflected wave

(31) Radiation characteristic

(32) Voiceless consonant

(33) Closed-tube resonator

(34) Spectral frequencies

(35) Stress

(36) Radiated spectrum

(37) Formant frequency

(38) Resonator (filter)

(39) Incidence wave

(40) Fricative

(41) Loudness

(42) Stop, plosive

(43) Quality

(44) Damping

(45) Diphthong

(46) Noise segment

(47) Glottal-source spectrum

(48) Steady-state

(49) Pitch

(50) Acoustic noninvariance

(51) First formant

(52) Noise-source spectrum

(53) Formant transition

(54) Spectral intensity

(55) Noise burst

(56) Contexual variation

(57) Spectral duration

(58) Second format

(59) Voiced consonant

(60) Nasal murmur

(61) Silence segment

(62) Sonorant

Acoustic Application Question 1

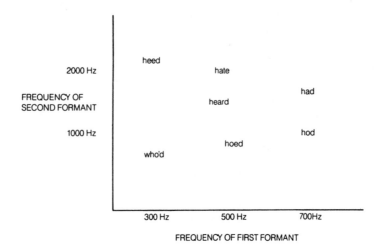

Acoustic Application Question 2

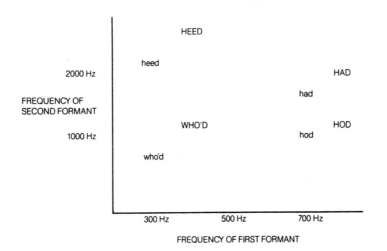

Acoustic Application Question 3

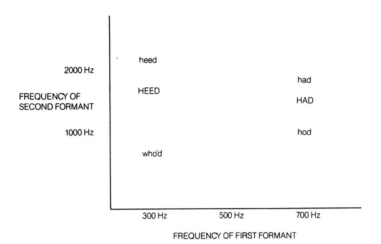

Acoustic Application Question 4

seed	noise + formant transition + vowel steady state + formant transition + silence + (release burst)
moose	nasal murmur + formant transition + vowel steady state + formant transition + noise
sand	noise + formant transition + vowel steady state + formant transition + nasal murmur + silence + (release burst)
stab	noise + *silence* + release burst + formant transition + *vowel steady state* + silence + (release burst)
bass	release burst + *formant transition* + vowel steady state + formant transitions + *noise*
west	long formant transition + vowel steady state + formant transition + noise + *silence* + *(release burst)*
wish	long formant transition + vowel steady state + *formant transition* + *noise*
sheep	*noise* + *formant transition* + vowel steady state + formant transition + silence + *(release burst)*
bob	*release burst* + formant transition + *vowel steady state* + formant transition + *silence* + (release burst)
meets	nasal murmur + formant transition + *vowel steady state* + *formant transition* + silence + *noise*
mast	*nasal murmur* + *formant transition* + vowel steady state + formant transition + noise + silence + (release burst)

CHAPTER 9

Self-Study Illustrations

(A) Pinna, auricle
(B) External ear
(C) External auditory canal
(D) Tympanic membrane
(E) Malleus, hammer
(F) Incus, anvil
(G) Stapes, stirrup
(H) Inner ear
(I) Auditory nerve
(J) Cochlea
(K) Eustachian tube
(L) Middle ear
(M) Utricle
(N) Semicircular canals
(O) Oval window
(P) Round window
(Q) Reissner's membrane
(R) Basilar membrane
(S) Scala tympani
(T) Cochlear duct
(U) Scala vestibuli
(V) Helicotrema
(W) Saccule
(X) Vestibular mechanism

(a) Pillar of Corti
(b) Spiral ligament
(c) Cells of Hensen
(d) Reticular lamina
(e) Tectorial membrane
(f) Reissner's membrane
(g) Cilia
(h) Hair cell
(i) Phalangeal cell
(j) Scala vestibuli
(k) Cochlear duct
(l) Scala tympani
(m) Perilymph
(n) Endolymph
(o) Perilymph
(p) Auditory nerve
(q) Modiolus
(r) Basilar membrane
(s) Spiral lamina
(t) Limbus

Self-Study Test of Terminology

(1) Middle ear
(2) Annular ligament
(3) Vestibule
(4) Outer ear
(5) Saccule
(6) Stapedius muscle
(7) Membranous labyrinth
(8) Incus (anvil)
(9) Auricle (pinna)
(10) Inner ear
(11) Cochlea
(12) Tensor tympani muscle
(13) Vestibular mechanism
(14) Oval window
(15) Cerumen
(16) Stapes (stirrup)
(17) Annulus
(18) Malleus (hammer)
(19) Eustachian tube
(20) Cilia
(21) External auditory meatus (ear canal)
(22) Footplate of the stapes
(23) Perilymph
(24) Utricle
(25) Semicircular canals
(26) Acoustic reflex
(27) Auditory ossicles
(28) Tympanic membrane
(29) Endolymph
(30) Scala tympani
(31) Cochlear duct
(32) Scala vestibuli
(33) Hair cells
(34) Hair cell supports
(35) Modiolus
(36) Limbus
(37) Round window
(38) Organ of Corti
(39) Reissner's membrane
(40) Helicotrema
(41) Tectorial membrane
(42) Basilar membrane
(43) Spiral ligament
(44) Phalangeal cells

Speech Reception Functions of the Ear

(1) External auditory canal
(2) Ossicular chain
(3) Stapedius muscle
(4) Large tympanic membrane acting on small footplate of the stapes
(5) Outer ear to middle ear
(6) Middle ear to inner ear
(7) Organ of Corti
(8) Basilar membrane
(9) Organ of Corti (shearing force of tectorial membrane bending hair cell cilia)

CHAPTER 10

Self-Study Test of Terminology

(1) Bone conduction
(2) Tuning curve
(3) Basilar membrane tuning
(4) Contralateral path
(5) Frequency encoding
(6) Auditory signal generation
(7) Intensity encoding
(8) Frequency analysis
(9) Place of excitation
(10) Descending auditory pathway
(11) Volley theory
(12) Shearing force
(13) Traveling wave
(14) Cochlear microphonic
(15) Ipsilateral path
(16) Frequency of excitation
(17) Wave envelope
(18) Tonotopic organization
(19) Complex wave analysis
(20) Ascending auditory pathway

Self-Study Test of Understanding

(A) Traveling waves
(B) Basilar membrane
(C) Stiffness
(D) Frequency analysis

(E) Complex
(F) Wave envelope
(G) Shearing force
(H) Tectorial
(I) Cilia
(J) Auditory signal
(K) Cochlear microphonic
(L) Frequency
(M) Ascending auditory pathway
(N) Cochlear nucleus
(O) Contralaterally
(P) Medial geniculate body
(Q) Primary auditory area
(R) Place of excitation
(S) Frequency of excitation
(T) Volleys
(U) Tonotopic organization
(V) Tuning curves
(W) Intensity
(X) Amplitudes
(Y) Cochlear microphonics
(Z) Descending auditory pathway

CHAPTER 11

Self-Study Illustrations

(A) Peripheral nervous system
(B) Cranial nerves
(C) Spinal nerves
(D) Central nervous system, CNS
(E) Brain
(F) Spinal cord
(G) Myelin
(H) Dendrites
(I) Cell bodies
(J) Axons
(K) Terminal arbors, axon terminal
(L) Absolute refractory period
(M) Presynaptic neuron
(N) Postsynaptic neuron
(O) Dendrite
(P) Neurotransmitters
(Q) Axon terminal, terminal arbor

(R) Axon
(S) Synaptic vesicles
(T) Synaptic gap, cleft
(U) Cell body
(V) Lower motor neuron

Self-Study Test of Terminology

(1) Autonomic nervous system (ANS)
(2) Terminal arbor, axon terminal
(3) Neural pulse
(4) Myelin sheath
(5) Synaptic vesicles
(6) Central nervous system (CNS)
(7) Threshold of excitation
(8) Neuron
(9) Synapse
(10) Peripheral nervous system
(11) Surface membrane
(12) Excitatory synapse
(13) Nodes of Ranvier
(14) Absolute refractory period
(15) Neurotransmitters
(16) Presynaptic neuron
(17) Inhibitory synapse
(18) Postsynaptic neuron
(19) Neuroreceptor

Neural Transmission Functions

(1) Threshold of excitation
(2) Dendrites
(3) Cell body
(4) Terminal arbors
(5) Neurotransmitters
(6) Axon terminal arbor
(7) Synaptic gap
(8) Dendrite
(9) Receptor
(10) ⌐Facilitate
(11) ⌐Inhibit
(12) Peripheral nervous system
(13) ⌐Autonomic nervous system
(14) ⌐Peripheral nervous system
(15) Central nervous system

CHAPTER 12

Self-Study Illustrations

(A) Central nervous system, CNS
(B) Peripheral nervous system
(C) Brain
(D) Spinal cord
(E) Cranial nerves
(F) Spinal nerves
(G) Autonomic nervous system, ANS
(H) Sympathetic division
(I) Parasympathetic division
(J) V, trigeminal
(K) VII, facial
(L) VIII, acoustic
(M) IX, glossopharyngeal
(N) X, vagus
(O) XI, accessory
(P) XII, hypoglossal
(Q) Dorsal horn, posterior horn
(R) Efferent, motor neuron
(S) Afferent, sensory neuron
(T) Dorsal root
(U) Ventral horn
(V) Dorsal root ganglion
(W) Spinal nerve
(X) Lower motor neuron
(Y) Ventral root

(a) Cranial
(b) Cervical
(c) Thoracic
(d) Lumbar
(e) Sacral
(f) Coccygeal
(g) Sympathetic ganglia
(h) Parasympathetic division
(i) Parasympathetic division
(j) Sympathetic division
(k) Sympathetic division
(l) Sympathetic division
(m) Parasympathetic division

Self-Study Test of Terminology

(1) Dorsal horn (posterior horn)
(2) Spinal nerves
(3) Dorsal root ganglion
(4) Ventral horn (anterior horn)
(5) Lower motor neuron
(6) Dorsal root
(7) Ventral root
(8) Cranial nerves
(9) I, Olfactory
(10) II, Optic nerve
(11) III, Oculomotor nerve (eye muscles)
(12) IV, Trochlear nerve (eye muscle)
(13) VI, Abducens nerve (eye muscle)
(14) X, Vagus nerve
(15) IX, Glossopharyngeal nerve
(16) VII, Facial nerve
(17) **XII, Hypoglossal nerve**
(18) V, Trigeminal nerve
(19) VIII, Acoustic nerve
(20) XI, Accessory nerve
(21) Parasympathetic division of ANS
(22) Sympathetic division of ANS
(23) Autonomic Nervous System (ANS)
(24) Sympathetic ganglia
(25) White matter
(26) Sensory fiber
(27) Gray matter
(28) Motor fiber

Speech Functions of Peripheral Nervous System

(1) Cervical, thoracic, and lumbar spinal nerves
(2) Cranial nerve X, vagus
(3) Recurrent laryngeal branch
(4) Recurrent laryngeal branch
(5) Recurrent laryngeal branch
(6) Superior laryngeal branch
(7) Cranial nerve XII, hypoglossal
(8) Cranial nerve IX, glossopharyngeal
(9) Cranial nerve XI, accessory
(10) Cranial nerve XI, accessory
(11) Cranial nerve XII, hypoglossal
(12) Cranial nerve V, trigeminal

(13) Cranial nerve VII, facial

(14) Cranial nerve VIII, acoustic

CHAPTER 13

Self-Study Illustrations

(A) Forebrain

(B) Midbrain

(C) Hindbrain

(D) Telencephalon

(E) Diencephalon

(F) Mesencephalon

(G) Metencephalon

(H) Myelencephalon

(I) Spinal cord

(J) Medulla

(K) Pons

(L) Cerebellum

(M) Midbrain

(N) Thalamus

(O) Basal ganglia, corpus striatum

(P) Cerebrum

(Q) Pyramidal decussation

(R) Medulla

(S) Pyramidal tract, pathway

(T) Thalamus

(U) Internal capsule

(V) Basal ganglia, corpus striatum

(W) Primary motor cortex

(a) Red nucleus

(b) Substantia nigra

(c) Brachium conjunctivum, superior cerebellar peduncle

(d) Restiform body, inferior cerebellar peduncle

(e) Brachium pontis, middle cerebellar peduncle

(f) Inferior colliculi

(g) Thalamus

(h) Lenticular nucleus

(i) Caudate nucleus

(j) Pons

(k) Brachium pontis, middle cerebellar peduncle

(l) Restiform body, inferior cerebellar peduncle

(m) Cerebellum

(n) Brachium conjunctivum, superior cerebellar peduncle

(o) Reticular formation

(p) Olfactory bulbs

(q) Uncus

(r) Amygdala

(s) Mammillary bodies

(t) Hippocampus

(u) Fornix

(v) Cingulate gyrus

(w) Limbic system

(aa) Fissure of Rolando

(bb) Primary somatic sensory cortex

(cc) Postcentral gyrus

(dd) Parietal lobe, supramarginal gyrus

(ee) Occipital lobe

(ff) Angular gyrus

(gg) Wernicke's area

(hh) Planum temporale

(ii) Temporal lobe

(jj) Primary auditory cortex

(kk) Transverse gyrus of Heschl

(ll) Fissure of Sylvius

(mm) Inferior frontal gyrus

(nn) Broca's area

(oo) Frontal lobe

(pp) Precentral gyrus

(qq) Primary motor cortex

(rr) Angular gyrus

(ss) Wernicke's area

(tt) Arcuate fasciculus

(uu) Broca's area

Self-Study Test of Terminology

(1) Brainstem

(2) Pons

(3) Mesencephalon

(4) Brachium conjunctivum

(5) Myelencephalon

(6) Telencephalon

(7) Spinal cord

(8) Novelty

(9) Metencephalon

(10) Quadrigeminal bodies
(11) Brain
(12) Red nucleus
(13) Midbrain
(14) Cerebrum
(15) Diencephalon
(16) Brachium pontis
(17) Restiform body
(18) Substantia nigra
(19) Medial geniculate body
(20) Internal capsule
(21) Supplementary motor area
(22) Thalamus
(23) Projection fibers
(24) Reticular formation
(25) Basal ganglia
(26) Wernicke's area
(27) Supramarginal gyrus
(28) Commissural fibers
(29) Hypothalamus
(30) Primary auditory cortex
(31) Reticular activating system (RAS)
(32) Cerebral cortex
(33) Angular gyrus
(34) Limbic system
(35) Temporal lobe
(36) Association fibers
(37) Fissure of Sylvius
(38) Proprioception
(39) Primary motor cortex
(40) Primary somatic sensory cortex
(41) Fissure of Rolando
(42) Arcuate fasciculus
(43) Cerebellum
(44) Longitudinal cerebral fissure
(45) Occipital lobe
(46) Broca's area
(47) Parietal lobe
(48) Frontal lobe
(49) Inferior colliculi
(50) Stroke, CVA
(51) Circle of Willis
(52) Middle cerebral artery
(53) Diploë
(54) Ventricles
(55) Fontanelle
(56) Meninges

Speech Functions of the Central Nervous System

(1) Auditory
(2) Proprioceptive
(3) Medulla
(4) Myelencephalon
(5) Inferior colliculi
(6) Midbrain
(7) Mesencephalon
(8) Medial geniculate bodies
(9) Thalamus
(10) Diencephalon
(11) Reticular activating system
(12) Spinal cord
(13) Brainstem
(14) Primary auditory
(15) Transverse gyrus of Heschl
(16) Temporal
(17) Cerebrum
(18) Telencephalon
(19) Projection
(20) Broca's
(21) Inferior frontal
(22) Dominant
(23) Corpus callosum
(24) Commissural
(25) Wernicke's
(26) Planum temporale
(27) Temporal
(28) Dominant
(29) Limbic
(30) Reticular
(31) Frontal
(32) Hypothalamus
(33) Restiform body
(34) Cerebellar
(35) Cerebellum
(36) Metencephalon
(37) Primary somatic
(38) Postcentral
(39) Parietal
(40) Wernicke's area

(41) Broca's area
(42) Arcuate fasciculus
(43) Association
(44) Supplementary motor area
(45) Supramarginal gyrus
(46) Parietal
(47) Sylvius
(48) Anglar gyrus
(49) Occipital
(50) Primary motor area
(51) Precentral
(52) Rolando
(53) Frontal
(54) Basal ganglia
(55) Caudate
(56) Lenticular
(57) Internal capsule
(58) Cortex
(59) Brachium pontis
(60) Middle
(61) Cerebellum
(62) Brachium conjunctivum
(63) Superior
(64) Red nucleus
(65) Substantia nigra

CHAPTER 14

Self-Study Test of Terminology

(1) Auditory pathway
(2) Neuromuscular system
(3) Transmission system
(4) Limbic system
(5) Reticular activating system (RAS)
(6) Descending sensory control pathway
(7) Input system
(8) Novelty
(9) Input processing
(10) Integrative system
(11) Verbal transformation
(12) Speech perception
(13) Top-down theory (active theory)
(14) Phonemic restoration
(15) Passive theory (bottom-up theory)

Self-Study Test of Understanding

(A) An input
(B) Transmission system
(C) Auditory pathway
(D) Reticular
(E) Novelty
(F) Limbic
(G) Reticular activating system
(H) Descending sensory control mechanism
(I) Primary cortical auditory
(J) Auditory pathway
(K) Reticular activating system
(L) Limbic
(M) Neuromuscular system
(N) Input processing
(O) Descending sensory control
(P) Integrative

CHAPTER 15

Self-Study Test of Terminology

(1) Supramarginal gyrus
(2) Cerebral dominance
(3) Wernicke's area
(4) Nondominant hemisphere
(5) Cross-modal sense
(6) Subcortical speech mechanisms
(7) Supplementary motor cortex
(8) Central processing
(9) Arcuate fasciculus
(10) Dominant hemisphere
(11) Sensory modality
(12) Message intent
(13) Broca's area
(14) Supramodal sense
(15) Time label
(16) Motor theory of speech perception
(17) Propositional message
(18) Angular gyrus
(19) Functional cerebral distance
(20) Brodmann areas
(21) Memory
(22) Short-term memory

Self-Study Test of Understanding

(A) Sensory modality
(B) Cross-modal
(C) Propositional
(D) Nondominant
(E) Dominant
(F) Motor theory of speech perception
(G) Central processing
(H) Time label
(I) Supramodal
(J) Message intent
(K) Propositional message
(L) Subcortical speech mechanisms
(M) Nondominant hemisphere
(N) Dominant hemisphere
(O) Functional cerebral distance
(P) Cerebral dominance
(Q) Dominant hemisphere
(R) Brodmann
(S) Wernicke's
(T) Planum temporale
(U) Temporal
(V) Broca's
(W) Arcuate fasciculus
(X) Supplementary motor cortex
(Y) Supramarginal gyrus
(Z) Nondominant

CHAPTER 16

Self-Study Test of Terminology

(1) Left (dominant) hemisphere
(2) Paralinguistic elements
(3) Linguistic speech planning
(4) Motor-speech patterning
(5) Automatic movement
(6) Muscle tone
(7) Working memory
(8) Propositional speech
(9) Cerebellum
(10) Volitional movement
(11) Limbic system
(12) Stages of speech processing
(13) Thalamus
(14) Right (nondominant) hemisphere
(15) Lower motor neuron
(16) Broca's area
(17) Automatic speech
(18) Motor schema
(19) Supramarginal gyrus
(20) Neural rhythms
(21) Extrapyramidal motor system
(22) Wernicke's area
(23) Motor mechanisms
(24) Coarticulation
(25) Pyramidal motor system
(26) Reticular formation
(27) Reflex
(28) Plan schema
(29) Sucking reflex

Self-Study of Understanding

(A) Working memory
(B) Coarticulation
(C) Limbic system
(D) Paralinguistic
(E) Cortical
(F) Automatic (planned automatically)
(G) Automatic movements
(H) Cortical control loops
(I) Wernicke's area
(J) Temporal lobe
(K) Arcuate fasciculus
(L) Primary somatic cortex
(M) Volitional movement
(N) Limbic system
(O) Basal ganglia
(P) Cerebellum
(Q) Thalamus
(R) Pyramidal motor system
(S) Extrapyramidal motor system
(T) Lower motor neurons